FAIRPOR
FA

DEFINING DOCUMENTS
IN AMERICAN HISTORY

Manifest Destiny & The New Nation

(1803-1859)

DEFINING DOCUMENTS
IN AMERICAN HISTORY

Manifest Destiny & The New Nation
(1803-1859)

Volume 1

SALEM PRESS
A Division of EBSCO Information Services
Ipswich, Massachusetts

GREY HOUSE PUBLISHING

Cover photo: Judgment in the U.S. Supreme Court Case *Dred Scott v. John F.A. Sanford,* March 6, 1857; Case Files 1792-1995; Record Group 267; Records of the Supreme Court of the United States; National Archives.

Copyright ©2013, by Salem Press, A Division of EBSCO Information Services, Inc.

All rights reserved. No part of this work may be used or reproduced in any manner whatsoever or transmitted in any form or by any means, electronic or mechanical, including photocopy, recording, or any information storage and retrieval system, without written permission from the copyright owner. For permissions requests, contact proprietary-publishing@ebscohost.com.

Defining Documents in American History: Manifest Destiny & The New Nation (1803-1859), 2013, published by Grey House Publishing, Inc., Amenia, NY, under exclusive license from EBSCO Information Services, Inc.

∞ The paper used in these volumes conforms to the American National Standard for Permanence of Paper for Printed Library Materials, Z39.48 1992 (R1997).

Library of Congress Cataloging-in-Publication Data

Manifest destiny and the new nation (1803-1859).
volumes cm. -- (Defining documents in American history)
Includes bibliographical references and index.
ISBN 978-1-4298-3742-2 (set) -- ISBN 978-1-4298-3743-9 (volume 1) -- ISBN 978-1-4298-3744-6 (volume 2)
1. Manifest Destiny--Sources. 2. United States--Territorial expansion--Sources. 3. United States--History--1783-1865--Sources.
E338.M25 2013
973.5--dc23

2013020044

ebook ISBN: 978-1-4298-3745-3

PRINTED IN THE UNITED STATES OF AMERICA

Contents

VOLUME 1

Complete List of Contents

VOLUME 1

Native American Land and Autonomy 623

Appendixes 663

Publisher's Note

Defining Documents in American History, by Salem Press, offers primary sources and analytical essays that explore the historical narratives of authors and the events and ideas of their period. The two-volume set *Manifest Destiny and the New Nation: 1803-1859* covers a period of expansion and exploration westward, which would more than double the size of the new nation. The transformation from colonial to a new American identity is reflected in a wide range of developments in the areas of religion, ethnic diversity, and social reform. Political developments would also mark a period of growing divisions that would lead the new nation toward civil war. Designed for college-age students, the aim of the series is to advance historical document studies as an important activity in learning about history. The selection draws upon the major documents of the period, including the governing documents that directed the country westward, as well documents representing the emerging abolitionist and women's rights movements. In addition, the collection offers less known yet essential primary sources from a diverse collection of authors viewing the new nation from multiple perspectives. The analysis of primary sources will establish the currency of the social and political meaning in primary source documents for today's researchers.

Essay and Volume Format

Manifest Destiny and the New Nation contains 61 complete and excerpted primary source documents and analytical essays. Each essay is 6,000 words, consisting of a 4,000 word analysis and a 2,000 word primary source. Readers will appreciate the diversity of the collected texts, including journals, letters, speeches, and political sermons, among other genres. Critical essays, written by historians and teachers, begin by introducing readers to the historical period, followed by a brief biography of the author and the events that occasion the composition of the document. An important feature of the essays is a close reading of the primary source that develops evidence of broader themes, such as author's rhetorical purpose, social or class position, point of view, and other relevant issues. In addition, essays are organized by chapter themes, highlighting major issues in the period, many of which extend across eras and continue to shape American life. Each chapter begins with an introduction that will explain the questions and problems, in some cases the dilemmas, underlying the subjects in the historical documents. A brief glossary highlights keywords important in the study of the primary source. Each essay offers a section of Additional Reading for further research.

Special Features

- **80 Lesson Plans** follow national history standards for learning designed to guide students and educators in document analysis and historical comprehension. Study questions, activities, and suggested author pairings will establish the legacy of documents and authorship for readers today. In addition, comparative analysis highlights how documents often emerge from a myriad of influences.
- Three historical **maps** illustrate developments in the early nineteenth century. The Louisiana Purchase Treaty of 1803 and the Lewis and Clark Expedition of 1804 show the transformation of the new nation's territorial boundaries. Creek and Cherokee Land Cessions in Colonial Georgia provides a graphic overview of the succession of treaties that would lead to the removal of Native Americans from their land in the southeast.
- **Historical Timeline** and **Chronological List** of titles will support readers in understanding the broader events and subjects in the period.
- A **Bibliography** lists helpful supplemental readings for further study.

Contributors

Salem Press would like to extend its appreciation to all involved in the development and production of this work. The essays have been written and signed by scholars of history, humanities, and other disciplines related to the essay's topics. Without these expert contributions, a project of this nature would not be possible. A full list of contributor's names and affiliations appears as front matter of this volume.

Introduction

America between the Revolutionary and Civil Wars feels like an adolescent, growing at a remarkable rate, overconfident, and full of contradictions. Committed to the principals of individual liberty and equal rights, Americans also held millions in permanent bondage. With a strong belief in the principle of private property, they disregarded the right of American Indians and Mexicans to occupy their own lands. A nation proud of its early settlers was also deeply suspicious of new immigrants. Charismatic religious figures jockeyed for position as the leaders of mass movements while promoting the individual spiritual experience. All over the country, the key question behind all of these issues was just who, exactly, was an American and what that meant. Women, people of color, ethnic minorities, immigrants, Indians, all sought an answer, and used the language of individual liberty and equality codified in the Constitution to argue for protection and justice. The "blessings of liberty" were unevenly granted, and many demanded to know why. To those who were born with the social standing to confidently declare themselves the real Americans—the white native-born men whose lineage was long established—the question could only be answered by identifying those who were excluded and then making the case for why it should be so.

Overshadowing and informing this national dialogue were two other outstanding questions: How do we take best advantage of the land that it is our God-given destiny to control, and what role does the government play in this new nation? Bravery and foolishness, cruelty and generosity, and above all, a desire to keep growing speak loudly from the answers in the pages of this book. As settlers pushed westward, they came into conflict with Indians who were reluctant to give up their traditional homelands. By mid-century, it was clear that the aboriginal Americans had lost their claim and would be increasingly marginalized. By then, the conversation about slavery had become a shouting match on the cusp of turning violent. A look at the growing chorus of protest that preceded the Civil War, and the political and legal wrangling that attempted to forestall it, is necessary to understand how the issue of American identity was worked out.

This volume begins with a primary source document drawn from the political maneuvering that began during the War of 1812. At first glance, it may seem that this is simply a plea to fund a flagging wartime effort, but it contains language that sets the tone for the period. Henry Clay is outraged by the impressment of American seamen by the British Navy, even those who were not born in the United States. He invokes the "sacred rights of the American freeman," and "the rights of the person." In fact, he uses the term "rights" seven times in several paragraphs, and "independence" and "liberty" several times each. He argues not only for the war, but for an America composed of native and foreign-born citizens whose rights are defended by a vigorous military, which relies on a strong federal government. It was a rousing speech, and Henry Clay got his troops; and, though he never explicitly intended as much, the War of 1812 sped the rise of the federal government, the reach of which was defined and broadened in the coming years with the help of the Supreme Court.

It quickly became evident that the Supreme Court would have a say in more than just the regulation of trade and commerce. It also helped to define who was an American with rights entitled to be defended. Throughout this period, the courts refused to offer protection to vulnerable people who were marginalized by their race or ethnicity. The California Supreme Court declared that Chinese eyewitnesses could not testify against white men, even in cases of murder. The Supreme Court refuted the claim that American Indians were a separate nation with concurrent rights, and also did not afford them the protections of citizenship; it was their in-between status as domestic dependant nations that allowed much egregious land theft to take place. The court's 1857 decision that the slave Dred Scott was not free even in a free state, and that as a black man, he had "no rights that the white man was bound to accept," laid plain the total vulnerability of even those who had made their way to freedom or been released by their masters. It was a startling decision, even in its time, and pushed the country further down the path that led to war.

For women active in the abolitionist movement, objecting to the enslavement and repression of African Americans led to a greater awareness of their own disadvantaged condition. Since social causes were considered part of their expanded private sphere, women who would not have mounted a stage to argue for women's rights did so to protest slavery, and then found themselves wondering aloud whether *their* treatment was also unjust and un-American. The principal of freedom, taken further and inward, led to the rethinking of the meaning of work, the role of education, the nature of religion, and the performance of civic duties. For some, it meant a wholesale rejection of social norms, but for many it meant that at least there was room to think in new ways, to imagine oneself as part of a uniquely progressive time. The compelling aspect of these documents is not necessarily the argument that they make; indeed, many of these voices sound, at first reading, hopelessly antiquated, as when Hannah Mather Crocker urged in 1818 that women be educated primarily so that they might provide a better crop of sons. Students may roll their eyes and wonder what this has to do with them. However, these documents become compelling when the reader is brought to understand the newness of the idea being put forward; an idea that seems innocuous today, like that women should be entitled to vote, was initially very radical, and had to be approached gradually, couched in the language of deference, and then slowly edged onto a greater stage, until Elizabeth Cady Stanton could get up in 1848, tuck her hair back in her hat, and demand the vote.

Alongside the spiritual and social expansion of the time, the physical expansion of the United States provided opportunity for some, oppression for others, and another element against which American identity could be measured. The Louisiana Purchase, which doubled the size of the country overnight, and the Monroe Doctrine's declaration that the Americas were no longer open to colonization by European powers, opened up vast new territory to be explored and eventually settled by the United States. Like the Puritans, most nineteenth-century American settlers saw the land as God-given, ownerless territory, and the people living on it already as an inconvenience at best, a threat to be eliminated at worst. There was no lack of bravery among the settlers, and the narratives of the westward journey are among the most gripping and immediate documents in this collection. However, early reports from areas that were opening to settlement had painted native Texans and Californians as dirty and lazy, and American Indians as wild savages. It is small wonder, therefore, that these groups' claims to their land were easily dismissed, and the virtuous white settler seen as a necessary, civilizing influence in those areas. Even when the intruder was not so civilizing, as was the case during the California Gold Rush, white Americans believed in their right to claim the land for themselves. American Indians were removed from their traditional lands as those lands became more desirable to settlers, and though they protested with force and moral suasion, treaties between the Indians and the US government were repeatedly broken, and Indians were moved to less valuable land in the West, at great cost to their culture and people. The question of slavery also haunted territorial expansion, as every new state admitted to the Union threatened to upset the delicate balance between free-state and slave-state representation in Congress.

In another contradiction, as Americans' desire to migrate west and claim territory there reached a fever pitch, those same Americans began to look with suspicion upon immigrants from other countries who saw the United States as a place that valued freedom and equality. Nativist groups formed to combat what they saw as the effluvia of the world being deposited at American's doorstep. Though we live in a nation of immigrants, they said, our ancestors had to work harder to get here and so we are entitled to a larger share of the rights of citizenship. Immigrants from Catholic countries were viewed with additional suspicion, as their loyalty to the Pope made them appear less patriotic. Americans entitled to full citizenship were once again defined by who they were not. They were not Indian, Mexican, Texan, or Californian. They were not women. They were not Catholic immigrants. They were not Chinese, and they were certainly not black.

Slavery defined the national conversation during this time like nothing else, and was the one issue that most clearly divided those whose identity as Americans was otherwise assured. Pro- and antislavery activists both saw their issue as fundamental to their identity. Proslavery elements focused on property rights with slaves as valuable possessions, and on the natural inferiority of the race. Antislavery elements focused on human rights, and felt that the liberty and equality that were so fundamental to the founding of the nation applied as well to enslaved and free blacks. Former slaves provided extraordinary insight into the reality of slavery, describing a system that treated livestock better than people. Slave narratives are among the most compelling primary sources in this volume. They gave voice to individuals whose experiences differed, but who provide the reader with examples of labor, resistance, family relationships, and religious belief that shaped enslaved life. Leaders in free black communities worked tirelessly to prove that they were worthy not only of freedom, but of full citizenship, by demonstrating the religious feeling and moral virtues of their members. When the Fugitive Slave Law came into effect in 1850, threatening escaped slaves and free blacks alike, the threat to those who spoke publically or allowed their story to be published increased tremendously, but these sources were also tremendously effective in bolstering support for the abolitionist cause. Many former slaves risked their freedom in support of the cause, and John Brown and his followers gave their lives.

Other documents chart the changing face of America during this time. The widespread development of industry provided often hazardous employment to the burgeoning immigrant population. People rushed to camp meetings to experience an ecstatic, physical religious conversion, and other reformers proclaimed that alcohol was at the root of all societal evils.

Taken individually, these documents address disparate movements and ideals. Taken together, however, they give voice to a nation whose primary task was figuring out who it was and what it was meant to do. Though Americans most often defined themselves by who was excluded from their ranks, and therefore the full benefits of liberty, they also considered progress, growth, and reform as central to the promise of the new nation. It is this struggle, this eagerness, and the very real progress that was made toward realizing the ideals of liberty and equality, that makes this one of the most important periods in American history.

Bethany Groff

Contributors

Anna Accettola, MA
Wilton, California

Michael Auerbach, MA
Marblehead, Massachusetts

Emily Bailey, MA
University of Pittsburgh

Adam Berger, PhD
New York, New York

Amanda Beyer-Purvis, MA
University of Florida

Steven L. Danver, PhD
Walden University

Jonathan Den Hartog, PhD
Northwestern College (St. Paul, Minnesota)

Tracey M. DiLascio, JD
Framingham, Massachusetts

Kevin E. Grimm, PhD
Beloit College

Bethany Groff
Historic New England

Jennifer L. Henderson Crane, PgDip
Fife, Scotland

Micah Issitt, MS
Philadelphia, Pennsylvania

Mark S. Joy, PhD
Jamestown College

Laurence W. Mazzeno, PhD
Alvernia University

Wendy Rouse, PhD
San Jose State University

Matthew D. Smith, PhD
Miami University Hamilton

Lee Tunstall, PhD
University of Calgary

Christopher Allen Varlack, MFA
Morgan State University

Vanessa E. Vaughn, MA
Chicago, Illinois

Donald A. Watt, PhD
McGovern Center for Leadership and Public Service

Maddie Weissman, MA
California State University, Los Angeles

Maps

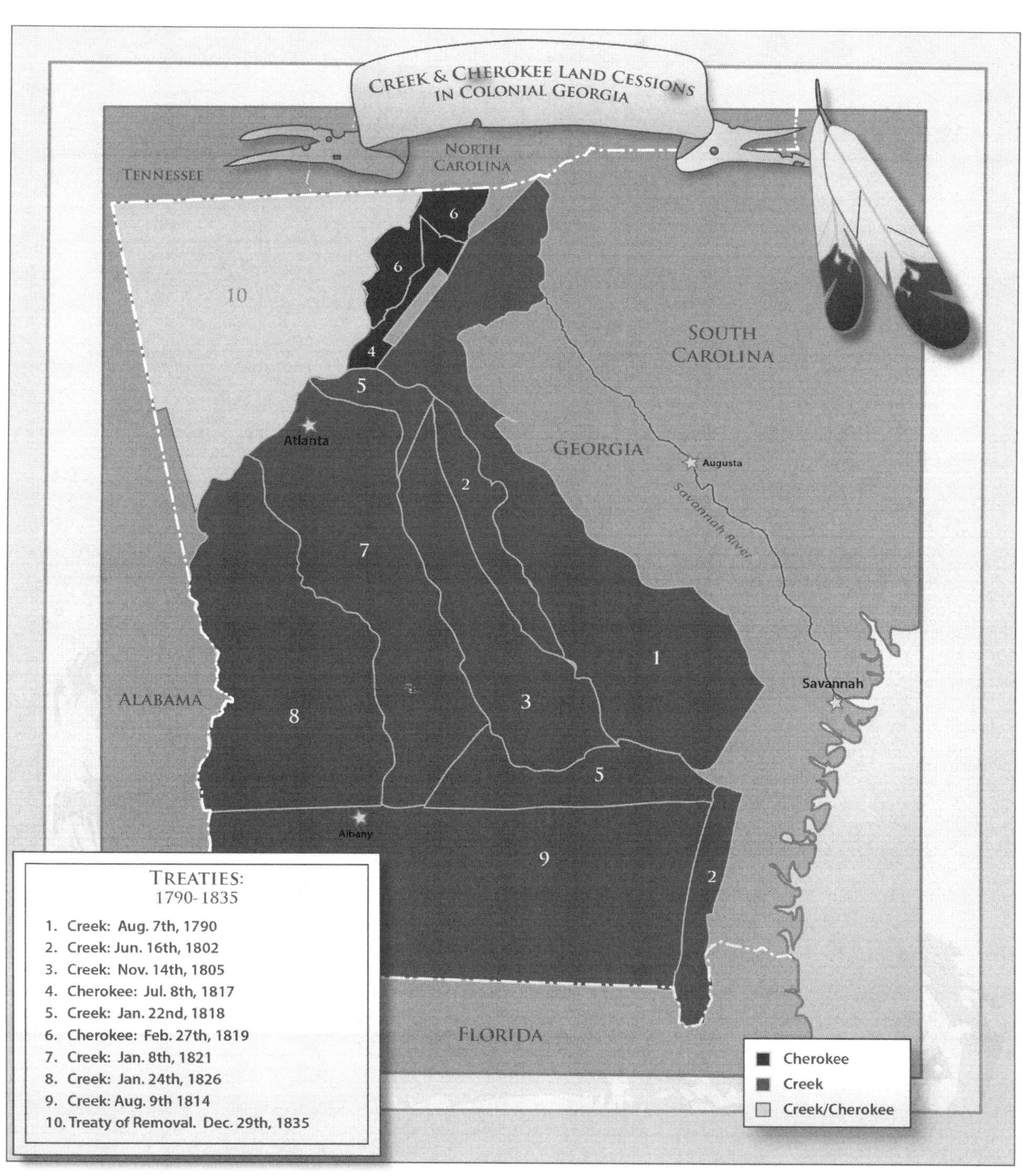
CREEK & CHEROKEE LAND CESSIONS IN COLONIAL GEORGIA
TENNESSEE
NORTH CAROLINA
SOUTH CAROLINA
GEORGIA
ALABAMA
FLORIDA
Atlanta
Augusta
Savannah River
Savannah
Albany
TREATIES:
1790-1835
1. Creek: Aug. 7th, 1790
2. Creek: Jun. 16th, 1802
3. Creek: Nov. 14th, 1805
4. Cherokee: Jul. 8th, 1817
5. Creek: Jan. 22nd, 1818
6. Cherokee: Feb. 27th, 1819
7. Creek: Jan. 8th, 1821
8. Creek: Jan. 24th, 1826
9. Creek: Aug. 9th 1814
10. Treaty of Removal. Dec. 29th, 1835
Cherokee
Creek
Creek/Cherokee

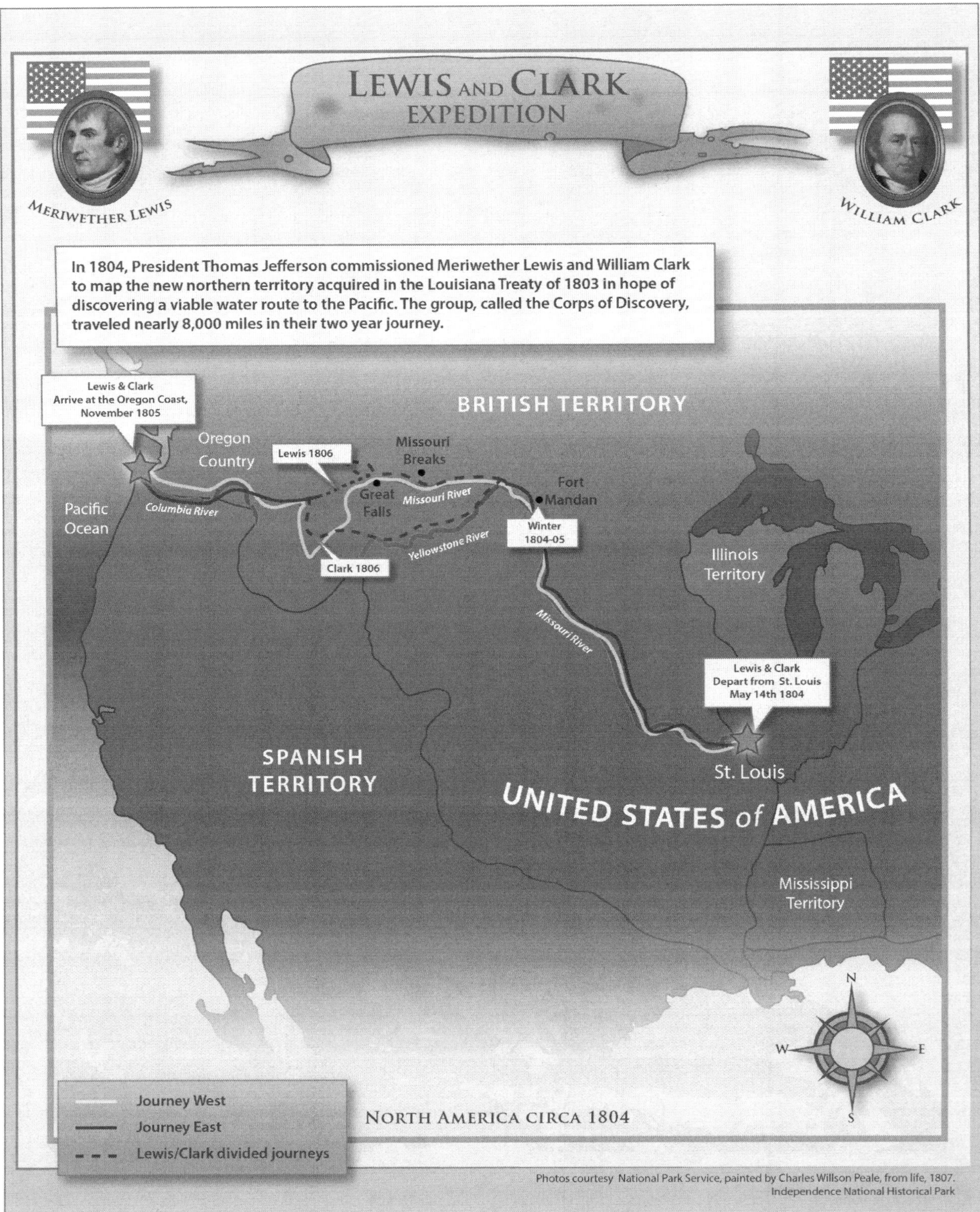
LEWIS AND CLARK
EXPEDITION
MERIWETHER LEWIS
WILLIAM CLARK
In 1804, President Thomas Jefferson commissioned Meriwether Lewis and William Clark to map the new northern territory acquired in the Louisiana Treaty of 1803 in hope of discovering a viable water route to the Pacific. The group, called the Corps of Discovery, traveled nearly 8,000 miles in their two year journey.
Lewis & Clark Arrive at the Oregon Coast, November 1805
BRITISH TERRITORY
Oregon Country
Lewis 1806
Missouri Breaks
Fort Mandan
Pacific Ocean
Columbia River
Great Falls
Missouri River
Winter 1804-05
Yellowstone River
Clark 1806
Illinois Territory
Missouri River
Lewis & Clark Depart from St. Louis May 14th 1804
St. Louis
SPANISH TERRITORY
UNITED STATES of AMERICA
Mississippi Territory
N
W
E
S
Journey West
Journey East
Lewis/Clark divided journeys
NORTH AMERICA CIRCA 1804
Photos courtesy National Park Service, painted by Charles Willson Peale, from life, 1807.
Independence National Historical Park

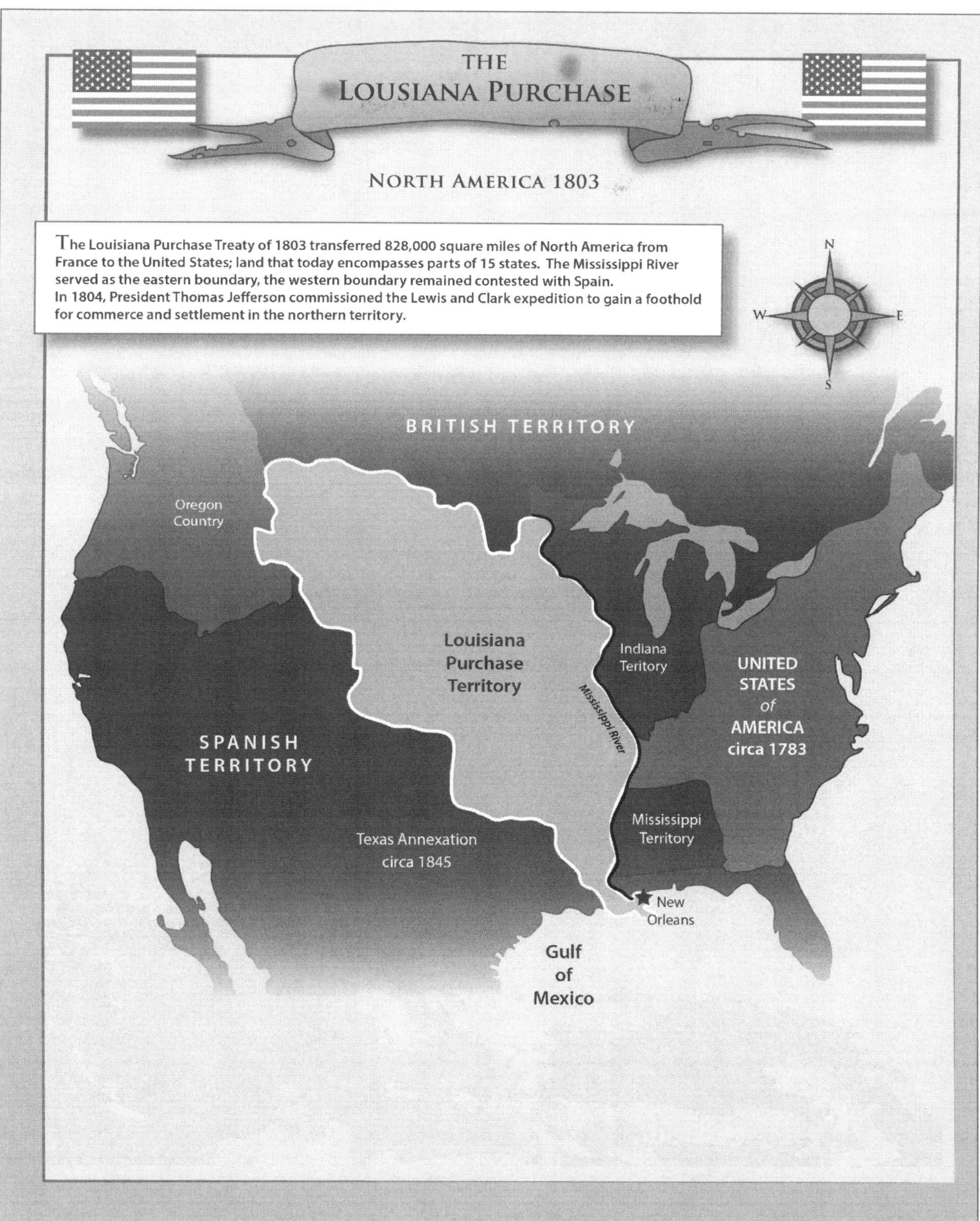
THE
LOUSIANA PURCHASE
NORTH AMERICA 1803
The Louisiana Purchase Treaty of 1803 transferred 828,000 square miles of North America from France to the United States; land that today encompasses parts of 15 states. The Mississippi River served as the eastern boundary, the western boundary remained contested with Spain.
In 1804, President Thomas Jefferson commissioned the Lewis and Clark expedition to gain a foothold for commerce and settlement in the northern territory.
N
W
E
S
BRITISH TERRITORY
Oregon Country
Louisiana Purchase Territory
Indiana Teritory
UNITED STATES of AMERICA circa 1783
Mississippi River
SPANISH TERRITORY
Mississippi Territory
Texas Annexation circa 1845
New Orleans
Gulf of Mexico

DEFINING DOCUMENTS
IN AMERICAN HISTORY

Manifest Destiny & The New Nation

(1803-1859)

Antebellum Law and Politics

The political and legal landscape in the first decades of the nineteenth century reflected a nation struggling to define itself and what it meant to be a citizen of the United States. The War of 1812 tested the military resolve of the new nation, and forced the British to respect US sovereignty. When Henry Clay referred to the "sacred rights of the American freeman" in his speech to Congress in 1813, his audience understood that he did not include American Indians or African Americans in this category. He did, however, include people who were not born in the United States but had become citizens. Indeed, the question of who was an American at all, and whose rights were bound to be respected, drove political and legal action during this period.

A vexing issue to the new nation involved the delicate balance between states' rights and the powers of the federal government. Colonies with unique characteristics and traditions before the Revolution became states that were expected to be able to operate together as a unified nation under a narrowly defined central government. The memory of the Revolutionary War was still fresh, and many Americans were wary of centralized power. The authority of the federal government to regulate trade, settlement, and commerce was tested repeatedly. Throughout this period, the Supreme Court defined and broadened its reach. State laws could not contradict or countermand federal laws, and when South Carolina rejected trade tariffs in 1833, armed federal intervention was threatened.

The newly muscular federal government was able to push forward with westward and southern expansion, declaring under the Monroe Doctrine that the continents of North and South America were no longer available for colonization by European powers, and acquiring vast swaths of territory from Mexico, France, and Spain. The stage was also set for the removal of native tribes, whose traditional lands were coveted by white settlers, and whose rights were hotly debated, with calls for Indian resettlement winning out in the end.

States were also deeply divided over the issue of slavery, and attempts at compromise during this period forestalled, but could not prevent, a final collapse of the Union. The increasingly antislavery North was enraged by the Fugitive Slave Act, which required the capture and return of escaped slaves discovered in free states. This was part of the Compromise of 1850, which sought to keep the Union together by accommodating both pro- and antislavery interests. The 1854 Kansas-Nebraska Act allowed the citizens of those two territories to choose whether to allow slavery or not, which set the stage for bloody pre–Civil War conflicts there. The 1857 *Dred Scott* Supreme Court decision, which concluded, essentially, that slaves were considered property even in free states, and that free blacks could never be citizens, further increased tension in the divided nation.

Bethany Groff

Speech in Congress on the War of 1812

Date: January 8, 1813
Author: Clay, Henry
Genre: address

"A nation ought but seldom to go to war. When it does, it should be for clear and essential rights alone . . . who is prepared to say that American seamen shall be surrendered, the victims to the British principle of impressment?"

Summary Overview

Henry Clay was a member of the House of Representatives and one of the most adamant proponents for declaring what became known as the War of 1812 (June 18, 1812–December 24, 1814) when it was debated in June of that year. Many had assumed the American forces would easily and quickly defeat the British and their allies, since the majority of the British forces were tied up in Europe in the war with Napoleon. When the anticipated success failed to come, support for the war declined. Following some naval victories, Congress passed bills authorizing additional naval forces. However, a bill proposed by President James Madison in December 1812 to increase the size of the American army by fifty thousand men stalled in part because the army had failed to achieve any significant victories against the British. In response to strong antiwar speeches, Henry Clay delivered speeches over a two-day period to strengthen support for the war effort and to ensure passage of the bill on January 11, 1813.

Defining Moment

Conflict continued between the Americans and the British after the formal conclusion of the Revolutionary War. The Jay Treaty, signed in 1794, relieved some pressure by granting Britain most-favored-nation status in terms of trade, but British and American interests still differed. This treaty was supported by President George Washington, but it was actively opposed by Thomas Jefferson and James Madison. Toward the end of his second term, Jefferson encouraged Congress to pass legislation moving away from the Jay Treaty, allowing Americans to trade with everyone in Europe, including Britain's enemy, the French. This policy, which was continued under President Madison, antagonized the British and led to them physically stopping American ships. When inspecting the American ships to confiscate goods going to or from France, the British at times used the opportunity to kidnap American sailors, as they needed more sailors for their war effort. In addition, the British were encouraging American Indians in the Northwest Territory to stop the influx of American settlers. As a result, in 1812, President Madison proposed war with Great Britain. Henry Clay, one of the two most outspoken supporters of this proposal in Congress, helped secure passage of the declaration.

In 1812, there were relatively few well-trained American troops. This resulted in a disastrous beginning to the war for the United States. The general at Detroit surrendered without a battle, and plans to invade Canada across the Niagara River failed to come to fruition. State militias did not want to fight outside their home states, and the northeastern part of the United States was against the war. President Madison, a Democratic-Republican, desperately needed additional troops if the United States was going to win the war. Members of the Federalist Party gave strong speeches in Congress that questioned why the war was continuing, since Britain had agreed to free trade. On January 8, Clay temporarily stepped down from his position as Speaker of the House to debate the issue. In his response, he emphasized what he saw as the heart of the struggle: the impressment, or kidnapping, of American sailors by the British to man their ships. The strength of this speech not only allowed the bill to pass but also created more popular support for the war. Following the Federalists' loss on this issue, they became increasingly marginalized. By the end of the war, in 1815, they were no longer a major factor in national politics. After decisively losing the election in 1816, they did not even field a candidate for the 1820 election.

Author Biography

Henry Clay, the seventh of nine children, was born on April 12, 1777. His parents, Reverend John Clay and Elizabeth Hudson Clay, lived in Virginia. Clay worked in the legal profession at an early age, originally as a secretary and clerk. His employees noticed his abilities and tutored him, allowing him to pass the bar in 1797. He then moved to Lexington, Kentucky, where he established a law practice. On April 11, 1799, he married Lucretia Hart, with whom he had eleven children.

Clay's successful law practice brought him attention that resulted in his election to the state legislature in 1803, where he served until 1809. In 1806, he was appointed to fill the last year of a US Senate term, even though he was not constitutionally old enough. He was seated for the last year of the term but did not run for election to that position, instead returning to the state legislature and becoming Kentucky's Speaker of the House. In early 1810, Clay was again selected to fill the last year of a US Senate term.

The 1810 elections took Clay to the US House of Representatives. He was part of the War Hawk wing of the Democratic-Republican Party, which was strongly anti-British. In a unique move, the returning and new members of the House elected Clay to the position of Speaker of the House on his first day in Congress. He transformed the position into one of power by appointing all his political allies to key committee assignments. In 1812, he assisted President Madison in passing the declaration of war for the War of 1812. Toward the end of the war, Clay resigned from the House to be part of the committee negotiating the Treaty of Ghent (1814). The following year, he helped negotiate a second treaty with Great Britain, this one regarding trade. After returning to the House, he strongly supported anti-European activities throughout the Americas. In 1820, one of his most notable legislative successes was securing the passage of the Missouri Compromise.

In 1824, Clay was one of four candidates for the presidency throwing his support to John Quincy Adams, who subsequently appointed him secretary of state. Later, strongly opposed to Adams's successor, Andrew Jackson, Clay returned to the Senate. He was on the national ticket as the presidential candidate for the National Republican Party in 1832 and the Whig Party in 1844. The second major legislative success of his career was developing the Compromise of 1850, which was intended to avoid secession and civil war. Like the Missouri Compromise, the Compromise of 1850 dealt with issues of slavery, statehood, and regulations for the Western territories. During this crisis, Clay was in declining health, suffering from tuberculosis, which caused his death on June 29, 1852.

HISTORICAL DOCUMENT

The war was declared because Great Britain arrogated to herself the pretension of regulating our foreign trade under the delusive name of retaliatory orders in council, a pretension by which she undertook to proclaim to American enterprise—"Thus far shalt thou go, and no farther"—Orders which she refused to revoke after the alleged cause of their enactment had ceased; because she persisted in the practice of impressing American seamen; because she had instigated the Indians to commit hostilities against us; and because she refused indemnity for her past injuries upon our commerce. I throw out of the question other wrongs.

The war in fact was announced, on our part, to meet the war which she was waging on her part. So undeniable were the causes of the war—so powerfully did they address themselves to the feelings of the whole American people—that when the bill was pending before this House, gentlemen in the opposition, although provoked to debate, would not, or could not, utter one syllable against it. It is true they wrapped themselves up in sullen silence, pretending that they did not choose to debate such a question in secret session. Whilst speaking of the proceedings on that occasion, I beg to be permitted to advert to another fact that transpired, an important fact, material for the nation to know, and which I have often regretted had not been spread upon our journals. My honorable colleague moved, in committee of the whole, to comprehend France in the war; and when the question was taken upon the proposition, there appeared but ten votes in support of it, of whom seven belonged to this side of the House and three only to the other!

It is said that we were inveigled into the war by the perfidy of France; and that had she furnished the document in time, which was first published in England in May last, it would have been prevented. I will concede to gentlemen every thing they ask about the injustice of France towards this country . . . All the world knows that the repeal of the Orders in Council resulted from the inquiry, reluctantly acceded to by the ministry, into the effect upon their manufacturing establishments of our non-importation law, or to the warlike attitude assumed by this government, or to both. But it is said that the Orders in Council are done away, no matter from what cause; and that having been the sole motive for declaring the war, the relations of peace ought to be restored. This brings me into an examination of the grounds for continuing the war.

I am far from acknowledging that, had the Orders in Council been repealed, as they have been, before the war was declared, the declaration would have been prevented. In a body so numerous as this is, from which the declaration emanated, it is impossible to say with any degree of certainty what would have been the effect of such a repeal. Each member must answer for himself. I have no hesitation, then, in saying that I have always considered the impressment of American seamen as much the most serious aggression. But, sir, how have those orders at last been repealed? Great Britain, it is true, has intimated a willingness to suspend their practical operation, but she still arrogates to herself the right to revive them upon certain contingencies, of which she constitutes herself the sole judge. She waives the temporary use of the rod, but she suspends it in terror over our heads. Supposing it was conceded to gentlemen that such a repeal of the Orders in Council as took place on the 23rd of June last, exceptionable as it is being known before the war, would have prevented the war, does it follow that it ought to induce us to lay down our arms without the redress of any other injury? Does it follow, in all cases, that that which would have prevented the war in the first instance should terminate the war? By no means. It requires a great struggle for a nation, prone to peace as this is, to burst through its habits and encounter the difficulties of war. Such a nation ought but seldom to go to war. When it does, it should be for clear and essential rights alone, and it should firmly resolve to extort, at all hazards, their recognition. The war of the revolution is an example of a war began for one object and prosecuted for another. It was waged, in its commencement, against the right asserted by the parent country to tax the colonies. Then no one thought of absolute independence. The idea of independence was repelled. But the British government would have relinquished the principle of taxation. The founders of our liberties saw, however, that there was no security short of independence, and they achieved our independence.

When nations are engaged in war, those rights in controversy which are not acknowledged by the Treaty of Peace are abandoned. And who is prepared to say that American seamen shall be surrendered, the victims to the British principle of impressment? And, sir, what is this principle? She contends that she has a right to the services of her own subjects; that, in the exercise of this right, she may lawfully impress them, even although she finds them in our vessels, upon the high seas, without her jurisdiction. Now, I deny that she has any right, without her jurisdiction, to come on board our vessels upon the high seas for any other purpose but in pursuit of enemies, or their goods, or goods contraband of war. But she further contends that her subjects cannot renounce their allegiance to her and contract a new obligation to other sovereigns. I do not mean to go into the general question of the right [of] expatriation. If, as is contended, all nations deny it, all nations at the same time admit and practice the right of naturalization. G. Britain herself does. Great Britain, in the very case of foreign seamen, imposes, perhaps, fewer restraints upon naturalization than any other nation. Then, if subjects cannot break their original allegiance, they may, according to universal usage, contract a new allegiance.

What is the effect of this double obligation? Undoubtedly, that the sovereign having the possession of the subject would have the right to the services of the subject. If he return within the jurisdiction of his primitive sovereign, he may resume his right to his services, of which the subject by his own act could not divest himself. But his primitive sovereign can have no right to go in quest of him out of his own jurisdiction into the jurisdiction of another sovereign, or upon the high seas, where there exists either no jurisdiction or it belongs to the nation owning the ship navigating them. But, sir, this discussion is altogether useless. It is not to the British principle, objectionable as it is, that we are alone to look;—it is to her practice—no matter what guise she puts on. It is in vain to assert the inviolability of the obligation of allegiance. It is in vain to set up the plea of necessity and to allege that she cannot exist without the impression of her seamen. The naked truth is, she comes, by her press-gangs, on board of our vessels, seizes our native seamen as well as naturalized, and drags them into her service. . . .

If there be a description of rights which, more than any other, should unite all parties in all quarters of the Union, it is unquestionably the rights of the person. No matter what his vocation, whether he seeks subsistence amidst the dangers of the deep, or draws it from the bowels of the earth, or from the humblest occupations of mechanic life, whenever the sacred rights of an American freeman are assailed, all hearts ought to unite and every arm should be braced to vindicate his cause. . . .

The disasters of the war admonish us, we are told, of the necessity of terminating the contest. If our achievements upon the land have been less splendid than those of our intrepid seamen, it is not because the American soldier is less brave. On the one element organization, discipline, and a thorough knowledge of their duties exist on the part of the officers and their men. On the other, almost every thing is yet to be acquired. We have however the consolation that our country abounds with the richest materials and that in no instance when engaged in an action have our arms been tarnished. At Brownstown and at Queenstown the valor of veterans was displayed and acts of the noblest heroism were performed. It is true, that the disgrace of Detroit remains to be wiped off. That is a subject on which I cannot trust my feelings, it is not fitting I should speak. But this much I will say, it was an event which no human foresight could have anticipated, and for which administration cannot be justly censured. It was the parent of all the misfortunes we have experienced on land. But for it the Indian war would have been in a great measure prevented or terminated; the ascendency on Lake Erie acquired, and the war pushed perhaps to Montreal. With the exception of that event, the war, even upon the land, has been attended by a series of the most brilliant exploits, which, whatever interest they may inspire on this side of the mountains, have given the greatest pleasure on the other. . . .

It is alleged that the elections in England are in favor of the ministry and that those in this country are against the war. If in such a cause (saying nothing of the impurity of their elections) the people of that country have rallied around their government, it affords a salutary lesson to the people here, who at all hazards ought to support theirs, struggling as it is to maintain our just rights. But the people here have not been false to themselves; a great majority approve the war, as is evinced by the recent reelection of the chief magistrate. Suppose it were even true that an entire section of the Union were opposed to the war, that section being a minority, is the will of the majority to be relinquished? In that section the real strength of the opposition had been greatly exaggerated. Vermont has, by two successive expressions of her opinion, approved the declaration of war. In New Hampshire, parties are so nearly equipoised that out of 30 or 35 thousand votes, those who approved and are for supporting it lost the election by only 1,000 or 1,500 votes. In Massachusetts alone have they obtained any considerable accession. If we come to New York, we shall find that other and local causes have influenced her elections.

What cause, Mr. Chairman, which existed for declaring the war has been removed? We sought indemnity for the past and security for the future. The Orders in Council are suspended, not revoked; no compensation for spoliations; Indian hostilities, which were before secretly instigated, now openly encouraged; and the practice of impressment unremittingly persevered in and insisted upon. Yet administration has given the strongest demonstrations of its love of peace. On the 29th June, less than ten days after the declaration of war, the Secretary of State writes to Mr. Russell, authorizing him to agree to an armistice upon two conditions only, and what are they? That the Orders in Council should be repealed and the practice of impressing American seamen cease, those already impressed being released. . . . In return, the enemy is offered a prohibition of the employment of his seamen in our service, thus removing entirely all pretext for the practice of impressment. The very proposition which the gentleman from Connecticut (Mr. Pitkin) contends ought to be made has been made. How are these pacific advances met by the other party? Rejected as absolutely inadmissible . . . An honorable peace is attainable only by an efficient war. My plan would be to call out the ample resources of the country, give them a judicious direction, prosecute the war with the utmost vigor, strike wherever we can reach the enemy, at sea or on land, and negotiate the terms of a peace at Quebec or Halifax. We are told that England is a proud and lofty nation, that disdaining to wait for danger, meets it half way. Haughty as she is, we once triumphed over her, and if we do not listen to the councils of timidity and despair we shall again prevail. In such a cause, with the aid of Providence, we must come out crowned with success; but if we fail, let us fail like men, lash ourselves to our gallant tars, and expire together in one common struggle, fighting for "seamen's rights and free trade."

GLOSSARY

arrogated: claimed a right from another

chief magistrate: president

disgrace of Detroit: the surrender of forces without a fight by General Hull during the Siege of Detroit in August 1812

impressment: the forcible removal of sailors from one ship to another to serve as part of the crew on the new ship, based on the perceived nationality of the sailors

inveigled: coaxed or won over by flattery

Orders in Council: a series of British decrees from 1783 to 1812 that outlined a commerce policy aligned in support of their current military policy

perfidy: a breach of trust or faith

press-gangs: officially sanctioned groups that forced men into military or naval service

primitive sovereign: a person's native country

Document Analysis

At one of the low points of the War of 1812, Henry Clay not only maintained his support for the war but pushed to strengthen the effort against the British and their American Indian allies. Acknowledging the changes that had occurred since the declaration of war on June 18, 1812, Clay outlined the issues that were still pertinent to the continuation of the war. In addition, he argued that the British had not changed their positions on the policies that had led to the declaration of war, thus mandating that the war should continue to be prosecuted. The bill that this speech supported would greatly expand the American army, which generally had performed poorly during 1812.

In order to understand the difficult situation of the United States, one should briefly look at the battles that Clay mentions in his speech. At the Battle of Brownstown (August 5, 1812), an American wagon train with supplies was advancing toward Detroit when its passengers spotted Shawnee allies of the British, and possibly British troops as well. They contacted the fort at Detroit, and General William Hull sent two hundred members of the Ohio militia to escort the supply train. While approaching the supply train, the soldiers were ambushed by twenty-four Shawnees, led by Tecumseh. The Ohio militia fled back toward the fort with losses of eighteen dead, twelve wounded, and seventy missing in action.

The Battle of Queenstown (October 13, 1812), also known as Queenston Heights, was an attempt by the Americans to invade Canada across the Niagara River. The initial goal was to take the high ground at Queenstown, where the British had cannons that could be used to fire on any troops trying to cross the river. The first stages of the early-morning attack went well, resulting in the New York militia, led by Major General Stephen Van Rensselaer, taking the high ground. This was to be followed up by a much larger invading force, composed of regular army and militia troops, which would then move toward Fort George, the primary British fortification overlooking the river. The regular army troops never arrived, as their commander did not believe it was acceptable for him to take orders from an officer in the militia. During the morning, Mohawk and Chippewa troops arrived to support the British, making their presence known with war cries, which scared members of the militia. With Fort George free from attack, all the British troops in the area could respond to the incursion. They also moved up more artillery to fire on the American troops and any boats crossing the river. When the expected American reinforcements failed to arrive, the American general crossed back to New York to force the rest of his militia to cross. However, having heard the cries of the American Indians, none of the militia members on the American side were willing to cross into Canada. Even the boatmen refused to row across to help rescue the outnumbered Americans. The leader of the American forces saw that no help was coming, and with no possible route of escape, he surrendered to the superior British forces. After the surrender, he and the British commander were surprised by additional New York militia soldiers also surrendering, for a total of about nine hundred American troops captured and about two hundred dead. Small groups of them had been hiding all around the area of the battle to avoid being a part of it. For the next two days, the American general in New York tried to rally the troops to again attack across the Niagara River, but they refused to move because it was raining.

The "disgrace of Detroit"(August 16, 1812), which ended the two-day Siege of Detroit, was an even greater military and psychological defeat for the Americans. General Hull had invaded Canada from Detroit, spending several weeks just across the river in what is now Windsor, Ontario. Withdrawing to Fort Detroit, he was followed by Shawnee and British troops. British artillery shelled the fort from Canada, and the Shawnee circled past the fort in such a manner that they appeared to number several times as many as were actually present. At some point, all the Michigan militia troops deserted. Believing that his forces were badly outnumbered, Hull surrendered the fort and his regular army troops without a fight to a force that was actually only about half as large as his own. The Ohio militia at Fort Detroit agreed to go home and not fight, allowing the British to capture the fort, with its much-needed supplies, and gain control of the northwestern part of the United States.

Such poor performances caused many to doubt that the United States should continue its war effort. Clay wanted to try to convince doubters of the war's necessity by supporting the bill with his skillful oration. In this speech, he moves directly to the four issues that had been the basis for the war. Great Britain, having been involved in the Napoleonic Wars for several years, had created a policy of controlling trade with France as one step toward winning that conflict. The United States, as a neutral party in the war, felt it was free to trade with any country in Europe. This is the issue

Clay refers to when he begins by stating that "Great Britain arrogated to herself the pretention of regulating our foreign trade." The second issue was "impressing American seaman," that is, forcibly taking sailors off American ships to work on the British ships. The third ongoing issue was the British support of American Indian resistance to American settlement in the Northwest Territory, land ceded to the United States at the end of the Revolutionary War. The final point in Clay's list of British wrongs is the fact that they refused to pay for damages caused by their policies.

Moving in his speech to the process by which war had been declared, Clay refers to the closed sessions of the House and Senate in June 1812 in which the proposal had been discussed. As he states, Clay believed the declaration of war by the United Sates was passed "to meet the war which [Britain] was waging on her part." For Clay, the restriction of trade and the impressment of American sailors were acts of war by Britain, even if undeclared. Clay may be stretching his case when he claims that no one spoke against the declaration in June because there was no support for remaining at peace. The Federalist legislators said they refused to "debate such a question in secret session," but Clay pretends not to believe them. Historically, Clay and President Madison's party, the Democratic-Republicans, had supported the French in their conflicts with the British. Clay's reference to the proposed amendment to the declaration of war that would have included France as an enemy state is to illustrate his view that everyone understood Great Britain was the enemy. The amendment only getting ten votes from the 142 members of the House showed its general lack of support, as did the fact that most of those came from Democratic-Republican legislators.

Clay then moves on to address one of the major objections to the continuation of the war, in addition to France's role in the conflict. He says he will "concede to gentlemen every thing they ask about the injustice of France towards this country." However, Clay rejects the proposition that France caused the war by tricking the Americans into a conflict with the British. The Orders in Council were a series of British decrees that increasingly limited trade with France and others on the continent. Belatedly recognizing that this was an increasing cause of conflict with the United States, on June 16, 1812, two days before the United States' formal declaration of war, the British government suspended the enforcement of the last three decrees regarding the Americans. Clay saw this as the result of pressure from British merchants and manufacturers not wanting to lose the American market, rather than a true change in the British government's position. Thus, even though later the British government said the decrees had been repealed, Clay neither accepted this nor believed it was grounds for ending the war. He cites the Revolutionary War as an example, stating that it began "against the right asserted by the parent country to tax the colonies" and ended only when the Americans "achieved [their] independence." For Clay, once a war had begun, the desired outcome often changed.

The change in this case, as Clay describes it, was not the addition of a new goal but rather the clarification of what had been, or should have been, the central point of the war from the beginning: "the impressment of American seamen as much the most serious aggression" by the British. Rough surveys of the time, as well as later estimates, indicate that in 1812, about eleven thousand American sailors had been born in other countries. Of those individuals, probably more than 80 percent of them were of British origin. With American merchant ships having an estimated total of about seventy thousand sailors, it is clear that a substantial portion of American sailors were at risk of impressment by the British.

The need for more sailors on British ships was the result of the Napoleonic Wars. A massive increase in the number of naval vessels was mandated by the British decision to blockade French and other continental ports. This placed great stress upon the navy to recruit seamen for the 130,000 to 150,000 naval positions, in addition to their own merchant fleet. Failing to meet this goal, the navy used other means to secure enough sailors. Britain did not accept the idea that its citizens could immigrate to other countries and renounce their British citizenship; the government believed that Americans who had been born in Great Britain remained British citizens and should serve on British ships. They did this by stopping American merchant ships and taking anyone they believed to be originally British. Due to the lack of clear documents for many sailors, the British ended up also taking some sailors who had actually been born in the United States. In either event, the United States recognized the individual right to immigrate and change citizenship, so they believed that all the sailors were Americans, with the rights of American citizens. Clay believed that Britain also recognized the naturalization process because, as he says, they had "fewer restraints upon naturalization than any other nation."

Clay did understand the logic behind the country where a person was born, the individual's "primitive sovereign," demanding that any former citizen physically present inside that country could be forced to serve the country of his or her birth. However, the fact that these actions were being taken not in British ports or British waters but "upon the high seas" made this action totally unacceptable to Clay and enough of a provocation for war to be declared. At the height of the British effort, they stationed ships near major ports to search all ships entering and leaving the port. Thus, in Clay's opinion, the fact that Britain had changed its Orders of Council did not amount to enough of a change in policy to end the war.

In the abridged edition of the speech presented in this document, Clay's responses to specific points made by other speakers are not included. Therefore, his discussion of the possible annexation of Canada at the conclusion of a successful war is not a part of this edition of the speech. However, the passages not included in this text do not have a bearing upon Clay's understanding of the essential reasons for the war and for the continuation of the war. The impressment of American sailors was the most obvious example of the British ignoring "the rights of the person." Clay's impassioned plea is that "whenever the sacred rights of an American freeman are assailed, all hearts ought to unite and every arm should be braced to vindicate his cause."

Even though Madison had requested the expansion of American military forces in 1810, the American army and navy were very small compared to the British. After the Revolutionary War, the national army shrank to almost nothing, as it was assumed that state militias would serve the needs of the country. Because the American merchant fleet had grown rapidly during the first decades of nationhood, the navy had continued to be somewhat adequately funded and was much better trained than the army. Thus, when Clay moves on to briefly discuss the military situation in which the United States found itself, most of the report is bad. He recognizes that the failure to achieve early successes in the effort to move into Canada caused some to think about "terminating the contest." However, Clay has confidence that, in the long run, the United States will prevail. He accepts the common American view that "our country abounds with the richest materials," which will ultimately be used to support the war effort.

While Clay puts a positive spin on the army's engagements against the British, it was clear from battles such as those described earlier that the additional forces authorized by the bill under debate were necessary. Members of the state militias were unreliable. They were willing to defend their individual states but were not very willing to be part of an offensive operation. In addition, the lack of cooperation between the militias and the regular army was very destructive. On the other hand, on the ocean, the ship-to-ship battles that had been fought had gone fairly well for the Americans. These battles included the two by the USS *Constitution* in which it destroyed HMS *Guerriere* and HMS *Java*, as well as the USS *United States'* capture of the HMS *Macedonia*. The American frigates were armed as well as or better than their British counterparts, and the commanders understood the tactics necessary to win.

In the next-to-last paragraph of his speech, Clay refers to the political landscape of January 1813. Leadership of the British government had passed to Robert Jenkinson in May 1812, and he remained in office for the next fifteen years. Thus, there was no change in British politics that Americans might see as indicating any change in British policy. Those who thought the war was losing support in America were rebutted by Clay's statement that the reelection of President Madison proved differently. Clay recognized the fact that the northeastern region of the United States generally did not support the war, although he did not give this much merit. It should be noted that in the Twelfth Congress, which voted to go to war, the Democratic-Republicans held 74 percent of the seats in the House, while after the elections in the fall of 1812, the Democratic-Republican membership of the House fell to 62 percent.

In the final section of this speech, Clay returns to the causes of the war and the need for additional troops to prosecute the war. Clay asserts that none of the original reasons for the war have ended. "The Orders in Council are suspended, not revoked," is his response on that major issue. Everyone recognized that the impressment of sailors continued, and no compensation had been made for previous injustices, as judged by the Americans. Clay notes that early in the conflict an overture was made to the British for peace, but this was not accepted by them. Their offer had also been found to be unacceptable to the American leadership. Thus Clay states that "an honorable peace is attainable only by an efficient war." In his view, this was the reason the House should pass the bill for additional troops. Clay was certain that just as the Revolutionary War had been successful, "we shall again prevail." He was willing to stake the existence of the United States and its entire future on the proposition that together the Americans could "prevail." "If we fail," Clay says, "let us fail like men, lash ourselves to our gallant tars, and expire together in one common struggle, fighting for 'seamen's rights and free trade.'"

Essential Themes

The central tenet of Clay's speech to members of the House of Representatives in support of the bill to increase the size of the army by twenty thousand men was the need for these troops to support the rights of all American citizens, whether native born or naturalized. His assertion that everyone should support the "sacred rights of an American freeman" has been echoed down through the centuries. While the issues of free trade and the interference of the British in the northwestern part of the United States were certainly strong issues in initiating the conflict, the War of 1812 has come to stand for the rights of Americans in whatever location. While the situation at that time only involved sailors on American ships traveling across the ocean, the arguments made by Clay apply to American citizens in any location and at any time.

As a nation whose population has always been mainly immigrants or the descendants of immigrants, the United States continued to have a strong interest in the laws regarding immigration and the naturalization of citizens. In most eras, the country sought immigrants to help with territorial expansion or for a more diverse labor force. Thus, another country not recognizing the citizenship of those who had moved to the United States and renounced their former citizenship was a major issue. Forcing the British to accept the naturalization process in 1812 was a major step toward true American independence. Establishing the fact that it was the American government that decided the status of an individual seeking to live in the United States, and not a foreign government, was of vital importance. From the time the war was successfully concluded, the United States has been able to set its own policy regarding immigration, naturalization, and citizenship, without outside interference.

Donald A. Watt, PhD

Bibliography

Caffrey, Kate. *The Twilight's Last Gleaming: Britain vs. America, 1812–1815*. New York: Stein, 1977. Print.

Drexler, Kenneth, comp. "Henry Clay: A Resource Guide." *Library of Congress*. LOC, 25 Aug. 2010. Web. 1 Apr. 2013.

Giddens, Sandra, and Owen Giddens. *A Timeline of the War of 1812*. New York: Rosen, 2004. Print.

Heidler, David S., and Jeanne T. Heidler. *Henry Clay: The Essential American*. New York: Random, 2010. Print.

Smith, Derek. "Disaster at Queenston Heights." *American History* 36.5 (2001): 38-44. Print.

Additional Reading

Duncan, Katherine. "Henry Clay: American Statesman." *Bicentennial of the War of 1812*. US Navy, n.d. Web. 1 Apr. 2013.

Hickey, Donald R. *The War of 1812: A Forgotten Conflict*. Urbana: U of Illinois P, 1989. Print.

Remini, Robert Vincent. *Henry Clay: Statesman for the Union*. New York: Norton, 1991. Print.

Schurz, Carl. *Henry Clay*. Vol. 1. New York: Chelsea, 1980. Print.

Stagg, John C. A. *Mr. Madison's War: Politics, Diplomacy, and Warfare in the Early American Republic*. Princeton: Princeton UP, 1983. Print.

LESSON PLAN: **Henry Clay Argues the Case for War**

Students analyze a speech by Henry Clay to trace events of the War of 1812 and consider its impact on American politics and identity.

Learning Objectives

Analyze the multiple causes that led to the War of 1812; compare and contrast different views on about the war; examine the influence of ideas on America's developing position in the early 1800s.

Materials: Henry Clay, "Speech in Congress on the War of 1812" (1813).

Overview Questions

Why does Clay urge Congress to continue the War of 1812? What hostilities does the United States face across multiple fronts? Why does Clay think war must go on, despite defeats? How does Clay think the war will impact American politics and national identity in the nineteenth century?

Step 1: Comprehension Questions

Why was war declared against Britain? What factors caused tensions with Britain to escalate? According to Clay, what is the United States fighting for?

- **Activity:** Pair students to list the reasons for declaring war. Have them identify where fighting occurred, across the continent and the Atlantic. Have students use their lists to discuss whether they agree or disagree with Clay's call to keep fighting.

Step 2: Comprehension Questions

How did Americans view the war? How did their views change over time? How might his arguments have swayed Congress and public opinion?

- **Activity:** Have students review paragraph two and discuss perspectives on the war. Ask students to locate passages about opinions at the time of Clay's speech and draw inferences about how perspective on the war might have changed over time.

Step 3: Context Questions

What "disasters" has the United States faced? Why is Clay confident that America will overcome these obstacles? According to his view, how might this fighting shape the country in the 1800s?

- **Activity:** Have students locate passages in which Clay describes US losses. Divide students into two groups, one to speculate how winning might impact the United States and one to discuss effects of losing. Have groups share their conclusions with the class.

Step 4: Explorations Questions

What factors does Clay think unite Americans? How do these issues bring the country together during war? How does this view lead Clay to maintain that this war must be fought, no matter the costs?

- **Activity:** Have students read aloud paragraph four and discuss what Clay means by "the rights of the person." Have students consider how these rights were violated and whether this justified war. Remind students to address the symbolic reasons for fighting Britain once again.

Step 5: Response Paper

Word length and additional requirements set by Instructor. Students answer the research question in the *Overview Questions*. Students state a thesis and use as evidence passages from the primary source document as well as support from the secondary historical document/s assigned in the lesson.

McCulloch v. Maryland

Date: March 6, 1819
Author: Marshall, John
Genre: court opinion

> *"Let the end be legitimate, let it be within the scope of the constitution, and all means which are appropriate, which are plainly adapted to that end, which are not prohibited, but consist with the letter and spirit of the constitution, are constitutional."*

Summary Overview

McCulloch v. Maryland is a US Supreme Court case that was decided on March 6, 1819, under the leadership of Chief Justice John Marshall. The Second Bank of the United States was operating a branch in Baltimore when the state of Maryland passed legislation effectively taxing its operation. James McCulloch, an officer of the Baltimore branch, refused to pay the tax and appealed to the US Supreme Court after the Maryland state courts decided the issue in favor of Maryland. *McCulloch v. Maryland* specifically addresses whether the United States Congress has the power under the US Constitution to establish a federal bank, and whether the states have the authority to tax a federal bank's operation within their borders. However, this case carries significance beyond these facts, because its rulings affected the balance of power between the federal government and the states, and shaped the future of US expansion during the nineteenth century.

Defining Moment

During the drafting of the US Constitution, the division of power between the federal and state governments was a hotly debated issue, with respected leaders holding strong opinions on both sides. Some, including the first US treasury secretary, Alexander Hamilton, and future US Supreme Court chief justice John Marshall, argued that a strong federal government was necessary to unite the people of the new nation. Others, including future president Thomas Jefferson, hesitated to give a centralized government too much control, still wary after the recent struggles against England's heavy-handed rule from afar.

In the end, perhaps as a matter of compromise, the Constitution addressed this matter in a rather vague way: it grants only a few specific powers to the federal government, and places only a few clear limitations on those powers. This is further complicated by a clause in article 1, section 8 known as the "Necessary and Proper Clause," which states that Congress has the authority to "make all Laws which shall be necessary and proper for carrying into Execution" the powers granted to it by the Constitution. From the early days of the United States, opinion was divided as to whether this clause should be interpreted as affirmatively granting Congress the power to pass any laws it deems necessary to carry out its constitutional duties, or intentionally limiting Congress's power to write only those laws that are deemed absolutely necessary to carry out its duties.

This interpretive difference has great meaning, because the Tenth Amendment reserves to the states any powers not explicitly granted to the federal government, and article 1, section 10 forbids the states from interfering with the exercise of those explicit federal powers.

Thus, the broader "granting" interpretation of the Necessary and Proper Clause effectively reduces the states' autonomy in favor of stronger national regulation that states cannot challenge. By contrast, the narrower "limiting" interpretation skews the balance of power more toward the states.

On its face, the Supreme Court in *McCulloch v. Maryland* simply needed to decide whether the Constitution authorized Congress to charter a federal bank, and whether the state of Maryland had the right to tax its operation. However, all parties involved knew that the case would have a far-reaching impact on the ideological split between those who favored a strong, centralized federal government, and those who championed more autonomous states.

Author Biography

John Marshall was born near Germantown, Virginia, on September 24, 1755. His formal education on the Virginia frontier was sparse but classical, consisting of one year at a private academy and some home tutoring. At age twenty, he joined a Virginia militia as a lieutenant to fight in the Revolutionary War. In 1780, he left the military and returned to Virginia, where he briefly studied law at the College of William and Mary. He was admitted to the Virginia bar and moved to Richmond, where he set up a law practice and established a strong reputation for his work in the state's appeals court. Marshall also served in a legislative capacity as a member of the Virginia House of Delegates from 1782 to 1789, and in 1788 he was appointed as a delegate to the Virginia convention charged with ratifying or rejecting the newly proposed US Constitution.

Marshall's first federal appointment in the young United States government was to a diplomatic mission to France in 1797 under President John Adams. Upon his return, at the request of former president George Washington, Marshall successfully ran for the Richmond seat in the US House of Representatives as a member of the Federalist Party. He took this seat in late 1799, and by May of the following year, President Adams had appointed him secretary of state. In 1801, Adams appointed Marshall chief justice of the Supreme Court of the United States.

Marshall served on the Supreme Court for thirty-four years, during which time he wrote 519 of the 1,215 opinions issued by the court, including several landmark cases defining the court's powers to interpret the Constitution, such as *Marbury v. Madison* (1803). During the early years of his tenure, Marshall had considerable influence among his fellow justices, reflected in the strong Federalist leaning of many decisions from that time. This started to change around 1804, when President Thomas Jefferson, a distant cousin of Marshall's and a strong anti-Federalist, appointed the first of three new justices to the court. The country's rapid economic growth and western expansion in the 1810s and early 1820s led to many decisions on the balance of power between the federal and state governments, including *McCulloch v. Maryland*. By the late 1820s, Marshall's influence further declined as President Andrew Jackson's appointees arrived on the court, skewing the bench further in favor of states' rights.

Chief Justice John Marshall continued to serve on the US Supreme Court until his death in Philadelphia on July 6, 1835.

HISTORICAL DOCUMENT

Chief Justice Marshall delivered the opinion of the Court.

In the case now to be determined, the defendant, a sovereign State, denies the obligation of a law enacted by the legislature of the Union, and the plaintiff, on his part, contests the validity of an act which has been passed by the legislature of that State. The constitution of our country, in its most interesting and vital parts, is to be considered; the conflicting powers of the government of the Union and of its members, as marked in that constitution, are to be discussed; and an opinion given, which may essentially influence the great operations of the government. No tribunal can approach such a question without a deep sense of its importance, and of the awful responsibility involved in its decision. But it must be decided peacefully, or remain a source of hostile legislation, perhaps of hostility of a still more serious nature; and if it is to be so decided, by this tribunal alone can the decision be made. On the Supreme Court of the United States has the constitution of our country devolved this important duty.

The first question made in the cause is, has Congress power to incorporate a bank?

It has been truly said that this can scarcely be considered as an open question, entirely unprejudiced by the former proceedings of the nation respecting it. The principle now contested was introduced at a very early period of our history, has been recognized by many successive legislatures, and has been acted upon by the judicial department, in cases of peculiar delicacy, as a law of undoubted obligation. . . .

The power now contested was exercised by the first Congress elected under the present constitution. The bill for incorporating the Bank of the United States did not steal upon an unsuspecting legislature, and pass unobserved. Its principle was completely understood, and was opposed with equal zeal and ability. After being resisted, first in the fair and open field of debate, and afterwards in the executive cabinet, with as much persevering talent as any measure has ever experienced, and being supported by arguments which convinced minds as pure and as intelligent as this country can boast, it became a law. The original act was permitted to expire; but a short experience of the embarrassments to which the refusal to revive it exposed the government, convinced those who were most prejudiced against the measure of its necessity, and induced the passage of the present law. It would require no ordinary share of intrepidity to assert that a measure adopted under these circumstances was a bold and plain usurpation, to which the constitution gave no countenance.

These observations belong to the cause; but they are not made under the impression that, were the question entirely new, the law would be found irreconcilable with the constitution.

In discussing this question, the counsel for the State of Maryland have deemed it of some importance, in the construction of the constitution, to consider that instrument not as emanating from the people, but as the act of sovereign and independent States. The powers of the general government, it has been said, are delegated by the States, who alone are truly sovereign; and must be exercised in subordination to the States, who alone possess supreme dominion.

It would be difficult to sustain this proposition. The Convention which framed the constitution was indeed elected by the State legislatures. But the instrument, when it came from their hands, was a mere proposal, without obligation, or pretensions to it. It was reported to the then existing Congress of the United States, with a request that it might "be submitted to a convention of delegates, chosen in each State by the people thereof, under the recommendation of its legislature, for their assent and ratification." This mode of proceeding was adopted; and by the convention, by Congress, and by the State legislatures, the instrument was submitted to the people. They acted upon it in the only manner in which they can act safely, effectively, and wisely, on such a subject, by assembling in convention. It is true, they assembled in their several States—and where else should they have assembled? No political dreamer was ever wild enough to think of breaking down the lines which separate the States, and of compounding the American people into one common mass. Of consequence, when they act, they act in their States. But the measures they adopt do not, on that account, cease to be the measures of the people themselves, or become the measures of the State governments.

From these conventions the constitution derives its whole authority. The government proceeds directly from the people; is "ordained and established" in the name of the people; and is declared to be ordained, "in order to form a more perfect union, establish justice, ensure domestic tranquility, and secure the blessings of liberty to themselves and to their posterity." The assent of the States, in their sovereign capacity, is implied in calling a convention, and thus submitting that instrument to the people. But the people were at perfect liberty to accept or reject it; and their act was final. It required not the affirmance, and could not be negatived, by the State governments. The constitution, when thus adopted, was of complete obligation, and bound the State sovereignties. . . .

This government is acknowledged by all to be one of enumerated powers. The principle, that it can exercise only the powers granted to it . . . is now universally admitted. But the question respecting the extent of the powers actually granted, is perpetually arising, and will probably continue to arise, as long as our system shall exist. . . .

Among the enumerated powers, we do not find that of establishing a bank or creating a corporation. But there is no phrase in the instrument which, like the articles of confederation, excludes incidental or implied powers; and which requires that everything granted shall be expressly and minutely described. Even the 10th amendment . . . omits the word "expressly," and declares only, that the powers "not delegated to the United States, nor prohibited to the states, are reserved to the states or to the people." . . . A constitution, to contain an accurate detail of all the subdivisions of which its great powers will admit, and of all the means by which they may be carried into execution . . . would, probably, never be understood by the public. Its nature, therefore, requires, that only its great outlines should be marked.

Although, among the enumerated powers of government, we do not find the word "bank" or "incorporation," we find the great powers, to lay and collect taxes; to borrow money; to regulate commerce; to declare and conduct a war; and to raise and support armies and navies. . . . But it may with great reason be contended, that a government, entrusted with such ample powers . . . must also be entrusted with ample means for their execution. The power being given, it is the interest of the nation to facilitate its execution. . . .

But the constitution of the United States has not left the right of Congress to employ the necessary means, for the execution of the powers conferred on the government, to general reasoning. To its enumeration of powers is added that of making "all laws which shall be necessary and proper for carrying into execution the foregoing powers, and all other powers vested by this constitution, in the government of the United States, or in any department thereof."

The counsel for the State of Maryland have urged various arguments, to prove that this clause, though in terms a grant of power, is not so in effect; but is really restrictive of the general right, which might otherwise be implied, of selecting means for executing the enumerated powers. . . .

Let this be done in the case under consideration. The subject is the execution of those great powers on which the welfare of a nation essentially depends. It must have been the intention of those who gave these powers, to insure, as far as human prudence could insure, their beneficial execution. This could not be done by confiding the choice of means to such narrow limits as not to leave it in the power of Congress to adopt any which might be appropriate, and which were conducive to the end. This provision is made in a constitution intended to endure for ages to come, and, consequently, to be adapted to the various crises of human affairs. To have prescribed the means by which government should, in all future time, execute its powers, would have been to change, entirely, the character of the instrument, and give it the properties of a legal code. It would have been an unwise attempt to provide, by immutable rules, for exigencies which, if foreseen at all, must have been seen dimly, and which can be best provided for as they occur. To have declared that the best means shall not be used, but those alone without which the power given would be nugatory, would have been to deprive the legislature of the capacity to avail itself of experience, to exercise its reason, and to accommodate its legislation to circumstances. If we apply this principle of construction to any of the powers of the government, we shall find it so pernicious in its operation that we shall be compelled to discard it. . . .

Let the end be legitimate, let it be within the scope of the constitution, and all means which are appropriate, which are plainly adapted to that end, which are not prohibited, but consist with the letter and spirit of the constitution, are constitutional. . . .

Should Congress, in the execution of its powers, adopt measures which are prohibited by the constitution; or should Congress, under the pretext of executing its powers, pass laws for the accomplishment of objects not entrusted to the government; it would become the painful duty of this tribunal, should a case requiring such a decision come before it, to say that such an act was not the law of the land. But where the law is not prohibited, and is really calculated to effect any of the objects entrusted to the government, to undertake here to inquire into the degree of its necessity, would be to pass the line which circumscribes the judicial department, and to tread on legislative ground. This court disclaims all pretensions to such a power.

After this declaration, it can scarcely be necessary to say that the existence of State banks can have no possible influence on the question. No trace is to be found in the constitution of an intention to create a dependence of the government of the Union on those of the States, for the execution of the great powers assigned to it. Its means are adequate to its ends; and on those means alone was it expected to rely for the accomplishment of its ends. To impose on it the necessity of resorting to means which it cannot control, which another government may furnish or withhold, would render its course precarious, the result of its measures uncertain, and create a dependence on other governments, which might disappoint its most important designs, and is incompatible with the language of the constitution. But were it otherwise, the choice of means implies a right to choose a national bank in preference to State banks, and Congress alone can make the election.

After the most deliberate consideration, it is the unanimous and decided opinion of this Court, that the act to incorporate the Bank of the United States is a law made in pursuance of the constitution, and is a part of the supreme law of the land. . . .

It being the opinion of the Court, that the act incorporating the bank is constitutional; and that the power of establishing a branch in the State of Maryland might be properly exercised by the bank itself, we proceed to inquire—

Whether the State of Maryland may, without violating the constitution, tax that branch? . . .

There is no express provision for the case, but the claim has been sustained on a principle which so entirely pervades the constitution. . . . This great principle is, that the constitution and the laws made in pursuance thereof are supreme; that they control the constitution and laws of the respective states, and cannot be controlled by them. From this . . . other propositions are deduced as corollaries. . . .

That the power to tax involves the power to destroy. . . . If the states may tax one instrument, employed by the government in the execution of its powers, they may tax any and every other instrument. They may tax the mail; they may tax the mint; they may tax patent-rights; they may tax the papers of the custom-house; they may tax judicial process; they may tax all the means employed by the government, to an excess which would defeat all the ends of government. This was not intended by the American people. They did not design to make their government dependent on the states. . . .

The result is a conviction that the states have no power, by taxation or otherwise, to retard, impede, burden, or in any manner control, the operations of the constitutional laws enacted by congress to carry into execution the powers vested in the general government. This is, we think, the unavoidable consequence of that supremacy which the constitution has declared. We are unanimously of opinion, that the law passed by the legislature of Maryland, imposing a tax on the Bank of the United States, is unconstitutional and void.

GLOSSARY

affirmance: affirmation

charter: legal document establishing a corporation and defining its operations

devolved: passed on to

enumerated powers: powers explicitly granted to Congress in the US Constitution, primarily in article 1, section 8

intrepidity: fearlessness

nugatory: inconsequential; without force

plaintiff: an individual, business, or other entity suing another in a court of law

sovereign: having supreme power

Document Analysis

In the early days of the United States, there was much debate about whether a national bank should be established, and whether doing so would be permissible under the US Constitution. In 1791, the Congress chartered the First Bank of the United States, with the goals of establishing a consistent and stable currency, extending credit to encourage further expansion of US territory, and facilitating the collection of taxes from the states for the benefit of the newly founded nation. The bank was championed by those in the administration of President George Washington with Federalist leanings, including Treasury Secretary Alexander Hamilton, but was opposed by those who supported states' rights, including Secretary of State Thomas Jefferson. Under its charter, the First Bank of the United States was limited to twenty years of operation; in 1811, Congress debated renewing the charter, and the bank's opponents won the day: the charter was not renewed, and the First Bank of the United States ceased operations.

However, the War of 1812 and the Napoleonic Wars led to worldwide financial instability, and it became clear that some intervention was needed to keep the fledgling US economy on track. Some of the national bank's earlier opponents conceded that the bank had served a useful function during its tenure, and in 1817, the Second Bank of the United States began operations under a new twenty-year charter. The Second Bank's headquarters were in Philadelphia, Pennsylvania, but the bank established branch locations in a number of cities across the United States.

The Second Bank had opened and was operating a branch in Baltimore, Maryland, in 1817 when the state passed legislation that amounted to a tax on the operations of any bank not chartered in Maryland, which included the Second Bank. The new law required that out-of-state banks must print their notes on special paper purchased from the state, or pay $15,000 per year to be exempt from the requirement. Noncompliant banks would face stiff fines. This law was controversial, as it was reminiscent of the stamp taxes that England had forced upon legal documents prepared in the United States prior to the American Revolution.

James McCulloch, who was then acting as the head of the Baltimore branch of the Second Bank, refused to pay the tax. He was reported to the state and ordered to pay the fine for noncompliance, but the Second Bank fought back. The fine was first appealed in the Maryland state court, where a judge ruled against McCulloch and the Second Bank on the grounds that the entire notion of a federal bank was unconstitutional, as the Constitution did not explicitly authorize Congress to establish such a bank. The case was then appealed to the US Supreme Court—which, in its decision, reaffirmed the court's authority to determine the constitutionality of state and federal legislative actions with respect to the US Constitution.

The Trial

Oral argument in *McCulloch v. Maryland* began before the US Supreme Court on February 22, 1819, and lasted for nine days. The members of the Supreme Court, as well as the Congress and numerous state leaders, were quite interested in the arguments and the outcome of the case. So, moreover, was the general public: a quote from the letters of Justice Joseph Story noted that the arguments took place before "a crowded audience of ladies and gentlemen; the hall was full almost to suffocation, and many went away for want of room" (325). Indeed, it was widely recognized that this case held more significance than the simple taxation of a single bank branch.

Altogether, six attorneys argued before the Supreme Court. Arguing on behalf of McCulloch and the Second Bank of the United States was Daniel Webster, a well-respected attorney from Massachusetts who frequently appeared before the court; William Wirt, the attorney general of the United States; and William Pinkney, former US attorney general under President James Madison. Arguing on behalf of the state of Maryland was Joseph Hopkinson, a well-known attorney from Philadelphia; Walter Jones, a private attorney from Washington, DC, with a reputation for extensive legal knowledge; and Luther Martin, attorney general for the state of Maryland.

The Supreme Court issued its opinion on March 6, 1819, just three days after the conclusion of oral arguments—impressively fast for an opinion that filled more than 150 written pages. Chief Justice John Marshall wrote the opinion, which, to the surprise of many observers, was unanimous. The ruling established that Congress did indeed have the authority to charter a federal bank, and that Maryland did not have the power to tax that bank's operations. However, the legal justification behind the decision gave the case significant and long-lasting impact.

The Decision

In writing for the court, Chief Justice Marshall lays out four arguments explaining why Congress did in fact have the authority to establish a national bank. First, the court states that, since Congress had created the First Bank of the United States, it likewise had the authority to create the second. This logic seems dubious, but Chief Justice Marshall explains that the decision to create the First Bank was made by "minds as pure and as intelligent as this country can boast." He notes that "its principle was completely understood, and was opposed with equal zeal and ability," and that Congress nonetheless voted to charter the First Bank. He reasoned that, since the decision to charter a federal bank was not made lightly the first time around, the judgment of those who made that decision should be trusted and allowed to stand. Chief Justice Marshall further noted that the chartering of the Second Bank occurred after a "short experience of the embarrassments to which the refusal to revive it exposed the government"; in other words, the Second Bank was chartered in a somewhat rushed manner. Marshall acknowledges that laws passed in this way might be more suspect than those that are extensively debated, but that fact alone does not mean the law is "irreconcilable with the constitution." This is particularly true in this case, since the First Bank was chartered only after lengthy discussion.

Second, the court rejected Maryland's argument that the states retain full sovereignty because they were the entities that ratified the Constitution in the first place. Drafted in 1787 at the Constitutional Convention held in Philadelphia, the Constitution was then ratified over a period of two years by state-level ratification conventions. The fact that the Constitution was ratified at the state level formed the basis of Maryland's argument that it was really the states, not the people, who adopted the Constitution, therefore making the states the locus of sovereignty from which federal power is derived. Chief Justice Marshall writes, however, that "it is true, [the ratification conventions] assembled in their several States," but that "the measures they adopt do not, on that account, cease to be the measures of the people themselves."

The third and fourth arguments are tied closely together, and address the provisions of the Constitution directly. The court agreed that the power to charter a national bank was not explicitly granted to Congress in article 1, section 8 of the Constitution. However, Marshall writes that "there is no phrase in the instrument which . . . requires that everything granted shall be expressly and minutely described." In other words, there was nothing in the Constitution that restricted Congress's powers to that which was specifically enumerated. He further elaborates that the Constitution does provide for "great powers, to lay and collect taxes; to borrow money; to regulate commerce; to declare and conduct a war; and to raise and support armies and navies," and that as a result Congress "must also be entrusted with ample means for their execution." So while Congress may not explicitly have the power to establish a national bank, it implicitly has that power if establishing such a bank will help to execute constitutional duties such as collecting taxes and borrowing money. Marshall particularly emphasized that, because the Constitution was meant to be a living document subject to interpretation, any rulings on the extent of its provisions must be considered in a broader context, and not limited to a strict reading of the text.

This led into Marshall's final argument, which relied upon the Necessary and Proper Clause. This clause, which is found in article 1, section 8, clause 18, states that Congress can pass any law that is "necessary" and "proper" to carry out the powers granted to it by the Constitution. However, the word "necessary" led to disagreement over its interpretation: Maryland argued that it meant Congress could only enact laws that were absolutely necessary in order to carry out its powers, and that establishing a national bank was not absolutely necessary for the government to function. However, Chief Justice Marshall ultimately said that it referred to "all means which are appropriate" and was not intended to limit Congress to actions that were essentially a last resort. He justified this interpretation by noting that the Necessary and Proper Clause was listed among Congress's powers in article 8, rather than among its limitations in article 9, and also by noting again that the US Constitution was intended to be a flexible document subject to contextual interpretation. If this were not the case, he argues, it would "deprive the legislature of the capacity to avail itself of experience, to exercise its reason, and to accommodate its legislation to circumstances."

The decision on this point was significant in the long-running battle between federalism and states' rights. Chief Justice Marshall stated that the Necessary and Proper Clause was meant to be "an additional power" granted to Congress, rather than "a restriction on those already granted." This gave Congress broad authority to pass many specific provisions not explicitly addressed in the Constitution, as long as they could be justifiably related to a power that Congress *was* specifically granted by the Constitution. Further complicating the issue is that the Tenth Amendment, which was ratified as part of the Bill of Rights in 1791, states that any power "not delegated to the United States by the Constitution, nor prohibited by it to the States, are reserved to the States respectively, or to the people." This meant that any decision that expanded the power of the federal government necessarily limited the power of the states to legislate in that same area.

This tension informed the second part of the court's decision in *McCulloch v. Maryland*: once it was determined that the federal government had the authority to create the Second Bank of the United States, the Supreme Court had to decide whether it was permissible for the state of Maryland to tax the operations of the Baltimore branch.

On this point, the court established that Maryland did not have the power to tax the operation of the federal bank within its borders. Chief Justice Marshall clearly stated that "the power to tax involves the power to destroy," and that a state cannot "retard impede, burden, or in any manner control, the operations of the Constitutional laws enacted by congress to carry into execution" its powers and duties. To support this ruling, Marshall makes what is commonly referred to as a "slippery slope" argument: he suggests that, if the state is allowed to tax the bank, next it will tax the mail, the mint, the judicial process, the patent system, and any other federal government operation that occurs within its borders. He notes that this would effectively allow a state to shut down the operation of the federal government in that state, which would directly contradict the will of the people as expressed in the ratification of the US Constitution.

Reaction

The decision in *McCulloch v. Maryland* was not well received in states known for anti-Federalist views, primarily in the South. The decision was widely criticized in newspapers, including the *Richmond Enquirer*, of Marshall's own hometown. Within a few days of the court's opinion being issued, a writer using the pen name "Amphictyon" wrote an editorial criticizing Marshall on several points, including the issuance of a single court opinion (when, until a few years prior, each justice had generally issued his own opinion), and suggesting that his ruling might have been a result of political influence. The writer likewise noted that the ruling would have broad implications for the future development of the United States, particularly with respect to westward expansion and the creation of railroads, canals, and other matters affecting interstate travel and commerce; the decision in *McCulloch v. Maryland* would ensure that the federal government could always have the final say on these matters if it so desired. In a rare move, Marshall felt it necessary to defend the ruling in the popular media, publishing a piece titled "A Friend to the Union" in the Philadelphia newspapers. This piece reiterated a significant point in the original opinion, namely that it was the people and not the states who had ratified the Constitution, and expressed Marshall's belief that it was within the federal government's authority to take any actions necessary to preserve the nation on behalf of the people that had chosen to form it.

Alas, there was no clear resolution of this ideological split, either at the time of the *McCulloch* decision, or at present; the issue of the division of power between the federal and state governments continues to be debated.

Essential Themes

McCulloch v. Maryland was a landmark case for the US Supreme Court because of its ruling on the balance of power between federal and state governments, and the constitutional justifications provided for its decision. In the early days of the United States, opinion was starkly divided between those who favored strong federal regulation and those who favored state autonomy. This issue was addressed only vaguely in the Constitution itself. The federal government was granted several specifically enumerated powers, with only a few explicit limitations. Any power not specifically granted to the federal government was reserved for the states by operation of the Tenth Amendment. However, the Necessary and Proper Clause of article 1, section 8 complicated the interpretation of these provisions, and the balance of federal power and state autonomy hinged upon whether that clause was interpreted in a broad "power-granting" sense or a narrow "power-limiting" sense.

McCulloch v. Maryland was significant because, in writing for the court, Chief Justice Marshall stated that the Necessary and Proper Clause should be interpreted broadly. This meant that Congress did indeed have authority to pass laws on matters not explicitly mentioned in the Constitution, as long as those laws were "necessary and proper" to carrying out its constitutional duties. This extended to the establishment of the Second Bank of the United States, because Congress did have explicit authority in several related areas, including levying taxes, lending money, and funding armies and navies. Additionally, by prohibiting the state from taxing the national bank, the court clearly established a limit on states' power: a state cannot take an action that interferes with the federal government's exercise of its constitutionally authorized powers.

The ruling in *McCulloch v. Maryland* had far-reaching consequences for the growth and development of the United States and its government. This theme was present quite often during the early days of the United States, as common infrastructure was being established. For example, it frequently arose in the context of the Interstate Commerce Clause, a clause of the US Constitution that granted Congress the authority to regulate any economic activity that would cross state lines. This effectively gave the federal government ultimate authority over the establishment of railroads, canals, and roadways in new states and territories, which was vitally important as the United States expanded across North America. Additionally during Franklin D. Roosevelt's presidency, much of the legislation that formed the New Deal was upheld as constitutional because of the precedent establishing broad powers for the federal government. This expansiveness has been called into question many times throughout history, and sometimes Congress's acts are struck down as unconstitutional if they are deemed insufficiently closely related to its enumerated powers. But since the established precedent is for broad legislative authority, any reduction in this power must be justified by the court, rather than the other way around. As a result, this ideology and the US Supreme Court's decision in *McCulloch v. Maryland* had a significant impact on the federal-state balance of power throughout the history of the United States.

Tracey M. DiLascio, JD

Bibliography

Crompton, Samuel Willard. McCulloch v. Maryland: *Implied Powers of the Federal Government*. New York: Infobase, 2007. Print. Harrison, Maureen, and Steve Gilbert, eds. *Landmark Decisions of the United States Supreme Court IV*. La Jolla: Excellent, 1994. Print.

Killenbeck, Mark R. M'Culloch v. Maryland: *Securing a Nation*. Lawrence: UP of Kansas, 2006. Print.

Story, Joseph. *Life and Letters of Joseph Story*. Boston: Little, 1851. Print.

Additional Reading

Catterall, Ralph C. H. *The Second Bank of the United States*. Chicago: U of Chicago P, 1968. Print.

Cushman, Clare, Ed. *The Supreme Court Justices: Illustrated Biographies, 1789–1993*. Washington, DC: Congressional Quarterly, 1993. Print.

Gunther, Gerald, Ed. *John Marshall's Defense of McCulloch v. Maryland*. Stanford: Stanford UP, 1969. Print.

Hall, Kermit L., ed. *The Oxford Guide to United States Supreme Court Decisions*. New York: Oxford UP, 1999. Print.

LESSON PLAN: **Powers Under the Constitution**

Students analyze a Supreme Court decision in a landmark case that set a precedent in US history.

Learning Objectives

Assess the importance of the Supreme Court in making precedent-setting decisions based on interpretations of the Constitution; appraise the decision in *McCulloch v. Maryland, written by Chief Justice John Marshall,* in establishing the Supreme Court as an independent and equal branch of government; formulate examples of how a different ruling might have led to different consequences; draw comparisons across eras to evaluate the influence of the court's ruling in the case.

Materials: *McCulloch v. Maryland* (1819); US Constitution.

Overview Questions

What precedent did the Supreme Court set in its ruling in *McCulloch v. Maryland*? Why was it important? Which amendment would states' rights advocates cite to refute the court's decision? How might the outcome have been different if the court had ruled in favor of the state of Maryland? What other Supreme Court cases in US history strengthened the power of the federal government?

Step 1: Comprehension Questions

What precedent did the Supreme Court set in its ruling in *McCulloch v. Maryland*? Why was it important? How did Chief Justice Marshall support his opinion? What impact did this ruling have on the role of the Supreme Court?

- **Activity:** Select students to read aloud from Marshall's opinion in the case; ask them to underline references to the Constitution and to read those references in the Constitution.

Step 2: Comprehension Questions

What effect did this decision have on the power of the Supreme Court?

- **Activity:** Engage students in a class discussion on the effects of the court's decision and what precedent the ruling in the case set.

Step 3: Context Questions

Which amendment would states' rights advocates cite to refute Marshall's argument? How might the outcome have been different if the court had ruled in favor of the state of Maryland?

- **Activity:** Have students work in pairs to review the first ten amendments to the Constitution, identifying which amendment states' rights supporters would use against Marshall's decision; then ask them to write a paragraph to explain the possible effects of a different ruling.

Step 4: Exploration Questions

What other Supreme Court cases in US history strengthened the power of the federal government?

- **Activity:** Have students work in small groups to research other Supreme Court cases that have strengthened the power of the federal government, such as *Marbury v. Madison* (1803) and *Gibbons v. Ogden* (1824); ask students to each write a summary to explain the results of their research.

Step 5: Response Paper

Word length and additional requirements set by Instructor. Students answer the research question in the *Overview Questions*. Students state a thesis and use as evidence passages from the primary source document as well as support from supplemental materials assigned in the lesson.

■ The Monroe Doctrine

Date: December 2, 1823
Author: Monroe, James
Genre: speech

"The American continents, by the free and independent condition which they have assumed and maintain, are henceforth not to be considered as subjects for future colonization by any European powers."

Summary Overview

Since its creation, the Monroe Doctrine has been one of the pivotal foreign policy statements by the US government. It has been used to shield Central and South America from European intervention and, with the addition of the Roosevelt Corollary in 1904, as the justification for American intervention into the affairs of countries in these areas. President James Monroe, having been persuaded by then Secretary of State John Quincy Adams, announced the doctrine to deter Spain and France from trying to reacquire control of Spain's former colonies in South America. In addition, Russia was expanding its territorial claims on the west coast of North America. The Monroe Doctrine was a unilateral American response to the international forces that seemed to be hemming in the United States. It has remained in force ever since it was announced in 1823 and is a foundation for American policy with other nations in the Western Hemisphere.

Defining Moment

Once Christopher Columbus's discovery of the "New World" became widely known throughout Europe, the European push to acquire the lands and resources of the Western Hemisphere resulted in the colonization of the North and South American continents and the adjacent islands. In 1776, the first colonies proclaimed and secured their independence, creating the United States. Beginning with Haiti in 1804, independent nations began to emerge from former European colonies in Central and South America. By the early 1820s, virtually all of Spain's mainland colonies had been successful in their revolutions. The United States recognized the new nations. Even though it was less than a decade after the end of the War of 1812, the relationship between the United States and Great Britain had warmed considerably. There was a strong common economic interest in trading with the nations that were emerging in Central and South America. However, at the same time, other changes were underway in Europe. After the Napoleonic Wars (1803–15), many continental European countries and governments were trying to reconstitute themselves. Several countries assisted in the solidification of power by the Bourbon royal family in Spain and were advocating that Spain retake its former colonies.

In response to this, Great Britain contacted the United States to work together to thwart the Spanish and French plans. Britain's desire to work against France and Spain stemmed from both political and economic interests. The British government proposed sending a joint message with the United States that colonization was not acceptable. The good relations evolving between the United States and Great Britain made President Monroe interested in the British proposition. He consulted his predecessors (Thomas Jefferson and James Madison) who believed working with the British would be beneficial. However, Adams was strongly against making any joint statements with the British. Over the last few months of 1823, Adams swayed Monroe to the position that a unilateral statement would be best.

Thus, in his seventh State of the Union address to Congress, President Monroe included the passage that came to be known as the Monroe Doctrine. The European powers were not impressed, as they knew that the United States did not have a strong military. However, Great Britain accepted President Monroe's declaration and let the other European powers know of its support. Thus, for its first few decades, the Monroe Doctrine was actually enforced by the strength of the British navy. The result of Monroe's pronouncement was that neither Spain nor any other European power tried to retake the newly independent countries.

Author Biography

James Monroe was born on April 28, 1858, to Spencer and Elizabeth Jones Monroe in Westmoreland County, Virginia. He graduated from Campbelltown Academy at age sixteen, the year his father died. He attended the College of William and Mary leaving school after a year to join the Third Virginia Regiment. As a planter owning more than twenty slaves, Monroe was automatically made an officer. During the Revolutionary War, he was wounded at the Battle of Trenton and then left the army in 1780.

Monroe believed that the legal profession would be the quickest way to financial success, so he studied law under Jefferson. After passing the bar in 1783, he remained in Virginia; however, he had to sell his family's plantation to establish his legal practice. He married Elizabeth Kortright in 1786, and they had three children, two of whom survived to become adults.

During the 1780s Monroe served in Virginia's House of Delegates and in three sessions of the Continental Congress. During the fight for Virginia's ratification of the Constitution in 1788, Monroe was one of the swing voters, finally voting for the new system of government, accepting the promise that a Bill of Rights would be added immediately. He became a senator in 1790. After serving about three and a half years, Monroe resigned to become ambassador to France. Sympathetic to the French Revolution, Monroe was able to free all the Americans who had been jailed during the turmoil. After serving for three years, and having policy disagreements with President George Washington, he returned to the United States, where he once again became active in the Democratic-Republic political movement headed by Jefferson.

In 1799, Monroe was elected to the first of his four nonsequential terms as governor of Virginia. He then accepted a commission from President Jefferson to return to France to negotiate the Louisiana Purchase. After completing that task in 1803, he was appointed ambassador to Great Britain. Returning to the United States in 1807, Monroe refused an offer to run against Jefferson's handpicked successor, Madison, accepting instead the position of secretary of state. He served in that position until October, 1914, when he was appointed secretary of war. However, no one filled his state position, so he unofficially filled two cabinet posts until the end of the War of 1812 when he resigned from the secretary of war position and was reappointed to the State Department. In 1817, he became the fifth president of the United States with only token opposition, due to the rapid decline of the Federalist Party. For his 1820 reelection he had no opposition. Retiring from politics in 1825, he died on July 4, 1831.

HISTORICAL DOCUMENT

At the proposal of the Russian Imperial Government, made through the minister of the Emperor residing here, a full power and instructions have been transmitted to the minister of the United States at St. Petersburg to arrange by amicable negotiation the respective rights and interests of the two nations on the northwest coast of this continent. A similar proposal has been made by His Imperial Majesty to the Government of Great Britain, which has likewise been acceded to. The Government of the United States has been desirous by this friendly proceeding of manifesting the great value which they have invariably attached to the friendship of the Emperor and their solicitude to cultivate the best understanding with his Government. In the discussions to which this interest has given rise and in the arrangements by which they may terminate the occasion has been judged proper for asserting, as a principle in which the rights and interests of the United States are involved, that the American continents, by the free and independent condition which they have assumed and maintain, are henceforth not to be considered as subjects for future colonization by any European powers . . .

It was stated at the commencement of the last session that a great effort was then making in Spain and Portugal to improve the condition of the people of those countries, and that it appeared to be conducted with extraordinary moderation. It need scarcely be remarked that the results have been so far very different from what was then anticipated. Of events in that quarter of the globe, with which we have so much intercourse and from which we derive our origin, we have always been anxious and interested spectators. The citizens of the United States cherish sentiments the most friendly in favor of the liberty and happiness of their fellow-men on that side of the Atlantic. In the wars of the European powers in matters relating to themselves we have never taken any part, nor does it comport with our policy to do so. It is only when our rights are invaded or seriously menaced that we resent injuries or make preparation for our defense. With the movements in this hemisphere we are of necessity more immediately connected, and by causes which must be obvious to all enlightened and impartial observers. The political system of the allied powers is essentially different in this respect from that of America. This difference proceeds from that which exists in their respective Governments; and to the defense of our own, which has been achieved by the loss of so much blood and treasure, and matured by the wisdom of their most enlightened citizens, and under which we have enjoyed unexampled felicity, this whole nation is devoted.

We owe it, therefore, to candor and to the amicable relations existing between the United States and those powers to declare that we should consider any attempt on their part to extend their system to any portion of this hemisphere as dangerous to our peace and safety. With the existing colonies or dependencies of any European power we have not interfered and shall not interfere. But with the Governments who have declared their independence and maintain it, and whose independence we have, on great consideration and on just principles, acknowledged, we could not view any interposition for the purpose of oppressing them, or controlling in any other manner their destiny, by any European power in any other light than as the manifestation of an unfriendly disposition toward the United States. In the war between those new Governments and Spain we declared our neutrality at the time of their recognition, and to this we have adhered, and shall continue to adhere, provided no change shall occur which, in the judgement of the competent authorities of this Government, shall make a corresponding change on the part of the United States indispensable to their security.

The late events in Spain and Portugal show that Europe is still unsettled. Of this important fact no stronger proof can be adduced than that the allied powers should have thought it proper, on any principle satisfactory to themselves, to have interposed by force in the internal concerns of Spain. To what extent such interposition may be carried, on the same principle, is a question in which all independent powers whose governments differ from theirs are interested, even those most remote, and surely none of them more so than the United States. Our policy in regard to Europe, which was adopted at an early stage of the wars which have so long agitated that quarter of the globe, nevertheless remains the same, which is, not to interfere in the internal concerns of any of its powers; to consider the government de facto as the legitimate government for us; to cultivate friendly relations with it, and to preserve those relations by a frank, firm, and manly policy, meeting in all instances the just claims of every power, submitting to injuries from none. But in regard to those continents circumstances are eminently and conspicuously different.

It is impossible that the allied powers should extend their political system to any portion of either continent without endangering our peace and happiness; nor can anyone believe that our southern brethren, if left to themselves, would adopt it of their own accord. It is equally impossible, therefore, that we should behold such interposition in any form with indifference. If we look to the comparative strength and resources of Spain and those new Governments, and their distance from each other, it must be obvious that she can never subdue them. It is still the true policy of the United States to leave the parties to themselves, in hope that other powers will pursue the same course.

GLOSSARY

acceded: in international law, to become a party to an agreement

allied powers: The Holy Alliance, formed in 1815, of Austria, Prussia, and Russia to push a conservative agenda in domestic policies and international relations

interposition: to forcibly exert influence into a situation

minister of the United States: the US ambassador

movements in this hemisphere: the revolutionary movements against Spain

new governments: in this context, governments being formed in the former Spanish colonies in Central and South America

this hemisphere: the Western Hemisphere, another way of referring to North and South America and the related islands. The small portion of Africa and the part of Great Britain that are actually in the Western Hemisphere are not usually included in this designation.

Document Analysis

In his seventh State of the Union address, President Monroe spent an extensive amount of time focusing on foreign relations. After the usual patriotic and conciliatory statements that open any State of the Union address, Monroe transitioned directly to US relations with other countries and the changed situation in the Western Hemisphere. He sought to give Congress and the American people, "a precise knowledge of our relations with foreign powers." While Monroe went well beyond simply stating the Monroe Doctrine, which is only about 15 percent of the speech, most of the speech did deal with related issues. Monroe understood that the 1820s were a pivotal time for the United States, during which the country could increase its political security and economic opportunities. Even though the Monroe Doctrine was not known by that name until the 1840s, the ideals set forth were immediately accepted by Americans. Monroe was the last president who is considered a Founding Father as well as the last president who had participated in the Revolutionary War. Because he had witnessed the birth of the nation and its initial steps toward true independence, Monroe knew that it was vital for the United States to claim a role for itself among the leading nations of the global community and also to help create a place in this system for the other new nations of Central and South America.

The first paragraph of the portion of the speech that is specifically considered the Monroe Doctrine can be found about one-fifth of the way through. After the greeting and introductory section of the speech, President Monroe specifically discussed portions of the Treaty of Ghent, which ended the War of 1812. Certain provisions of that treaty established commissions to deal with specific issues of long term importance. Monroe did not report that agreement had been reached on the three areas under discussion. However, it can be inferred that the fact that Great Britain and the United States were continuing to discuss these issues was mentioned by Monroe in order to indicate the close relationship that was beginning to develop between the two former adversaries. After that relationship was lifted, Monroe went on to mention problems with France over "several important subjects." Again, this was a signal that although Monroe had favored France a decade or more earlier, this was no longer the case. Following the chastisement of France, Monroe moved into the situation with Russia, which is the opening paragraph of the Monroe Doctrine.

Although Central and South America were the main focus of the Monroe Doctrine, what was actually the most pressing issue in 1823 was the possible expansion of Russian colonial activities on the West Coast of North America. During the eighteenth century, the Russian Empire had pushed eastward from Siberia to the islands and mainland of what is now Alaska. The desire for valuable furs enticed the Russians first to trade with the native population and then to establish settlements in Alaska. As with other European incursions into North America, the relations between the natives and Russians were not always peaceful, but eventually an agreement was reached allowing for good relations. As fur prices fell, larger quantities were needed for any possible profit. This meant moving further south to areas where sea otters had not been overhunted. This foray took the Russians as far south as Fort Ross in California, where a permanent settlement was established in 1812. Thus, from that point north, the coastal region was being claimed by Russia, Great Britain, and the United States. These were the issues referred to in the first paragraph of the text.

President Monroe acknowledged that Russia had invited both the United States and Great Britain to bilateral talks regarding this territory. Thus, President Monroe looked forward to "discussions to which this interest has given rise and the arrangements by which they may terminate the occasion." The prospect of a treaty for a peaceful conclusion to Russian claims beyond their historic claim in Alaska was important for Monroe. Later in the doctrine, he stated that regarding existing colonies, the United States has "not interfered and shall not interfere." As Russia had been in Alaska since before the United States existed, its claim to that territory was not covered by the doctrine. However, claims further south were less certain, thus the desire for a treaty. It took less than five months from the time President Monroe gave this speech for an agreement to be reached between Russia and the United States. Russia gave up all claims to territory below what is now the southern tip of Alaska's panhandle. (This did not include Fort Ross in California because, even though the exact northern border of California had yet to be determined, Fort Ross was clearly in what had been Spanish and what became Mexican territory.) Within a year after signing the treaty with the United States, Russia signed virtually the same treaty with Great Britain, leaving the United States and Great Britain to work out who would control what became Oregon, Washington, and British Columbia.

The first paragraph of the Monroe Doctrine concluded with a statement that was the key to the rest of the document. It said, "the American continents, by the free and independent condition which they have assumed and maintain, are henceforth not to be considered as subjects for future colonization by any European powers." This has been understood to be the fundamental position of the United States ever since the day it was proclaimed. Although technically slighted by the American refusal to issue a joint statement with them, the British did not respond negatively to Monroe's statement. What was important to the British was that the new nations remain open to British trade and other economic interests. American merchants wanted similar opportunities, but the dominant concern for the United States was not to be pulled into the European conflicts that had unleashed massive destruction throughout that continent. President Washington had warned against getting entangled in European affairs, and if the restructured European powers were going to attempt to expand their holdings in the Western Hemisphere, US isolationist policy would be in jeopardy. Thus, President Monroe believed that a statement of US policy toward the new countries was necessary.

After the dramatic statement at the close of the first paragraph of what is considered the Monroe Doctrine, President Monroe then spent a considerable amount of time outlining the situation with specific nations and the ongoing trend in US foreign policy. He then dealt with a number of appropriations for the military, as well as actions taken by the military during the preceding year. President Monroe then spent just over 20 percent of his speech on domestic issues, including the post office, roads, a proposed canal from the Chesapeake Bay to the Ohio River, and various harbor infrastructure upgrades. Next, he returned to foreign affairs, mentioning his support for those in Greece seeking to win their independence from the Ottoman Empire. The rest of the speech continued his presentation of the Monroe Doctrine.

Monroe began by briefly describing part of the situation in Europe, and the errors that had been made in previous predictions. The Iberian Peninsula had been in turmoil since the invasion of Napoleon. The monarch had stepped aside for Napoleon, but the people, with British assistance, had continued to fight. In 1812, a liberal constitution was written, establishing a national assembly and limitations on any future monarch. When Ferdinand VI returned to the throne in 1814, he abolished the constitution. This led to a series of revolts, and in 1820, he was forced to accept the constitution. This was the "liberty and happiness" to which Monroe referred. However, "the results have been so far very different from what was then anticipated" was Monroe's way of pointing to the restoration of a Spanish absolute monarchy by French forces, as authorized by the Holy Alliance, which consisted of Austria, Prussia, and Russia. (This political philosophy of these absolute monarchies was mentioned by Monroe through his statement, "political system of the allied powers is essentially different in this respect from that of America.") Monroe indicated that, as regarded European wars, the United States has, "never taken any part, nor does it comport with our policy to do so." The full restoration of the Spanish monarchy had occurred earlier in 1823. Ferdinand wanted not only to reestablish the old form of government but also to bring the empire back to its former glory. He was warned not to do this when Monroe stated that events in the Western Hemisphere "are of necessity more immediately connected" with the concerns of the United States.

In the next section, Monroe amplified his warning by stating that the United States would see as a threat to its security any attempts by European powers to pull former American colonies back into any country's sphere of political and economic influence. He began this section by stating that the United States had good relations with the European countries, even though they had a different system of government. Thus, the United States was willing to cooperate with them and to allow them to continue to keep any existing colonies. However, by the time President Monroe announced this doctrine, all mainland Spanish and Portuguese colonies had declared their independence and were well on their way to achieving it. Monroe reminded Spain, and other European powers, that the United States had not participated in the wars of independence. However, once the new nations were established, the United States would not stand by and let any European power take actions "for the purpose of oppressing" the former colonies, nor would the United States stand by if Spain tried to make changes in its relationship with its former colonies that caused concerns for "their security."

President Monroe went on to comment on the situation in Europe and what it said about the various nations. Using Spain and Portugal as examples, Monroe referred to the unsettled conditions in those countries. Portugal was in the midst of several changes, all stemming from the Napoleonic Wars. During those conflicts, the royal family had fled to Brazil and seemed quite content to rule from there. However, Portugal believed it was superior to Brazil and therefore demanded the royal family return to rule from Lisbon, with Brazil returned to colonial status. In 1821, the king returned as a constitutional monarch, and in 1822, his son declared Brazil independent. This left a void in Portugal's government, as there was no heir for the crown, and resulted in ongoing struggles between those who wanted a constitutional monarchy and those who wanted one with absolute powers. Similarly, in Spain the turmoil and conflict continued between those who advocated for an absolute monarchy and those who desired a constitutional government. Monroe spoke of his beliefs regarding the inappropriateness of the Holy Alliance "to have interposed by force in the internal concerns of Spain." Monroe questioned how far these countries were willing to go to try to change others.

Even with these concerns, however, Monroe stated that he still followed the foreign policy that "was adopted at an early stage of the wars," the policy first advocated by President Washington. In addition, it was the American policy "to consider the government de facto as the legitimate government for us." This meant that no matter how a government had come into power, or what political system was used by the government, the United States was willing to work with whatever government was ruling a country at that point in time. The United States would try to develop good relations with governments of all countries, accepting "just claims of every power" while allowing "injuries from none." This was the norm for Europe, with whom the United States had its dealings when independence was achieved. However, in the last sentence of this section Monroe noted that things had changed; with other independent countries existing in North and South America. Monroe asserted, "in regard to those continents circumstances are eminently and conspicuously different."

President Monroe closed the Monroe Doctrine with a warning to the Holy Alliance, as Spain had been wracked by wars and would not have had the power to try to regain its former colonies without assistance. Monroe asserted that the people of Central and South America would not freely choose to return to being colonies or return to being governed by European absolute monarchs. Thus, if the European powers tried to force their views on the former colonies, the United States could not view this "with indifference." President Monroe believed that Spain "can never subdue them," thus it would need assistance. He closed with the hope that the policy of noninterference that the United States tended to follow would be followed by all nations of the world.

Monroe closed his State of the Union address with references to the large increase in both the population and territory of the United States. He asserted that these increases not only made the nation stronger but also allowed the federal system to work more effectively. He believed that the United States was stronger and more unified than at any time in the past, which was a veiled warning to any European country that might want to support Spain's thoughts of regaining its colonies. Throughout his speech to Congress, President Monroe made it clear that the United States was adamant in its views supporting the new nations of the Western Hemisphere and asserted that it had the power to carry out the Monroe Doctrine. Fortunately, it was a few decades before the country was tested as to its resolve and strength.

Essential Themes

There is one central theme in the Monroe Doctrine: the continents of North and South America, and the nearby islands, were no longer to be considered available for colonization or conquest by European powers. Underlying this was the almost continuous warfare that had been taking place in Europe ever since the beginning of Washington's presidency. The United States had been drawn into the War of 1812, in part, because of the restrictions that Britain had placed on trade. As the United States wanted the opportunity to trade with the emerging nations of the Western Hemisphere, President Monroe wanted to be clear about American intentions. In addition, at the conclusion of the Napoleonic Wars, conservative monarchies developed an alliance that pushed its agenda not only in its own countries but also in places such as Spain. The United States was willing to accept other forms of government in Europe but did not believe the former colonies wanted, or would accept, an absolute monarchy forced on them from the outside.

Leaders of the Latin American countries responded positively to Monroe's statement, as they were in the midst of their last battles for full independence in South America. However, they recognized that this was a national policy for the United States and as such would be used in the interests of United States, not of the emerging nations. Secretary of State Adams advocated this policy to Monroe as a statement of total opposition to colonization. It seems that Monroe, and most others, did not hold views as extreme as Adams's. In just over a decade, the policy spelled out in the Monroe Doctrine was used to keep Britain from developing strong ties with Texas, and within three decades, it was used to keep the British out of Hawaii, so that the United States could control that area. Theodore Roosevelt extended the policy even further by asserting that the Monroe Doctrine gave the United States the right, and the duty, to intervene when problems arose in Latin America. Although it has been interpreted differently down through the decades, the Monroe Doctrine has been one of the most enduring policies of the American government.

Donald A. Watt, PhD

Bibliography

"American President: James Monroe (1758-1831)." *Miller Center, University of Virginia*. Rector and Visitors of the University of Virginia, 2013. Web. 26 Aug. 2012.

Cunningham, Noble E. *The Presidency of James Monroe*. Lawrence: UP of Kansas, 1996. Print.

Office of the Historian. "Monroe Doctrine, 1823." *Office of the Historian*. Office of the Historian, Bureau of Public Affairs, US Department of State, n.d. Web. 26 Aug. 2012.

---. "Roosevelt Corollary to the Monroe Doctrine, 1904." *Office of the Historian*. Office of the Historian, Bureau of Public Affairs, US Department of State, n.d. Web. 26 Aug. 2012.

Additional Reading

Bemis, Samuel Flagg. *John Quincy Adams and the Foundations of American Foreign Policy*. New York: Knopf, 1949. Print.

Borgens, Edward G. *Background of the Monroe Doctrine*. New York: Vantage, 2004. Print.

Hart, Gary. *James Monroe*. New York: Times Books, 2005. Print.

May, Ernest R. *The Making of the Monroe Doctrine*. Cambridge: Belknap-Harvard UP, 1975. Print.

LESSON PLAN: **President Monroe's Warning**

Students analyze a speech by James Monroe to consider developing American foreign policy in the early nineteenth century.

Learning Objectives

Analyze the influence of the Monroe Doctrine to reconstruct patterns of historical succession and duration; evaluate the implementation of Monroe's call for US involvement in foreign affairs; assess the continuing importance of the doctrine to American foreign policy.

Materials: James Monroe, "The Monroe Doctrine" (1823).

Overview Questions

What does the Monroe Doctrine declare? Why does Monroe think it necessary to issue this warning? How does the doctrine reflect the changing role of the United States in the early 1800s? How did the doctrine stand to shape American policy and identity for centuries to follow?

Step 1: Comprehension Questions

What warning does Monroe issue in this doctrine? What message did it send to European powers? What events led Monroe to make this declaration?

- **Activity:** Pair students to review paragraphs two and three and write a summary of Monroe's message to Portugal and Spain. Have students use their summaries to discuss what events with Spain and Portugal led Monroe to send this message.

Step 2: Context Questions

Why does Monroe think it necessary to overturn President George Washington's policy of neutrality? What factors does he think justify American involvement in foreign affairs?

- **Activity:** Remind students that Washington thought the United States should not become involved in foreign affairs. Have students draw inferences about why Monroe reverses this policy, citing passages to support their claims.

Step 3: Context Questions

What does the doctrine suggest about the US position in North and South America? How did it reflect the country's increasing power across the continent? Why might it have been interpreted as an assertion of US hegemony?

- **Activity:** Divide students into two groups. Have one group give a speech advocating for the prominent position of the United States in the Americas. Have the other group give a speech criticizing the United States for this role. Remind groups to include information from the doctrine in their speeches.

Step 4: Historical Connections Questions

Why might the doctrine have proved a defining document in US history? How did it stand to impact the Americas in the nineteenth century? Why might future presidents have continued to invoke the doctrine when making foreign policy decisions?

- **Activity:** Have students discuss what they know about US involvement in the Americas in the twentieth century. Ask them how the Monroe Doctrine might have been used to justify American involvement in other countries. Based on these examples, have students consider the impact of this document over time.

Step 5: Response Paper

Word length and additional requirements set by Instructor. Students answer the research question in the *Overview Questions*. Students state a thesis and use as evidence passages from the primary source document as well as support from supplemental materials assigned in the lesson.

Gibbons v. Ogden

Date: March 2, 1824
Author: Marshall, John
Genre: court opinion; constitution; law

"When a State proceeds to regulate commerce with foreign nations, or among the several States, it is exercising the very power that is granted to Congress, and is doing the very thing which Congress is authorized to do."

Summary Overview

The decision by Chief Justice John Marshall in the 1824 Supreme Court case of *Gibbons v. Ogden* was a landmark ruling that ended the steamboat navigation monopoly originally granted to Robert R. Livingston and Robert Fulton by the New York State legislature. The Livingston-Fulton monopoly controlled all steamboat traffic between New York City and Albany along the Hudson River. Their successful manufacture and operation of steamboats on the Hudson River revolutionized the speed and efficiency, not to mention the cost, at which goods and passengers could be transported regionally. A crucial channel for interstate trade and travel, the New York monopoly prevented any outside steam-powered vessel from entering New York waterways. The monopoly held by Livingston and Fulton, therefore, was widely reviled and after years of litigation defending the steamboat monopoly, the *Gibbons v. Ogden* decision declared the state-granted monopoly to be in conflict with Congress's right to regulate commerce. The *Gibbons* decision abolished the right of any state to protect transportation monopolies that affected interstate commerce.

Defining Moment

In 1808, American engineer Robert Fulton succeeded in launching the *Clermont*, a steamboat able to move upriver faster than five miles per hour. The *Clermont* made it possible to travel from New York City to Albany on the Hudson River within thirty-two hours. The New York legislature, impressed by the success of this joint venture by Fulton and his business partner Robert Livingston, not only provided them with a monopoly on state steamboat transportation, but included provisions in the monopoly that expanded their entitlement for thirty years and dictated that any steamboat entering New York waters without the consent of Livingston and Fulton be seized by the state. The monopoly kept out other entrepreneurial steamboat ventures that sought navigational routes in New York waterways and forced peripheral routes to pay significant licensing fees to operate. The Livingston-Fulton monopoly was deeply unpopular with regional business and the public alike, and the monopoly endured a significant number of legal challenges while in effect. The strong familial and political connections of Robert Livingston in the New York legislature and court system, however, secured the injunction's legacy until challenged in the Supreme Court in 1824. Though Livingston and Fulton were often the direct targets of cases challenging their exclusive navigation rights, the case that ultimately reached the Supreme Court and dismantled these exclusive rights involved neither of the men so famously associated with the monopoly.

The complainant in the critical constitutional case was Aaron Ogden, a former governor of New Jersey, who held the majority interest in a steamboat line between New York City and Elizabethtown, New Jersey. Although he had at one point been an aggressive challenger of the Livingston-Fulton monopoly, Ogden was unsuccessful in his efforts and instead joined the monopoly as a licensed operator. Thomas Gibbons had moved from Georgia to Elizabethtown, New Jersey, and entered into a business venture with Ogden upon his arrival. The contentious relationship that developed between Ogden and Gibbons, however, had as much to do with personal animosity as with business matters. Gibbons had long been involved in a family conflict over matters of inheritance with his daughter and her husband. Ogden, at one point, inserted himself into the Gibbons' family matter, taking the side of Gibbons's daughter against Gibbons himself. After this event, the two men's relationship devolved quickly. The following year, Gibbons began a steamboat operation that ran the same route Ogden had claimed under the Livingston-Fulton monopoly. Ogden took Gibbons to court for violating the dictates of the monopoly, and the two men pursued their case all the way to the Supreme Court. The decision handed down in *Gibbons v. Ogden* presented a broad interpretation of what constituted interstate commerce, and ultimately reserved for the Supreme Court the right to determine when state law was in violation of congressional power to regulate interstate commerce. Marshall's majority opinion in the case employed his well-known use of narrow constitutional interpretation, which worked to strengthen the authority of the federal government without dismantling the rights of the states.

Author Biography

John Marshall, the fourth chief justice of the US Supreme Court, was born in 1755 and grew up in the developing counties of Virginia's frontier territories. Marshall's formative years were spent engaged in the political challenges and physical battles of the Revolutionary War. He became an officer in the Continental army in his early twenties and experienced firsthand the challenges and hardships that accompanied fighting a war in a new country that had yet to form a central government authoritative enough to draw military provisions and resources from its states to relieve suffering troops. Despite the organizational challenges, Marshall was profoundly influenced by the nationalistic goals of the Revolutionary War.

Marshall's only formal training in the legal profession came from George Wythe, a prominent Virginia judge. The future Supreme Court justice attended a brief course taught by Wythe in Williamsburg, Virginia, while he was on leave from his duties with the army. Though aspiring for a career in law, the disruption of the Revolutionary War prevented Marshall from starting his own law practice. Instead, Marshall joined the Virginia legislature. Though unsatisfied with the slow process of the legislature, Marshall spent a good portion of his career in and out of office in Virginia. Marshall's experiences with the Revolutionary War, both positive and negative, as well as his familiarity with the important but often inefficient function of state legislatures profoundly influenced Marshall's conviction in the need for a federalist system supported by a strong, centralized government.

Marshall held positions in both legislative and legal institutions for twenty years in the state of Virginia. In 1799, however, Marshall embarked on a national political career. Marshall served in the House of Representatives and as President John Adams's secretary of state. Marshall retained that position for only one year, however, before he was appointed by Adams to the position of chief justice of the Supreme Court in 1801. Over the course of his career, Marshall wrote the deciding opinions for several landmark Supreme Court cases. Marshall's legacy as chief justice has proven to be one of the most enduring and significant in the history of the Supreme Court. The Marshall Court advanced foundational court opinions that continue to shape constitutional law through the present.

HISTORICAL DOCUMENT

The appellant contends that this decree is erroneous because the laws which purport to give the exclusive privilege it sustains are repugnant to the Constitution and laws of the United States. They are said to be repugnant: first, to that clause in the Constitution which authorizes Congress to regulate commerce; second, to that which authorizes Congress to promote the progress of science and useful arts.

As preliminary to the very able discussions of the Constitution which we have heard from the bar, and as having some influence on its construction, reference has been made to the political situation of these states, anterior to its formation. It has been said that they were sovereign, were completely independent, and were connected with each other only by a league. This is true. But, when these allied sovereigns converted their league into a government, when they converted their congress of ambassadors, deputed to deliberate on their common concerns, and to recommend measures of general utility, into a legislature, empowered to enact laws on the most interesting subjects, the whole character in which the states appear underwent a change, the extent of which must be determined by a fair consideration of the instrument by which that change was effected.

This instrument contains an enumeration of powers expressly granted by the people to their government. It has been said that these powers ought to be construed strictly. But why ought they to be so construed? Is there one sentence in the Constitution which gives countenance to this rule? In the last of the enumerated powers, that which grants, expressly, the means for carrying all others into execution, Congress is authorized *to make all laws which shall be necessary and proper* for the purpose. But this limitation on the means which may be used is not extended to the powers which are conferred; nor is there one sentence in the Constitution, which has been pointed out by the gentlemen of the bar, or which we have been able to discern, that prescribes this rule. We do not, therefore, think ourselves justified in adopting it. . . .

We know of no rule for construing the extent of such powers other than is given by the language of the instrument which confers them, taken in connection with the purposes for which they were conferred.

The words are: *Congress shall have power to regulate commerce with foreign nations, and among the several states, and with the Indian tribes*. The subject to be regulated is commerce; and our Constitution being, as was aptly said at the bar, one of enumeration and not of definition, to ascertain the extent of the power it becomes necessary to settle the meaning of the word. . . .

Commerce, undoubtedly, is traffic, but it is something more—it is intercourse. It describes the commercial intercourse between nations, and parts of nations, in all its branches, and is regulated by prescribing rules for carrying on that intercourse. The mind can scarcely conceive a system for regulating commerce between nations which shall exclude all laws concerning navigation, which shall be silent on the admission of the vessels of the one nation into the ports of the other, and be confined to prescribing rules for the conduct of individuals in the actual employment of buying and selling or of barter. If commerce does not include navigation, the government of the Union has no direct power over that subject, and can make no law prescribing what shall constitute American vessels, or requiring that they shall be navigated by American seamen.

Yet this power has been exercised from the commencement of the government, has been exercised with the consent of all, and. has been understood by all to be a commercial regulation. All America understands, and has uniformly understood, the word *commerce* to comprehend navigation.

If the opinion that "commerce," as the word is used in the Constitution, comprehends navigation also, requires any additional confirmation, that additional confirmation is, we think, furnished by the words of the instrument itself. . . .

The word used in the Constitution, then, comprehends, and has been always understood to comprehend, navigation within its meaning, and a power to regulate navigation is as expressly granted as if that term had been added to the word "commerce". . . .

This principle is, if possible, still more clear, when applied to commerce "among the several States". . . . What is commerce "among" them, and how is it to be conducted? Can a trading expedition between two adjoining

States, commence and terminate outside of each? And if the trading intercourse be between two States remote from each other, must it not commence in one, terminate in the other, and probably pass through a third? . . . The power of Congress, then, whatever it may be, must be exercised within the territorial jurisdiction of the several States. . . .

We are now arrived at the inquiry—What is this power? It is the power to regulate, that is, to prescribe the rule by which commerce is to be governed. This power, like all others vested in Congress, is complete in itself, may be exercised to its utmost extent, and acknowledges no limitations other than are prescribed in the Constitution. . . .

When a State proceeds to regulate commerce with foreign nations, or among the several States, it is exercising the very power that is granted to Congress, and is doing the very thing which Congress is authorized to do. There is no analogy, then, between the power of taxation and the power of regulating commerce. . . .

We must first determine whether the act of laying "duties or imposts on imports or exports" is considered in the Constitution as a branch of the taxing power, or of the power to regulate commerce. We think it very clear that it is considered as a branch of the taxing power. . . . The power of imposing duties on imports is classed with the power to levy taxes, and that seems to be its natural place. But the power to levy taxes could never be considered as abridging the right of the States on that subject, and they might, consequently, have exercised it by levying duties on imports or exports, had the Constitution contained no prohibition on this subject. This prohibition, then, is an exception from the acknowledged power of the States to levy taxes, not from the questionable power to regulate commerce. . . .

So, if a State, in passing laws on subjects acknowledged to be within its control . . . shall adopt a measure of the same character with one which Congress may adopt, it does not derive its authority from the particular power which has been granted, but from some other, which remains with the State and may be executed by the same means. . . .

Since, in exercising the power of regulating their own purely internal affairs the States may sometimes enact laws the validity of which depends on their interfering with, and being contrary to, an act of Congress passed in pursuance of the Constitution, the Court will enter upon the inquiry whether the laws of New York, as expounded by the highest tribunal of that State, have, in their application to this case, come into collision with an act of Congress and deprived a citizen of a right to which that act entitles him. . . . In one case and the other, the acts of New York must yield to the law of Congress, and the decision sustaining the privilege they confer against a right given by a law of the Union must be erroneous. . . .

It will at once occur that, when a Legislature attaches certain privileges and exemptions to the exercise of a right over which its control is absolute, the law must imply a power to exercise the right. The privileges are gone if the right itself be annihilated. It would be contrary to all reason, and to the course of human affairs, to say that a State is unable to strip a vessel of the particular privileges attendant on the exercise of a right, and yet may annul the right itself; that the State of New York cannot prevent an enrolled and licensed vessel, proceeding from Elizabethtown, in New Jersey, to New York, from enjoying, in her course, and on her entrance into port, all the privileges conferred by the act of Congress, but can shut her up in her own port, and prohibit altogether her entering the waters and ports of another State. To the Court, it seems very clear that the whole act on the subject of the coasting trade, according to those principles which govern the construction of statutes, implies unequivocally an authority to licensed vessels to carry on the coasting trade. . . .

If, as our whole course of legislation on this subject shows, the power of Congress has been universally understood in America to comprehend navigation, it is a very persuasive, if not a conclusive, argument to prove that the construction is correct, and if it be correct, no clear distinction is perceived between the power to regulate vessels employed in transporting men for hire and property for hire. . . . A coasting vessel employed in the transportation of passengers is as much a portion of the American marine as one employed in the transportation of a cargo. . . .

Vessels have always been employed to a greater or less extent in the transportation of passengers, and have never been supposed to be, on that account, withdrawn from the control or protection of Congress. . . .

If, then, it were even true that the *Bellona* and the *Stoudinger* were employed exclusively in the conveyance of passengers between New York and New Jersey, it would not follow that this occupation did not constitute a part of the coasting trade of the United States, and was not protected by the license annexed to the answer. . . .

The laws of New York, which grant the exclusive privilege set up by the respondent, take no notice of the employment of vessels, and relate only to the principle by which they are propelled. Those laws do not inquire whether vessels are engaged in transporting men or merchandise, but whether they are moved by steam or wind. If by the former, the waters of New York are closed against them, though their cargoes be dutiable goods, which the laws of the United States permit them to enter and deliver in New York. If by the latter, those waters are free to them though they should carry passengers only. . . .

The questions, then, whether the conveyance of passengers be a part of the coasting trade and whether a vessel can be protected in that occupation by a coasting license are not, and cannot be, raised in this case. The real and sole question seems to be whether a steam machine in actual use deprives a vessel of the privileges conferred by a license. . . .

The first idea which presents itself is that the laws of Congress for the regulation of commerce do not look to the principle by which vessels are moved. That subject is left entirely to individual discretion, and, in that vast and complex system of legislative enactment concerning it . . . there is not . . . one word respecting the peculiar principle by which vessels are propelled through the water, except what may be found in a single act granting a particular privilege to steamboats. . . .

But all inquiry into this subject seems to the Court to be put completely at rest by the act already mentioned, entitled, "An act for the enrolling and licensing of steamboats."

This act authorizes a steamboat employed, or intended to be employed, only in a river or bay of the United States, owned wholly or in part by an alien, resident within the United States, to be enrolled and licensed as if the same belonged to a citizen of the United States.

This act demonstrates the opinion of Congress that steamboats may be enrolled and licensed, in common with vessels using sails. They are, of course, entitled to the same privileges, and can no more be restrained from navigating waters and entering ports which are free to such vessels than if they were wafted on their voyage by the winds, instead of being propelled by the agency of fire. . . .

Powerful and ingenious minds, taking as postulates that the powers expressly granted to the government of the Union are to be contracted by construction into the narrowest possible compass and that the original powers of the States are retained if any possible construction will retain them may, by a course of well digested but refined and metaphysical reasoning founded on these premises, explain away the Constitution of our country and leave it a magnificent structure indeed to look at, but totally unfit for use. They may so entangle and perplex the understanding as to obscure principles which were before thought quite plain, and induce doubts where, if the mind were to pursue its own course, none would be perceived. In such a case, it is peculiarly necessary to recur to safe and fundamental principles to sustain those principles, and when sustained, to make them the tests of the arguments to be examined.

GLOSSARY

alien: nonresident

appellant: party appealing a court decision

***Belladona* and *Stoudinger*:** names of the steamboats owned by Thomas Gibbons

coasting trade: commerce operating via waterway between adjacent harbors within the same nation, as opposed to international or long-distance commerce.

levy: to impose charges

postulates: presumptions without supporting evidence

sovereignty: absolute statutory power inside territorial boundaries

steam machine: steamboat

Document Analysis

The *Gibbons v. Ogden* opinion, considered to be one of the most important Supreme Court decisions in the nation's history, allowed Chief Justice John Marshall to affirm the government's authority over interstate commerce by asserting a broad definition of commerce while also providing a narrow legal basis for his decision, which endeavored to preserved the equilibrium between state and federal power. The opinion delivered by Marshall in the *Gibbons v. Ogden* case clearly demonstrates Marshall's tendency toward making measured and narrow decisions in controversial cases. Certainly, the chief justice was a proponent of a strong central government and a defender of the Supreme Court's role in judicial review, which allowed the Supreme Court to nullify the actions of the executive and judiciary branches as well as state laws deemed to be unconstitutional. Understanding the delicate balance of power in a federalist system that granted simultaneous sovereignties to both the state and federal governments, Marshall was careful in writing the *Gibbons* opinion to assert the primacy of federal law while also managing to avoid establishing a legal precedent that would make significant restrictions on states' rights. As such, Marshall's opinion in the *Gibbons* case avoided making any sweeping claims about the commerce clause's ability to grant absolute exclusivity to Congress in implementing laws concerning commerce and trade. Instead, Marshall's decision rested on the conflict between the New York steamboat law and the federal Coasting Act of 1793. The Coasting Act was a congressional act that enrolled and licensed seafaring vessels engaged in trade and fishing along the coast. Marshall's opinion rested on the conflict between the New York monopoly and the federal government's authority to regulate the vessels involved in transportation and trade according to the Coasting Act. The supremacy of the federal law lay in Congress's power to regulate commerce. Granted by the Commerce Clause of the Constitution, Congress holds the power "to regulate commerce with foreign nations, and among the several states, and with the Indian Tribes" (Section I, Article 8, Clause 3).

In framing the court decision, Marshall directly addressed the arguments advanced by the attorneys for both Thomas Gibbons and Aaron Ogden. Gibbons was represented by Daniel Webster and William Wirt, who argued for Gibbons's right to run his steamboats freely due to the unconstitutional nature of the New York monopoly. They argued for the exclusive right of Congress to regulate interstate commerce under the Commerce Clause. To support their argument for federal exclusivity, they sought to make a clear distinction between the powers of the state, which regulated the health, safety, and well-being of its residents, and the powers of the federal government, which were put in place to regulate national concerns such as commerce. Webster and Wirt also contended that the New York monopoly violated the federal Coasting Act of 1793, which required all vessels involved in coastal trade to register with the federal government. The attorneys argued that the Coasting Act provided ship captains with right of entry to all American ports. Ogden's lawyers, Thomas J. Oakley and Thomas A. Emmet, provided a counterargument that defended states' rights by claiming that the state and federal governments held concurrent power over regulating commerce. In other words, the states had the right to regulate commerce within their borders as they saw fit, as long as their commerce laws did not conflict with federal regulations. They also sought to portray the legislature's allowance of a steamboat monopoly not as a commercial statute, but instead as a navigation law, permissible under the powers reserved for the states. Additionally, Ogden's lawyers sought to define commerce narrowly, to be applied only to the transport and sale of merchandise.

When examining Marshall's decision, the opinion clearly shows the influence of both arguments submitted before the Court. Chief Justice Marshall appeared to integrate into his opinion both the concept of concurrent state and federal power over commerce presented by Ogden's attorneys, as well as the argument that the state of New York's monopoly was in violation of the federal Coasting Act of 1793, as presented by Gibbons's lawyers. The narrowly defined decision by Marshall allowed him to assert the supremacy of federal over state law by upholding the Coasting Act while avoiding making any constitutional claims to the federal exclusivity over commerce law.

Concurrent Commerce Power

In tackling the issues brought to bear in the *Gibbons v. Ogden* case, Marshall carefully addressed the relationship between the federal government and state governments on the issue of commerce law. Chief Justice Marshall delineated the way in which state and federal law were to operate in relation to one another. Marshall took pains to outline the idea that each states was free to make laws concerning its own operation and well-being, even if the laws the state enacted were "of the same character with one which Congress may adopt." If, however, the state adopted a law that came into conflict with laws passed by Congress under the authority of the Constitution, the state law "must yield to the law of Congress, and the decision sustaining the privilege they confer against a right given by a law of the Union must be erroneous." In the *Gibbons* case, ruled Marshall, the New York steamboat monopoly directly conflicted with the federal Coasting Act of 1793 and was therefore in violation of a federal law regulating commerce. The state law, therefore, had to yield to the supremacy of the federal law.

What Marshall failed to touch on in his opinion, however, was whether or not state laws regulating interstate commerce were automatically in violation of Congress's power to regulate commerce, even if Congress had passed no contradictory law. His affirmation of the states' ability to pass laws "of the same character with one which Congress may adopt" seemed to indicate that as long as Congress adopted no conflicting law, the states were free to regulate commerce as their needs dictated. The Supreme Court, therefore, did not rule in *Gibbons v. Ogden* that the power to regulate commerce was exclusive to Congress, but instead that the federal government and the states held concurrent powers. Marshall preserved, in his decision, a sense of balance between the authority of states and the federal government over the issue of commerce, and tasked the Court with deciding on a case-by-case basis whether a state law infringed on the congressional authority over regulating commerce. Knowing the limits to the federal government's ability to address the individual needs of the states in regulating transportation, communication, and trade—especially as the nation expanded further west—Marshall's decision made room for the states to control unique problems that might arise related to matters of commerce. Despite this careful balance struck by Marshall in the *Gibbons* case, in avoiding addressing the nature of the commerce clause, his opinion left open the possibility that, in the future, the Supreme Court could rule that Congress retained a discrete right to regulate commerce and that states were prohibited from enacting any laws of that nature.

Expanding the Meaning of "Commerce"

Marshall's opinion in Gibbons is most widely known for the legal longevity of his broad definition of commerce. Ogden's attorneys appealed to a narrow understanding of commerce, which encompassed only the movement and sale of goods. As steamboats were a system of navigation and not goods themselves, and as they most often transported passengers and not just goods, Ogden's attorneys argued that the regulation of steamboat routes was outside the purview of federal regulation of commerce. Marshall rejected this line of reasoning and instead defined commerce in expansive terms. Marshall noted firmly in his opinion that "the mind can scarcely conceive a system for regulating commerce between nations which shall exclude all laws concerning navigation." This statement by the chief justice worked to establish the authority of the federal government to regulate navigational routes that traversed state boundaries. Nodding to the popular interest in the case, as well as the legitimacy of his assessment, Marshall stated definitively that "all America understands, and has uniformly understood, the word *commerce* to comprehend navigation." The restricted use of steamboats on waterways was not only an issue of navigation, Marshall acknowledged, but also an issue of the expanding uses of technology.

The basis on which New York restricted boats entering it waters was based solely on the technology used to propel it, as sail boats were not restricted from New York waterways under the steamboat monopoly. If the actions of New York state, in granting Livingston—and, by proxy, Ogden—a monopoly on the use of steamboat technology, became the standard in all states, the possibility of restricting advancing transportation technology across the nation was a genuine possibility. If every state were able to grant exclusive rights over transportation to different parties in every state, the conflict between states would only grow as means of transportation expanded. Marshall's opinion served to diminish these potential conflicts, but also managed to expand the reach of the federal government beyond the limits of technological advancements. Marshall's expansion of the constitutional definition of commerce beyond trade and subsequently even beyond navigation can be seen in the passage which asserts that, "commerce, undoubtedly, is traffic, but it is something more—it is intercourse. It describes the commercial intercourse between nations, and parts of nations, in all its branches, and is regulated by prescribing rules for carrying on that intercourse." The use of the vague and sweeping term "intercourse" provided an incomparably wide category under which myriad forms of interstate dealings could be regulated by the federal government. This far-reaching definition of commerce provided the possibility for the government to expand its regulatory authority over the advancing transportation and communication technology that was rapidly emerging just as the nation was about to begin its westward expansion.

Though careful to preserve the legal balance between state and federal authority, Marshall concluded his majority opinion by leveling an impassioned warning against the excessive advocacy of state authority in matters clearly under the purview of the federal government. Chief Justice Marshall cautioned those within the nation's legal institutions to avoid trying to find ways to diminish the powers that the Constitution bestows to Congress. Always a commanding advocate for a strong central government, Marshall took to task those who would reduce federal powers into "the narrowest possible compass" while finding "any possible construction" through which states may assert their regulatory rights. For Marshall, a continual expansion of regulatory rights retained by the states could "explain away the Constitution of our country and leave it a magnificent structure indeed to look at, but totally unfit for use." Marshall's call for preservation of fundamental constitutional principles and the acknowledgement of the federal government's primary authority in broadly defined matters of commerce resulted in one of the most important and influential Supreme Court decisions on federal power in the nation's history.

Essential Themes

The immediate aftermath of the *Gibbons v. Ogden* decision resulted in widespread popular support for the decision. The cost of using steamboat transportation fell significantly as the number of active steamboats between Baltimore and New York City increased from four to forty-three in just one year. Commerce in Hudson River ports expanded measurably in the wake of opening the waterway to significant growth in the number of steamboat lines. Beyond the immediate benefits, however, Marshall's broad interpretation of interstate commerce in the *Gibbons* decision had a lasting impact on the government's ability to regulate the rapidly expanding transportation and communication technology facilitating the swift national expansion into western territory. The *Gibbons* decision also had incredible longevity in providing the constitutional authority to expand the regulatory powers of government. The Great Depression and the subsequent implementation of the New Deal by the Roosevelt administration created new legal importance for the *Gibbons v. Ogden* decision. The broad reading of commerce allowed the federal government to expand its regulatory powers to national labor, industry, agricultural, and banking issues. Considered one of the most important cases in constitutional history, the *Gibbons v. Ogden* decision reinforced the primacy of federal laws that conflicted with those implemented by the states, assisted the rapid expansion of national transportation and communication, and paved the way for an expanding definition of what constituted commerce under the regulatory power of the federal government.

Amanda Beyer-Purvis, MA

Bibliography

Baxter, Maurice G. *The Steamboat Monopoly:* Gibbons V. Ogden, *1824*. New York: Knopf, 1972. Print.

Cooke, Fred'k H. "The *Gibbons v. Ogden* Fetish." *Michigan Law Review* 9.4 (1911): 324–33. Print.

Cox, Thomas H. Gibbons v. Ogden, *Law, and Society in the Early Republic*. Athens: Ohio UP, 2009. Print.

Johnson, Herbert A. Gibbons v. Ogden: *John Marshall, Steamboats, and the Commerce Clause*. Lawrence: UP of Kansas, 2010. Print.

Mendelson, Wallace. "New Light on *Fletcher v. Peck* and *Gibbons v. Ogden*." *Yale Law Journal* 58.4 (1949): 567–73. Print.

Additional Reading

Coenen, Dan T. *Constitutional Law: The Commerce Clause*. New York: Foundation, 2004. Print.

Fribourg, Marjorie G. *The Supreme Court in American History: Ten Great Decisions; the People, the Times and the Issues*. Philadelphia: Macrae, 1965. Print.

May, Christopher N, and Allan Ides. *Constitutional Law, National Power and Federalism: Examples and Explanations*. New York: Aspen, 2007. Print.

Paskoff, Paul F. *Troubled Waters: Steamboat Disasters, River Improvements, and American Public Policy, 1821–1860*. Baton Rouge: Louisiana State UP, 2007. Print.

"Steamboats on the Hudson: An American Saga: Two Bobs, Three Johns, Three Jims, a Nick, an Aaron, a Tom and a Boat." *New York State Library Database*. New York State Library, 2012. Web. 29 Oct. 2012.

LESSON PLAN: **The Federal Government's Supremacy over Commerce**

Students analyze Supreme Court Chief Justice John Marshall's 1824 landmark opinion in *Gibbons v. Ogden* regarding the commerce clause and consider its enduring influence today.

Learning Objectives

Examine the influence of ideas behind the balance of powers established by the Constitution in Chief Justice Marshall's opinion; assess the importance of individual rights to appraise Marshall's opinion in *Gibbons v. Ogden*; explain historical continuity to trace the influence of the *Gibbons v. Ogden* ruling today.

Materials: *Gibbons v. Ogden*: Supreme Court opinion by John Marshall (1824); US Constitution: Article 1, Section 8 (1787)

Overview Questions

How does Marshall define commerce, and why is this important? What arguments does Marshall make to support the court's decision in *Gibbons v. Ogden*? What precedent did Marshall's opinion establish? How did his opinion influence other Supreme Court decisions and acts of Congress? How does his opinion influence the United States today?

Step 1: Comprehension Questions

According to Marshall, what is the significance of Congress's authorization "to make all laws which shall be necessary and proper"? According to Marshall's opinion in *Gibbons v. Ogden*, what types of commerce does Congress have the power to regulate? Why is Marshall's definition of *commerce* central to his arguments?

▶ **Activity:** Ask students to read aloud passages that highlight Marshall's explanation of the commerce clause; have students discuss the effectiveness of Marshall's use of language in explaining Congress's power to regulate commerce.

Step 2: Comprehension Questions

How does Marshall dismiss the claim that state governments can "regulate commerce with foreign nations"? Why does Marshall state that "New York must yield to the law of Congress"?

▶ **Activity:** Have students circle any references related to states' powers and underline those related to Congress's powers; have students summarize these powers and then discuss their views on the differences between the powers of the state and the federal governments.

Step 3: Context Questions

How did Marshall's opinion establish a precedent for a stronger federal government? Based on your reading of the commerce clause, do you agree with Marshall's opinion? Why or why not?

▶ **Activity:** Ask students to explore historical events that were influenced by Marshall's opinion, such as the Civil Rights Act of 1964; have students create an annotated timeline of these events.

Step 4: Exploration Questions

How does Marshall's opinion continue to influence the relationship between the states and the federal government? Should the Supreme Court revisit Marshall's decision? Why or why not?

▶ **Activity:** Have students debate whether Marshall's opinion should be revisited; have them make an outline for an essay that traces Marshall's influence on the Supreme Court from the 1820s to today.

Step 5: Response Paper

Word length and additional requirements set by Instructor. Students answer the research question in the *Overview Questions*. Students state a thesis and use as evidence passages from the primary source document as well as support from supplemental materials assigned in the lesson.

President Andrew Jackson's Message to Congress "On Indian Removal"

Date: December 6, 1830
Author: Jackson, Andrew
Genre: speech; report

"We now propose to acquire the countries occupied by the red men of the South and West by a fair exchange, and, at the expense of the United States, to send them to land where their existence may be prolonged and perhaps made perpetual."

Summary Overview

This document is a portion of President Andrew Jackson's annual message to Congress, submitted to Congress in written form in December 1830. These annual messages correspond to what came to be called the "State of the Union Address," but beginning with Thomas Jefferson's administration (1801–1809), presidents did not deliver these addresses, but submitted them in written form. It was not until Woodrow Wilson's presidency that the practice of an orally delivered speech was revived. In this document, Jackson surveys the progress of the government's program to move American Indians out of the eastern parts of the United States to the Great Plains, beyond the Mississippi River. Such removals had begun before Jackson's time, but they became an official policy of the government with the passage of the Indian Removal Act in May, 1830. Jackson firmly supported the removal program, and in this message he cites several points which he believed justified the relocation of the American Indians.

Defining Moment

Frontier settlers moving into the lands between the Appalachian Mountains and the Mississippi River called for the American Indians in this region to be relocated into the Great Plains regions beyond the Mississippi. Many believed that white people would never settle the Plains region because the semiarid climate of much of that area was not suitable for the type of agriculture American farmers practiced. Even before Jackson's presidency, many removal treaties were negotiated with various tribes, but the major resettlement of eastern tribes into the West came as a result of the Indian Removal Act, passed in May 1830, during Jackson's first administration. The government intended to exchange the lands the American Indians occupied in the east for lands in the West. The American Indians would be paid for improvements made on their land, and the government would pay the expenses of moving them. These terms were not always followed faithfully, and perhaps most importantly, some tribes or tribal factions were eventually forced to move, although the bill had said nothing about moving anyone against their will. American politicians and opinion makers justified removal on humanitarian grounds, suggesting that it would enable the Indians to go on living as distinct people, pursuing their traditional lifestyles, unhampered by settler pressure in the West. The Indian Removal Act was bitterly debated in Congress. Not surprisingly, it was supported by states that still had large American Indian populations within their borders, and opposed by Northeastern and

New England states where this was not the case. Support for the bill generally followed party lines as well, with most of Jackson's Democratic Party supporting it, while the opposition Whig Party was critical of the bill. While many supported removal just because they wanted access to American Indian lands, many humanitarians and missionaries supported removal because they believed that in the long run, it would be in the best interest of the American Indians. In this message to Congress, Jackson comments on the progress of the removal effort up to that point. Perhaps because the debate over the removal bill had been so acrimonious, Jackson was anxious to present evidence to Congress and the American people about the successes of the removal program, and gives many arguments justifying the policy. Including removals before Jackson's administration, and those carried out after the passage of the Indian Removal Act, over seventy thousand American Indians were moved from the Southeast and the Upper Midwest, into the "Indian Territory" in what is now the states of Kansas, Oklahoma, and part of Nebraska.

Author Biography

Andrew Jackson rose from an obscure background to become a wealthy planter, a military officer, politician, and finally the seventh president of the United States. He was born in Waxhaw, South Carolina, on March 15, 1767. He served briefly in the last years of the American War of Independence. Although he had little formal education, Jackson studied law with a lawyer in Salisbury, North Carolina and was admitted to the bar in that state in 1787.

Jackson was appointed to serve as a prosecuting attorney in the western district of North Carolina, which included what is now the state of Tennessee. Thus began his association with the state that became central to his life and career. When Tennessee was preparing for statehood, Jackson served in the state constitutional convention, and then was elected as the first US congressman from the new state. He was elected to the US Senate in 1797 but served only briefly before being appointed a justice on the Tennessee Supreme Court. Serving as a major general in the Tennessee militia during the War of 1812, Jackson won a significant victory over the Creek Indians at the Battle of Horseshoe Bend in present-day Alabama in March, 1814. As a reward for this achievement, he was appointed a brigadier general in the US Army. In January 1815, he won a significant victory against the British at the Battle of New Orleans. These military exploits made him a national hero. In 1817, he was recalled to military duty to lead a campaign against the Seminole Indians, who were making raids out of Spanish Florida into Georgia. Jackson's invasion of Florida almost embroiled the United States in a confrontation with Spain and Britain, and although President James Monroe and much of his Cabinet were ready to censure Jackson, he was defended by Secretary of State John Quincy Adams, who persuaded Spain to concede Florida and allow an extension of the Louisiana Territory's western border to the Pacific. After Florida was annexed to the United States, Jackson served briefly as the territorial governor. He was elected to the US Senate from Tennessee in 1823.

Jackson ran for president in 1824, but because no candidate won a majority of the Electoral College vote, the House of Representatives selected the president. Speaker of the House Henry Clay, who had been a presidential candidate himself, supported John Quincy Adams, who was elected. Adams then made Clay the secretary of state, which had become a stepping stone to the presidency. Jackson's supporters charged that a "corrupt bargain" had been struck. In 1828, Jackson defeated Adams in a deeply personal, hard-fought campaign. He was reelected in 1832, defeating Henry Clay. After leaving office in 1837, he remained influential in Democratic politics, but primarily retired to the Hermitage, his plantation near Nashville, Tennessee. He died there on June 8, 1845.

HISTORICAL DOCUMENT

It gives me pleasure to announce to Congress that the benevolent policy of the Government, steadily pursued for nearly thirty years, in relation to the removal of the Indians beyond the white settlements is approaching to a happy consummation. Two important tribes have accepted the provision made for their removal at the last session of Congress, and it is believed that their example will induce the remaining tribes also to seek the same obvious advantages.

The consequences of a speedy removal will be important to the United States, to individual States, and to the Indians themselves. The pecuniary advantages which it promises to the Government are the least of its recommendations. It puts an end to all possible danger of collision between the authorities of the General and State Governments on account of the Indians. It will place a dense and civilized population in large tracts of country now occupied by a few savage hunters. By opening the whole territory between Tennessee on the north and Louisiana on the south to the settlement of the whites it will incalculably strengthen the southwestern frontier and render the adjacent States strong enough to repel future invasions without remote aid. It will relieve the whole State of Mississippi and the western part of Alabama of Indian occupancy, and enable those States to advance rapidly in population, wealth, and power. It will separate the Indians from immediate contact with settlements of whites; free them from the power of the States; enable them to pursue happiness in their own way and under their own rude institutions; will retard the progress of decay, which is lessening their numbers, and perhaps cause them gradually, under the protection of the Government and through the influence of good counsels, to cast off their savage habits and become an interesting, civilized, and Christian community.

What good man would prefer a country covered with forests and ranged by a few thousand savages to our extensive Republic, studded with cities, towns, and prosperous farms embellished with all the improvements which art can devise or industry execute, occupied by more than 12,000,000 happy people, and filled with all the blessings of liberty, civilization and religion?

The present policy of the Government is but a continuation of the same progressive change by a milder process. The tribes which occupied the countries now constituting the Eastern States were annihilated or have melted away to make room for the whites. The waves of population and civilization are rolling to the westward, and we now propose to acquire the countries occupied by the red men of the South and West by a fair exchange, and, at the expense of the United States, to send them to land where their existence may be prolonged and perhaps made perpetual.

Doubtless it will be painful to leave the graves of their fathers; but what do they more than our ancestors did or than our children are now doing? To better their condition in an unknown land our forefathers left all that was dear in earthly objects. Our children by thousands yearly leave the land of their birth to seek new homes in distant regions. Does Humanity weep at these painful separations from everything, animate and inanimate, with which the young heart has become entwined? Far from it. It is rather a source of joy that our country affords scope where our young population may range unconstrained in body or in mind, developing the power and facilities of man in their highest perfection.

These remove hundreds and almost thousands of miles at their own expense, purchase the lands they occupy, and support themselves at their new homes from the moment of their arrival. Can it be cruel in this Government when, by events which it can not control, the Indian is made discontented in his ancient home to purchase his lands, to give him a new and extensive territory, to pay the expense of his removal, and support him a year in his new abode? How many thousands of our own people would gladly embrace the opportunity of removing to the West on such conditions! If the offers made to the Indians were extended to them, they would be hailed with gratitude and joy.

And is it supposed that the wandering savage has a stronger attachment to his home than the settled, civilized Christian? Is it more afflicting to him to leave the graves of his fathers than it is to our brothers and children? Rightly considered, the policy of the General Government toward the red man is not only liberal, but generous. He is unwilling to submit to the laws of the States and mingle with their population. To save him from this alternative, or perhaps utter annihilation, the General Government kindly offers him a new home, and proposes to pay the whole expense of his removal and settlement.

GLOSSARY

consummation: coming to an intended end or completion

General Government: US federal government

pecuniary: referring to financial matters

red men: American Indians

rude: rudimentary or primitive

Document Analysis

In this annual message submitted to Congress in December 1830 (the equivalent of the modern State of the Union address, although not delivered orally) Jackson sought to update Congress on the progress of the program of removing American Indians from the eastern parts of the United States into the "Indian Territory" that had been created in what is now Kansas and Oklahoma. The debate in Congress over the passage of the Indian Removal Act, which Jackson signed on May 28, 1830, had been bitter, so perhaps part of Jackson's purpose in this message was to assure opponents that the policy was just and beneficial to the American Indians. He notes that relocating them from the eastern parts of the country to lands "beyond the white settlements" had been the policy of the government for nearly thirty years, and he projects that this process was nearing its completion. It is correct to note that many tribes had moved to the West before Jackson's administration, under terms of individual treaties. Also, in some cases, even without any formal treaties, tribes simply fled westward from the pressure of white settlement. But the Indian Removal Act has made this process a clearly defined policy of the federal government, and the pace of removals picked up dramatically after this legislation was passed. In his prediction that this process was nearing completion, Jackson was somewhat premature, because the last removals from east of the Mississippi would not be completed until the late 1850s.

After the Indian Removal Act was passed, the federal government sent representatives to the central Plains region to negotiate treaties with the American Indians who already lived in this region. The government bought land from these tribes, and promised other treaty benefits. In return the western tribes agreed to give up some of their lands for the resettlement of the tribes being removed out of the East, and promised not to molest the eastern tribes being relocated into the region. What became known as the Indian Territory included most of what is now Oklahoma, Kansas, and part of Nebraska. Including removals that began before Jackson's administration, eventually about ten thousand American Indians were removed from the Great Lakes and Upper Midwest region; most of these tribes were settled in present-day Kansas. Between 1830 and 1840, about sixty thousand American Indians from the southeast, including the tribes that white people in the nineteenth century referred to as the "Five Civilized Tribes," were moved into what is now Oklahoma. The Five Civilized Tribes included the Cherokees, the Choctaws, the Creeks or Muskogee people, the Chickasaws, and the Seminoles.

Jackson argued that further progress in relocating American Indians to the West would be beneficial to the federal government, to the individual states from which the tribes were removed, and to the American Indians themselves. For the federal government, there will be "pecuniary advantages" as Jackson phrased it—meaning savings in federal spending. Moving the

American Indians away from white settlement should decrease the chances of military conflict, which would save the federal government the funds that would have to be spent on such fighting. But Jackson concedes that these financial benefits are the least significant of the benefits of the removal program. He is also concerned about the wider possibilities for deterring foreign attacks on the United States. While the territory of the Louisiana Purchase had been obtained from France in 1803, the far Southwest, including Texas, was still in Spanish hands. Jackson argued that a "dense and civilized population" in the region that now makes up Alabama and Mississippi would serve as a deterrent to possible Spanish designs on that region, or to any potential threat from foreign nations that might be launched from the Gulf of Mexico. Jackson believed there would be numerous advantages to seeing white settlement take the place of the "few savage hunters" that now inhabited this region. His use of a term like "savage" here, and the later reference to "rude institutions" of the American Indians reflect the racist stereotypes that were common among white Americans at this time. Historians have often pictured Jackson as an Indian hater, but it perhaps is more accurate to suggest his view of the American Indians was paternalistic—they were, to Jackson as to many Americans, a backward people who needed the care and oversight of the federal government. In suggesting that it would be better for extensive white settlement to replace a few nomadic hunters in this region, Jackson is expressing an idea that was very common among white settlers and government policy makers. Many of those who supported American Indian removal had developed a novel argument to support their position. The American Indians had a surplus of land—they often farmed small portions but hunted over large expanses of land that was otherwise unsettled and unused. But since they refused to give up this land, it was the American Indians, as this argument went, who were the greedy or stingy party. They refused to "share" their lands with European American settlers that would actually put it use in farming. This argument ignored the fact that since many of the tribes lived by a mixed economy of agriculture combined with hunting and gathering, the land they hunted on was essential to their ways of life, even though it was not used as white settlers might use it.

Mississippi (admitted to statehood in 1817) and Alabama (made a state in 1819) were relatively new states, and Jackson argues that moving the American Indians out of the boundaries of these states will allow economic and political development there to proceed more quickly. As cotton production expanded into these regions, many Southern politicians argued that the presence of large numbers of American Indians in these new states was hampering the development of plantations and large scale agricultural production.

Another advantage that Jackson sees in removal is that it will "separate the Indians from immediate contact with the settlements of whites." This might be seen as a defensive argument, suggesting that the white settlers would be less vulnerable to American Indian attacks if the tribes were moved farther away. But Jackson saw it primarily as something that protected the American Indians. Many supporters of removal argued that if American Indians lived too close to white settlements, they tended to pick up bad habits from the settlers (like the use of alcohol). Also, they were often subject to being cheated in business transactions or other types of mistreatment at the hands of white people. Many people who supported removal nevertheless also believed that the American Indians would eventually have to assimilate and be absorbed into the general culture of the nation. But, ironically, they were arguing that it was best for the American Indians, at this point, to be moved away from the white settlements. Frontier white settlers, apparently, were not thought to be particularly good role models of the superiority of European American civilization.

If the American Indians were moved to the West, they would not be within the boundaries of any state, so they would be free from the interference of any state government. Many of the states in the Southeast had been very aggressive in trying to move the American Indians out of their states. Political leaders on the state level did not like having American Indians living in their boundaries who were not subject to the jurisdiction of the state government, as American Indian affairs were supposed to be handled only by the federal government. The Cherokees had taken a legal challenge all the way to the Supreme Court, arguing that Georgia had no right to legislate over American Indian lands. But the Supreme Court ruled in the case *Cherokee Nation v. Georgia* (1831) that the case was outside of the Court's jurisdiction because the Cherokee nation, like other American Indian nations, was not strictly a "foreign nation" under the US Constitution.

Jackson says that if the American Indians moved to the West, they could continue to live as they wish, according to "their own rude institutions." Removal would "retard the progress of decay, which is lessening their numbers." This is another reference to the belief that living too close to white settlements had a deleterious effect on the American Indians, and was a factor in the decline of their populations. While removal would allow the American Indians, at least for a time, to pursue their traditional ways of life, the ultimate goal was still civilization and assimilation—as Jackson indicates when he suggests that gradually, through "the influences of good counsels," they might abandon their old ways of life and become a "civilized and Christian community." Under the Indian Removal program, missionaries—who would be one example of the kind of people Jackson had in mind in his reference to "good counsels," would only be allowed in the American Indian lands with the permission of the tribes. Many missionaries opposed removal as an unjust policy, but some supported it, believing it would ultimately be in the best interest of the Indians. Some missionaries believed that the Indian Territory would be a kind of controlled environment, where missionaries, educators, and other humanitarians could influence the American Indians, but whiskey sellers and dishonest traders would not be allowed to corrupt them . Assimilation and conversion to Christianity would still be the goal, but could be pursued more gradually, without the pressure of white settlement intruding on American Indian communities.

Jackson could not imagine that any person of good will could prefer a situation where a few thousand American Indians roamed and hunted over land that could support a large population of settlers with prosperous farms and industrious towns and cities. As the tide of frontier settlement moved inexorably westward, the Indians were being engulfed. Since this had proven to be destructive to American Indian cultures and a threat to even their very existence, Jackson argued that it was only just to acquire their land by "a fair exchange," and to move them at government expense to new lands in the West. In those new western lands, they would not be molested, and their very existence as distinct nations and peoples "may be prolonged and perhaps made perpetual."

Jackson admits it might be painful for American Indians to leave their traditional homelands and the graves of their fathers. But he notes that Europeans coming to America, and American frontier settlers, had been doing this very thing for generations. Jackson believed that rather than grieving at the fact that these European American settlers had left their homelands, humanity rejoiced at the opportunities that migration provided for these immigrants or frontier settlers. These settlers moved at their own expense, and bought their land either from the government or from land dealers. Could it be thought cruel, then, Jackson asks, for the government to exchange lands with American Indians, and to move the tribes at government expense to the West? Jackson argued that many white Americans or European immigrants would "gladly embrace" an opportunity to do precisely what the government is doing for the American Indians. Jackson poses the rhetorical question, "Is it supposed that the wandering savage has a stronger attachment to his home than the settled civilized Christian" does? He seems to believe the answer could only be no, but many anthropologists today would argue that American Indians did indeed have a stronger tie to their homelands and to the places where their ancestors were buried than most European Americans did. Much of their tribal culture was centered on the environment where their people had lived for many generations. Many American Indian religious beliefs were clearly entwined with the environment of the people's homelands, and would lose some of their meaning or spiritual "power" outside of the context of those lands.

In the concluding statement of this excerpt, Jackson argues that when "rightly considered," the government's policy toward the American Indians "is not only liberal, but generous." Since they were unwilling to mix with non-Indian peoples, and become subject to state jurisdiction, the alternative of moving them west to an area outside the boundaries of any state seemed to be a just solution. This policy, Jackson suggests, might ultimately save the American Indian nations from "utter annihilation." With the benefit of hindsight, it is obvious that Indian removal, in the long run, had a disastrous impact on many of the tribes removed. Knowing this, comments like Jackson's protestations that the government's policy toward the American Indians was just, beneficial, and even "generous," tend to be dismissed as simply political rhetoric. To some extent, it may well have been, and some politicians clearly did support removal simply because it opened the eastern lands to white settlement. But one of the great ironies of the US government's policies toward the American Indians in the early 1800s is that many politicians and policy makers seemed to have genuinely believed that they could deal justly and peacefully with them, and yet at the same time, dispossess them of virtually all of their original lands. The white politicians and policy makers did not seem to see the inherent inconsistency in these goals, and the impossibility of achieving both goals simultaneously. People can be treated justly, or their lands can be taken from them—but it is simply not possible to do both at the same time.

American Indian removal was based on one flawed premise: the idea that European American settlers would never want the land in the Great Plains. Much of the Plains region is dry, treeless, and somewhat barren. Therefore, it was thought the American Indians could be relocated there, and they would be left alone indefinitely. The removal treaties promised that these new western lands would be theirs "forever." Not only were the Great Plains seen as a somewhat inhospitable environment for European American farmers, the Indian Territory was on the far western edge of US territory. Texas had not yet been annexed, and the American southwest was still under Mexican control. So it seemed the Indians were being moved to an out-of-the way, undesirable land on the extreme edge of the American domain. Therefore, they could be left unmolested, and the so-called "Indian problem" was thought to be solved. But of course, the premise that this land would never be desired by European American settlers was simply not true. Land that could not support crop farming might well be profitable for cattle ranching, and while the typical early European American settler was a corn farmer, wheat farming would eventually boom on the Great Plains. When the government was trying to negotiate removal treaties with some of the eastern tribes, they occasionally organized exploratory expeditions, during which government agents would escort tribal leaders to see the lands in Kansas or Oklahoma, and let them see that it was good land. Therefore, their people should have no fear of moving there. But some of the American Indian leaders seemed to read the handwriting on the wall more clearly than the government's representatives could. Yes, they admitted, this is good land—but then they posed the question of whether the white man would eventually want it as well.

Although the federal government promised the relocating tribes that the western lands would be theirs forever "forever" as early as 1854, the Indian Territory was under assault from new government policies. The Kansas-Nebraska Act, passed in 1854, separated what became the states of Kansas and Nebraska from the Indian Territory. Many of the Indians who had been moved to Kansas were moved again, to Oklahoma. Tribes that had been resettled to Oklahoma had to give up some of their lands for the use of these refugees from Kansas. What is now Oklahoma remained the Indian Territory until 1890, when the Oklahoma Territory Organic Act began the process of creating the state of Oklahoma. Under this legislation, Oklahoma Territory encompassed most of the western half of what is now Oklahoma while the eastern half remained the Indian Territory. However, the federal government's jurisdiction over these American Indian lands was increasing even before Oklahoma statehood, as was settler encroachment on American Indian lands. Finally in 1907, the region became the state of Oklahoma. A large Indian population remained in Oklahoma, as it still does today, but there was no longer a separate American Indian homeland as had been promised in the Indian Removal Act.

Essential Themes

Jackson's explanation of the American Indian removal policy and his arguments justifying it illustrate several major themes in the federal government's relationship with native peoples in the early nineteenth century. Jackson expresses a firm belief that what the government is doing is just, humane, and even generous. Indians who opposed removal, of course, saw it in no such terms. But European American policy makers in this era were convinced of the superiority of their customs and institutions, so they did not believe it was necessary to take into consideration what the American Indians might have wanted. Because of the widespread racism and ethnocentrism among European American politicians and opinion makers, the American Indians were seen as a backward people, and it was assumed that the government would know what was best for them. The policy of removing the American Indians out of the eastern parts of the United States and relocating them into the Great Plains region west of the Mississippi was based on what white Americans thought was a fair exchange—the Indians would give up some land, and be given other land to replace it. They would be paid for improvements that had been made on the land they were leaving, and the government would pay the costs of relocating them. To government officials and potential settlers, looking only at the value of the land and its potential productivity, this appeared to be a fair policy. In this document, Jackson seems to express amazement that anyone could raise objections to it. But to the American Indians, the lands they were being asked (and eventually forced in some cases) to leave were an important part of their cultural heritage, and it could not simply be "replaced" by other land, even with monetary payments also added into the formula. It is obvious that many white Americans of that era supported removal only because it would clear the American Indian population out of lands that were wanted for farming and settlement. But, ironically, many people who supported removal genuinely believed it would be best for the American Indians, in the long run. Where they lived in the East, they would be engulfed by the tide of white migration and settlement, and this usually had a negative impact on American Indian communities. Since that was the case, many thought it would be preferable to move them to the West, to an area where they would be left alone "forever." The fatal flaw in this argument, of course, was that there was virtually no place where, ultimately, the Indians would be left alone. The continued growth of the white American population and the demand for land would eventually press into the Indian Territory that had been created in the West, and the policy of removal would generally be seen as a failure that had a tragic impact on American Indian nations.

Mark S. Joy, PhD

Bibliography

Foreman, Grant. *Indian Removal*. Norman: U of Oklahoma P, 1953. Print.

Perdue, Theda, and Michael D. Green. *The Cherokee Nation and the Trail of Tears*. New York: Viking, 2007. Print.

---. *The Cherokee Removal: A Brief History with Documents*. Boston: Bedford, 2005. Print.

Prucha, Francis Paul. *The Great Father: The United States Government and the American Indians*. 2 vols. Lincoln: U of Nebraska P, 1984. Print.

Remini, Robert V. *The Legacy of Andrew Jackson: Essays on Democracy, Indian Removal, and Slavery*. Baton Rouge: Louisiana State UP, 1988. Print.

Additional Reading

Ehle, John. *Trail of Tears: The Rise and Fall of the Cherokee Nation*. New York: Anchor, 1988. Print.

Prucha, Francis Paul. "Andrew Jackson's Indian Policy: A Reassessment." *Journal of American History* 56 (1969): 537–39. Print.

Rogin, Michael Paul. *Fathers and Children: Andrew Jackson and the Subjugation of the American Indians*. New York: Transactions, 1991. Print.

Satz, Reginald N. *American Indian Policy in the Jacksonian Era*. Lincoln: U of Nebraska P, 1975. Print.

Wallace, Anthony F. C. *The Long Bitter Trail: Andrew Jackson and the Indians*. New York: Hill, 1993. Print.

LESSON PLAN: **Jackson's Removal of American Indians**

Students analyze Jackson's speech and what it reveals about his policies toward American Indians, and explore its impact on westward expansion and sectional tensions.

Learning Objectives

Consider multiple perspectives on Jackson's policy and the removal of American Indians; compare and contrast differing ideas on economic policies related to westward expansion; analyze the multiple causation of the formation of political parties and sectional tensions.

Materials: Andrew Jackson, "President Andrew Jackson's Message to Congress 'On Indian Removal'" (1830); Tecumseh, "Tecumseh's Speech, of August 11, 1810, to Governor William Harrison" (1810).

Overview Questions

What reasons and evidence does Jackson present to support his policy of removing American Indians living east of the Mississippi River? What counterarguments does Jackson present to refute opponents of his policy? How does Jackson's speech reflect different sectional interests and growing sectional tensions? What does Jackson's speech tell us about westward expansion and relations between European American settlers and American Indians?

Step 1: Comprehension Questions

Why does Jackson claim that his policy will "enable [the southeast] to advance rapidly in population, wealth, and power"? According to Jackson, why does his policy benefit American Indians as well?

- **Activity:** Invite students to read aloud key passages; have students list Jackson's reasons and evidence to support his claims of the necessity of American Indian removal.

Step 2: Comprehension Questions

How does Jackson refute arguments by those who claim that his policy was unfair and cruel to American Indians? Do you think his counter-arguments are effective? Why or why not?

- **Activity:** Have student identity the rhetorical questions Jackson asks to refute opponents of his policy; ask students to evaluate the strengths and weaknesses of Jackson's use of rhetorical devices, including counterarguments.

Step 3: Context Questions

At the time of Jackson's speech, the North was industrializing while the South's economy remained mostly agriculture based. How does Jackson's speech reveal growing political and sectional differences? How does Jackson's speech support further westward expansion?

- **Activity:** Have students explore other historical sources related to supporters and opponents of Jackson's American Indian policies; have them present their findings.

Step 4: Exploration Questions

Jackson claims that his policy is "benevolent"; Tecumseh, speaking twenty years earlier, states that his people have "little confidence in the promises of Americans." What do these speeches reveal about differing perspectives on past, current, and future relations between American Indians and other Americans?

- **Activity:** Have students summarize the similarities and differences between the speeches; have students present oral arguments that support or counter the idea that American Indian removal was historically inevitable.

Step 5: Response Paper

Word length and additional requirements set by Instructor. Students answer the research question in the *Overview Questions*. Students state a thesis and use as evidence passages from the primary source document as well as support from supplemental materials assigned in the lesson.

Liberty and Union, Now and Forever, One and Inseparable

Date: January 26, 1830
Author: Webster, Daniel
Genre: speech

"Everywhere, spread all over in characters of living light, blazing on all its ample folds, . . . that other sentiment, dear to every true American heart–Liberty and Union, now and forever, one and inseparable!"

Summary Overview

The Constitution and the Bill of Rights provided general rules regarding how the state and national governments should relate to one another. Differences of interpretation on this issue have existed ever since. When debating a Senate resolution regarding the disposition of federal lands, Senator Robert Y. Hayne, from South Carolina, expanded the debate to include states' rights and his belief that these were superior to the rights of the national government. In response, Daniel Webster gave this speech on the origins of the United States and the relative positions of the national and state governments within the federal system. Webster transformed the discussion on whether states had the right to nullify federal law to one on the origins of political power for the US government, and in what extreme circumstances this power might be withdrawn. Webster spoke so forcefully that President Andrew Jackson was swayed to Webster's point of view on the broader issues of the debate.

Defining Moment

In 1830, Webster was completing the second decade of his political career, which would span nearly four decades. In the first half of his career, he had seen a reversal in the regional views of relationships with the United States government. During the War of 1812, New England was uneasy with the federal government, and some leaders spoke of secession, or at least rewriting parts of the Constitution. By 1830, New England was mainly supportive of the federal government, while states in the South spoke of secession, or at least of taking the initiative to not allow the enforcement of federal laws with which they disagreed. It was at this moment that Webster, the junior senator from Massachusetts, took to the floor of the US Senate to proclaim his vision of what the United States should be.

The thirteen colonies that came together to oppose British rule in the 1770s had all been created separately and had their own histories and heritages. Under the Articles of Confederation, it became clear that greater unity among the colonies was necessary. With the adoption of the Constitution, the mechanism for a strong central government was created; however, there were many different views of how the national and state governments should work together. The South, especially South Carolina, had been strongly affected by the 1819 recession. More than 10 percent of its population moved west, and the cotton industry had a hard time recovering. The federal government was blamed, with tariffs acts from 1816 through 1828 being the focus of the blame. South Carolina had already flouted a federal judge's ruling on the status of African sailors on foreign ships in port at Charleston. The "nullification" movement, as this pro-states' rights group was called, asserted that each state could pick and choose which federal law to enforce and obey. Their position was forcefully presented in 1828 by Vice President John C. Calhoun, who later stepped down from the position of vice president in order to freely present his views on this issue. Webster was a strong advocate for national unity, and he spoke up when the issue was raised in the debates of January 1830. This speech went far beyond carrying the day in the Senate, with thousands of printed copies distributed throughout the nation. It has been seen as one of the greatest speeches in the history of the Senate and was used as a prime example of a persuasive speech by teachers of rhetoric for the rest of the century.

Author Biography

Webster was born in Salisbury (now Franklin), New Hampshire, on January 18, 1782. One of the nine children of Ebenezer and Abigail Webster, he grew up while his father, a strong Federalist, worked as a small farmer and innkeeper. Webster had a substantial formal education, first at Phillips Exeter Academy and then at Dartmouth College. He studied law in New Hampshire and Massachusetts, passed the bar, and started his practice in New Hampshire. In 1807, Webster began to be more active in political affairs, through writing and giving speeches. He married Grace Fletcher in 1808. His public speaking led to his 1812 election to the House of Representatives as an antiwar Federalist representing New Hampshire. After two terms, he decided to leave Congress, and New Hampshire, in order to establish a lucrative law practice in Boston.

While he had been a well-known lawyer prior to entering Congress, Webster became known as a preeminent scholar on the Constitution. As a result, he handled many of the highest-profile cases of that period, including arguing more than two hundred cases before the Supreme Court. In 1822, he was elected to the House of Representatives from Massachusetts, serving until he was elected to the Senate. His legislation included reforming the criminal codes and blocking actions to undermine the treaty with the Creek Indians. In 1828, he was elected to the Senate, where he would serve until 1841, and again from 1845 to 1850. From 1841 to 1843, and again beginning in 1850, Webster served as secretary of state.

Once in the Senate, he supported the 1828 tariff bill, although he had opposed earlier ones and normally advocated free trade. Through this, he became allied with Henry Clay on the issues of federal land and roads. Opposing President Jackson, Webster was one of the founders of the Whig Party. Throughout his Senate service, Webster strongly advocated American unity. As secretary of state, he negotiated a treaty finalizing the border between Maine and New Brunswick. Returning to the Senate in 1845, he opposed Texas joining the union because he thought it would lead to war (it did) and because it would increase the number of slave states. He supported the Compromise of 1850, which included the Fugitive Slave Act of 1850. Most New England leaders were shocked by his support of the Fugitive Slave Act portion of the compromise. Returning to the position of secretary of state, Webster was outspoken on many international issues, even though the United States technically remained neutral. He died, while serving as secretary of state, on October 24, 1852.

HISTORICAL DOCUMENT

There yet remains to be performed, Mr. President, by far the most grave and important duty which I feel to be devolved on me by this occasion. It is to state, and to defend, what I conceive to be the true principles of the Constitution under which we are here assembled. I might well have desired that so weighty a task should have fallen into other and abler hands. I could have wished that it should have been executed by those whose character and experience give weight and influence to their opinions, such as cannot possibly belong to mine. But, sir, I have met the occasion, not sought it; and I shall proceed to state my own sentiments, without challenging for them any particular regard, with studied plainness, and as much precision as possible.

I understand the honorable gentleman from South Carolina to maintain, that it is a right of the state legislatures to interfere whenever, in their judgment, this government transcends its constitutional limits and to arrest the operation of its laws.

I understand him to maintain this right as a right existing under the Constitution, not as a right to overthrow it on the ground of extreme necessity, such as would justify violent revolution.

I understand him to maintain an authority, on the part of the states, thus to interfere for the purpose of correcting the exercise of power by the general government, of checking it, and of compelling it to conform to their opinion of the extent of its powers.

I understand him to maintain that the ultimate power of judging of the constitutional extent of its own authority is not lodged exclusively in the general government, or any branch of it; but that, on the contrary, the states may lawfully decide for themselves, and each state for itself, whether, in a given case, the act of the general government transcends its power.

I understand him to insist that if the exigency of the case, in the opinion of any state government, require it, such state government may, by its own sovereign authority, annul an act of the general government which it deems plainly and palpably unconstitutional. . . .

What he contends for is that it is constitutional to interrupt the administration of the Constitution itself, in the hands of those who are chosen and sworn to administer it, by the direct interference, in form of law of the states, in virtue of their sovereign capacity. The inherent right in the people to reform their government I do not deny; and they have another right, and that is to resist unconstitutional laws without overturning the government. It is no doctrine of mine that unconstitutional laws bind the people. The great question is- Whose prerogative is it to decide on the constitutionality or unconstitutionality of the laws? On that, the main debate hinges.

The proposition that, in case of a supposed violation of the Constitution by Congress, the states have a constitutional right to interfere and annul the law of Congress is the proposition of the gentleman. I do not admit it. If the gentleman had intended no more than to assert the right of revolution for justifiable cause, he would have said only what all agree to. But I cannot conceive that there can be a middle course, between submission to the laws, when regularly pronounced constitutional, on the one hand, and open resistance, which is revolution or rebellion, on the other.

I say, the right of a state to annul a law of Congress cannot be maintained but on the ground of the inalienable right of man to resist oppression; that is to say, upon the ground of revolution. I admit that there is an ultimate violent remedy, above the Constitution and in defiance of the Constitution, which may be resorted to when a revolution is to be justified. But I do not admit that, under the Constitution and in conformity with it, there is any mode in which a state government, as a member of the Union, can interfere and stop the progress of the general government, by force of her own laws, under any circumstance whatever.

This leads us to inquire into the origin of this government and the source of its power. Whose agent is it? Is it the creature of the state legislatures, or the creature of the people? If the government of the United States be the agent of the state governments, then they may control it, provided they can agree in the manner of controlling it; if it be the agent of the people, then the people alone can control it, restrain it, modify, or reform it. It is observable enough that the doctrine for which the honorable gentleman contends leads him to the necessity of maintaining, not only that this general government is the creature of the states, or that it is the creature of each of the states severally, so that each may assert the power for itself of determining whether it acts within the limits of its authority. It is the servant of four-and-twenty masters, of different wills and different purposes, and yet bound to obey all.

This absurdity (for it seems no less) arises from a misconception as to the origin of this government and its true character. It is, sir, the people's Constitution, the people's government, made for the people, made by the people, and answerable to the people. The people of the United States have declared that this Constitution shall be the supreme law. We must either admit the proposition or dispute their authority. The states are, unquestionably, sovereign, so far as their sovereignty is not affected by this supreme law. But the state legislatures, as political bodies, however sovereign, are yet not sovereign over the people. So far as the people have given power to the general government, so far the grant is unquestionably good, and the government holds of the people and not of the state governments. We are all agents of the same supreme power, the people. The general government and the state governments derive their authority from the same source. Neither can, in relation to the other, be called primary, though one is definite and restricted, and the other general and residuary. The national government possesses those powers, which it can be shown the people have conferred on it, and no more. All the rest belongs to the state governments, or to the people themselves. So far as the people have restrained state sovereignty, by the expression of their will, in the Constitution of the United States, so far, it must be admitted, state sovereignty is effectually controlled.

I do not contend that it is, or ought to be, controlled farther. The sentiment to which I have referred propounds that state sovereignty is only to be controlled by its own "feeling of justice"; that is to say, it is not to be controlled at all, for one who is to follow his own feelings is under no legal control. . . .

I must now beg to ask, sir, whence is this supposed right of the states derived? Where do they find the power to interfere with the laws of the Union? Sir, the opinion which the honorable gentleman maintains is a notion founded in a total misapprehension, in my judgment, of the origin of this government, and of the foundation on which it stands. I hold it to be a popular government, erected by the people; those who administer it, responsible to the people; and itself capable of being amended and modified, just as the people may choose it should be. It is as popular, just as truly emanating from the people, as the state governments. It is created for one purpose; the state governments for another. It has its own powers; they have theirs. There is no more authority with them to arrest the operation of a law of Congress than with Congress to arrest the operation of their laws. . . .

This government, sir, is the independent offspring of the popular will. It is not the creature of state legislatures; nay, more, if the whole truth must be told, the people brought it into existence, established it, and have hitherto supported it for the very purpose, among others, of imposing certain salutary restraints on state sovereignties. The states cannot now make war; they cannot contract alliances they cannot make, each for itself, separate regulations of commerce; they cannot lay imposts; they cannot coin money. If this Constitution, Sir, be the creature of state legislatures, it must be admitted that it has obtained a strange control over the volitions of its creators. . . .

Sir, I deny this power of state legislatures altogether. It cannot stand the test of examination. Gentlemen may say that, in an extreme case, a state government might protect the people from intolerable oppression. Sir, in such a case, the people might protect themselves, without the aid of the state governments. Such a case warrants revolution. It must make, when it comes, a law for itself. A nullifying act of a state legislature cannot alter the case, nor make resistance any more lawful. In maintaining these sentiments, sir, I am but asserting the rights of the people. I state what they have declared and insist on their right to declare it. They have chosen to repose this power in the general government, and I think it my duty to support it, like other constitutional powers. . . .

To avoid all possibility of being misunderstood, allow me to repeat again, in the fullest manner, that I claim no powers for the government by forced or unfair construction. I admit that it is a government of strictly limited powers; of enumerated, specified, and particularized powers; and that whatsoever is not granted, is withheld. But notwithstanding all this, and however the grant of powers may be expressed, its limit and extent may yet, in some cases, admit of doubt; and the general government would be good for nothing, it would be incapable of long existing, if some mode had not been provided in which those doubts, as they should arise, might be peaceably but authoritatively solved. . . .

Mr. President, I have thus stated the reasons of my dissent to the doctrines which have been advanced and maintained. I am conscious of having detained you and the Senate much too long. I was drawn into the debate with no previous deliberation, such as is suited to the discussion of so grave and important a subject. But it is a subject of which my heart is full, and I have not been willing to suppress the utterance of its spontaneous sentiments. I cannot, even now, persuade myself to relinquish it without expressing once more my deep conviction that, since it respects nothing less than the Union of the States, it is of most vital and essential importance to the public happiness.

I profess, sir, in my career hitherto, to have kept steadily in view the prosperity and honor of the whole country, and the preservation of our federal Union. It is to that Union we owe our safety at home, and our consideration and dignity abroad. It is to that Union that we are chiefly indebted for whatever makes us most proud of our country-that Union we reached only by the discipline of our virtues in the severe school of adversity. It had its origin in the necessities of disordered finance, prostrate commerce, and mined credit. Under its benign influences, these great interests immediately awoke, as from the dead, and sprang forth with newness of life. Every year of its duration has teamed with fresh proofs of its utility and its blessings. And although our territory has stretched out wider and wider, and our population spread farther and farther, they have not outrun its protection or its benefits. It has been to us all a copious fountain of national, social, and personal happiness.

I have not allowed myself, sir, to look beyond the Union, to see what might be hidden in the dark recess behind. I have not coolly weighed the chances of preserving liberty when the bonds that unite us together shall be broken asunder. I have not accustomed myself to hang over the precipice of disunion, to see whether, with my short sight, I can fathom the depth of the abyss below; nor could I regard him as a safe counselor in the affairs in this government whose thoughts should be mainly bent on considering, not how the Union may be best preserved but how tolerable might be the condition of the people when it should be broken up and destroyed. While the Union lasts, we have high, exciting, gratifying prospects spread out before us, for us and our children. Beyond that I seek not to penetrate the veil.

God grant that in my day, at least, that curtain may not rise! God grant that on my vision never may be opened what lies behind! When my eyes shall be turned to behold for the last time the sun in heaven, may I not see him shining on the broken and dishonored fragments of a once glorious Union; on states dissevered, discordant, belligerent; on a land rent with civil feuds, or drenched, it may be, in fraternal blood! Let their last feeble and lingering glance rather behold the gorgeous ensign of the republic, now known and honored throughout the earth, still full high advanced, its arms and trophies streaming in their original luster, not a stripe erased or polluted, nor a single star obscured, bearing for its motto, no such miserable interrogatory as "What is all this worth?" nor those other words of delusion and folly, "Liberty first and Union afterwards"; but everywhere, spread all over in characters of living light, blazing on all its ample folds, as they float over the sea and over the land, and in every wind under the whole heavens, that other sentiment, dear to every true American heart-Liberty and Union, now and forever, one and inseparable!

GLOSSARY

arrest: to stop

ensign: flag, in this case the American flag

exigency: a situation when immediate action is needed

general government: in this speech it refers to the federal government of the United States

lay imposts: levy a duty on imports

nullify: to make a law invalid

that curtain: in this instance, Webster was referring to the "veil" that hid the destruction that would occur if the unity of the United States was challenged

Document Analysis

What is called the Webster-Hayne debate was actually a series of four speeches during the period of January 19–27, 1830. The first speech by each man dealt fairly directly with the western land resolution under consideration. However, in his second speech, Senator Hayne expanded the discussion to include the relative role of state governments versus that of the national government. The day after Hayne's second speech, Webster began a two-day response, excerpts of which are the text in the historical document section. Webster claimed that the United States was not a collection of states but one political system founded upon the consent of the people. He asserted that the national government had the right to expect that all constitutional laws would be observed in all parts of the nation. He believed that the people had given the federal government rights and powers to carry out policies in the best interest of the nation as a whole, and that these powers should not be limited by one region's desire to follow another policy. Webster proudly proclaimed that the United States had become a respected power in the world because of its unity and that any division would only come from a civil war, which, if successful, would lead to the ruin of all parts of the nation.

The beginning of the excerpt of Webster's speech is located more than three-fifths of the way through the full speech. The last four paragraphs of the excerpt are the last paragraphs of his speech. Prior to presenting the philosophical arguments of the excerpt, which in the Senate records is subtitled "The True Principles of the Constitution," Webster dealt with many of the substantive issues of the resolution and of Hayne's speeches. Webster's speech included many passages dealing with the history of certain issues, as well as Webster's previous views on many of these issues such as the creation of the Northwest Territory, slavery, and New England's relationship with the western states and territories. Webster continued with various discussions regarding perceived regional political differences as represented in tariffs, the national debt, and what types of infrastructure projects should be the responsibility of the national government. Having argued these points forcefully, Webster then turned to a more general view of the Constitution and its interpretation regarding the relationship between the national government and the states.

During his legal career, Webster had studied the Constitution quite closely in order to appeal cases to the Supreme Court. Although in the opening paragraph of the speech Webster stated that he wished the "task should have fallen into other and abler hands," there was no other senator who was actually recognized as being more able than Webster. In fact, once it became clear he would respond a second time to Hayne on January 26, interested observers packed the session, filling the visitors' gallery. One person in the gallery was a friend of Webster who, on Webster's instructions, was to use shorthand to take down the full speech. Webster was not as modest as he claimed to be. Webster stated that he did not seek this debate, which was partially true, because Hayne initiated the series of speeches. However, once engaged, Webster was more than happy to continue the discussion. Webster had little doubt that he understood the "true principles of the Constitution."

Within the first section of the speech, Webster continued with short statements regarding Hayne's views of the Constitution and the federal system. Webster stated that Hayne believed that "it is a right of the state legislatures to interfere whenever, in their judgment, this government transcends its constitutional limits." Because one can find points where Hayne, and others, interrupted Webster's speech to clarify or correct a position he said they held, one can assume that these, and the following points, are essentially correct interpretations of Hayne's position. It is interesting to note that it was the state legislature—rather than the chief executive of a state—which could decide whether or not the national government was acting properly. This was in line with two points of early nineteenth-century American political thought. The first point was that the king and executive branch of the British government, not the British people, had provoked the American colonies to engage in the American Revolution. Thus, chief executives were somewhat suspect within any government. The second point was the thought that the legislature was closer than the executive branch to the people and, thus, better able to judge and carry out the will of the people. According to the argument Webster said Hayne put forward, if the state legislature was certain the national government was not acting in accordance to the Constitution, the legislature had the authority to stop the implementation of whatever national law was causing the problem.

The second point Webster said Hayne presented was that this right to block the implementation of a federal law was "a right existing under the Constitution." This meant that the state could block a federal law on its own, without seceding from the Union. As he clearly stated later in the speech, Webster did believe in the right of the people to revolt in extreme circumstances. This point he saw as something clearly different from blocking the implementation of a law by a particular state legislature.

Continuing his list of strongly related, but slightly different, points of Hayne's argument, Webster moved to his third point: Hayne advocated that states had the right to limit the federal (general) government's power and to force the national government to limit its actions to those the states find acceptable. This clearly would make the state level of government the more powerful than the federal level. In Webster's mind, allowing states to have this type of power would have been a move back toward the power structure of the Articles of Confederation.

In the fourth point listed by Webster, he made it clear that to accept Hayne's position would be to give each state veto power over the actions of the national government. Contrary to the understanding that only the Supreme Court had the power to rule on cases of constitutionality, Hayne would extend this power to each state. Webster's last point in this section of the speech was his assertion that Hayne believed that the state's power was not only to ignore national laws but also to officially declare them void. In the speech, but not the excerpt, Webster went on to declare that these points were the essence of Hayne's arguments and that while many in South Carolina might disagree with the federal tariffs, Webster did not believe a majority of South Carolinians accepted Hayne's argument. Hayne then interrupted and read a statement from a document known as the Virginia Resolution that supported states' rights. After Webster spoke briefly about the times when armed revolution might be necessary, in a second point of information, Hayne clearly stated that his view was not limited to times of revolution; rather, he believed that a state could constitutionally block any action by the national government. This meant that Hayne believed that the Constitution granted states the right to annul national laws.

After this second clarification by Hayne, the speech resumed at the next section of the excerpt. Webster initiated his argument by asking whether one could claim to be upholding the Constitution by not allowing the government outlined within it to function. Webster did not deny that it was possible to change the structure of the government or to object to unconstitutional laws. The focal point of the discussion, for Webster, was, what part of the American system of government had the right to judge the constitutionality of laws? As to the states' right to do this, Webster was clear in his response. "I do not admit it." Webster said there might be times, as in 1776, when an armed revolution might be justified. But for the states to ignore, or call unconstitutional, laws that met the normal standard of constitutionality, was totally wrong from Webster's point of view.

Webster repeatedly made the point that there was normal acceptance of a law and there was the extreme case when violent revolution was justified, but nothing in between. Continuing in the text, Webster rejected the idea that people's right "to resist oppression . . . the ground of revolution" gave states the right to "annul a law of Congress." For Webster, it was an either/or situation. Either one was operating under the Constitution in which the national government was given various rights and powers or one was not operating under the Constitution, which would mean using "an ultimate violent remedy." There was no middle ground for states to partially accept the governmental structure of the Constitution. This interpretation was held by Webster, but not by Hayne, because of their differing assumptions regarding who had created the American system of government. For Webster, the Constitution and the government of the United States was the "creature of the people," while the statement that Hayne read from the Virginia Resolution stated the basis of "the federal government . . . result[ed] from the compact to which the States are parties." This difference as to the basis of the national government was the issue on which Webster spent considerable time.

Webster called it absurd that anyone would believe that it was not "the people's Constitution, the people's government, made for the people, made by the people, and answerable to the people." Webster agreed that state governments did have a role to play within the federal system, but he disagreed that they were "sovereign over the people." By this Webster meant that states could not interfere with the Constitution, as its power came from the people. The supreme power, in Webster's political theory, was the people. Even though the legitimacy of state and national governments come from the same source, there were differences in their roles. According to Webster, while states had an essential role to play within the federal system, "In the Constitution of the United States, so far, it must be admitted, state sovereignty is effectually controlled." Thus, although Webster admitted that the national government did not have unlimited powers, its power came from the people and not the states. Therefore, any limitation of power came from the people and not from the states. Whether states should be limited in their power, and if so, where the limits should be drawn, was not at the heart of this discussion, according to Webster. He said he was dealing with the present system outlined in the Constitution.

During the next portion of the speech (which is not in the excerpt), Webster illustrated several areas in which the Constitution, and therefore the people, gave the powers to national government and not to the states. He continued by dealing with the Carolina Doctrine (the states' ability to nullify federal laws), listing the current and some previous regional disagreements on national laws, and asking how differences in opinion among the states would be resolved when some accepted a federal law and others did not.

Returning to the issue of where the foundation of political power is, Webster reasserted that the power came from the people. The system of government was "erected by the people," and the people had the right and power to change it, if they desired. The division of power between the state and federal governments was because of what he called a division of labor between the two. Webster then went on to advance his claim of federal superiority over state governments by asserting that the people have supported the national government in order to impose "restraints on state sovereignties." Listing powers reserved to the national government, Webster remarked that if the state governments really were the entities that created the national government, then it was strange that so many powers were taken away from the states and given to the national government.

In a passage not included in the excerpt Webster outlined the role of the Supreme Court and how granting it the power to decide on constitutionality made the current system a government and not a confederation. Because of this, as the excerpt continues, Webster asserted that state governments did not have the ability to "protect the people from intolerable oppression." Webster argued that anytime oppression was so extreme that the states might contribute to the protection of the people, the people would already have taken steps to protect themselves. "A nullifying act of a state legislature cannot alter the case," was Webster's statement regarding the inadequacies of state governments. Webster maintained that his argument clearly supported people's rights, some of which the people had voluntarily given to the national government. Webster then went on to confirm that there was only one body, at the federal level rather than the state level, which had the power to determine whether an action was proper. Webster again reminded the senators that he accepted the idea that the national government had "limited powers." However, this did not make it possible for states to nullify an act of the national government.

In the closing section of the speech, Webster apologized for speaking so long, and he repeated his claim that, while the topic was of great concern to him, this speech was not something for which he had prepared. He recalled his Federalist background, asserting that he had always worked for the interests of the entire United States. He recalled that the United States had come into existence because of "great adversity" and, in its initial years, was far from solid. However, Webster proclaimed that everyone could be proud of what the Union had achieved and that each year its achievements were even greater, just as its territory and population continued to grow. Webster was convinced that liberty could only be preserved by the preservation of the United States. He proclaimed, "while the Union lasts, we have high, exciting, gratifying prospects spread out before us, for us and our children." He felt that only through unity was happiness and prosperity possible. Webster offered a prayer that he would never see events move beyond debates, to "civil feuds . . . drenched . . . in fraternal blood!" His hope was that throughout his life and beyond, the country would remain united, without "a single star obscured." Rather, Webster prayed that what would always be seen was the image "dear to every true American heart—Liberty and Union, now and forever, one and inseparable!"

Essential Themes

Ultimately, Webster was on the winning side of the debate over states' rights versus the power of the national government. While not everyone has agreed with the relative powers of the national versus state governments, it is clear that throughout the decades since Webster's speech his point of view has prevailed. States do not have the right to unilaterally reject a federal law, just as he so eloquently argued. This debate and this speech did not end the "issue of whether a state could nullify a national law. The nullification debate continued for three more years, but Webster had asserted his philosophical position so forcefully that it became widely accepted. This was helped by the fact that more than forty thousand copies of his speech were printed across the United States.

At the end of the Nullification Crisis, President Jackson foresaw that the next regional crisis would be over slavery. The same strong pro-Union views that Webster held and proclaimed in the 1830s, and fear of massive bloodshed if secession were attempted by the South, were the reasons he accepted the Compromise of 1850, even though it cost him politically. Webster desperately sought ways to help cement the unity of the United States. Eventually the regional disagreements became so great that words alone could not solve the problem, and the two sides could not envision any more compromises. However, after the close of the Civil War, perhaps even bloodier than Webster had foreseen, Webster's vision of a strong, prosperous United States, made possible by the unity of the nation, came to be better understood by all.

Donald A. Watt, PhD

Bibliography

Baxter, Maurice G. *One and Inseparable: Daniel Webster and the Union.* Cambridge: Harvard UP, 1984. Print.

Byrd, Robert C. *The Senate, 1789–1989: Classic Senate Speeches.* Washington, DC: US Senate, 1994. Print.

Remini, Robert V. *Daniel Webster: The Man and His Time.* New York: Norton, 1997. Print.

Additional Reading

Bartlett, Irving H. *Daniel Webster.* New York: Norton, 1978. Print.

Kartalopoulos, William S. "Daniel Webster: Dartmouth's Favorite Son." *Dartmouth College.* Dartmouth College, 1995. Web. 3 Sept. 2012.

McDonald, Forrest. *States' Rights and the Union: Imperium in Imperio.* Lawrence: UP of Kansas, 2000. Print.

Webster, Daniel, et al. *The Webster-Hayne Debate on the Nature of the Union.* Indianapolis: Liberty Fund, 2000. Print.

LESSON PLAN: **The Debate Over States' Rights**

Students analyze Webster's speech, examine its impact on rising sectional differences and conflicts over states' rights, and evaluate its place among political speeches in American history.

Learning Objectives

Compare and contrast differing sets of ideas related to political and sectional differences; analyze cause-and-effect relationships to understand how economic growth affected life in the North, South, and West; analyze multiple causation of the formation of political parties, including sectional factors; evaluate the importance of Webster's speech in US history.

Materials: Excerpts from: Daniel Webster's "Liberty and Union, Now and Forever, One and Inseparable" (1830); Andrew Jackson's "Message to the Senate and House Regarding South Carolina's Nullification" (1833)

Overview Questions

Why does Webster support a strong federal government? Why does Webster consider the Constitution the "supreme law"? How did Webster's speech reflect the growing divide between political parties and regions of the country? Did Webster's speech have a lasting impact on the United States? Why or why not?

Step 1: Comprehension Questions

What are Webster's reasons for claiming that states don't have the right to "annul the law of Congress"? Why does Webster state that the Constitution was "made for the people, made by the people, and answerable to the people"?

- **Activity:** Have students discuss passages related to Webster's main arguments; have student pairs list Webster's reasons in support of a strong federal government.

Step 2: Comprehension Questions

Why does Webster assert that the Union is "a copious fountain of national, social, and personal happiness"? What is the significance of Webster's conclusion: "Liberty and Union, now and forever, one and inseparable"?

- **Activity:** Have students summarize Webster's views on government power; ask volunteers to read aloud their summaries; have students debate the proper balance of federal and state power.

Step 3: Context Questions

Webster and Jackson represented different political parties; why did they both argue for a strong federal government? Why did Jackson call for force if necessary to preserve the Union while Webster did not?

- **Activity:** Have students create a Venn diagram to compare and contrast the two speeches; have students present their diagrams; have students explore other historical documents to evaluate how economics contributed to political and sectional differences.

Step 4: Exploration Questions

Many historians consider Webster's speech one of the most important in US history; do you agree? Why or why not?

- **Activity:** Have students list five speeches they consider the most influential in US history and their reasons why; have students present and evaluate their lists in small groups.

Step 5: Response Paper

Word length and additional requirements set by Instructor. Students answer the research question in the *Overview Questions*. Students state a thesis and use as evidence passages from the primary source document as well as support from supplemental materials assigned in the lesson.

■ *Cherokee Nation v. Georgia*

Date: March 18, 1831
Author: Marshall, John
Genre: court opinion; law

"An Indian tribe or nation within the United States is not a foreign state, in the sense of the constitution, and cannot maintain an action in the courts of the United States."

Summary Overview

On March 18, 1831, the US Supreme Court handed down a decision to the Cherokee Nation denying its petition to prevent the state of Georgia from extending legal authority into Cherokee territory. In 1829 and 1830, Georgia's state legislature had enacted a series of legislative acts stripping the Cherokees residing within its borders of their constitutional, judicial, and legal autonomy. The Cherokee Nation, receiving negligible support in countering Georgia's actions from either the newly elected President Andrew Jackson or the US Congress, turned to the Supreme Court to seek recognition of its status as a sovereign nation.

Writing the majority opinion for the court in *Cherokee Nation v. Georgia*, John Marshall dismissed the Cherokees' case on the grounds that American Indian tribes were not considered foreign nations under the Constitution and therefore could not bring suit directly to the Supreme Court without going through the process of lower court appeals. Unable to receive an injunction against the actions of the state of Georgia, the Cherokee Nation remained increasingly vulnerable to the coercive tactics of the state government in bringing Cherokee territory under its authority. The Cherokees were ultimately expelled from their tribal lands in the Southeast and removed to land west of the Mississippi in an episode now known as the Trail of Tears.

Defining Moment

The relationship of the United States government to American Indian nations was complex and inconsistent. The designs of the growing nation on Indian lands led to many instances of conflict and negotiation, which in turn led to many signed and broken treaties. Early government policy, however, did not necessarily foreshadow the direction that Indian relations would take in the mid-nineteenth century. George Washington's administration, and particularly his secretary of war, Henry Knox, implemented a policy that recognized tribal sovereignty and the right of native peoples to their lands. In addition, the government implemented a "civilization" initiative that encouraged American Indians to convert from hunting and gathering to farming and animal husbandry.

The Cherokee Nation in particular embraced the civilization initiative. Early on, the Cherokees modeled their tribal system around the institutional structures of the United States. By the mid-eighteenth century, the Cherokees established a primary chief to act as their nation's figurehead and elected a national council to assist in conducting negotiations with the United States federal government. The tribe had established a legal and judicial system and police force by 1810 and ratified a constitution in 1827. In the early nineteenth century, Cherokee territory occupied land located within the states of North Carolina, Tennessee, Georgia, and Alabama. By the 1820s, the state of Georgia had begun to put intense pressure on native peoples to cede their land and relocate out of the state in order to allow white Georgians access to the valuable territory. After the Creeks were pushed out of state land via the 1826 Treaty of Washington, Georgia set its sights on removing the Cherokees.

Encountering resistance to removal by the Cherokee nation, Georgia began to use legislative acts to extend the state's legal powers into Cherokee territory. John Ross, the Cherokees' principle chief, immediately sought legal assistance against the encroachments of the state. The tribe contracted William Wirt, a nationally renowned lawyer, as their attorney. Wirt saw his first opportunity to challenge Georgia's actions when a Cherokee man, George "Corn" Tassel, was arrested by Georgia police for murdering another Cherokee man on Cherokee territory. Though the Cherokee Nation disputed the jurisdiction of the case, a tribunal of appellate judges within the state overruled the Cherokee contestation and allowed the Tassel trial to proceed. Tassel was found guilty and sentenced to death. Wirt appealed Tassel's conviction and asked the Supreme Court for an injunction to suspend Tassel's execution. Chief Justice John Marshall granted the request and subpoenaed Georgia's governor to appear before the court. Georgia's governor and the state legislature decided to ignore the subpoena and carry out the execution, defying the Supreme Court's instruction. On December 24, 1830, Tassel was hanged; William Wirt filed the case that would become *Cherokee Nation v. Georgia* three days later.

Author Biography

Born in Germantown, Virginia, in 1755, John Marshall experienced firsthand the often-violent contests over land between western Virginian settlers and American Indians. Despite being steeped in frontier life from a very young age, he was encouraged by his father to read poetry, history, and classical texts. His childhood was a mixture of pioneer living and genteel education. Marshall came of age surrounded by the philosophy and patriotism of the Revolutionary War. At age nineteen, he was appointed lieutenant in the Continental Army and later spent the infamous winter of 1777–78 with George Washington at Valley Forge. While on extended leave from the war, Marshall began the only formal legal training of his career when he attended a three-month-long course in law taught by George Wythe at the College of William and Mary. Soon after, Marshall resigned his commission in the Continental Army, passed the bar exam, and attempted to begin practicing law. The disruption of the war, however, had closed the courts temporarily. His career in law delayed, Marshall won a seat in the Virginia House of Delegates in 1782. Finding the House of Delegates chaotic and unproductive, Marshall spent time in and out of office sporadically over the years due to his ambivalence about the efficiency of the legislature. His experience in legislative government, coupled with the nationalistic feelings he developed in the Revolution, began to shape Marshall's belief in the need for a Federalist system driven by a strong central government.

Marshall held prominent positions in the political and legal institutions of Virginia for nearly two decades until President John Adams began to recruit him to national office. Serving first as a special envoy to France during the XYZ Affair and then as Adams's secretary of state, Marshall was ultimately appointed by Adams to the position of chief justice of the United States Supreme Court in 1801. Marshall's legacy as chief justice would prove to be one of the most enduring and influential in the history of the court. Marshall died in 1835, after thirty-four years as chief justice.

HISTORICAL DOCUMENT

This bill is brought by the Cherokee nation, praying an injunction to restrain the state of Georgia from the execution of certain laws of that state, which, as is alleged, go directly to annihilate the Cherokee as a political society, and to seize for the use of Georgia, the lands of the nation which have been assured to them by the United States, in solemn treaties repeatedly made and still in force.

If courts were permitted to indulge their sympathies, a case better calculated to excite them can scarcely be imagined. A people, once numerous, powerful, and truly independent, found by our ancestors in the quiet and uncontrolled possession of an ample domain, gradually sinking beneath our superior policy, our arts and our arms, have yielded their lands, by successive treaties, each of which contains a solemn guarantee of the residue, until they retain no more of their formerly extensive territory than is deemed necessary to their comfortable subsistence. To preserve this remnant, the present application is made.

Before we can look into the merits of the case, a preliminary inquiry presents itself. Has this court jurisdiction of the cause? The third article of the constitution describes the extent of the judicial power. The second section closes an enumeration of the cases to which it is extended, with "controversies between a state or citizens thereof, and foreign states, citizens or subjects." A subsequent clause of the same section gives the Supreme Court original jurisdiction, in all cases in which a state shall be a party. The party defendant may then unquestionably be sued in this court. May the plaintiff sue in it? Is the Cherokee nation a foreign state, in the sense in which that term is used in the constitution?

The counsel for the plaintiffs have maintained the affirmative of this proposition with great earnestness and ability. So much of the argument as was intended to prove the character of the Cherokees as a state, as a distinct political society, separated from others, capable of managing its own affairs and governing itself, has in the opinion of a majority of the judges, been completely successful. They have been uniformly treated as a state, from the settlement of our country. The numerous treaties made with them by the United States, recognize them as a people capable of maintaining the relations of peace and war, of being responsible in their political character for any violation of their engagements, or for any aggression committed on the citizens of the United States, by any individual of their community. Laws have been enacted in the spirit of these treaties. The acts of our government plainly recognise the Cherokee nation as a state, and the courts are bound by those acts.

A question of much more difficulty remains. Do the Cherokees constitute a foreign state in the sense of the constitution? The counsel have shown conclusively, that they are not a state of the Union, and have insisted that, individually, they are aliens, not owing allegiance to the United States. An aggregate of aliens composing a state must, they say, be a foreign state; each individual being foreign, the whole must be foreign.

This argument is imposing, but we must examine it more closely, before we yield to it. The condition of the Indians in relation to the United States is, perhaps, unlike that of any other two people in existence. In general, nations not owing a common allegiance, are foreign to each other. The term foreign nation is, with strict propriety, applicable by either to the other. But the relation of the Indians to the United States is marked by peculiar and cardinal distinctions which exist nowhere else. The Indian territory is admitted to compose a part of the United States. In all our maps, geographical treaties, histories and laws, it is so considered. In all our intercourse with foreign nations, in our commercial regulations, in any attempt at intercourse between Indians and foreign nations, they are considered as within the jurisdictional limits of the United States, subject to many of those restraints which are imposed upon our own citizens. They acknowledge themselves, in their treaties, to be under the protection of the United States; they admit, that the United States shall have the sole and exclusive right of regulating the trade with them, and managing all their affairs as they think proper; and the Cherokees in particular were allowed by the treaty of Hopewell, which preceded the constitution, "to send a deputy of their choice, whenever they think fit, to congress." Treaties were made with some tribes, by the state of New York, under a then unsettled construction of the confederation, by which they ceded all their lands to that state, taking back a limited grant to themselves, in which they admit their dependence. Though the Indians are acknowledged to have an unquestionable, and heretofore unquestioned, right to the lands they occupy, until that right shall be extinguished by a voluntary cession to our government; yet it may well be doubted, whether those tribes which reside within the acknowledged boundaries of the United States can, with accuracy, be denominated foreign nations. They may, more correctly, perhaps, be denominated domestic dependent nations. They occupy a territory to which we assert a title independent of their will, which must take effect in point of possession, when their right of possession ceases. Meanwhile, they are in a state of pupilage; their relation to the United States resembles that of a ward to his guardian. They look to our government for protection: rely upon its kindness and its power; appeal to it for relief to their wants; and address the president as their great father. They and their country are considered by foreign nations, as well as by ourselves, as being so completely under the sovereignty and dominion of the United States, that any attempt to acquire their lands, or to form a political connection with them would be considered by all as an invasion of our territory and an act of hostility. These considerations go far to support the opinion, that the framers of our constitution had not the Indian tribes in view, when they opened the courts of the Union to controversies between a state or the citizens thereof and foreign states.

In considering this subject, the habits and usages of the Indians, in their intercourse with their white neighbors, ought not to be entirely disregarded. At the time the constitution was framed, the idea of appealing to an American court of justice for an assertion of right or a redress of wrong, had perhaps never entered the mind of an Indian or of his tribe. Their appeal was to the tomahawk, or to the government. This was well understood by the statesmen who framed the constitution of the United States, and might furnish some reason for omitting to enumerate them among the parties who might sue in the courts of the Union. Be this as it may, the peculiar relations between the United States and the Indians occupying our territory are such, that we should feel much difficulty in considering them as designated by the term foreign state, were there no other part of the constitution which might shed light on the meaning of these words. But we think that in construing them, considerable aid is furnished by that clause in the eighth section of the third article, which empowers congress to "regulate commerce with foreign nations, and among the several states, and with the Indian tribes." In this clause, they are as clearly contradistinguished by a name appropriate to themselves, from foreign nations, as from the several states composing the Union. They are designated by a distinct appellation; and as this appellation can be applied to neither of the others, neither can the application distinguishing either of the others be, in fair construction, applied to them. The objects to which the power of regulating commerce might be directed, are divided into three distinct classes-foreign nations, the several states, and Indian tribes. When forming this article, the convention considered them as entirely distinct. We cannot assume that the distinction was lost, in framing a subsequent article, unless there be something in its language to authorize the assumption.

The counsel for the plaintiffs contend, that the words "Indian tribes" were introduced into the article, empowering congress to regulate commerce, for the purpose of removing those doubts in which the management of Indian affairs was involved by the language of the ninth article of the confederation. Intending to give the whole of managing those affairs to the government about to be instituted, the convention conferred it explicitly; and omitted those qualifications which embarrassed the exercise of it, as granted in the confederation. This may be admitted, without weakening the construction which has been intimated. Had the Indian tribes been foreign nations, in the view of the convention, this exclusive power of regulating intercourse with them might have been, and most probably, would have been, specifically given, in language indicating that idea, not in language contradistinguishing them from foreign nations. Congress might have been empowered "to regulate commerce with foreign nations, including the Indian tribes, and among the several states." This language would have suggested itself to statesmen who considered the Indian tribes as foreign nations, and were yet desirous of mentioning them particularly.

It has been also said, that the same words have not necessarily the same meaning attached to them, when found in different parts of the same instrument; their meaning is controlled by the context. This is undoubtedly true. In common language, the same word has various meanings, and the peculiar sense in which it is used in any sentence, is to be determined by the context. This may not be equally true with respect to proper names. "Foreign nations" is a general term, the application of which to Indian tribes, when used in the American constitution, is, at best, extremely questionable. In one article, in which a power is given to be exercised in regard to foreign nations generally, and to the Indian tribes particularly, they are mentioned as separate, in terms clearly contradistinguishing them from each other. We perceive plainly, that the constitution, in this article, does not comprehend Indian tribes in the general term "foreign nations;" not, we presume, because a tribe may not be a nation, but because it is not foreign to the United States. When, afterwards, the term "foreign state" is introduced, we cannot impute to the convention, the intention to desert its former meaning, and to comprehend Indian tribes within it, unless the context force that construction on us. We find nothing in the context, and nothing in the subject of the article, which leads to it.

The court has bestowed its best attention on this question, and, after mature deliberation, the majority is of opinion, that an Indian tribe or nation within the United States is not a foreign state, in the sense of the constitution, and cannot maintain an action in the courts of the United States.

A serious additional objection exists to the jurisdiction of the court. Is the matter of the bill the proper subject for judicial inquiry and decision? It seeks to restrain a state from the forcible exercise of legislative power over a neighboring people, asserting their independence; their right to which the state denies. On several of the matters alleged in the bill, for example, on the laws making it criminal to exercise the usual powers of self-government in their own country, by the Cherokee nation, this court cannot interpose; at least, in the form in which those matters are presented.

That part of the bill which respects the land occupied by the Indians, and prays the aid of the court to protect their possession, may be more doubtful. The mere question of right might, perhaps, be decided by this court, in a proper case, with proper parties. But the court is asked to do more than decide on the title. The bill requires us to control the legislature of Georgia, and to restrain the exertion of its physical force. The propriety of such an interposition by the court may be well questioned; it savors too much of the exercise of political power, to be within the proper province of the judicial department. But the opinion on the point respecting parties makes it unnecessary to decide this question.

If it be true, that the Cherokee nation have rights, this is not the tribunal in which those rights are to be asserted. If it be true, that wrongs have been inflicted, and that still greater are to be apprehended, this is not the tribunal which can redress the past or prevent the future. The motion for an injunction is denied.

STORY, J. and THOMPSON, J. dissenting.

GLOSSARY

appellation: name

injunction: a court order preventing an action from advancing

jurisdictional limits: in this context, the territorial boundaries within which US law applies

ninth article of the confederation: refers to the Article of Confederation that gave Congress the right to resolve international disputes

pupilage: a period of supervision by an authoritative body

sovereignty: absolute statutory power inside territorial boundaries

Treaty of Hopewell: treaty signed in 1785 between the Continental Congress and the Cherokee Nation agreeing to limits on the expansion of White settlement

Document Analysis

The case of *Cherokee Nation v. Georgia* defined the relationship between the United States and the American Indian nations inhabiting the land. In writing the majority opinion in the case, John Marshall articulated maturing ideas on constitutionally defined relationships between Indian nations and US federal and state governments. He also explored the right of Indian nations to bring suit in original jurisdiction cases and conceived of native nations' status as "domestic dependent nations." The *Cherokee Nation* court opinion reflects Marshall's attempts to navigate the increasingly precarious position of native peoples in the Southeast, the hostile political environment surrounding the court, and the limitations set by the Constitution.

Original Jurisdiction

When deciding on how to best address the Cherokee Nation's legal case, the tribe's attorney, William Wirt, presented John Ross, the Cherokee principle chief, with three options. An individual suit could be made against a state official to challenge the restrictive Cherokee codes of the state legislature, but Wirt was wary of seeking legal recourse from the lower courts. The state and the Cherokee Nation could jointly present the case to the Supreme Court to determine the laws' constitutionality, a proposal the Georgia governor rejected outright. The Cherokees could appeal a case tried in Georgia to the Supreme Court, but after the collapse of the Tassel case, Wirt decided to press forward with the last option: Wirt would attempt to convince the Supreme Court to hear the case on the basis of original jurisdiction. In article 3, section 2, clause 2 of the US Constitution, the Supreme Court is given original jurisdiction—the right to try previously untried cases—only in circumstances involving suits between states and foreign governments. All other cases the Supreme Court adjudicates must be heard on appeal. Wirt framed his case to the court by arguing for the sovereignty of the Cherokees as a foreign nation. To argue for their status as a foreign nation, Wirt used the US government's history of signing treaties with the Cherokees, just as they would any other foreign nation, as evidence that they held sovereignty over their own governmental structure and controlled their own lands. Additionally, Wirt contested Georgia's actions by pointing to the supremacy clause of the Constitution, which prevents states from superseding national laws and treaties.

Marshall's interpretation of original jurisdiction in this case demonstrated his understanding of the limits set by the Constitution on the court. Though Marshall used the *Cherokee Nation* opinion to explore the constitutionality of several aspects of Cherokee claims to sovereignty, the case ultimately came down to the question of whether they had standing to exercise original jurisdiction. In addressing this issue, Marshall looks directly to the language of the Constitution. While he notes that, according to article 3, section 2 of the Constitution, the state of Georgia could clearly be a party to an original jurisdiction case, he questions whether "the Cherokees constitute a foreign state in the sense of the constitution." Marshall acknowledges the independence and self-governance of the Cherokees and notes that the Cherokees are not citizens of the United States, but instead citizens of their own nation. What complicates their status as "foreign" nations, according to Marshall, is that "Indian territory is admitted to compose a part of the United States." Marshall also points to the language contained within many treaties between the US government and American Indians in which native tribes had agreed "to be under the protection of the United States." For Marshall, these pieces of evidence indicate that, traditionally, neither the US government nor Indian nations themselves had considered their relationship to be one between foreign nations. In making the final determination on the issue of original jurisdiction, however, Marshall looks to article 3, section 8 of the Constitution, which gives Congress the right to "regulate commerce with foreign nations, and among the several states, and with the Indian tribes." This passage, according to the chief justice, made a clear distinction between foreign nations and Indian tribes by listing them separately. For Marshall, then, the Cherokees made up a distinct nation, just not a foreign one.

His decision to throw the case out on these grounds, however, raised questions for the Cherokees and their allies about the political reasons for allowing the case to turn on a jurisdictional issue. Both the hostility of the Jackson administration to the power of the court and the administration's support for Indian removal made the *Cherokee Nation* case politically challenging for Marshall to navigate. At the conclusion of his opinion, Marshall notes that a decision favoring the Cherokees would require the Supreme Court to control the actions of a state. Marshall notes that the "propriety of such an interposition by the court may be well questioned; it savors too much of the exercise of political power, to be within the proper province of the judicial department." This statement reveals Marshall's acute understanding that the exercise of such power was under intense scrutiny at the time. Democrats in Congress, with the support of Andrew Jackson, had proposed a bill that would strip the Supreme Court of its ability to review the constitutionality of state court decisions. Moreover, Jackson had based much of his campaign for president on promises to diminish federal authority and strip Indians of their remaining hold on eastern land. Knowing the political climate and the looming threats to judicial power, some Cherokees and their advocates accused Marshall of avoiding a controversial decision by citing a simple lack of constitutional authority in the *Cherokee Nation* decision.

Domestic Dependent Nations

Despite the dismissal of the case on jurisdictional grounds, Marshall did manage to include important contributions to the definition of native nations' sovereignty and, perhaps most significantly, defined their relationship to the federal government within the *Cherokee Nation* opinion. One of the most enduring aspects of Marshall's decision was the demarcation of native tribes as "domestic dependent nations." This designation, articulated for the first time in *Cherokee Nation v. State of Georgia*, persists as the legal categorization of the relationship between native tribes and the US government. Marshall's reasoning for creating the category of "domestic dependent nation" rested on his interpretation not only of the physical fact of native nations residing within US borders, but more importantly on the power dynamic he saw operating between the United States and native tribes. For Marshall, the United States occupied the role of "guardian" to native nations, and while independent, these nations could not persevere without the authority of the United States protecting and guiding them. Marshall gave several reasons for this assessment of the relationship. He saw the acknowledgment by native tribes of US governmental power over their interests, along with the familial language by which they addressed the nation's president, as signs of native deference to the supremacy of the United Sates. In an irony Marshall does not highlight, the mere use of governmental systems and organizations by native tribes to seek resolution of their disputes was also evidence of their "state of pupilage." Finally, the inability of native nations to make territorial or political deals with any country other than the US government provides for Marshall conclusive proof that their status was dependent.

Even while initiating a new status for native tribes on US land, Marshall also takes time in the opinion to recognize that the court fully acknowledges the constitutional right and ability of native nations to construct political and social systems separate from those of the United States. The Cherokees, according to the court, could govern their own affairs as a separate state. For the chief justice, the decision by the Cherokees to draft their own constitution, set up their own system of policing and adjudication, elect their own executive officials, and even declare "peace and war" against the United States is perfectly within their rights as an independent "political society." Marshall's apparent acknowledgement of the rights held by the Cherokees indicates that the court understood the state of Georgia to be violating these same rights. For some Cherokees, including John Ross, the *Cherokee Nation* opinion, though unsuccessful, provided hope that with a suitable case the Supreme Court could alleviate the pressure being placed on them by the Georgia legislature.

In the end, however, John Marshall's opinion in *Cherokee Nation v. Georgia* was a decision that neither satisfied the Cherokees, who hoped to halt Georgia's encroaching authority, nor the Jackson administration, which sought a quick removal of native peoples from southeastern lands. Marshall walked a fine political line in the *Cherokee Nation* decision, acknowledging that the Cherokees enjoyed a level of independence over their own police powers and land use, but also establishing the precedent that American Indian nations are distinct in their status as "domestic dependent nations" to the United States. Marshall's categorization left the status of native sovereignty legally ambiguous. The most poignant issue for the Cherokees, however, was that the chief justice's exploration of these issues in the court opinion was purely cerebral. Ultimately, the *Cherokee Nation* decision did little to resolve the question of American Indians' legal relationship to the individual states. Marshall dismissed the case on the grounds that American Indian grievances could not be brought to the court as original jurisdiction cases. That dismissal on jurisdictional grounds consequently prevented the court from being able to consider fully the Cherokee Nation's claims that Georgia was illegally infringing upon its sovereignty.

Scholars continue to argue over the extent to which Marshall's ruling in the case was an act of political strategy. Marshall was intent on preserving the Supreme Court's authority as a branch of government. Knowing that Andrew Jackson's administration was hostile to judicial power and that the administration would likely undermine a decision that restrained the action of the state of Georgia and protected the Cherokee claims, Joseph C. Burke and others have argued that Marshall avoided adjudicating a case that could have potentially led to a weakening of the authority of the court. Others such as Tim A. Garrison have noted that John Marshall's understanding of Indian sovereignty had shown an intellectual evolution over the course of several Supreme Court cases. Marshall's 1810 opinion in *Fletcher v. Peck* suggested that natives' rights to possession of their land may be overridden by states in certain circumstances. *Johnson v. McIntosh*, decided in 1823, again saw Marshall espousing the possibility that native rights to lands could be extinguished, but this time only by the federal government. By the time of *Cherokee Nation*, however, Marshall's interpretation of native sovereignty had expanded significantly. For Garrison and others, Marshall's changing understanding of native sovereignty provides evidence that Marshall truly believed native tribes could not be considered foreign nations under the Constitution and therefore lacked standing for original jurisdiction.

Essential Themes

Though the Cherokee Nation did not get the ruling it wanted in its case against Georgia, many remained hopeful that Marshall's acknowledgment of the Cherokees' independence as a nation could potentially result in a favorable ruling "in a proper case, with proper parties." Encouraged to continue litigation until a case emerged in which the court had jurisdiction, the Cherokees finally received the adjudication they had hoped for in 1832 with the decision handed down in *Worcester v. Georgia*. In writing the majority opinion, Marshall finally codified into law the sovereignty of the Cherokee Nation and confirmed that the tribe was protected under the laws and treaties they negotiated with the federal government, which no state had a right to subvert.

Although a major legal victory for the Cherokees, the state of Georgia refused to recognize the court's authority in the matter and did nothing to reverse its Indian policies. The Jackson administration likewise refused to enforce the court's decision or overturn the Indian Removal Act passed by Congress two years prior. The state of Georgia remained free to exercise authority over the native people and lands within its borders. With no tangible federal assistance, the Cherokee Nation became increasingly divided over whether to succumb to state pressure and move to reserved lands west of the Mississippi River.

John Ross and the Cherokee National Council continued to resist the pressure to remove, but in 1835, a group of Cherokees identifying themselves as the Treaty Party, signed the Treaty of New Echota with officials from the US government. The treaty ceded all Cherokee lands in Georgia and agreed to removal. Though the majority party of the Cherokee Nation challenged the legality of the treaty, it became the legal basis of their expulsion from Georgia lands. Even in the face of their near-total territorial loss, the Cherokees and other native nations in the United States persist even today in claiming and fighting for their status as sovereign nations.

Amanda Beyer-Purvis, MA

Bibliography

Burke, Joseph C. "The Cherokee Cases: A Study in Law, Politics, and Morality." *Stanford Law Review* 21.3 (1969): 500–31. Print.

Conser, Walter H., Jr. "John Ross and the Cherokee Resistance Campaign, 1833–1838." *Journal of Southern History* 44.2 (1978): 191–212. Print.

Davis, Ethan. "An Administrative Trail of Tears: Indian Removal." *American Journal of Legal History* 50.1 (2008–10): 49–100. Print.

Garrison, Tim A. *The Legal Ideology of Removal: The Southern Judiciary and the Sovereignty of Native American Nations*. Athens: U of Georgia P, 2002. Print.

Magliocca, Gerard N. "The Cherokee Removal and the Fourteenth Amendment." *Duke Law Journal* 53.3 (2003): 875–965. Print.

Norgren, Jill. *The Cherokee Cases: Two Landmark Federal Decisions in the Fight for Sovereignty*. Norman: U of Oklahoma P, 2004. Print.

---. "Lawyers and the Legal Business of the Cherokee Republic in Courts of the United States,1829–1835." *Law and History Review* 10.2 (1992): 253–314. Print.

Perdue, Theda, and Michael D. Green. *The Cherokee Nation and the Trail of Tears*. London: Viking, 2007. Print.

Williams, Walter L. "Cherokee History: An Analysis of Recent Studies." *American Indian Quarterly* 5.4 (1979): 347–54. Print.

Additional Reading

Agnew, Brad. *Fort Gibson, Terminal on the Trail of Tears*. Norman: U of Oklahoma P, 1980. Print.

Ehle, John. *Trail of Tears: The Rise and Fall of the Cherokee Nation*. New York: Doubleday, 1988. Print.

Foreman, Grant. *Indian Removal: The Emigration of the Five Civilized Tribes of Indians*. Norman: U of Oklahoma P, 1953. Print.

Perdue, Theda, and Michael D. Green. *The Cherokee Removal: A Brief History with Documents*. Boston: Bedford/St. Martin's, 1995. Print.

Remini, Robert V. *Andrew Jackson & His Indian Wars*. New York: Viking, 2001. Print.

Wilkinson, Charles F. *American Indians, Time, and the Law: Native Societies in a Modern Constitutional Democracy*. New Haven: Yale UP, 1987. Print.

LESSON PLAN: **The Supreme Court Rules against the Cherokee Nation**

Students analyze John Marshall's majority opinion against the Cherokee Nation, examine its impact on the Cherokee people, and explore the Cherokee people's strategies to keep their homelands.

Learning Objectives

Consider multiple perspectives on American Indian policy; analyze cause-and-effect relationships that affected territorial expansion and life in the South and West; compare and contrast differing sets of ideas to explore strategies for survival forged by the Cherokee people and other American Indians.

Materials: Chief Justice John Marshall, *Cherokee Nation v. Georgia* (1831); Cherokee Nation delegation, "Address of the Committee and Council of the Cherokee Nation to the People of the United States" (1830).

Overview Questions

Why does Marshall rule that the Supreme Court has no jurisdiction in this case? What impact did this ruling have on the Cherokee people, and on the South and West? What strategies did the Cherokee people use to keep their homelands? How effective were these strategies?

Step 1: Comprehension Questions

Why does Marshall argue that the Cherokee Nation is not a foreign state "in the sense in which the term is used in the constitution"? Is this argument central to Marshall's decision against the Cherokee Nation? Why or why not?

- **Activity:** Invite students to read aloud key passages. Have students list Marshall's reasons for arguing that the Cherokee Nation is not a foreign state and evaluate their validity.

Step 2: Comprehension Questions

What is the significance of Marshall describing the Cherokees' relationship to the United States as that "of a ward to his guardian"? How does Marshall's use of language enhance his argument?

- **Activity:** Have student identify passages that demonstrate Marshall's use of language. Ask students to paraphrase these passages and discuss their meaning and importance.

Step 3: Context Questions

Why did Marshall's ruling pave the way for the Cherokees' removal from their homelands? How did this ruling affect the Cherokee people? How did it change the South and West?

- **Activity:** Have students explore historical sources related to this ruling's impact on the Cherokee Nation, the South, and the West, and present their findings.

Step 4: Exploration Questions

How do Marshall's arguments compare with those in the Cherokee delegation's speech before Congress? The Cherokee people went to court and before Congress to try to keep their land. Were their strategies effective? Why or why not?

- **Activity:** Have students present arguments that support or counter Marshall's ruling. Have students explore alternative courses of action that the Cherokee people used or could have considered.

Step 5: Response Paper

Word length and additional requirements set by Instructor. Students answer the research question in the *Overview Questions.* Students state a thesis and use as evidence passages from the primary source document as well as support from supplemental materials assigned in the lesson.

Fugitive Slave Act

Date: September 18, 1850
Author: US Congress
Genre: Law

"Upon affidavit made by the claimant . . . he has reason to apprehend that such fugitive will be rescued by force from . . . their possession before he can be taken beyond the limits of the State in which the arrest is made."

Summary Overview

Signed into law in September of 1850 as one of the five major compromise measures of the sweeping Compromise of 1850, the Fugitive Slave Act quickly emerged as that series' most controversial and divisive pieces of legislation. Intended to placate Southern slaveholding interests and thus ease the growing tensions between the free states of the North and the slave states of the South, the Fugitive Slave Act had precisely the opposite effect by dramatically increasing animosity between the regions. The act built upon the existing Fugitive Slave Act of 1793 to require Northerners to actively cooperate with runaway slave catchers and placed the decision on the legal status of captured African Americans firmly in the hands of federal judges. The law also punished those who failed to maintain control of captured African Americans or who helped them escape from bondage. The severity of the act immediately inflamed Northerners and bolstered the antislavery movement, but the law itself remained on the books until 1864.

Defining Moment

Tensions over slavery had been rising for decades before the creation of the Compromise of 1850 and the accompanying Fugitive Slave Act. From colonial times, the use of unfree labor had been vital to the economies of the agricultural regions of the American Southeast, where European settlers employed contractually bounded indentured servants and captured African slaves and their descendents as unfree workers. Although slavery had been legal and active in the North during the colonial period, economic shifts, urbanization, and sociopolitical ideas helped make bonded labor less valuable there; states such as Vermont and Massachusetts barred slavery soon after independence, and the institution was prohibited altogether in the Northern frontier of the Northwest Territory. At the same time, however, the growing value of cash crops—particularly cotton—made enslaved labor an ever larger component of the Southern economy. Even after the transatlantic slave trade ended in 1808, the number of slaves in South grew as a result of natural increase. Slavery became ever more entwined with economics in the places where it was practiced.

At the same time, Southern concerns over the issue of fugitive slaves were also rising. Running away was one common form of slave resistance, and the rising number and declining treatment of enslaved African Americans only made the act more likely to occur. Although slaves who escaped with little planning often enjoyed liberty for only a few days before they either returned voluntarily or were captured in the local area, well-planned escapes by those who were unencumbered by family ties—typically young, single men—had a better chance of success. The rise of the Underground Railroad during the first half of nineteenth century also encouraged those who wished to flee slavery, particularly those enslaved in states geographically near free states. Thus, slaveholders strongly desired a new fugitive slave law to repress such attempts.

In January of 1850 and in response to California's application to join the union as a free state, Senator Henry Clay of Kentucky proposed a series of measures aimed at quelling the rising tensions over slavery and thus keeping the nation intact. The resulting Compromise of 1850, passed piecemeal the following September, contained five major provisions. First, California was admitted to the union as a free state. The disputed boundaries of the slave state of Texas were fixed, and, further, the remainder of the previously Mexican land was organized into territories in which voters would determine whether the territory was slave or free. Fourth—and most controversially—a new, stringent Fugitive Slave Act would be adopted to ease the process of recapturing escaped slaves. Finally, the domestic slave trade would be banned in the nation's capital, Washington, DC.

Author Biography

The US Congress that passed the Fugitive Slave Act in 1850 was one divided along sectional and political lines, largely over the defining political issue of the era—slavery. For decades, Congress had sought to maintain the delicate balance between slave and free states within its halls by selectively admitting states according to their status. In 1820, for example, the Missouri Compromise had sought to prevent an outbreak of sectional tensions by admitting both the slave state of Missouri and the free state of Maine at the same time, thus preventing any one faction from gaining a majority in the Senate. This compromise assured sectional balance in the legislature for several years, but the competing ideologies of political parties grew. From the single-party control of Democratic-Republicans during the so-called Era of Good Feelings during the late 1810s and early 1820s emerged a Congress divided among the Democrats, Whigs, and, by the late 1840s, the Free-Soilers, who opposed the expansion of slavery to the territories.

These political differences were on full display in the votes on all of the measures contained within the Compromise of 1850, but none more so than the passage of the Fugitive Slave Act. In total, just thirty-nine of the Senate's sixty members voted on the law; whether those abstaining from the vote, which included both Northern and Southern members of the body, were simply unable to attend the vote or preferred not have their name attached to the measure in any way remains a question of history. Interestingly, the three senatorial architects of the compromise were among those who did not vote on it; Daniel Webster had left office in late July, while Clay and Stephen Douglas simply declined to cast ballots. Voting patterns on the bill largely followed sectional lines, with all twenty-four Southern senators who cast votes favoring the measure and twelve of fifteen Northern senators who cast votes opposing it. Of the three Northern votes for the measure, all came from Democrats.

The members of the 223-member House of Representatives voted along similar lines. More than 10 percent of the total body chose to abstain from voting, the majority of whom represented free states. Of the 109 total votes in favor of the Fugitive Slave Act, seventy-eight of them came from Southern representatives, none of whom opposed the measure. The remaining support came from Northern representatives, although more than double the number of Northern supporters opposed the law; in fact, just two more Northerners voted in favor of the bill than declined to vote at all. From the beginning, the Fugitive Slave Act was clearly a measure that lacked nationwide support.

HISTORICAL DOCUMENT

An Act to amend, and supplementary to, the Act entitled "An Act respecting Fugitives from Justice, and Persons escaping from the Service of their Masters," approved February twelfth, one thousand seven hundred and ninety-three.

Be it enacted by the Senate and House of Representatives of the United States of America in congress assembled, That the persons who have been, or may hereafter be, appointed commissioners, in virtue of any act of Congress, by the Circuit Courts of the United States and who, in consequence of such appointment, are authorized to exercise the powers that any justice of the peace, or other magistrate of any of the United States, may exercise in respect to offenders for any crime or offence against the United States, by arresting, imprisoning, or bailing the same under and by virtue of the thirty-third section of the act of the twenty-fourth of September seventeen hundred and eighty- nine, entitled "An Act to establish the Judicial courts of the United States," shall be, and are hereby, authorized and required to exercise and discharge all the powers and duties conferred by this act.

SEC. 2. And be it further enacted, That the Superior Court of each organized Territory of the United States shall have the same power to appoint commissioners to take acknowledgements of bail and affidavits and to take depositions of witnesses in civil cases, which is now possessed by the Circuit Court of the United States; and all commissioners who shall hereafter be appointed for such purposes by the Superior Court of any organized Territory of the United States, shall possess all the powers, and exercise all the duties, conferred by law upon the commissioners appointed by the Circuit Courts of the United States for similar purposes, and shall moreover exercise and discharge all the powers and duties conferred by this act.

SEC. 3. And be it further enacted, That the Circuit Courts of the United States, and the Superior Courts of each organized Territory of the United States, shall from time to time enlarge the number of commissioners, with a view to afford reasonable facilities to reclaim fugitives from labor, and to the prompt discharge of the duties imposed by this act.

SEC. 4. And be it further enacted, That the commissioners above named shall have concurrent jurisdiction with the judges of the Circuit and District Courts of the United States, in their respective circuits and districts within the several States, and the judges of the Superior Courts of the Territories, severally and collectively, in term-time and vacation; and shall grant certificates to such claimants, upon satisfactory proof being made, with authority to take and remove such fugitives from service or labor, under the restrictions herein contained, to the State or Territory from which such persons may have escaped or fled.

SEC. 5. And be it further enacted, That it shall be the duty of all marshals and deputy marshals to obey and execute all warrants and precepts issued under the provisions of this act, when to them directed; and should any marshal or deputy marshal refuse to receive such warrant, or other process, when tendered, or to use all proper means diligently to execute the same, he shall, on conviction thereof, be fined in the sum of one thousand dollars, to the use of such claimant, on the motion of such claimant, by the Circuit or District Court for the district of such marshal; and after arrest of such fugitive, by such marshal or his deputy, or whilst at any time in his custody under the provisions of this act, should such fugitive escape, whether with or without the assent of such marshal or his deputy, such marshal shall be liable, on his official bond, to be prosecuted for the benefit of such claimant, for the full value of the service or labor of said fugitive in the State, Territory, or District whence he escaped: and the better to enable the said commissioners, when thus appointed, to execute their duties faithfully and efficiently, in conformity with the requirements of the Constitution of the United States and of this act, they are hereby authorized and empowered, within their counties respectively, to appoint, in writing under their hands, anyone or more suitable persons, from time to time, to execute all such warrants and other process as may be issued by them in the lawful performance of their respective duties; with authority to such commissioners, or the persons to be appointed by them, to execute process as aforesaid, to summon and call to their aid the bystanders, or posse comitatus of the proper county, when necessary to ensure a faithful observance of the clause of the Constitution referred to, in conformity with the provisions of this act; and all good citizens are hereby commanded to aid and assist in the prompt and efficient execution of this law, whenever their services may he required, as aforesaid, for that purpose; and said warrants shall run, and be executed by said officers, anywhere in the State within which they are issued.

SEC. 6. And be it further enacted, That when a person held to service or labor in any State or Territory of the United States, ha: heretofore or shall hereafter escape into another State or Territory of the United States, the person or persons to whom such service 01 labor may be due, or his, her, or their agent or attorney, duly authorized, by power of attorney, in writing, acknowledged and certified under the seal of some legal officer or court of the State or Territory in which the same may be executed, may pursue and reclaim such fugitive person, either by procuring a warrant from some one of the courts, judges, or commissioners aforesaid, of the proper circuit, district, or county, for the apprehension of such fugitive from service or labor, or by seizing and arresting such fugitive, where the same can be done without process, and by taking, or causing such person to be taken, forthwith before such court, judge, or commissioner, whose duty it shall be to hear and determine the case of such claimant in a summary manner; and upon satisfactory proof being made, by deposition or affidavit, in writing, to be taken and certified by such court, judge, or commissioner, or by other satisfactory testimony, duly taken and certified by some court, magistrate, justice of the peace, or other legal officer authorized to administer an oath and take depositions under the laws of the State or Territory from which such person owing service or labor may have escaped, with a certificate of such magistracy or other authority, as aforesaid, with the seal of the proper court or officer thereto attached, which seal shall be sufficient to establish the competency of the proof, and with proof, also by affidavit, of the identity of the person whose service or labor is claimed to be due as aforesaid, that the person so arrested does in fact owe service or labor to the person or persons claiming him or her, in the State or Territory from which such fugitive may have escaped as aforesaid, and that said person escaped, to make out and deliver to such claimant, his or her agent or attorney, a certificate setting forth the substantial facts as to the service or labor due from such fugitive to the claimant, and of his or her escape from the State or Territory in which he or she was arrested, with authority to such claimant, or his or her agent or attorney, to use such reasonable force and restraint as may be necessary, under the circumstances of the case, to take and remove such fugitive person back to the State or Territory whence he or she may have escaped as aforesaid. In no trial or hearing under this act shall the testimony of such alleged fugitive be admitted in evidence; and the certificates in this and the first [fourth] section mentioned, shall be conclusive of the right of the person or persons in whose favor granted, to remove such fugitive to the State or Territory from which he escaped, and shall prevent all molestation of such person or persons by any process issued by any court, judge, magistrate, or other person whomsoever.

SEC. 7. And be it further enacted, That any person who shall knowingly and willingly obstruct, hinder, or prevent such claimant, his agent or attorney, or any person or persons lawfully assisting him, her, or them, from arresting such a fugitive from service or labor, either with or without process as aforesaid, or shall rescue, or attempt to rescue, such fugitive from service or labor, from the custody of such claimant, his or her agent or attorney, or other person or persons lawfully assisting as aforesaid, when so arrested, pursuant to the authority herein given and declared; or shall aid, abet, or assist such person so owing service or labor as aforesaid, directly or indirectly, to escape from such claimant, his agent or attorney, or other person or persons legally authorized as aforesaid; or shall harbor or conceal such fugitive, so as to prevent the discovery and arrest of such person, after notice or knowledge of the fact that such person was a fugitive from service or labor as aforesaid, shall, for either of said offences, be subject to a fine not exceeding one thousand dollars, and imprisonment not exceeding six months, by indictment and conviction before the District Court of the United States for the district in which such offence may have been committed, or before the proper court of criminal jurisdiction, if committed within any one of the organized Territories of the United States; and shall moreover forfeit and pay, by way of civil damages to the party injured by such illegal conduct, the sum of one thousand dollars for each fugitive so lost as aforesaid, to be recovered by action of debt, in any of the District or Territorial Courts aforesaid, within whose jurisdiction the said offence may have been committed.

Sec. 8. And be it further enacted, That the marshals, their deputies, and the clerks of the said District and Territorial Courts, shall be paid, for their services, the like fees as may be allowed for similar services in other cases; and where such services are rendered exclusively in the arrest, custody, and delivery of the fugitive to the claimant, his or her agent or attorney, or where such supposed fugitive may be discharged out of custody for the want of sufficient proof as aforesaid, then such fees are to be paid in whole by such claimant, his or her agent or attorney; and in all cases where the proceedings are before a commissioner, he shall be entitled to a fee of ten dollars in full for his services in each case, upon the delivery of the said certificate to the claimant, his agent or attorney; or a fee of five dollars in cases where the proof shall not, in the opinion of such commissioner, warrant such certificate and delivery, inclusive of all services incident to such arrest and examination, to be paid, in either case, by the claimant, his or her agent or attorney. The person or persons authorized to execute the process to be issued by such commissioner for the arrest and detention of fugitives from service or labor as aforesaid, shall also be entitled to a fee of five dollars each for each person he or they may arrest, and take before any commissioner as aforesaid, at the instance and request of such claimant, with such other fees as may be deemed reasonable by such commissioner for such other additional services as may be necessarily performed by him or them; such as attending at the examination, keeping the fugitive in custody, and providing him with food and lodging during his detention, and until the final determination of such commissioners; and, in general, for performing such other duties as may be required by such claimant, his or her attorney or agent, or commissioner in the premises, such fees to be made up in conformity with the fees usually charged by the officers of the courts of justice within the proper district or county, as near as may be practicable, and paid by such claimants, their agents or attorneys, whether such supposed fugitives from service or labor be ordered to be delivered to such claimant by the final determination of such commissioner or not.

SEC. 9. And be it further enacted, That, upon affidavit made by the claimant of such fugitive, his agent or attorney, after such certificate has been issued, that he has reason to apprehend that such fugitive will be rescued by force from his or their possession before he can be taken beyond the limits of the State in which the arrest is made, it shall be the duty of the officer making the arrest to retain such fugitive in his custody, and to remove him to the State whence he fled, and there to deliver him to said claimant, his agent, or attorney. And to this end, the officer aforesaid is hereby authorized and required to employ so many persons as he may deem necessary to overcome such force, and to retain them in his service so long as circumstances may require. The said officer and his assistants, while so employed, to receive the same compensation, and to be allowed the same expenses, as are now allowed by law for transportation of criminals, to be certified by the judge of the district within which the arrest is made, and paid out of the treasury of the United States.

SEC. 10. And be it further enacted, That when any person held to service or labor in any State or Territory, or in the District of Columbia, shall escape therefrom, the party to whom such service or labor shall be due, his, her, or their agent or attorney, may apply to any court of record therein, or judge thereof in vacation, and make satisfactory proof to such court, or judge in vacation, of the escape aforesaid, and that the person escaping owed service or labor to such party. Whereupon the court shall cause a record to be made of the matters so proved, and also a general description of the person so escaping, with such convenient certainty as may be; and a transcript of such record, authenticated by the attestation of the clerk and of the seal of the said court, being produced in any other State, Territory, or district in which the person so escaping may be found, and being exhibited to any judge, commissioner, or other officer authorized by the law of the United States to cause persons escaping from service or labor to be delivered up, shall be held and taken to be full and conclusive evidence of the fact of escape, and that the service or labor of the person escaping is due to the party in such record mentioned. And upon the production by the said party of other and further evidence if necessary, either oral or by affidavit, in addition to what is contained in the said record of the identity of the person escaping, he or she shall be delivered up to the claimant. And the said court, commissioner, judge, or other person authorized by this act to grant certificates to claimants or fugitives, shall, upon the production of the record and other evidences aforesaid, grant to such claimant a certificate of his right to take any such person identified and proved to be owing service or labor as aforesaid, which certificate shall authorize such claimant to seize or arrest and transport such person to the State or Territory from which he escaped: Provided, That nothing herein contained shall be construed as requiring the production of a transcript of such record as evidence as aforesaid. But in its absence the claim shall be heard and determined upon other satisfactory proofs, competent in law.

GLOSSARY

abet: to encourage or help another person in an action

affidavit: a formal written statement used as evidence in court

attestation: testimony

claimants: people who make a legal claim or motion

conferred: granted

conformity: state of being in accordance with rules or standards

conviction: the act of finding a person guilty

indictment: a formal accusation

marshal: a federal official charged with capturing fugitives, serving court documents, and performing other federal law-enforcement duties

posse comitatus: a group of men raised by a sheriff to execute the law

Document Analysis

Passed in September of 1850, the Fugitive Slave Act was one component of the Compromise of 1850 unequivocally aimed at appeasing proslavery Southern interests. Unlike the other measures of the compromise—which allowed states and territories including California, New Mexico, and Utah to pursue was what expected to be an antislavery future in the United States; settled disputes surrounding the boundaries of Texas and New Mexico; and ended the slave trade in Washington, DC—the Fugitive Slave Act offered no benefit for the antislavery North. Instead, the act sought to fulfill something that Southerners had wanted for years: a stronger measure with which to legally demand the return of enslaved human property if that property successfully escaped from bondage.

The Fugitive Slave Act of 1850 was not the first measure to address the issue of runaway slaves. The US Constitution had asserted that any person "held in service or labor" in a given state could not be freed under the laws of another state if he or she reached the latter location as a fugitive. Instead, the Constitution affirmed that an escaped slave remained enslaved, and should legally be returned to the appropriate slave owner. What the Constitution did not specify, however, was any means by which this provision could be enacted.

To fill this void, the US Congress passed the nation's first Fugitive Slave Act in 1793. This law proclaimed that Southern slaveholders or slave catchers had the right to seek out escaped slaves in other states, and then to reclaim them as property after presenting evidence to that effect to a magistrate or judge. Under the federal law, captured African Americans had no right to a jury trial, nor did they have the right to present evidence in their own defense. Passed at a time when antislavery sentiment was on the rise—Northern states had already begun abolishing slavery, antislavery societies were growing in number in both the United States and Great Britain, and early abolitionists were beginning to agitate for emancipation—the law surely sought to address a growing problem, from the perspective of Southern slaveholders, of Northern support for what was likely an increasing number of enslaved African Americans.

The law failed to stop escapes, however, and in some ways even encouraged their success. Northerners largely opposed the Fugitive Slave Act as being antithetical to American ideals of liberty, equality, and justice. Even those who did not consider slavery a moral question did take issue with the law's refusal of a jury trial or even a proper defense when resolving an African American's status. Before long, antislavery Northerners were resisting the law in a variety of ways. Northern state legislatures passed personal liberty laws that restored some rights to accused fugitive slaves. In some states, convicted African Americans had the right to a jury trial upon appeal. In others, governments provided defense attorneys to aid the accused. Throughout the North, individual action also rose. Antislavery activists in individual communities formed committees that sought to help fugitive slaves and to resist the slave catchers sent to find them. On a broader scale, abolitionists helped organize the Underground Railroad to provide an informal network of safe havens to fugitive slaves traveling from the South to safety in Canada, where slavery was illegal.

Unsurprisingly, Northern resistance to the Fugitive Slave Act of 1793 angered Southerners, who saw it as an assault of their constitutional property rights. By Southern logic, the US Constitution guaranteed their right to own and hold property, in this case, humans; by escaping, slaves were essentially stealing themselves, and by protecting or aiding them, Northerners were violating the Constitution. Personal liberty laws were a particular sticking point, and in 1842, the US Supreme Court addressed the issue in the case of *Prigg v. Pennsylvania*. This ruling, over a Pennsylvania law that barred taking African Americans out of the state in order to enslave them, found that the law was unconstitutional under the constitutional supremacy clause granting precedence to federal over state laws. However, the ruling also found that Northern states had no responsibility to enforce Southern laws that had been enacted to capture fugitive slaves across state lines, and it suggested that states could make laws dictating how or whether their own state officials were required to enforce the federal Fugitive Slave Act. As a result, Northern states passed new laws that removed state-level officials from the process of seeking or convicting fugitive slaves altogether. The Fugitive Slave Act stood, but was enforced only by federal agents.

This turn of events further inflamed Southerners. The refusal of Northern states to enforce Southern property rights seemed to Southerners a direct attack by their countrymen on their lives and livelihoods. Calls for a new, more stringent federal fugitive slave law that would create an environment more conducive to the easy capture and conviction of fugitive slaves throughout the nation arose in the South. After California applied to join the Union as a free state in 1849 and the admission of New Mexico and Utah along the same lines seemed imminent, political leaders realized that Southerners would reject such a major expansion of organized free US territory without concessions to proslavery interests. One of those concessions was the adoption of the Compromise of 1850's Fugitive Slave Act, a law that directly built upon the embattled 1793 measure.

The new Fugitive Slave Act set the process of capturing, trying, and returning suspected fugitive slaves firmly into the federal arena. At its outset, the law asserted the right of federal officials to be the new national slave catchers as the law's primary enforcers. The opening section affirms that federal commissioners had the powers of "arresting, imprisoning, or bailing" any criminals so defined within the law—in other words, fugitive slaves. It further both "authorized and required" these commissioners to complete their duties, in contrast to the state officials whom had been found to not be required to execute the federal law. This time, Congress wanted to ensure that the law was enforced. Furthermore, in its second section the law named the territorial superior courts equal to the US circuit courts for the purposes of enforcing the law. Like circuit courts, territorial superior courts gained the power to appoint the special commissioners charged with executing the Fugitive Slave Act; all these courts also gained the ability to "exercise and discharge all the powers and duties conferred by this act." In other words, state courts, attached as they were to state legislatures that were sometimes antislavery, no longer had any role in the process of trying fugitive slaves. Instead, the federal government reigned supreme.

The next few sections of the law addressed further administrative details of the execution of the act. Section 3 empowered the US Circuit Courts and their territorial equivalents to hire more commissioners as needed to adequately pursue and try accused fugitives. The following section granted the federal commissioners jurisdiction throughout the circuit, district, or territorial division in which they were appointed; further, it granted these commissioners the power to bestow the certificates upon which the legal process surrounding the capture of fugitive slaves was based. Section 5 of the law charged federal marshals and deputy marshals with the enforcement of warrants and other relevant legal orders in fugitive slave cases, taking them out of the hands of state officials. Marshals who refused to perform their duties were subject to a substantial fine, and those who lost custody of an accused fugitive slave either willingly or accidentally were financially liable to the escapee's alleged owner for that person's market value in the slave owner's state. This same section also permitted federal commissioners to deputize any "one or more suitable persons" to carry out fugitive slave warrants and even to summon others living in the area to assist in the process. In no way could proslavery forces argue that the new Fugitive Slave Act failed to provide for adequate manpower to carry out its strictures.

After putting in place both the federal supremacy in the enforcement of the law and a structure of specially charged federal officials to carry it out, the Fugitive Slave Act moves to the central issue: how to find, claim, try, and restore slave owners' errant human property. Section 6 of the law declares that the owner or properly authorized agent of a runaway slave who crossed from his or her home state or territory into another had the right to "pursue and reclaim" that fugitive in the state or territory to which he or she had fled. After capture, the fugitive slave was tried and, as the later portions of the law assure, most likely convicted; the act continues that owners or agents could present a written affidavit of the fugitive's identity and status as an enslaved, rather than free, African American and as a piece of property held by the slave owner bringing the action. The slave owner or agent had the right to present a great deal of evidence supporting the claim that the accused was, in fact, a fugitive slave; the accused, however, was expressly forbidden from entering testimony in his or her own defense. Instead, the certificates asserting the slave owner's claims about the fugitive's status "shall be conclusive . . . to remove such fugitive to the State or Territory from which he escaped, and shall prevent all molestation of such person or persons by any process issued by any court, judge, magistrate, or other person whomsoever."

The process for issuing these vital certificates is detailed in the Fugitive Slave Act's final section. Under the law, a slave owner, or that person's representative, could seek a certificate in the court of his choice. That court was responsible for recording details that were used to identify the accused fugitive slave—little more than "a general description"—and that told about the events of the accused person's escape. These details were provided by the claimant to the court and served to provide the "full and conclusive evidence" of the escape, the identity of the fugitive, and the fact that the person in question was legitimately owned by the slaveholder asserting the claim. This certificate served as a legal basis to seize, try, and transport the accused fugitive in any US state or territory and acted as the main evidence in any trial.

These actions clearly stacked the legal deck against African Americans, fugitive slaves and free blacks alike. The certificates of proof could be issued by a court in the slave owner's home state and carried the force of law wherever they were taken; the certificates were the sole permissible form of evidence in a fugitive slave trial. Thus, a free African American kidnapped and accused of being a fugitive slave lacked the legal right to present documentation in his or her own defense. The accused lacked any way to prove their identities or display manumission papers or other records to show either that they were not the persons named in any certificates or that the statements made by the certificates were invalid. To be captured and tried was practically as good as being captured and sent to slavery, with only something of a sham legal proceeding intervening. The earlier actions of Northern state courts to help keep possible fugitives from being quickly sent South were thus impeded.

The Fugitive Slave Act also outlawed individual action in support of fugitive slaves. Anyone who "knowingly and willingly" interfered with the efforts of a slave owner, or any of that owner's agents or representatives, to seize and try a suspected fugitive faced legal penalty, as did anyone who worked to help a fugitive slave escape from the slave catchers' "justice" by helping that fugitive travel or hide, as on the Underground Railroad. These penalties were steep; convicted white sympathizers faced a fine of up to one thousand dollars—as much as twenty-five thousand dollars in modern terms—and a term in prison of up to six months. A person convicted of helping a fugitive slave successfully escape was also held financially liable for the slave owner's loss of property in the amount of one thousand dollars per head. The chain of forced responsibility did not end with capture. The arresting officer was legally bound by section 9 to ensure that the fugitive slave did not escape his custody, and was charged "to employ so many persons as he may deem necessary to overcome" anyone who might try to help the fugitive get away. No longer could Northerners show opposition to Southern slavery through this type of activism, or even through benign apathy, without facing serious potential consequences. Even those opposed to slavery were now legally required to support slave owners living in distant slave states.

Further, the Fugitive Slave Act incentivized the capture and conviction of African Americans regardless of their actual status as fugitive slaves or free blacks through its system of payment. Under the law, the slave owner who made the legal claim was responsible for paying the commissioners and others in the process, as well as for the food, shelter, and other basic needs of an accused fugitive held in custody. Federal commissioners who tried and convicted a fugitive slave received ten dollars for their services; commissioners who tried, but did not convict, a fugitive slave were paid only five dollars. Those who caught and arrested a suspected fugitive received five dollars per head. A convicted fugitive slave was worth more to a commissioner than a freed defendant. The seizure of essentially any African American could generate income for the person who performed the arrest. Thus, the financial structure of the law encouraged the arrest of anyone as a suspected fugitive, rather than the actual person in question, so long as the slave owner was not too particular. It further urged federal commissioners to take the easy route of finding that person guilty of being a fugitive slave.

Unsurprisingly, these measures terrified free blacks living in the North and appalled all people committed to the American ideals of justice. Northern opposition to the practice of capturing and returning fugitive slaves without adequate legal protections was obvious in the region's history of personal liberty laws and lack of concerted effort to execute the Fugitive Slave Act of 1793. Yet the law now made all Northerners active members of the slaveholding society by forcing them to carry out the law or face direct personal penalty. It also allowed for the easy conviction of any accused fugitive with essentially no opportunity for defense. As part of the Compromise of 1850, the Fugitive Slave Act showed that the expansion of free US territory was in no way an invitation for African Americans to live freely in it.

Essential Themes

In theory, the Fugitive Slave Act had been created to ease tensions over slavery. The law granted Southerners something that they deeply desired—stronger legal action against escaped slaves—in exchange for the prospect of a growing number of free territories. The reality of the Fugitive Slave Act was quite different than the theory, however. In practice, the law enraged Northerners who were forced not merely to tolerate the existence of slavery across their borders but also to work directly to support slave owners through the active policing and threatened consequences of neglecting to capture and to hold a suspected runaway. The law's structure for managing the status of captured African Americans suspected of being fugitives was quickly and accurately viewed as overly weighted in favor of the slaveholders; over the next several years, more than three hundred captured African Americans were sent to the South. In contrast, just a handful of people managed to maintain their freedom after being taken into custody. The law, in effect, began what escaped slave and Northerner Harriet Jacobs called "the beginning of a reign of terror to the colored population" (286). African Americans in the North who had escaped from slavery decades previously faced the possibility of being captured and re-enslaved; children and young people who had, they believed, been born free could be taken because their mother had been an escaped slave. Even those who had gained freedom legally lacked the ability to prove their case in court, and thus could be wrongfully re-enslaved. Unsurprisingly, numerous African Americans fled the North to the safety of Canada.

The law energized the abolition movement and persuaded more Northerners to support the cause of abolition. Previously, black abolitionists had been on the whole more vocal and more radical than their white counterparts. The Fugitive Slave Act changed all that as white abolitionists lashed out against what they saw as enforced complicity in slavery. The operations of the Underground Railroad improved as the ranks and dedication of abolitionists increased. Several Northern states also responded to the act by passing personal liberty laws that sought to contravene its most extreme measures. These laws allowed suspected fugitives to appeal their case before a jury, for example, and placed harsh punishments on those who took African Americans illegally or lied to force them to return to slavery. Such laws further angered Southern leaders, who saw them as an attack on their rights to maintain slavery. Writing in December of 1860, just ten years after the passage of the Fugitive Slave Act, the leaders of South Carolina declared that these laws were evidence of the breached contract among the states guaranteed in the US Constitution and one of the main reasons that the state was declaring its secession from the United States. Ultimately, the Fugitive Slave Act contributed directly to the very conflict that it sought to prevent: the breakup of the United States of America and the beginning of the Civil War that followed.

Vanessa E. Vaughn, MA

Bibliography

Hamilton, Holman. *Prologue to Conflict: The Crisis and Compromise of 1850*. New York: Norton, 1964. Print.

Horton, James Oliver, and Lois E. Horton. *Slavery and the Making of America*. New York: Oxford UP, 2005. Print.

Jacobs, Harriet. *Incidents in the Life of a Slave Girl*. Boston, 1861. Print.

"*Prigg v. Pennsylvania*." *Oyez*. The Oyez Project at IIT Chicago-Kent College of Law, 27 Mar. 2013. Web. 29 Mar. 2013.

Ransom, Roger L. *Conflict and Compromise: The Political Economy of Slavery, Emancipation, and the American Civil War*. New York: Cambridge UP, 1989. Print.

Remini, Robert V. *At the Edge of the Precipice: Henry Clay and the Compromise That Saved the Union*. New York: Perseus, 2010. Print.

Additional Reading

Brown, William Wells. *From Fugitive Slave to Free Man: The Autobiographies of William Wells Brown*. New York: Mentor, 1993. Print.

Thompson, John. *The Life of John Thompson, a Fugitive Slave: Containing His History of Twenty-Five Years in Bondage and His Providential Escape*. 1856. New York: Penguin, 2011. Print.

LESSON PLAN: **The Fugitive Slave Act and the Compromise of 1850**

Students will analyze the Fugitive Slave Act of 1850 and explore its significance as a polarizing event before the Civil War.

Learning Objectives

Consider and appreciate multiple historical perspectives of slaveholders, abolitionists, and African Americans; interrogate historical data to understand the Fugitive Slave Act; support interpretations of the Fugitive Slave Act with historical evidence; establish temporal order from the Compromise of 1850 to the Civil War.

Materials: The Fugitive Slave Act (1850); the Compromise of 1850.

Overview Questions

What were the main provisions of the Fugitive Slave Act? Why was it passed? Why was the law controversial? How did it impact escaped slaves seeking freedom in the North, free African Americans, and relations between the North and the South?

Step 1: Comprehension Questions

What problem does Section 6 of this legislation indicate it was passed to address? What role does it assign to federal officials in carrying it out? What incentives does it provide to encourage those persons to do so?

- **Activity:** Remind students that the Fugitive Slave Act was part of the Compromise of 1850. Have students identify the other provisions of the compromise.

Step 2: Comprehension Questions

What procedures does the law create for the capture and return of fugitive slaves? What provisions does it make to prevent others from hindering the law's enforcement? What specific actions to help escaped slaves does the law make crimes?

- **Activity:** Have students create flow charts to detail and illustrate the step-by-step process in the capture and return of escaped slaves.

Step 3: Context Questions

What does the phrase in Section 6 "without process" mean? What is the significance of the last sentence in the section? To where could an African American in the North have turned for help if suspected or accused of being an escaped slave?

- **Activity:** Discuss the concept of due process of law. Explore with students the implications of these two provisions for all African Americans in the North, whether free or escaped slaves.

Step 4: Historical Connections Questions

Why was passage of this law so important to Southerners? How effective do its provisions seem to be in addressing the concerns that motivated its passage? How do you think Northerners, and especially abolitionists, felt about this law? For what reasons would they have held these feelings?

- **Activity:** Have students take the role of a Southern slaveholder, an abolitionist, a free Northern African American, or an escaped slave in the North and write a letter to the editor expressing their views on the Fugitive Slave Act. Call on students to read their letters to the class.

Step 5: Response Paper

Word length and additional requirements set by Instructor. Students answer the research question in the Overview Questions. Students state a thesis and use as evidence passages from the primary source document as well as support from supplemental materials assigned in the lesson.

Compromise of 1850

Date: January 29, 1850; passed August–September 1850
Author: Clay, Henry
Genre: speech; law

"It being desirable, for the peace, concord, and harmony of the Union of these States, to settle and adjust amicably all existing questions of controversy between them arising out of the institution of slavery upon a fair, equitable and just basis."

Summary Overview

Comprising a series of five laws passed during the late summer of 1850, the Compromise of 1850 was a bold but ultimately unsuccessful attempt to placate sectional interests and bind together the North and South in a lasting, if legally and economically divergent, Union. Brought on by the application of California to enter the nation as a free state in late 1849, the compromise sought to meet both Northern interests in the expansion of the United States into additional free territory and Southern interests in offering the possibility of the extension of slavery into the territories and in protecting slave owners' human property through a strengthened fugitive slave law. The final compromise allowed for the admission of California, the usage of popular sovereignty to determine the slavery question in the territories, the end of the slave trade in the nation's capital, and the passage of a stringent Fugitive Slave Act. Despite its provisions, the compromise failed to prevent the looming national crisis of the Civil War, barely more than a decade away.

Defining Moment

Slavery was the subject of numerous compromises during the early history of the United States. The framers of the Constitution had faced the issue during the writing of the nation's plan for government, establishing guidelines for the counting of enslaved individuals for the purposes of representation, affirming the legality of the return of fugitive slaves, and postponing the legal end of the transatlantic slave trade until the year 1808. Forty years later, the Missouri Compromise of 1820 sought to ease the tensions that arose over Missouri's application for admission to the Union as a slave state by allowing for the concurrent entry of Maine as a free state—a duality that permitted the balance of slave and free state representation in the Senate to remain equal—and by barring the expansion of slavery further into the territory acquired under the Louisiana Purchase.

However, the issue of slavery remained unsettled at best. The nation continued to expand west as American settlers entered lands previously controlled by American Indians or foreign powers. The admission of slave states was routinely balanced by that of free states, so that no one region overtook the other in power and influence. Nevertheless, conflict arose. One of the leading issues behind the Texas Revolution, for example, was the settlers' desires to own slaves in territory under the jurisdiction of emancipated Mexico.

That event led to the Mexican-American War, which itself generated a new source of debate: how to determine the slave or free status of the vast territory acquired under the Treaty of Guadalupe Hidalgo.

In December of 1849, the territory of California applied for admission to the Union as a free state. This application kicked off a new sectional crisis, for the approval of such as a measure would again disrupt the delicate balance between slave and free states in Congress. The addition of another state also reflected the issues inherent in the debate over the expansion of slavery through the growing United States. Because proslavery Southerners greatly opposed the Wilmot Proviso, a proposed measure that would bar the expansion of slavery into any territory, the issue of slavery again required a substantive compromise to prevent disagreements, or worse, disunion. Thus began the debates that would create the Compromise of 1850, an effort to appease antislavery Northerners, mollify proslavery expansionist Southerners, and create a lasting status quo in the style of the Missouri Compromise three decades previously.

Author Biography

Known as the "Great Compromiser" for his numerous efforts to effect compromise over the issue of slavery, statesman Henry Clay was the primary force behind the congressional effort to enact the Compromise of 1850. Of particular assistance to the aging senator from Kentucky—in 1850, Clay was in his early seventies—were both a fellow congressional veteran Massachusetts senator Daniel Webster and a rising star, Illinois senator Stephen Douglas. Webster was a famed orator, a former US congressman and secretary of state, and a longtime senator. Douglas, one of the Senate's youngest members, was a Democrat who espoused the theory of popular sovereignty, or the practice of allowing a territory's people decide whether to permit or ban slavery within its borders.

By 1850, Clay was one of Congress's most respected statesmen. Born in Virginia in 1777 and raised in that state, he entered state government as a teenager and gained admission to the bar at the age of twenty. He then moved to Kentucky, where his mother lived, and established himself in legal practice in Lexington. Within a few years his public-speaking skills had helped him win a seat in the Kentucky legislature; in 1806, he entered the Senate through special appointment to serve the last few months of the term of disgraced Senator John Adair. Clay spent a few more years in the Kentucky legislature before returning to the US Senate, again through appointment, in 1810. He won election in his own right to the House of Representatives later that year, and immediately upon his entry to that body was named Speaker of the House.

Clay used his position to promote a nationalist agenda he termed the "American System," and he was highly regarded by his peers. Clay used this political capital to help end the crises that arose after Missouri applied for admission to the Union as a slave state—an act that would allow for the expansion of slavery into the territories and give slaveholding states an advantage in Congress. Clay helped broker the Missouri Compromise, preserving the balance and stemming major sectional conflict for some years. He spent much of the next several decades in national government, mounting a failed bid for the presidency, serving as secretary of state under John Quincy Adams, and filling one of Kentucky's two seats in the US Senate for much of the 1830s and early 1840s. He returned to the Senate shortly before a new sectional crisis arose in 1849. Clay died in 1852, just a few years after the Compromise was passed.

HISTORICAL DOCUMENT

CLAY'S RESOLUTIONS, January 29, 1850

It being desirable, for the peace, concord, and harmony of the Union of these States, to settle and adjust amicably all existing questions of controversy between them arising out of the institution of slavery upon a fair, equitable and just basis: therefore,

1. Resolved, That California, with suitable boundaries, ought, upon her application to be admitted as one of the States of this Union, without the imposition by Congress of any restriction in respect to the exclusion or introduction of slavery within those boundaries.

2. Resolved, That as slavery does not exist by law, and is not likely to be introduced into any of the territory acquired by the United States from the republic of Mexico, it is inexpedient for Congress to provide by law either for its introduction into, or exclusion from, any part of the said territory; and that appropriate territorial governments ought to be established by Congress in all of the said territory, not assigned as the boundaries of the proposed State of California, without the adoption of any restriction or condition on the subject of slavery.

3. Resolved, That the western boundary of the State of Texas ought to be fixed on the Rio del Norte, commencing one marine league from its mouth, and running up that river to the southern line of New Mexico; thence with that line eastwardly, and so continuing in the same direction to the line as established between the United States and Spain, excluding any portion of New Mexico, whether lying on the east or west of that river.

4. Resolved, That it be proposed to the State of Texas, that the United States will provide for the payment of all that portion of the legitimate and bona fide public debt of that State contracted prior to its annexation to the United States, and for which the duties on foreign imports were pledged by the said State to its creditors, not exceeding the sum of- dollars, in consideration of the said duties so pledged having been no longer applicable to that object after the said annexation, but having thenceforward become payable to the United States; and upon the condition, also, that the said State of Texas shall, by some solemn and authentic act of her legislature or of a convention, relinquish to the United States any claim which it has to any part of New Mexico.

5. Resolved, That it is inexpedient to abolish slavery in the District of Columbia whilst that institution continues to exist in the State of Maryland, without the consent of that State, without the consent of the people of the District, and without just compensation to the owners of slaves within the District.

6. But, resolved, That it is expedient to prohibit, within the District, the slave trade in slaves brought into it from States or places beyond the limits of the District, either to be sold therein as merchandise, or to be transported to other markets without the District of Columbia.

7. Resolved, That more effectual provision ought to be made by law, according to the requirement of the constitution, for the restitution and delivery of persons bound to service or labor in any State, who may escape into any other State or Territory in the Union. And,

8. Resolved, That Congress has no power to promote or obstruct the trade in slaves between the slaveholding States; but that the admission or exclusion of slaves brought from one into another of them, depends exclusively upon their own particular laws.

GLOSSARY

bona fide: genuine

inexpedient: not profitable or beneficial

marine league: measure of distance equaling three nautical miles

obstruct: block or bar

restitution: return of property to its original owner

Document Analysis

On January 29, 1850, Clay set forth a series of eight resolutions that formed the heart of the Compromise of 1850, a group of laws that sought to quell sectional anxieties and assure national "peace, concord, and harmony" over the controversial issues of slavery and its expansion into the territories in much the same way that the Clay-engineered Missouri Compromise had done three decades previously. His resolutions related to three major issues: westward expansion, the practice of slavery and the slave trade in the District of Columbia, and the creation of a new and more stringent Fugitive Slave Act.

In ongoing conflict over the continued practice of slavery in general, the expansion of US territory into lands previously held by Mexico, where slavery was illegal, provided a new battleground. These lands included California, New Mexico, Utah, and Texas, with the latter carrying its own associated set of border disputes and debt. Because much of this area had a non-slaveholding past—and because the geographical features of Utah were thought not to be conducive to the agricultural practices with which US slavery was closely tied—it was widely accepted that California, New Mexico, and Utah would become free territories or states. Expansion in this way would essentially prevent the South from growing west, further isolating it from the remainder of the Union and creating a general sense of unease among proslavery Southerners. One of the main factors behind Southern anxiety was the 1846 proposal known as the Wilmot Proviso. This measure would have banned the expansion of slavery into any territory acquired from Mexico. Although it passed the House on several occasions, the Wilmot Proviso failed to clear the Senate. Nevertheless, its specter informed all debate about the western territories.

Thus, Clay began his resolutions by addressing the event that had instigated the revival of sectional debate that the proposed compromise sought to address: the application by California to enter the United States. That event had revived rumbles of discontent and led to new calls in the House of Representatives that the South's interests must be acknowledged and protected or that the union of states should be dissolved entirely. California's situation was an unusual one. The area had been under US control for a relatively short period of time before the discovery of gold made its population rapidly surge from just six thousand to some eighty-five thousand. Sitting president Zachary Taylor, a Southerner and hero of the Mexican-American War, encouraged California and nearby New Mexico to organize constitutional conventions and apply for statehood without undergoing the usual territorial stage. Taylor then suggested that Congress make no decisions on the slavery issue until the western regions submitted their applications, hoping that this would forestall what was certain to be contentious debate. Taylor's plan was an impractical one, however; as all three states were expected to organize free state constitutions, proslavery Southerners would never accept the addition of so many new states covering so great a territory without some concessions in return.

Clay sought to address the California question by simply taking Congress out of the equation. California, he argued, should be admitted to the Union "without the imposition by Congress of any restriction in respect to the exclusion or introduction of slavery." The people of California, he later argued, had chosen not to include slavery in their state constitution, and Congress had no place to reverse that decision. Over the next several months, the admission of California remained the most popular and least debated of the measures associated with the compromise—so much so that some suggested that California's admission be separated from the rest of the compromise. Yet without the carrot of California statehood little incentive existed for North and South to resolve the other sectional issues at stake; thus, leaders kept California attached to the compromise as a whole.

This same absence of congressional involvement, Clay argued in his second resolution, should be extended to the remainder of the Mexican territory: New Mexico and Utah. Both of these regions were expected to apply for statehood in short order, and New Mexico's history of liberty and Utah's Mormon opposition for slavery made it unlikely that either would permit slavery. Thus, Clay suggested, the direct congressional creation of an antislavery measure in the vein of the Wilmot Proviso was not necessary. Free-Soilers and other Northerners opposed to the expansion of slavery were almost certain to see the practice barred in California, New Mexico, and Utah, after all, and the passage of the Wilmot Proviso would only enrage Southerners. Thus, it was "inexpedient" in Clay's opinion to pursue that route. Instead, Congress should permit the territories to organize without interference. The actual outcome of this proposal was perhaps unexpected. Although the issues surrounding the admission of New Mexico and Utah contributed greatly to the demise of the proposed omnibus bill containing all of the measures of the compromise in July of 1850, the territories won admission after Douglas split the measure into several independent segment. Neither Utah nor New Mexico became a state at that time, however. New Mexico was acknowledged as not sufficiently prepared for the challenges of statehood and instead chose to pursue a territorial organization; with its cultural practice of polygamy, Utah could not win sufficient support for full statehood until 1896, well after the slavery question had been decided by the Civil War.

Clay next turned to the issues surrounding Texas. Texas was already a state, having been added in 1845. Despite this, its formal boundaries remained unsettled, and a land dispute was underway between Texas and New Mexico, primarily over the area surrounding Santa Fe. Texas's admission had also permitted for the possibility that the massive territory be divided into several smaller states. Further complicating matters was Texas's high debt load, which stemmed from both borrowing during the state's Mexican and republican periods and the loss of customs revenue resulting from its addition to the United States. Together, these sums amounted to some $11 million, a figure equal to hundreds of millions of dollars in modern terms. According to Texans, the United States was at least partially responsible for that debt because of the decline in customs revenue. The state's fate was therefore undetermined in a number of ways, and the proposed admission of New Mexico directly affected Texas's future.

Clay offered two proposals to resolve the Texas question. First, he suggested that Texas's border follow the Rio Grande from its mouth to the southern line of New Mexico, and then travel eastward to the line set by the US-Spain Treaty of 1819. This proposal would have resulted in a much smaller Texas than the one that actually was established, with the northern border of the state roughly level with the city of El Paso. At the same time, Clay proposed that the United States assume that portion of Texas's public debt which had accrued before the state became part of the United States. In exchange, Texas would give up its claims to the lands slated for inclusion in the territory of New Mexico. These proposals proved contentious. Texans sought greater debt relief and more land; at one point, Texans even threatened to establish a military presence in Santa Fe to assert their claim. Several competing proposals for the boundaries of Texas emerged. Not until August was an accepted compromise reached—one that was more favorable to Texan interests without impeding New Mexico's independence. The United States granted Texas $10 million, nearly enough to settle its public debts. The state's new borders held more than thirty thousand square miles of land than had Clay's proposed boundaries—and Santa Fe remained in New Mexico.

Clay's fifth and sixth resolutions were also interrelated. In the fifth, he argued that slavery should remain legal in the nation's capital because of a variety of factors, including Washington, DC's geographic position between two slave states, Virginia and Maryland; the inadvisability of enacting a federal measure for the district without consulting its residents or those of nearby Maryland, which would become a slave state largely disconnected from its Southern slaveholding neighbors were the district made free; and without a plan for payment to the district's slave owners for the emancipation of their valuable human property. These arguments refuted efforts by Northern Whigs and Free-Soilers to end slavery in the district, an action strongly opposed by proslavery Southerners who argued that abolition in Washington, DC, was further a violation of the good faith of Maryland and Virginia, which had given up the land needed to create the capital. Debate also took place over whether Congress had the right under the Constitution to actually pass such a measure, but Clay neatly skirted this question in his fifth resolution, mentioning only that such an action was "inexpedient" because of the factors described above. In a speech given several days later, Clay affirmed that he did believe that a congressional bar on slavery in the capital was constitutional—but continued to argue that it was impolitic.

In contrast, Clay stated in his sixth resolution that the slave trade should be ended in the District of Columbia. At that time, Washington, DC, was the site of the some of the nation's largest and most infamous slave markets; one open-air pen where slaves were held before sale was located just outside the Capitol building and visible from its halls. Free blacks around the district faced the possibility of being illegally kidnapped and sold into slavery by unscrupulous slave traders. For decades, the practice had generated opposition, and calls for the end of the slave trade in the capital were nothing new; the apparent hypocrisy of the sale of human beings in a country claiming itself dedicated to liberty even drew derision from foreign observers. Thus, Northerners, and even some Southerners, opposed the continued existence of slave markets, and Clay believed that making this concession to antislavery interests would greatly help smooth rising sectional tensions. The measure became the fifth and final law contained within the overall compromise to successfully pass Congress, garnering votes from Northerners, a fair number of Southern Whigs, and even a handful of Southern Democrats.

Although this law abolished the practice of wholesale, long-distance slave trading, it did not eliminate all slave sales. Slave transactions among buyers and sellers within the district remained legal, and the rights of district slave owners to leave its boundaries for the purchase of slaves to bring back to their property within the district were protected. It thereby addressed antislavery concerns while affirming proslavery practices. This idea was reflected in Clay's eighth, and final, proposal, which was a simple statement in support of states' rights—that Congress lacked the power to either "promote or obstruct" the slave trade between the states. Rather, he argued, this could be regulated "exclusively upon [states'] own particular laws." This assertion, like the law ending the slave trade in Washington, DC, protected states' rights to conduct slavery in a way that aimed to mollify Southerners who believed that the federal government wished to abolish the practice altogether.

Clay's seventh proposal for a "more effectual provision . . . for the restitution and delivery of persons bound to service or labor in any State" became the most galvanizing of all of the measures contained within the final compromise. Enacted as the fourth of the five laws within the full compromise, the Fugitive Slave Act built upon the existing Fugitive Slave Act of 1793 to greatly enhance the power of Southern slaveholders to demand full federal complicity in the search and seizure of any suspected fugitive slave regardless of his or her present location or even the duration of time that he or she had been at large. The law was passed along almost exclusively sectional lines. Many legislators abstained from voting on the measure, either forced to be away from the capital at that time or voluntarily declining to register their opinion on the matter. Of those who did vote, all Southerners and just a few Northerners supported the measure. Regional interests trumped political affiliation.

Clearly intended to appease proslavery interests as a trade-off for the expansion of the Union without an assurance of the extension of slavery, the measure was more notable for its effects on Northerners. Because the final Fugitive Slave Act legally penalized all people who refused to actively assist in the seizure and return of escaped slaves, it angered even those white Northerners who were not abolitionists by requiring them to directly take part in the institution of slavery. The Fugitive Slave Act's barring of testimony by accused African Americans in their own defense also violated Northern ideals of judicial fairness, as did the law's provision for trial not by jury but by a judge. The law further provided higher financial incentives for the conviction and return of an accused fugitive than for the formal recognition of the freedom of a suspected runaway. Altogether, these measures made the North almost as dangerous and hostile to the civil liberties of African Americans as the South; unsurprisingly, many Northern blacks—including free blacks who held that status by birthright or through legally obtaining liberty—fled for the safer land of Canada.

White Northerners also sought to reject the letter of Clay's seventh resolution through their state legislatures. After the Compromise of 1850, Northern legislatures passed state laws that essentially nullified portions of the Fugitive Slave Act by allowing for the appeal of fugitive slave convictions before a jury, enacting harsh punishments for perjury in fugitive slave cases, and preventing state officials from acting on fugitive slave claims. These laws in turn became a point of contention with proslavery Southerners who saw them as an assault of their property rights.

Overall, the story of the Compromise of 1850 is one that shows this failure of its parts to truly serve the needs of the whole by bringing about the peace and harmony that Clay and other compromise proponents so greatly hoped to achieve. On the whole, the Compromise of 1850 did seem to largely serve Northern interests—California had won entry, and slavery was possible but by no means guaranteed in the new territories of the Southwest. While this was not the firmly antislavery measure that the failed Wilmot Proviso had been, it did settle the matter for the time. Southerners made immediate gains as well, however. The Fugitive Slave Act was an apparent proslavery victory. Slavery was, in fact, practiced in the new territories of New Mexico and Utah and even retained a measure of legality in California after 1850. Most of the new California legislators were Democrats sympathetic to Southern interests. The compromise further protected slavery and even a small-scale slave trade in the District of Columbia while ending only its most obvious and repugnant outlets. In attempting to ease sectional tensions, Clay's resolutions actually set the stage for the rapid growth of ill will between the North and South that took place during the 1850s.

Essential Themes

Like its political predecessor, the Missouri Compromise of 1820, the Compromise of 1850 was largely an effort to restore stability to a nation pulled apart by sectional tensions stemming from social, political, and economic differences. In this way it reflected the leading issues of its day. The question of slavery—the South's "peculiar institution"—had long created a rift between North and South. Over time, that rift had spread despite the best efforts of federal legislators to quell conflict through measures such as the Missouri Compromise. The Compromise of 1850 bore substantial resemblance to the spirit of Clay's earlier success of the Missouri Compromise. Again, the measure allowed for the expansion of the United States with an attempt at balancing slave and free interests in the legislature, and again, it aimed to placate all sides without substantially changing the existing law of the land.

Indeed, these increased sectional tensions owed a debt to one of the other significant contemporary issues then facing the nation: westward expansion. As the United States made the steady march toward the Pacific in the name of Manifest Destiny, broadly supported by its people, the nation inevitably faced the challenge of determining whether its future was one of liberty, bondage, or an uneasy combination of the two. The national desire to become the master of the continent was apparent in the Compromise of 1850, however, as it worked to grow and to organize formal US territory despite the potential political consequences.

However, unlike the Missouri Compromise, the Compromise of 1850 failed to achieve lasting peace. Within just a few years, the doctrine of popular sovereignty sparked the violence that was termed "Bloody Kansas" as pro- and antislavery forces struggled to achieve their desired outcome on the vote over slavery in that territory. Far from being a way for territorial voices to democratically determine their own destiny, popular sovereignty served only to drag those territories even more directly into the heated fray. The Fugitive Slave Act, added to appease proslavery Southern politicians and landowners, proved an even more dismal failure. Northerners were angered by their new legal duties as slave catchers and slavery supporters, and some Northern state legislatures responded by passing personal-liberty laws that fueled Southern anger and were ultimately cited as one of the causes of South Carolina's secession. At the same time, widespread white support for the radical abolition movement grew. Rather than achieving Clay's goals of preserving the Union, the Compromise of 1850 served to heighten violence, highlight differences, and encourage already inflamed tensions. The Missouri Compromise had purchased the nation three decades of relative peace; its successor, little more than a decade.

Vanessa E. Vaughn, MA

Bibliography

Hamilton, Holman. *Prologue to Conflict: The Crisis and Compromise of 1850*. New York: Norton, 1964. Print.

Horton, James Oliver, and Lois E. Horton. *Slavery and the Making of America*. New York: Oxford UP, 2005. Print.

Johnson, Charles, et al. *Africans in America: America's Journey through Slavery*. New York: Harcourt, 1998. Print.

Ransom, Roger L. *Conflict and Compromise: The Political Economy of Slavery, Emancipation, and the American Civil War*. New York: Cambridge UP, 1989. Print.

Remini, Robert V. *At the Edge of the Precipice: Henry Clay and the Compromise that Saved the Union*. New York: Perseus, 2010. Print.

---. "Henry Clay." *American National Biography*. American National Biography Online, 17 Sept. 2012. Web. 11 Mar. 2013.

Additional Reading

Apple, Lindsey. *The Family Legacy of Henry Clay: In the Shadow of a Kentucky Patriarch*. Lexington: UP of Kentucky, 2011. E-book.

Remini, Robert V. *Henry Clay: Statesman for the Union*. New York: Norton, 1991. Print.

Rozwenc, Edwin C., ed. *The Compromise of 1850*. Boston: Heath, 1957. Print.

LESSON PLAN: **The Compromise of 1850**

Students will explore divisions over slavery by analyzing Henry Clay's resolutions and the bills that were the basis for the Compromise of 1850.

Learning Objectives

Identify central questions regarding the allowance of slavery in some states but not others; draw comparisons across regions to define enduring issues over slavery; interrogate historical data in the resolutions and statutes that led to the Compromise of 1850; analyze cause-and-effect relationships regarding the Compromise of 1850; challenge arguments of historical inevitability.

Materials: The Compromise of 1850; Henry Clay, "Clay's Resolutions January 29, 1850."

Overview Questions

With what issues does the Compromise of 1850 deal? How does the Compromise resolve them? How do these resolutions constitute a compromise?

Step 1: Comprehension Questions

What topics do Clay's resolutions address? Why was the question of slavery in California an issue between the North and the South? How does Clay propose to resolve it? How does he propose to deal with slavery in the rest of the Mexican Cession?

- **Activity:** Have students write one-sentence summaries of Clay's proposals. For each one, call on students to read their summaries to the class.

Step 2: Comprehension Questions

What resolutions are made about slavery in Washington, DC? Why are they a compromise? How does Clay fear that making Washington, DC, free soil will affect Maryland? How does he propose to deal with slaves escaping to free soil?

- **Activity:** Organize students into groups. Have each group decide which proposals were concessions by the North to the South, and which were concessions by the South to the North. Have a spokesperson for each group report their judgments to the class.

Step 3: Context Questions

Why would the boundaries of Texas have been an issue between the North and the South? What incentive does Clay offer Texas to give up some of its territory? How might losing this territory affect any slavery there?

- **Activity:** Have students take the role of a proslavery southerner or a northern abolitionist and write ten-second "sound bites" reacting to the Compromise of 1850. Have students present their sound bites to the class.

Step 4: Historical Connections Questions

Why did the war with Mexico (1846–48) intensify the debate over slavery? What territories did the United States gain from the war? How did this expansion further polarize the North and the South over the slavery issue? Why did California's petition for admission to the Union in 1849 create the crisis that led to the compromise outlined in Clay's document?

- **Activity:** Challenge students with this proposition: The war with Mexico was a cause of the Civil War. Discuss the sequence of events from the Mexican Cession to the Gold Rush and California's resultant rapid readiness for statehood in exploring any possible cause-and-effect relationship.

Step 5: Response Paper

Word length and additional requirements set by Instructor. Students answer the research question in the *Overview Questions*. Students state a thesis and use as evidence passages from the primary source document as well as support from supplemental materials assigned in the lesson.

Dred Scott v. Sandford

Date: March 6, 1857
Author: Taney, Roger B.
Genre: court opinion

"Dred Scott was not a citizen of Missouri within the meaning of the Constitution of the United States, and not entitled as such to sue in its courts."

Summary Overview

Delivered in a heated atmosphere of sectional tensions over slavery, the US Supreme Court decision in *Dred Scott v. Sandford* delighted proslavery forces, horrified antislavery activists, and unquestionably pushed the nation closer to the looming crisis of the Civil War. Written by Chief Justice Roger B. Taney, the ruling not only denied liberty to the plaintiff, an African American man who claimed that his temporary residence in a free state had earned him his freedom, but also declared that the US Constitution failed to grant the right of citizenship to any black American. The decision fueled the rise of the antislavery Republican Party and provided a rallying point for those opposed to the institution throughout the United States. As a result, sectional divides grew even larger, and within only a few years, the peace that some politicians had hoped the decision would assure had come to a complete end.

Defining Moment

By the time the US Supreme Court issued its decision in *Dred Scott v. Sandford*—also written as *Dred Scott v. Sandford* due to a typographical error in the original court ruling—the United States was inflamed by sectional tensions over slavery. Although the Compromise of 1850 had sought to ease rising sectional issues over the westward spread of slavery and the continued existence of the institution itself by throwing out the Wilmot Proviso, supporting the doctrine of popular sovereignty, and making a concession to proslavery interests in the form of a harsh Fugitive Slave Act, the hoped-for era of peace had failed to materialize.

Instead, sectional tensions greatly worsened. The debate over the expansion of slavery into the territories, fueled by the breaking of the Missouri Compromise line in favor of popular sovereignty under the Kansas-Nebraska Act of 1854, created the violent era known as Bleeding Kansas, which lasted until 1861. The application of the Fugitive Slave Act enraged Northerners, who were forced to become active participants in Southern slavery through the law's requirement that they actively assist in the capture and return of suspected fugitives to their owners, without a fair or equitable judicial system to hear claims. The publication of Harriet Beecher Stowe's enormously popular antislavery novel *Uncle Tom's Cabin* in 1852 persuaded a great number of Northerners that the institution should be abolished. Political rifts over slavery led to the fall of the long-standing Whig Party and the rise of the new Republican Party, which opposed the expansion of slavery into new territories or states. In the spring of 1856, congressional debate over slavery exploded into violence when Southern congressman Preston Brooks physically attacked Northern senator Charles Sumner over the content of a speech that the abolitionist Sumner had delivered.

In November of 1856, voters elected James Buchanan to the presidency. A Democrat who had spent much of the era of rising tensions serving in government posts abroad, Buchanan had little grasp of the volatility of the national situation. Believing that the measures of the past would serve to resolve the sectional tensions of the present, he appointed Northern and Southern officials to his administration and assumed that the debate over slavery could be solved by appeals to Americans' belief in their Constitution. The issuance of the *Dred Scott* decision by the Supreme Court just two days into his term showed how wrong Buchanan was. In his inaugural address, the new president—who presumably had an inkling of what the court's ruling would be—had argued that the impending Supreme Court decision would settle the question of slavery once and for all. Instead, it fed sectional antagonism and moved the nation inexorably closer to civil war.

Author Biography

Although each the justices of the US Supreme Court issued individual opinions on the ruling, the opinion of Chief Justice Roger B. Taney is generally considered the most historically significant. A native of Maryland, Taney was a member of one of the state's leading planter families. He studied law in his youth and served briefly in the Maryland state legislature in his early twenties, remaining interested in politics even after losing office in 1800. Despite conflicts with the Federalist Party over its lack of support for the War of 1812, he nevertheless became a leading voice in the state Federalist Party and returned to the Maryland legislature as a state senator in 1816. Over the next several years, Taney became attached to the Democratic Party under Andrew Jackson, and in 1831, he became attorney general in the Jackson administration. In this role, Taney helped lead the legal fight against the Second Bank of the United States. In 1835, Jackson nominated Taney to the Supreme Court seat left vacant by the death of Chief Justice John Marshall. Considerable opposition was mounted in Congress to his appointment, but Taney eventually won confirmation. He assumed his new office in 1836 and held it until his death in 1864.

Taney's court opinions and the events of his life indicate a man deeply uncomfortable with the existence of the slave trade and institution of slavery, yet also firmly convinced of the moral, intellectual, and political inferiority of African Americans. In 1819, he spoke out against slavery as an "evil" and "a blot on our national character" when he defended a preacher charged with inciting a slave insurrection. By the 1820s, he had freed all of his own slaves. Yet his legal record shows his acceptance of slavery as a fact of life. While serving in the Supreme Court, he tended to support states' rights in matters involving slavery while upholding the doctrine of federalism as established under the Marshall court. Like Marshall, for example, Taney tended to believe that the federal Bill of Rights did not apply to the states. When dealing with slavery, he hoped that it would be ended as a moral wrong, but he preferred and trusted that this could be done via gradual emancipation by the states in which slavery existed rather than through direct and, he thought, unconstitutional federal action against slave owners' property rights. Nevertheless, he also held clearly racist opinions about the capabilities of blacks—opinions made evident in his most famous decision, the *Dred Scott* case.

HISTORICAL DOCUMENT

This case has been twice argued. After the argument at the last term, differences of opinion were found to exist among the members of the court, and as the questions in controversy are of the highest importance, and the court was at that time much pressed by the ordinary business of the term, it was deemed advisable to continue the case and direct a re-argument on some of the points in order that we might have an opportunity of giving to the whole subject a more deliberate consideration. It has accordingly been again argued by counsel, and considered by the court; and I now proceed to deliver its opinion.

There are two leading questions presented by the record:

1. Had the Circuit Court of the United States jurisdiction to hear and determine the case between these parties? And

2. If it had jurisdiction, is the judgment it has given erroneous or not?

The plaintiff in error, who was also the plaintiff in the court below, was, with his wife and children, held as slaves by the defendant in the State of Missouri, and he brought this action in the Circuit Court of the United States for that district to assert the title of himself and his family to freedom.

The declaration is in the form usually adopted in that State to try questions of this description, and contains the averment necessary to give the court jurisdiction; that he and the defendant are citizens of different States; that is, that he is a citizen of Missouri, and the defendant a citizen of New York.

The defendant pleaded in abatement to the jurisdiction of the court, that the plaintiff was not a citizen of the State of Missouri, as alleged in his declaration, being a negro of African descent, whose ancestors were of pure African blood and who were brought into this country and sold as slaves.

To this plea the plaintiff demurred, and the defendant joined in demurrer. The court overruled the plea, and gave judgment that the defendant should answer over. And he thereupon put in sundry pleas in bar, upon which issues were joined, and at the trial the verdict and judgment were in his favor. Whereupon the plaintiff brought this writ of error. . . .

The question then arises, whether the provisions of the Constitution, in relation to the personal rights and privileges to which the citizen of a State should be entitled, embraced the negro African race, at that time in this country or who might afterwards be imported, who had then or should afterwards be made free in any State, and to put it in the power of a single State to make him a citizen of the United States and endue him with the full rights of citizenship in every other State without their consent? Does the Constitution of the United States act upon him whenever he shall be made free under the laws of a State, and raised there to the rank of a citizen, and immediately clothe him with all the privileges of a citizen in every other State, and in its own courts? . . .

In the opinion of the Court the legislation and histories of the times, and the language used in the Declaration of Independence, show that neither the class of persons who had been imported as slaves nor their descendants, whether they had become free or not, were then acknowledged as a part of the people nor intended to be included in the general words used in that memorable instrument.

It is difficult at this day to realize the state of public opinion in relation to that unfortunate race which prevailed in the civilized and enlightened portions of the world at the time of the Declaration of Independence and when the Constitution of the United States was framed and adopted. But the public history of every European nation displays it in a manner too plain to be mistaken.

They had for more than a century before been regarded as beings of an inferior order and altogether unfit to associate with the white race, either in social or political relations; and so far inferior that they had no rights which the white man was bound to respect; and that the Negro might justly and lawfully be reduced to slavery for his benefit. He was bought and sold and treated as an ordinary article of merchandise and traffic whenever a profit could be made by it. This opinion was at that time fixed and universal in the civilized portion of the white race. It was regarded as an axiom in morals as well as in politics which no one thought of disputing or supposed to be open to dispute, and men in every grade and position in society daily and habitually acted upon it in their private pursuits, as well as in matters of public concern, without doubting for a moment the correctness of this opinion. . . .

No one, we presume, supposes that any change in public opinion or feeling, in relation to this unfortunate race, in the civilized nations of Europe or in this country should induce the Court to give to the words of the Constitution a more liberal construction in their favor than they were intended to bear when the instrument was framed and adopted. . . .

What the construction was at that time we think can hardly admit of doubt. We have the language of the Declaration of Independence and of the Articles of Confederation, in addition to the plain words of the Constitution itself; we have the legislation of the different States, before, about the time, and since the Constitution was adopted; we have the legislation of Congress, from the time of its adoption to a recent period; and we have the constant and uniform action of the Executive Department, all concurring together, and leading to the same result. And if anything in relation to the construction of the Constitution can be regarded as settled, it is that which we now give to the word "citizen" and the word "people."

And, upon a full and careful consideration of the subject, the court is of opinion, that, upon the facts stated in the plea in abatement, Dred Scott was not a citizen of Missouri within the meaning of the Constitution of the United States, and not entitled as such to sue in its courts, and consequently that the Circuit Court had no jurisdiction of the case, and that the judgment on the plea in abatement is erroneous.

We are aware that doubts are entertained by some of the members of the court, whether the plea in abatement is legally before the court upon this writ of error; but if that plea is regarded as waived, or out of the case upon any other ground, yet the question as to the jurisdiction of the Circuit Court is presented on the face of the bill of exception itself, taken by the plaintiff at the trial, for he admits that he and his wife were born slaves, but endeavors to make out his title to freedom and citizenship by showing that they were taken by their owner to certain places, hereinafter mentioned, where slavery could not by law exist, and that they thereby became free, and, upon their return to Missouri, became citizens of that State. . . .

We proceed, therefore, to inquire whether the facts relied on by the plaintiff entitled him to his freedom.

The case, as he himself states it, on the record brought here by his writ of error, is this:

The plaintiff was a negro slave, belonging to Dr. Emerson, who was a surgeon in the army of the United States. In the year 1834, he took the plaintiff from the State of Missouri to the military post at Rock Island, in the State of Illinois, and held him there as a slave until the month of April or May, 1836. . . .

The act of Congress, upon which the plaintiff relies, declares that slavery and involuntary servitude, except as a punishment for crime, shall be forever prohibited in all that part of the territory ceded by France, under the name of Louisiana, which lies north of thirty-six degrees thirty minutes north latitude and not included within the limits of Missouri. And the difficulty which meets us . . . is whether Congress was authorized to pass this law under any of the powers granted to it by the Constitution. . . .

As there is no express regulation in the Constitution defining the power which the general government may exercise over the person or property of a citizen in a territory thus acquired, the Court must necessarily look to the provisions and principles of the Constitution, and its distribution of powers, for the rules and principles by which its decisions must be governed.

Taking this rule to guide us, it may be safely assumed that citizens of the United States who migrate to a territory...cannot be ruled as mere colonists, dependent upon the will of the general government, and to be governed by any laws it may think proper to impose. . . .

For example, no one, we presume, will contend that Congress can make any law in a Territory respecting the establishment of religion, or the free exercise thereof, or abridging the freedom of speech or of the press, or the right of the people of the Territory peaceably to assemble and to petition the Government for the redress of grievances. . . .

These powers, and others, . . . are . . . denied to the general government; and the rights of private property have been guarded with equal care. . . .

An act of Congress which deprives a citizen of the United States of his liberty or property, without due process of law, merely because he came himself or brought his property into a particular territory of the United States...could hardly be dignified with the name of due process of law.

The powers over person and property of which we speak are not only not granted to Congress but are in express terms denied and they are forbidden to exercise them. . . . And if Congress itself cannot do this . . . it could not authorize a territorial government to exercise them. . . .

It seems, however, to be supposed that there is a difference between property in a slave and other property and that different rules may be applied to it in expounding the Constitution of the United States. And the laws and usages of nations, and the writings of eminent jurists upon the relation of master and slave and their mutual rights and duties, and the powers which Governments may exercise over it have been dwelt upon in the argument. . . .

Now, as we have already said in an earlier part of this opinion upon a different point, the right of property in a slave is distinctly and expressly affirmed in the Constitution. The right to traffic in it, like an ordinary article of merchandise and property, was guarantied to the citizens of the United States in every State that might desire it for twenty years. And the Government in express terms is pledged to protect it in all future time if the slave escapes from his owner. This is done in plain words—too plain to be misunderstood. And no word can be found in the Constitution which gives Congress a greater power over slave property or which entitles property of that kind to less protection that property of any other description. The only power conferred is the power coupled with the duty of guarding and protecting the owner in his rights.

Upon these considerations, it is the opinion of the court that the act of Congress which prohibited a citizen from holding and owning property of this kind in the territory of the United States north of the line therein mentioned is not warranted by the Constitution, and is therefore void, and that neither Dred Scott himself nor any of his family were made free by being carried into this territory, even if they had been carried there by the owner with the intention of becoming a permanent resident.

We have so far examined the case, as it stands under the Constitution of the United States, and the powers thereby delegated to the Federal Government.

GLOSSARY

abatement: the ending of a legal claim

axiom: a generally accepted rule

erroneous: in error; wrong

express: explicit and direct

guarantied: assured; protected

writ of error: an action to reverse a judgment due to a mistaken ruling

Document Analysis

With each of the nine justices submitting different opinions on the matter, despite forming an overall 7–2 majority against the plaintiff, the US Supreme Court case of *Dred Scott v. Sandford* was one of the most contentious rulings in the court's history. It has also come to be widely regarded as one of the worst. In an opinion that went far beyond the scope necessary to address his conclusion in the case, Chief Justice Roger B. Taney offered a strong argument for institutionalized racism that stated that African Americans could not, under the US Constitution, be citizens; that the Congress had no right to restrict slavery in the territories, thus revoking the Missouri Compromise of 1820; that slavery was entirely legal under the Constitution; and, finally, that Scott lacked the right to sue in the federal courts, as he was not a US citizen, thus affirming his status as a slave.

Although the court did not rule on the case until March 1857, the matter had been wending its way through the judicial process for many years, and the events that inspired the legal claim dated back even further. The facts of the case, however, were undisputed. Born in about 1795, Dred Scott was originally owned by the Blow family of Virginia. With this household, he moved to Saint Louis in the slave state of Missouri in 1827. Six years later, the Blow family sold Scott to an army surgeon, Dr. John Emerson. Soon after, Emerson's work took him and Scott to Rock Island in the free state of Illinois and, later, to the free territory of Wisconsin. In total, Scott lived as a part of Emerson's household in free lands for some five years, during which time Scott married Harriet Robinson, and Emerson married a woman named Irene Sanford (whose family name would later be misspelled in court as "Sandford"). The expanded household returned to Missouri, where Emerson died in 1843. Scott then sought to buy his freedom from Emerson's widow, but she refused his offer. Scott and his wife decided to seek their freedom through the courts, which had previously emancipated enslaved claimants on similar grounds. Dred and Harriet Scott filed separate court cases in Missouri in 1846, arguing that their long-term residency in free Illinois and Wisconsin meant they were no longer bound to slavery. Harriet Scott's individual claim was soon dropped and made contingent on the ruling in her husband's case, *Dred Scott v. Irene Emerson*, which proceeded slowly through the state courts.

In 1850, the Saint Louis Circuit Court ruled in Scott's favor, supporting the plaintiff's argument that the voluntary decision to bring them to free soil had freed them over the defendant's assertion that Emerson's status as a military doctor made the household subject to military rather than civil law. Irene Emerson filed an appeal, and in time the case reached the Missouri Supreme Court; by this time, however, she had remarried, moved out of Missouri, and passed ownership of the Scotts to her brother, John Sanford. The political climate surrounding slavery was also quite different in 1852, when that court ruled on the matter, from what it had been in 1846 or even early 1850, when Scott had won the day in Saint Louis. The passage of the Compromise of 1850 had stirred sectional tensions, and the resistance of Northern states to measures such as the Fugitive Slave Act and the expansion of slavery westward had angered Southerners. As a result, Missouri's highest court overturned the circuit court's decision, arguing that the state's willingness to honor similar claims in the past had been based on a mutual reciprocity of respect for laws among the states. Because Northern states opposed Southern states' property laws, the court asserted, Missouri was no longer willing to extend the in-kind recognition of the laws of Illinois and Wisconsin that would have established Scott's freedom. Under this ruling, Dred Scott was a Missourian, subject only to the laws of Missouri, and therefore still a slave.

The situation also seemed increasingly pessimistic for the Scotts on a personal level. The Sanford family was affiliated with strong proslavery views. The Scotts and their two young daughters had been hired out by Sanford to work for another Saint Louis family, but the slave owner had previously sold a number of Missouri slaves whom he had inherited from his father. The possibility that the Scotts could be sold to another owner or even split up and sold to separate owners was very real. Thus the Missouri Supreme Court decision did not end Scott's legal journey. Because John Sanford, the Scotts' new owner, lived in New York City, Scott's case was eligible for trial at the federal levels as a dispute between citizens of different states. In 1853, Scott's lawyer filed a new suit, *Dred Scott v. Sanford*, with the federal circuit court. Sanford took a different defense from his sister's in the earlier case, arguing that Scott was not a citizen of Missouri due to his race, and therefore his claim of freedom based on his shifting citizenship was not a valid one. However, the judge presiding over the case rejected this argument, asserting that free blacks, while lacking many rights of white citizens, did have the right to sue in federal courts; therefore, if Scott were in fact free, then he was bringing his claim legitimately. But the same judge did not support Scott's assertion of freedom based on his time in Illinois and Wisconsin, instructing the jury to consider it only a temporary condition that gave way to enslavement once Scott returned to Missouri. Following these instructions, the jury ruled against Scott.

With this defeat, the case had but one venue for appeal: the US Supreme Court (where "Sanford" became "Sandford"). Supported by Northern abolitionists, Scott's case came before that body in early 1856 for the first of the two arguments mentioned by Taney in his published opinion. After those oral arguments, the court deliberated but did not reach a conclusion. Instead, the justices agreed to hear another round of arguments in December of 1856. Over the course of the year between these rounds, three significant political events that shaped the sectional debate occurred. First, violence erupted in Kansas over that territory's planned vote on whether to allow or bar slavery, with both proslavery and abolitionist forces wreaking havoc around the territory. Next, Congressman Preston Brooks beat Senator Charles Sumner with a cane on the floor of the Senate over perceived slights against his cousin, the Southern proslavery senator Andrew Butler. Tensions between opposing legislators had finally exploded into actual bloodshed, and Sumner required years to recover from the attack. Finally, Northern Democrat James Buchanan was elected to the presidency. Taney issued his opinion two days after Buchanan—who declared that the court ruling would end the question of slavery altogether—assumed office.

The Opinion

Taney began his opinion by setting forth the two essential questions that the court had been asked to consider. First, he sought to address the issue of whether the federal court that had rejected Scott's appeal had jurisdiction to hear the case at all—essentially a matter of whether Scott, as a citizen of Missouri, had the right to sue Sanford, a citizen of New York. The answer to the next question rested on the answer to the first. If yes, then the court had to determine whether the lower court's decision was correct under the US Constitution. If no, then the matter was settled. Taney then briefly recapped the question of whether Scott, as the black descendant of African slaves, was legitimately a citizen of Missouri entitled to sue in the federal courts.

To answer these questions, Taney first addressed the issue of whether the US Constitution enabled states to grant free blacks national citizenship that must be accepted by all of the other states, which would include the right to sue in federal courts. He drew upon both the language of the Constitution and that of the preceding Declaration of Independence to answer the question with a firm denial. The combined US political history, he argued, "show[ed] that neither the class of persons who had been imported as slaves nor their descendants, whether they had become free or not, were then acknowledged as a part of the people" included in the broad assertions of equality in the nation's founding documents. The framers, he believed, had never intended for any black person to be considered a part of "the people," or the body politic of the United States.

Taney supported this assertion by pointing to the historical opinion of people of African descent as "beings of an inferior order . . . unfit to associate with the white race, either in social or political relations." Furthermore, he stated that the framers' opinions of black Americans placed them "so far inferior that they had no rights which the white man was bound to respect," as evidenced by the practice of enslavement by Europeans and their American counterparts. The mere toleration of the existence of slavery was enough to show that the men who wrote the US Constitution had no interest in extending national membership to their black coresidents. To further bolster his claims of original intent, Taney called on other national and state-level documents of the early American era, including the Articles of Confederation, claiming that these equally showed an original intent for the practice of slavery. He concluded that "if anything in relation to the construction of the Constitution can be regarded as settled, it is that which we now give to the word 'citizen' and the word 'people.'"

That a minority of early Europeans in the Americas and later colonial leaders actually did question the morality of slavery went ignored. Thomas Jefferson, the author of the Declaration of Independence, stated his moral opposition to slavery, despite owning numerous slaves and being avowedly unconvinced that whites and blacks had equal human capabilities; founder John Adams opposed slavery; and Benjamin Franklin even called for its abolition. Under the early American government set up by the Articles of Confederation, Congress passed a Northwest Ordinance to organize its growing territory and exclude slavery from those new boundaries. The language of the Constitution, itself a compromise measure meant to draw together the dissimilar former colonies, failed to reflect this division of opinion, however, and Taney argued that nothing suggested "any change in public opinion or feeling" in either Europe or the United States. Apparently, he believed that the growth of the US abolitionist movement and the actual end of slavery in nations such as Great Britain and Spain did not reflect a shift toward the acceptance of black personhood. Therefore, he argued, Scott had no right to sue in the courts because, as a black man, he could not possibly hold citizenship.

Taney could have ended his opinion there, determining that the court could not rule because Scott was not a citizen. However, he continued to discuss the issues raised by the case to determine, in effect, whether Scott would have been free if he had indeed had the right to sue for his liberty. After restating the facts of the case, Taney next turned to the question of whether Congress had the constitutional right to bar slavery in the territories—a central tenet of the Missouri Compromise, which had outlawed slavery in the territories north of a set compromise line. This line had not been violated until the passage of the Kansas-Nebraska Act in 1854, and rumblings about its constitutionality had emerged from proslavery voices in the federal government in the years preceding the Dred Scott decision. In his opinion, Taney set forth several arguments of original intent to support his decision. He recalled the conclusion that the framers of the US Constitution had meant slavery to be legal in the United States due to the inclusion of a clause barring discussion of the transatlantic slave trade for twenty years after the document's creation and an article asserting the right of slave owners to reclaim fugitive slaves across state lines. "This is done in plain words—too plains to be misunderstood," Taney stated. He continued that the Constitution, which protected slavery through its guarantee of property rights, did not make a special exemption in this case that would allow Congress to legislate that protection away.

Thus, Taney concluded that the congressional ban on the institution of slavery in the territories north of the Missouri Compromise line was unconstitutional. Property rights, he suggested, could not be dissolved in this manner, in much the same way that the rights to the freedoms of religion, speech, press, and assembly could not be taken away by Congress. Revocation of a citizen's property rights without due process of law could not take place simply because that citizen traveled from one state to another, Taney argued, and the Constitution strongly sought to ensure that such revocation did not take place. If Congress lacked the right to put these types of federal restrictions on property, so, logically, did territorial governments under its jurisdiction. Taney rejected the argument that enslaved humans were a different form of property from any other type of personal holding.

As a result of these conclusions, according to Taney, "neither Dred Scott himself nor any of his family were made free by being carried into this territory"—that is, Wisconsin—because the legislation outlawing slavery there was not valid. To address the question of whether Scott's residence in the free state of Illinois would have granted him freedom if the court had held that he had the right to sue, Taney asserted in a section not reproduced here that the answer was again no. Citing the 1850 US Supreme Court decision in *Strader et al. v. Graham*, Taney argued that enslaved persons taken willingly from a slave state to a free state remained subject to the laws of their home slave state. Because Scott was taken as a slave to the free state of Illinois, he remained a slave there, according to the laws of Missouri.

Taney thus rejected every possible argument for Scott's freedom in favor of a constitutional viewpoint that went far beyond the scope of what even the most ardent proslavery proponent might have expected. Slavery was not only legal but protected under the US Constitution, so firmly that Congress had no power to legislate against it in federal territories. African Americans, whether enslaved or free, lacked even the most basic rights asserted in the Constitution. In short, black Americans were not even second-class citizens; they were less than citizens, because the framers had denied them even the possibility of becoming citizens. Racism, according to Taney, was the natural and intended state of affairs in the United States.

Essential Themes

It is nearly impossible to overstate the importance of the *Dred Scott* decision. Although the decision was not the immediate cause of the Civil War, it certainly served to increase sectional tensions and radicalize opposition to slavery in the North. Buchanan, and possibly the Supreme Court, may have believed that issuing a ruling that unquestionably affirmed the constitutionality of slavery would quell the calls for emancipation by antislavery activists by appealing to their sense of duty to the nation's founding document. These leaders may have thought that if they removed slavery from the federal political sphere, the issue would recede back into a question handled at the state level. The actual result was quite the opposite, however, because of the sweeping constitutional statements that Taney made in his opinion. If he had merely stated that Scott was not a citizen of Missouri and thus his claim was invalid, Taney may have avoided sparking the outrage that followed the decision. Instead, he inadvertently encouraged the rise to power of the Republican Party and added to the chain of events culminating in the outbreak of the Civil War. In the long run, the Dred Scott decision has remained among the most studied in US history. Its arguments exemplify the intense racism built into the early national system and underscore the complete lack of regard proslavery advocates had for African Americans.

The court's decision to essentially strip African Americans of citizenship was particularly pivotal. Certainly institutionalized racism had been present in the United States since its inception. The Declaration of Independence and the US Constitution hailed the virtues of liberty and equality while making national allowances for the practice of slavery and even banning discussion of the transatlantic slave trade during the nation's early years. Slave codes that barred racial intermarriage, made it illegal to provide slaves with even a basic education, and greatly restricted blacks' civil liberties had been on the books even in colonial times. Yet none of these measures had previously gone so far as to deny African Americans citizenship altogether and in perpetuity. In the Dred Scott decision, the US Supreme Court—the highest legal voice in the land—formally declared that black Americans were not Americans at all and, as such, had no expectation of even basic legal protections under the Constitution. Although some of the court's justices strongly dissented from this view in their own opinions, it was

Taney's argument that was seized on by pro- and antislavery voices alike. Not until the ratification of the Fourteenth and Fifteenth Amendments in 1868 and 1870, respectively, were black Americans formally assured birthright citizenship and granted the political rights associated with that status.

On a smaller scale, but no less vital to the participants in the case, Scott and his family remained enslaved—but not for long. The Blow family, who had originally owned Scott and for whom he had worked on loan while owned by Sanford, purchased the family and freed them in May 1857. Scott had little time to enjoy his liberty, however, as he died of tuberculosis in September of the following year.

Vanessa E. Vaughn, MA

Bibliography

Beschloss, Michael R., and Hugh Sidey. "James Buchanan." *The Presidents of the United States of America*. Washington: White House Hist. Assn., 2009. N. pag. *The White House*. Web. 11 Mar. 2013.

Finkelman, Paul. *Dred Scott v. Sandford: A Brief History with Documents*. Boston: Bedford, 1997. Print.

Greenberg, Ethan. *Dred Scott and the Dangers of a Political Court*. Lanham: Lexington, 2009. Print.

Horton, James Oliver, and Lois E. Horton. *Slavery and the Making of America*. New York: Oxford UP, 2005. Print.

VanBurkleo, Sandra F., and Bonnie Speck. "Taney, Roger Brooke." *American National Biography Online*. Amer. Council of Learned Societies, Feb. 2000. Web. 11 Mar. 2013.

Additional Reading

Graber, Mark A. *Dred Scott and the Problem of Constitutional Evil*. New York: Cambridge UP, 2006. Print.

Johnson, Charles, et al. *Africans in America: America's Journey through Slavery*. New York: Harcourt, 1998. Print.

Kutler, Stanley I., ed. *The Dred Scott Decision: Law or Politics?* Boston: Houghton, 1967. Print.

LESSON PLAN: **The Dred Scott Decision**

Students analyze the Dred Scott Supreme Court case decision and Abraham Lincoln's "House Divided" speech to assess the decision's significance in the coming of the Civil War.

Learning Objectives

Identify central questions addressed in the documents regarding African Americans' status in US territories, property rights, and federal versus states' rights; analyze cause-and-effect relationships and the influence of ideas in terms of how the Dred Scott decision influenced the outbreak of the Civil War; challenge arguments of historical inevitability; hypothesize the influence of the past.

Materials: Chief Justice Roger B. Taney, *Dred Scott v. Sanford* (1857); Abraham Lincoln, "House Divided" speech (1858).

Overview Questions

What was the Supreme Court's decision in *Dred Scott v. Sanford*? What was the court's reasoning in the decision? What were its legal ramifications? How did the case contribute to sectional polarization?

Step 1: Comprehension Questions

Who was the plaintiff in this case? Who was the defendant? What dispute was the Supreme Court being asked to decide? How did Lincoln summarize the events that led to the case? What constitutional question did the court raise about Dred Scott?

- **Activity:** Call on students to read aloud the paragraph in the court's decision that states the constitutional question it must decide. Then have them identify and read aloud its answer to that question.

Step 2: Comprehension Questions

What opinion does Lincoln voice about the court's decision in his 1858 speech? What views does he offer about the court's timing of its decision?

- **Activity:** Point out that Lincoln did not expect the "house" to remain divided. Have students create short speeches that revise this famous passage to include the implications of the court's decision, following, "It will become all one thing, or all the other."

Step 3: Context Questions

How was the Scott case about property rights? In what way was it a case about citizenship? What role did the case's citizenship aspects play in the Supreme Court's decision? What decision did the court make about property rights? Why did Lincoln believe that decision would cause the spread of slavery?

- **Activity:** Write these questions on the board: Does the Bill of Rights apply to African Americans? Does the Constitution limit the property rights of slaveholders? Have students write one-paragraph summaries of the court's answer to each question.

Step 4: Historical Connections Questions

How might the 1856 election have been affected had the Supreme Court announced this decision before rather than after it? What effect might the election of a Republican instead of Southern Democrat James Buchanan have had on the coming of the Civil War?

- **Activity:** Have students take the role of a Northern abolitionist or a Southern slaveholder and write letters to the editor opposing or supporting the court's decision.

Step 5: Response Paper

Word length and additional requirements set by Instructor. Students answer the research question in the *Overview Questions*. Students state a thesis and use as evidence passages from the primary-source document as well as support from supplemental materials assigned in the lesson.

Lincoln's "House Divided" Speech

Date: June 16, 1858
Author: Lincoln, Abraham
Genre: speech

"I believe this government cannot endure, permanently half slave and half free.

I do not expect the Union to be dissolved—I do not expect the house to fall—but I do expect it will cease to be divided."

Summary Overview

In the early summer of 1858, members of the recently formed Republican Party of Illinois gathered in a state convention. One of their chief goals was to nominate a candidate for US Senate. This was not usually done, since the decision would be made by state legislators, rather than majority vote of the party. Still, to head off confusion (including the raising of other candidates' names) and to present a clear choice for Republicans against the nationally known Democrat Stephen Douglas, the convention nominated Abraham Lincoln. Lincoln had been working on a taut, terse, combative speech that would provide both his acceptance of the nomination and the grounds on which he intended to contest the election. That speech has come to be called the "House Divided" speech, because of a metaphor Lincoln used in the introduction, speaking of the nation as a house divided over the issue of slavery. In the speech, Lincoln masterfully wove together his philosophical opposition to slavery while working to achieve the short-term political end of building the Republican Party and getting himself elected to the Senate.

Defining Moment

Lincoln entered the lists in 1858 at a critical moment for the nation and amid a number of significant contexts that established how the speech would be received. One key context was the westward expansion of the United States, fueled by visions of Manifest Destiny, which had touched off the Mexican-American War in 1846. That war had added large swaths of new territory, and what place slavery would have in those new lands remained to be decided. As a result of this indeterminacy, sectional conflict increased, played out in party politics at the national level. Both expansionists and those who wished to limit slavery realized the stakes were growing significantly.

The conflict received greater expression as political parties sharpened their stances. For Lincoln, this meant supporting the emerging Republican Party. The Republicans had surfaced in reaction to the Kansas-Nebraska Act of 1854. They represented an amalgam of Whigs (a party on its last legs, divided over the issue of the expansion of slavery), Free-Soil parties, Know-Nothings (American Party members), abolitionists, and immigrant groups. Sites in both Wisconsin and Michigan claim to be the birthplace of the Republican Party, but in truth, the party coalesced across the North by appealing to multiple constituencies. Although the Republican candidate for president in 1856, John C. Frémont, did not win, he ran well throughout the North. Lincoln had shown clear attachment to the

Republican Party, and the party was strengthened by the nomination of Lincoln at its convention in June 1858. Such party unanimity was essential because, in the nineteenth century (and until the passage of the Seventeenth Amendment in the twentieth), US senators were chosen by the state legislatures. In Illinois, this meant the combined vote of both houses. Thus, Lincoln set out to make the campaign a true choice between parties—symbolized by himself and Douglas—regarding national issues.

In the "House Divided" speech, Lincoln identified significant issues of the previous five years that he believed threatened to shift the balance of slavery in the nation. These issues began with the Kansas-Nebraska Act of 1854, which had been authored by none other than his opponent Douglas. The act left the issue of slavery in territories like Kansas up to "popular sovereignty," meaning the people of a given territory would decide the issue, not the federal government. The end result, though, was "Bleeding Kansas," as pro- and antislavery forces dueled through both politics and open violence to gain control of the state. One key result of this clash was the Lecompton Constitution, a proslavery constitution sent to Washington, DC, as proof of the territory's intent. Douglas broke with President James Buchanan over the Lecompton Constitution, but to Lincoln it symbolized the antidemocratic forces lurking behind the claims of popular sovereignty. This belief was only strengthened when the Supreme Court issued its *Dred Scott v. Sandford* decision, declaring that the slave Dred Scott, even though he had been taken into free territory, remained the property of his master. He had no standing before the court and so could not sue for his freedom. To Lincoln, this represented a grave judicial threat to dealing with slavery. Taking these issues together, 1858 was a moment ripe for Illinois (and by extension the nation) to confront the issue of slavery and its expansion.

Author Biography

In 1858, Lincoln was not the famous figure he would become. He had established himself in Illinois, and some Republicans on the national level had heard of him. At this point, though, he was decidedly a regional figure. Lincoln was born in Kentucky in 1809. His family moved several times when he was a child, so he was raised in Indiana and then Illinois. As a young man he demonstrated the "Free Labor" ideal, whereby men were free to use their physical labor as a stepping stone to greater accomplishments in life. In his early twenties he built and took a flatboat of goods down the Mississippi to New Orleans. There, he was horrified by the slave market, seeing the brutal realities of people buying and selling other people. Returning to Illinois, he worked hard and engaged in multiple activities. He served in the military during the Black Hawk War in 1831 and became a captain. In New Salem he ran a general store, served as town postmaster, and worked as a surveyor. When these activities failed to produce a career, he began to study law, gaining admission to the bar in 1836. He then moved to Springfield (the new state capital) to practice law. He took on a wide variety of cases, especially as he rode the legal circuit through the state, although he gave special attention to business and railroad cases. He soon married Mary Todd and started a family.

In the 1830s, Lincoln also began his political career, serving multiple terms in the Illinois House of Representatives. As a Whig, he served one term in the US House of Representatives (1847–49). He opposed the Mexican-American War, believing President James K. Polk had misled the American people as to whether actual territorial aggression had been perpetrated by the Mexican army. To prove this point, Lincoln introduced "spot resolutions" in Congress to demand on what "spot" American blood had been shed. Lincoln's stance proved unpopular, and he was not reelected. Lincoln withdrew from politics for several years, but he was reenergized with the debate over the Kansas-Nebraska Act. He was an early supporter of the new Republican Party, and he even received votes to be its vice presidential candidate in 1856. Remaining active in Republican politics, he was ready to challenge Douglas for the US Senate seat in 1858.

HISTORICAL DOCUMENT

Mr. President and Gentlemen of the Convention.

If we could first know where we are, and whither we are tending, we could then better judge what to do, and how to do it.

We are now far into the fifth year, since a policy was initiated, with the avowed object, and confident promise, of putting an end to slavery agitation.

Under the operation of that policy, that agitation has not only, not ceased, but has constantly augmented.

In my opinion, it will not cease, until a crisis shall have been reached, and passed.

"A house divided against itself cannot stand."

I believe this government cannot endure, permanently half slave and half free.

I do not expect the Union to be dissolved—I do not expect the house to fall—but I do expect it will cease to be divided.

It will become all one thing, or all the other.

Either the opponents of slavery, will arrest the further spread of it, and place it where the public mind shall rest in the belief that it is in course of ultimate extinction; or its advocates will push it forward, till it shall become alike lawful in all the States, old as well as new—North as well as South.

Have we no tendency to the latter condition?

Let anyone who doubts, carefully contemplate that now almost complete legal combination—piece of machinery so to speak—compounded of the Nebraska doctrine, and the Dred Scott decision. Let him consider not only what work the machinery is adapted to do, and how well adapted; but also, let him study the history of its construction, and trace, if he can, or rather fail, if he can, to trace the evidences of design, and concert of action, among its chief bosses, from the beginning.

But, so far, Congress only, had acted; and an endorsement by the people, real or apparent, was indispensable, to save the point already gained, and give chance for more.

The new year of 1854 found slavery excluded from more than half the States by State Constitutions, and from most of the national territory by Congressional prohibition.

Four days later, commenced the struggle, which ended in repealing that Congressional prohibition.

This opened all the national territory to slavery; and was the first point gained.

This necessity had not been overlooked; but had been provided for, as well as might be, in the notable argument of "squatter sovereignty," otherwise called "sacred right of self government," which latter phrase, though expressive of the only rightful basis of any government, was so perverted in this attempted use of it as to amount to just this: That if any one man, choose to enslave another, no third man shall be allowed to object.

That argument was incorporated into the Nebraska bill itself, in the language which follows: "*It being the true intent and meaning of this act not to legislate slavery into any Territory or state, nor to exclude it there from; but to leave the people thereof perfectly free to form and regulate their domestic institutions in their own way, subject only to the Constitution of the United States.*"

Then opened the roar of loose declamation in favor of "Squatter Sovereignty," and "Sacred right of self government." "But," said opposition members, "let us be more specific—let us amend the bill so as to expressly declare that the people of the territory may exclude slavery." "Not we," said the friends of the measure; and down they voted the amendment.

While the Nebraska bill was passing through congress, a law case, involving the question of a negroe's freedom, by reason of his owner having voluntarily taken him first into a free state and then a territory covered by the congressional prohibition, and held him as a slave, for a long time in each, was passing through the U.S. Circuit Court for the District of Missouri; and both Nebraska bill and law suit were brought to a decision in the same month of May, 1854. The negroe's name was "Dred Scott," which name now designates the decision finally made in the case.

Before the then next Presidential election, the law case came to, and was argued in the Supreme Court of the United States; but the decision of it was deferred until after the election. Still, before the election, Senator Trumbull, on the floor of the Senate, requests the leading advocate of the Nebraska bill to state his opinion whether the people of a territory can constitutionally exclude slavery from their limits; and the latter answers, "That is a question for the Supreme Court."

The election came. Mr. Buchanan was elected, and the endorsement, such as it was, secured. That was the second point gained. The endorsement, however, fell short of a clear popular majority by nearly four hundred thousand votes, and so, perhaps, was not overwhelmingly reliable and satisfactory.

The outgoing President, in his last annual message, as impressively as possible echoed back upon the people the weight and authority of the endorsement. The Supreme Court met again; did not announce their decision, but ordered a re-argument. The Presidential inauguration came, and still no decision of the court; but the incoming President, in his inaugural address, fervently exhorted the people to abide by the forthcoming decision, whatever it might be.

Then, in a few days, came the decision.

The reputed author of the Nebraska bill finds an early occasion to make a speech at this capitol indorsing the Dred Scott Decision, and vehemently denouncing all opposition to it.

The new President, too, seizes the early occasion of the Silliman letter to indorse and strongly construe that decision, and to express his astonishment that any different view had ever been entertained.

At length a squabble springs up between the President and the author of the Nebraska bill, on the mere question of fact, whether the Lecompton constitution was or was not, in any just sense, made by the people of Kansas; and in that squabble the latter declares that all he wants is a fair vote for the people, and that he cares not whether slavery be voted down or voted up. I do not understand his declaration that he cares not whether slavery be voted down or voted up, to be intended by him other than as an apt definition of the policy he would impress upon the public mind—the principle for which he declares he has suffered much, and is ready to suffer to the end...

The several points of the Dred Scott decision, in connection with Senator Douglas' "care not" policy, constitute the piece of machinery, in its present state of advancement. This was the third point gained.

The working points of that machinery are:

First, that no negro slave, imported as such from Africa, and no descendant of such slave can ever be a citizen of any State, in the sense of that term as used in the Constitution of the United States.

This point is made in order to deprive the negro, in every possible event, of the benefit of this provision of the United States Constitution, which declares that—

"The citizens of each State shall be entitled to all privileges and immunities of citizens in the several States."

Secondly, that "subject to the Constitution of the United States," neither Congress nor a Territorial Legislature can exclude slavery from any United States territory. This point is made in order that individual men may fill up the territories with slaves, without danger of losing them as property, and thus to enhance the chances of permanency to the institution through all the future.

Thirdly, that whether the holding a negro in actual slavery in a free State, makes him free, as against the holder, the United States courts will not decide, but will leave to be decided by the courts of any slave State the negro may be forced into by the master. This point is made, not to be pressed immediately; but, if acquiesced in for a while, and apparently indorsed by the people at an election, then to sustain the logical conclusion that what Dred Scott's master might lawfully do with Dred Scott, in the free State of Illinois, every other master may lawfully do with any other one, or one thousand slaves, in Illinois, or in any other free State.

Auxiliary to all this, and working hand in hand with it, the Nebraska doctrine, or what is left of it, is to educate and mould public opinion, at least Northern public opinion, to not care whether slavery is voted down or voted up.

This shows exactly where we now are; and partially also, whither we are tending.

It will throw additional light on the latter, to go back, and run the mind over the string of historical facts already stated. Several things will now appear less dark and mysterious than they did when they were transpiring. The people were to be left "perfectly free" "subject only to the Constitution." What the Constitution had to do with it, outsiders could not then see. Plainly enough now, it was an exactly fitted niche, for the Dred Scott decision to afterwards come in, and declare the perfect freedom of the people, to be just no freedom at all.

Why was the amendment, expressly declaring the right of the people to exclude slavery, voted down? Plainly enough now, the adoption of it, would have spoiled the niche for the Dred Scott decision . . .

While the opinion of the Court, by Chief Justice Taney, in the Dred Scott case, and the separate opinions of all the concurring Judges, expressly declare that the Constitution of the United States neither permits Congress nor a Territorial legislature to exclude slavery from any United States territory, they all omit to declare whether or not the same Constitution permits a state, or the people of a State, to exclude it.

Possibly, this was a mere omission; but who can be quite sure, if McLean or Curtis had sought to get into the opinion a declaration of unlimited power in the people of a state to exclude slavery from their limits, just as Chase and Macy sought to get such declaration, in behalf of the people of a territory, into the Nebraska bill—I ask, who can be quite sure that it would not have been voted down, in the one case, as it had been in the other.

The nearest approach to the point of declaring the power of a State over slavery is made by Judge Nelson. He approaches it more than once, using the precise idea, and almost the language too, of the Nebraska act. On one occasion his exact language is, "except in cases where the power is restrained by the Constitution of the United States, the law of the State is supreme over the subject of slavery within its jurisdiction."

In what cases the power of the states is so restrained by the U.S. Constitution, is left an open question, precisely as the same question, as to the restraint on the power of the territories was left open in the Nebraska act. Put that and that together, and we have another nice little niche, which we may, ere long, see filled with another Supreme Court decision, declaring that the Constitution of the United States does not permit a state to exclude slavery from its limits.

And this may especially be expected if the doctrine of "care not whether slavery be voted down or voted up," shall gain upon the public mind sufficiently to give promise that such a decision can be maintained when made.

Such a decision is all that slavery now lacks of being alike lawful in all the States.

Welcome or unwelcome, such decision is probably coming, and will soon be upon us, unless the power of the present political dynasty shall be met and overthrown.

We shall lie down pleasantly dreaming that the people of Missouri are on the verge of making their State free; and we shall awake to the reality, instead, that the Supreme Court has made Illinois a slave State.

To meet and overthrow the power of that dynasty is the work now before all those who would prevent that consummation.

That is what we have to do. But how can we best do it?

There are those who denounce us openly to their own friends, and yet whisper us softly, that Senator Douglas is the aptest instrument there is, with which to effect that object . . .

He has done all in his power to reduce the whole question of slavery to one of a mere right of property; and as such, how can he oppose the foreign slave trade—how can he refuse that trade in that "property" shall be "perfectly free"—unless he does it as a protection to the home production? And as the home producers will probably not ask the protection, he will be wholly without a ground of opposition.

Senator Douglas holds, we know, that a man may rightfully be wiser to-day than he was yesterday—that he may rightfully change when he finds himself wrong.

But, can we for that reason, run ahead, and infer that he will make any particular change, of which he, himself, has given no intimation? Can we safely base our action upon any such vague inference?

Now, as ever, I wish to not misrepresent Judge Douglas' position, question his motives, or do aught that can be personally offensive to him. Whenever, if ever, he and we can come together on principle so that our great cause may have assistance from his great ability, I hope to have interposed no adventitious obstacle.

But clearly, he is not now with us—he does not pretend to be—he does not promise to ever be.

Our cause, then, must be entrusted to, and conducted by its own undoubted friends—those whose hands are free, whose hearts are in the work—who do care for the result.

Two years ago the Republicans of the nation mustered over thirteen hundred thousand strong.

We did this under the single impulse of resistance to a common danger, with every external circumstance against us.

Of strange, discordant, and even, hostile elements, we gathered from the four winds, and formed and fought the battle through, under the constant hot fire of a disciplined, proud, and pampered enemy.

Did we brave all then, to falter now?—now—when that same enemy is wavering, dissevered and belligerent?

The result is not doubtful. We shall not fail—if we stand firm, we shall not fail.

Wise councils may accelerate or mistakes delay it, but, sooner or later the victory is sure to come.

GLOSSARY

Chase and Macy: Senator Salmon P. Chase of Ohio and Representative Daniel Macy of Indiana, both opponents of the Kansas-Nebraska Act

mould: to shape or form

mustered: gathered and organized for battle

niche: a small opening, used from the perspective of carpentry

prohibition: legal limit

squatter: a land settler, especially one without legal right

whither: where

Document Analysis

Lincoln launched into his speech by identifying the stakes of the political contest, which he believed were nothing less than the character of the American nation in its relationship to slavery. The problem originated in the division of the United States over slavery and the actions of certain political leaders to expand slavery's presence in the nation. To describe the significance of the dispute, Lincoln reached for a biblical metaphor, claiming, "A house divided against itself cannot stand." His hearers would have immediately recognized the reference, as Lincoln was quoting Jesus from Matthew 12:25 (repeated in Mark 3:25). As historian Richard Carwardine has noted, much of the antislavery sentiment in Illinois originated in churches, and so Lincoln was using a familiar turn of biblical phrase to demonstrate the seriousness of the issue and the moral significance of the debate. But this disunion could not remain: "I believe this government cannot endure, permanently half slave and half free," Lincoln told his audience. He continued, "I do not expect the Union to be dissolved—I do not expect the house to fall—but I do expect it will cease to be divided. It will become all one thing or all the other."

Lincoln then presented two alternatives: "Either the opponents of slavery, will arrest the further spread of it, and place it where the public mind shall rest in the belief that it is in course of ultimate extinction; or its advocates will push it forward, till it shall become alike lawful in all the States." Lincoln believed—and stated elsewhere—that slavery had been tolerated by the founding generation of the county because people believed it would ultimately disappear, that the country would evolve away from using slaves. Since slavery was accepted in the Constitution, Lincoln was willing to accept it where it already existed. However, he refused to accept the expansion of slavery, especially when underhanded, undemocratic means were used to bring it about. This led to his claim, throughout the speech, of a conspiracy to expand slavery throughout the entire nation. Near the end of the speech, Lincoln portrayed the danger this way: "We shall lie down pleasantly dreaming that the people of Missouri are on the verge of making their State free; and we shall awake to the reality, instead, that the Supreme Court has made Illinois a slave State." Lincoln believed this would be as abhorrent to all the citizens of Illinois as it was to himself.

In the speech, Lincoln masterfully wove together his philosophical opposition to slavery while working to achieve short-term political ends. Philosophically, Lincoln indicated his distaste for slavery's expansion. Self-government demanded the ability to oppose the expansion of slavery. On a moral level, Lincoln suggested that it was insufficient (as Douglas had already declared) simply not to care. Politically, Lincoln hoped to rally Republicans, Free-Soilers, and former Whigs to his candidacy. Thus, he was building political support for his candidacy, just as he had encouraged the holding of a Republican convention to nominate him. Further, Lincoln sought to detach eastern Republicans from any flirtation with Douglas. When Douglas broke with President Buchanan over the Lecompton Constitution, easterners such as Horace Greeley believed he could be lured away from the Democrats and brought into the Republican fold. Lincoln wanted those outsiders to see the Illinois Republicans' perspective: Douglas had actually contributed to the problems surrounding the issue of slavery, and so long as he refused to take a moral position on the issue, he could never be more than an occasional and accidental ally. From this stance, Lincoln hoped to confront all Illinoisans with Douglas's inconsistencies and involvement in slavery's expansion—which Lincoln believed was unpopular in the state, even though many still tolerated slavery's existence.

Lincoln reached out to a wide audience—first those in the convention hall but also, more importantly, all the Illinois citizens who would read or hear the speech. Lincoln was trying to shape interpretation of the political landscape. To do so, he laid out his outline at the very first: "If we could first know where we are, and whither we are tending, we could then better judge what to do, and how to do it." This provided the division of his speech, as he predicated his ultimate call for action on his previous diagnosis of recent events.

Where We Are and Whither We Are Tending

In describing his contemporary conditions, Lincoln charged that a conspiracy to advance slavery existed. He used multiple words to describe this: a "combination," "a piece of machinery," with "evidences of design and concert of action." Later, he used a carpentry analogy, that when framed timbers gathered by multiple people are joined together to construct a building, with all the pieces in place, it is hard to believe that a common plan was not guiding them. Lincoln's logic was that if things appeared to be a conspiracy and worked together as a conspiracy, with things fitting together as if they had been planned, then it was reasonable to assume some sort of design or conspiracy was at work. Lincoln went further and identified the four major contributors to this design, which he portrayed as the "workmen": "Stephen [Douglas], Franklin [Pierce], Roger [B. Taney], and James [Buchanan]."

Lincoln then traced how he saw this design coming together in a series of steps, beginning in 1854. The first step involved the "Nebraska bill" (Kansas-Nebraska Act), authored by Douglas. The bill had multiple pernicious effects. First, it "opened all the national territory to slavery." By undoing the Missouri Compromise, this was a marked departure of national policy and laid the groundwork for subsequent problems. Second, Lincoln pointed to the philosophy underlying the Kansas-Nebraska Act. To Douglas, the approach represented a type of popular sovereignty, a democratic endorsement of the settlers' views on slavery. Lincoln mocked this, though, calling it "squatter sovereignty" and claiming that it perverted a true definition of self government to instead mean "That if any one man, choose to enslave another, no third man shall be allowed to object." Third, Lincoln insisted that the Nebraska act had a negative effect "to educate and mould public opinion . . . to not care whether slavery is voted down or voted up." Douglas had already tried to ignore the morality of slavery, and his bill was training Northerners to do the same thing.

The other steps involved national politics around the *Dred Scott* Supreme Court case. As the case was argued (and reargued) before the court, successive Democratic presidents Pierce (1853–57) and Buchanan (1857–61) worked to prepare public opinion to accept the court's ruling. In his final year as president, Pierce spoke in favor of accepting the forthcoming decision. Buchanan, who was alerted of the final decision before it was made public, used his inaugural address to endorse what the court would hand down. Then, Buchanan further lent his support to the decision when he responded to the "Silliman Letter." Benjamin Silliman was a respected professor of natural sciences at Yale, and he enlisted forty signatories to protest publicly the proslavery activity of Kansas's territorial governor. Buchanan responded with a public letter of his own, published in the Washington, DC, newspaper the *Union*. In the letter, he not only endorsed those activities in Kansas but belittled anyone who might dare dispute the *Dred Scott* vision of slavery in the territories. Lincoln saw all of this as further conspiring to prepare the country to go along with the expansion of slavery, which he and the Republicans refused to do.

These presidential utterances were meant to advance the *Dred Scott* majority decision. The ruling, written by Chief Justice Taney, laid a legal groundwork for the permanence of slavery and expansion of the institution. In Lincoln's telling, the ruling's three main components all contributed to strengthen slavery. First, it declared that no slave or descendent of a slave can ever be a citizen of a state or the United States. This would prevent the protections afforded to free blacks in free states from traveling with them to slave states. Second, the ruling denied to both Congress and any territorial legislature the ability to exclude slavery from any US territory. To Lincoln this meant opening up all western territories to slavery and that no territory settled by antislavery Northerners could keep slavery out. To Lincoln's mind, this was not just judicial activism but judicial revolution, as it denied the validity of both the Northwest Ordinance and the Missouri Compromise. Finally, any disputes about the condition of a slave taken into a free state would be decided by a slave state (in Dred Scott's case, Missouri), rather than a free state.

Given this background, Lincoln believed he could also say something about where the country was heading. He observed that there was no clear statement in *Dred Scott* about whether a state could exclude slavery. Supreme Court justices John McLean and Benjamin Robbins Curtis had dissented from the Taney decision but not addressed this question, nor had Supreme Court justice Samuel Nelson. Lincoln saw an opening—"another nice little niche"—for another Supreme Court decision that could declare that states had no power to exclude slavery. Lincoln ventured to suggest that this was likely, especially after Americans were educated for long enough in the "don't care" attitude of Douglas. As Lincoln saw it, the end result would be, through judicial power, to expand slavery across the entire United States.

What to Do and How to Do It

After reviewing the *Dred Scott* decision, Lincoln turned to the question of how Republicans should respond. His answer was, "To meet and overthrow the power of that dynasty is the work now before all those who would prevent that consummation." Claiming that these proslavery actors were part of a political dynasty was a serious charge in the American republic. In using that strong language, Lincoln was again pointing to the need to oppose the antidemocratic conspiracy to spread slavery. Thus, Republicans would stand as a bulwark against the shadowy plans of proslavery politicians.

Lincoln states clearly that Douglas is not the leader Illinois needed, based on his stance on slavery. Perhaps eastern Republicans would whisper "that Senator Douglas is the aptest instrument there is," but Lincoln argued against any rapprochement. Yes, Douglas may have been right on the Lecompton Constitution, and Lincoln was glad if Douglas was "wiser to-day than he was yesterday." Still, to Lincoln, he remained wrong on the fundamental moral question of slavery, as he continued to insist that he did not care whether it should be allowed or forbidden. As a result, he was in no position to advance the Republican position about slavery. Douglas was a "caged and toothless" lion, without standing to counter the slave conspiracy. By extension, Lincoln was making clear that he opposed slavery's expansion, and that this was the only legitimate moral position. This position led Lincoln to assert with great finality, "But clearly, he is not now with us—he does not pretend to be—he does not promise to ever be." Lincoln wanted to make clear that he was the only viable Republican choice.

Lincoln then would lead the charge of organizing Illinois Republicans for the election. In 1856, the Republicans had done well, and Lincoln hoped to build upon their success. Therefore, he ended his speech with a call to courage and action: "We shall not fail—if we stand firm, we shall not fail . . . sooner or later the victory is sure to come." With these words, Lincoln and the Republicans were ready to contest the senatorial election throughout the state.

Essential Themes

Lincoln's speech had significant effects both immediately in Illinois and for later debates about slavery and the trajectory of the nation. Initially, the speech received a warm response at the convention and from dedicated Republicans. However, it also issued terms that were too stark for many. It ran the risk of scaring away as many voters as it might attract. The moral certainty of the speech also seemed to threaten disunion over the slavery issue. Despite Lincoln's subsequent insistence that he was not inviting conflict, his pleas were not enough to deflate this charge. Indeed, one of Douglas's lines of attack was that Lincoln was a radical abolitionist unwilling to compromise.

Politically, the speech kicked off the senatorial election season. After exchanging subsequent speeches (often with Lincoln following Douglas around the state), the candidates agreed to a series of debates, which would gain fame as the Lincoln-Douglas debates. Stretching from August through October, the two men debated each other throughout Illinois. In these debates, Lincoln returned often to the themes he had sketched in the "House Divided" speech, especially attacking Douglas as one who did not care about slavery and whose support for popular sovereignty on the issue was incoherent in light of the *Dred Scott* decision. In the election, Lincoln won the popular vote, but Democrats (and hence Douglas) won the majority of state legislative seats, including key "swing" counties around Springfield in the center of the state. Although he had lost, Lincoln had firmly articulated a Republican position against the expansion of slavery and raised his national profile.

Subsequently, the "House Divided" speech continued to serve as a touchstone for the divides of the late 1850s. As the Civil War approached, Southerners pointed back to the speech as evidence of Lincoln's radicalism and desire for conflict, even though Lincoln rejected such labels. In the twentieth century, scholars have noted the significance of the themes that Lincoln advanced in the speech. For political philosopher Harry Jaffa, Lincoln encapsulated the moral debate at the heart of the sectional split that would ultimately lead to the Civil War. For Jaffa, the divide was nothing less than a "Crisis of the House Divided." More recently, historian Allen Guelzo portrayed the "House Divided" speech as the kickoff to the Lincoln-Douglas debates, which, in his interpretation, defined the country. The "House Divided" speech has continued to retain its power as a rhetorical presentation, as a significant marker on the path to Civil War, and as a touchstone for issues of fundamental significance in the American political tradition.

Jonathan Den Hartog, PhD

Bibliography

Carwardine, Richard. *Lincoln: A Life of Purpose and Power*. New York: Vintage, 2006. Print.

Finkelman, Paul. *Dred Scott v. Sandford: A Brief History with Documents*. Boston: Bedford, 1997. Print.

Guelzo, Allen. *Abraham Lincoln: Redeemer President*. Grand Rapids, MI: Eerdmans, 1999. Print.

---. "Houses Divided: Lincoln, Douglas, and the Political Landscape of 1858." *Journal of American History* 94.2 (2007): 391–417. Print.

---. *Lincoln and Douglas: The Debates That Defined America*. New York: Simon, 2008. Print.

Jaffa, Harry. *Crisis of the House Divided: An Interpretation of the Issues in the Lincoln-Douglas Debates*. 1959. Chicago: U of Chicago P, 1982. Print.

Additional Reading

Foner, Eric. *The Fiery Trial: Abraham Lincoln and American Slavery*. New York: Norton, 2010. Print.

Holzer, Harold, ed. *The Lincoln-Douglas Debates: The First Complete, Unexpurgated Text*. New York: HarperCollins, 1993. Print.

Johannsen, Robert, ed. *The Lincoln-Douglas Debates of 1858*. New York: Oxford UP, 2008. Print.

Lincoln, Abraham. "The War with Mexico: Speech in the United States House of Representatives." *TeachingAmericanHistory.Org*. Ashbrook Center, 2006–12. Web. 13 Mar. 2013.

McPherson, James. *Battle Cry of Freedom: The Civil War Era*. New York: Oxford UP, 2003. Print.

Potter, David. *The Impending Crisis, 1848–1861*. New York: Harper, 1977. Print.

Zarefsky, David. *Lincoln, Douglas, and Slavery: In the Crucible of Public Debate*. Chicago: U of Chicago P, 1990. Print.

LESSON PLAN: **Lincoln and the Spread of Slavery**

Students analyze Abraham Lincoln's House Divided speech to gain understanding of the Dred Scott decision and other issues that led to the Civil War.

Learning Objectives

Identify issues and problems in the past; compare and contrast differing sets of ideas; identify central questions and narrative addresses; differentiate between historical fact and historical interpretation; analyze cause-and-effect relationships; formulate an opinion on an issue.

Materials: Lincoln's "House Divided" Speech (1858)

Overview Questions

What federal government actions is Lincoln objecting to? What views does Lincoln have about how these actions might impact the nation? How does Lincoln propose to counter these actions? How do the views Lincoln expresses in this speech compare to abolitionist views about slavery?

Step 1: Comprehension Questions

What opinion of the state of the Union does Lincoln offer at the beginning of his speech? What 1854 event is Lincoln referring to in his speech? Why does he feel that event marked the beginning of a struggle to keep the "house" divided?

- **Activity:** Have students write a paragraph explaining why the passage of the Kansas-Nebraska Act was a controversial event in the 1850s.

Step 2: Comprehension Questions

What was "squatter sovereignty" and how is it related to the "right of self government"? What opinion of "squatter sovereignty" does Lincoln seem to hold? Why?

- **Activity:** Explore the concept of popular sovereignty with the class. Ask whether it is a legitimate expression of democracy. As they discuss this question, have them contemplate a scenario in which the majority by popular vote might deprive a group of certain rights or freedoms.

Step 3: Context Questions

What opinion does Lincoln voice about the Supreme Court's Dred Scott decision? What impact does he fear it will could on the "house divided"? Why should he have had such concerns?

- **Activity:** Have students write a one-paragraph summary of Lincoln's summary of the Dred Scott decision. Call on students to read their summaries to the class.

Step 4: Historical Connection Questions

Why did the Dred Scott decision make Lincoln's issues with "squatter sovereignty" irrelevant? What suggestion does he make about how popular sovereignty might be used to block the Supreme Court's ruling?

- **Activity:** Organize the class into small groups. Have each group discuss and decide whether, on the basis of this speech, it would categorize Lincoln as an abolitionist. Have a spokesperson from each group explain its position to the class.

Step 5: Response Paper

Word length and additional requirements set by Instructor. Students answer the research question in the *Overview Questions*. Students state a thesis and use as evidence passages from the primary source document as well as support from the secondary historical documents assigned in the lesson.

On the Irrepressible Conflict

Date: October 25, 1858
Author: Seward, William H.
Genre: speech

"No aristocracy of any kind, much less an aristocracy of slaveholders, shall ever make the laws of the land in which I shall be content to live."

Summary Overview

This document is an excerpt from a speech the Republican Senator William H. Seward delivered in Rochester, New York, on October 25, 1858. He portrayed the United States as a nation divided between regions based on free and slave systems of labor, regions he predicted would inevitably clash. In what quickly became known as his "On the Irrepressible Conflict" speech, Seward voiced the fears of Northern Republicans who were wary of the expansion of the Southern Slave Power, articulated the free-labor worldview that had developed in the North by the 1850s, and even posed the opening argument in the later debate among historians over the inevitability of the American Civil War.

Defining Moment

By the 1850s, Seward was more radical on the issue of slavery than most Northerners, who typically only wanted to ban slavery in the territories. For instance, during the debate over the Compromise of 1850, which extended the line of the 1820 Missouri Compromise between slave and free territories all the way to California, Seward delivered an inflammatory speech on the floor of the Senate. He declared that the Constitution opposed slavery, believed Congress should ban slavery in the territories, and portrayed slavery as a threat to democracy. One of his statements, delivered in his March 11, 1850, speech "Freedom in the New Territories," that "there is a higher law than the Constitution," especially triggered Southern animosity since, as historian Sean Wilentz notes, a Northerner seemed to be invoking extralegal religious sentiment as justification for a potential end to slavery. Moving through the National Republican, Anti-Masonic, Whig, and Republican parties throughout the antebellum period, Seward consistently sought to combat immorality and aristocracy in politics. Furthermore, in his eyes, the system of slavery corrupted American politics, specifically through the Democratic Party. When deep fissures over the opening of further territories to the expansion of slavery under the 1854 Kansas-Nebraska Act destroyed the Whig Party, Seward enthusiastically helped the nascent Republican Party establish itself in New York in late 1855. Long before his most famous speech, "On the Irrepressible Conflict," Seward's readiness to combat slavery formed from his involvement in the Protestant religious fervor of the Second Great Awakening, the subsequent Protestant reform societies, and the political parties that favored stronger government intervention in economic and social matters. As an indication of his consistent and in fact deepening antislavery sentiments, when he learned of the Supreme Court's 1857 decision in *Dred Scott v. Sandford*, which in part declared the Missouri Compromise of 1820 unconstitutional and opened up the entire West to slavery, Seward delivered a blistering harangue against the decision in the Senate.

Thus, by 1858, Northerners loved Seward for his consistent antislavery stance and his remarkably articulate and passionate speeches. Unsurprisingly, Southerners despised him. Therefore, after winning a new six-year term in the Senate in 1854, he went on the campaign trail in the North in 1858 to bolster support for his fellow Republican candidates. At the front of a packed Corinthian Hall in Rochester, New York, on October 25, 1858, Seward delivered what would become his most famous speech against what Republicans by then termed the "Slave Power." As usual, many Northern Republicans embraced the speech and Democrats in both the North and South lambasted Seward as a warmonger, an agitator who would cause slaves to rise in rebellion, and a threat to slavery itself. For instance, the *New York Herald-Tribune* labeled him an "arch agitator" and said he was one of the "more dangerous" abolitionists. Antislavery abolitionists praised the speech, but moderate papers such as the *New York Times* suggested his language was dangerous. Southerners viewed Seward's speech as further evidence that the central objective of the new Republican Party was the elimination of slavery. While Seward had not explicitly mentioned ending slavery where it existed, his portrayal of an inevitable conflict suggested that soon slavery itself would become the target of the Republican Party. In the minds of Southerners, the Republicans would only need to take a small step from objecting to the expansion of slavery into the territories, which they openly did in the late 1850s, to seeking to destroy slavery everywhere in the United States. Indeed, the primary trigger to South Carolinian, and broadly Southern, secession was that in 1860, Republican leader Abraham Lincoln won the presidency without a single Southern electoral vote. With the slaveholding states now a permanent minority in the United States, Southerners believed they could no longer protect themselves from a North dominated by the Republican Party, led by men such as Seward, that would likely, Southerners believed, target their peculiar institution for elimination.

Author Biography

After Abraham Lincoln, William Seward was one of the most important Northern Republicans of the Civil War era. Seward was born in 1801 into a wealthy family in rural Orange County, New York. Although his family initially owned a few slaves, he came to dislike slavery, and the family's slaves gained their freedom as New York slowly ended the institution during the early 1800s. After graduating from Union College in Schenectady, he became a lawyer and settled in Auburn, New York, where he joined a law practice and married Frances Miller, the daughter of the senior partner in his firm.

Seward soon became involved in the rough-and-tumble politics of antebellum New York, leaving the short-lived National Republican Party for the Anti-Masonic Party when the latter formed in the late 1820s. Despite his wealthy upbringing and comfortable income, Seward was attracted to any movement he deemed moral at its core, as the Anti-Masons seemed to be in their determination to combat what they saw as the corrupt influence of Freemasons in politics and government. By the mid-1830s, however, Seward moved to the Whig Party because, as Wilentz writes, he "envisaged government as a lever for commercial improvement and as a weapon to combat social ills, from crime in the cities to inadequate schooling in the countryside" (482–83). Thus, Seward's belief in the utility of government both to expand economic opportunity and to reform society placed him firmly on an ideological trajectory that during the antebellum period would find him in the National Republican, Anti-Mason, Whig, and then Republican parties. These political movements generally believed government should aid in the construction of infrastructure such as canals, railroads, and national roads and should also provide funds and legislation to aid the social-reform movements emerging from the Second Great Awakening of the early nineteenth century. The latter included the temperance movement, poor relief, and abolitionism, among others.

Running as a Whig, Seward was elected governor of New York in 1838 and reelected two years later, but he faced opposition from both the Democratic Party and conservatives in his own party who did not like his reform agenda. Next, Seward was elected to the US Senate in the tumultuous year of 1849 when the nation was deciding how to treat the vast new territory acquired from Mexico. He would remain in Congress first as a Whig and then a Republican, until Lincoln appointed him secretary of state in early 1861. In that position, he presided over the purchase of Alaska from Russia in 1867. He also constructed a grand vision for the expansion of American power into the Pacific and the Caribbean that would not be realized until the very end of the nineteenth century. He retired in 1869 and died on October 10, 1872.

HISTORICAL DOCUMENT

The unmistakable outbreaks of zeal which occur all around me show that you are earnest men—and such a man am I. Let us, therefore, at least for a time, pass all secondary and collateral questions, whether of a personal or of a general nature, and consider the main subject of the present canvass. The Democratic party, or, to speak more accurately, the party which wears that attractive name—is in possession of the federal government. The Republicans propose to dislodge that party, and dismiss it from its high trust.

The main subject, then, is whether the Democratic party deserves to retain the confidence of the American people. In attempting to prove it unworthy, I think that I am not actuated by prejudices against that party, or by prepossessions in favor of its adversary; for I have learned, by some experience, that virtue and patriotism, vice and selfishness, are found in all parties, and that they differ less in their motives than in the policies they pursue.

Our country is a theatre, which exhibits, in full operation, two radically different political systems; the one resting on the basis of servile or slave labor, the other on voluntary labor of freemen. The laborers who are enslaved are all negroes, or persons more or less purely of African derivation. But this is only accidental. The principle of the system is, that labor in every society, by whomsoever performed, is necessarily unintellectual, groveling and base; and that the laborer, equally for his own good and for the welfare of the State, ought to be enslaved. The white laboring man, whether native or foreigner, is not enslaved, only because he cannot, as yet, be reduced to bondage . . .

The slave system is one of constant danger, distrust, suspicion, and watchfulness. It debases those whose toil alone can produce wealth and resources for defense, to the lowest degree of which human nature is capable, to guard against mutiny and insurrection, and thus wastes energies which otherwise might be employed in national development and aggrandizement. The free-labor system educates all alike, and by opening all the fields of industrial employment and all the departments of authority, to the unchecked and equal rivalry of all classes of men, at once secures universal contentment, and brings into the highest possible activity all the physical, moral, and social energies of the whole state. In states where the slave system prevails, the masters, directly or indirectly, secure all political power, and constitute a ruling aristocracy. In states where the free-labor system prevails, universal suffrage necessarily obtains, and the state inevitably becomes, sooner or later, a republic or democracy . . .

Hitherto, the two systems have existed in different States, but side by side within the American Union. This has happened because the Union is a confederation of States. But in another aspect the United States constitute only one nation. Increase of population, which is filling the States out to their very borders, together with a new and extended network of railroads and other avenues, and an internal commerce which daily becomes more intimate, is rapidly bringing the States into a higher and more perfect social unity or consolidation. Thus, these antagonistic systems are continually coming into closer contact, and collision results . . .

Unlike too many of those who in modem time invoke their authority, they had a choice between the two. They preferred the system of free labor, and they determined to organize the government, and so direct its activity, that that system should surely and certainly prevail. For this purpose, and no other, they based the whole structure of the government broadly on the principle that all men are created equal, and therefore free—little dreaming that, within the short period of one hundred years, their descendants would bear to be told by any orator, however popular, that the utterance of that principle was merely a rhetorical rhapsody; or by any judge, however venerated, that it was attended by mental reservation, which rendered it hypocritical and false . . .

It remains to say on this point only one word, to guard against misapprehension. If these States are to again become universally slaveholding, I do not pretend to say with what violations of the constitution that end shall be accomplished. On the other hand, while I do confidently believe and hope that my country will yet become a land of universal freedom, I do not expect that it will be made so otherwise than through the action of the several States co-operating with the federal government, and all acting in strict conformity with their respective constitutions.

The strife and contentions concerning slavery, which gently disposed persons so habitually deprecate, are nothing more than the ripening of the conflict which the fathers themselves not only thus regarded with favor, but which they may be said to have instituted.

It is not to be denied, however, that thus far the course of that contest has not been according to their humane anticipations and wishes. In the field of federal politics, slavery, deriving unlooked-for advantages from commercial changes, and energies unforeseen from the facilities of combination between members of the slaveholding class and between that class and other property classes, early rallied, and has at length made a stand, not merely to retain its original defensive position, but to extend its sway throughout the whole Union. It is certain that the slaveholding class of American citizens indulge this high ambition, and that they derive encouragement for it from the rapid and effective political successes which they have already obtained. The plan of operation is this: By continued appliances of patronage and threats of disunion, they will keep a majority favorable to these designs in the Senate, where each State has an equal representation.

Through that majority they will defeat, as they best can, the admission of free States and secure the admission of slave States. Under the protection of the judiciary, they will, on the principle of the Dred Scott case, carry slavery into all the territories of the United States now existing and hereafter to be organized. By the action of the President and Senate, using the treaty-making power, they will annex foreign slaveholding States. In a favorable conjuncture they will induce Congress to repeal the act of 1808 which prohibits the foreign slave trade, and so they will import from Africa, at a cost of only twenty dollars a head, slaves enough to fill up the interior of the continent. Thus relatively increasing the number of slave States, they will allow no amendment to the constitution prejudicial to their interest; and so, having permanently established their power, they expect the federal judiciary to nullify all State laws which shall interfere with internal or foreign commerce in slaves. When the free States shall be sufficiently demoralized to tolerate these designs, they reasonably conclude that slavery will be accepted by those States themselves.

I shall not stop to show how speedy or how complete would be the ruin which the accomplishment of these slaveholding schemes would bring upon the country. For one, I should not remain in the country to test the sad experiment. Having spent my manhood, though not my whole life, in a free State, no aristocracy of any kind, much less an aristocracy of slaveholders, shall ever make the laws of the land in which I shall be content to live. Having seen the society around me universally engaged in agriculture, manufactures, and trade, which were innocent and beneficent, I shall never be a denizen of a State where men and women are reared as cattle, and bought and sold as merchandise.

When that evil day shall come, and all further effort at resistance shall be impossible, then, if there shall be no better hope for redemption than I can now foresee, I shall say with Franklin, while looking abroad over the whole earth for a new and more congenial home, "Where liberty dwells, there is my country."

You will tell me that these fears are extravagant and chimerical. I answer, they are so; but they are so only because the designs of the slaveholders must and can be defeated. But it is only the possibility of defeat that renders them so. They cannot be defeated by inactivity. There is no escape from them compatible with non-resistance. How, then, and in what way, shall the necessary resistance be made? There is only one way. The Democratic party must be permanently dislodged from the government.

The reason is, that the Democratic party is inextricably committed to the designs of the slaveholders, which I have described. Let me be well understood. I do not charge that the Democratic candidates for public office now before the people are pledged to—much less that the Democratic masses who support them really adopt—those atrocious and dangerous designs. Candidates may, and generally do, mean to act justly, wisely, and patriotically, when they shall be elected; but they become the ministers and servants, not the dictators, of the power which elects them. The policy which a party shall pursue at a future period is only gradually developed, depending on the occurrence of events never fully foreknown. The motives of men, whether acting as electors or in any other capacity, are generally pure.

Nevertheless, it is not more true that "hell is paved with good intentions," than it is that earth is covered with wrecks resulting from innocent and amiable motives.

The very constitution of the Democratic party commits it to execute all the designs of the slaveholders, whatever they may be. It is not a party of the whole Union, of all the free States and of all the slave States; nor yet is it a party of the free States in the North and in the Northwest; but it is a sectional and local party, having practically its seat within the slave States, and counting its constituency chiefly and almost exclusively there. Of all its representatives in Congress and in the electoral colleges, two-thirds uniformly come from these States. Its great element of strength lies in the vote of the slaveholders, augmented by the representation of three-fifths of the slaves. Deprive the Democratic party of this strength, and it would be a helpless and hopeless minority, incapable of continued organization. The Democratic party, being thus local and sectional, acquires new strength from the admission of ever new slave State, and loses relatively by the admission of every new free State into the Union . . .

This dark record shows you, fellow-citizens, what I was unwilling to announce at an earlier stage of this argument, that of the whole nefarious schedule of slaveholding designs which I have submitted to you, the Democratic party has left only one yet to be consummated—the abrogation of the law which forbids the African slave-trade.

I know—few, I think, know better than I—the resources and energies of the Democratic party, which is identical with the slave power. I do ample justice to its traditional popularity. I know further—few, I think, know better than I—the difficulties and disadvantages of organizing a new political force, like the Republican party, and the obstacles it must encounter in laboring without prestige and without patronage. But, understanding all this, I know that the Democratic party must go down, and that the Republican party must rise into its place. The Democratic party derived its strength, originally, from its adoption of the principles of equal and exact justice to all men. So long as it practiced this principle faithfully it was invulnerable.

It became vulnerable when it renounced the principle, and since that time it has maintained itself, not by virtue of its own strength, or even of its traditional merits, but because there as yet had appeared in the political field no other party that had the conscience and the courage to take up, and avow, and practice the life-inspiring principle which the Democratic party had surrendered. At last, the Republican party has appeared. It avows, now, as the Republican party of 1800 did, in one word, its faith and its works, "Equal and exact justice to all men." Even when it first entered the field, only half organized, it struck a blow which only just failed to secure complete and triumphant victory. In this, its second campaign, it has already won advantages which render that triumph now both easy and certain.

The secret of its assured success lies in that very characteristic which, in the mouth of scoffers, constitutes its great and lasting imbecility and reproach. It lies in the fact that it is a party of one idea; but that is a noble one—an idea that fills and expands all generous souls; the idea of equality—the equality of all men before human tribunals and human laws, as they all are equal before the divine tribunal and divine laws.

I know, and you know, that a revolution has begun. I know, and all the world knows, that revolutions never go backward. Twenty senators and a hundred representatives proclaim boldly in Congress to-day sentiments and opinions and principles of freedom which hardly so many men, even in this free State, dared to utter in their own homes twenty years ago. While the government of the United States, under the conduct of the Democratic party, has been all that time surrendering one plain and castle after another to slavery, the people of the United States have been no less steadily and perseveringly gathering together the forces with which to recover back again all the fields and all the castles which have been lost, and to confound and overthrow, by one decisive blow, the betrayers of the constitution and freedom forever.

GLOSSARY

aggrandizement: an increase in size or stature

chimerical: illusory

derivation: descent, lineage

Dred Scott case: *Dred Scott v. Sandford* (1857), a Supreme Court decision that favored the rights of slave owners

fathers: in this case, the Founding Fathers of the United States

slave power: term used by Northerners to describe what they saw as the threatening political power of Southern slaveholders

universal suffrage: voting rights for all adult citizens

Document Analysis

To Seward, two completely divergent societies had come into being in the United States. Opposite sources of labor had created "two radically different political systems," one free and the other slave. This was quite a drastic portrayal of the increasingly sharp and violent sectional divide that was plaguing the United States. Most American leaders in the 1850s, both in the North and the South, still emphasized the ideals Americans had in common, including belief in the Constitution, liberty, private property, individual rights, and the voting franchise, for white men at least. Of course, some abolitionists argued the Constitution was in fact an evil, proslavery document, but such voices constituted a minority of Northerners even up to the advent of the Civil War. Seward, however, viewed the situation differently. He portrayed the North and the South as two different societies based on two different economic systems, constituted by two different systems of labor, and that would soon clash. His arguments echoed the warnings of other Republicans that the expansion of the Slave Power threatened Northern white rights, but his clear, hard-hitting style and clever phrasing helped his words stick in the minds of his audience. In addition, the inevitability of a coming conflict seemed alarmingly new to both Northerners and Southerners.

Threats to Northern White Rights

While setting up the initial framework for his argument, Seward described Southern slavery in an interesting way. He noted its racial character but also claimed that "this is only accidental." He argued that the very nature of the slave system required workers, of any race, to be enslaved for the good of society and then hinted this meant that whites could soon find themselves under the yoke of slavery as well. Claiming the white man "cannot, as yet, be reduced to bondage," indicated his fear that the slave-owning aristocracy of the South might one day place whites in chains to serve their own purposes. Seward saw slavery as fundamentally unconcerned with race. He believed the South had only adopted African slaves because of the particular nature of American history. Therefore, Seward was subtly warning his white audience that the Slave Power and the system of slavery in the South could one day threaten their rights. By claiming this threat to white rights, Seward was contributing to the already well-established Republican argument that the Slave Power threatened the rights of Northern white men. Expansion of slavery into the territories, Republicans argued, would keep whites from the opportunity and freedom they sought. Events such as the gag rule in Congress during the late 1830s and early 1840s, when speaking of slavery was officially prohibited, and the Fugitive Slave Act of 1850, which required Northerners to help Southern slave catchers or face fines or imprisonment, seemed to threaten Northern whites' freedom, claimed Republicans throughout the 1850s. Thus, Seward's speech tapped into the ongoing Republican argument that slavery was not merely an issue contained in the South. The system threatened to expand nationally and trample white rights.

In addition to warning of the threats to white freedom, Seward argued that slavery undermined the economic opportunity of individual whites and slowed the economic growth of the nation as a whole. Seward pointed out that to maintain the system of slavery, whites had "to guard against mutiny and insurrection, and thus [slavery] wastes energies which otherwise might be employed in national development and aggrandizement." The slave system not only threatened to trample on the rights of whites but also made whites into guardsmen and robbed the entire nation of their potential economic productivity. For Seward, the free-labor system he and the Republican Party advocated was far superior. In such a system, individual farmers and workers gained direct profit from their hard work and simultaneously contributed to national wealth and development. In such a free-labor system, human capacities were unleashed for good purposes and all men, in theory, could receive equal education and be equal in politics. On the contrary, in the slave system, according to Seward, "the masters, directly or indirectly, secure all political power, and constitute a ruling aristocracy." Seward was not completely correct, because while large landowners often held political office, most white men in the South from any class did have the franchise and therefore could vote for their desired candidate. Returning the Southern elite to office repeatedly indicated that the rest of the Southern white male population often agreed with the goals, arguments, and views of their slaveholding neighbors. For instance, the Southern states would declare secession in 1860 and 1861 through special conventions to which delegates were democratically elected. In some places in the South, property-holding requirements for voting remained in place, and more commonly, owning land was required to hold office; however, compared to the rest of the world in the mid-nineteenth century, the South was a relatively democratic political system, for white men at least. Thus, Seward's attempt to portray a conflict between a democracy and an aristocracy was not entirely accurate, although it played well to Northern audiences. In addition, while the South was democratic in nature, this simply meant the entire white population, even nonslaveholders, supported the institution of slavery.

The Coming Collision

For Seward, the conflict between two fundamentally divergent social systems had reached a decision point. Because of a growing populace, the economic expansion the United States had experienced in the previous decades, and the internal improvements that Whigs and then Republicans championed (such as national roads, railroads, and canals), "these antagonistic systems are continually coming into closer contact, and collision results." Although slavery and free labor had existed separately for a while, the two systems were interacting more closely. For Seward, the remarkable growth the United States had experienced during the first half of the nineteenth century in terms of the development of infrastructure, the expansion and integration of regional and national markets, and new achievements in travel and communications, including the train and the telegraph, was creating a crisis situation in which the slave and free-labor societies were beginning to clash and to maneuver for expansion into the newly acquired territories from Mexico and to gain control, at each other's expense, of states that already existed. The market, communications, and transportation revolutions of the antebellum period, identified and given causal strength by various historians, seemed to Seward to be forcing the American population to make a decision about what type of society the United States would be in the future.

Seward then enlisted the original founders of the United States in support of his arguments. Seward seemed to believe that the Constitution was antislavery in nature. Thus, the Founding Fathers had intended that slavery would wither away and die. He even noted that the deep divisions over slavery Americans witnessed during the 1850s were actually a logical extension of the "conflict which the fathers themselves not only thus regarded with favor, but which they may be said to have instituted." Did Seward mean the first generation of American statesmen had intended to create such deep sectional strife? On the contrary, Seward believed the Founding Fathers had assumed that by constructing a Constitution and a political system based on equality, slavery would die a natural death. Unfortunately, said Seward, "thus far the course of that contest has not been according to their humane anticipations and wishes." Without noting the actual crop, cotton, that produced the deepening hold of slavery in the South during the antebellum decades, Seward spoke of the "commercial changes" that had created the cotton empire in the southern United States. Indeed, few Americans in the late eighteenth century had predicted the switch from tobacco to cotton in the South that subsequently produced an agricultural system centered on one of the most profitable raw materials in the world at the time. Seward's point, however, was that the Founding Fathers' intention for slavery was for it to end slowly and quietly through the extension of the ideals of freedom and free labor. Economic changes, however, had helped prevent such an extinction of the peculiar institution.

The Threatened Expansion of Slavery

Seward pointed out that those who benefited from the slave system also actively protected it. Seward first mentioned "the rapid and effective political successes which they have already obtained," which invoked a number of Northern resentments against the South that stemmed from the nation's antebellum political history. The three-fifths clause of the Constitution, whereby a slave counted as three-fifths of a person for purposes of state representation in the House of Representatives and the Electoral College, had long given the Southern states, especially Virginia, a political advantage in national elections. For instance, between 1788 and 1828, only one non-Virginian held the presidency: John Adams of Massachusetts, from 1796 to 1800. Such Southern control of the White House, and often of Congress, had created animosity among Northerners because of the way the South used the people they oppressed to further their own political control.

Seward then voiced the increasing fear held by Republicans and Northerners throughout the 1850s that the Slave Power would extend its sway into all the western territories. In fact, blocking the extension of slavery into the territories was the central organizing principle of the Republican Party in the 1850s. While the Compromise of 1850 had extended westward the line between slave and free states of the original Missouri Compromise of 1820, the 1854 Kansas-Nebraska Act had opened up vast areas in the northern plains and northern Rockies to the possibility of slavery. Seward also condemned "the principle of the Dred Scott case." In 1857, the Supreme Court had not only declared the former slave Dred Scott to not be a person but also had also ruled that the original Missouri Compromise was unconstitutional, thus threatening to, as Seward put it, "carry slavery into all the territories of the United States now existing and hereafter to be organized." Throughout the 1850s, Northerners came to believe that the Slave Power of the South intended to expand slavery into the entire area of the old Louisiana Purchase and the newly acquired regions from Mexico. Halting such expansion was a core goal of the Republican Party, and Seward warned his constituents that dire consequences would result if they were unsuccessful in that objective.

Seward went on to warn that the slaveholders would reopen the international slave trade and abuse the power of the federal and state courts to allow slavery wherever they wanted. He even claimed that one day "when the free States shall be sufficiently demoralized to tolerate these designs, they reasonably conclude that slavery will be accepted by those States themselves." Thus, Seward went even farther than most Republican leaders and tried to convince his listeners that even their very freedom in their own home states was at stake in blocking the Democrats and the Slave Power. Seward then passionately declared that he would never live in a place controlled by an "aristocracy of any kind, much less an aristocracy of slaveholders" and claimed he would travel the world in search of such a free place. He was hinting that there actually was no such place in the world at the time other than the United States and was thus portraying the liberty found in the United States, at least in the North, according to him, as an experiment of historical importance for humanity. Indeed, in the mid-nineteenth century, few places in the world valued individual and property rights as highly as the United States, and most Americans, while they continued to be wary of direct involvement in the affairs of nations across the oceans, wanted the world to see the country as a beacon of liberty and freedom. Seward was suggesting that slavery undermined the historical importance of the United States.

Republicans Must Resist

Much of what Seward said during his speech seemed alarmist. He had accused the slaveholders of subverting the Constitution, of wanting to reopen the Atlantic slave trade, of oppressing their fellow white citizens, and of threatening to extend slavery even into the free states. When he addressed the charge that "these fears are extravagant and chimerical," he openly admitted "they are so." He did not hide the fact he was trying to scare his audience, but he was doing so, he claimed, "because the designs of the slaveholders must and can be defeated." In order to combat such a powerful enemy, Seward believed, he had to warn of the potentially dire consequences that could result from further electoral victories by the Democrats. He claimed "inactivity" and "non-resistance" were not options, since such courses of action would only aid in the Slave Power's oppression of Northern whites. The solution for Seward was Republican electoral victory. He mentioned that many Democratic officeholders and the population who supported the Democrats were not at fault, although this seemed to contradict much of what he had already said in his speech. He claimed the elite slaveholders had hijacked the Democratic Party for their own evil designs. He argued the Democrats were a "sectional and local party" and needed to be confined to the South and not permitted to expand elsewhere. If slavery expanded into the western territories, new slave states would be added to the nation, which would augment the power of the slave states in Congress. To Seward, the Democrats had "renounced the principle" of "equal and exact justice to all men" that had been the original central idea of the party. According to Seward, the Republicans should carry the banner of "the idea of equality—the equality of all men before human tribunals and human laws, as they are all equal before the divine tribunal and divine laws." Seward declared this idea a "revolution" and claimed the Republicans would emerge victorious because "revolutions never go backward." The above excerpt ended with heated words against the Democrats. Seward believed the clash between the slave states and free states, between the Republicans and Democrats, indeed between freedom and equality on one hand and aristocracy and oppression on the other, was now an inevitable "irrepressible conflict."

Essential Themes

One of the central debates in the study of the Civil War focuses on whether or not the United States could have avoided such a bloody showdown. Seward issued the opening salvo in that debate even before the Civil War occurred. Historian Kenneth M. Stampp, in *The Imperiled Union* (1980), has noted, "After the Civil War Seward's concept of an irrepressible conflict involving issues of fundamental importance became, in various forms, the predominant view among historians of the sectional crisis" (193). While some historians and politicians argued the tragedy could have been averted, many more adopted Seward's view that, because of the central moral issues involved in slavery, the war had been unavoidable. While modern historians hold mixed views on the inevitability of the war, Seward's conception of the sectional struggle cast a long shadow over the work of historians into the early part of the twentieth century. Although Stampp, in *And the War Came* (1964), notes that Seward "himself vigorously denied the inevitability of the war when the final crisis came" (2–3), his 1858 speech has remained a classic statement of the position that the Civil War would one day arrive, and was always going to happen, as long as slavery remained in the United States.

Thus, Seward's speech not only contributed to Republican electoral victories in 1858 but also helped frame one of the debates about the coming of the Civil War. In addition, the excerpt above provides a window into the minds of many Northern Republicans during the 1850s, as they feared the expansion of the Slave Power into the territories and worried what the expansion of slavery meant for Northern white rights. While Seward was a bit more radical than the average Northerner, he nevertheless addressed many of their concerns when he rose to speak in Rochester in October 1858. Therefore, his speech was either widely praised or condemned in his contemporary context because he clearly spelled out the Northern Republican worldview. His speech remains an important part of the discussion of the onset of the Civil War, because of his clear stance on the "irrepressible" and inevitable nature of a coming conflict between economic, social, and political systems based on either slave labor or free labor. Thus, he was a part of the events surrounding the Civil War, and his views and speech have contributed to the ongoing discussion of those events up to the present.

Kevin E. Grimm, PhD

Bibliography

Bancroft, Frederic. *The Life of William Henry Seward.* Vol. 1. New York: Harper, 1900. Print.

Foner, Eric. *Free Soil, Free Labor, Free Men: The Ideology of the Republican Party before the Civil War.* New York: Oxford UP, 1995. Print.

Goodwin, Doris Kearns. *Team of Rivals: The Political Genius of Abraham Lincoln.* New York: Simon, 2005. Print.

Herring, George C. *From Colony to Superpower: US Foreign Relations since 1776.* New York: Oxford UP, 2008. Print.

Stampp, Kenneth M. *And the War Came: The North and the Secession Crisis, 1860–61.* Chicago: U of Chicago P, 1964. Print.

---. *The Imperiled Union: Essays on the Background of the Civil War.* New York: Oxford UP, 1980. Print.

Wilentz, Sean. *The Rise of American Democracy: Jefferson to Lincoln.* New York: Norton, 2005. Print.

Additional Reading

Howe, Daniel Walker. *What Hath God Wrought: The Transformation of America, 1815–1848.* New York: Oxford UP, 2007. Print.

McPherson, James M. *Battle Cry of Freedom: The Civil War Era.* New York: Oxford UP, 1988. Print.

Rozwenc, Edwin C. *The Causes of the American Civil War.* 2nd ed. Lexington, MA: Heath, 1972. Print.

Sellers, Charles S. *The Market Revolution: Jacksonian America, 1815–1846.* New York: Oxford UP, 1991. Print.

Stampp, Kenneth M., ed. *The Causes of the Civil War.* Englewood Cliffs, NJ: Prentice, 1965. Print.

LESSON PLAN: **Sectional Conflict and Party Politics**

Students analyze a speech by William Seward to better understand the sectional polarization that contributed to the Civil War.

Learning Objectives

Assess a historical document's credibility; identify the central questions a document addresses; appreciate historical perspectives; distinguish between unsupported expressions of opinion and informed hypotheses grounded in historical evidence.

Materials: William Seward, "On the Irrepressible Conflict" (1858)

Overview Questions

Why did Seward make this speech? What views did Seward have about the state of the Union in 1858? What fears does Seward have? How accurate were the conditions and situations Seward described?

Step 1: Comprehension Questions

What opinions does Seward hold about slavery? What does Seward think of slaveholders? What is Seward's stated purpose in this speech? What do you think are his long-term goals in making the speech? What fears have motivated him to make it?

- **Activity:** Create two columns on the board, labeled "Similarities" and "Differences." Have students identify the comparisons and contrasts Seward makes between slavery and free labor. List their responses in the appropriate column on the board. Then discuss whether Seward's views on this subject were accurate.

Step 2: Comprehension Questions

How does Seward characterize the political and social system that exists in the South? Why does he consider slaveholders to be an aristocracy? What comparison does he make to the society that exists in the North?

- **Activity:** Discuss Seward's views in paragraph six about the nation's framers and founding. Have students identify statements they would dispute and explain why.

Step 3: Context Questions

Why does Seward think that the Democratic Party should be "permanently" removed from government? What connection does he make between Democrats and slaveholders? What plan does he charge they have to take control of the nation and spread slavery?

- **Activity:** Have students work in groups to investigate the accuracy of Seward's charges that the Democratic Party (1) was not truly a national party, (2) supported slavery and its spread, (3) was controlled by Southern slaveholders, and (4) enabled the South to control Congress. Have groups report their findings to the class.

Step 4: Historical Connection Questions

Why do you think Seward titled his speech "On the Irrepressible Conflict"? What conflict is he talking about? What role does he foresee for his party in resolving that conflict?

- **Activity:** Discuss the concept of propaganda with the class. Have students write position papers on whether Seward's speech should be considered a propaganda piece.

Step 5: Response Paper

Word length and additional requirements set by Instructor. Students answer the research question in the *Overview Questions*. Students state a thesis and use as evidence passages from the primary source document as well as support from the secondary historical document/s assigned in the lesson.

Supplemental Historical Documents

HISTORICAL DOCUMENT

Message to the Senate and House Regarding South Carolina's Nullification Ordinance

Date: January 16, 1833
Author: Jackson, Andrew
Genre: address

By these various proceedings, therefore, the State of South Carolina has forced the General Government, unavoidably, to decide the new and dangerous alternative of permitting a State to obstruct the execution of the laws within its limits or seeing it attempt to execute a threat of withdrawing from the Union. That portion of the people at present exercising the authority of the State solemnly assert their right to do either and as solemnly announce their determination to do one or the other.

In my opinion, both purposes are to be regarded as revolutionary in their character and tendency, and subversive of the supremacy of the laws anal of the integrity of the Union. The result of each is the same, since a State in which, by an usurpation of power, the constitutional authority of the Federal Government is openly defied and set aside wants only the form to be independent of the Union.

The right of the people of a single State to absolve themselves at will and without the consent of the other States from their most solemn obligations, and hazard the liberties and happiness of the millions composing this Union, can not be acknowledged. Such authority is believed to be utterly repugnant both to the principles upon which the General Government is constituted and to the objects which it is expressly formed to attain.

Against all acts which may be alleged to transcend the constitutional power of the Government, or which may be inconvenient or oppressive in their operation, the Constitution itself has prescribed the modes of redress. It is the acknowledged attribute of free institutions that under them the empire of reason and law is substituted for the power of the sword. To no other source can appeals for supposed wrongs be made consistently with the obligations of South Carolina; to no other can such appeals be made with safety at any time; and to their decisions, when constitutionally pronounced, it becomes the duty no less of the public authorities than of the people in every case to yield a patriotic submission.

That a State or any other great portion of the people, suffering under long and intolerable oppression and having tried all constitutional remedies without the hope of redress, may have a natural right, when their happiness can be no otherwise secured, and when they can do so without greater injury to others, to absolve themselves from their obligations to the Government and appeal to the last resort, needs not on the present occasion be denied.

The existence of this right, however, must depend upon the causes which may justify its exercise. It is the ultima ratio, which presupposes that the proper appeals to all other means of redress have been made in good faith, and which can never be rightfully resorted to unless it be unavoidable. It is not the right of the State, but of the individual, and of all the individuals in the State. It is the right of mankind generally to secure by all means in their power the blessings of liberty and happiness; but when for these purposes any body of men have voluntarily associated themselves under a particular form of government, no portion of them can dissolve the association without acknowledging the correlative right in the remainder to decide whether that dissolution can be permitted consistently with the general happiness. In this view it is a right dependent upon the power to enforce it. Such a right, though it may be admitted to preexist and can not be wholly surrendered, is necessarily subjected to limitations in all free governments, and in compacts of all kinds freely and voluntarily entered into, and in which the interest and welfare of the individual become identified with those of the community of which he is a member. In compacts between individuals, however deeply they may affect their relations, these principles are acknowledged to create a sacred obligation; and in compacts of civil government, involving the liberties and happiness of millions of mankind, the obligation can not be less.

Without adverting to the particular theories to which the federal compact has given rise, both as to its formation and the parties to it, and without inquiring whether it be merely federal or social or national, it is sufficient that it must be admitted to be a compact and to possess the obligations incident to a compact; to be "a compact by which power is created on the one hand and obedience exacted on the other; a compact freely, voluntarily, and solemnly entered into by the several States and ratified by the people thereof, respectively; a compact by which the several States and the people thereof, respectively, have bound themselves to each other and to the Federal Government, and by which the Federal Government is bound to the several States and to every citizen of the United States." To this compact, in whatever mode it may have been done, the people of South Carolina have freely and voluntarily given their assent, and to the whole and every part of it they are, upon every principle of good faith, inviolably bound. Under this obligation they are bound and should be required to contribute their portion of the public expense, and to submit to all laws made by the common consent, in pursuance of the Constitution, for the common defense and general welfare, until they can be changed in the mode which the compact has provided for the attainment of those great ends of the Government and of the Union. Nothing less than causes which would justify revolutionary remedy can absolve the people from this obligation, and for nothing less can the Government permit it to be done without violating its own obligations, by which, under the compact, it is bound to the other States and to every citizen of the United States. . . .

For this purpose it might be proper to provide that whenever by any unlawful combination or obstruction in any State or in any port it should become impracticable faithfully to collect the duties, the President of the United States should be authorized to alter and abolish such of the districts and ports of entry as should be necessary, and to establish the custom-house at some secure place within some port or harbor of such State, and in such cases it should be the duty of the collector to reside at such place, and to detain all vessels and cargoes until the duties imposed by law should be properly secured or paid in cash deducting interest; that in such cases it should be unlawful to take the vessel and cargo from the custody of the proper officer of the customs unless by process from the ordinary judicial tribunals of the United States, and that in case of an attempt otherwise to take the property by a force too great to be overcome by the officers of the customs it should be lawful to protect the possession of the officers by the employment of the land and naval forces and militia, under provisions similar to those authorized by the eleventh section of the act of the 8th of January, 1809.

This provision, however, would not shield the officers and citizens of the United States, acting under the laws, from suits and prosecutions in the tribunals of the State which might thereafter be brought against them, nor would it protect their property from the proceeding by distress, and it may well be apprehended that it would be insufficient to insure a proper respect to the process of the constitutional tribunals in prosecutions for offenses against the United States and to protect the authorities of the United States, whether judicial or ministerial, in the performance of their duties. It would, moreover, be inadequate to extend the protection due from the Government to that portion of the people of South Carolina against outrage and oppression of any kind who may manifest their attachment and yield obedience to the laws of the Union.

It may therefore be desirable to revive, with some modifications better adapted to the occasion, the sixth section of the act of the 3rd March, 1815, which expired on the 4th March, 1817, by the limitation of that of 27th April, 1816, and to provide that in any case where suit shall be brought against any individual in the courts of the State for any act done under the laws of the United States he should be authorized to remove the said cause by petition into the circuit court of the United States without any copy of the record, and that the court should proceed to hear and determine the same as if it had been originally instituted therein; and that in all cases of injuries to the persons or property of individuals for disobedience to the ordinance and laws of South Carolina in pursuance thereof redress may be sought in the courts of the United States. It may be expedient also, by modifying the resolution of the 3rd March, 1791, to authorize the marshals to make the necessary provision for the safe-keeping of prisoners committed under the authority of the United States.

Provisions less than these, consisting as they do for the most part rather of a revival of the policy of former acts called for by the existing emergency than of the introduction of any unusual or rigorous enactments, would not cause the laws of the Union to be properly respected or enforced. It is believed these would prove adequate unless the military forces of the State of South Carolina authorized by the late act of the legislature should be actually embodied and called out in aid of their proceedings and of the provisions of the ordinance generally. Even in that case, however, it is believed that no more will be necessary than a few modifications of its terms to adapt the act of 1795 to the present emergency, as by that act the provisions of the law of 1792 were accommodated to the crisis then existing, and by conferring authority upon the President to give it operation during the session of Congress, and without the ceremony of a proclamation, whenever it shall be officially made known to him by the authority of any State, or by the courts of the United States, that within the limits of such State the laws of the United States will be openly opposed and their execution obstructed by the actual employment of military force, or by any unlawful means whatsoever too great to be otherwise overcome.

In closing this communication, I should do injustice to my own feelings not to express my confident reliance upon the disposition of each department of the Government to perform its duty and to cooperate in all measures necessary in the present emergency.

The crisis undoubtedly invokes the fidelity of the patriot and the sagacity of the statesman, not more in removing such portion of the public burden as may be necessary than in preserving the good order of society and in the maintenance of well-regulated liberty.

While a forbearing spirit may, and I trust will, be exercised toward the errors of our brethren in a particular quarter, duty to the rest of the Union demands that open and organized resistance to the laws should not be executed with impunity.

The rich inheritance bequeathed by our fathers has devolved upon us the sacred obligation of preserving it by the same virtues which conducted them through the eventful scenes of the Revolution and ultimately crowned their struggle with the noblest model of civil institutions. They bequeathed to us a Government of laws and a Federal Union founded upon the great principle of popular representation. After a successful experiment of forty-four years, at a moment when the Government and the Union are the objects of the hopes of the friends of civil liberty throughout the world, and in the midst of public and individual prosperity unexampled in history, we are called to decide whether these laws possess any force and that Union the means of self-preservation. The decision of this question by an enlightened and patriotic people can not be doubtful. For myself, fellow-citizens, devoutly relying upon that kind Providence which has hitherto watched over our destinies, and actuated by a profound reverence for those institutions I have so much cause to love, and for the American people, whose partiality honored me with their highest trust, I have determined to spare no effort to discharge the duty which in this conjuncture is devolved upon me. That a similar spirit will actuate the representatives of the American people is not to be questioned; and I fervently pray that the Great Ruler of Nations may so guide your deliberations and our joint measures as that they may prove salutary examples not only to the present but to future times, and solemnly proclaim that the Constitution and the laws are supreme and the *Union indissoluble*.

LESSON PLAN: **Jackson and the Doctrine of Nullification**

Students analyze Andrew Jackson's response to the nullification crisis and South Carolina's threat to secede from the Union, and examine the legacy of Jackson's vision for America.

Learning Objectives

Compare and contrast differing sets of ideas about states' rights; compare and contrast differing sets of ideas about economic policies that contributed to sectional differences; analyze cause-and-effect relationships of the nullification crisis; draw comparisons across eras to evaluate Jackson's speech and Madison's writings; hypothesize the influence of the past by assessing Jackson's ideas.

Materials: Andrew Jackson, "Message to the Senate and House Regarding South Carolina's Nullification Ordinance" (1833); James Madison, "*The Federalist* No. 10" (1787).

Overview Questions

How did Jackson respond to South Carolina's attempt to nullify federal laws? Why did Jackson argue that no state has the right to secede from the Union? How did Jackson's speech exacerbate sectional differences? How are Jackson's speech and Madison's ideas on federalism alike and different? What relevance does Jackson's speech have for Americans today, and why?

Step 1: Comprehension Questions

Why does Jackson call South Carolina's actions "dangerous," "subversive," and "utterly repugnant"? Why does Jackson consider the state-federal relationship "a sacred obligation"?

- **Activity:** Have students read aloud passages that highlight Jackson's reasons for opposing nullification. Next, ask students to summarize Jackson's views on the state-federal relationship and discuss their summaries.

Step 2: Comprehension Questions

Why does Jackson claim that he has the right to employ "land and naval forces and militia" against any state that obstructs federal law? Are his reasons for this claim convincing? Why or why not?

- **Activity:** Ask students to discuss Jackson's purposes for writing; have students work in small groups to examine Jackson's use of language and its effectiveness.

Step 3: Context Questions

Southerners felt that federal tariff laws hurt their economy while benefiting the North's economy. How did Jackson's speech contribute to growing sectional differences? Why would Jackson defend a federal law that hurt the common people, the source of his popular support?

- **Activity:** Have students review other primary and secondary sources for greater insights into the nullification crisis; ask students to present their findings.

Step 4: Exploration Questions

Jackson's speech presents a vision for America similar to Madison's ideas on federalism. How relevant is this shared vision in American politics today, and why? What idea from Jackson's speech is most important for Americans today, and why?

- **Activity:** Have students complete Venn diagrams to compare and contrast Jackson's and Madison's views. Then have students write brief articles about Jackson's influence on politics today.

Step 5: Response Paper

Word length and additional requirements set by Instructor. Students answer the research question in the *Overview Questions*. Students state a thesis and use as evidence passages from the primary source document as well as support from supplemental materials assigned in the lesson.

Manifest Destiny

Manifest Destiny was the idea that the new United States was destined to spread its progressive government and civilizing influence to all corners of North America. Westward expansion proceeded at breakneck speed throughout the century, beginning with the Louisiana Purchase in 1803, which doubled the size of the country overnight. Texas, California, and everything in between were acquired between 1845 and 1853, mostly as a result of the Mexican-American War. Lewis and Clark's goal of finding a contiguous water route to the Pacific failed, but they mapped, described, and claimed most of the continent for the United States, and their journey inspired generations eager for land to settle the West. Many settlers who made the overland trek with their families discovered an inhospitable wilderness, and their narratives provide poignant proof of their struggle to establish themselves on the western frontier.

Central to the idea of Manifest Destiny was the belief that the American people and their traditions and government were uniquely advanced, that it was their right and responsibility to spread this enlightenment across the continent, and that this was part of God's revealed plan for the nation. Manifest Destiny relied on people who were already occupying new lands understanding that their claims were weaker and their cultures inferior to those of the newcomers. Reports from California and Texas were filled with the racial ideology that buttressed this idea, allowing settlers to believe that they were performing a civilizing service to the people they encountered. Mexicans, Native Americans, and Asians were all part of these lesser cultures, and could not be allowed to participate as citizens. In the case of *People v. Hall*, the California Supreme court decided that Asians could not even to testify against white settlers, thus stripping them of any legal recourse. Often land that was held by families for generations was taken because they could not officially prove their ownership. Voices of protest were heard from those who suffered as part of this aggressive land acquisition. The discovery of gold in California in 1848 only hastened the rush of settlers, both short and long term, who believed that the land was theirs for the taking.

When Texas founder Stephen Austin advocated for Texan independence, he made a uniquely American argument: that the oppression the settlers felt under the Mexican government was the same as those felt by the colonists under British rule, and that rights afforded to white Americans were universal, even on land belonging to another sovereign nation. He also argued that the settlement of Texas would provide a bulwark against incursions by Indian tribes and Mexico. The colonization of Texas was, in his opinion, the best way to ensure the success of the United States. As settlers gained control of Texas, they enforced a system of racial and ethnic bias that forced many native Texans to feel like foreigners in the land of their birth.

Bethany Groff

Louisiana Purchase Treaty

Date: 1803
Author: Jefferson, Thomas
Genre: treaty

The inhabitants of the ceded territory [Louisiana] shall be incorporated in the Union of the United States and admitted . . . to the enjoyment of all these rights, advantages and immunities of citizens of the United States. . . .

Summary Overview

By a vote of twenty-four to seven, the United States Senate doubled the size of the country on October 20, 1803, with the ratification of the Louisiana Purchase Treaty. The purchase of the Louisiana Territory from France did away with one threat of foreign intervention in US affairs. Domestically, despite a variety of objections, President Thomas Jefferson expanded the constitutional powers of the federal government by acquiring new territory through the Louisiana Purchase and granting automatic citizenship to its inhabitants. Jefferson had run for the presidency on a platform of limiting the size of government and reducing the national debt. However, the opportunity to acquire the entire region overcame his political inclinations, and the purchase of the Louisiana Territory rapidly accelerated the growth of the United States. Although it would be decades before the idea of Manifest Destiny would be vocalized, the Louisiana Purchase was a major step in the process of expanding the United States from the Atlantic to the Pacific Ocean.

Defining Moment

During the early years of the United States, Great Britain, Spain, and France were still imperial rivals for territorial claims and political influence in North America, particularly in Florida and the Louisiana Territory. At the same time, the growth of the population of the United States led to an increasing number of settlements west of the Appalachian Mountains. As a result, the river that formed the western boundary of the young nation, the Mississippi, had become a vital route for the transportation of commodities produced by the western states; however, the United States had little control over this waterway. In 1798, the Spanish governor of Louisiana prohibited the transport of US goods through New Orleans, crippling the US economy. In 1800, France quietly regained control of Louisiana, which had been given to Spain after the Seven Years' War. The French subsequently reopened New Orleans to US trade. However, there was still great uneasiness in the western states as to the reliability of this trade route.

At about the same time France regained the Louisiana Territory from Spain, the French colony of Saint-Domingue, now the nation of Haiti, declared its full independence from France after a decade of fighting. Saint-Domingue had been the economic linchpin of French Caribbean interests, and without it there was no reason to expend resources in the region. Unable to permanently subdue the Haitian revolt and tied down by war in Europe, French leader Napoleon Bonaparte found Louisiana to be of no great value. In 1802, President Jefferson sent diplomats Robert R. Livingston and

James Monroe to France to purchase New Orleans and the immediate vicinity. In March 1803, Napoleon instructed his finance minster, François Barbé-Marbois, to sell Louisiana to the United States in order to fund a series of military campaigns across Europe that would come to be known as the Napoleonic Wars. In April 1803, Barbé-Marbois offered the entire territory of Louisiana to the United States for fifteen million dollars. Although not authorized to spend that much, Livingston and Monroe recognized a good bargain. On April 30, 1803, they signed the Louisiana Purchase Treaty, a copy of which arrived in the United States ten weeks later.

Jefferson readily accepted the expanded purchase and pushed for ratification. With the purchase, the economic growth of the western states was assured, and one possible base for foreign interference was removed. The issues raised by the opponents of the treaty were real, in that the Louisiana Territory had ill-defined boundaries, the purchase raised new, issues related to slavery, and the automatic citizenship granted to the inhabitants of the territory disrupted the east-west political balance of power in the United States and created anxiety regarding how well the population of the region would integrate into US society. However, the advantages of the purchase outweighed the potential problems. With ratification, three million dollars in gold were sent to France, with the rest of the purchase being financed through British and Dutch banks.

Author Biography

Thomas Jefferson, the third president of the United States, was born on April 13, 1743, in Shadewell, Virginia. The elder son of Peter and Jane Randolph Jefferson, he was born into a wealthy family. Having studied with tutors as a young child, Jefferson began his formal education at a local school at the age of nine. At age sixteen, Jefferson entered the College of William and Mary and graduated within two years. From 1762 until 1767, he read law for five years as a clerk under George Wythe, a prominent judge, while also studying political philosophy. He married Martha Wayles Skelton in 1772 and they had six children, although only two daughters survived childhood. Both Jefferson and his wife inherited extensive landholdings from their fathers. Martha died in 1782.

Jefferson's political career began in Virginia's House of Burgesses in 1769. In 1775, he was elected to the Second Continental Congress. John Adams, also a delegate to the Second Continental Congress, convinced Jefferson to write a draft of a document declaring American independence. After minor revisions by a committee and other modifications by the full Congress, Jefferson's creation, the Declaration of Independence, was ratified.

Jefferson returned to the Virginia legislature in 1776, authoring a significant number of bills to revise the state's laws. He served two years as governor of Virginia beginning in 1779. Following the American Revolution, he served in the Congress of the Confederation before he was appointed minister to France in 1785. He returned to the United States in 1789 and accepted the appointment as secretary of state during President George Washington's first term. During this time, he began to have major disagreements with the Federalists, the political party supporting a strong, centralized federal government. When Washington retired, Jefferson ran for president as a Democratic-Republican, losing to John Adams, a Federalist. However, Jefferson, as runner-up, became the vice president, serving from 1797 to 1801. Jefferson became president in 1801, defeating Adams and then being chosen by the House of Representatives to be president over his running mate, Aaron Burr. These two elections caused Congress to put forward what became the Twelfth Amendment, establishing separate ballots for president and vice-president.

Jefferson began his presidency by cutting government expenditures; however, external challenges quickly forced him in the other direction. He increased the military, created the United States Military Academy at West Point, and used naval operations to confront the Barbary states of North Africa, where a number of US ships had been captured and held for ransom. The Louisiana Purchase also greatly expanded the country and the national government's role. After his second term as president, Jefferson retired to Monticello, working to found the University of Virginia, a nonsectarian university. Jefferson died on July 4, 1826, in Charlottesville, Virginia.

HISTORICAL DOCUMENT

The President of the United States of America and the First Consul of the French Republic in the name of the French People desiring to remove all Source of misunderstanding relative to objects of discussion mentioned in the Second and fifth articles of the Convention of the 8th Vendémiaire an 9 (30 September 1800) relative to the rights claimed by the United States in virtue of the Treaty concluded at Madrid the 27 of October 1795, between His Catholic Majesty & the Said United States, & willing to Strengthen the union and friendship which at the time of the Said Convention was happily reestablished between the two nations have respectively named their Plenipotentiaries to wit The President of the United States, by and with the advice and consent of the Senate of the Said States; Robert R. Livingston Minister Plenipotentiary of the United States and James Monroe Minister Plenipotentiary and Envoy extraordinary of the Said States near the Government of the French Republic; And the First Consul in the name of the French people, Citizen Francis Barbé Marbois Minister of the public treasury who after having respectively exchanged their full powers have agreed to the following Articles.

Article I

Whereas by the Article the third of the Treaty concluded at St Ildefonso the 9th Vendémiaire an 9 (1st October) 1800 between the First Consul of the French Republic and his Catholic Majesty it was agreed as follows.

"His Catholic Majesty promises and engages on his part to cede to the French Republic six months after the full and entire execution of the conditions and Stipulations herein relative to his Royal Highness the Duke of Parma, the Colony or Province of Louisiana with the Same extent that it now has in the hand of Spain, & that it had when France possessed it; and Such as it Should be after the Treaties subsequently entered into between Spain and other States."

And whereas in pursuance of the Treaty and particularly of the third article the French Republic has an incontestible title to the domain and to the possession of the said Territory—The First Consul of the French Republic desiring to give to the United States a strong proof of his friendship doth hereby cede to the United States in the name of the French Republic for ever and in full Sovereignty the said territory with all its rights and appurtenances as fully and in the Same manner as they have been acquired by the French Republic in virtue of the above mentioned Treaty concluded with his Catholic Majesty.

Article II

In the cession made by the preceeding article are included the adjacent Islands belonging to Louisiana all public lots and Squares, vacant lands and all public buildings, fortifications, barracks and other edifices which are not private property.—The Archives, papers & documents relative to the domain and Sovereignty of Louisiana and its dependances will be left in the possession of the Commissaries of the United States, and copies will be afterwards given in due form to the Magistrates and Municipal officers of such of the said papers and documents as may be necessary to them.

Article III

The inhabitants of the ceded territory shall be incorporated in the Union of the United States and admitted as soon as possible according to the principles of the federal Constitution to the enjoyment of all these rights, advantages and immunities of citizens of the United States, and in the mean time they shall be maintained and protected in the free enjoyment of their liberty, property and the Religion which they profess.

Article IV

There Shall be Sent by the Government of France a Commissary to Louisiana to the end that he do every act necessary as well to receive from the Officers of his Catholic Majesty the Said country and its dependances in the name of the French Republic if it has not been already done as to transmit it in the name of the French Republic to the Commissary or agent of the United States.

Article V

Immediately after the ratification of the present Treaty by the President of the United States and in case that of the first Consul's shall have been previously obtained, the commissary of the French Republic shall remit all military posts of New Orleans and other parts of the ceded territory to the Commissary or Commissaries named by the President to take possession—the troops whether of France or Spain who may be there shall cease to occupy any military post from the time of taking possession and shall be embarked as soon as possible in the course of three months after the ratification of this treaty.

Article VI

The United States promise to execute such treaties and articles as may have been agreed between Spain and the tribes and nations of Indians until by mutual consent of the United States and the said tribes or nations other Suitable articles Shall have been agreed upon.

Article VII

As it is reciprocally advantageous to the commerce of France and the United States to encourage the communication of both nations for a limited time in the country ceded by the present treaty until general arrangements relative to commerce of both nations may be agreed on; it has been agreed between the contracting parties that the French Ships coming directly from France or any of her colonies loaded only with the produce and manufactures of France or her Said Colonies; and the Ships of Spain coming directly from Spain or any of her colonies loaded only with the produce or manufactures of Spain or her Colonies shall be admitted during the Space of twelve years in the Port of New-Orleans and in all other legal ports-of-entry within the ceded territory in the Same manner as the Ships of the United States coming directly from France or Spain or any of their Colonies without being Subject to any other or greater duty on merchandize or other or greater tonnage than that paid by the citizens of the United States.

During that Space of time above mentioned no other nation Shall have a right to the Same privileges in the Ports of the ceded territory—the twelve years Shall commence three months after the exchange of ratifications if it Shall take place in France or three months after it Shall have been notified at Paris to the French Government if it Shall take place in the United States; It is however well understood that the object of the above article is to favour the manufactures, Commerce, freight and navigation of France and of Spain So far as relates to the importations that the French and Spanish Shall make into the Said Ports of the United States without in any Sort affecting the regulations that the United States may make concerning the exportation of the produce and merchandize of the United States, or any right they may have to make Such regulations.

Article VIII

In future and for ever after the expiration of the twelve years, the Ships of France shall be treated upon the footing of the most favoured nations in the ports above mentioned.

Article IX

The particular Convention Signed this day by the respective Ministers, having for its object to provide for the payment of debts due to the Citizens of the United States by the French Republic prior to the 30th Sept. 1800 (8th Vendémiaire an 9) is approved and to have its execution in the Same manner as if it had been inserted in this present treaty, and it Shall be ratified in the same form and in the Same time So that the one Shall not be ratified distinct from the other.

Another particular Convention Signed at the Same date as the present treaty relative to a definitive rule between the contracting parties is in the like manner approved and will be ratified in the Same form, and in the Same time and jointly.

Article X

The present treaty Shall be ratified in good and due form and the ratifications Shall be exchanged in the Space of Six months after the date of the Signature by the Ministers Plenipotentiary or Sooner if possible.

In faith whereof the respective Plenipotentiaries have Signed these articles in the French and English languages; declaring nevertheless that the present Treaty was originally agreed to in the French language; and have thereunto affixed their Seals.

Done at Paris the tenth day of Floreal in the eleventh year of the French Republic; and the 30th of April 1803.

Robt R Livingston [seal]

Jas. Monroe [seal]

Barbé Marbois [seal]

GLOSSARY

appurtenances: a general legal term referring to any rights or responsibilities attached to a piece of property or a position

commissaries: commissioners or envoys who represent their government in diplomatic affairs

Convention of the 8th Vendemiaire an 9: an inconclusive treaty between the United States and France, containing a statement of friendship and peace between the two nations but mainly dealing with economic issues, free trade, and restitution for captured vessels and cargo

First Consul of the French Republic: the title held by Napoleon at the time of the treaty, prior to his being crowned emperor in 1804

His Catholic Majesty: the king of Spain

particular convention: refers to either of the two documents also signed and to be ratified with the treaty

plenipotentiaries: diplomats with full powers to represent one government in its dealings with another

treaty concluded at Madrid: a treaty between the United States and Spain setting the boundary between the colonies of East and West Florida and the United States.

Treaty of St. Ildefonso: the treaty in 1800 that returned Louisiana Territory to France from Spain

Document Analysis

For twenty years, the boundaries of the United States had been set by the Treaty of Paris, the document that officially ended the Revolutionary War between Great Britain and the United States. Even though the United States had sought to stay neutral regarding conflicts in Europe, those conflicts nevertheless had a major impact upon the US economy and security. Surrounded by European colonies, the United States had to be wary not only of North American events, but of what was happening on the other side of the Atlantic. Thus, any step that could decrease European influence in the United States was seen as a positive development. In addition, Jefferson was one of the earliest leaders to understand the possibilities of what lay west of the Appalachians. Jefferson understood that retaining the original boundary at the Mississippi River was not in the best interests of the United States. The temporary closure of the port of New Orleans to US goods in the late 1790s caused many settlers in the west to advocate war against Spain. Already, Jefferson had shown resolve in standing up to foreign interests by refusing the demands of the Barbary states and sending military forces to protect US shipping interests in the Mediterranean. As one of the weakest European nations, Spain's control of New Orleans and Louisiana did not cause major concern. However, once it became known that France had reacquired Louisiana, Jefferson sought to acquire New Orleans and the southern tip of the territory in order to assure vital US economic interests. While historically, France and the United States had had good relations, Napoleon's rise to power created greater uncertainty. To have France begin to build a strong North American colony or to have Great Britain capture New Orleans from France would be devastating for the United States. Thus, Jefferson instructed his representatives to begin the process of trying to acquire New Orleans.

The agreement was drawn up in the names of the leaders of the two countries, President Thomas Jefferson of the United States of America and First Consul Napoleon Bonaparte of France. The preamble of the treaty lists the credentials of the individuals representing the two countries. As leaders of their respective governments, these individuals had the power to enter into agreements with other nations, even though the United

States required an additional ratification process for these agreements to be completely binding. The representatives of the United States, Robert R. Livingston and James Monroe, were political allies of Jefferson. Livingston came to know Jefferson during the Second Continental Congress. Livingston was appointed minister to France by Jefferson in 1801 and, as such, was given instructions to negotiate for the purchase of New Orleans, with an initial budget of two million dollars. James Monroe had been minister to France for two years during Washington's presidency. In 1803, on his way to serve as minister to Great Britain, Monroe was directed to France specifically to negotiate a treaty allowing the United States to obtain New Orleans, with the budget increased to ten million dollars and with a fallback option to negotiate an agreement with Great Britain allowing the United States a free hand in the southern part of the Louisiana Territory. Representing France was François Barbé-Marbois, the French treasury minister, who was well acquainted with the United States. He had served as a diplomat to the United States from 1779 to 1785, and had communicated with Jefferson, then governor of Virginia, at that time. Thus, those involved in the final negotiations all knew Jefferson well and were known to each other. Jefferson used this to his advantage, sending different information to various individuals to help his goal of obtaining New Orleans.

The Treaty

In the preamble, the treaty also mentions agreements that the United States had previously made with France and Spain. The Convention of the 8th Vendémiaire an 9 was an agreement made between France and the United States in 1800 that sought to solve issues related to an unofficial conflict between France and the United States. In the late 1790s, French privateers were allowed by their government to attack United States shipping. This resulted in US naval vessels being dispatched. By 1800, Napoleon Bonaparte wanted to end this conflict, as he had other, more pressing military concerns. The 1800 convention ended the unofficial conflict and made provisions for the repayment of damages, although the agreement's "second and fifth articles," referred to in the preamble of the Louisiana Purchase Treaty, clearly stated that, while the debts owed to US citizens for goods confiscated by French privateers would be paid, the negotiators were "not being able to agree at present" on the payments that should be made. This was to be taken care of within the framework of the Louisiana Purchase Treaty. In addition, the 1795 Treaty of Madrid between the United States and Spain had set the boundary between the United States and the Spanish colonies. However, when Spain gave Louisiana back to France, there had been an understanding that part of West Florida would go with the territory. Thus, this boundary was also subject to debate, and was to be addressed within the context of the Louisiana Purchase Treaty and related conventions.

Article 1 of the treaty clarifies the right of France to the territory. In 1763, at the end of the Seven Years' War, known in America as the French and Indian War, France had given up its colonies in North America. Quebec went to the British and Louisiana went to Spain. However, by the end of the century, with Spain feeling increasingly pressured militarily by France, it agreed to return the territory to France in the Treaty of St. Ildefonso of 1800. In the quote from that treaty contained in the text of the Louisiana Purchase Treaty, the reference to "his Royal Highness the Duke of Parma" indicates that, in exchange for Louisiana, France would give the Duke of Parma (a grandson of the king of Spain) a portion of what is now northern Italy. The uncertainty regarding the border between Louisiana and Florida appears in the following passage about other agreements "subsequently entered into between Spain and other States." However, as far as the negotiators were concerned, the important point in this article is that there had been an agreement between Spain and France giving clear title to the territory to France, even if the boundaries were unclear.

Article 2 clarifies these boundaries somewhat, while establishing the rights of property owners in Louisiana. This purchase "included the adjacent Islands belonging to Louisiana." Thus, at least the southern boundary was clarified as the Gulf of Mexico. The United States gained title to "all public lots and Squares, vacant lands and all public buildings, fortifications, barracks and other edifices which are not private property." Although the emphasis seems to be upon what was now owned by the government of the United States, it is important to note that property owned by individuals was not affected. This was in line with American belief in the private ownership of property. The various papers needed to document ownership also became the property of the United States. This would help to ensure the property that had been given to various individuals in the territory would be documented and their rights upheld.

The most important article for those living in the colony was article 3. This article granted the free inhabitants of the Louisiana Territory citizenship in the United States. Going beyond that, they were promised admission into full statehood "as soon as possible according to the principles of the federal Constitution." Four new states had been admitted into the union prior to the ratification of this treaty, so the terms and procedures for statehood were well understood. While a territory, the inhabitants of Louisiana were guaranteed "free enjoyment of their liberty, property and the Religion which they profess." As all of these rights were guaranteed to any citizen in the United States, it was not difficult for the American negotiators to include these provisions in the treaty.

Article 4 reflects upon the fact that France's reacquisition of Louisiana had not been publicized, and was even kept secret from some government officials. Thus, France's promise to send a special envoy to Louisiana to assist in the transfer of power from France to the United States includes mention of the "Officers of his Catholic Majesty." Some Spanish troops and officials had remained in Louisiana, many without knowledge of the transfer from Spain to France because Spain had been slow in turning over the territory. Also, from the two governments' point of view, the Spanish officials remained in order not to alert others to the transfer of power. The special "Commissary" sent by France would assist in making certain everything was in order as the transfer of the territory to the United States progressed. This process is outlined further in article 5. Once the treaty had been ratified by both countries, the special envoy sent by Napoleon would turn over everything "to the Commissary or Commissaries named by the President." The armed forces in the territory would leave within "three months after the ratification of this treaty."

Article 6 gives the American Indians in the territory the same rights they had had under Spanish rule. In reality, because most of the territory had not been settled, most of the tribes there did not have formal agreements with the Spanish. Thus, in journeys such as the Lewis and Clark expedition, American settlers had to devise their own agreements with the indigenous population. Although it was not uniformly enforced, in 1769 Spain had outlawed holding American Indians in slavery. In later years, this Spanish law and article 6 of the treaty were used by some slaves of mixed African and American Indian ancestry to try to gain their freedom, a few successfully. As with previous provisions in the treaty, article 6 was essentially a statement maintaining the status quo.

Articles 7 and 8 deal with similar topics, but within a longer time frame. Just as trade concerns were the major reason most Americans were interested in obtaining the Louisiana Territory, France and Spain had similar concerns. Thus in article7, French and Spanish ships carrying French or Spanish cargo are assured that the port of New Orleans would remain open to them for a transitional twelve-year period. This would ensure a continuity of economic interests, because the French and Spanish merchants in New Orleans, St. Louis, and other cities would have been dealing with manufacturers from their home countries or getting raw materials from other colonies. Thus, the merchants would not be cut off from their normal source of supply. The twelve-year period was an arbitrary time frame, but long enough that new sources of supplies could be established if necessary. The only way the supply chain could be ended prior to that period would be if the US government stopped trade between the people in the Louisiana Territory and the rest of the United States, but this, of course, was not foreseeable. Article 8 guarantees that after the twelve-year period, French ships would not be treated any differently than any other foreign ships. Thus, if the United States allowed any foreign ships to dock in New Orleans, it had to allow French ships, as well. Spain, however, is not mentioned in this article.

Article 9 deals with the two conventions that were "Signed this day by the respective Ministers." Because this treaty was seen as one that sought to "Strengthen the union and friendship . . . between the two nations," the details of what was being given to France in exchange for Louisiana were not included in the main treaty. As stated in the treaty, the conventions and the treaty "shall be ratified in the same form and in the Same time So that the one Shall not be ratified distinct from the other." Thus, if all three documents were not ratified at the same time, the agreement would no longer be valid. The first convention noted in the treaty is the one that fulfilled the previous convention, the Convention of the 8th Vendémiaire an 9, which had been signed on September 30, 1800. That convention ended hostilities between French privateers and the United States. While an agreement had been reached that restitution should be paid, as previously mentioned, the amount and how this was to be done had not been settled. In this convention, the United States said that it would take care of repaying its own citizens for their losses, which was stated to be the equivalent of about $3.75 million. The second convention mentioned in article 9 of the Louisiana Purchase Treaty specifically states that a payment of $11.25 million would be paid directly to France. This amount was to be paid over time, with the total being guaranteed by interests in London, Amsterdam, or Paris. France would have the right to hold any American bonds to cover the amount due, at 6 percent interest, or to sell the bonds to any individual or entity. Thus the financial arrangements for the purchase were covered in the two conventions signed at the same time as the treaty. The total of the two conventions was $15 million, in excess of what Livingston and Monroe had been authorized to spend. However, they were no longer purchasing just New Orleans and the southern part of the Louisiana Territory, but the entire territory. Thus, in line with their powers as plenipotentiaries, Livingston and Monroe signed the treaty and conventions and Jefferson accepted what they had accomplished.

As with all formal treaties, the final article deals with the process of ratification and which copy was the official one. In this case, it was "the present Treaty . . . originally agreed to in the French language." Thus, if there were disputes between the English and French versions, the French was the one that would be enforced. While the time period of six months for the exchange of ratified treaties might seem long, given the speed of transportation of the early 1800s, this was necessary.

When the treaty and conventions were presented to the Senate for ratification, there were major disputes. During the debate, opponents raised the issues regarding the ill-defined boundaries of the purchase (which included an understanding that Spain had a claim on part of the territory), the extension of slavery into the western territories, the disruption to the established east-west political balance of power, and the integration of the population of the region into American society. Many members of the House of Representatives were upset with the purchase proposal and voted against its implementation. However, by two votes, the House sided with Jefferson and the treaty. In the Senate, most senators saw the advantages of the purchase, and the treaty easily garnered the two-thirds vote needed to pass.

Essential Themes

In the history of the United States, the Louisiana Purchase was a pivotal step toward the country's development into a world power. In 1803, the majority of North America was colonized by European powers and, except for the Atlantic Ocean on its eastern border, the United States was surrounded by Spanish, French, and British colonies. The easiest trade route from the western states to any market was controlled by the Spanish-French alliance. With the purchase of the Louisiana Territory, the entire Mississippi River system and the port of New Orleans came under the control of the United States. In addition, the growing population east of the Mississippi River was now shielded from possible foreign incursions from the west. The dream of American dominance in North America was beginning to be fulfilled.

Politically, the fact that the federal government exercised powers beyond those specifically enumerated in the Constitution had been accepted as a result of this purchase by all major political groups in the United States. While the Northwest Ordinance of 1787 had previously established a pattern for the ownership and administration of United States territory that was not a part of a state, the Louisiana Purchase set the precedent for the expansion of the United States beyond its original boundaries. Never again was the constitutionality of American expansion seriously questioned. In retrospect, some note that the various American Indian claims to this territory should have been considered more seriously than they were. However, many leaders, including Jefferson, believed that these claims could only be taken seriously if the American Indians fully adopted the European way of life. Thus, ignoring Indian claims in the Louisiana Territory was no different from the way other tribes were being treated in the existing US states and territories. Nevertheless, the Louisiana Purchase was a major accomplishment, opening up new venues for economic and scientific pursuits.

Donald A. Watt, PhD

Bibliography

Cerami, Charles A. *Jefferson's Great Gamble*. Naperville: Sourcebooks, 2003. Print.

Malone, Dumas. *Jefferson, the President: First Term 1801–1805*. Vol. 4. Boston: Little, Brown, 1970. Print.

Thomas Jefferson's Monticello. Thomas Jefferson Foundation, 2012. Web. 2 Apr. 2013.

Additional Reading

Beschloss, Michael, and Hugh Sidey. "Thomas Jefferson." *The Presidents of the United States of America*. WhiteHouse.gov, 2009. Web. 20 Sept. 2012.

DeConde, Alexander. *This Affair of Louisiana*. New York: Scribner's, 1976. Print.

Fleming, Thomas. *The Louisiana Purchase*. Hoboken: Wiley, 2003. Print.

Kastor, Peter J., ed. *The Louisiana Purchase: Emergence of an American Nation*. Washington, DC: CQ, 2002. Print.

LESSON PLAN: **The Louisiana Purchase Hastens Westward Expansion**

Students analyze the Louisiana Purchase Treaty and Congress's decision to ratify it, evaluate the treaty's impact on the United States and on the concept of Manifest Destiny, and explore its legacy.

Learning Objectives

Evaluate the implementation of President Thomas Jefferson's decision to purchase the Louisiana Territory and its subsequent effects; explain historical continuity to assess how the Louisiana Purchase affected Native Americans and other inhabitants of the territory; examine the influence of ideas to explain the roots of Manifest Destiny and its effects on westward expansion; hypothesize the influence of the treaty and of Manifest Destiny on Americans today.

Materials: The Louisiana Purchase Treaty (1803); "The Voice of Warning to the Native Born Patriots of Our Country" by the Louisiana Native American Association (1839)

Overview Questions

What does the Louisiana Purchase Treaty reveal about Jefferson's decision to buy the Louisiana Territory? What were the treaty's consequences for the United States, particularly Native Americans and other inhabitants in the territory? How did the treaty further western expansion and the development of Manifest Destiny? How do the Louisiana Purchase Treaty and Manifest Destiny continue to shape the United States today?

Step 1: Comprehension Questions

Based on your reading of the Louisiana Purchase Treaty, why do you think Jefferson agreed to it? How would France and the United States each benefit from the treaty? Were there any drawbacks to the treaty for either country? Why or why not?

- **Activity:** Have students complete graphic organizers identifying the treaty's advantages and disadvantages for each country; have small groups discuss their organizers.

Step 2: Comprehension Questions

What were the obligations of the United States to the "inhabitants of the ceded territory"? To "the tribes and nations of Indians"? To "French Ships" and "Ships of Spain" coming to New Orleans?

- **Activity:** Have students summarize the US government's obligations agreed to in the treaty; have students debate the pros and cons of these obligations; have students discuss New Orleans's importance to France and the United States.

Step 3: Context Questions

Based on "*The Voice of Warning*," how might acquiring New Orleans have affected Native Americans and others in the territory? Why would the authors of "The Voice" want to slow immigration to the United States?

- **Activity:** Have students examine "The Voice of Warning" to evaluate the treaty's impact on the United States in the early 1800s.

Step 4: Exploration Questions

How did the Louisiana Purchase Treaty influence westward expansion? How did it contribute to the development of Manifest Destiny?

- **Activity:** Have students discuss how the treaty and Manifest Destiny influence Americans culturally, politically, and economically today.

Step 5: Response Paper

Word length and additional requirements set by Instructor. Students answer the research question in the *Overview Questions*. Students state a thesis and use as evidence passages from the primary source document as well as support from supplemental materials assigned in the lesson.

The Journals of Lewis and Clark

Date: 1805
Author: Lewis, Meriwether; Clark, William
Genre: journal

"Great joy in camp we are in View of the Ocian."

Summary Overview

In 1804, Meriwether Lewis, William Clark, and the Corps of Discovery Expedition, organized by President Thomas Jefferson after the purchase of the Louisiana Territory, set off to find a water route that would link the Columbia River to the Mississippi River system. Lewis and Clark's expedition would open commercial routes between the developing northwestern United States and the East and, at the same time, help hasten westward expansion. Lewis documented the trip, providing details of the terrain of this vast region, yet unseen by European American eyes, as well as his encounters with American Indians and, ultimately, the Pacific Ocean.

Defining Moment

In 1803, President Jefferson succeeded in purchasing from France the vast region known as the Louisiana Territory. This area stretched across the American midsection, from what is now southeastern Louisiana to western Montana. Seeking to open the area to westward expansion, Jefferson ordered that an expedition to the territory's westernmost regions be organized. The primary purpose of the mission, which would be dubbed the Corps of Discovery Expedition, was to find a link between the Columbia River in the Pacific Northwest and the Missouri River (which flows from the Rocky Mountains to the Mississippi River near what is now St. Louis).

The Corps of Discovery Expedition was no mere voyage of discovery and exploration. The link Jefferson sought would in effect link the Pacific Ocean with the Missouri and Mississippi Rivers as well as the other major waterways of the eastern half of the country. This expedition would make it much easier to establish commercial routes with the undeveloped Northwest. It would therefore also open the door for westward expansion.

Because success meant a potentially enormous return on the investment of resources, Jefferson wanted to make sure that the expedition's leaders were highly capable and trustworthy. He turned to his personal secretary, Meriwether Lewis, who was both highly intelligent and experienced on the American frontier. Lewis looked to another skilled frontiersman, William Clark, to help him command the expedition. Along with more than three dozen men, the group trained and organized their supplies in Missouri, collecting weapons and gifts for American Indians they would inevitably meet along the way.

In 1804, the corps left their staging area in Illinois and met Lewis in St. Charles, Missouri, before embarking on a course up the Missouri River. They would follow the course of the Missouri, stopping occasionally in remote outposts and trapping camps before waiting out the winter months. In the spring of 1805, the expedition continued onward, coming to the Jefferson (a tributary of the Missouri). With the help of an Indian tribe, the group followed the Jefferson until it linked with the Columbia River. At the end of the year, the Expedition reached the mouth of the Columbia River and the Pacific Ocean, their mission a success. Lewis and Clark would compile a journal of their trip for the return east. The journal included maps, accounts of their Indian encounters, and other important information about the new route to the Pacific Northwest.

Author Biography

Meriwether Lewis

Meriwether Lewis was born on August 18, 1774, at a plantation in Albemarle County, Virginia. His father, William, was a highly decorated officer in the American Revolution. His mother (who was also William Lewis's cousin) was Lucy Meriwether, a well-known cook. Lewis's family was among the first to settle in the southern Virginia region. William Lewis died of pneumonia when Meriwether was five, leaving Lucy to care for him as he grew up.

After helping manage his family's estate, Lewis joined the Virginia state militia and participated in suppressing the Whiskey Rebellion in 1794. He proved a successful officer while stationed in the frontier regions of Ohio and Tennessee, rising to the rank of captain by 1801. At that point, President Jefferson, a close friend of Lewis's family, appointed Lewis his private secretary. Because of his experience on the frontier, Lewis was involved in the planning for the corps's expedition to the Northwest. In 1808, after his return from the expedition, Lewis was appointed (by Jefferson again) governor of the Louisiana Territory. He held the post for under a year, however, dying in a shooting in 1809 while traveling back to Washington, DC. Most historians believe his death was a suicide, but whether it was suicide or murder remains a topic of some debate.

William Clark

William Clark was born on August 1, 1770, on a plantation in Caroline County, Virginia, to John Clark III and Ann Rogers. Unlike his older brothers' classical educations in Virginia, William's education was less elite, a product of his family's move to the frontier of Kentucky. He enlisted in the army in 1789 and took part in the campaign to protect Kentucky and Ohio settlers from Indian attacks. He later served with Lewis, and the two became friends.

Clark retired from the military in 1796 due to an illness and returned home to attend to his family's property. Shortly thereafter, he married Julia Hancock before departing with Lewis on the expedition to the Northwest. When he returned, he took a position as the principal Indian agent for the Louisiana Territory. In 1813, he became governor of the newly formed Missouri Territory. Losing his seat in 1820, he assumed the role of superintendent of Indian affairs in St. Louis. His wife died in 1820, as did several of his children. Clark remarried in 1821, but his second wife died in 1831. He held the post of superintendent until his death in 1838.

HISTORICAL DOCUMENT

William Clark:

November 7th Thursday 1805

A cloudy foggey morning Some rain. we Set out early proceeded under the Stard Shore under a high rugid hills with Steep assent the Shore boalt and rockey, the fog So thick we could not See across the river, two Canos of Indians met and returned with us to their village which is Situated on the Stard Side behind a cluster of Marshey Islands, on a narrow chanl. of the river through which we passed to the *Village* of 4 Houses, they gave us to eate Some fish, and Sold us, fish. *Wap pa to* roots three *dogs* and 2 otter Skins for which we gave fish hooks principally of which they were verry fond.

Those people call themselves *War-ci-â-cum* and Speake a language different from the nativs above with whome they trade for the *Wapato* roots of which they make great use of as food. their houses differently built, raised entirely above ground eaves about 5 feet from the ground Supported and covered in the same way of those above, dores about the Same size but in the Side of the house in one Corner, one fire place and that near the opposit end; around which they have their beads raised about 4 feet from the flore which is of earth, under their beads they Store away baskets of dried fish Berries & *wappato,* over the fire they hang the flesh as they take them and which they do not make immediate use. Their Canoes are of the Same form of those above. The Dress of the men differ verry little from those above, The womin altogether different, their robes are Smaller only Covering their Sholders & falling down to near the hip— and Sometimes when it is Cold a piec of fur curiously plated and connected So as to meet around the body from the arms to the hips— "The garment which occupies the waist and thence as low as the knee before and mid leg behind, cannot properly be called a petticoat, in the common acception of the word; it is a *Tissue* formed of white Cedar bark bruised or broken into Small Strans, which are interwoven in their center by means of Several cords of the Same materials which Serves as well for a girdle as to hold in place the Strans of bark which forms the tissue, and which Strans, Confined in the middle, hand with their ends pendulous from the waiste, the whole being of Suffcent thickness when the female Stands erect to conceal those parts useally covered from familiar view, but when she stoops or places herself in any other attitudes this battery of Venus is not altogether impervious to the penetrating eye of the amorite. This tissue is Sometims formed of little Strings of the Silk grass twisted and knoted at their ends" &c. Those Indians are low and ill Shaped all flat heads . . .

after delaying at this village one hour and a half we Set out piloted by an Indian dressed in a Salors dress, to the main Chanel of the river, the tide being in we Should have found much dificuelty in passing into the main Chanel from behind those islands, if without a pilot, a large marshey Island near the middle of the river near which Several Canoes Came allong Side with Skins, roots fish &c. to Sell, and had a temporey residence on this Island, here we See great numbers of water fowls about those marshey Islands; here the high mountanious Countrey approaches the river on the Lard Side, a high mountn. to the S W. about 20 miles, the high mountans. Countrey Continue on the Stard Side, about 14 miles below the last village and 18 miles of this day we landed at a village of the Same nation. This village is at the foot of the high hills on the Stard Side back of 2 Small Islands it contains 7 indifferent houses built in the Same form of those above, here we purchased a Dog Some fish, *wappato* roots and I purchased 2 beaver Skins for the purpose of makeing me a *roab*, as the robe I have is rotten and good for nothing. opposit to this Village the high mountaneous Countrey leave the river on the Lard Side below which the river widens into a kind of Bay & is Crouded with low Islands Subject to be Covered by the tides— we proceeded on about 12 miles below the Village under a high mountaneous Countrey on the Stard. Side. Shore boald and rockey and Encamped under a high hill on the Stard. Side opposit to a rock Situated half a mile from the Shore, about 50 feet high and 20 feet Diamieter, we with dificuelty found a place Clear of the tide and Sufficiently large to lie on and the only place we could get was on round Stones on which we lay our mats rain Continud. moderately all day & Two Indians accompanied us from the last village, they we detected in Stealing a knife and returned, our Small Canoe which got Seperated in the fog this morning joined us this evening from a large Island Situated nearest the Lard Side below the high hills on that Side, the river being too wide to See either the form Shape or Size of the Islands on the Lard Side.

Great joy in camp we are in *View* of the *Ocian*, this great Pacific Octean which we been So long anxious to See. and the roreing or noise made by the waves brakeing on the rockey Shores (as I Suppose) may be heard distinctly . . .

November 8th Friday 1805

A Cloudy morning Some rain, we did not Set out untill 9 oClock, haveing Changed our Clothing— proceeded on Close under the Stard. Side, the hills high with Steep assent, Shore boald and rockey Several low Islands in a Deep bend or Bay to the Lard Side, river about 5 or 7 miles wide. three Indians in a Canoe overtook us, with Salmon to Sell, passed 2 old villages on the Stard. Side and at 3 miles entered a nitch of about 6 miles wide and 5 miles deep with Several Creeks makeing into the Stard Hills, this nitch we found verry Shallow water and Call it the Shallow nitch we came too at the remains of an old village at the bottom of this nitch and dined, here we Saw great numbers of fowl, Sent out 2 men and they killed a Goose and two *Canves back* Ducks here we found great numbers of flees which we treated with the greatest caution and distance; after Diner the Indians left us and we took the advantage of a returning tide and proceeded on to the Second point on the Std. here we found the Swells or waves So high that we thought it imprudent to proceed; we landed unloaded and drew up our Canoes. Some rain all day at intervales; we are all wet and disagreeable, as we have been for Several days past, and our present Situation a verry disagreeable one in as much; as we have not leavel land Sufficient for an encampment and for our baggage to lie Cleare of the tide, the High hills jutting in So Close and Steep that we cannot retreat back, and the water of the river too Salt to be used, added to this the waves are increasing to Such a hight that we cannot move from this place, in this Situation we are compelled to form our Camp between the hite of the Ebb and flood tides, and rase our baggage on logs— We are not certain as yet if the whites people who trade with those people or from whome they precure ther goods are Stationary at the mouth, or visit this quarter at Stated times for the purpose of trafick &c. I believe the latter to be the most probable conjucture— The Seas roled and tossed the Canoes in Such a manner this evening that Several of our party were Sea Sick.

Novr. 9th Saturday 1805
The tide of last night obliged us to unload all the Canoes one of which Sunk before She was unloaded by the high waves or Swells which accompanied the returning tide, The others we unloaded, and 3 others was filled with water Soon after by the Swells or high Sees which broke against the Shore imediately where we lay, rained hard all the fore part of the day, the [tide] which rose untill 2 oClock P M to day brought with it Such emence Swells or waves, added to a hard wind from the S W South which Loosened the Drift trees which is verry thick on the Shores, and tossed them about in Such a manner, as to endanger our Canoes very much, with every exertion and the Strictest attention by the party was Scercely Suffient to defend our Canoes from being Crushed to pieces between those emensely large trees maney of them 200 feet long and 4 feet through. The tide of this day rose about [*blank*] feet & 15 Inches higher than yesterday this is owing to the wind which Sets in from the ocian, we are Compelled to move our Camp from the water, as also the loading every man as wet all the last night and this day as the rain Could make them which Contind. all day. at 4 oClock the wind Shifted about to the S. W imediately from the ocian and blew a Storm for about 2 hours, raised the tide verry high all wet & cold Labiech killed 4 Ducks very fat & R. Fields Saw Elk Sign.

not withstanding the disagreeable time of the party for Several days past they are all Chearfull and full of anxiety to See further into the ocian. the water is too Salt to Drink, we use rain water. The Salt water has acted on some of the party already as a Pergitive. rain continus . . .

November 11th 1805
a hard rain all the last night we again get wet the rain continue at intervals all day. Wind verry high from S W and blew a Storm all day Sent out Jo. Fields & Collins to hunt. at 12 oClock at a time the wind was verry high and waves tremendeous five Indians Came down in a Canoe loaded with fish of Salmon Spes. Called *Red Charr,* we purchased of those Indians 13 of these fish, for which we gave, fishing hooks & some trifling things, we had Seen those Indians at a village behind Some marshey Islands a few days ago. they are on their way to trade those fish with white people which they make Signs live below round a point, those people are badly Clad, one is dressd. in an old Salors Jacket & Trouses, the others Elk Skin robes. we are truly unfortunate to be Compelled to lie 4 days nearly in the Same place at a time that our day are precious to us, The Wind Shifted to [*blank*] the Indians left us and Crossed the river which is about 5 miles wide through the highest Sees I ever Saw a Small vestle ride, their Canoe is Small, maney times they were out of Sight before the were 2 miles off Certain it is they are the best canoe navigators I ever Saw The tide was 3 hours later to day than yesterday and rose much higher, the trees we camped on was all on flote for about 2 hours from 3 untill 5 oClock P M, the great quantities of rain which has fallen losenes the Stones on the Side of the hill & the Small ones fall on us, our Situation is truly a disagreeable one our Canoes in one place at the mercy of the waves our baggage in another and our Selves & party Scattered on drift trees of emense Sizes, & are on what dry land they can find in the Crevices of the rocks & hill Sides

November 12th Tuesday 1805
A Tremendious wind from the S. W. about 3 oClock this morning with Lightineng and hard claps of Thunder, and Hail which Continued untill 6 oClock a. m. when it became light for a Short time, then the heavens became Sudenly darkened by a black Cloud from the S. W. and rained with great violence untill 12 oClock, the waves tremendious brakeing with great fury against the rocks and trees on which we were encamped. our Situation is

dangerous. we took the advantage of a low *tide* and moved our camp around a point to a Small wet bottom at the mouth of a Brook, which we had not observed when we Came to this cove; from it being verry thick and obscured by drift trees and thick bushes It would be distressing to See our Situation, all wet and Colde our bedding also wet, (and the robes of the party which Compose half the bedding is rotten and we are not in a Situation not to supply their places) in a wet bottom Scercely large enough to contain us, with our baggage half a mile from us and Canoes at the mercy of the waves, altho Secured as well as possible, Sunk with emence parcels of Stone to wate them down to prevent their dashing to pieces against the rocks; one got loose last night and was left on a rock a Short distance below, without rciving more dammage than a Split in her bottom—Fortunately for us our men are healthy. 3 men Gibson Bratten & Willard attempted to go aroud the point below in our Indian Canoe, much Such a canoe as the Indians visited us in yesterday, they proceeded to the point from which they were oblige to return, the waves tossing them about at will I walked up the branch and giged 3 Salmon trout. the party killed 13 Salmon to day in a branch about 2 miles above. rain Continued

GLOSSARY

lard: port, left side

nitch: niche, bay

pergitive: purgative, laxative

stard: starboard, right side

wapato: flowering plant whose root was a food staple for Lewis and Clark's expedition.

Document Analysis

The journals of Lewis and Clark, compiled over the course of the two years during which the corps traveled, provide great details of the sights and people encountered by the expedition. These images were important for officials back in Washington, DC, not only because they gave an illustration of a region that had never before been seen by white Americans, but also because they gave the American government a detailed course to follow during subsequent expeditions. To be sure, Americans had visited and established encampments in the Pacific Northwest, and they had established a number of towns, settlements, and forts along the Missouri and Mississippi Rivers (the country's two longest rivers, respectively). However, no link between the main river of the Northwest, the Columbia River, and the major eastern river system had yet been found. Should the expedition be successful, the United States would finally have the key to major westward expansion.

Documenting the journey from Illinois to the Pacific and back initially fell to Lewis, the more educated of the expedition's two leaders. However, Clark and others in the corps kept journals as well. When Lewis died, the task of compiling the various accounts fell to Clark, who kept detailed records but whose writing style was rougher than Lewis's.

During the summer of 1804, Lewis, Clark, and the Corps of Discovery Expedition traveled north and west along the Missouri River, arriving at Fort Mandan (in what is now western North Dakota). There, they set up camp and prepared for a continued journey westward, which would occur in the spring of 1805 once the river waters had risen again. When the waters became favorable, they traveled along the Jefferson River, the westernmost tributary of the Missouri. With them were the Shoshone Indian woman Sacagawea, who was used as a guide and interpreter. Sacagawea, who was a slave and wife to the corps's steersman, Toussaint Charbonneau, became invaluable to Lewis and Clark, helping the corps make the treacherous journey on foot and horseback from the end of the Jefferson over the Bitterroot Mountains (between what is now Montana and Idaho). Once they crossed the mountains, they found food and supplies with the help of the Nez Percé Indians. In October of 1805, they hollowed out new canoes and set off on the Clearwater River, a branch of the Snake and Columbia Rivers.

On November 7, 1805, Clark writes in his journal of an encounter with a group of Indians along the Columbia River. The group was traveling along the "stard" (starboard, or right side) of the river during a particularly foggy and rainy morning. While drifting beneath some high, rocky hills, they met two canoes containing Indians Clark identifies as "War-ci-â-cum"—most likely the small Wahkiakum tribe of the Chinook Indians. Lewis and Clark followed the Indians back to their village in a narrow channel off the river.

While at the village, Clark says that the Wahkiakum gave the members of the corps fish to eat and then sold them fish, three dogs, and two otter skins in exchange for new fishing hooks. The Indians also sold the men wapato root. Lewis and Clark had never encountered this root before, but during their travels, Lewis observed American Indians digging in the mud beneath these flowering plants. The root found beneath the riverside muck reminded Lewis of a small potato. When the wapato root was dried, pounded into meal, and formed into cakes, it presented a starchy side dish that became a staple food for the corps.

Clark continues his observations of the Wahkiakum village, which in a number of ways was distinctive in comparison to the lifestyles of other Indians with whom the expedition came into contact. In a typical home, the Wahkiakum had a fireplace in one corner. On the opposite side of the house, Clark observed, were baskets with dried fish, wapato, berries, and other food sources. Clark also takes note of the clothing preferences of his Wahkiakum hosts. In particular, Clark seems interested in the women's garments. The women's robes were shorter than those he had observed in other tribes. However, when it was cold, the Wahkiakum women used a curious, petticoat-like dressing to keep themselves warm. This garment was a piece of white cedar bark that had been softened and woven together with fur. This accessory could be attached to the robe and, Clark observes, it was sturdy and firm enough to act as both a petticoat and a girdle.

The Wahkiakum's language, according to Clark's account, was different from the other Indians with whom the corps traded. This dialect, according to experts, was known as Kathlamet, and was a style typical of the Chinook tribes that lived in the upper Columbia River watershed. The fact that Clark observed the distinctiveness of the Wahkiakum dialect suggests that it was considerably different from other Chinook dialects in both the upper and lower Columbia regions; the Wahkiakum could therefore be considered distinctive to the "middle Chinook" territory.

After their visit to the Wahkiakum village, the expedition set out through a series of "marshey islands" and back to the Columbia, aided by the piloting skills of one of their hosts. As they came upon a larger one of these islands (based on the maps drawn by Clark, some historians believe this island to be what is now referred to as Tenasillahe Island, located at a curve in the river), they were joined by more Wahkiakum Indians in canoes, with whom they traded. As the journey continued, Clark took account of the high, mountainous country. They encountered more Wahkiakum along the way, at one point trading for supplies (which included a new robe for Clark). They later paddled toward what is now known as Pillar Rock, a massive stone that, according to Clark, was close to fifty feet in height. They found a suitable campsite near the rock and away from the shoreline. The river, he observes, was becoming wider in this region.

Later in the same journal entry, Clark reports that they had just passed another Wahkiakum village while paddling through a thick morning fog. When the fog lifted, Lewis, Clark and the rest of the corps were greeted with a most welcome sight. "We are in view of the Ocian [Ocean]," he joyfully states, "which we had been So long anxious to See." Although it is more likely that they had reached the mouth of the Columbia River at this point and not the Pacific Ocean itself, the ocean was indeed close. Clark adds that he and his companions were excited at the prospect of soon hearing the Pacific's waves crashing on the rocks, a sound he had been anticipating throughout the journey.

On November 8, 1805, Clark's journal states that the group started late, having encountered rain that morning and needing a change of clothes before embarking. According to Clark's log, they traveled toward an area known as "Cape Disappointment" (so called because British sea captain and fur trader John Meares, while seeking the mouth of the Columbia in 1788, missed the river and concluded that it did not exist). The river continued to widen considerably. As it expanded, it also became choppy, with large swells making travel difficult for the canoes. They stayed relatively close to the right ("stard") side of the river. They encountered several canoes of Indians from whom they purchased salmon. They also came across two Indian villages along with a number of bays and inlets of varying size.

The corps soon came upon an old Indian village, where they set up camp, killed some fowl, and proceeded to dine with a group of Indians. After their meal, the tide had returned, working to the advantage of the expedition. Lewis, Clark, and the group set out again (the Indians went their separate ways).

Unfortunately, Clark says, the group's time on the water was short-lived, as the waves had become too difficult to navigate. The expedition therefore returned to the shore, where they offloaded their supplies and carried their canoes along the river's edge. Rain had been soaking them for the previous few days, and on this day, Clark says, the rain continued. These conditions made life difficult for the group. The situation was already challenging for the expedition's members, as the high water along the river's edge had made it extremely difficult to find a suitable campground (they were surrounded by steep cliffs and rocks, and they could not turn around to return to more favorable resting areas). The fact that the high tidewater contained a great deal of salt meant that, despite the high volume of water, none of it could be used. The group was thus tired, dirty, thirsty, cold, and wet. Nevertheless, this unpleasant set of circumstances notwithstanding, the men needed to portage and carry their supplies onward. Clark suggests that the men were in a foul mood.

To adapt, the expedition would camp during the brief periods between the tide's ebb and flow, putting their baggage on logs to keep them from becoming soaked on the ground. When the group returned to the river, it was just as unpleasant an experience as it had been on land. The rough seas tossed the light canoes violently, making several of the men (who were seasoned enough to never get seasick) extremely nauseated.

The difficult conditions led Clark to wonder about other white visitors to this region. There were trappers and other white people in the area, trading with the Indians with whom Lewis and Clark came into contact. However, the expedition found no trading encampments or outposts. Clark asked himself if the corps would eventually come across such trading stations closer to the mouth of the river, or if these white traders simply visited the region during specific times. Clark supposed the latter scenario, and was right to do so—no trading station would be established in this region until 1811, when the Astorian fur traders arrived.

On November 9, 1805, Clark writes, the weather and tides were becoming more of a danger than before. A storm had intensified the strength and size of the river's waves, and the high tides only exacerbated conditions. Clark reports that the expedition needed to unload the canoes (one of which sank and three more of which were swamped during the previous night's high tide). Lewis and Clark's party and supplies were not much safer on land, either—the high winds, coming from the southwest, were causing the immense trees by the river side to bend deeply. With the high tide eroding the soil beneath the roots, Clark worries that these trees would topple, destroy the camp, and kill his men. Clark says that the party was forced to move their encampment away from the river's edge, transporting all of their supplies further inland. The men were soaked and tired, making the task of moving everything even more difficult.

Nevertheless, Clark says, the men remained in good spirits and anxious to reach their goal of the Pacific Ocean. Despite the fact that they were cold and wet, the men willingly moved on. They made the best of their situation as well—although they were running out of potable water, they were able to collect and drink the rainwater. They even made use of the plentiful salt water, using it as a laxative ("pergitive") to encourage good health. Furthermore, there was wildlife in abundance (including, Clark says, elk), ensuring that the expedition would not go hungry so close to the ocean.

On November 11, Lewis and Clark's expedition remained cold and wet amid harsh rain, wind, and tidal conditions. Even the hillsides and mountains above became treacherous, as the rain loosened rocks and soil—in addition to falling trees, the men were now concerned with being caught in a landslide or avalanche. They did, however, encounter another group of Indians, with whom they exchanged fishing hooks and a few trinkets for fish (what Clark called "red charr," commonly known as sockeye salmon). Although he is not particularly fond of their mode of dress (elk skin robes and old sailor's jackets, for example), he is taken aback by their prowess in a canoe. They "are the best canoe navigators I ever saw," he exclaims, noting how these Indians were able to manage the dangerous waters in small boats. These Indians were likely Kathlamets, who shared the river with the Wahkiakums.

On November 12, 1805, the weather took an even greater turn for the worse. As the expedition party rested at a campsite within sight of Mount Hood, a new storm came in from the southwest. The men awoke at 3 a.m. to thunder and lightning, along with hail and heavy rain. The storm, according to Clark, lasted three hours and was followed by a short reprieve. As the men recovered from this violent storm, yet another black cloud moved in from the southwest. The rain that came with it lasted for six more hours, and the driving winds continued to churn the river water. The men moved their camp further inland, leaving their canoes along the shore, weighted down by large rocks to prevent them from being carried into the water. The men's situation, in the words of Clark, was "distressing"—they were cold and wet and their bedding was rotten beyond repair. There was no way to replace any of the expedition's supplies at this point.

Still, Clark says, the men were healthy in spite of the lack of rest and warmth. Their canoes (which were crafted by Indians they had met along their travels), which had been used in challenging waters, remained relatively undamaged. More Indians arrived to trade, and Clark again seems impressed by their ability to navigate the rough waters of the Columbia. After bidding farewell to these Indians, the corps moved onward toward their goal of the Pacific.

Essential Themes

The Corps of Discovery Expedition, led by Lewis and Clark, was a pivotal voyage in early American history. To be sure, white people had visited the northwestern regions of the newly established United States, but their stays in the region were short, focusing on the acquisition of fur and other resources rather than on settlement. On the eastern half of the country, white people were moving into the frontier, along the Mississippi and Missouri Rivers. However, no one had yet found what was assumed to be a link that could help hasten American expansion into the West. The acquisition of the Louisiana Territory made it possible for this link to be established. For this reason, Jefferson was able to shepherd the Louisiana Purchase through Congress and quickly assemble the Corps of Discovery. Jefferson then turned to his most trusted man (who in turn hired *his* most trusted man) to lead the expedition up the Missouri toward the Columbia.

When Lewis and Clark's party left its staging area near St. Louis, their demeanor was positive, particularly in light of the prospect of eventually reaching their goal of the Columbia River and the Pacific Ocean. Upon leaving the outposts and encampments of the Upper Midwest, the expedition moved into uncharted territory. They were fortunate, however, to have in their group American Indians who knew not only the land they would soon enter but also how to survive in that land.

Indians would play a vital role in the expedition's survival along both the Missouri and the Columbia Rivers. Crossing the northern Rockies (the Bitterroots) was accomplished with the guidance of the Indians in their group as well as the local tribes. Clark's journal of November 1805 provides countless more examples of the party's interactions with Indians, who assisted the expedition with supplies (particularly durable canoes), guidance, and hospitality. The Indians also inspired the white travelers to continue their quest. As Lewis and Clark's party struggled against the powerful tides, currents, and waves of the Columbia River, they were amazed by the local Indians' ability to navigate these often treacherous waters.

Lewis and Clark's journals were not just simple accounts of the expedition's transcontinental adventures. The two drew detailed maps, described countless landmarks and dangerous areas, and documented the characteristics of the American Indian tribes in this region. In this light, the journals served as a comprehensive and invaluable guide for westward-bound Americans. The millions of words written by the two leaders (and the party's other members) also serve as a testament to the bravery and fortitude of the men (and women) who, despite being battered and worn by several days of harsh Northwest weather, continued to push ahead with high morale and zeal for their difficult mission.

Michael Auerbach, MA

Bibliography

"Deadly Crossing: The Bitterroots." *National Geographic*. National Geographic Society, n.d. Web. 9 Feb. 2013.

Fifer, Barbara. "Wapato and Cous Roots." *Discovering Lewis and Clark*. Lewis and Clark Fort Mandan Foundation, Aug. 2006. Web. 9 Feb. 2013.

The Journals of the Lewis and Clark Expedition. U of Nebraska–Lincoln, n.d. Web. 8 Feb. 2013.

"Lewis and Clark Expedition Time Line." *National Geographic*. National Geographic Society, n.d. Web. 9 Feb. 2013.

"Meriwether Lewis." *The West Film Project*. PBS.org, 2001. Web. 8 Feb. 2013.

Perry, Douglas. "Teaching with Documents: The Lewis and Clark Expedition." *National Archives*. US National Archives and Records Administration, n.d. Web. 9 Feb. 2013.

"William Clark." *The West Film Project*. PBS.org, 2001. Web. 8 Feb. 2013.

"William Clark." University of Virginia, n.d. Web. 8 Feb. 2013.

Additional Readings

Ambrose, Stephen. *Undaunted Courage*. New York: Simon, 1997. Print.

Jones, Landon Y. *The Essential Lewis and Clark*. New York: HarperCollins, 2002. Print.

Josephy, Alvin M, Jr. *Lewis and Clark through Indian Eyes*. Hopkinton, MA: Vintage, 2007. Print.

Kirby, Don. "The Great Northern Plains as Viewed by the Lewis and Clark Expedition." *Rangelands* 32.5 (2010): 2–4. Print.

Knapp, Paul. "Lewis and Clark's Tempest: The 'Perfect Storm' of November 1805, Oregon, USA." *Holocene* 21.4 (2011): 693–97. Print.

LESSON PLAN: **Lewis and Clark and Northwest Expansion**

Students analyze excerpts from the *Journals*, evaluate the Lewis and Clark expedition's impact on westward expansion and the concept of Manifest Destiny, and explore the expedition's legacy.

Learning Objectives

Evaluate the implementation of the decision to purchase the Louisiana Territory and its subsequent effects; explain historical continuity and change to assess how the Louisiana Purchase affected Native Americans; analyze cause-and-effect relationships of US trading interests and continental expansion; hypothesize the influence of the expedition on Americans today.

Materials: Excerpts from *The Journals of Lewis and Clark* (1805); *Regarding Oregon Statehood* by Governor George L. Curry (1857)

Overview Questions

What do the *Journals* reveal about the natural resources of the Pacific Northwest? What do the *Journals* tell us about American Indians in the Northwest? How did the Lewis and Clark expedition influence westward expansion and the concept of Manifest Destiny? Why should this expedition matter to Americans today?

Step 1: Comprehension Questions

What natural resources does Clark list? Why was it important to record these? What insights does Clark provide into the Pacific Northwest's climate and geography?

- **Activity:** Have students summarize passages that reveal scientific and geographic information about the Northwest; have small groups discuss why this information was needed in the early 1800s.

Step 2: Comprehension Questions

What do these excerpts reveal about the lives of American Indians in the Pacific Northwest? Why would this information be important to record? In his November 8 entry, Clark makes a brief note about trade; why would he record this? What was its significance at the time?

- **Activity:** Have students speculate as to who "the white people who trade with those people" are; have students explore other historical documents to learn more about American Indians in the Northwest.

Step 3: Context Questions

What can we learn from *Regarding Oregon Statehood* about the Lewis and Clark expedition's impact on the Pacific Northwest? How did this expedition contribute to westward expansion and shape the concept of Manifest Destiny?

- **Activity:** Have small groups discuss how opportunities to trade across the Pacific also helped propel westward expansion; have students create graphic organizers that explain the reasons for westward expansion.

Step 4: Exploration Questions

From a global economic perspective, how important is the Pacific Northwest to the US economy, and why? Suppose Lewis and Clark never explored this area; how might that have changed US history?

- **Activity:** Have students write a journal entry on the importance of the Pacific Northwest today; have students present and discuss their entries.

Step 5: Response Paper

Word length and additional requirements set by Instructor. Students answer the research question in the *Overview Questions*. Students state a thesis and use as evidence passages from the primary source document as well as support from supplemental materials assigned in the lesson.

■ California and Its Inhabitants

Date: 1840
Author: Dana, Richard Henry, Jr.
Genre: diary; memoir

"By the close of the summer I had . . . acquired some knowledge of the character and habits of the people, as well as of the institutions under which they live."

Summary Overview

This document, written by Richard Henry Dana Jr., is a chapter from his book *Two Years before the Mast*, published in 1840. Dana was a sailor for two years during his recovery from measles, and during that time he kept a diary of his observations of life aboard ship and in the areas he visited. In the preface to the book, Dana explains that his purpose in writing is to show what life is like for the average sailor and to fill what he saw as a void in maritime literature. According to his own words, he did his best to relate events as he saw them, without interpreting them or evaluating the morality of those individuals he met. This specific chapter (chapter 21), "California and Its Inhabitants," shows what life was like for Mexicans and American Indians living in California at the time Dana visited, in 1834. It is one of the few surviving primary sources from before the gold rush.

Defining Moment

After the California gold rush began in 1848, people rushed to the West Coast in order to "strike it rich"; many documents about California life during this time exist because of the increase in population. Reliable sources about daily life and customs before the gold rush, however, are scarce. One of the only remaining documents is that of Richard Henry Dana Jr. Dana was an outsider, a sailor raised on the East Coast with no ties to the local people, which makes his account even rarer. In the preface to *Two Years before the Mast*, Dana even states that his intention in writing his account is to provide an unbiased recording of local cultures as he encountered them. While biases can never be totally removed from a person's recollection of an event, Dana does his best not to pass too much judgment on local people, which helps historians gain a better understanding of the time period and the relationships between different cultural groups.

This excerpt gives details about the Mexican, Spanish, Anglo, and native residents of California, the establishment of the Jesuit missions and *presidios* (Spanish military garrisons) that governed California and its inhabitants, and the changes in power and culture from the 1600s to Dana's visit in 1834. The hierarchy of power in the territory, which was originally in the hands of the Jesuits, was given to Mexican *administradores* after Mexico's independence from Spain in 1821. Even though the administradores technically governed California, there was no formal system of law in the territory, or at least no immediate system of justice—those who governed California were often far away in Mexico. Since the people of California could not rely on the Mexican government to help them, they frequently took matters into their own hands. American Indians, the lowest social group, who were made to be serfs of the missions, were treated the most harshly.

Author Biography

Richard Henry Dana Jr. was born in 1815 in Cambridge, Massachusetts, to Richard and Ruth Dana. Dana was a dedicated student, even though illness sometimes required that he leave school. During his academic life, he was exposed to many influences, such as the preaching of Reverend Nehemiah Adams and participation in protests at Harvard College. Dana was following in his father's and grandfather's distinguished footsteps when he entered Harvard. In his third year of school, however, he came down with the measles, and one of the side effects was a severe loss of vision. While he recovered, he decided to leave school and became a sailor, and then a fur trader for a brief time in California. In the two years he spent aboard ship, Dana maintained a diary chronicling his experiences and observations of the people he met. Upon his return to Massachusetts in 1836, Dana reenrolled at Harvard and finished his degree, became a lawyer, married Sarah Watson, and eventually opened his own law office in Boston. During this period, he revisited his diary and published his observations and experiences under the title *Two Years before the Mast*.

Dana's work strongly reflects his experiences as a young man at sea. He would sail again in 1859, this time around the world as a passenger. His trip took him once again to California, which he wrote about in "Twenty Fours Years After," published in later editions of *Two Years before the Mast*. Many of Dana's clients were seamen, and he became known for his staunch defense of their rights, especially against captains and shipmasters. He also defended the rights of several fugitive slaves and became involved in the anti-slavery Free Soil Party, which was founded in 1848. This began his political career, which culminated in his appointment as United States district attorney by President Abraham Lincoln; he served in this role during the Civil War. One of his cases at this time, argued in front of the Supreme Court in 1863, concerned the seizure of property at sea during wartime. Dana was a recognized expert of maritime law.

When President Andrew Johnson came to office, Dana resigned as district attorney and went back to his private law practice. He also served in the Massachusetts legislature from 1867 to 1868. Dana was considered for an appointment as a US ambassador and a nomination for senator in the 1870s, but he had his own views and did not stray from them, which prevented him from acquiring either position. He retired from American politics and moved to Italy in order to work on a book about international law. He died in Rome in 1882, shortly after starting his work. Although remembered as a relatively minor figure of the nineteenth century, Dana's literary contribution provides a rare look at a common seaman's life and life in California before—and after—the drastic changes made by the gold rush (1848–1855).

HISTORICAL DOCUMENT

We kept up a constant connection with the presidio, and by the close of the summer I had added much to my vocabulary, besides having made the acquaintance of nearly everybody in the place, and acquired some knowledge of the character and habits of the people, as well as of the institutions under which they live.

California was discovered in 1534 by Ximenes, or in 1536 by Cortes, I cannot settle which, and was subsequently visited by many other adventurers, as well as commissioned voyagers of the Spanish crown. It was found to be inhabited by numerous tribes of Indians, and to be in many parts extremely fertile; to which, of course, were added rumors of gold mines, pearl fishery, etc. No sooner was the importance of the country known, than the Jesuits obtained leave to establish themselves in it, to Christianize and enlighten the Indians. They established missions in various parts of the country toward the close of the seventeenth century, and collected the natives about them, baptizing them into the Church, and teaching them the arts of civilized life. To protect the Jesuits in their missions, and at the same time to support the power of the crown over the civilized Indians, two forts were erected and garrisoned, —one at San Diego, and the other at Monterey. These were called presidios, and divided the command of the whole country between them. Presidios have since been established at Santa Barbara, San Francisco, and other places, dividing the country into large districts, each with its presidio, and governed by a commandante. The soldiers, for the most part, married civilized Indians; and thus, in the vicinity of each presidio, sprung up, gradually, small towns. In the course of time, vessels began to come into the ports to trade with the missions and received hides in return; and thus began the great trade of California. Nearly all the cattle in the country belonged to the missions, and they employed their Indians, who became, in fact, their serfs, in tending their vast herds. In the year 1793, when Vancouver visited San Diego, the missions had obtained great wealth and power, and are accused of having depreciated the country with the sovereign, that they might be allowed to retain their possessions. On the expulsion of the Jesuits from the Spanish dominions, the missions passed into the hands of the Franciscans, though without any essential change in their management. Ever since the independence of Mexico, the missions had been going down; until, at last, a law was passed, stripping them of all their possessions, and confining the priests to their spiritual duties, at the same time declaring all the Indians free and independent *Rancheros*. The change in the condition of the Indians was, as may be supposed, only nominal; they are virtually serfs, as much as they ever were. But in the missions the change was complete. The priests have now no power, except in their religious character, and the great possessions of the missions are given over to be preyed upon by the harpies of the civil power, who are sent there in the capacity of *administradores*, to settle up the concerns; and who usually end, in a few years, by making themselves fortunes, and leaving their stewardships worse than they found them. The dynasty of the priests was much more acceptable to the people of the country, and, indeed, to everyone concerned with the country, by trade or otherwise, than that of the administradores. The priests were connected permanently to one mission, and felt the necessity of keeping up its credit. Accordingly the debts of the missions were regularly paid, and the people were, in the main, well treated, and attached to those who had spent their whole lives among them. But the administradores are strangers sent from Mexico, having no interest in the country; not identified in any way with their charge, and, for the most part, men of desperate fortunes, —broken-down politicians and soldiers, —whose only object is to retrieve their condition in as short a time as possible. The change had been made but a few years before our arrival upon the coast, yet, in that short time, the trade was much diminished, credit impaired, and the venerable missions were going rapidly to decay.

The external political arrangements remain the same. There are four or more presidios, having under their protection the various missions, and the pueblos, which are towns formed by the civil power and containing no mission or presidio. The most northerly presidio is San Francisco, the next Monterey, the next Santa Barbara, including the mission of the same, San Luis Obispo, and Santa Buenaventura, which is said to be the best mission in the whole country, having fertile soil and rich vineyards. The last, and most southerly, is San Diego, including the mission of the same, San Juan Capistrano, the Pueblo de los Angeles, the largest town in California, with the neighboring mission of San Gabriel. The priests, in spiritual matters, are subject to the Archbishop of Mexico, and in temporal matters to the governor-general, who is the great civil and military head of the country.

The government of the country is an arbitrary democracy, having no common law, and nothing that we should call a judiciary. Their only laws are made and unmade at the caprice of the legislature, and are as variable as the legislature itself. They pass through the form of sending representatives to the congress at Mexico, but as it takes several months to go and return, and there is very little communication between the capital and this distant province, a member usually stays there as permanent member, knowing very well that there will be revolutions at home before he can write and receive an answer; and if another member should be sent, he has only to challenge him, and decide the contested election in that way.

Revolutions are matters of frequent occurrence in California. They are got up by men who are at the foot of the ladder and in desperate circumstances, just as a new political organization may be started by such men in our own country. The only object, of course, is the loaves and fishes; and instead of caucusing, paragraphing, libelling, feasting, promising, and lying, they take muskets and bayonets, and, seizing upon the presidio and customhouse, divide the spoils, and declare a new dynasty. As for justice, they know little law but will and fear. A Yankee, who had been naturalized, and become a Catholic, and had married in the country, was sitting in his house at the

Pueblo de los Angeles, with his wife and children, when a Mexican, with whom he had had a difficulty, entered the house, and stabbed him to the heart before them all. The murderer was seized by some Yankees who had settled there, and kept in confinement until a statement of the whole affair could be sent to the governor-general. The governor-general refused to do anything about it, and the countrymen of the murdered man, seeing no prospect of justice being administered, gave notice that, if nothing was done, they should try the man themselves. It chanced that, at this time, there was a company of some thirty or forty trappers and hunters from the Western States, with their rifles, who had made their head-quarters at the Pueblo; and these, together with the Americans and Englishmen in the place, who were between twenty and thirty in number, took possession of the town, and, waiting a reasonable time, proceeded to try the man according to the forms in their own country. A judge and jury were appointed, and he was tried, convicted, sentenced to be shot, and carried out before the town blindfolded. The names of all the men were then put into a hat, and each one pledging himself to perform his duty, twelve names were drawn out, and the men took their stations with their rifles, and, firing at the word, laid him dead. He was decently buried, and the place was restored quietly to the proper authorities. A general, with titles enough for an hidalgo, was at San Gabriel, and issued a proclamation as long as the fore-top-bowline, threatening destruction to the rebels, but never stirred from his fort; for forty Kentucky hunters, with their rifles, and a dozen of Yankees and Englishmen, were a match for a whole regiment of hungry, drawling, lazy half-breeds. This affair happened while we were at San Pedro (the port of the Pueblo), and we had the particulars from those who were on the spot. A few months afterwards, another man was murdered on the high-road between the Pueblo and San Luis Rey by his own wife and a man with whom she ran off. The foreigners pursued and shot them both, according to one story. According to another version, nothing was done about it, as the parties were natives, and a man whom I frequently saw in San Diego was pointed out as the murderer. Perhaps they were two cases that had got mixed.

When a crime has been committed by Indians, justice, or rather vengeance is not so tardy. One Sunday afternoon, while I was at San Diego, an Indian was sitting on his horse, when another, with whom he had had some difficulty, came up to him, drew a long knife, and plunged it directly into the horse's heart. The Indian sprang from his falling horse, drew out the knife, and plunged it into the other Indian's breast, over his shoulder, and laid him dead. The fellow was seized at once, clapped into the calabozo, and kept there until an answer could be received from Monterey. A few weeks afterwards I saw the poor wretch, sitting on the bare ground, in front of the calabozo, with his feet chained to a stake, and handcuffs about his wrists. I knew there was very little hope for him. Although the deed was done in hot blood, the horse on which he was sitting being his own, and a favorite with him, yet he was an Indian, and that was enough. In about a week after I saw him, I heard that he had been shot. These few instances will serve to give one a notion of the distribution of justice in California.

In their domestic relations, these people are not better than in their public. The men are thriftless, proud, extravagant, and very much given to gaming; and the women have but little education, and a good deal of beauty, and their morality, of course, is none of the best; yet the instances of infidelity are much less frequent than one would at first suppose. In fact, one vice is set over against another; and thus something like a balance is obtained. If the women have but little virtue, the jealousy of their husbands is extreme, and their revenge deadly and almost certain. A few inches of cold steel has been the punishment of many an unwary man, who has been guilty, perhaps, of nothing more than indiscretion. The difficulties of the attempt are numerous, and the consequences of discovery fatal, in the better classes. With the unmarried women, too, great watchfulness is used. The main object of the parents is to marry their daughters well, and to this a fair name is necessary. The sharp eyes of a dueña, and the ready weapons of a father or brother, are a protection which the characters of most of them—men and women—render by no means useless; for the very men who would lay down their lives to avenge the dishonor of their own family would risk the same lives to complete the dishonor of another.

Of the poor Indians very little care is taken. The priests, indeed, at the missions, are said to keep them very strictly, and some rules are usually made by the alcaldes to punish their misconduct; yet it all amounts to but little. Indeed, to show the entire want of any sense of morality or domestic duty among them, I have frequently known an Indian to bring his wife, to whom he was lawfully married in the church, down to the beach, and carry her back again, dividing with her the money which she had got from the sailors. If any of the girls were discovered by the alcalde to be open evil-livers, they were whipped, and kept at work sweeping the square of the presidio, and carrying mud and bricks for the buildings; yet a few reals would generally buy them off. Intemperance, too, is a common vice among the Indians. The Mexicans, on the contrary, are abstemious, and I do not remember ever having seen a Mexican intoxicated.

Such are the people who inhabit a country embracing four or five hundred miles of sea-coast, with several good harbors; with fine forests in the north; the waters filled with fish, and the plains covered with thousands of herds of cattle; blessed with a climate than which there can be no better in the world; free from all manner of diseases, whether epidemic or endemic; and with a soil in which corn yields from seventy to eighty fold. In the hands of an enterprising people, what a country this might be! we are ready to say. Yet how long would a people remain so, in such a country? The Americans (as those from the United States are called) and Englishmen, who are fast filling up the principal towns, and getting the trade into their hands, are indeed more industrious and effective than the Mexicans; yet their children are brought up Mexicans in most respects, and if the "California fever" (laziness) spares the first generation, it is likely to attack the second.

GLOSSARY

administrador: administrator or manager; government official

alcalde: a judge

calabozo: jail

caucusing: the meeting of any group organized to further a special interest or cause

commandante: commander, leader

dueña: female form of *dueño,* master

fore-top-bowline: part of a sail on a ship

hidalgo: a man of lower nobility; one who owns considerable property or is otherwise esteemed

libelling: defamation by written or printed words, or in any form other than words or gestures

presidio: a garrisoned fort; military post

ranchero: ranch owner; person who runs a ranch, typically for the purpose of raising cattle

real: silver coin used in Spain and Spanish America

serf: a person in servitude, required to give their services to a lord

sovereign: British gold coin

Yankee: somewhat derogatory word for an American

Document Analysis

Richard Henry Dana begins *Two Years before the Mast* with a preface in which he informs his audience that he is trying to write a true account of his experiences and life in the places he visited, focusing on California in this excerpt. What people experience and share with others is always affected by their own morals and opinions, so learning the truth about historical events is difficult, at best, and requires readers to separate facts from the overtones conveyed in the text. Dana wrote "California and Its Inhabitants" in order to help relay information about life in California in 1834 to an audience who had never seen it for themselves. This period of time was fraught with tensions between the ethnic groups who populated California and the institutions that controlled the land and the people. Dana helps to illustrate those tensions and does his best to maintain a neutral tone, but his own values are still present in his writing and have to be examined separately from the text.

Without an understanding of California's history, Dana's work has no context and loses its impact. While he does spend a significant portion of his chapter explaining the history of California, the validity of this information should be questioned. One can do so by reviewing other primary sources for comparison, to help piece together the most accurate account of Californian history. The main sources to look at from this time period are accounts recorded by Jesuit and Franciscan monks for their Spanish overseers. There is also, in a rare example, an account about the arrival of the Spanish written by a Luiseño American Indian named Pablo Tac (1822–1841), who was born and educated at Mission San Luis Rey (Gutierrez and Orsi, 197–198). The history includes information about the mission as well as the life of the Luiseño. Through the information provided in such records, readers can trust that Dana's retelling of the local history is as accurate as he was able to produce.

California has been inhabited for approximately fourteen thousand years and was first colonized in the sixteenth century by Spain, but it was a slow colonization, mostly controlled by Spanish missionaries. As Dana states in the second paragraph of his chapter, California was fertile and rich in resources, which made it very attractive for explorers, missionaries, and traders. Soon after the Jesuits came to California, the Spanish Crown set up presidios, or garrisoned forts, in nearby areas in order to provide protection. The presidios, the towns, and the missions worked together to consolidate Spanish control in its territories; however, these buildings were only built and maintained because the American Indians who lived there were forced into working for the Spanish, becoming serfs, as Dana calls them.

Once Mexican independence was achieved in 1821, life in California was altered, as Spanish domination fell away and the new Mexican government took control. Especially affected were the priests, who were stripped of their power and possessions. Dana tells most of this history in accurate detail; it was likely relayed to him through oral stories and the memories of the people he met. Something Dana includes, which is an invaluable part of this primary source, is the views of the people from whom he learned this history. When he begins his section on the Mexican administradores, Dana adds the opinions of the "people of the country." Because administradores lacked a permanent connection to the missions of California and to the local area, they did not care about what state they left the land and the people in when they returned to Mexico. This disregard for the local and native populations resulted in a decline in the overall well-being of the territory and its inhabitants, in turn leading to an increase in unrest and tension between the ethnic groups. Dana reveals this unrest while detailing his own experiences in the territory in 1834, nearly fifteen years after the introduction of the administradores.

Tensions between Ethnic Groups

Since the beginning of Spanish movement into California, tension existed between the native population and the colonizing population. Dana describes these changes several times in his work, beginning with the earliest movement of the Spanish into California. The Jesuits took it upon themselves to leave Spain and "to Christianize and enlighten the Indians." The belief that native populations need to be converted to Christianity is a common theme of this time period. European powers in general felt that civilization came through Christianity, and, therefore, colonized peoples were expected to convert. But even after conversion, the native populations were not considered to be the same social status as the Spanish, or even the Mexicans. The "civilized Indians," as Dana calls them, were better off than the uncivilized who made up the serfs, but they were still treated as inferior to anyone with European bloodlines.

Even throughout the changes in government and leadership during the nineteenth century, the American Indians were not really affected, because they were essentially always on the bottom of the social hierarchy. Dana comments on this fact after noting that the priests lost their power to the administradores after the Mexican Revolution. While everyone else's quality of life suffered, the American Indians went on much as they had before. The government in California, however, was unstable at best. Because of the loose structure of control under the administradores, and the frequent turnover as they returned to Mexico, laws were created and ignored on a regular basis.

Justice at this time was mostly in the hands of the people, which made for dangerous and uncertain times. Dana relates that a Yankee (a mildly derogatory Spanish term for a person born in the United States), could be taken from his house by a Mexican man and murdered over a disagreement, and there would be no official action taken by someone in the government. The only justice that he would gain was if his own countrymen would then take the Mexican into custody and try him themselves, which is not justice so much as vengeance. Dana also reports a story about a man murdered by his wife and her lover. One version he heard said that the Mexicans shot the murderers; in another, the Mexicans did not react, because the incident involved Californians—and nothing was done by the Californians, either. If Dana's account is to be believed in its entirety, it would show that laws, or rules rather, existed that made violence within an ethnic and social group more acceptable than violence that crossed social strata. This in and of itself would have created tension in a time when people already viewed each other on unequal terms.

American Indians, however, were treated much more harshly. Dana relates one event in which an American Indian man killed another American Indian who had killed his horse; he was immediately taken into custody and, after being imprisoned, was shot for his crime. Dana himself says, "When a crime has been committed by Indians, justice, or rather vengeance is not so tardy." This statement reveals that Dana, and most likely everyone else, knew this system was heavily weighted against the American Indians, but nothing was done to correct it. A strong delineation between American Indians and all other people would have to be long standing and quite extreme to produce such a definitive difference in treatment. This pervasive attitude affected Dana as well, as he would have learned much of his knowledge of California from locals while he worked in the fur trade. This comes through quite clearly in the last third of his chapter, in which he talks more about the personalities of the Mexicans and American Indians, revealing his own feelings about these people and his own values and upbringing.

Dana's Prejudices

Dana shows some prejudice when speaking about life in California, mainly regarding the mannerisms of the Mexicans and the American Indians. This is not to say that Dana harbored any ill will against any of them personally, just that his writing reflects a common mindset of his time, as well as his own "Eastern superiority," as it is labeled by Robert Gale in his biography of Dana. Most people at this time, especially the Mexicans and white Americans, felt that they were superior to and more civilized than the native peoples. Dana's phrasing and word choices show this. His phrasing also shows his distaste for the Mexicans. After Dana talks about the failings of the California justice system—an overall negative judgment against the Mexicans, whom he even calls "hungry, drawling, lazy half-breeds"—he moves to another subject, the personalities and mannerisms of those who live in California.

At the start of this section, Dana calls the Mexican men "thriftless, proud, [and] extravagant" and the women of low morals. He goes on to say that the women's lack of virtue is balanced by their husbands' jealousy, which serves to keep the women in check. In the first one hundred words, not a single positive aspect of these people is mentioned, let alone expanded upon. While an overabundance of positive attributes would be equally suspect, the entire lack of them clearly shows how Dana and other eastern Americans viewed the Mexicans. He also expresses the idea that these jealous husbands are overly emotional and reactionary, neither of which are favorable traits, because they use murder to punish a man who commits "nothing more than [an] indiscretion." His next statement, that parents have only one goal, to arrange good marriages for their daughters, is also explained in a somewhat judgmental tone, even though this was not an unusual circumstance in many places in the world, including England and even Dana's own upper-class East Coast home. Without trying to understand these ideas in a wider context, Dana condemns the Californian families and their ways of life, even though they are not so different from Dana's own background. The only positive trait that Dana attributes to the Mexicans is that they do not drink and that he has never seen a Mexican drunk. This passing reference comes only after a paragraph explaining the moral evils of the American Indians.

In his second-to-last paragraph, Dana explains in more detail the character of the American Indians, who up to this point have only been described as serfs and as generally having the same status no matter who ran the missions and presidios. American Indians who lived near the towns were almost completely under the control of the monks and the administadores, and they were also viewed in the harshest light. This control over them was necessary, in the view of Dana and those around him, because without it, their "entire want of any sense of morality or domestic duty" could not be controlled. Adultery and prostitution were apparently not uncommon, nor was drunkenness. Just as with his description of the Mexicans, Dana has no words of praise for the American Indians, nor does he seem to have any pity for them. Even when describing the punishment of "evil-livers," whipping and physical work, his tone is without any compassion. In his view, it seems, the American Indians were wrong in the way they lived their life and, therefore, whatever punishment is given to them is deserved, or not enough.

Prejudice is evident in nearly every author's writing, and while it can skew the validity of an account, it also provides necessary information about the social tensions and constructs of the time. California under the priests and administradores was heavily influenced by religion and the morals of the time. This is reflected in Dana's writing, as he also had a religious background and would view the world through these moral strictures. Nevertheless, for the most part, Dana wrote a thorough account of his time in a foreign land without blurring his experiences with heavy-handed expressions of the evils of any non-Christian groups.

In the decades following the publication of Dana's book, as early as 1888, people began to misunderstand his intentions and lose sight of the fact that *Two Years before the Mast* is not a work of fiction. While it is an edited and rewritten version of Dana's journal, he told the truth of life in California as he saw it. *Two Years before the Mast* provides information about unknown parts of the world to people who had never been or would never visit, and it does so from the point of view of a common sailor and trader, instead of the more pampered and privileged view—despite Dana's privileged upbringing. This style of history was not common for years after his publication. Even though it has been reduced to a minor work of literature, Dana's book set the stage for the major works that followed.

Essential Themes

Because Dana was brought up on the East Coast in a well-to-do family, he looked down on some of the inhabitants of California, seeing them as uncultured and uncivilized. But his nature, exemplified by his protection of his fellow students and sailors both before and after his time at sea, shows how he had a more balanced view of the world than many others of his time. Dana shares this uncommon point of view with his audience through his book. While partially critical of Mexicans and American Indians, the chapter has no overwhelming tone of censure or distaste. Dana reflects the local attitudes of the time and, through this, adds to the work's overall significance and historical impact.

While *Two Years before the Mast* may not be remembered as a major work of literature, it is a progressive book that reflects the character of the man who wrote it and its own time period. The central themes of the book, to relate facts in the most honest way possible and to inform people about a world they have never experienced, are not confined to this work alone, or even to this genre. Dana was simply notable for bringing honesty and a common viewpoint to a published work concerning one man's travels. The look at the world of pre–gold rush California and the understanding of the social tensions in the region are almost extras when the work is viewed in this manner. This excerpt is historically significant because of its contribution to an area of history that is lacking in personal accounts. *Two Years before the Mast*, however, goes beyond what each of its chapters can provide: it opened readers' minds to a new approach to historical writing.

Anna Accettola, MA

Bibliography

Dana, Richard Henry, Jr. *Two Years Before the Mast and Other Voyages*. Ed. Thomas L. Philbrick. New York: Library of America, 2005. Print.

Gale, Robert L. *Richard Henry Dana Jr*. New York: Twayne, 1969. Print.

Gutiérrez, Ramón A., and Richard J. Orsi, eds. *Contested Eden: California before the Gold Rush*. Berkeley: U of California P, 1998. Print.

Hart, James D. "Richard Henry Dana Jr., 1815–1882 by Samuel Shapiro." *American Literature* 34.3 (1962): 418–19. Print.

Additional Reading

Jackson, Robert H., and Edward D. Castillo. *Indians, Franciscans, and Spanish Colonization: The Impact of the Mission System on California Indians*. Albuquerque: U of New Mexico P, 1995. Print.

McWilliams, Carey. *Factories in the Field: The Story of Migratory Farm Labor in California*. 1939. Berkeley: U of California, 2000. Print.

---. *Southern California: An Island on the Land*. Santa Barbara: Peregrine Smith, 1973. Print.

Rice, Richard B., William A. Bullough, and Richard J. Orsi. *The Elusive Eden: A New History of California*. 3rd ed. Boston: McGraw, 2002. Print.

Shapiro, Samuel. *Richard Henry Dana Jr., 1815–1882*. East Lansing: Michigan State UP, 1961. Print.

Washburn, Wilcomb E., and William C. Sturtevant, eds. *Handbook of North American Indians*. Vol. 4. Washington: Smithsonian Institution, 1988. Print.

Weber, David J. *The Mexican Frontier, 1821–1846: The American Southwest under Mexico*. Albuquerque: U of New Mexico P, 1982. Print.

LESSON PLAN: **"What a Country This Might Be!"**

Students analyze Richard Henry Dana's observations about California under Mexican rule and evaluate his writings' influence on westward expansion, the concept of Manifest Destiny, and the Mexican-American War.

Learning Objectives

Analyze cause-and-effect relationships of US trading interests and continental expansion to the Pacific; examine the influence of ideas to explain the roots of Manifest Destiny and how this concept influenced westward expansion; consider multiple perspectives on the Mexican-American War.

Materials: Richard Henry Dana Jr., "California and Its Inhabitants," Chapter XXI from *Two Years before the Mast* (1840); Treaty of Guadalupe Hidalgo (1848).

Overview Questions

What do Dana's observations reveal about the importance of California's natural resources? What do his observations tell us about how Mexican rule affected California's inhabitants? How might Dana's writings have influenced westward expansion and the concept of Manifest Destiny? How might Dana's writings have helped justify the Mexican-American War?

Step 1: Comprehension Questions

Dana observes that California is "in many parts extremely fertile." How did California's natural resources shape its founding and subsequent development? What was the "great trade" that Dana notes? What was its significance?

- **Activity:** Have students explain the importance of trade to California's early development. Next, have students examine other historical documents for different perspectives on California's founding and early history.

Step 2: Comprehension Questions

What reasons and evidence does Dana provide to support his claim that American Indians under Mexican rule are "virtually serfs"? What reasons and evidence does he provide to support his claim that Mexican rule is "arbitrary"?

- **Activity:** Have students analyze what biases, if any, are revealed in Dana's writing. Have small groups discuss Dana's point of view on the Mexican rule of California.

Step 3: Context Questions

Dana notes that there are "rumors of gold mines [and] pearl fishery." Why would rumors such as these help fuel westward expansion? Dana states that "in the hands of an enterprising people, what a country this might be." How would statements such as these have contributed to Americans' sense of Manifest Destiny?

- **Activity:** Have small groups discuss how opportunities, real or imagined, in California influenced westward expansion. Have students write two advertisements for a wagon trip west: one based on rumor, and one based on fact.

Step 4: Exploration Questions

How might Dana's writings have contributed to support for the Mexican-American War? What do his observations and the Treaty of Guadalupe Hidalgo reveal about different perspectives on the Mexican-American War?

- **Activity:** Have students debate whether Dana's observations helped justify the Mexican-American War. Have students research and present their findings about the treaty's consequences on California's inhabitants.

Step 5: Response Paper

Word length and additional requirements set by Instructor. Students answer the research question in the *Overview Questions*. Students state a thesis and use as evidence passages from the primary source document as well as support from supplemental materials assigned in the lesson.

On Texan Independence

Date: March 7, 1836
Author: Austin, Stephen F.
Genre: speech

"Our cause is just, and is the cause of light and liberty:—the same holy cause for which our forefathers fought and bled:—the same that has an advocate in the bosom of every freeman, no matter in what country, or by what people it may be contended for."

Summary Overview

On March 7, 1836, Stephen F. Austin, the most successful empresario (one who recruited settlers) of Texan colonization, gave a speech in Louisville, Kentucky, imploring Americans to lend their support and assistance in Texas's quest for independence from Mexico. His speech was methodical, detailing the history of Mexican involvement with Texas, the desire to raise colonies of respectable citizens—to do so was a deterrent to invading Native American tribes such as the Comanche—and the escalating issues with the Mexican government, culminating in the denial of basic rights. On two occasions, Austin strategically reminds his audience of the similar feelings of oppression that drove their forefathers to revolt against Great Britain only sixty years before, thus recalling a central part of American history still within living memory. It is important to note that Austin was not asking for Texas to be admitted into the Union; rather, he was seeking the assistance of one nation for another in its quest for self-government.

Defining Moment

This speech of Stephen F. Austin's presents a powerful message, even to a modern reader. His words were written not in haste but with careful thought and preparation. There is much evidence to suggest he wished to represent Texas's pursuit for independence as thoroughly and honestly as possible; to this end, Austin was particular with dates and other details. Although not included below, found within the unabridged speech is a list of reasons Austin gave to prove that the Mexican government had failed in its federal duties to Texas and its people, principally the recent dissolution of the government by General Santa Anna. The following is an exceptionally emphatic example of Austin's message regarding this: "The people of Texas firmly adhered to the last moment, to the constitution which they and the whole nation had sworn to support. The government of Mexico have not—the party now in power have overturned the constitutional government and violated their oaths—they have separated from their obligations, from their duty and from the people of Texas; and, consequently, they are the true rebels." Although this section does not include a reference to the American Revolution, similarities may be drawn between the two conflicts. Governments have obligations to their constituents and, therefore, should be held responsible when they fail. For Austin, this particular failure could only be remedied by the secession of Texas.

The entirety of Austin's speech makes a number of references to the American Revolution; no doubt this was done specifically to generate sympathy for Texas's fight.

Austin implored his listeners to recognize the justifiable reasons he and his people had for complete separation from Mexico, arguing that they, too, had been ill used by those in power and were no longer willing to endure it.

Author Biography

Stephen Fuller Austin, despite the many years that have passed since his death, is still fondly remembered and hallowed within the state of Texas, where he is popularly regarded as the father of the state. He was born in Virginia on November 3, 1793, to Moses and Maria Austin and was raised in Missouri. The career of Texan empresario was not the path Stephen chose for himself; rather, the vision of colonization throughout Texas was the dream of his father. Moses Austin, who originally dealt with the Spanish with regard to Texas, knew that Spain wished the land settled and had attempted to do so repeatedly in the past in order to "keep interlopers and Indians at bay and lend credibility to Spanish claims of possession" (Brands 21). Soon after permission for his colony was granted, Moses died, leaving his son Stephen in charge of carrying out his dream.

Settlement of Texas may not have been Stephen's life goal, but it was a promise to his father that he successfully fulfilled, despite tangles with the Mexican government after Mexico won its independence from Spain. In time, he came to hold his own vision for Texas, which included a capital city: "The Texas of his dreams was not a collection of isolated homesteads but a community of cooperating individuals and families" (Brands 91).

The last year of Austin's life—1836, the same year as his speech—saw the establishment of the Republic of Texas on March 2, followed the next month by the momentous victory against General Santa Anna at the Battle of San Jacinto. He passed away from pneumonia on December 27, 1836, at the age of forty-three. Sam Houston, a general of the Texan army and later the first president of the new republic, lamented, "The Father of Texas is no more! The first pioneer of the wilderness has departed!" (qtd. in Brands 478). Since his death, Stephen F. Austin has continued to be hailed throughout the land he led toward independence.

HISTORICAL DOCUMENT

It is with the most unfeigned and heartfelt gratitude that I appear before this enlightened audience, to thank the citizens of Louisville, as I do in the name of the people of Texas, for the kind and generous sympathy they have manifested in favor of the cause of that struggling country; and to make a plain statement of facts explanatory of the contest in which Texas is engaged with the Mexican Government.

The public has been informed, through the medium of the newspapers, that war exists between the people of Texas and the present government of Mexico. There are, however, many circumstances connected with this contest, its origin, its principles and objects which, perhaps, are not so generally known, and are indispensable to a full and proper elucidation of this subject.

When a people consider themselves compelled by circumstances or by oppression, to appeal to arms and resort to their natural rights, they necessarily submit their cause to the great tribunal of public opinion. The people of Texas, confident in the justice of their cause, fearlessly and cheerfully appeal to this tribunal. In doing this the first step is to show, as I trust I shall be able to do by a succinct statement of facts, that our cause is just, and is the cause of light and liberty:—the same holy cause for which our forefathers fought and bled:—the same that has an advocate in the bosom of every freeman, no matter in what country, or by what people it may be contended for.

But a few years back Texas was a wilderness, the home of the uncivilized and wandering Comanche and other tribes of Indians, who waged a constant warfare against the Spanish. These settlements at that time were limited to the small towns of Bexar, (commonly called San Antonio) and Goliad, situated on the western limits. The incursions of the Indians also extended beyond the Rio Bravo del Norta, and desolated that part of the country.

In order to restrain these savages and bring them into subjection, the government opened Texas for settlement. Foreign emigrants were invited and called to that country. American enterprise accepted the invitation and promptly responded to the call. The first colony of Americans or foreigners ever settled in Texas was by myself. It was commenced in 1821, under a permission to my father, Moses Austin, from the Spanish government previous to the Independence of Mexico, and has succeeded by surmounting those difficulties and dangers incident to all new and wilderness countries infested with hostile Indians. These difficulties were many and at times appalling, and can only be appreciated by the hardy pioneers of this western country, who have passed through similar scenes.

The question here naturally occurs, what inducements, what prospects, what hopes could have stimulated us, the pioneers and settlers of Texas, to remove from the midst of civilized society, to expatriate ourselves from this land of liberty, from this our native country, endeared to us as it was, and still is, and ever will be, by the ties of nativity, the reminiscences of childhood and youth and local attachments, of friendship and kindred? Can it for a moment be supposed that we severed all these ties—the ties of nature and of education, and went to Texas to grapple with the wilderness and with savage foes, merely from a spirit of wild and visionary adventure, without guarantees of protection for our persons and property and political rights? No, it cannot be believed. No American, no Englishman, no one of any nation who has a knowledge of the people of the United States, or of the prominent characteristics of the Anglo-Saxon race to which we belong—a race that in all ages and in all countries wherever it has appeared has been marked for a jealous and tenacious watchfulness of its liberties, and for a cautious and calculating view of the probable events of the future—no one who has a knowledge of this race can or will believe that we removed to Texas without such guarantees, as free born and enterprising men naturally expect and require.

The fact is, we had such guarantees; for, in the first place the government bound itself to protect us by the mere act of admitting us as citizens, on the general and long established principle, even in the dark ages, that protection and allegiance are reciprocal—a principle which in this enlightened age has been extended much further; for its received interpretation now is, that the object of government is the well being, security, and happiness of the governed, and that allegiance ceases whenever it is clear, evident, and palpable, that this object is in no respect effected.

But besides this general guarantee, we had others of a special, definite, and positive character—the colonization laws of 1823, '24, and '25, inviting emigrants generally to that country, especially guaranteed protection for person and property, and the right of citizenship.

When the federal system and constitution were adopted in 1824, and the former provinces became states, Texas, by her representative in the constituent congress, exercised the right which was claimed and exercised by all the provinces, of retaining within her own control, the rights and powers which appertained to her as one of the unities or distinct societies, which confederated together to form the federal republic of Mexico. But not possessing at that time sufficient population to become a state by herself, she was with her own consent, united provisionally with Coahuila, a neighbouring province or society, to form the state of COAHUILA AND TEXAS, "until Texas possessed the necessary elements to form a separate state of herself." I quote the words of the constitutional or organic act passed by the constituent congress of Mexico, on the 7th of May, 1824, which establishes the state of Coahuila and Texas. This law, and the principles on which the Mexican federal compact was formed, gave to Texas a specific political existence, and vested in her inhabitants the special and well defined rights of self-government as a state of the Mexican confederation, so soon as she "possessed the necessary elements." Texas consented to the provisional union with Coahuila on the faith of this guarantee. It was therefore a solemn compact, which neither the state of Coahuila and Texas, nor the general government of Mexico, can change without the consent of the people of Texas.

In 1833 the people of Texas, after a full examination of their population and resources, and of the law and constitution, decided, in general convention elected for that purpose, that the period had arrived contemplated by said law and compact of 7th May, 1824, and that the country possessed the necessary elements to form a state separate from Coahuila. A respectful and humble petition was accordingly drawn up by this convention, addressed to the general congress of Mexico, praying for the admission of Texas into the Mexican confederation as a state. I had the honor of being appointed by the convention the commissioner or agent of Texas to take this petition to the city of Mexico, and present it to the government. I discharged this duty to the best of my feeble abilities, and, as I believed, in a respectful manner. Many months passed and nothing was done with the petition, except to refer it to a committee of congress, where it slept and was likely to sleep. I finally urged the just and constitutional claims of Texas to become a state in the most pressing manner, as I believed it to be my duty to do; representing also the necessity and good policy of this measure, owning to the almost total want of local government of any kind, the absolute want of a judiciary, the evident impossibility of being governed any longer by Coahuila, (for three fourths of the legislature were from there,) and the consequent anarchy and discontent that existed in Texas. It was my misfortune to offend the high authorities of the nation—my frank and honest exposition of the truth was construed into threats.

At this time (September and October, 1833,) a revolution was raging in many parts of the nation, and especially in the vicinity of the city of Mexico. I despaired of obtaining anything, and wrote to Texas, recommending to the people there to organize as a state de facto without waiting any longer. This letter may have been imprudent, as respects the injury it might do me personally, but how far it was criminal or treasonable, considering the revolutionary state of the whole nation, and the peculiar claims and necessities of Texas, impartial men must decide. It merely expressed an opinion. This letter found its way from San Antonio de Bexar, (where it was directed) to the government. I was arrested at Saltillo, two hundred leagues from Mexico, on my way home, taken back to that city and imprisoned one year, three months of the time in solitary confinement, without books or writing materials, in a dark dungeon of the former inquisition prison. At the close of the year I was released from confinement, but detained six months in the city on heavy ball. It was nine months after my arrest before I was officially informed of the charges against me, or furnished with a copy of them. The constitutional requisites were not observed, my constitutional rights as a citizen were violated, the people of Texas were outraged by this treatment of their commissioner, and their respectful, humble and just petition was disregarded.

These acts of the Mexican government, taken in connection with many others and with the general revolutionary situation of the interior of the republic, and the absolute want of local government in Texas, would have justified the people of Texas in organizing themselves as a State of the Mexican confederation, and if attacked for so doing in separating from Mexico. They would have been justifiable in doing this, because such acts were unjust, ruinous and oppressive, and because self-preservation required a local government in Texas suited to the situation and necessities of the country, and the character of its inhabitants. Our forefathers in '76 flew to arms for much less. They resisted a principle, "the theory of oppression," but in our case it was the reality—it was a denial of justice and of our guarantied rights—it was oppression itself.

Texas, however, even under these aggravated circumstances forbore and remained quiet. The constitution, although outraged and the sport of faction and revolution, still existed in name, and the people of Texas still looked to it with the hope that it would be sustained and executed, and the vested rights of Texas respected. I will now proceed to show how this hope was defeated by the total prostration of the constitution, the destruction of the federal system, and the dissolution of the federal compact.

It is well knows that Mexico has been in constant revolutions and confusion, with only a few short intervals, ever since its separation from Spain in 1821. This unfortunate state of things has been produced by the effects of the ecclesiastical and aristocratical party to oppose republicanism, overturn the federal system and constitution, and establish a monarchy, or a consolidated government of some kind.

In 1834, the President of the Republic, Gen. Santa Anna, who heretofore was the leader and champion of the republican party and system, became the head and leader of his former antagonists—the aristocratic and church party. With this accession of strength, this party triumphed. The constitutional general Congress of 1834, which was decidedly republican and federal, was dissolved in May of that year by a military order of the President before its constitutional term had expired. The council of government composed of half the Senate which, agreeably to the constitution, ought to have been installed the day after closing the session of Congress, was also dissolved; and a new, revolutionary, and unconstitutional Congress was convened by another military order of the President. This Congress met on the 1st of January, 1835. It was decidedly aristocratic, ecclesiastical and central in its politics. A number of petitions were presented to it from several towns and villages, praying that it would change the federal form of government and establish a central form. These petitions were all of a revolutionary character, and were called "pronunciamientos," or pronouncements for centralism. They were formed by partial and revolutionary meetings gotten up by the military and priests. Petitions in favour of the federal system and constitution, and protests against such revolutionary measures, were also sent in by the people and by some of the State Legislatures, who still retained firmness to express their opinions. The latter were disregarded and their authors persecuted and imprisoned. The former were considered sufficient to invest Congress with plenary powers. It accordingly, by a decree, deposed the constitutional Vice President, Gomez Farias, who was a leading federalist, without any impeachment or trial, or even the form of a trial, and elected another of their own party, Gen. Barragan, in his place. By another decree it united the Senate with the House of Representatives in one chamber, and thus constituted, it declared itself invested with full powers as a national convention. In accordance with these usurped powers, it proceeded to annul the federal constitution and system, and to establish a central or consolidated government. How far it has progressed in the details of this new system is unknown to us. The decree of the 3d of October last, which fixes the outlines of the new government, is however sufficient to show that the federal system and compact is dissolved and centralism established. The States are converted into departments.

GLOSSARY

appertained: rightfully belonged

Bexar: short form of San Antonio's original name, San Antonio de Béxar

Gen. Barragan: Miguel Barragán (1789–1836), a Mexican general who also served as interim president

Gen. Santa Anna: Antonio López de Santa Anna (1794–1876), president of Mexico both before and after Barragán, best remembered for his infamous clash with the Texans at the Alamo

organic act: an act that institutes a fundamental aspect of government, such as establishing a territory

plenary: absolute and unchecked

Rio Bravo del Norta: the Mexican name for the Rio Grande, the river that forms the present-day border between Mexico and Texas

Document Analysis

Stephen F. Austin spoke before a crowd in Louisville, Kentucky, describing the plight of the newly declared Republic of Texas and making the case for its complete independence from Mexico. To him, the government of Mexico had no recourse to challenge the Texans' decision; in fact, the government's actions had precipitated the colonists' pursuit of freedom. The available resources make it difficult to determine who exactly made up the audience for this speech, but it is clear that Austin possessed a strong desire to set the record straight. He opened by saying, "The public has been informed, through the medium of the newspapers, that war exists between the people of Texas and the present government of Mexico"; although his speech then describes how this has been misconstrued, Texas was indeed at war with Mexico. A crucial event in Texan history had occurred the day before Austin gave this speech, though he made no references to it; it is unclear whether he had yet received news of the Battle of the Alamo.

The Alamo

The Alamo is an integral part of Texas, both its history and its culture. Originally a mission, the Alamo, also referred to as the Mission San Antonio de Valero, was for the Texan side a symbol of the battle lines in the ensuing conflicts with the Mexican army. For two of the three men most associated with its defense, there was mixed communication from the start as to what exactly to do with the old mission. James Bowie, under direction from General Sam Houston, was determined to destroy it before leaving, as he saw the Alamo as difficult to defend; however, his attitude soon changed. William Barret Travis wanted to defend the fort, but he, like Bowie before him, realized it held far too few men to do so. In a letter later echoed by pleas from Travis, Bowie wrote, "Our force is very small; the returns this day to the commandant is only hundred and twenty officers and men. . . . It would be a waste of men to put our brave little band against thousands" (qtd. in Brands 340). Bowie and Travis, who held joint leadership over those stationed at the Alamo, were severely outnumbered by Santa Anna and the Mexican army, which has been estimated at approximately five thousand troops.

In the end, the men defending the Alamo could not fend off the troops surrounding them. Historian Richard Flores details the scene at the old mission: "Upon arriving, Santa Anna orders the men in the Alamo to surrender. Unwilling to do so, Travis answers with a canon [*sic*] shot aimed at the Mexican forces" ("Alamo" 93). The men in the Alamo made their choice, and surrender was not an option. The final battle on March 6, 1836, saw the fall of approximately two hundred men, including Travis and Bowie, as well as the illustrious Davy Crockett. In his detailed account of Texas's fight against Mexico for freedom, historian H. W. Brands states that while Santa Anna proved his military might against the mission in San Antonio de Béxar that day, his success was a veneer, as it merely handed the Texans "a rallying cry that lifted their political struggle against Santa Anna to the moral realm. . . . Santa Anna's great blunder at Béxar was not to lose so many of his own men but to kill so many of the enemy (and after the battle to burn their bodies, which added to the sacrificial significance)" (378).

Texas from Wilderness to Colonization

Although hostilities with the Mexican army were known to Austin at the time of his speech, he chose instead to focus on what he and others had brought to the Mexican territory of Texas. He may have chosen this approach in order to present Texas's bid for independence as a measured decision, rather than as simply the result of provocation due to armed conflict. This approach lent more credibility to their cause, especially given Austin's past: he had led the first legal settlement within the territory; therefore, no one else possessed more authority to speak on the subject than he. In his speech, Austin said, "The government opened Texas for settlement. Foreign emigrants were invited and called to that country. American enterprise accepted the invitation and promptly responded to the call. The first colony of Americans or foreigners ever settled in Texas was by myself." Historian Sam W. Haynes writes that the Mexican government was highly interested and invested in empresarios bringing in settlers; each empresario was obligated to "bring at least one hundred families to settle the area within a six-year period," and to fulfill their mission, the empresarios were given vast land grants (57). In an effort to preserve heritage and cultural values, the government issued two stipulations that the settlers were to abide by and that, presumably, each individual empresario was required to enforce: they had to be Roman Catholics (or agree to convert), and they had to become Mexican citizens. Given the generous endowments of land the Mexican government was offering in order to bring in a population, most were willing to adhere to these requirements. However, as time went on and more settlers began arriving, more and more of them proved resistant to the government's conditions. Haynes writes that Austin tried valiantly to carry out his obligations as an empresario, but "the challenge of turning [the settlers] into loyal Mexican citizens . . . proved more difficult. . . . Anglo-Texans possessed neither the resources nor the inclination to abide by the Mexican government's insistence on building Spanish-speaking schools and Catholic churches" (57).

Immigration from the United States into Texas came to a halt in April 1830, nearly a decade after Austin's first settlement. A Mexican official, Manuel de Mier y Terán, had made a visit to the territory two years before and was appalled by what he saw; there had been little attempt by the colonists to observe the precepts set down by the officials and particularly a lack of respect toward acculturation, inclining the colony dangerously toward what Mexico did not want to happen: the acquisition of Texas by the United States. Haynes closes his article by stating that the banning of new settlements in the territory, as well as the abolition of slavery—then a highly heated topic within the US government—led directly to the fight for Texan independence.

Texans vs. the Mexican Government: Who Was to Blame?

In Austin's speech, he averred that he had done much for the Mexican government, turning Texas from a "wilderness" to a civilized society where the people had no fear of Indian raids; his speech specifically named the Comanche tribe as one that caused problems. He also brought the settlers the Mexican government had requested, thereby creating a thriving population of fresh Mexican citizens. Mexico failed to uphold its end of the bargain by not providing a stable government: "The constitutional general Congress of 1834 . . . was dissolved in May of that year by a military order of the President before its constitutional term had expired. The council of government composed of half the Senate . . . was also dissolved." To Austin's way of thinking, what good would the colonies be if there was not a proper overall structure and legislation in place for the populace?

However, Stephen Austin's claim that Mexico was pushing Texas toward independence leaves out a critical detail. Austin, like his father before him, had assured Mexican officials that those signed on to move to the settlements either would already be professed Roman Catholics or would become so, and that they would become Mexican citizens, with the attendant adoption of associated cultural factors. As Mier y Terán had observed, these conditions had not been upheld. In this regard, whether due to the empresarios' reluctance to hold the new colonists to the rules requested by the government or the colonists' resistance to such regulations, Stephen Austin and the other empresarios had not fulfilled their part of the bargain.

Despite this, Austin's argument about being let down by officials holds the most sway. No society can adequately be provided for without the support of a stable government. The repeated actions of the Mexican officials left the settlers with little confidence in those in power, as the balance shifted again and again among a mix of faces and offices. As already mentioned, Mexico greatly feared the annexation of Texas by the United States, which would have cost the nation a great territory. However, given the lack of a consistent administration, the loss of Texas was perhaps not surprising.

Essential Themes

There are recurring references throughout Austin's speech to "our forefathers." His choice of words is clever: by using the word "our," he includes his audience in the Texans' plight. The audience, hearing the references to the revolution, may have held that parallel in their minds throughout his speech, ensuring empathy in the hearts of his listeners. Here was semiautonomous, English-speaking Texas being oppressed by Mexico, its parent country. The people of the United States, previously under the yoke of England, had risen up and broken away; such a nation would sympathize with the plight of Texas. At one point in his speech, Austin went further, suggesting that the Texans had a stronger case for independence: "Our forefathers in '76 flew to arms for much less. They resisted a principle, 'the theory of oppression,' but in our case it was the reality—it was a denial of justice and of our guarantied rights—it was oppression itself." Although it is unknown how effective Austin's speech would have been if the tragedy at the Alamo had not occurred, or even what it lent to their cause overall along with the massacre, the Texans did find their support. The Republic of Texas was a separate entity in North America for nine years before being granted US statehood in 1845. The endeavors of Stephen Austin, William Travis, James Bowie, Davey Crockett, and Sam Houston have not been forgotten in the state. Their names have been enshrined in history, and Texans continue to hold them in the highest esteem.

Jennifer L. Henderson Crane, PgDip

Bibliography

Austin, Stephen F. "Address of the Honorable S. F. Austin, Delivered at Louisville, Kentucky, March 7, 1836." *PBS: New Perspectives on the West*. West Film Proj. and WETA, 2001. Web. 13 Mar. 2013.

Barker, Eugene C. "Austin, Stephen Fuller." *The Handbook of Texas Online*. Texas State Hist. Assn., n.d. Web. 13 Mar. 2013.

The Biographical Encyclopedia of Texas. New York: Southern, 1880. *The Portal to Texas History*. Web. 13 Mar. 2013.

Brands, H. W. *Lone Star Nation: The Epic Story of the Battle for Texas Independence*. New York: Anchor, 2005. Print.

Flores, Richard R. "The Alamo: Myth, Public History, and the Politics of Inclusion." *Radical History Review* 77 (2000): 91–103. Print.

---. "Memory-Place, Meaning, and the Alamo." *American Literary History* 10.3 (1998): 428–45. Print.

Haynes, Sam W. "'To Colonize 500 Families . . . Catholics, and of Good Morals': Stephen Austin and the Anglo-American Immigration to Texas, June 4, 1825." *OAH Magazine of History* 19.6 (2005): 57. Print.

Sherrod, Rick. "The Road from Nacogdoches to Natchitoches: John Sprowl & the Failed Fredonian Rebellion." *East Texas Historical Journal* 48.2 (2010): 9–40. Print.

"Stephen F. Austin." *San Jacinto Museum of History*. San Jacinto Museum of Hist., n.d. Web. 13 Mar. 2013.

Additional Readings

Barton, Betty. "Stephen F. Austin's Arrest and Imprisonment in Mexico, 1834–1835." *Texana* 11.1 (1973): 1–17. Print.

Davis, William C. *Three Roads to the Alamo: The Lives and Fortunes of David Crockett, James Bowie, and William Barret Travis*. New York: Harper, 1998. Print.

Donovan, James. *The Blood of Heroes: The 13-Day Struggle for the Alamo—and the Sacrifice That Forged a Nation*. New York: Little, 2012. Print.

Fehrenbach, T. R. *Lone Star: A History of Texas and the Texans*. Boulder: Da Capo, 2000. Print.

Jones, Robert, and Pauline H. Jones. "Stephen F. Austin in Arkansas." *Arkansas Historical Quarterly* 25.4 (1966): 336–53. Print.

---. "Stephen F. Austin in Missouri." *Texana* 3.1 (1965): 44–59. Print.

LESSON PLAN: **Independent Nation or New State?**

Students analyze Stephen Austin's speech, examine Texas's struggles for independence, and evaluate Texas's path to statehood and its impact on sectional differences and Manifest Destiny.

Learning Objectives

Analyze multiple causation of the Texas War for Independence and the Mexican-American War; consider multiple perspectives on the Mexican-American War; compare and contrast differing sets of ideas to analyze how debates over slavery strained national cohesiveness; differentiate between historical facts and interpretations to assess democracy in the West.

Materials: Stephen Austin's "On Texan Independence" (1836); excerpts from William Henry Seward's "On the Irrepressible Conflict" (1858)

Overview Questions

How does Austin justify Texas's War for Independence? How does Austin's speech provide insight into the causes of the Mexican-American War? Who does Austin consider a Texan? Why is this important in the context of events leading up to the Civil War? From Austin's speech, what can we learn about democracy in the West? About Manifest Destiny's influence on the nation?

Step 1: Comprehension Questions

What evidence does Austin provide to justify his claim that "our cause . . . is the cause of light and liberty"? Is Austin's argument effective? Why or why not?

- **Activity:** Have students identify and evaluate Austin's use of language; have small groups use Austin's speech as a starting point for a close examination of Texas's War for Independence.

Step 2: Comprehension Questions

How does Austin connect Texas's War for Independence to the American Revolution? How valid are Austin's connections and why? What insights into the Mexican-American War can we gain from Austin's speech?

- **Activity:** Have students complete Venn diagrams to compare and contrast Texas's War for Independence and the American Revolution; have students present and discuss their diagrams in small groups.

Step 3: Context Questions

Austin characterizes Texans as belonging to "the Anglo-Saxon race"; how does Austin's characterization help us better understand sectional differences leading up to the Civil War? What insights into sectional differences do we gain from Seward's speech?

- **Activity:** Have students compare and contrast the two speeches; have students explore other historical documents to evaluate how Texas's path to statehood affected national cohesion.

Step 4: Exploration Questions

Does Austin's speech reveal limits to democracy in the West? Why or why not? What does it tell us about Manifest Destiny's influence on Americans in the 1800s?

- **Activity:** Assign small groups a Western state to research and evaluate its political democracy; have groups present their findings; hold a class discussion about the degree to which democracy was characteristic of the West.

Step 5: Response Paper

Word length and additional requirements set by Instructor. Students answer the research question in the *Overview Questions*. Students state a thesis and use as evidence passages from the primary source document as well as support from supplemental materials assigned in the lesson.

■ A Foreigner in My Own Land

Date: 1842
Author Name: Seguin, Juan Nepomuceno
Genre: memoir; diary

"I had to leave Texas, abandon all, for which I fought and spent my fortune, then become a wanderer . . . I was in this country a being out of the pale of society, and when she could not protect the rights of her citizens, they seek protection elsewhere. I had been tried by a rabble, condemned without a hearing, and consequently was at liberty to provide for my own safety."

Summary Overview

Seguín's memoir illustrates how a prominent figure in Texas history became denigrated and marginalized in the grand historical narrative; it exposes the shifting sociocultural and political milieu occurring in the Southwest as American foreign policy called for westward expansion during the nineteenth century. Authored by Juan Nepomuceno Seguín—a native and former mayor of San Antonio, Texas—this excerpt attempts to vindicate his purported betrayal of Texas through a detailed recounting of the events that occurred and the players responsible for the decline of his public image.

Once a reliable compatriot in the fight for Texan independence, Seguín quickly became viewed as a traitor and was forced out of Texas without due process. He alludes to the racial undertones of his treatment, which reflects the broader sociocultural trends occurring during this period of rapid expansion when white colonists clashed with natives on the North American continent. Several Tejanos (Mexican Texans) bravely fought for independence for Texas but were subsequently relegated to second-class status in the new Republic of Texas. The desire for white hegemony and an Anglo (i.e., Anglo-American) culture necessitated the removal of Tejanos like Seguín who possessed political clout. This excerpt alludes to Seguín's value to Texas during the revolution and insinuates that the cause of his downfall lay in his status as a Tejano who possessed power in a land the Anglos so desperately wanted. His detailed account of the events surrounding his abrupt transformation into a foreigner in his own land elucidates the shifting political, socioeconomic, and cultural structures wrought by Manifest Destiny and its detrimental effects on nonwhite citizens. Such structures left an enduring legacy on the land and illustrate the roots of a racial status quo that many feel has endured into the present day.

Defining Moment

During the nineteenth century, the United States experienced significant internal tensions brought about by a foreign policy of expansion and conquest, symbolized in the 1872 allegorical painting *American Progress* by artist John Gast.

The term "Manifest Destiny," first coined by John O'Sullivan in a 1845 newspaper article, is the belief that the United States was destined and divinely ordained to expand across the North American continent to cover the land from the Atlantic Ocean to the Pacific Ocean. This concept necessitated a reimagination of land as vacant despite the presence of peoples who had resided on it for centuries. Seguín's excerpt alludes to the adverse affects of westward movement and the thirst for land and power that resulted in heightened tensions between Anglos and native peoples.

Antagonism towards Seguín and his fellow Tejanos undergirded the complicated and contested image of Seguín as a traitor, despite his heroism and his role in the Texas Revolution. As the United States expanded westward, Texas had a unique political function, and the imminent battles over the territory provided a stage for Seguín to craft his identity in the minds of Texans and Mexicans.

The Texas Revolution of the 1830s and the events that followed serve to demonstrate American exceptionalism and the swiftly changing political, social, and cultural milieu occurring on the American frontier. The shifting conditions were caused primarily by heavy Anglo migration into Texas, which altered the balance of power and created a venue for white hegemony. Following the Texas Revolution (and after Seguín fled to Mexico), the remaining Tejanos who had fought for Texan independence at first enjoyed some political clout in the new republic. Before long, however, they suffered from arbitrary governmental seizures of their land, livestock, and food. They were treated as second-class citizens, and after Mexico twice invaded Texas during the 1840s, Tejanos—by virtue of their ethnicity—were viewed as aliens in their homeland. The new constitution codified this second-class citizenship by denying the protection of guaranteed rights and land grants to those who did not support the revolution. All Tejanos were categorized as traitors unless they could show clear proof they were not. Additionally, Tejanos who left Texas during the revolution were considered aliens upon their return.

The stipulations set forth in the constitution engendered violence against Tejanos, including lynchings and riots, that ultimately led to the reduction of the Tejano population in Texas. This serves as a microcosm for the changes wrought by Manifest Destiny and the chafing of clashing cultures. The acquisition of land became central to the ideology of Manifest Destiny, and land occupation produced serious sociocultural and political changes. After the annexation of Mexican territory at the conclusion of the Mexican-American War, an anti-Mexican sentiment permeated US society and stigmatized Mexican Americans as perpetual others within American culture. Such sentiments implied that Mexican culture was separate from American culture, thus creating tensions in a region Mexicans had once owned and were native to.

Author Biography

Juan Nepomuceno Seguín was born into a respected and wealthy Tejano family on October 27, 1806, in San Antonio, Texas, to Juan José Maria Erasmo Seguín and María Josefa Becerra during a time when Texas was important politically. Seguín's father and mother operated the post office in the city of Bexar. Juan was the oldest of three children: Tomas, a younger brother who died during infancy, and a younger sister who was born in 1809. Information regarding his early childhood remains scant due to a scarcity of records.

At a young age, Seguín became a provisional mayor, or *alcade*, of San Antonio, and after holding various political offices he played an active role in the Texas Revolution or War for Independence against Mexico. After banding together Tejanos sympathetic to the Anglo cause, Seguín led them against Mexican General Santa Anna in 1835 and participated in the siege of the Alamo the following year, narrowly escaping death. His engagement in the battle risked his family property and fortune, revealing his loyalty to Texas and its severing from Mexican control. Sympathetic to the Anglos in the wake of the revolution, Seguín campaigned for the controversial Texan senator and Anglo military general Sam Houston, which fostered skepticism and feelings of betrayal in the eyes of some Tejanos; Houston ordered Seguín to protect the Mexican frontier from the encroaching Mexican army. Seguín and his Tejano legion contributed to the defeat of Santa Anna's army at the Battle of San Jacinto, which brought the Texan Revolution to an end. The residual effects of the revolution, however, greatly impacted Seguín's position and the place of other Tejanos within Anglo society and the new republic. Mexican armies continued to attempt invasions into Texas, which alienated the Tejanos living there and rendered them suspect as traitors or potential traitors in the eyes of the Anglo government. In 1842, Mexican General Ráfael Vásquez briefly seized control of San Antonio, of which Seguín was then mayor. Although Seguín led a force in pursuit of the retreating Vásquez, he was blamed for the attack and forced to flee to Mexico, dashing his dreams of securing freedom for all Texans, Tejano and Anglo alike. Such realities exasperated Seguín and prompted him to write about his intense feelings of betrayal by those he had perceived as loyal countrymen and comrades.

The Mexican government did not welcome Seguín when he arrived at Nuevo Laredo in 1842. Police officials arrested him and gave him an ultimatum: either he serve in the Mexican army or be sent away for a very long prison sentence. Choosing to join the army, Seguín fought in the Mexican-American War starting in 1846 against the United States. Despite switching sides, Seguín is hailed as a hero for his contributions during the Battle of the Alamo and at San Jacinto. At the conclusion of the war in 1848, Seguín moved back north to his hometown in Texas, but he returned to Mexico in 1867 after continued threats on his life. He then began authoring his *Personal Memoirs of Juan N. Seguín* in an attempt to rectify and rehabilitate his reputation in the eyes of Americans. Concurrently he voiced his aversion to the nebulous position and status of Tejanos in American society; he had become what ethnic studies professor Mae Ngai terms an "impossible subject," or an individual without a country. Unprotected by their US citizenship because of their race, Tejanos exercised minimal political clout and suffered from identity crises as a result of their culture and citizenship. Throughout much of his political and military career, Seguín battled being labeled a traitor by both Anglos and Tejanos. In 1890, Seguín died in Mexico near the Rio Grande and across from the land he had fought so hard to liberate.

HISTORICAL DOCUMENT

The tokens of esteem, arid evidences of trust and confidence, repeatedly bestowed upon me by the Supreme Magistrate, General Rusk, and other dignitaries of the Republic, could not fail to arouse against me much invidious and malignant feeling. The jealousy evinced against me by several officers of the companies recently arrived at San Antonio, from the United States, soon spread amongst the American straggling adventurers, who were already beginning to work their dark intrigues against the native families, whose only crime was, that they owned large tracts of land and desirable property.

John W. Smith, a bitter enemy of several of the richest families of San Antonio, by whom he had been covered with favors, joined the conspiracy which was organized to ruin me.

I will also point out the origin of another enmity which on several occasions, endangered my life. In those evil days, San Antonio was swarming with adventurers from every quarter of the globe. Many a noble heart grasped the sword in the defence of the liberty of Texas, cheerfully pouring out their blood for our cause, and to them everlasting public gratitude is due; but there were also many bad men, fugitives from their country, who found in this land an open field for their criminal designs.

San Antonio claimed then, as it claims now, to be the first city of Texas; it was also the receptacle of the scum of society. My political and social situation, brought me into continual contact with that class of people. At every hour of the day and night, my countrymen ran to me for protection against the assaults or exactions of those adventurers. Sometimes, by persuasion, I prevailed on them to desist; some times, also, force had to be resorted to. How could I have done other wise? Were, not the victims my own countrymen, friends and associates? Could; I leave them defenceless, exposed to the assaults of foreigners, who, on the pretext that they were Mexicans, treated them worse than brutes. Sound reason and the dictates, of humanity would, have precluded a different conduct on my part. . . .

1842. After the retreat of the Mexican army under Santa Anna, until Vasquez invasion in 1842, the war between Texas and Mexico ceased to be carried on actively. Although open commercial intercourse did not exist, it was carried on by smuggling, at which the Mexican authorities used to wink, provided it was not carried on too openly, so as to oblige them to notice it, or so extensively as to arouse their avarice.

In the beginning of this year, I was elected Mayor of San Antonia. Two years previously a gunsmith, named Goodman, had taken possession of certain houses situated on the Military Plaza, which were the property of the city. He used to shoe the horses of the volunteers who passed, through San Antonio, and thus accumulated a debt against the Republic, for the payment of which he applied to the President to give him possession of the buildings referred to, which had always been known as city property.

The board of Aldermen passed a resolution to the effect, that Goodman should be compelled to leave the premises; Goodman resisted, alleging that the houses had been given to him by the President, in payment for public services. The Board could not, of course, acknowledge in the President any power to dispose of the city property, and consequently directed me to carry the resolution into effect. My compliance with the instructions of the Board caused Goodman to become my most bitter and inveterate enemy in the city.

The term for the mortgage that Messrs. Ogden and Howard held on my property, had run out. In order to raise money and comply with my engagements, I determined to go to Mexico for a drove of sheep. But fearful that this new trip would prove as fatal as the one already alluded to, I wrote to General Vasquez, who was then in command of the Mexican frontier, requesting him to give me a pass. The tenor of Vasquez' answer caused me to apprehend that an expedition was preparing against Texas, for the following month of March.

I called, a session of the Board of Aldermen, (of which the Hon. S. A. Maverick was a member,) and laid before them the communication of General Vasquez, stating, that according to my construction of the letter we might soon the approach of the Mexicans.

A few days afterwards, Don José Maria Garcia, of Laredo, came to San Antonio; his report was so circumstantial, as to preclude all possible doubts as to the near approach of Vasquez to San Antonio. Notice was immediately sent to the Government of the impending danger. In the various meetings held to devise means of defence, I expressed my candid opinion as to the impossibility of defending San Antonio. I observed, that for myself; I was going to the town of Seguin, and advised everyone to do the same.

On leaving the city, I passed through a street where some men were making breastworks; I stated to them that I was going to my ranch, and thence to Seguin, in case the Mexican forces should take possession of San Antonio.

From the Nueces river, Vasquez forwarded a proclamation by Arista, to the inhabitants of Texas. I received at my ranch, a bundle of those proclamations, which I transmitted at once to the Corporation of San Antonio.

As soon as Vasquez entered the city, those who had determined upon defending the place, withdrew to Seguin. Amongst them were Dunn and Chevallie, who had succeeded in escaping from the hands of the Mexicans, into which they had fallen while on a reconnoitering expedition on the Medina. The latter told me that Vasquez and his officers stated that I was in favor of the Mexicans; and Chevallie further added that, one day as he was talking with Vasquez, a man, named Sanchez, came within sight, whereupon the General observed: "You see that man! Well, Colonel Seguin sent him to me, when he was at Rio Grande. Seguin is with us." He then drew a letter from his pocket, stating that it was from me. Chevallie asked to be allowed to see it, as he knew my handwriting, but the General refused and cut short the interview.

On my return to San Antonio, several persona told me that the Mexican officers had declared that I was in their favor. This rumor, and some threats uttered against me by Goodman, left me but little doubt that my enemies would try to ruin me.

Some of the citizens of San Antonio had taken up arms in favor of the enemy. Judge Hemphill advised me to have them arrested and tried, but as I started out with the party who went in pursuit of the Mexicans, I could not follow his advice.

Having observed that Vasquez gained ground on us, we fell back on the Nueces river. When we came back, to San Antonio, reports were widely spreading about my pretended treason. Captain Manuel Flores, Lieutenant Ambrosio Rodriguez, Matias Curbier, and five or six other Mexicans, dismounted with me to find out the origin of the imposture. I went out with several friends leaving Curbier in my house. I had reached the Main Plaza, when several persons came running to inform me, that some Americans were murdering Curbier. We ran back to the house, where we found poor Curbier covered with blood. On being asked who assaulted him, he answered, that the gunsmith. Goodman, in company with several Americans, had struck him with a rifle. A few minutes afterwards, Goodman returned to my house, with about thirty volunteers, but, observing that we were prepared to meet them, they did not attempt to attack us. We went out of the house and then to Mr. Guilbeau's, who offered me his protection. He went out into the street, pistol in hand, and succeeded in dispersing the mob, which had formed in front of my house. Mr. John Twohig offered me a shelter for that night; on the next morning, I went under disguise to Mr. Van Ness' house; Twohig, who recognised me in the street, warned me to "open my eyes." I remained one day at Mr. Van Ness'; next day General Burleson arrived at San Antonio, commanding a respectable force of volunteers. I presented myself to him, asking for a Court of Inquiry; he answered, that there were no grounds for such proceedings. In the evening I went to the camp, and jointly with Colonel Patton, received a commission to forage for provisions in the lower ranchos. I complied with this trust.

I remained, hiding from rancho to rancho, for over fifteen days. Every party, of volunteers en route to San Antonio declared, "they wanted to kill Seguin." I could no longer go from farm to farm, and determined to go to my own farm and raise fortifications, &c.

Several of my relatives and friends joined me. Hardly a day elapsed without receiving notice that a party was preparing to attack me; we were constantly kept under arms. Several parties came in sight, but, probably seeing that we were prepared to receive them, refrained from attacking. On the 30th of April, a friend from San Antonio sent me word that Captain Scott, and his company were coming down by the river, burning the ranchos on their way. The inhabitants of the lower ranchos called on us for aid against Scott. With those in my house, and others to the number of about 100, I started to lend them aid. I proceeded, observing the movements of Scott, from the function of the Medina to Pajaritos. At that place we dispersed and I returned to my wretched life. In those days I could not go to San Antonio without peril of my life.

Matters being in this state, I saw that it was necessary to take some step which would place me in security, and save my family from constant wretchedness. I had to leave Texas, abandon all, for which I had fought and spent my fortune, to become a wanderer. The ingratitude of those, who had assumed to themselves the right of convicting me; their credulity in declaring me a traitor, on mere rumors, when I had to plead, in my favor the loyal patriotism with which I had always served Texas, wounded me deeply.

But, before leaving my country, perhaps for ever, I determined to consult with all those interested in my welfare. I held a family council. All were in favor of my removing for some time to the interior of Texas. But, to accomplish this, there were some unavoidable obstacles. I could not take one step from my ranch; towards the Brazos, without being exposed to the rifle of the first person who might meet me, for, through the whole country, credit had been given to the rumors against me. To emigrate with my family was impossible, as I was a ruined man, from the time of the invasion of Santa Anna and our flight to Nacogdoches, furthermore, the country of the Brazos was unhealthier than that of Nacogdoches, and what might, we not expect to suffer from disease in a new country, and without friends or means.

Seeing that all these plans were impracticable, I resolved to seek a refuge amongst my enemies, braving all dangers. But before taking this step, I sent in my resignation to the Corporation of San Antonio, as Mayor of the city, stating to them, that, unable any longer to suffer the persecutions of some ungrateful Americans, who strove to murder me, I had determined to free my family and friends from their continual misery on my account; and go and live peaceably in Mexico. That for these reasons I resigned my office, with all my privileges and honors as a Texan.

I left Bexar without any engagements towards Texas, my services paid by persecutions, exiled and deprived of my privileges as a Texan citizen, I was in this country a being out of the pale of society, and when she could not protect the rights of her citizens, they seek protection elsewhere. I had been tried by a rabble, condemned without a hearing, and consequently was at liberty to provide for my own safety.

GLOSSARY

breastwork: fortifications for defense against an impending attack

credulity: the quality of quickly trusting someone without good reason; the quality of being gullible

enmity: hatred, animosity, or ill will

evince: to show or make clear

inveterate: established, enduring, or persistent

invidious: causing resentment or jealousy

rabble: crowd of disorderly individuals; mob

reccoiter: to inspect in order to gather information for military purposes

Document Analysis

The contradictory image of Juan Nepomuceno Seguín as a traitor and a hero in Texas during the nineteenth century has been debated by historians up to the present day. Seguín's memoir regarding his controversial political and military career illustrates the changes that occurred during a time of expansion across the North American continent that resulted in shifting socioeconomic, political, and cultural structures. As the title suggests, land—Texas and Mexican territory—became crucial to the fulfillment of Manifest Destiny, or the idea that Americans are divinely ordained to expand across the North American continent. Such an ideology called for Anglo settlers to come into contact with native Mexicans, which led to mounting sociocultural tensions as a result of political and economic imperatives. Settlers, or "adventurers," carried with them notions of white hegemony over natives as the American political domain expanded. As a result, nonwhite individuals such as Seguín who possessed status, political clout, and land faced mounting opposition and contempt from their Anglo compatriots.

Around age thirty-five, Seguín was the mayor of San Antonio, a city that was integral to Anglo dreams of fulfilling their Manifest Destiny. Marked a traitor for the majority of his adult life, Seguín sought to clear his name through this deeply passionate memoir in which he elucidated not only the origin of his branding as a traitor but also conveyed his loyalty to his family as a reason for his perceived divided loyalties (which many other Tejanos conveyed and continue to demonstrate into the present day). He uses vivid language that sets up a binary between criminal and hero in order to rehabilitate his legacy as a hero of Texas and a Tejano leader. In this way he seeks to subvert the image of the angelic Anglo settler set against the criminal, brutish native Mexican.

Cultural artifacts produced during the nineteenth century articulated various political sentiments, racial stereotypes, and salient historical inquiries that permeated this period. John Gast's painting *American Progress* conveyed ubiquitous ideas that undergirded Manifest Destiny and Anglo relations with nonwhite natives; Seguín subtly alludes to such ideas in his vindication of his tarnished legacy. Gast's depiction conveys how social characteristics became inscribed on real and imagined space emanating from the notion of Manifest Destiny. He portrays the US nation-state in the symbol of a sexualized, angelic, and white mother figure whose aggressive movement westward conveys a protective posture; built into the construction of whiteness is the notion of purity. She holds books in her hands to demonstrate her knowledge as she moves into corners of the word depicted and racialized as dark and in need of enlightenment. The painting contrasts a progressive, cultured, and divine white race with the dark, backwards, savage, nonwhite, and uncivilized natives. Such attitudes regarding native Mexicans undergirded US treatment of them after the moment of contact and subsequent conquest. The ideology of Manifest Destiny spawned the increasingly tense interactions between westward moving Anglos and the natives residing in formerly Mexican territory in the Southwest as a result of occupied land and racial and cultural differences.

Seguín sets a binary of Anglo settlers as the true "criminals" against the sovereignty of native Tejanos as a way of elevating his heroic status and contesting his image as a traitor. Furthermore, he stressed his loyalty to Texas, to his fellow Tejanos, and to his family, despite constant questioning of his moral character; he left Texas not out of betrayal but to protect his family from the suffering they were enduring as a result of Anglo oppression. Seguín fervently believed in the idea that a Tejano could be proud of his or her national heritage while remaining a "loyal Tejano" (Montejano 26). He heroically fought for Texas during the Texas Revolution out of his loyalty to and love for his native land. However, many Anglo "adventurers" migrating into the land fought for the "liberty of Texas" as a part of their "criminal designs" to steal the land once independence was achieved; Tejano property and life were therefore not secure during this turbulent period. Seguín subverts the image of himself as a traitorous criminal by deflecting such a delineation onto encroaching Anglo settlers through his use of vivid and explicit diction. On the other hand, he also used his position in the government to protect his defenseless countrymen from the criminal activity of and the force used by Anglo adventurers. Seguín does so to emphasize a moral code based on the justice he lived by and acted on. Furthermore, he alludes to the racial undertones of the Anglos' perceived prerogatives in the region as depicted by Gast; Mexicans were viewed and treated as savage "brutes" who were not self-possessed or worthy of owning "desirable property." Additionally, Seguín articulates an image of himself as a victim of this Anglo hatred, brutish treatment, and oppression by top officials to garner sympathy; he left Texas not by choice but out of necessity, to save his family from "enemies trying to ruin" him, and it was he who warned city officials of the advancing Mexican army towards the city, thus constructing himself as a heroic figure.

As a prominent Tejano senator who sympathized with the Anglo government during the Texas Revolution, Seguín endured accusations of being traitor by his fellow Tejanos, while Anglo "dignitaries of the Republic" concurrently treated him with vigilant suspicion. His position as mayor of San Antonio gave him political clout to which Tejanos generally did not have access during this period of American expansion. Although his prominent political position fostered Anglo aversion toward him, most of his purported transgressions emanated out of his actions as a leader in the military. Such disdain and "jealousy" demonstrated by prominent Anglos within the army toward him and his fellow Tejanos for owning land that they felt was ordained for them fostered similar attitudes in the Anglo masses. Property and land formed the roots of his enemies' disdain toward him and other Tejanos, whose "only crime was that they owned large tracts of land and desirable property."

Seguín's work as a land speculator combined with the centrality of land to the ideology of Manifest Destiny also played a huge role in sullying his public image. As a land speculator, Seguín worked for several Anglo detractors who accused him of fraud in his selling land. Many alleged that he would not return money he had confiscated when residing in San Antonio. Seguín asserts that he dealt with land and property disputes according to Texas law and maintained compliance with the directions of the board. However, several of his decisions regarding the land of prominent Anglo families incurred him bitter enemies despite his adherence to legal standards. Following the Texas Revolution, Mexican families living along the Guadalupe and San Antonio rivers experienced high rates of expulsion and land seizures by the Texas government (Montejano 26); Mexicans who remained loyal to Texas rather than Mexico nonetheless endured random acts of violence, land and livestock seizures, and acts of humiliation by people who held anti-Mexican sentiments. By the 1840s, the majority of the prominent Mexican families with Spanish ties had left Texas, either by force or under threat of murder.

The role of land during US expansion with regard to American Indians further helps explain Anglo sentiments toward Seguín and the complicated image he inherited as a result of his social status and land ownership. The colonial relationship between American Indians and Anglo-Americans enabled the US government to strip American Indians of their tribal sovereignty through the dispossession of their culturally sacred, ancestral lands; to do so, a racialized public discourse helped to support various legal precepts that maintained the myth of American Indians as, increasingly, a "vanishing race." Bolstered by the ideological conceits of the myth, white sellers perceived natives as infantilized and impotent in order to refute indigenous land claims and justify European domination. For the United States to become a country ruled by the masculinized "Yankee spirit" of the Euro-American colonist required the extermination of indigenous people, both physically and culturally, from the American landscape. Ultimately, it was the unequal relationship established upon contact that provided the colonists the tools to wipe the American Indians off of their native landscape and ultimately from the American consciousness through reimagining space with regard to racial hierarchies (Espiritu 46). The reimagining of land and space within the United States thus reinforced the white hegemony over the natives' sociocultural systems of native groups and provided an impetus for the cultural genocide of American Indians.

Such processes began to take place upon Anglo advancement into Texan land and infusion into the existing socioeconomic and political systems. Rumors of Seguín's loyalty to the Mexicans destroyed his reputation in the eyes of Texans, both Anglo and Tejano. Seguín describes in anguish the severe danger he and his family faced as the Mexican army threatened to seize San Antonio and several of the surrounding cities. Such daily affliction and peril caused by "mere rumors" forced him to move his family and become "a wanderer" in the land he had served and fought for. His former friends and colleagues turned on him, forcing his family to flee to Mexico while he faced incarceration and forced military service against his former homeland during the Mexican-American War. Seguín invokes his military accolades in the service of Texas and his political accomplishments to emphasize his loyalty and garner more sympathy for his adverse treatment. A loyal and productive citizen, Seguín was betrayed and abandoned by the country he served, and his anguish resonates with the many other Mexican American families betrayed by a country they too served and inhabited for generations.

Throughout this excerpt from Seguín's memoir, it is clear that the sociocultural and political landscapes were drastically shifting as a result of US expansion westward. Mexican Americans became increasingly subordinated to the status of second-class citizens, and they saw their citizenship rights violated without due process. Land grants were violated frequently, and force was often used to seize desired land plots from Mexican families, leaving them no choice but to flee their native land. This process of arbitrarily rendering Mexican Americans stateless for Anglo gain exposes the salient racial antagonisms that characterized this period. A legacy of white supremacy and dispossession rather than one of liberty and justice as the foundation of America emerged out of this hotly contested time. Citizenship for nonwhite individuals—event prominent political figures such as Seguín—did not guarantee the protection of rights codified by the US constitution.

Essential Themes

Juan Nepomuceno Seguín was a Tejano who possessed unusual socioeconomic status and political clout. He lived a patriotic life fighting for Texas, his native land that he served ardently both in the military and in politics. Additionally, he combated an image of himself as a traitor both to his own Mexican heritage and to the land that he served. His conflicted life represents a microcosm of the Tejano experience in Texan regions to the present day, which has inspired cultural articulations of such struggles. In the face of Anglo-American colonization and hegemony in the American Southwest, author Americo Paredes's *George Washington Gomez* (1990) details the struggles of Mexicotexans, as he calls them, to preserve their culture and identity in the face of growing Anglo hegemony in the American Southwest in the early twentieth century.

With the development of railroads in Texas, Anglos migrated into borderland towns and displaced the Tejano power structure; as a result, this demographic shift led to drastic sociocultural and political changes. Paredes's novel centers around a young Mexican-American boy who struggles with his identity while living in Jonesville, a fictional, rural town on the border between Texas and the United States in which the Anglo migrants displaced the Tejanos (Mexicotexans) through settler-colonialism. The colonial processes that take place in Paredes's novel demonstrate that, while this novel typifies the American story between the 1910s and 1940s, the history of Mexicans living in the Southwest suffering violence at the hands of Anglo-Americans shaped an idiosyncratic narrative rooted in vicious oppression that is symbolic of the region and the rendering of native Mexicans as foreigners in their own land. Paredes's novel depicts the idiosyncrasies of life on the borderland caused by colonial structures as a result of Anglo migration and hegemony in a predominately rural region. Nonetheless, the themes and issues raised in *George Washington Gómez*—although set on the Texas borderlands—convey a typical American story by dramatizing the extent to which nativist sentiment undergirded US government policies between the 1910s and the 1940s; thus, Paredes portrays national sociocultural trends on a local level that took root during the period in which Seguín lived; his experiences represented the experiences of Tejanos living in a region in transition.

The violent history between Anglos and Mexicans in the American Southwest resulting in colonial social structures renders regional economic trends as exceptional in comparison to national trends. Paredes's depiction of race in the American Southwest implicates a social system structured by "internal colonialism" that discriminates against individuals of Mexican descent (Ngai). This colonial structure took in the antagonistic relationship between Mexico and the United States as a result of the US annexation of Mexican land following the Mexican-American War in 1848; Paredes's protagonist Feliciano expresses extreme rage over the "gringos" taking Mexican land by force (102). Settler-colonialism is the process by which a hegemonic population occupies space by forcibly removing an inhabiting population. Paredes implicates these colonial processes that structure life for Mexican Americans at the borderland when discussing the significance of chaparral (the shrubland of southern California) to Mexicotexans. Indigenous to the Southwest, chaparral represented the Mexicotexan's "guarantee of freedom" from "alien law" and allowed small farmers to work their own land independently (42). However, once the Americans annexed the Southwest, they developed the land by eradicating the chaparral, which did not benefit them economically; using Mexican labor and paying them barely enough money to subsist, American farmers replaced the chaparral with cotton and citrus orchards (42). American policies such as this suggest that they sought to integrate this region into the global economy both ethnically and economically, and to do so required an eradication of the traditional Mexican way of life. Paredes's projection of Mexicans as colonized individuals within America renders them as an oppressed people in their native land and implicates their subjection to prejudice and violence. The notion that the Mexican family's standard of living was much lower than the Anglo's portrays Mexicans in the rural Southwest as an inferior stock of people compared with their Anglo oppressors (200).

This nativist sentiment experienced by Seguín in his transition into an "impossible subject" survived into the twentieth century and translated into gross civil rights violations during the 1930s and 1940s. Paredes dramatizes the dialogue between the police and a Mexican worker who did not have his documentation papers with him, resulting in his forced repatriation back to Mexico (197). Between five hundred thousand and one million Mexicans and Mexican Americans in California alone had their citizens' rights violated through forced repatriation during the 1930s as a result of job competition during the Great Depression. Economic uncertainties "inflamed racial hostility toward Mexicans," which prompted the deportation and repatriation of Mexicans regardless of citizenship status (Ngai 71). This legacy of nonwhite Americans arbitrarily becoming foreigners in their own land has persisted well into the twentieth and twenty-first centuries. Through his emotional memoirs, Seguín articulated the grief and anger over his tarnished image and second-class citizenship and expressed the experiences of many Tejanos and other nonwhite groups due to Anglo discrimination, which in some ways endures into the present day.

Maddie Weissman, MA

Bibliography

Espiritu, Yen Le. *Home Bound: Filipino American Lives across Cultures, Communities, and Countries*. Berkeley: U of California P, 2009. Print.

Galdeano, Daniel. "Juan Seguín: A Paradox in the Annals of Texas History." *Seguín Family Historical Society*. Seguín Family Historical Society, n.d. Web. 14 Mar. 2013.

Montejano, David. *Anglos and Mexicans in the Making of Texas, 1836–1986*. Austin: U of Texas P, 1994. Print.

Ngai, Mae M. *Impossible Subjects: Illegal Aliens and the Making of Modern America*. Princeton: Princeton UP, 2004. Print.

Paredes, Américo. *George Washington Gómez: A Mexicotexan Novel*. Houston: Arte Publico, 1990. Print.

Seguín, Juan N. "The Fate of the Tejanos, 1858." *American History 135, Primary Documents*. U. of South Alabama, 2009. Web. 14 Mar. 2013.

Additional Reading

Chemerka, William R. *Juan Seguín: Tejano Leader*. Houston: Bright Sky, 2012. Print.

Henderson, Timothy J. *A Glorious Defeat: Mexico and Its War with the United States*. New York: Farrar, 2007. Print.

Weber, David J., ed. *Foreigners in Their Native Land: Historical Roots of the Mexican Americans*. Albuquerque: U of New Mexico P, 1973. Print.

LESSON PLAN: **Who Is a Texan?**

Students analyze Juan Seguín's writings, explore community and citizenship in Texas and the West, and examine different perspectives on the Mexican-American War, Manifest Destiny, and national identity.

Learning Objectives

Examine the influence of ideas to explain Manifest Destiny and how it influenced westward expansion and national identity; consider multiple perspectives on the Mexican-American War; analyze cause-and-effect relationships of expansion and community in the West; differentiate between historical facts and interpretations to assess democracy in the West.

Materials: Juan Seguín, "A Foreigner in My Own Land," from *Personal Memoirs of John N. Seguín* (1842); Stephen Austin, "On Texan Independence" ("Address of the Honorable S. F. Austin, Delivered at Louisville, Kentucky, March 7,1836").

Overview Questions

Why does Seguín believe that he must resign and leave Texas? What insights into the Mexican-American War do Seguín's writings provide? What does Seguín's perspective reveal about community, citizenship, and democracy in the West? Based on Seguín's writing and Austin's speech, how did Manifest Destiny shape westward expansion and America's national identity?

Step 1: Comprehension Questions

According to Seguín, who is "swarming" into Texas and why? What are the effects of this "swarming" on Texas?

- **Activity:** Have students identify examples of Seguín's use of persuasive language; have small groups discuss and evaluate them.

Step 2: Comprehension Questions

After Texas's independence, Mexico recaptured San Antonio and rumors spread that Seguín was "in favor of the Mexicans." What effects did these rumors have on Seguín? Why was Seguín "resolved to seek refuge amongst [his] enemies" rather than seek justice in Texas?

- **Activity:** Have students make a chronological outline of the events Seguín cites as reasons for leaving Texas. Have students define *treason* and discuss how a society can balance security and individual rights.

Step 3: Context Questions

As a *Tejano*, or person of Spanish heritage who calls Texas home, what perspectives on Manifest Destiny can we learn from Seguín? What insights into democracy and citizenship in the West do we learn from Seguín? Why should historians study Seguín's perspectives?

- **Activity:** Have students complete Venn diagrams to compare and contrast the two documents in terms of what they tell us about Manifest Destiny and national identity; have students present and discuss their diagrams in small groups.

Step 4: Exploration Questions

Why would Seguín want Texas to remain an independent country rather than seek statehood? If Texas remained independent, would that have prevented the Mexican-American War? Why or why not?

- **Activity:** Assign small groups other historical documents in order to examine different perspectives on the Mexican-American War, Manifest Destiny, and national identify before the Civil War. Have groups present their findings and discuss them as a class.

Step 5: Response Paper

Word length and additional requirements set by Instructor. Students answer the research question in the *Overview Questions*. Students state a thesis and use as evidence passages from the primary source document as well as support from supplemental materials assigned in the lesson.

Across the Plains in 1844

Date: 1844
Author: Pringle, Catherine Sager
Genre: autobiography; memoir

"Poor child! What will become of you?"

Summary Overview

The piece provided below is from the first chapter of the memoir of Catherine Sager Pringle, written around 1860, though it centers upon events in 1844. Pringle, along with her parents and six siblings, joined hundreds of other families in migrating across the plains in the early 1840s, headed for Oregon. Not yet a part of the United States (it would not achieve statehood until 1859), Oregon was presented as a healthful country with fertile fields. The Sager family, originally from Ohio, set off on their westward trek from St. Joseph, Missouri, a city along the Missouri River that was a popular jumping-off point for the trails toward Oregon and California.

Pringle's memories of the journey westward are highly visual, and they resonate with other journals of those who followed the Overland Trail, a more southern alternative to the Oregon Trail. Her words are even more intriguing given her age of nine years at the time of her family's travels. While her family endured tragedy and heartache, Pringle and three of her siblings did eventually succeed in their mother's hope that they would reach Oregon and a better life, though it was not in the way that Naomi Sager had envisioned.

Defining Moment

For Catherine Sager Pringle's father, Henry, the dream of the West held much promise, and he fully intended that he and his family would reach it and erect a family home that would endure for generations. The climate, advertised as good for one's health and well-being, would greatly improve his wife's strength, and his children would grow with vitality. As he possessed skills both in farming and as a blacksmith, Henry Sager could easily have slotted into a comfortable role within a new community; after all, Pringle wrote that her father "had a wide reputation for ingenuity." Sadly, like so many others who preceded them on the trail west, and the others that followed, Sager did not live to set foot upon Oregon, and neither did his wife. The Sagers planned well, travelling during the optimum time (late spring and summer), but, just like the weather, illness and accidents could not be foreseen.

Oregon Country, later a territory in 1846, was the land held aloft as fresh and open. The fields were lush with flora and fauna, a more picturesque area not to be found elsewhere. The alluring descriptions of Oregon were widespread through the 1830s and 1840s, and soon it reached such a crescendo, as historian Frank McLynn wrote, "that it almost seemed as that the laws of God's universe had been breached and that missionaries had found themselves back in the Garden of Eden" (33). Ginger Wadsworth, in her work *Words West: Voices of Young Pioneers* (2003), quotes Edward Lenox, who rode the Overland Trail with his father, as hearing that, "they do say that out in Oregon, the pigs are running about under the great acorn trees, round and fat, and already cooked, with knives and forks sticking in them" (44).

It is left to history what stories or hyperbole Henry Sager may have heard. Whatever prompted him to relocate his family from Missouri to Oregon, there is little doubt that he held only the best intentions for his family. However, as described by his daughter, the Sagers' overland trip was laden with accidents and tragedy. Knowing his end imminent as he lay dying of typhoid, or what his daughter terms "camp fever," he despaired, "Poor child! What will become of you?" The Sagers did not travel with any relatives, nor did any relatives live in Oregon or other reaches west. Pringle wrote, "His wife was ill, the children small, and one likely to be a cripple," in reference to an injury explained below. It would be left to the charity of strangers among the other travellers and those already in Oregon to care for Sager's seven children.

Author Biography

Catherine Sager Pringle, born on the fifteenth of April in 1835, holds a secure place in the history of American westward migration. Though she provides history with a rich recounting of her journey, she neglects or simply chooses not to include a narrative of her life before the family's decision to relocate. One of seven children (two sons, five daughters) born to Henry and Naomi Sager, Pringle survived the trek to Oregon, but at a severe price. Accidents were certainly common enough in everyday life, but even more so along the Overland Trail, especially for those unused to a nomadic life as part of a caravan. Parents were busy with a variety of duties—aside from driving the wagons and animals—to get their families through each day. On the first of August, roughly four months along the trail, Pringle leaped from the wagon while it was still in motion, but the hem of her dress "caught on an axe handle and the wagon wheels ran over her, crushing her legs" (McFlynn 208). Of the accident, Pringle wrote that her father "picked me up and saw the extent of the injury when the injured limb hung dangling in the air. In a broken voice he exclaimed, 'My dear child, your leg is broken all to pieces!'" Though the leg was set, Pringle had to ride inside the wagon for the duration of the trip. Within less than a month, worse occurrences followed.

Both parents died of typhoid within weeks of each other, leaving Pringle and her siblings orphans. Before Henry Sager's death, he spoke to the wagon train's captain, William Shaw, and begged that he bring his family to the mission run by Dr. Marcus Whitman and Narcissa Whitman in Oregon, which was established in the region of Waiilatpu. Following Naomi Sager's death in September of 1844, the Shaws installed themselves as temporary guardians of the seven orphans until they met with the Whitmans the following month. Sadly, the tragedy of the Sager orphans did not end with their adoption by the Whitmans. Three years later, in November 1847, the Whitman mission was attacked by a branch of the Cayuse Indian tribe. Both Dr. and Mrs. Whitman were among the dead, as were the two Sager boys, John and Francis. Louisa, still a young child, succumbed to disease, leaving Catherine, Elizabeth, Matilda, and Henrietta, the baby born on the trail. Catherine, along with Elizabeth and Matilda, lived to old age, passing away in 1910 in her mid-seventies.

HISTORICAL DOCUMENT

CHAPTER I: ON THE PLAINS IN 1844

My father was one of the restless ones who are not content to remain in one place long at a time. Late in the fall of 1838 we emigrated from Ohio to Missouri. Our first halting place was on Green River, but the next year we took a farm in Platte County. He engaged in farming and blacksmithing, and had a wide reputation for ingenuity. Anything they needed, made or mended, sought his shop. In 1843, Dr. Whitman came to Missouri. The healthful climate induced my mother to favor moving to Oregon. Immigration was the theme all winter, and we decided to start for Oregon. Late in 1843 father sold his property and moved near St. Joseph, and in April, 1844, we started across the plains. The first encampments were a great pleasure to us children. We were five girls and two boys, ranging from the girl baby to be born on the way to the oldest boy, hardly old enough to be any help.

STARTING ON THE PLAINS

We waited several days at the Missouri River. Many friends came that far to see the emigrants start on their long journey, and there was much sadness at the parting, and a sorrowful company crossed the Missouri that bright spring morning. The motion of the wagon made us all sick, and it was weeks before we got used to the seasick motion. Rain came down and required us to tie down the wagon covers, and so increased our sickness by confining the air we breathed.

Our cattle recrossed in the night and went back to their winter quarters. This caused delay in recovering them and a weary, forced march to rejoin the train. This was divided into companies, and we were in that commanded by William Shaw. Soon after starting Indians raided our camp one night and drove off a number of cattle. They were pursued, but never recovered.

Soon everything went smooth and our train made steady headway. The weather was fine and we enjoyed the journey pleasantly. There were several musical instruments among the emigrants, and these sounded clearly on the evening air when camp was made and merry talk and laughter resounded from almost every camp-fire.

INCIDENTS OF TRAVEL

We had one wagon, two steady yoke of old cattle, and several of young and not well-broken ones. Father was no ox driver, and had trouble with these until one day he called on Captain Shaw for assistance. It was furnished by the good captain pelting the refractory steers with stones until they were glad to come to terms.

Reaching the buffalo country, our father would get someone to drive his team and start on the hunt, for he was enthusiastic in his love of such sport. He not only killed the great bison, but often brought home on his shoulder the timid antelope that had fallen at his unerring aim, and that are not often shot by ordinary marksmen. Soon after crossing South Platte the unwieldy oxen ran on a bank and overturned the wagon, greatly injuring our mother. She lay long insensible in the tent put up for the occasion.

August 1st we nooned in a beautiful grove on the north side of the Platte. We had by this time got used to climbing in and out of the wagon when in motion. When performing this feat that afternoon my dress caught on an axle helve and I was thrown under the wagon wheel, which passed over and badly crushed my limb before father could stop the team. He picked me up and saw the extent of the injury when the injured limb hung dangling in the air.

THE FATHER DYING ON THE PLAINS

In a broken voice he exclaimed: "My dear child, your leg is broken all to pieces!" The news soon spread along the train and a halt was called. A surgeon was found and the limb set; then we pushed on the same night to Laramie, where we arrived soon after dark. This accident confined me to the wagon the remainder of the long journey.

After Laramie we entered the great American desert, which was hard on the teams. Sickness became common. Father and the boys were all sick, and we were dependent for a driver on the Dutch doctor who set my leg. He offered his services and was employed, but though an excellent surgeon, he knew little about driving oxen. Some of them often had to rise from their sick beds to wade streams and get the oxen safely across. One day four buffalo ran between our wagon and the one behind. Though feeble, father seized his gun and gave chase to them. This imprudent act prostrated him again, and it soon became apparent that his days were numbered. He was fully conscious of the fact, but could not be reconciled to the thought of leaving his large and helpless family in such precarious circumstances. The evening before his death we crossed Green River and camped on the bank. Looking where I lay helpless, he said: "Poor child! What will become of you?" Captain Shaw found him weeping bitterly. He said his last hour had come, and his heart was filled with anguish for his family. His wife was ill, the children small, and one likely to be a cripple. They had no relatives near, and a long journey lay before them. In piteous tones he begged the Captain to take charge of them and see them through. This he stoutly promised. Father was buried the next day on the banks of Green River. His coffin was made of two troughs dug out of the body of a tree, but next year emigrants found his bleaching bones, as the Indians had disinterred the remains.

We hired a young man to drive, as mother was afraid to trust the doctor, but the kindhearted German would not leave her, and declared his intention to see her safe in the Willamette. At Fort Bridger the stream was full of fish, and we made nets of wagon sheets to catch them. That evening the new driver told mother he would hunt for game if she would let him use the gun. He took it, and we never saw him again. He made for the train in advance, where he had a sweetheart. We found the gun waiting our arrival at Whitman's. Then we got along as best we could with the doctor's help.

Mother planned to get to Whitman's and winter there, but she was rapidly failing under her sorrows. The nights and mornings were very cold, and she took cold from the exposure unavoidably. With camp fever and a sore mouth, she fought bravely against fate for the sake of her children, but she was taken delirious soon after reaching Fort Bridger, and was bed-fast. Travelling in this condition over a road clouded with dust, she suffered intensely. She talked of her husband, addressing him as though present, beseeching him in piteous tones to relieve her sufferings, until at last she became unconscious. Her babe was cared for by the women of the train. Those kind-hearted women would also come in at night and wash the dust from the mother's face and otherwise make her comfortable. We travelled a rough road the day she died, and she moaned fearfully all the time. At night one of the women came in as usual, but she made no reply to questions, so she thought her asleep, and washed her face, then took her hand and discovered the pulse was nearly gone. She lived but a few moments, and her last words were, "Oh, Henry! If you only knew how we have suffered." The tent was set up, the corpse laid out, and next morning we took the last look at our mother's face. The grave was near the road; willow brush was laid in the bottom and covered the body, the earth filled in—then the train moved on.

Her name was cut on a headboard, and that was all that could be done. So in twenty-six days we became orphans. Seven children of us, the oldest fourteen and the youngest a babe. A few days before her death, finding herself in possession of her faculties and fully aware of the coming end, she had taken an affectionate farewell of her children and charged the doctor to take care of us. She made the same request of Captain Shaw. The baby was taken by a woman in the train, and all were literally adopted by the company. No one there but was ready to do us any possible favor. This was especially true of Captain Shaw and his wife. Their kindness will ever be cherished in grateful remembrance by us all. Our parents could not have been more solicitous or careful. When our flour gave out they gave us bread as long as they had any, actually dividing their last loaf. To this day Uncle Billy and Aunt Sally, as we call them, regard us with the affection of parents. Blessings on his hoary head!

At Snake River they lay by to make our wagon into a cart, as our team was wearing out. Into this was loaded what was necessary. Some things were sold and some left on the plains. The last of September we arrived at Grande Ronde, where one of my sister's clothes caught fire, and she would have burned to death only that the German doctor, at the cost of burning his hands, saved her. One night the captain heard a child crying, and found my little sister had got out of the wagon and was perishing in the freezing air, for the nights were very cold. We had been out of flour and living on meat alone, so a few were sent in advance to get supplies from Dr. Whitman and return to us. Having so light a load we could travel faster than the other teams, and went on with Captain Shaw and the advance. Through the Blue Mountains cattle were giving out and left lying in the road. We made but a few miles a day. We were in the country of "Dr. Whitman's Indians," as they called themselves. They were returning from buffalo hunting and frequented our camps. They were loud in praise of the missionaries and anxious to assist us. Often they would drive up some beast that had been left behind as given out and return it to its owner.

One day when we were making a fire of wet wood Francis thought to help the matter by holding his powder-horn over a small blaze. Of course the powder-horn exploded, and the wonder was he was left alive. He ran to a creek nearby and bathed his hands and face, and came back destitute of winkers and eyebrows, and his face was blackened beyond recognition. Such were the incidents and dangerous and humorous features of the journey.

We reached Umatilla October 15th, and lay by while Captain Shaw went on to Whitman's station to see if the doctor would take care of us, if only until he could become located in the Willamette. We purchased of the Indians the first potatoes we had eaten since we started on our long and sad journey. October 17th we started for our destination, leaving the baby very sick, with doubts of its recovery. Mrs. Shaw took an affectionate leave of us all, and stood looking after us as long as we were in sight. Speaking of it in later years, she said she never saw a more pitiful sight than that cartful of orphans going to find a home among strangers.

We reached the station in the forenoon. For weeks this place had been a subject for our talk by day and formed our dreams at night. We expected to see log houses, occupied by Indians and such people as we had seen about the forts. Instead we saw a large white house surrounded with palisades. A short distance from the doctor's dwelling was another large adobe house, built by Mr. Gray, but now used by immigrants in the winter, and for a granary in the summer. It was situated near the mill pond, and the grist mill was not far from it. . . .

GLOSSARY

camp fever: typhoid, a disease common on the Overland Trail, and often fatal

Dutch doctor: Theophilos Dagen, the doctor who attended Catherine's injury

Grande Ronde: a valley in Oregon near the Blue Mountains; sometimes referred to as "La Grande Ronde"

Laramie: a fort on the North Platte River, today in Wyoming, that served as a stop on the trail

Snake River: a river that flows through the states of Idaho, Oregon, Washington, and Wyoming

South Platte: a river running through Colorado and Nebraska

St. Joseph: a city in Missouri found along the Missouri River, which functioned as a starting-off point

Umatilla: a river in Oregon

Whitman, Dr.: Marcus Whitman, who with his wife established a mission in the Oregon territory; Catherine's adopted parents

Willamette: a valley in northwest Oregon

William Shaw: captain of the wagon train of which the Sager family was a part

Document Analysis

When Henry and Naomi Sager set out on their journey in April of 1844 from St. Joseph, Missouri, they had with them their six children—John, Francis, Catherine, Elizabeth, Matilda, and Louisa—who ranged in age from three to thirteen years. Months into the trail, Naomi gave birth to a fifth daughter, Henrietta. This venture into the unknown eventually led to both Henry and Naomi's deaths from typhoid, termed by Pringle "camp fever," as well as a variety of accidents to Pringle and her siblings. With Henry's death in August of that year, Naomi—whose own demise closely followed his—and her seven children were left on the trail with the others in their caravan, trusting to charity for their support and maintenance. As they were so far along the trail, turning back was not possible, nor did the Sagers have any relatives joining them on the trek or ahead of them in Oregon.

Pringle's details, namely the tragedies and various accidents, including that of her leg being run over by a wagon wheel, reveal a forthright description of progress along the trail, yet there is a measure of detachment in her memoir. This may be read in a variety of ways, such as simply the passage of time. The events of 1844 occurred when Pringle was only nine years old, whereas she recorded her memories around the age of twenty-five.

Despite the eclipse of approximately sixteen years from the events to her writing of them, Pringle is very clear on particulars, such as the rivers she passed and the people she met. This would suggest, though the resources do not account for it, that she may have had help during the writing process, or, at some point after settling in Oregon, was moved to record her memories. Either way, her memoir provides modern readers with valuable insight into her experience and that of countless others.

Life on the Trail

A journey along the Overland Trail, despite the daily hard work, all the hours of travelling, and the consequent stresses, presented itself as a big adventure to the hundreds of children making their way across the plains with their parents. As the majority of those on the trail were of farming families, their children would not have been strangers to hard work; they would already have been used to heavy chores throughout their daily routines. Adapting such duties to the outdoor spectrum on the dusty plains took getting used to, especially for those involved in the family's cooking and washing. Here, men, women, and children performed their various chores while exposed to torrential rains and sweeping winds, excessive heat, and, if delayed, snow and hail storms.

Travelling westward required great fortitude and hardiness, and it came with a heavy price tag. The journey itself would take months, but the planning stages could take that or longer. Supplies had to be bought, gathered, or made, enough to sustain an entire family for the trek west. Posts and forts were located along the trail that sold various goods and supplies, but typically their prices were at a premium. Francis Parkman, a historian from Boston, Massachusetts, travelled the Oregon Trail in the 1840s—around the same time as the Pringle family—and was not impressed with the actions of storekeepers: "They [emigrants on the trail] were plundered and cheated without mercy. In one bargain, concluded in my presence, I calculated the profits that accrued to the fort, and found that at the lowest estimate they exceeded *eighteen hundred percent*" (McLynn 106). Planning and saving for the emigration to Oregon might have taken a while, but, as shown by Parkman, it was far better than running out of supplies and losing money at forts.

A rather large item of necessity, and the iconic image of the western pioneer, was the wagon. The wagon served a number of purposes: conveyance, storage, shelter, sickroom, and pantry. It had to be structurally sturdy to withstand the rigors of the trip, and yet not too heavy, as it still needed to be pulled easily along by animals. Frank McLynn cites oak, hickory, and maple as some of the more popular types of wood used in construction, with elm and ash also favored (53). The top cover—typically made of "a heavy rainproof canvas, caulked, oiled, and painted, usually linen, sailcloth, or oilcloth" (53)—provided shelter to the goods inside. The oxen or mules (both were popular for teams) did not have an easy time; wagons could carry anywhere from 1,000 to 2,500 pounds, though 1,600 pounds was the recommended weight limit. Generally, the wagon was not used to carry all members of the family, as the back of the wagon was mainly for storage. Excepting the ill and the very young, all others walked alongside the wagon; it was not merely an issue of space, but extra weight for the animals at the head. Pringle, due to her leg accident, could not walk, so was allocated a spot in the wagon for the remainder of the journey. Given that the wagon would not have been built with suspension, her ride inside would not have been very comfortable or enviable, and all the bumps along the trail may have aggravated her injury further.

Gathering supplies for an entire family for a months-long journey into the relatively unknown took up the bulk of the preparation time, and it did not merely include food. The wagon was to be a home in miniature. With that in mind, all essential items had to be brought: tools for fixing the wagon, candles, soap, kitchen utensils, medicine and various other medical items, clothes, bedding, sewing materials, guns and ammunition, and other things deemed essential. Ginger Wadsworth cites the memory of a thirteen-year-old girl, Kit Scott, who recorded her memories of her family's westward preparation of clothes and other goods:

> [The] fingers of the women and girls all the winter, providing . . . bedding, blankets, of stockings and sunbonnets, of hickory shirts and gingham aprons . . . that the family might be outfitted for the trip. Ah! The tears that fell upon these garments, fashioned with trembling fingers by the flaring light of tallow [animal fat] candles; the heartaches that were stitched and knitted and woven into them, through the brief winter afternoons. (14)

While measures were taken for keeping warm and dry during the trip, many families spent much of their preparation time ensuring that their families would be well fed. Some practiced cooking over open fires so that they might be ready when the time came. Others put time into making what they could before the journey, such as the snack so often associated with Civil War soldiers, hardtack. John Roger James, cited by Wadsworth, remembered how he, his father, and his brothers spent much of their time in this occupation before setting out for Oregon:

> Father fixed up a place to mix up a lot of dough and knead it with a lever fastened to the wall. He would put a pile of dough into a trough . . . and would have us boys spend the evening kneading the dough thoroughly, then roll it out and cut it into cracker shape about four inches square and then bake them hard and fill them into seamless grain sacks. There would be no lard or butter used, as there would be danger of them spoiling. (16)

Hardtack was not known for being an epicurean delight, but it was food and it satisfied hunger, if not taste, especially if there was nothing else available.

It is very probable that the extra chores performed before a family made their way westward also served as trials for the children for the work they would be expected to do along the trail. As deemed by their sex, older daughters were babysitters from the start, along with assisting their mothers with the cooking, mending, and doctoring. While the various duties of children may have differed from family to family according to their needs, there was one chore that all historians document, the same chore remembered by many who made the journey as children: the collection of buffalo chips. Wood for fuel was not always readily available along the plains. The pioneers took to using whatever was plentiful and available, and one that filled both these criteria was the dried dung of buffalos, known as buffalo chips. McLynn states that the chips, "when dry . . . resembled rotten wood and would make a clear hot fire" (103). Marion Russell, a child on the trail, remembered being on the prairie and collecting buffalo chips:

> I would stand back and kick them, then reach down and gather them carefully, for under them lived spiders and centipedes. Sometimes scorpions ran from beneath them. I would fill my long full dress skirt with the evening's fuel and take it back to mother. (Wadsworth 84–85)

For others, the drudgery of chores held highlights, such as driving the teams pulling the wagons and cracking the whip. Taking part in such a grown-up activity, especially given the arduous life on the trail, must have indeed been a special treat.

Buffalo

Pringle's father, like many men, was anxious to score a buffalo (or bison) kill; according to Pringle, he did accomplish this, but there is no mention whether Mr. Sager made any use of the meat. Pringle wrote only that "he not only killed the great bison, but often brought home on his shoulder the timid antelope." Read at face value, Pringle presents her father as shooting for sport, rather than for the necessity of feeding his large family, particularly when faced with Pringle's comment that her father "was enthusiastic in his love of such sport." The buffalo, like the covered wagon an iconic image of the westward movement, roamed the plains in such large numbers so as to look like brown waves moving about the land. Although the assorted American Indian tribes were scrupulous in using every part of the animal, those on the trail were not so meticulous. Only a small portion of the buffalo was taken for food—the "tongues, hump meat, and marrow bones," the rest left to scavenger animals such as vultures and wolves, while the American Indians could fashion clothing, shelter, and food from the buffalo (Wadsworth 80). Buffalo hunting for sport came into vogue during this time, driving the animals nearly to extinction. The sport continued through the late nineteenth century, attracting the likes of future president Theodore Roosevelt.

The Sagers, like countless other families striving to make a fresh start in Oregon, met with tragedies they never could have foreseen. Plagued by accidents and then the deaths of their parents, the Sager children experienced the thrill of the trail, but also the trail at its most harsh and brutal. It would be impossible to estimate the number of families that did not arrive in the West without losing someone they loved. Despite the sadness of her story, Catherine Sager Pringle left for history the testimony of her experience, an experience shared by more people than she could have realized.

Essential Themes

As evidenced in Pringle's excerpt, accidents along the trail could occur easily, as when Pringle jumped off the moving wagon. Simple accidents and infections, though, particularly in a time of limited medical knowledge—much less being situated along the plains far from a doctor—could spell certain death.

For example, during the Civil War, twenty years after these events, more soldiers died from disease and infection than from gunshots. There were cases, such as those of Henry and Naomi Sager, in which even the presence of a doctor could not assuage bouts with typhoid. Typhoid and cholera, both prevalent along the plains (as well as in cities back East) could act swiftly, often with fatal results.

The Sagers' affliction with typhoid aside, accidents were what plagued the family the most. Before the mention of her own accident, Pringle recounts one of her mother. She states, "Soon after crossing South Platte the unwieldy oxen ran on a bank and overturned the wagon, greatly injuring our mother." This occurrence was also documented by McLynn; he states that in addition to injuring Naomi Sager, the overturning wagon also tore off Pringle's dress and that "Henry Sager's face was badly skinned" (209). The day did not end there for the Sager family, as "later, the girls went out for a midnight stroll and were nearly killed when a sentry shot at them, mistaking them for Indians" (209). Life on the trail, though filled with promise and excitement, was also filled with dread, as demonstrated by Pringle's memories.

Jennifer L. Henderson Crane, BA, PgDip

Bibliography

Frizzell, Lodisa. *Across the Plains to California in 1852: Journal of Mrs. Lodisa Frizzell*. Ed. Victor Hugo Paltsits. 1915. Project Gutenberg, 2010. E-book. Web. 25 Mar. 2013.

Gwartney, Debra. "Plucked from the Grave: The First Female Missionary to Cross the Continental Divide Came to a Gruesome End Partly Caused by Her Own Zeal. What Can Learn from Her?" *American Scholar* 80.3 (2011), 71–81. Print.

Jones, Karen. "'My Winchester Spoke to Her': Crafting the Northern Rockies as a Hunter's Paradise, c.1870–1910." *American Nineteenth Century History* 11.2 (2010), p. 183–203. Print.

Keyes, Sarah. "'Like a Roaring Lion': The Overland Trail as a Sonic Conquest." *Journal of American History* 96.1 (2009), 19–43. Print.

McLynn, Frank. *Wagons West: The Epic Story of America's Overland Trails*. London: Cape, 2002. Print.

Menard, Andrew. "Down the Santa Fe Trail to the City upon a Hill." *Western American Literature* 45.2 (2010): 162–188. Print.

Pringle, Catherine Sager. *Across the Plains in 1844*. c.1860. *Archives of the West*. West Film Project and WETA (PBS), 2001. Web. 25 Mar. 2013.

Royce, Sarah. *Across the Plains: Sarah Royce's Western Narrative*. Ed. Jennifer Dawes Adkison. Tucson: U of Arizona P, 2009. Print.

Wadsworth, Ginger. *Words West: Voices of Young Pioneers*. New York: Clarion, 2003. Print.

Additional Reading

Bagley, Will. *So Rugged and Mountainous: Blazing the Trails to Oregon and California, 1812–1848*. Norman: U of Oklahoma P, 2010. Print.

---. *With Golden Visions Bright before Them: Trails to the Mining West, 1849–1852*. Norman: U of Oklahoma P, 2012. Print.

"Diaries, Memoirs, Letters, and Reports along the Trails West." *The Overland Trail*. Elizabeth Larson, n.d. Web. 25 Mar. 2013.

Thompson, Erwin N. *Shallow Grave at Waiilatpu: The Sagers' West*. Portland: Western Imprints, 1985. Print.

Werner, Emmy E. *Pioneer Children on the Journey West*. Boulder: Westview P, 1995. Print.

LESSON PLAN: "One of the Restless Ones"

Students analyze Catherine Sager Pringle's *Across the Plains in 1844* and compare its value to that of William Porter's Oregon Trail diary (1848).

Learning Objectives

Identify Pringle's purpose in writing; appreciate the historical perspective of her account; reconstruct the literal meaning of the account; compare and contrast the historical value of her account and William Porter's.

Materials: Catherine Sager Pringle, *Across the Plains in 1844* (1860); William Porter, Oregon Trail diary (1848).

Overview Questions

What aspects of Pringle's narration suggest her purpose? How does Pringle's account differ from twenty-first–century assumptions about Oregon Trail journeys? What data does the account add to the understanding of those journeys? How does Porter's account of a similar journey complement Pringle's?

Step 1: Comprehension Questions

What does Pringle accomplish in telling her story? What does the publication date (1860) suggest about her purposes?

- **Activity:** Challenge students to find and read passages that suggest Pringle's purpose. Discuss what makes this narrative compelling. Have students speculate on how the time between the events and Pringle's writing of them might have affected details, her views, and her purpose.

Step 2: Comprehension Questions

What information about the trials of the Oregon Trail surprised you? What do Pringle's descriptions of her parents' deaths reveal about her, the journey, and the spirit of the people who moved westward?

- **Activity:** Have students read aloud passages that describe the Sagers' deaths. Discuss whether Pringle's narrative tone makes the passages more or less sorrowful and why. Discuss whether or not the narrative suggests that the Sagers were aware of their possible fates and what this reveals about those who embarked on the trail.

Step 3: Context Questions

What information does Pringle provide that can be verified through other sources? What do the less-verifiable details add to the historical record?

- **Activity:** Have students briefly outline the travel details that Pringle provides, such as dates, locations, river crossings, etc. Then have students list personal details of Sager family history that she provides. Have students discuss why each list is important to historians.

Step 4: Exploration Questions

How does Pringle's account of the trail west differ from Porter's? How do the two narratives complement each other?

- **Activity:** Have students read and characterize the nature of Porter's account. Ask which narrative most accurately gives a feel for life on the trail and why. Discuss why historians would find each account a valuable tool in understanding the practical challenges of moving west.

Step 5: Response Paper

Word length and additional requirements set by Instructor. Students answer the research question in the *Overview Questions*. Students state a thesis and use as evidence passages from the primary source document as well as support from supplemental materials assigned in the lesson.

Treaty of Guadalupe Hidalgo

Date: February 2, 1848
Author: Trist, Nicholas Philip
Genre: treaty

"There shall be firm and universal peace between the United States of America and the Mexican Republic, and between their respective countries, territories, cities, towns, and people, without exception of places or persons."

Summary Overview

In May 1846, the Mexican-American War officially began. Spain and the United States had signed a treaty regarding the boundaries between the Spanish colony of Mexico and the United States, which Mexican leaders honored when they gained independence. However, with Texas's annexation to the United States, there were issues regarding the western border of that state. President James Polk sought territorial expansion and pressed the issue, resulting in the beginning of hostilities. Although the United States forces had won all the major battles and virtually every confrontation when US diplomat Nicholas Trist arrived in mid-1847, the Mexican government refused to negotiate. However, toward the end of 1847, after another series of military defeats, including the American occupation of Mexico City, representatives of a new Mexican government accepted the invitation to negotiate and quickly reached an agreement to end the war. The treaty not only granted the United States' desire for all the territory west of Texas (known as the Mexican Cession), it set the framework for United States–Mexican relations for decades to come.

Defining Moment

The United States' granting of statehood to Texas in 1845 set the stage for the Mexican-American War. Mexico had never fully accepted the independence of the Republic of Texas, declared in 1836. Mexico asserted that the territory of Texas stopped at the Nueces River, while Texas claimed territory farther south and west with the Rio Grande as the border. During the process of the United States annexing Texas, Mexico broke off diplomatic relations but did not declare war. President Polk ordered troops into Texas and then subsequently into the territory between the Nueces and the Rio Grande. In April 1846, a month after the American forces arrived in the disputed territory, Mexican cavalry attacked a small American scouting party. General Zachary Taylor then began to push south, forcing the Mexican troops out of the disputed area and, within five months, capturing Monterrey, a major city in northeastern Mexico. While Taylor, facing stiff opposition, continued to move slowly south, General Winfield Scott convinced Polk to order most of the forces to go with him and invade Mexico through Veracruz, with Mexico City as the ultimate goal. Because the American forces were split into two armies, Taylor's and Scott's troops were always outnumbered. However, in spite of this, both continued to be successful on the battlefield. The plan to capture Mexico City succeeded, and on September 14, 1847, just under six months after the campaign started in Veracruz, Scott was in the Mexican capital.

Appointed in April 1847 to negotiate a peace treaty with Mexico, Nicholas Trist traveled to Veracruz and accompanied General Scott's army. When the opportunity arose for discussions with Antonio López de Santa Anna, the Mexican president and general, Santa Anna would not grant major concessions. In October 1847, Santa Anna was deposed, and the new government was open to negotiations with Trist. That same month, Polk decided to recall Trist to Washington. In mid-November, Trist received the orders to return but refused to leave and instead continued negotiating. In January 1848, an agreement was reached, and the treaty was signed on February 2. While Polk was upset that Trist had not followed his orders, Polk did read the treaty and saw that it accomplished most of what he wanted (though the treaty gave the United States about 55 percent of Mexico, and Polk had desired more.) Polk was ready for the war to end, so he accepted the pact and sent it to the Senate for ratification. The treaty and the war established that the United States expected to hold the superior position in its relationship with Mexico. This was the case for many decades and, to a certain extent, is still reflected in American foreign policy.

Author Biography

Born in 1800, in Charlottesville, Virginia, Nicholas Philip Trist was the son of Hore Browse Trist and Mary Louisa Brown Trist. His father was given the post of customs agent in Natchez, Louisiana, by President Thomas Jefferson when Trist was quite young. After finishing his formal education at the College of Orleans, Trist traveled to Monticello, where he met his future wife, Jefferson's granddaughter Virginia Jefferson Randolph. Trist briefly attended West Point but left to seek sufficient resources to marry. In 1823, following his mother's death, he began formal law studies with Jefferson and, a year later, married Virginia, with whom he had three children. After assisting Jefferson as a private secretary until Jefferson's death, Trist used his connections to obtain a post in the State Department.

From 1828 to 1833, Trist was a clerk in the State Department, except for a short period when he was a private secretary to President Andrew Jackson. He was then posted to Havana, Cuba, for eight years. During this time, his work as US consul received mixed reviews due to his strong support of slavery and questions regarding whether he was forging documents for slave traders. Although he returned to Washington under a cloud, he continued work with the State Department. In 1845, President Polk appointed him chief clerk, which, at that time, was the State Department's second-highest position. He served as chief clerk until April 1847, when he was sent by Polk as his personal envoy to the Mexican government to negotiate a peace treaty. This was to be the high point of Trist's career. Traveling toward Mexico City from the Gulf Coast with General Scott, Trist and Scott were able to negotiate a temporary truce in late August when American forces were poised to capture Mexico City. Because the Mexican government would not make any serious concessions, that round of negotiations failed. Scott captured the city, and Trist was then able to enter into negotiations with a new Mexican government. Because the August negotiations were not successful, Trist was officially recalled to Washington by Polk. Trist refused to go, writing a sixty-one-page letter in response. Trist and the Mexican negotiators were able to draw up the Treaty of Guadalupe Hidalgo, which eventually was accepted by both governments, after some amendments by the United States Senate.

When Trist returned to Washington, Polk, who by then had formally fired Trist, refused to pay him for his expenses or for his last several months of work. Trist never recovered financially from this setback, but was able to obtain clerical work at a railroad. In 1871, he was finally paid back wages for his work negotiating the treaty and was appointed postmaster of Alexandria, Virginia, by President Ulysses S. Grant. Trist died on February 11, 1874.

HISTORICAL DOCUMENT

TREATY OF PEACE, FRIENDSHIP, LIMITS, AND SETTLEMENT BETWEEN THE UNITED STATES OF AMERICA AND THE UNITED MEXICAN STATES CONCLUDED AT GUADALUPE HIDALGO, FEBRUARY 2, 1848; RATIFICATION ADVISED BY SENATE, WITH AMENDMENTS, MARCH 10, 1848; RATIFIED BY PRESIDENT, MARCH 16, 1848; RATIFICATIONS EXCHANGED AT QUERETARO, MAY 30, 1848; PROCLAIMED, JULY 4, 1848.

IN THE NAME OF ALMIGHTY GOD

The United States of America and the United Mexican States animated by a sincere desire to put an end to the calamities of the war which unhappily exists between the two Republics and to establish Upon a solid basis relations of peace and friendship, which shall confer reciprocal benefits upon the citizens of both, and assure the concord, harmony, and mutual confidence wherein the two people should live, as good neighbors have for that purpose appointed their respective plenipotentiaries, that is to say: The President of the United States has appointed Nicholas P. Trist, a citizen of the United States, and the President of the Mexican Republic has appointed Don Luis Gonzaga Cuevas, Don Bernardo Couto, and Don Miguel Atristain, citizens of the said Republic; Who, after a reciprocal communication of their respective full powers, have, under the protection of Almighty God, the author of peace, arranged, agreed upon, and signed the following: Treaty of Peace, Friendship, Limits, and Settlement between the United States of America and the Mexican Republic.

ARTICLE I

There shall be firm and universal peace between the United States of America and the Mexican Republic, and between their respective countries, territories, cities, towns, and people, without exception of places or persons. . . .

ARTICLE V

The boundary line between the two Republics shall commence in the Gulf of Mexico, three leagues from land, opposite the mouth of the Rio Grande, otherwise called Rio Bravo del Norte, or Opposite the mouth of its deepest branch, if it should have more than one branch emptying directly into the sea; from thence up the middle of that river, following the deepest channel, where it has more than one, to the point where it strikes the southern boundary of New Mexico; thence, westwardly, along the whole southern boundary of New Mexico (which runs north of the town called Paso) to its western termination; thence, northward, along the western line of New Mexico, until it intersects the first branch of the river Gila; (or if it should not intersect any branch of that river, then to the point on the said line nearest to such branch, and thence in a direct line to the same); thence down the middle of the said branch and of the said river, until it empties into the Rio Colorado; thence across the Rio Colorado, following the division line between Upper and Lower California, to the Pacific Ocean.

The southern and western limits of New Mexico, mentioned in the article, are those laid down in the map entitled "Map of the United Mexican States, as organized and defined by various acts of the Congress of said republic, and constructed according to the best authorities. Revised edition. Published at New York, in 1847, by J. Disturnell," of which map a copy is added to this treaty, bearing the signatures and seals of the undersigned Plenipotentiaries. And, in order to preclude all difficulty in tracing upon the ground the limit separating Upper from Lower California, it is agreed that the said limit shall consist of a straight line drawn from the middle of the Rio Gila, where it unites with the Colorado, to a point on the coast of the Pacific Ocean, distant one marine league due south of the southernmost point of the port of San Diego, according to the plan of said port made in the year 1782 by Don Juan Pantoja, second sailing-master of the Spanish fleet, and published at Madrid in the year 1802, in the atlas to the voyage of the schooners Sutil and Mexicana; of which plan a copy is hereunto added, signed and sealed by the respective Plenipotentiaries.

In order to designate the boundary line with due precision, upon authoritative maps, and to establish upon the ground land-marks which shall show the limits of both republics, as described in the present article, the two Governments shall each appoint a commissioner and a surveyor, who, before the expiration of one year from the date of the exchange of ratifications of this treaty, shall meet at the port of San Diego, and proceed to run and mark the said boundary in its whole course to the mouth of the Rio Bravo del Norte. They shall keep journals and make out plans of their operations; and the result agreed upon by them shall be deemed a part of this treaty, and shall have the same force as if it were inserted therein. The two Governments will amicably agree regarding what may be necessary to these persons, and also as to their respective escorts, should such be necessary.

The boundary line established by this article shall be religiously respected by each of the two republics, and no change shall ever be made therein, except by the express and free consent of both nations, lawfully given by the General Government of each, in conformity with its own constitution. . . .

ARTICLE VII

The river Gila, and the part of the Rio Bravo del Norte lying below the southern boundary of New Mexico, being, agreeably to the fifth article, divided in the middle between the two republics, the navigation of the Gila and of the Bravo below said boundary shall be free and common to the vessels and citizens of both countries; and neither shall, without the consent of the other, construct any work that may impede or interrupt, in whole or in part, the exercise of this right; not even for the purpose of favoring new methods of navigation. Nor shall any tax or contribution, under any denomination or title, be levied upon vessels or persons navigating the same or upon merchandise or effects transported thereon, except in the case of landing upon one of their shores. If, for the purpose of making the said rivers navigable, or for maintaining them in such state, it should be necessary or advantageous to establish any tax or contribution, this shall not be done without the consent of both Governments.

The stipulations contained in the present article shall not impair the territorial rights of either republic within its established limits.

ARTICLE VIII

Mexicans now established in territories previously belonging to Mexico, and which remain for the future within the limits of the United States, as defined by the present treaty, shall be free to continue where they now reside, or to remove at any time to the Mexican Republic, retaining the property which they possess in the said territories, or disposing thereof, and removing the proceeds wherever they please, without their being subjected, on this account, to any contribution, tax, or charge whatever.

Those who shall prefer to remain in the said territories may either retain the title and rights of Mexican citizens, or acquire those of citizens of the United States. But they shall be under the obligation to make their election within one year from the date of the exchange of ratifications of this treaty; and those who shall remain in the said territories after the expiration of that year, without having declared their intention to retain the character of Mexicans, shall be considered to have elected to become citizens of the United States.

In the said territories, property of every kind, now belonging to Mexicans not established there, shall be inviolably respected. The present owners, the heirs of these, and all Mexicans who may hereafter acquire said property by contract, shall enjoy with respect to it guarantees equally ample as if the same belonged to citizens of the United States.

ARTICLE IX

The Mexicans who, in the territories aforesaid, shall not preserve the character of citizens of the Mexican Republic, conformably with what is stipulated in the preceding article, shall be incorporated into the Union of the United States. and be admitted at the proper time (to be judged of by the Congress of the United States) to the enjoyment of all the rights of citizens of the United States, according to the principles of the Constitution; and in the mean time, shall be maintained and protected in the free enjoyment of their liberty and property, and secured in the free exercise of their religion without restriction.

ARTICLE X

[Stricken out]

ARTICLE XI

Considering that a great part of the territories, which, by the present treaty, are to be comprehended for the future within the limits of the United States, is now occupied by savage tribes, who will hereafter be under the exclusive control of the Government of the United States, and whose incursions within the territory of Mexico would be prejudicial in the extreme, it is solemnly agreed that all such incursions shall be forcibly restrained by the Government of the United States whensoever this may be necessary; and that when they cannot be prevented, they shall be punished by the said Government, and satisfaction for the same shall be exacted all in the same way, and with equal diligence and energy, as if the same incursions were meditated or committed within its own territory, against its own citizens.

It shall not be lawful, under any pretext whatever, for any inhabitant of the United States to purchase or acquire any Mexican, or any foreigner residing in Mexico, who may have been captured by Indians inhabiting the territory of either of the two republics; nor to purchase or acquire horses, mules, cattle, or property of any kind, stolen within Mexican territory by such Indians.

And in the event of any person or persons, captured within Mexican territory by Indians, being carried into the territory of the United States, the Government of the latter engages and binds itself, in the most solemn manner, so soon as it shall know of such captives being within its territory, and shall be able so to do, through the faithful exercise of its influence and power, to rescue them and return them to their country, or deliver them to the agent or representative of the Mexican Government. The Mexican authorities will, as far as practicable, give to the Government of the United States notice of such captures; and its agents shall pay the expenses incurred in the maintenance and transmission of the rescued captives; who, in the mean time, shall be treated with the utmost hospitality by the American authorities at the place where they may be. But if the Government of the United States, before receiving such notice from Mexico, should obtain intelligence, through any other channel, of the existence of Mexican captives within its territory, it will proceed forthwith to effect their release and delivery to the Mexican agent, as above stipulated.

For the purpose of giving to these stipulations the fullest possible efficacy, thereby affording the security and redress demanded by their true spirit and intent, the Government of the United States will now and hereafter pass, without unnecessary delay, and always vigilantly enforce, such laws as the nature of the subject may require. And, finally, the sacredness of this obligation shall never be lost sight of by the said Government, when providing for the removal of the Indians from any portion of the said territories, or for its being settled by citizens of the United States; but, on the contrary, special care shall then be taken not to place its Indian occupants under the necessity of seeking new homes, by committing those invasions which the United States have solemnly obliged themselves to restrain.

ARTICLE X

All grants of land made by the Mexican government or by the competent authorities, in territories previously appertaining to Mexico, and remaining for the future within the limits of the United States, shall be respected as valid, to the same extent that the same grants would be valid, if the said territories had remained within the limits of Mexico. But the grantees of lands in Texas, put in possession thereof, who, by reason of the circumstances of the country since the beginning of the troubles between Texas and the Mexican Government, may have been prevented from fulfilling all the conditions of their grants, shall be under the obligation to fulfill the said conditions within the periods limited in the same respectively; such periods to be now counted from the date of the exchange of ratification's of this treaty: in default of which the said grants shall not be obligatory upon the State of Texas, in virtue of the stipulations contained in this Article.

The foregoing stipulation in regard to grantees of land in Texas, is extended to all grantees of land in the territories aforesaid, elsewhere than in Texas, put in possession under such grants; and, in default of the fulfillment of the conditions of any such grant, within the new period, which, as is above stipulated, begins with the day of the exchange of ratifications of this treaty, the same shall be null and void.

GLOSSARY

appertaining: belonging

character of Mexicans: citizenship of Mexico

Guadalupe Hidalgo: the name of the Basilica of Guadalupe in Villa Hidalgo, where the treaty was signed

plenipotentiaries: diplomats or government representatives with full authority to act on behalf of the leaders who sent them

prejudicial in the extreme: a polite way of stating the incursions to which this phrase applied would devastate the area and cost many Mexicans their lives

redress: remedy; compensation

savage tribes: refers to the Comanches and, to a lesser extent, Apaches and Navajos, whose numerous raids throughout northern Mexico had destroyed the local economy and killed thousands of people prior to the war

Document Analysis

The Treaty of Guadalupe Hidalgo was an exhaustive attempt to outline the steps that should be taken not only to end the Mexican-American War, but also to create a stronger peace in the future. Nicholas Trist and the three Mexican negotiators clearly understood the balance of power between the two nations. However, Trist limited American demands to the goals that had been outlined prior to the war, as well as giving the Mexicans some assistance in rebuilding after the war. The impact of a country's losing more than half its territory cannot be minimized. However, the fact that neither President Polk nor Nicholas Trist listened to Americans who desired to annex all of Mexico indicated that their understanding of Manifest Destiny did not include incorporating all of North America into the United States. Although the United States Senate felt free to make changes to the document, and some provisions of the treaty were not upheld for Mexicans who became American citizens, the main points of the intergovernmental relationship were met by both nations. The relationship reflected in this treaty made possible the Gadsden Purchase, a roughly 30,000-square-mile area occupying present-day southern Arizona and southwestern New Mexico, acquired from Mexico in late 1853.

Obviously, the initial paragraph in the extract above was not a part of the original treaty, since it contains information about the ratification process by the United States after the treaty was signed on February 2, 1848. The designation of this treaty as a "Treaty of Peace, Friendship, Limits, and Settlement" is an attempt to describe the full content and intent of the agreement. It is more than a statement that the war was finished. As with most treaties, this one is better known by the designation of where it was signed, Guadalupe Hidalgo. From the time it was signed, it took just over a month for the United States Senate to amend and ratify it. These changes were referred to the Mexican ambassador to the United States, and he tentatively approved them. The statement "ratified by president, March 16, 1848" indicates that President Polk had accepted the changes made by the Senate. While this was happening, Mexico was formally approving the treaty as well. The meeting with Mexican leaders in Querétaro was to fulfill article 23, which states that representatives of the two governments would meet to exchange formal copies of the ratified treaty. Since the United States had made unilateral changes to the treaty (even though they had been provisionally accepted by the Mexican ambassador), a second agreement had to be drawn up to reflect these changes and to represent formal acceptance of them by the Mexican government. Thus, the Protocol of Querétaro was drawn up by representatives of the United States and the Mexican minister of foreign affairs. The points in the protocol each address one of the changes by the United States. The first is that the original article 9 (civil rights) was deleted and article 3 of the Treaty of Louisiana (Louisiana Purchase) was substituted. The protocol states that the United States "did not intend to diminish in any way what was agreed upon by the aforesaid article IX." Similarly, the United States claimed that in deleting article 10, it did not intend to take away the "grants of land made by Mexico." Finally, Mexico was assured that the deletion of the last part of article 12 did not change any rights Mexico had with regard to the money that the United States was going to pay. The formal acceptance of these three changes by the Mexican foreign minister made it possible for the agreement to go into effect immediately, without the Mexican government having to repeat its ratification process.

The preamble to the treaty identifies its goal, the nations that were party to the agreement, and who had been authorized to negotiate on behalf of the two nations. The United States of America and the United Mexican States (also called the Mexican Republic) had "a sincere desire to put an end to the calamities of the war which unhappily exists between the two Republics and to establish Upon a solid basis relations of peace and friendship." Thus, Trist and the Mexican representatives had authority from their two governments to make a formal agreement with the intention of creating an enduring peace. They sought to create a situation in which their countries could live together "as good neighbors."

Article 1 states the reason for the agreement: "firm and universal peace" between the two nations was the intent of both. Prior to the war, there had been military threats from both sides. Mexico had threatened war if the United States annexed Texas, which Mexico still claimed, and President Polk had put forward for the United States the idea of Manifest Destiny and began taking appropriate actions to ensure the fulfillment of this idea. Although Polk's campaign slogan of "Fifty-Four Forty or Fight" was directed toward the British, with whom he peacefully negotiated an agreement regarding Oregon territory, his campaign had made it clear that he had a similar goal of extending the United States to California. Because of the rebellion in Texas, there had not been a firm peace between the United States and Mexico for more than a decade.

The three articles not printed in this text (2, 3, and 4) all dealt with the disengagement of military forces, leaving Mexican military supplies and fortifications intact, reestablishing civilian rule, and a timely withdrawal of American troops from Mexico. While most of the moves were to be "at the earliest moment practicable," the withdrawal from Mexico City was to occur within a month from the time the military commander had been notified that the peace treaty had been ratified by both countries. Provisions for mutual support were a part of the treaty; for instance, if the American forces were not able to be withdrawn from the tropical ports on the Gulf of Mexico (Veracruz) by the "sickly season" (May through October), the forces would move inland away from the cities, as protection from the tropical diseases.

Article 5 outlined the new borders between the United States and Mexico. In many ways, this was the most important article in the treaty, as the lack of clarity regarding Texas's borders had initiated the war. It was clear from the descriptions of the new border that none of the negotiators had firsthand experience in that region. They did not even know if the Rio Grande had one or more channels where it entered the Gulf of Mexico or if the Gila River intersected the western border of New Mexico. In terms of the territory that had precipitated the war, the Texas border was set where the United States said it should be, at the Rio Grande. In places where there was uncertainty, reference maps were identified as authoritative for the treaty. In a region that had neither been formally surveyed nor mapped in detail, it was not easy to identify the border clearly. Thus, in the third paragraph of this article, provision is made for a joint surveying team to be appointed in order to identify and mark the boundary between the United States and Mexico. What the surveyors identified, following the directions in the first two paragraphs of this article, would stand as the border and be "religiously respected by each of the two republics." The surveyors did discover that the city of El Paso was actually about a hundred miles west of where the negotiators had assumed it was located, resulting in a dispute until the Gadsden Purchase was negotiated.

Article 6, not printed in this text, details the rights of American ships and boats to free transit through the Gulf of California and up the Colorado River to reach American territory. Prior to the damming of the Colorado and Gila Rivers, it was possible to navigate the sixty miles to what is now Yuma, although the city never developed into a seaport. Examining all possibilities, the treaty also states that if a road or railroad were built close to the Gila River by either country, it would be a cooperative venture to serve both nations. Similar considerations are contained in article 7, which states that rivers forming the boundary between the two nations would be open to navigation by both. However, as the land on each bank belonged to the respective nations, this freedom of movement did not apply to the "landing upon one of their shores." These articles were changed by the Gadsden Purchase's movement of the border further south.

Articles 8 and 9 refer to the rights given to Mexican citizens who would live in the United States as a result of the transfer of more than 525,000 square miles of territory west of the state of Texas. These articles of the treaty were the ones least observed by various jurisdictions in the United States, as the property of many former Mexican citizens was not respected. Article 8 gives Mexican citizens now in United States territory one year in which to decide whether they wanted to retain Mexican citizenship or accept American citizenship. The default was for them to become American citizens. If they chose to return to Mexico, they were free to dispose of their property and take "the proceeds wherever they please." This article also grants the right of property ownership in the United States to Mexican citizens "as if the same belonged to citizens of the United States." Article 9 was shortened by the US Senate, to bring it into greater conformity with the laws for all other territories. The shortened article 9 is a basic statement that the territory would become states in accordance with the laws governing this process, and in the meantime, the people would have "the free enjoyment of their liberty and property, and secured in the free exercise of their religion without restriction." The deleted text included a guarantee that they would keep any rights they had under Mexican law, rights matching those given to people in the former Louisiana or Florida territories; a guarantee regarding the freedom for religious officials "in the discharge of the offices of their ministry"; and a statement that Catholics in the new American territories would have free access to and unhindered communication with Catholic officials in Mexico.

Article 10 was deleted from the treaty but is printed here at the end of the excerpt above. Even though the Protocol of Querétaro states that "suppressing" this section did not "annul the grants of lands made by Mexico in the ceded territories," this was actually the intent of many who supported this change. In California, the very large haciendas (estates) granted by the Spanish and Mexican governments were not respected by the American settlers. In addition, during the decade between Texas obtaining its independence and its annexation to the United States, land grants had been made in that territory by the Mexican government. This article would have mandated that Texas and the United States respect these grants, some of which would have conflicted with deeds issued by Texas. Thus, for logistical reasons in Texas and by the desires of Americans more generally, article 10 was stricken by the Senate. The Protocol of Querétaro was a simple way of getting the treaty wording accepted by the Mexican government. While the American negotiators may have believed that the protocol would be supported in Washington, it was never really implemented by the US government.

The last article printed in this text, article 11, had to do with the predominant American Indian tribes in the region acquired by the United States. The Comanche confederation and two Apache tribes had become major problems for Mexico. Spain had made peace with most of the tribes in the eighteenth century, but that was not seen as applying to Mexico. Thus, since the 1820s, thousands of people had been killed and the economic ventures of the Mexicans had suffered greatly. Because the American settlers were willing to trade for the cattle and horses the American Indians had taken in their raids, many Mexicans believed the Americans were encouraging the American Indians to continue their raids on Mexican settlements. Since the traditional homelands of the tribes would become part of the United States, they became the problem of the United States. As such, the United States promises that "all such incursions shall be forcibly restrained by the government of the United States." This was easier to put into a document than to carry out. Many historians believe that this was the only positive thing to come out of the war for Mexico. In the first few years after the war, almost three-quarters of the US Army was assigned to this task, with limited success. Mexico was demanding more protection and/or reparations. When the treaty for the Gadsden Purchase was being negotiated, the United States paid Mexico to accept the negation of article 11.

Not printed in this text, article 12 states that the American government would pay Mexico fifteen million dollars for the land being acquired and gives a schedule for the payments. (This was less than half the money that had been offered prior to the war.) In addition, article 13 states that the United States will assume payment to United States citizens for American court judgments that had been made against Mexico, a sum of no more than $3.25 million, according to article 15. Article 14 states that no further claims could be made, and article 15 clarifies the process for paying the claims.

Article 16 allows both countries to "fortify whatever point within its territory it may judge proper." The next article renews an 1831 commerce treaty. Article 18 clarifies that money or goods sent to Mexico to support American troops would not be subject to any Mexican taxes. On a related topic, article 19 describes how taxes should be applied to nonmilitary goods that came into areas of Mexico not occupied by American forces during the war, and article 20 deals with the importation of goods between the time the treaty is signed and is ratified. Article 21 promises that if any "disagreement shall hereafter arise between the Governments of the two republics," they would try to resolve their differences peacefully. Article 22 lists certain rules that would be followed if another war were to break out. The final article, article 23, deals with the ratification and notification process for the treaty.

Trist and his Mexican counterparts strove to make certain that all contingencies were covered in the treaty. It passed this test in that President Polk—who, when he received it, had already fired Trist and was looking for any flaws—accepted the treaty and sent it on to the Senate. The Mexican officials had very little choice in the major provisions of the treaty. The most important point was that the treaty did end the war, on terms desired by the United States, and allowed the United States and Mexico to enter into a more peaceful, if not always harmonious, relationship.

Essential Themes

The Mexican-American War had come about because both the United States and Mexico had pushed toward the brink, allowing one small skirmish to result in a full-blown war. President Polk had tried to negotiate for the desired territory, while constant turmoil in the Mexican government did not allow for any substantive negotiations. Once the war started, the United States forces pushed back the Mexican army until Mexico had no real choice but to negotiate. For the United States, the most important point in the treaty was Mexico giving up any claim to the land from the eastern border of Texas to the Pacific coast in California. This is outlined in article 5, and the ceded territory contained everything that Trist had been told to request, from the Rio Grande to San Diego. While ending the war as soon as possible was essential and peaceful relations with Mexico were important, the key point in the treaty was what is known as the Mexican Cession, the territory acquired by the United States. Manifest Destiny, as envisioned by American leaders, was not to be stopped for any reason. Other points in the treaty, such as the rights of Mexican citizens in the new territories and property and commercial rights, represented items similar to what had been outlined in previous annexation treaties. Although it is doubtful that the US government agreed to these provisions without intending to fulfill all its obligations, these were of substantially lower importance than the territory. Since the ratification of the Treaty of Guadalupe Hidalgo, the two nations have not only peacefully coexisted, but have developed closer cooperation across many areas of mutual concern.

Donald A. Watt, PhD

Bibliography

Griswold del Castillo, Richard. "Appendix 1: The Original Text of Articles IX and X of the Treaty of Guadalupe Hidalgo and the Protocol of Querétaro." *The Treaty of Guadalupe Hidalgo: A Legacy of Conflict*. Norman: U of Oklahoma P, 1990. 179–82. Print.

Ohrt, Wallace. *Defiant Peacemaker: Nicholas Trist in the Mexican War*. College Station: Texas A & M UP, 1997. Print.

"Treaty of Guadalupe Hidalgo; February 2, 1848." *Treaties and Conventions between the United States of America and Other Powers since July 4, 1776*. Washington: GPO, 1871. *Avalon Project*. Web. 15 Mar. 2013.

U.S.-Mexican War: 1846–1848. KERA, 14 Mar. 2006. Web. 15 Mar. 2013.

Additional Reading

Bloom, John Porter, ed. *The Treaty of Guadalupe Hidalgo, 1848*. Las Cruces: Yucca Tree, 1999. Print.

Mahin, Dean B. *Olive Branch and Sword: the United States and Mexico, 1845–1848*. Jefferson: McFarland, 1997. Print.

Merry, Robert W. *A Country of Vast Designs: James K. Polk, the Mexican War, and the Conquest of the American Continent*. New York: Simon, 2009. Print.

"Milestones: 1830–1860." *Office of the Historian*. Bureau of Public Affairs, United States Department of State, 2010. Web. 15 Mar. 2013.

Schroeder, John H. *Mr. Polk's War: American Opposition and Dissent, 1846–1848*. Madison: U of Wisconsin P, 1973. Print.

LESSON PLAN: **A Line Is Drawn**

Students analyze the Treaty of Guadalupe Hidalgo and how Juan Nepomuceno Seguín's pre-treaty memoir anticipates the effects of the treaty after it was signed.

Learning Objectives

Identify the function of the document; analyze multiple perspectives represented in the treaty; interrogate historical data to judge the long-term impact of the treaty; compare the treaty to Seguín's writing to gauge the potential inevitability of the treaty's effects.

Materials: Nicholas P. Trist, Treaty of Guadalupe Hidalgo (1848); Juan Nepomuceno Seguín, "A Foreigner in My Own Land," from *Personal Memoirs of John N. Sequín* (1842)

Overview Questions

What actions did the treaty direct? What do its tone and details imply about the winners and losers of the war? How did it alter the destiny of each country? How do Seguín's personal observations suggest some treaty outcomes?

Step 1: Comprehension Questions

In what ways did the treaty propose to end the war between the United States and Mexico? How did sections of the treaty alter the map of the North America?

- **Activity:** Have students list specific conditions of peace. Direct them to use a map of North America to trace boundaries set by the treaty. Have students speculate about why compensation for individuals was built into the treaty.

Step 2: Comprehension Questions

How does this document reveal who won the war? How can the terms toward the defeated country be characterized?

- **Activity:** Have students read aloud passages that suggest the victor in the war. Discuss with students whether the treaty's terms seem fair. Discuss how the terms of the treaty might be judged differently today.

Step 3: Context Questions

How did the treaty's terms affect the long-term wealth and growth of both Mexico and the United States? How does the treaty still affect each country?

- **Activity:** Have students suggest sources they might use to gauge the effects of the treaty. Discuss how those sources might be used to explain the long-term fate of each country in the context of the treaty.

Step 4: Exploration Questions

How do Seguín's "A Foreigner in My Own Land" and the treaty anticipate the fate of many Mexican American citizens in the decades following the treaty? In what ways could stricter enforcement of the treaty's terms have eliminated some of those consequences?

- **Activity:** Have students review the challenges Seguín faced during the great changes in Texas in the 1830 and 1840s. Have students speculate about how the treaty's terms may have unintentionally guaranteed similar fates for Mexicans who became American citizens when the North American map was redrawn.

Step 5: Response Paper

Word length and additional requirements set by Instructor. Students answer the research question in the *Overview Questions*. Students state a thesis and use as evidence passages from the primary source document as well as support from supplemental materials assigned in the lesson.

People v. Hall

Date: 1854
Author: Murray, Hugh
Genre: court opinion

"A distinct people . . . whom nature has marked as inferior, and who are incapable of progress or intellectual development . . . for them is claimed, not only the right to swear away the life of a citizen, but . . . administering the affairs of our Government."

Summary Overview

George Hall was arrested and convicted for the 1853 murder of a Chinese immigrant miner in Nevada County, California. The Chinese immigrants who witnessed the murder provided the essential testimony that led to Hall's conviction. However, Hall appealed the court's decision, claiming that a Chinese immigrant should not be able to testify against a white man and citing a law that denied black individuals and Indians the right to testify. The case ultimately ended up in the California Supreme Court, where the justices were asked not only to consider the original intent of the law as it applied to Chinese immigrants but also, by default, to deliberate on the status of Chinese immigrants as members of American society. Chief Justice Hugh Murray delivered the majority opinion of the court, which concluded that Chinese immigrants were not entitled to the same rights and privileges as white people and therefore did not have the right to testify against a white man in court.

Defining Moment

After the discovery of gold in California, Chinese immigrants were among countless other immigrant groups who flocked to the gold mines seeking their fortune. Poverty, wars, and oppressive government policies pushed many Chinese families to send their sons looking for economic opportunities abroad. Chinese merchants and entrepreneurs recognized the lucrative potential of moving to California to establish businesses that provided goods and services for Chinese immigrants living and working in the goldfields. By 1852, approximately twenty-five thousand Chinese lived in the state. Initially they were welcomed by politicians and business owners, who saw their presence as a sign of the future wealth and prosperity of the state. Labor recruiters eagerly sought Chinese laborers to work in mining, manufacturing, and agricultural industries.

The initial welcome quickly faded, however. By the early 1850s, the placer deposits had dwindled, and mining became big business. Only those individuals with the capital to purchase heavy equipment and hire laborers to mine for gold were profiting. Companies employed Chinese immigrants partly because they were viewed as especially industrious workers and partly because they could pay them lower wages than white workers. Exasperated by limited job opportunities, white workingmen looked for scapegoats. Economic frustrations combined with rising racial tensions led to a backlash against foreign miners. This backlash manifested itself in the form of laws such as the Foreign Miner's Tax, which sought to force the Chinese from the mining camps by imposing a tax on them. Further oppressive laws followed. In some cases, tensions culminated in outright violence through efforts to forcibly remove Chinese immigrants from California towns and physical attacks on individual Chinese miners.

In 1853, George Hall and two other white men attempted to assault and rob a Chinese gold miner living and working along the Bear River in Nevada County, California. Ling Sing, another Chinese miner in the camp, was coming to the aid of his neighbor when Hall shot and killed him. Hall was promptly arrested and taken to court. The testimony of three Chinese witnesses led to Hall's conviction. The judge sentenced Hall to death by hanging. However, Hall challenged the conviction on the grounds that section 14 of California's Criminal Proceedings Act prohibited the testimony of "blacks, mulatto persons, or Indians" against a white person, insisting that the ban also extended to the Chinese. Hall appealed his case all the way to the California Supreme Court.

Author Biography

Chief Justice Hugh C. Murray, who delivered the majority opinion for the court in the case of *People v. Hall*, had a rather short but infamous career in law. Murray was born in Saint Louis, Missouri, in 1825. He was raised in Illinois and began to study law there in the 1840s. Murray served for a brief time as a second lieutenant in the United States infantry during the war with Mexico. Shortly after his admittance to the bar, he traveled to California to practice law. Murray reached San Francisco during the height of the gold rush in 1849 and found ample opportunities for personal and professional growth. The social connections he forged in San Francisco helped to build his career. Before long, he was serving as a justice of the Superior Court of San Francisco.

Murray continued his meteoric rise. In 1851, he was appointed to the State Supreme Court. The following year, he became chief justice after the resignation of H. A. Lyons. Murray was only twenty-seven years old when he became chief justice of the California Supreme Court and only twenty-nine years old when he rendered the decision in *Hall*, one of his most infamous decisions and the case for which he is perhaps most well known. Murray's career was cut short by consumption, which claimed his life in 1857.

Murray had a reputation for nativism as a member of the anti-immigrant, anti-Catholic American Party (also referred to as the Know-Nothing Party). This organization, composed primarily of Anglo-American Protestants, gained support and influence in the 1850s following a rapid increase in immigration to the United States. The gold rush only exacerbated the party's fears of an immigrant invasion. The party, platform sought to limit immigration and naturalization, especially of Germans and Irish, who were perceived as more loyal to the Catholic Church and the Pope than to democratic values. The American Party further sought to inhibit the power and political influence of all foreigners already living in the United States, including the Chinese. Murray's American Party background and his nativist sentiments are clearly reflected in the *Hall* decision. His zeal for protecting white Americans from the potential harmful influences of inferior races is clear in the language of the majority opinion.

HISTORICAL DOCUMENT

Mr. Ch. J. MURRAY delivered the opinion of the Court, Mr. J. HEYDENFELDT concurred.

The appellant, a free white citizen of this State, was convicted of murder upon the testimony of Chinese witnesses.

The point involved in this case, is the admissibility of such evidence.

The 394th section of the Act Concerning Civil Cases, provides that no Indian or Negro shall be allowed to testify as a witness in any action or proceeding in which a White person is a party.

The 14th section of the Act of April 16th, 1850, regulating Criminal Proceedings, provides that "No Black or Mulatto person, or Indian, shall be allowed to give evidence in favor of, or against a white man."

The true point, at which we are anxious to arrive, is the legal signification of the words, "Black, Mulatto Indian and White person," and whether the Legislature adopted them as generic terms, or intended to limit their application to specific types of the human species.

Before considering this question, it is proper to remark the difference between the two sections of our Statute, already quoted, the latter being more broad and comprehensive in its exclusion, by use of the word "Black," instead of Negro.

Conceding, however, for the present, that the word "Black," as used in the 14th section, and "Negro," in 394th, are convertible terms, and that the former was intended to include the latter, let us proceed to inquire who are excluded from testifying as witnesses under the term "Indian."

When Columbus first landed upon the shores of this continent, in his attempt to discover a western passage to the Indies, he imagined that he had accomplished the object of his expedition, and that the Island of San Salvador was one of those Islands of the Chinese sea, lying near the extremity of India, which had been described by navigators

Acting upon this hypothesis, and also perhaps from the similarity of features and physical conformation, he gave to the Islanders the name of Indians, which appellation was universally adopted, and extended to the aboriginals of the New World, as well as of Asia.

From that time, down to a very recent period, the American Indians and the Mongolian, or Asiatic, were regarded as the same type of the human species.

In order to arrive at a correct understanding of the intention of our Legislature, it will be necessary to go back to the early history of legislation on this subject, our Statute being only a transcript of those of older States.

At the period from which this legislation dates, those portions of Asia which include India proper, the Eastern Archipelago, and the countries washed by the Chinese waters, as far as then known, were denominated the Indies, from which the inhabitants had derived the generic name of Indians.

Ethnology, at that time, was unknown as a distinct science, or if known, had not reached that high point of perfection which it has since attained by the scientific inquiries and discoveries of the master minds of the last half century. Few speculations had been made with regard to the moral or physical differences between the different races of mankind. These were general in their character, and limited to those visible and palpable variations which could not escape the attention of the most common observer.

The general, or perhaps universal opinion of that day was, that there were but three distinct types of the human species, which, in their turn, were subdivided into varieties or tribes. This opinion is still held by many scientific writers, and is supported by Cuvier, one of the most eminent naturalists of modern times.

Many ingenious speculations have been resorted to for the purpose of sustaining this opinion. It has been supposed, and not without plausibility, that this continent was first peopled by Asiatics, who crossed Behring's Straits, and from thence found their way down to the more fruitful climates of Mexico and South America. Almost every tribe has some tradition of coming from the North, and many of them, that their ancestors came from some remote country beyond the ocean.

From the eastern portions of Kamtschatka, the Aleutian Islands form a long and continuous group, extending eastward to that portion of the North American Continent inhabited by the Esquimaux. They appear to be a continuation of the lofty volcanic ranges which traverse the two continents, and are inhabited by a race who resemble, in a remarkable degree, in language and appearance, both the inhabitants of Kamtschatka (who are admitted to be of the Mongolian type,) and the Esquimaux, who again, in turn, resemble other tribes of American Indians. The similarity of the skull and pelvis, and the general configuration of the two races; the remarkable resemblance in eyes, beard, hair, and other peculiarities, together with the contiguity of the two Continents, might well have led to the belief that this country was first peopled by the Asiatics, and that the difference between the different tribes and the parent stock was such as would necessarily arise from the circumstances of climate, pursuits, and other physical causes, and was no greater than that existing between the Arab and the European, both of whom were supposed to belong to the Caucasian race.

Although the discoveries of eminent Archeologists, and the researches of modern Geologists, have given to this Continent an antiquity of thousands of years anterior to the evidence of man's existence, and the light of modern science may have shown conclusively that it was not peopled by the inhabitants of Asia, but that the Aborigines are a distinct type, and as such claim a distinct origin, still, this would not, in any degree, alter the meaning of the term, and render that specific which was before generic.

We have adverted to these speculations for the purpose of showing that the name of Indian, from the time of Columbus to the present day, has been used to designate, not alone the North American Indian, but the whole of the Mongolian race, and that the name, though first applied probably through mistake, was afterwards continued as appropriate on account of the supposed common origin.

That this was the common opinion in the early history of American legislation, cannot be disputed, and, therefore, all legislation upon the subject must have borne relation to that opinion.

Can, then, the use of the word "Indian," because at the present day it may be sometimes regarded as a specific, and not as a generic term, alter this conclusion? We think not; because at the origin of the legislation we are considering, it was used and admitted in its common and ordinary acceptation, as a generic term, distinguishing the great Mongolian race, and as such, its meaning then became fixed by law, and in construing Statutes the legal meaning of words must be preserved.

Again: the words of the Act must be construed in *pari materia*. It will not be disputed that "White" and "Negro," are generic terms, and refer to two of the great types of mankind. If these, as well as the word "Indian," are not to be regarded as generic terms, including the two great races which they were intended to designate, but only specific, and applying to those Whites and Negroes who were inhabitants of this Continent at the time of the passage of the Act, the most anomalous consequences would ensue. The European white man who comes here would not be shielded from the testimony of the degraded and demoralized caste, while the Negro, fresh from the coast of Africa, or the Indian of Patagonia, the Kanaka, South Sea Islander, or New Hollander, would be admitted, upon their arrival, to testify against white citizens in our courts of law.

To argue such a proposition would be an insult to the good sense of the Legislature.

The evident intention of the Act was to throw around the citizen a protection for life and property, which could only be secured by removing him above the corrupting influences of degraded castes.

It can hardly be supposed that any Legislature would attempt this by excluding domestic Negroes and Indians, who not unfrequently have correct notions of their obligations to society, and turning loose upon the community the more degraded tribes of the same species, who have nothing in common with us, in language, country or laws.

We have, thus far, considered this subject on the hypothesis that the 14th section of the Act Regulating Criminal Proceedings, and the 394th section of the Practice Act, were the same.

As before remarked, there is a wide difference between the two. The word "Black" may include all Negroes, but the term "Negro" does not include all Black persons.

By the use of this term in this connection, we understand it to mean the opposite of "White," and that it should be taken as contradistinguished from all White persons.

In using the words, "No Black, or Mulatto person, or Indian shall be allowed to give evidence for or against a White person," the Legislature, if any intention can be ascribed to it, adopted the most comprehensive terms to embrace every known class or shade of color, as the apparent design was to protect the White person from the influence of all testimony other than that of persons of the same caste. The use of these terms must, by every sound rule of construction, exclude every one who is not of white blood.

The Act of Congress in defining what description of aliens may become naturalized citizens, provides that every "free white citizen," &c. &c. In speaking of this subject, Chancellor Kent says, that "the Act confines the description to "white" citizens, and that it is a matter of doubt, whether, under this provision, any of the tawny races of Asia can be admitted to the privileges of citizenship." 2 Kent's Com. 72.

We are not disposed to leave this question in any doubt. The word "White" has a distinct signification, which *ex vi termini*, excludes black, yellow, and all other colors. It will be observed, by reference to the first section of the second article of the Constitution of this State, that none but white males can become electors, except in the case of Indians, who may be admitted by special Act of the Legislature. On examination of the constitutional debates, it will be found that not a little difficulty existed in selecting these precise words, which were finally agreed upon as the most comprehensive that could be suggested to exclude all inferior races.

If the term "White," as used in the Constitution, was not understood in its generic sense as including the Caucasian race, and necessarily excluding all others, where was the necessity of providing for the admission of Indians to the privilege of voting, by special legislation?

We are of the opinion that the words "White," "Negro," "Mulatto," "Indian," and "Black person," wherever they occur in our Constitution and laws, must be taken in their generic sense, and that, even admitting the Indian of this Continent is not of the Mongolian type, that the words "Black person," in the 14th section must be taken as contradistinguished from White, and necessarily excludes all races other than the Caucasian.

We have carefully considered all the consequences resulting from a different rule of construction, and are satisfied that even in a doubtful case we would be impelled to this decision on grounds of public policy.

The same rule which would admit them to testify would admit them to all the equal rights of citizenship, and we might soon see them at the polls, in the jury box, upon the bench, and in our legislative halls.

This is not a speculation which exists in the excited and over-heated imagination of the patriot and statesman, but it is an actual and present danger.

The anomalous spectacle of a distinct people, living in our community, recognizing no laws of this State except through necessity, bringing with them their prejudices and national feuds, in which they indulge in open violation of law; whose mendacity is proverbial; a race of people whom nature has marked as inferior, and who are incapable of progress or intellectual development beyond a certain point, as their history has shown; differing in language, opinions, color, and physical conformation; between whom and ourselves nature has placed an impassable difference, is now presented, and for them is claimed, not only the right to swear away the life of a citizen, but the further privilege of participating with us in administering the affairs of our Government.

These facts were before the Legislature that framed this Act, and have been known as matters of public history to every subsequent Legislature.

There can be no doubt as to the intention of the Legislature, and that if it had ever been anticipated that this class of people were not embraced in the prohibition, then such specific words would have been employed as would have put the matter beyond any possible controversy.

For these reasons, we are of opinion that the testimony was inadmissible. The judgment is reversed and the cause remanded.

Mr. Justice WELLS dissented, as follows:

From the opinion of the Chief Justice, I must most respectfully dissent.

GLOSSARY

anomalous spectacle: strange sight

conformation: structure, appearance

convertible: interchangeable

degraded: inferior, pushed to a lower position

demoralized: morally corrupt

ex vi termini: by the force of the term

ingenious speculations: clever assumptions

mendacity: deceitfulness

Mongolian: an outdated term referring to all individuals of Asian descent, specifically Chinese

pari material: two laws analyzed together due to their similarity

signification: meaning, importance

Document Analysis

The majority opinion handed down by the California Supreme Court in the case of *People v. Hall* reflected not only the attempt of the court to provide a clear definition of racial categories in order to protect the interests of the white race but also reveals the racial anxieties and virulent anti-Chinese hostilities that existed in the United States at the time. The bulk of the testimony in the case against George Hall was provided by Chinese witnesses. The question before the court was whether or not such testimony should be admissible given that it was provided by nonwhite individuals. Section 14 of California's Criminal Proceedings Act, an 1850 act of the legislature that regulated criminal proceedings, had already established that "no Black or Mulatto person, or Indian," would be allowed to testify against a white man in a court of law. Since the law never specifically excluded the testimony of a Chinese individual, the justices sought to determine whether or not the law was intended to apply to the Chinese as well. Thus, they struggled first to define what the creators of the law intended by the terms *black*, *white*, and *Indian*. Second, they reflected on the implications of expanding rights and political power to nonwhite races. The text of the majority opinion clearly reflects the racial tensions and fears of the era and provides insight into the history of American race relations.

Defining Racial Categories

In the first section of the majority opinion, Murray turned to historical and scientific evidence to help deconstruct the meanings behind the racial categories defined by the 1850 law. Murray begins by making the argument that since the time of Columbus's first contact with the native people of San Salvador, the term *Indian* historically has been used to imply American Indians as well as Asians. Murray points out that Columbus, who was attempting to locate a passage to the Indies, assumed that the island was located in the Chinese sea near India and that its inhabitants were of Asian descent, and so he referred to the island's native people as Indians. Although Columbus's assumption was incorrect, the term *Indian* was henceforth applied generically to both Asians and American Indians.

Murray then moves to provide scientific evidence to buttress his argument. He claims that anthropological theories about the Asian origins of the ancestors of American Indians further seemed to validate the association between the two groups. Murray summarizes the ideas of ethnologists who had previously concluded that American Indian groups had originally migrated across the Bering Strait into North America. Although he admits that this theory had recently been challenged, Murray concludes that historical and scientific evidence confirms that "the name of Indian, from the time of Columbus to the present day, has been used to designate, not alone the North American Indian, but the whole of the Mongolian race."

Murray further defines the intent behind the use of the words *black* and *white* in the original 1850 legislation. The court argues the broadest definition of the terms. The word *black* is defined as "the opposite of 'white.'" Thus the court insists that the specific phrasing of the original legislation that denied any "Black or Mulatto person, or Indian," from testifying against a white person was intended "to embrace every known class or shade of color." Murray therefore concludes that the intent of the use of the term *Indian* in the law prohibiting Indians from testifying against white individuals was anticipated to apply to the Chinese as well. His intent here is to validate historically and scientifically the notion that white people have always viewed Chinese people as nonwhite and therefore not entitled to the same rights and privileges as white people.

Racial Anxieties

Clearly underlying the court's decision are the racial anxieties at play in American society at the time. An influx of immigrants from around the world contributed to heightened nativist sentiments. Heated discussions over the future of slavery and the question of the status of American Indians in American society raged in the political arena, and sectional tensions threatened to divide the nation. The case of *People v. Hall* reflected an overall concern about the future status of white people in the United States. The opinion clearly suggests that the court is concerned not only with protecting white people from the potentially damning testimony of untrustworthy "others" but also about the broader, potentially devastating implications of the decision to allow nonwhite individuals to testify in a court of law. Murray argues, for instance, that if the court allowed groups other than white people to testify in court, they might also be allowed the right to vote, serve on a jury, or gain positions of political power.

The potential of these groups to gain equal rights as citizens is imagined as a great threat to all of American society, in part because of the perception that these groups represented "inferior races." Murray argues,

> The anomalous spectacle of a distinct people, living in our community . . . whom nature has marked as inferior, and who are incapable of progress or intellectual development . . . differing in language, opinions, color, and physical conformation: between whom and ourselves nature has placed an impassable difference . . . is now presented, and for them is claimed, not only the right to swear away the life of a citizen, but the further privilege of participating with us in administering the affairs of our Government.

Here, Murray clearly outlines the type of scientific racism implicit in his overarching argument, which justifies racist laws by suggesting that anthropology has delineated the distinctions between the races and ordered them hierarchically. He uses this pseudoscientific theory to legitimize his decision to deny these groups access to the exercise of full social and political equality, arguing that the "scientifically" proven racial inferiority of certain groups necessitates the interpretation of laws to shield the superior race from the potential harm of too much power in the hands of intellectually incapable races. Murray's fear was that allowing nonwhite groups to testify against white people would open the door to allowing these same groups to gain "equal rights of citizenship" and participate in the administration of "the affairs of our government."

The immediate implication of the court's decision was the reversal of Hall's conviction. Hall literally got away with murder because the testimony of the three Chinese witnesses had to be disregarded. The broader implication was effectively to make the Chinese a target. The ruling itself seemed to encourage acts of violence against the Chinese, with perpetrators fully aware that their actions would likely go unpunished. Denied equal protection under the law, the Chinese immigrant community responded with outrage at the court's decision. They objected to being categorized the same as other racial groups. Letters of protest sent to the governor pointed out the racism of the majority opinion and demanded equal protection of the law. A letter written by Lai Chun-Chuen representing the Chinese merchants in San Francisco countered anti-Chinese arguments that labeled the Chinese as primitive and barbaric. Lai argued that the history of Chinese civilization pointed to the superiority of the Chinese over less developed races such as black people and Indians. Although grounded in some of the same racialized rhetoric espoused by Murray and the court, the argument effectively countered stereotypes of the Chinese as less civilized then Caucasians. This attempt to distance themselves from black people and Indians and more closely associate themselves with white people would prove to be a common and somewhat successful tactic of the Chinese American community when challenging future racist laws. Similarly, the merchant class recognized an advantage in pointing out their class status and distancing themselves from common laborers as a means of arguing against discriminatory laws and for greater political power in the years to come.

Despite the ruling in *People v. Hall*, the Chinese immigrant community continued to take their cases before the court in hopes of obtaining justice. Their efforts sometimes proved successful, depending in large part on the judge, the jury, and the acumen of their lawyers. Calling upon an extensive transnational network of support, Chinese immigrants relied on family, friends, and kinship and district organizations to protect their rights and freedoms. They persisted in their protests and efforts to reverse discriminatory laws. White allies, including big business leaders and Christian missionaries who supported Chinese immigration, often came to the aid of the Chinese and spoke out publicly on their behalf. Reverend William Speer, a Presbyterian missionary, publicly insisted that the Hall decision violated principles of democracy, Christianity, and common humanity. The political influence of white community leaders like Speer helped gain some degree of public support for the Chinese cause.

Although *People v. Hall* would be effectively overturned by federal civil rights legislation in the 1870s, by that point the anti-Chinese movement on the Pacific coast was gaining significant political momentum. Anti-Chinese lobbyists would succeed in lobbying Congress to pass significant measures to curb Chinese immigration and ultimately exclude Chinese laborers, culminating in the passage of the Chinese Exclusion Act in 1882. Chinese people living in the United States suffered countless acts of violence in a concerted effort to drive them out of towns throughout the West Coast. Even large urban ethnic enclaves provided limited protection against anti-Chinese hostilities. San Francisco's Chinese community fought extensive legal battles against efforts to drive them from certain industries, segregate their children in the schools, and prevent their families from joining them in the United States. The era of anti-Chinese exclusion and hostility continued well into the twentieth century. It was not until China became a US ally in World War II that Chinese exclusion as an immigration policy was repealed. Even then, the institutionalized discrimination established substantial barriers to social, political, and economic progress that would require decades to overcome.

Essential Themes

The case of *People v. Hall* highlights not only the extent of the racial tensions between Chinese immigrants and white miners but also the ways in which the judicial branch established a racialized system of justice that privileged white persons above all other groups. Justice Murray's opinion in *People v. Hall* echoed the racist rhetoric of the era and reflected larger tensions at play in the United States in the mid-nineteenth century as the nation struggled to come to terms with who would be allowed access to citizenship. Murray's writing reflects a common attitude held by white American nativists, who feared that the influx of large numbers of "inferior" classes of foreigners would lead to the ultimate downfall of the nation. Although it is clear that not all white Americans shared in this viewpoint, the political power exerted by individuals of Murray's status had far-reaching implications. The justices of the California Supreme Court had the power to validate discriminatory laws and extend the application of other laws, which ultimately codified racist sentiments into the US legal system, thus making the task of battling racism and injustice even more difficult for the generations of Chinese Americans that followed.

Wendy Rouse, PhD

Bibliography

Almaguer, Tomas. "'They Can Be Hired in Masses; They Can Be Managed and Controlled Like Unthinking Slaves.'" *Race and Racialization: Essential Readings*. Ed. Tania Das Gupta et al. Toronto: Canadian Scholars', 2007. 217–31. Print.

Camp, Edgar Whittlesey. "Hugh C. Murray: California's Youngest Chief Justice." *California Historical Society Quarterly* 20.4 (1941): 365–73. Print.

Daniels, Roger. *Asian America: Chinese and Japanese in the United States since 1850*. Seattle: U of Washington P, 1988. Print.

Limerick, Patricia Nelson. *The Legacy of Conquest: The Unbroken Past of the American West*. New York: Norton, 1987. Print.

McClain, Charles J. *In Search of Equality: The Chinese Struggle against Discrimination in Nineteenth-Century America*. Berkeley: U of California P, 1994. Print.

Pfaelzer, Jean. *Driven Out: The Forgotten War against Chinese Americans*. New York: Random, 2007. Print.

Rawls, James J., and Walton Bean. *California: An Interpretive History*. 9th ed. Boston: McGraw, 2008. Print.

Additional Reading

Aarim-Heriot, N. *Chinese Immigrants, African Americans & Racial Anxiety in the United States, 1848-82*. Urbana: U of Illinois P, 2006. Print.

Chan, Sucheng. *Asian Americans: An Interpretive History*. New York: Twayne, 1991. Print.

Lee, Erika. *At America's Gates: Chinese Immigration during the Exclusion Era, 1882–1943*. Chapel Hill: U of North Carolina P, 2007. Print.

Sandmeyer, Elmer Clarence. *The Anti-Chinese Movement in California*. Urbana: U of Illinois P, 1991. Print.

Takaki, Ronald. *A History of Asian Americans: Strangers from a Different Shore*. Boston: Little, 1998. Print.

Yung, J., G. H. Chang, and H. M. Lai, eds. *Chinese American Voices: From the Gold Rush to the Present*. Berkeley: U of California P, 2006. Print.

LESSON PLAN: **A Split Decision**

Students analyze Chief Justice Murray's opinion in *People v. Hall* and how Pun Chi's appeal rebuts it.

Learning Objectives

Identify the purpose of this document; analyze the influence of early nineteenth century ideas in Murray's opinion; draw comparisons across eras; appreciate the contrasting perspectives in Murray's opinion and Pun Chi's appeal.

Materials: Chief Justice Hugh Murray, *People v. Hall (1854)*; Pun Chi, "We Chinese Are Viewed Like Thieves and Enemies" (ca. 1860)

Overview Questions

How does the nature of this document affect its language? What evidence does Murray cite in making his case? What parts of this opinion would twenty-first century readers agree with? How does Pun Chi's appeal to Congress refute Murray's legal opinion?

Step 1: Comprehension Questions

What is the specific function of this document? How does its purpose affect its tone?

- **Activity:** Have students read aloud the stated purpose of the author of this document. Discuss with students how the document's linguistic style might affect readers. Discuss whether or not the tone would be the same even with a different conclusion and why or why not.

Step 2: Context Questions

What arguments does Murray make to support his conclusion? What evidence does he offer to substantiate his arguments?

- **Activity:** Have students summarize Murray's opinion. Direct students to list specific evidentiary facts he offers and the sources he uses to support them. Have students discuss which facts seem unsupported. Discuss what factors might have led Murray's contemporaries to accept his arguments as valid.

Step 3: Context Questions

What facts in Murray's argument would a modern reader assume are true? What evidence is there that not all of Murray's contemporaries shared his views?

- **Activity:** Have students list statements from the opinion that might generally be assumed as true today. Have students then list statements would be regarded as false. Have students cite evidence within the document that not all of Murray's contemporaries shared his view.

Step 4: Exploration Questions

How does Pun Chi's appeal reflect the probable effects of *People v. Hall?* How does it counter Murray's argument?

- **Activity:** Have students list specific statements in Pun Chi's appeal that suggest negative effects of the thinking supported in *People v. Hall.* Then direct students to create a two-column graph listing Murray's negative opinions of nonwhite people on one side and how Pun Chi's appeal either directly or indirectly refutes those opinions on the other side.

Step 5: Response Paper

Word length and additional requirements set by Instructor. Students answer the research question in the *Overview Questions*. Students state a thesis and use as evidence passages from the primary source document as well as support from supplemental materials assigned in the lesson.

On Seizing Land from Native Californians

Date: April 1855
Author: de la Guerra, Pablo
Genre: speech

"The [war of 1848] took place, and we . . . were sold like sheep, abandoned by our nation, and as it were, strangers on the very soil on which we were native . . . already we have suffered deeply; our property sacrificed."

Summary Overview

In his speech known as "On Seizing Land from Native Californians," Pablo de la Guerra—an influential nineteenth-century Mexican American politician in the California State Assembly—addresses the state Senate regarding a ratified bill known as the Land Law (1851), which allowed for the seizure of land by the US government if its Latino residents failed to provide official documentation of their land grants. Scant documentation of land rights existed during this era, leading to the unjust confiscation of land and, thus, an eradication of the rights codified by the Treaty of Guadalupe Hidalgo at the conclusion of the Mexican-American War (1846–48). As one of the only Mexican American citizens serving in the California State Assembly, de la Guerra used that political forum to voice his opposition to the blatant social injustice experienced by native Mexicans in the aftermath of the war. Although the Treaty of Guadalupe Hidalgo promised the protection of native land grants from American settlers migrating west, the US government ostensibly ignored the treaty with the onset of the California gold rush and allowed for the land to be claimed by settlers. De la Guerra subtly elucidates the racialization of Mexican Americans initiated by the treaty through poignant diction and language. During an epoch in which the ideology of Manifest Destiny guided US foreign policy, de la Guerra attempts to give a political voice to Mexican Americans by protecting their landholdings through legal means during an era of unequal representation in politics. He engages with ubiquitous tropes in the Latino counternarrative, dealing with issues surrounding race, citizenship, and multiculturalism in a country that claims its fundamental pillars to be liberty and democracy. De la Guerra's speech conveys a legacy of conflict and hardship wrought by the Treaty of Guadalupe Hidalgo and elucidates the origin of the Latino civil rights movement within the treaty itself and the social injustice that enabled the trend of land loss throughout annexed Mexican territory. The racial logic of white hegemony undergirded US foreign policy along with overt economic motives.

Defining Moment

The nineteenth century was an epoch of rapid westward US expansion as a result of "Manifest Destiny" and the reimagining of occupied land and space as available. Coined by John O'Sullivan, Manifest Destiny—the view that claimed God wanted the people of the United States to control all North American land from the Atlantic to the Pacific Oceans—became the central ideology for US foreign policy and expansion during the nineteenth century. The shifting frontier became associated with American identity of the "rugged individual" espoused by Frederick Jackson Turner, an American historian whose frontier thesis argued that up until the 1890s, the history of the United States had been characterized by territorial expansion, military conquest, and cultural amalgamation; westward expansion defined the United States and justified the divinely ordained American prerogative to seize control of the land despite the presence of native inhabitants whose claim to the land harked back centuries before the existence of the United States. De la Guerra's speech elucidates both how the myth of a vanishing frontier functioned and the material consequences it spawned: the illegal seizure of native Mexicans' land by the conquering United States in the aftermath of the Mexican-American War. The war centered on a dispute over land in the Rio Grande territory and resulted in US victory; the subsequent peace treaty shifted geopolitical borders of the United States and Mexico. Mexicans immediately became colonized persons within their homeland; this idea undergirded the Chicano movement during the twentieth century, as participants based their movement on the imagined homeland they called Aztlán, the American Southwest stolen from them at the conclusion of the Mexican-American War.

The colonization of the West and the expansion of the American frontier into previously Mexican territory complicated both the definition of American citizenship and who received its full privileges. With the ratification of the Treaty of Guadalupe Hidalgo, US borders quickly changed, rendering Mexicans living in the region subject to US rule with little protection despite the treaty's promises. De la Guerra emerged as one of the sole advocates for Mexican American land claims and sought to defend them against racial violence. Born a Mexican citizen, de la Guerra sympathized with the natives when land-seizure bills continued to be put forth in the Senate. His speech addressing an unsympathetic Senate questioned the "liberal myth" of the United States as founded on democratic principles of equality and liberty by highlighting the injustice undergirding the land-seizure bills targeting Mexicans as conquered citizens of color. Annexed by the United States as a result of the Mexican-American War, the American Southwest complicated and redefined the meanings of nationality and citizenship. Mexicans were given an ascriptive form of citizenship that the government used to deflect the reality that Mexicans were a conquered people. The negotiation of Mexican land that de la Guerra discusses serves as a microcosm for the experience of persons of color in the United States as the definition of citizenship was contested and reformulated throughout the nineteenth and twentieth centuries.

Author Biography

Pablo de la Guerra was born on November 29, 1819, in Santa Barbara, California—then a viceroyalty of Spain—into a distinguished household. He was born in a Spanish colony, worked for the Mexican government in what became the Mexican state of California after Mexican independence, and died a US citizen after his homeland came under US hegemony following the Mexican-American War. His father, José de la Guerra, migrated from Spain to Mexico during the 1790s and married Antonia Carrillo, a member of a well-to-do family residing in California. Born a Mexican citizen, de la Guerra chose to naturalize as an American citizen under the terms of the 1848 Treaty of Guadalupe Hidalgo.

Because of his family's prestige within the community, de la Guerra became an active public servant, serving in local and statewide government legislative bodies, including California's constitutional convention in 1849. This convention formally granted Mexicans citizenship rights enjoyed by whites, hinting at the racial prerequisites of "whiteness" for American citizenship. Delegates came to a consensus that "a small amount of Indian blood" was admissible for US citizenship, and Mexicans would be formally enfranchised while excluding both African Americans and American Indians. In 1850, California was officially recognized as a state, which conferred on de la Guerra US citizenship. During the 1860s, de la Guerra became the acting lieutenant governor of California and also served in the California state legislature. Legally defined as white, de la Guerra relished the privileges enjoyed by white citizens, especially in the political arena; his political clout—a rarity for individuals of Mexican descent during that era—gave him a forum for his advocacy of Mexican American rights. As a member of the California State Assembly and Senate, de la Guerra emerged as an advocate for Mexican American rights and was recognized as dependable by both Latinos and whites.

However, when de la Guerra was elected as a California state court judge in 1869, California filed a lawsuit that questioned his eligibility for the position based on his questionable citizenship because of the color of his skin. The prosecutor, M. M. Kimberly, argued that the California act of April 20, 1863, stipulated that only

US citizens retained eligibility for the elected office of district judge. Invoking several articles of the Treaty of Guadalupe Hidalgo, Kimberly argued that de la Guerra was not a US citizen, because the treaty never granted the power to render Mexicans or Americans Indians citizens and because he was not white. De la Guerra rebutted that he was white and therefore was excluded from the racial laws in practice in California. Although the California Supreme Court sided with de la Guerra by classifying him as white, and therefore exempt from racial laws, the decision reaffirmed citizenship as race-based; as a white citizen, de la Guerra had the privileges of citizenship under constitutional law protected while nonwhite Mexicans did not. Thus, the US government retained the power to distribute political privileges to individuals on the basis of race.

Despite his legal battles, de la Guerra remained a staunch advocate for Mexican American rights and claims under the stipulations of the Treaty of Guadalupe Hidalgo. He fought every land-seizure bill that entered the Senate and ultimately set the foundation for the Hispanic American civil rights movement during the twentieth century. Eventually, mounting political pressure defeated his efforts as white settlers migrating to California vehemently demanded reclamation of the "vacant" land. De la Guerra died on February 5, 1874.

HISTORICAL DOCUMENT

I hope the Senate will allow me to offer a few remarks upon the merits of the bill, and to state why, upon the principles of reason and justice I consider that the bill should be indefinitely postponed. :

Well, sir, the war took place, and we, after doing our duty as citizens of Mexico, were sold like sheep abandoned by our nation, and as it were, awoke from a dream, strangers on the very soil on which we were native and to the manor born. We passed from the hands of Mexico to that of the United States, but we had the consolation of believing that the United States, as a nation, was more liberal than our own. We had the greatest respect for an American. Every American who came to our country was held in higher estimation than even one of our countrymen. And I call upon every American who visited us to bear testimony to this fact. And after being abandoned by our own country and annexed to the United States, we thought that we belonged to a nation the most civilized, the most humane-a nation that was the foremost in planting the banner of liberty on every portion of its dominions-a nation that was the most careful in protecting the just rights of its citizens. Well, sir, in 1849, a great many emigrated to California, not to settle upon the land or to cultivate the soil, but to work in the mines and go home; and from '49 to '52 they had no other object, but many finding that it was hard work in the mines, and being told that the land in the State had not been separated from the public domain, had no boundaries and being probably further misled by lawyers, or interested persons, who stated that the land in this condition would never be confirmed to the owners by the Supreme Court of the United States, came and settled upon our lands. And I ask, are we to suffer for that?

I believe that I speak advisedly, when I say that three-fourths of the settlers upon the lands, have been aware that someone had a prior claim; they knew it by common report, that such a one and such a one had a claim upon the land; but they thought that even if it was confirmed to the owners, that the use of the land until the confirmation, would be worth more than the improvements that they would make. Perhaps one-fourth went upon the land in good faith. I do not know that such was the case, but I am willing to grant it; but now, when they find that it is probable that the Supreme Court of the United States will confirm these grants, and after deriving all the benefits for the use of the same, they apply to the Legislature, in order that a State Law may be set up as a bar against the action of the Court of the United States.

I say, sir, that already we have suffered deeply; our property has been sacrificed. The Bay of San Francisco alone, at one time, had more cattle than can now be found in the counties of Santa Clara, Monterey, Santa Cruz, San Luis Obispo, and Santa Barbara. Horses, at that time could be counted by the thousands; and I believe that many settlers have settled upon lands for the purposes of stealing the cattle and sending them to the San Francisco market for sale.

Now, sir, of the 113 members in this Legislature, I am the only native of this state; and the native population expect from me, and through me, that in my place in this Legislative Hall, that I shall call the attention of this body to the facts I have now stated, and to tell you that badly treated as they have been in every respect, they look around them and find no other aid except in the mercy of Heaven, and the justice of this Legislature; and now, in their name, I call upon you, Senators, to consider that if they are deprived of what is left to them, they have no other place to go to. They have been rejected by the Mexicans; they know no other country but California, and by depriving them of their rights, they will be compelled to be beggars in the streets; and in order to prevent this terrible calamity from overtaking them, they, through me, throw themselves upon your mercy and clemency; and they ask and expect from you protection that will justify before the eyes of the world the belief in justice of the American people. If the American settlers are deprived of what they have expended for their improvements, they can go home and meet the aid and sympathies of their friends and countrymen; but the Californian, what prospect has he before him, or where shall he go?

I wish to make one remark about the expression, "settled in good faith," and I am done. Sir, if this bill has effect, it will be from the countries of Santa Clara upward, because in the south we have no settlers; but in those counties I am now referring to, the settlers greatly outnumber the land claimants, and it is useless to say that juries are incorruptible. We know that such is not the case from our daily experience. And these juries will be formed by whom? Sir, they will consist of those very settlers. The Sheriff will summon such a jury as will suit their views. I have seen a good deal of juries in California. I have seen where proof, clear as noon day, would not alter the decision of a jury from their preconceived opinions.

And I will affirm that I believe that out of 100 cases tried between the settlers and the land owners that 99 will be given in favor of the settler.

And, sir, to conclude these remarks, permit me to assure you, upon my honor as a gentleman, that everything I have stated is true and as clear as conviction itself. I know that I am in the Senate chamber of California, where full liberty of speech is allowed, but if I were speaking to a barbarous people, I should still advocate the same sentiments, and even if I were killed for so doing, I should at least have the satisfaction of dying in a just cause, and should receive the reward from Him who has said, "Blessed are those who are persecuted, for righteousness sake, for of such is the kingdom of heaven."

GLOSSARY

calamity: catastrophe, disaster

clemency: forgiveness, mercifulness

consolation: comfort, solace

liberal: progressive, favorable to reform

the war: Refers to the Mexican-American War, in which the United States defeated Mexico and annexed the land that comprises the modern-day American Southwest (including California)

Document Analysis

De la Guerra's speech represents a defense of Mexican American civil rights and laid the foundation for the subsequent twentieth-century Chicano movement. The language he uses alludes to the racial undertones of US immigration and foreign policy during the nineteenth century; in a covert fashion, de la Guerra addresses and laments an American legal system supported by structural and institutional racism that denies persons of color the protections promised by US citizenship. Thus, his staunch defense of land rights highlights broader themes in US history regarding racial hegemony. Invoking a recurring theme of liberty, de la Guerra juxtaposes the actions of the US government with the rudimentary American value of liberty to elucidate the dissonance, and thus hypocrisy, of American values. Born a Mexican citizen into a well-to-do family, de la Guerra possessed political clout that he was willing to exercise in his fight for social justice for Mexican Americans. De la Guerra—the only California native serving in the state legislature—not only recognized the injustices occurring around him but also demonstrated the courage to stand up to a government comprising elite white men who possessed the salient racial attitudes that characterized the time period.

In the opening of his speech, de la Guerra describes native Mexicans as docile, compliant citizens despite their savage treatment at the hands of the US government during and after the Mexican-American War. Identifying himself at the outset with these native Mexicans despite his position in the California legislature, de la Guerra quickly establishes himself as an advocate for and defender of native rights despite his decision to naturalize as an American citizen. His goal in this speech is twofold: he seeks to subvert common knowledge in US public discourse and cultural attitudes toward Mexicans and subtly expose the fallacy of American values and character. He does so immediately by using specific diction associated with the mythos of the United States and its founding principles. The United States expanded westward by touting itself as a beacon of liberty, spreading democracy, equality, and freedom across the North American continent. Native Mexicans viewed the United States as a "humane . . . nation" that would welcome, embrace, and protect inhabitants of Mexico as equal citizens. These expectations articulated by de la Guerra mirror the sentiments held by immigrants throughout American history who seek refuge in a country that promises a better life and equal, just treatment.

Such expectations of the United States expressed by de la Guerra on behalf of the Mexican Americans he served emanate from the mythos in public discourse and public consciousness; myths transcend stereotypes and become deeply embedded within the social consciousness. Through his subtle assertion of Mexicans as second-class citizens, de la Guerra realizes the fallacy of the myth of a United States "more liberal" than Mexico in its approach to immigration and assimilation, and he conveys such sentiments through his exasperated tone at the outset of his speech.

The promised protection of citizenship rights of Mexican Americans and the ensuing violation of them contribute to de la Guerra's postulate that US values had become the antithesis of what they claimed to be through founding documents such as the Constitution. Prior to and during the Mexican-American War, American settlers were considered aliens in Mexico whose presence was not welcomed by the native Mexicans. Following American victory, the United States annexed the territory known as the Mexican Cession. Arbitrary land laws passed by the US government at the state and national levels made the "calamity" of loss of land and citizenship possible and left Mexicans in the annexed territory vulnerable to attacks on their rights. Laws such as those for which de la Guerra expresses disapproval in his speech thereby arbitrarily constructed Mexicans as illegal, rendering them "strangers" on their native soil. Mexicans living within the territorial borders of the United States had no legal status; "abandoned" by Mexico and betrayed by the United States. As de la Guerra notes, without their rights protected vis-à-vis land grants, Mexicans would become "beggars" in the street hoping for law courts to uphold justice. Therefore, de la Guerra contends that the hypocritical actions of the US government make its representatives the true "barbarians," rather than the Mexicans whom they ostensibly sought to enlighten.

Anglo-Americans never fully accepted Mexicans as racial equals despite allowing those living in the ceded territories to acquire US citizenship. Manifest Destiny—the ideology that guided US expansion throughout the nineteenth century—glorified the white settler. As historian Mae M. Ngai discusses, though US expansionists desired to control all of Mexico, racial suspicions led them to abandon such sentiments out of aversion to incorporating a nonwhite race into the United States. De la Guerra recognizes such racial attitudes and suspicions held by the US government in his speech and uses both metaphors and particular diction to convey the binary of civilized and uncivilized peoples, but he does so to subvert popular conceptions. Although viewed as barbarous, savage, and uncivilized, Mexicans, de la Guerra asserts, treated the United States and its citizens upon annexation with respect and fidelity. Conversely, however, rather than receive "humane" treatment, Mexicans had their land seized by the government and reclaimed by white settlers despite their knowledge of its rightful ownership. Furthermore, de la Guerra laments the institutional racism toward Mexican Americans underpinning the US legal system. Viewing juries comprising settlers as corruptible and possessing "preconceived opinions," de la Guerra critiques the inequities latent in law courts dealing with land-claim disputes. He thereby suggests that juries racialized Mexicans and rendered them second-class citizens because of their nationality and race; thus, Mexicans could never fully acculturate and become truly American. Therefore, Mexicans remained at the fringe of US citizenship because of their second-class treatment at the hands of a government that touted the values of equality and liberty for all.

The dissonance between the function of land in Mexican culture—a culture rooted in land as a sacred space to be protected and treasured—and its capitalistic role in American culture further explain the cruel actions of the American government that de le Guerra describes in his speech. De la Guerra outlines the emotional trauma of native Mexicans losing their land and having their property "sacrificed" and "stolen" for the economic gain of a conquering nation. Euro-American colonialism and expansion across the North American continent historically led to violent encounters between natives and the European colonists. The cultural divide between the natives and the colonists regarding the sanctity and importance of land within their respective worldviews catalyzed colonial antagonisms once the natives were uprooted from their sacred lands. The removal and dissociation of natives from their culturally sacred land—to which they had been tied both spatially and culturally for thousands of years—conveys how land lay at the heart of the violent colonial practices waged against indigenous communities in the American Southwest. Mexicans not only viewed land as the key to their survival but also as tied in to their spirituality and religious beliefs. De la Guerra laments how US capitalism led to the exploitation for the sake of profit of Mexican's once fertile lands. He thus highlights the primacy of capitalism—a profit-driven and amoral economic system—in the development of the United States. Capitalism required the alienation of native land claims by reimagining American land as unclaimed to enable white settlers to claim it as their own. Thus, de la Guerra implies, westward expansion was rooted in conquest, with latent political, economic, and cultural imperatives rather than the mere desire to "plant" and spread the "banner of liberty" in Mexican soil.

De la Guerra invokes religiosity to further highlight the hypocrisy of the government's actions in seizing native land. Rendered stateless and unprotected by a conquering US government that violated its own treaty, Mexican Americans became "beggars in the streets" whose livelihood depended on the mercy of a settler government who perceived Mexicans as lesser people. De la Guerra questions the moral basis of settlers occupying Mexican land "in good faith" by questioning the religious justification for stealing land. Such actions delineate the US government as "barbarous people" rather than the enlightened, righteous, and civilized individuals that they tout themselves to be. Thus, de la Guerra invokes the religious principles Americans claim fundamentally underpin the country's origin to expose the hypocrisy and irreligious behavior involved in stealing land and persecuting native Mexicans. Such sentiments subvert the images of the civilized Yankee and subhuman Mexican that dominated public attitudes and discourse during a turbulent epoch. The conquest and annexation of Mexican territory catalyzed a period of US foreign policy marked by colonialism and imperialism that had lasting consequences for the United States in terms of both its global relations and its internal structures.

Essential Themes

The US government continued to treat Mexicans as second-class citizens following the Treaty of Guadalupe Hidalgo; unequal political representation and the absence of protection for Mexican American citizenship rights through the seizure of land revealed such second-class treatment. Overtly racist stereotypes soon permeated public discourse, and anti-Mexican rhetoric resulted in a production of knowledge regarding the figure of the Mexican as dirty, incompetent, and subhuman. The emergence of scientific racism contributed to the degradation of Mexicans well into the twentieth century and underlay the efforts to restrict Mexican immigration during the 1920s despite the need for cheap labor in the agribusinesses of the Southwest. As Ngai notes, although racialized, Mexicans retained a legal status as white, although this category remained unstable because of their race. Their presence in regions once under Mexican control rendered them "racialized aliens" whose labor was needed but presence was resented because of the to the deep-seated antagonisms dating back to the Treaty of Guadalupe Hidalgo and subsequent land seizures.

De la Guerra delivered his speech on the seizure of native land prior to his legal debacle regarding his fitness for citizenship and service in California legislative bodies. Despite suffering from the injustice latent in government institutions toward citizens of Mexican descent, de la Guerra emerged as the sole advocate for native rights in the California Senate during a time when ideas connoted by Manifest Destiny permeated both elite circles and the public domain. Despite de la Guerra's efforts to advocate for and defend native rights, the system of white hegemony prevailed. Nonetheless, his efforts served as a foundation for a subsequent civil rights movement during the twentieth century known as the Chicano movement. This cultural movement during the 1960s sought to revive native Mexican culture and reclaim land that was rightfully theirs in the American Southwest. Members of the Chicano movement sought to reclaim their homeland of Aztlán, thereby aligning Mexican Americans with the American Indian cause. Furthermore, the psychological trauma of Mexican American loss of land led their descendants to negotiate a new identity for Mexican Americans that claimed indigeneity and resulted in the emergence of a nationalism based on culture rather than geopolitical borders and mythos.

Maddie Weissman, MA

Bibliography

Menchaca, Martha. *Recovering History, Constructing Race: The Indian, Black, and White Roots of Mexican Americans*. Austin: U of Texas P, 2001. Print.

Ngai, Mae M. *Impossible Subjects: Illegal Aliens and the Making of Modern America*. Princeton: Princeton UP, 2004. Print.

Smith, Andrea. *Conquest: Sexual Violence and American Indian Genocide*. Cambridge, MA: South End, 2005.

Additional Reading

Garcia y Griego, Manuel. "Persistence and Disintegration: New Mexico's Community Land Grants in Historical Perspective." *Natural Resources Journal* 48.4 (2008): 847–56. *Academic Search Premier*. Web. 12 Aug. 2012.

Hernández, Sonia. "The Legacy of the Treaty of Guadalupe Hidalgo on Tejanos' Land." *Journal of Popular Culture* 35.2 (2001): 101. Print.

Johnson, Kevin R. *Immigration, Citizenship, and U.S./Mexico Relations. Bilingual Review* 25.1 (2000): 23–39. Print.

"Pablo de la Guerra Speaks Out against Injustice." *Santa Barbara Independent*. Santa Barbara Independent, 2 Aug. 2007. Web. 12 Aug. 2012.

LESSON PLAN: **A Formal Plea**

Students analyze Pablo de la Guerra's speech "On Seizing Land from Native Californians" and compare it to articles within the Treaty of Guadalupe Hidalgo.

Learning Objectives

Identify the central question de la Guerra addresses; read the speech imaginatively; interrogate historical data; compare and contrast the promise of the *Treaty of Guadalupe Hidalgo* to the behaviors de la Guerra identifies.

Materials: Pablo de la Guerra, "On Seizing Land from Native Californians" (1855); Nicholas B. Trist, Treaty of Guadalupe Hidalgo (1848).

Overview Questions

What was de la Guerra's goal and how effective was his argument? How does the fact that this was a speech affect its content? How do historians know these are de la Guerra's literal words? What does de la Guerra's speech reveal about the effectiveness of the Treaty of Guadalupe Hidalgo?

Step 1: Context Questions

What is the specific purpose of this document? How does de la Guerra mount his argument?

- **Activity:** Direct a student to explain the bill de la Guerra is arguing against. Have students list his points against passage of the bill. Further discuss the logic of his argument in its contemporary context.

Step 2: Comprehension Questions

How do the rhetorical devices required in a speech affect de la Guerra's argument?

- **Activity:** Have students read passages aloud, giving their readings the oral emphasis a real speech would have. Ask students to identify practical and rhetorical devices that the genre requires. Discuss how those rhetorical needs helped or hurt de la Guerra's argument.

Step 3: Context Questions

What particular problems would a speech versus a written document present to historians? What additional sources might historians employ to verify the authenticity of this speech's content?

- **Activity:** Discuss with students how and if historians know these are the literal words that de la Guerra spoke in the California Senate. Have students suggest other sources that historians might use to confirm the speech's authenticity.

Step 4: Exploration Questions

How does de la Guerra specifically show the bill the California Senate is considering is inconsistent with the Treaty of Guadalupe Hidalgo? How might twenty-first century readers use this inconsistency as evidence in causes of modern-day problems?

- **Activity:** Have students review the list they created of the points in de la Guerra's argument. Direct students to identify specific articles within the treaty that de la Guerra believed were being violated. Challenge students to mount their own arguments about the potential long-term effects of the California Senate's apparent violation of the treaty.

Step 5: Response Paper

Word length and additional requirements set by Instructor. Students answer the research question in the *Overview Questions.* Students state a thesis and use as evidence passages from the primary source document as well as support from supplemental materials assigned in the lesson.

■ The Discovery of Gold in California

Date: November 1857
Author: Sutter, John A.
Genre: article; memoir

"Then the people commenced rushing up from San Francisco and other parts of California, in May, 1848: in the former village only five men were left to take care of the women and children. The single men locked their doors and left for 'Sutter's Fort,' and from there to the Eldorado."

Summary Overview

In *Hutchings' California Magazine* in 1857, John Augustus Sutter recounted the events surrounding the discovery of gold at his mill near Coloma, California, some nine years earlier. He explained how word of the discovery spread and how the discovery affected him personally. Sutter, a Swiss immigrant who became an early California landowner, could have become extremely wealthy as a result of the discovery of gold on his land, but it ran counter to his goals and eventually became the catalyst for a series of business failures that would characterize much of his later life. Within the context of American history, however, the discovery of gold in California helped to justify the country's belief in Manifest Destiny. It also set into motion large-scale and rapid immigration, and forced the nation to further address whether slavery would be allowed to expand westward.

Defining Moment

In January 1848, the United States was already preparing to expand its holdings in the Southwest. The war with Mexico was ending, and the goals of Manifest Destiny—the belief that the United States was destined by Providence to expand all the way across the North American continent—were becoming realities with the negotiation of the Treaty of Guadalupe Hidalgo, under which Mexico ceded to the United States all the land from Texas to the Pacific. This Mexican Cession, as it was called, included the territory of Alta California, or Upper California, a name the Americans shortened to California.

Prior to Mexican independence in 1821, Alta California was a Spanish colony, and the search to find wealth in the Southwest dates back to the earliest Spanish *entradas*, or explorations, in the 1530s and 1540s. Stories of riches such as the mythical Seven Cities of Cibola had fuelled the imagination of explorers like Francisco Vásquez de Coronado, but in truth, the Spanish colonies of Texas, New Mexico, and Alta California had been a drain on Spanish resources. The riches the Spanish had found in their other colonies, such as Peru and Mexico, seemed not to be in evidence in Spain's northern holdings. Therefore, relatively few Spaniards colonized Alta California, although a vibrant Hispanic culture, based around the large landholdings of a number of wealthy Californios (Spanish-speaking inhabitants of California) and the numerous Franciscan missions, was well established by the time the Americans arrived. Before US annexation, the future cities of San Diego, Los Angeles, and San Francisco (then called Yerba Buena) were nothing more than small towns in a region far from the corridors of Spanish, Mexican, or American power.

The events that John Sutter describes, however, would change everything. California would almost overnight go from a primitive expanse occupied by Mexican landowners to a bustling and wild frontier region dominated by mostly young, single men from the eastern United States, Europe, and China. Prior to the gold rush, Americans had gradually been moving across the continent. Afterward, as historian J. S. Holliday aptly put it, "the world rushed in." The gold that flowed out of California, which had remained hidden until just after the Americans took over, seemed to justify the American notion of Manifest Destiny and the country's preordained right to inhabit the continent.

Author Biography

Born in Baden, Germany, to Swiss parents in 1803, Johann August Sutter emigrated from Berne, Switzerland, to the United States in 1834 in order to avoid mounting debt, changing his first two names to John Augustus. He left his wife and family behind, though he hoped to bring them to the United States when his fortunes turned. He found his way to California in 1839, after stops in St. Louis, the Oregon Territory, and Hawaii. Along the way, Sutter relied on inflated stories of his past and his considerable "gift of gab" to get him out of financial difficulties and convince merchants to extend him credit and government officials to view him as a valuable new member of the community. Even the nickname "Captain" was the result of exaggerating his time as an under lieutenant in the Bernese reserve corps into service as a commander in the famed Swiss Guard (Hurtado 19–20). He tried his hand at trading along the Santa Fe Trail, raising horses and cattle, and building a hotel before leaving for California in order to avoid being sued for default on his debts in Missouri.

Once in California, Sutter impressed both American traders and Mexican government officials with his stories and apparent wealth, claiming, for instance, that he owned a ship. He applied for and received Mexican citizenship and then received a grant of 50,000 acres near present-day Sacramento, where he hoped to raise horses, cattle, and sheep. Once he made peace with the local Nisenan and Miwok Indians, whom he employed as laborers and as his own personal military force, his compound, which he named Sutter's Fort, became the social, political, and commercial center for the entire inland region. Because the area was so isolated from the centers of Mexican power closer to the coast, Sutter became the de facto authority of the region. But the events that would change the history of California and the United States as a whole occurred on another part of Sutter's land grant, about forty-five miles away from Sutter's Fort at a sawmill he had commissioned in the Coloma Valley, named for a nearby Maidu Indian settlement.

HISTORICAL DOCUMENT

It was in the first part of January, 1848, when the gold was discovered at Coloma, where I was then building a saw-mill. The contractor and builder of this mill was James W. Marshall, from New Jersey. In the fall of 1847, after the mill seat had been located, I sent up to this place Mr. P. L. Wimmer with his family, and a number of laborers, from the disbanded Mormon Battalion; and a little later I engaged Mr. Bennet from Oregon to assist Mr. Marshall in the mechanical labors of the mill. Mr. Wimmer had the team in charge, assisted by his young sons, to do the necessary teaming, and Mrs. Wimmer did the cooking for all hands.

I was very much in need of a new saw-mill, to get lumber to finish my large flouring mill, of four run of stones, at Brighton, which was commenced at the same time, and was rapidly progressing; likewise for other buildings, fences, etc., for the small village of Yerba Buena, (now San Francisco.) In the City Hotel, (the only one) at the dinner table this enterprise was unkindly called "another folly of Sutter's," as my first settlement at the old fort near Sacramento City was called by a good many, "a folly of his," and they were about right in that, because I had the best chances to get some of the finest locations near the settlements; and even well stocked rancho's had been offered to me on the most reasonable conditions; but I refused all these good offers, and preferred to explore the wilderness, and select a territory on the banks of the Sacramento. It was a rainy afternoon when Mr. Marshall arrived at my office in the Fort, very wet. I was somewhat surprised to see him, as he was down a few days previous; and then, I sent up to Coloma a number of teams with provisions, mill irons, etc., etc. He told me then that he had some important and interesting news which he wished to communicate secretly to me, and wished me to go with him to a place where we should not be disturbed, and where no listeners could come and hear what we had to say. I went with him to my private rooms; he requested me to lock the door; I complied, but I told him at the same time that nobody was in the house except the clerk, who was in his office in a different part of the house; after requesting of me something which he wanted, which my servants brought and then left the room, I forgot to lock the doors, and it happened that the door was opened by the clerk just at the moment when Marshall took a rag from his pocket, showing me the yellow metal: he had about two ounces of it; but how quick Mr. M. put the yellow metal in his pocket again can hardly be described.

The clerk came to see me on business, and excused himself for interrupting me, and as soon as he had left I was told, "now lock the doors; didn't I tell you that we might have listeners?" I told him that he need fear nothing about that, as it was not the habit of this gentleman; but I could hardly convince him that he need not to be suspicious. Then Mr. M. began to show me this metal, which consisted of small pieces and specimens, some of them worth a few dollars; he told me that he had expressed his opinion to the laborers at the mill, that this might be gold; but some of them were laughing at him and called him a crazy man, and could not believe such a thing.

After having proved the metal with aqua fortis, which I found in my apothecary shop, likewise with other experiments, and read the long article "gold" in the Encyclopedia Americana, I declared this to be gold of the finest quality, of at least 23 carats. After this Mr. M. had no more rest nor patience, and wanted me to start with him immediately for Coloma; but I told him I could not leave as it was late in the evening and nearly supper time, and that it would be better for him to remain with me till the next morning, and I would travel with him, but this would not do: he asked me only "will you come to-morrow morning?" I told him yes, and off he started for Coloma in the heaviest rain, although already very wet, taking nothing to eat. I took this news very easy, like all other occurrences good or bad, but thought a great deal during the night about the consequences which might follow such a discovery. I gave all my necessary orders to my numerous laborers, and left the next morning at 7 o'clock, accompanied by an Indian soldier, and vaquero, in a heavy rain, for Coloma. About half way on the road I saw at a distance a human being crawling out from the brushwood.

I asked the Indian who it was: he told me "the same man who was with you last evening." When I came nearer I found it was Marshall, very wet; I told him that he would have done better to remain with me at the fort than to pass such an ugly night here but he told me that he went up to Coloma, (54 miles) took his other horse and came half way to meet me; then we rode up to the new Eldorado. In the afternoon the weather was clearing up, and we made a prospecting promenade. The next morning we went to the tail-race of the mill, through which the water was running during the night, to clean out the gravel which had been made loose, for the purpose of widening the race; and after the water was out of the race we went in to search for gold. This was done every morning: small pieces of gold could be seen remaining on the bottom of the clean washed bed rock. I went in the race and picked up several pieces of this gold, several of the laborers gave me some which they had picked up, and from Marshall I received a part. I told them that I would get a ring made of this gold as soon as it could be done in California; and I have had a heavy ring made, with my family's cost of arms engraved on the outside, and on the inside of the ring is engraved, "The first gold, discovered in January, 1848." Now if Mrs. Wimmer possesses a piece which has been found earlier than mine Mr. Marshall can tell, as it was probably received from him. I think Mr. Marshall could have hardly known himself which was exactly the first little piece, among the whole.

The next day I went with Mr. M. on a prospecting tour in the vicinity of Coloma, and the following morning I left for Sacramento. Before my departure I had a conversation with all hands: I told them that I would consider it as a great favor if they would keep this discovery secret only for six weeks, so that I could finish my large flour mill at Brighton, (with four run of stones,) which had cost me already about from 24 to 25,000 dollars—the people up there promised to keep it secret so long. On my way home, instead of feeling happy and contented, I was very unhappy, and could not see that it would benefit me much, and I was perfectly right in thinking so; as it came just precisely as I expected. I thought at the same time that it could hardly be kept secret for six weeks, and in this I was not mistaken, for about two weeks later, after my return, I sent up several teams in charge of a white man, as the teamsters were Indian boys. . . .

Mr. Brannan made a kind of claim on Mormon Island, and put a tolerably heavy tax on "The Latter Day Saints." I believe it was 30 per cent, which they paid for some time, until they got tired of it, (some of them told me that it was for the purpose of building a temple for the honor and glory of the Lord.)

So soon as the secret was out my laborers began to leave me, in small parties first, but then all left, from the clerk to the cook, and I was in great distress; only a few mechanics remained to finish some very necessary work which they had commenced, and about eight invalids, who continued slowly to work a few teams, to scrape out the mill race at Brighton. The Mormons did not like to leave my mill unfinished, but they got the gold fever like everybody else. After they had made their piles they left for the Great Salt Lake. So long as these people have been employed by me they have behaved very well, and were industrious and faithful laborers, and when settling their accounts there was not one of them who was not contented and satisfied.

Then the people commenced rushing up from San Francisco and other parts of California, in May, 1848: in the former village only five men were left to take care of the women and children. The single men locked their doors and left for "Sutter's Fort," and from there to the Eldorado. For some time the people in Monterey and farther south would not believe the news of the gold discovery, and said that it was only a 'Ruse de Guerre' of Sutter's, because he wanted to have neighbors in his wilderness. From this time on I got only too many neighbors, and some very bad ones among them.

What a great misfortune was this sudden gold discovery for me! It has just broken up and ruined my hard, restless, and industrious labors, connected with many dangers of life, as I had many narrow escapes before I became properly established. . . .

At the same time I was engaged in a mercantile firm in Coloma, which I left in January, 1849—likewise with many sacrifices. After this I would have nothing more to do with the gold affairs. At this time, the Fort was the great trading place where nearly all the business was transacted. I had no pleasure to remain there, and moved up to Hock Farm, with all my Indians, and who had been with me from the time they were children. The place was then in charge of a Major Domo.

It is very singular that the Indians never found a piece of gold and brought it to me, as they very often did other specimens found in the ravines. I requested them continually to bring me some curiosities from the mountains, for which I always recompensed them. I have received animals, birds, plants, young trees, wild fruits, pipe clay, stones, red ochre, etc., etc., but never a piece of gold. Mr. Dana of the scientific corps of the expedition under Com. Wilkes' Exploring Squadron, told me that he had the strongest proof and signs of gold in the vicinity of Shasta Mountain, and furthers south. A short time afterwards, Doctor Sandels, a very scientific traveler, visited me, and explored a part of the country in a great hurry, as time would not permit him to make a longer stay.

He told me likewise that he found sure signs of gold, and was very sorry that he could not explore the Sierra Nevada. He did not encourage me to attempt to work and open mines, as it was uncertain how it would pay and would probably be only for a government. So I thought it more prudent to stick to the plow, notwithstanding I did know that the country was rich in gold, and other minerals. An old attached Mexican servant who followed me here from the United States, as soon as he knew that I was here, and who understood a great deal about working in placers, told me he found sure signs of gold in the mountains on Bear Creek, and that we would go right to work after returning from our campaign in 1845, but he became a victim to his patriotism and fell into the hands of the enemy near my encampment, with dispatches for me from Gen. Micheltorena, and he was hung as a spy, for which I was very sorry.

By this sudden discovery of the gold, all my great plans were destroyed. Had I succeeded for a few years before the gold was discovered, I would have been the richest citizen on the Pacific shore; but it had to be different. Instead of being rich, I am ruined, and the cause of it is the long delay of the United States Land Commission of the United States Courts, through the great influence of the squatter lawyers. Before my case will be decided in Washington, another year may elapse, but I hope that justice will be done me by the last tribunal—the Supreme Court of the United States. By the Land Commission and the District Court it has been decided in my favor. The Common Council of the city of Sacramento, composed partly of squatters, paid Adelpheus Felch, (one of the late Land Commissioners, who was engaged by the squatters during his office), $5,000, from the fund of the city, against the will of the tax-payers, for which amount he has to try to defeat my just and old claim from the Mexican government, before the Supreme Court of the United States in Washington.

GLOSSARY

aqua fortis: a solution of nitric acid that dissolves most metals other than gold

Eldorado: an area of great wealth, based on the Spanish legend of El Dorado, a city of gold

major domo: an administrator who acts on behalf of an absent landowner or supervises an owner's business

Mormon Battalion: a military unit made up of members of the Church of Jesus Christ of Latter-Day Saints, which were then known as Mormons, that served during the Mexican-American War, many of whom settled in California

Document Analysis

John Sutter had an ambition that was certainly as big as the events that swept through his land grant starting in January 1848, and though he personally did not profit from the gold rush that followed, he was an integral member of the drama that played out in California, transforming the area from a sparsely populated Mexican backwater to one of the economic engines of the United States in a matter of less than five years.

One might think that someone with Sutter's ambitions who also had the good fortune to have gold discovered on his land would be well positioned to profit from the discovery. However, Sutter achieved all he had more by force of personality and slyness than business acumen, and this became readily apparent in the years following the discovery. By the time Sutter told his story to a popular journal—nearly a decade after the discovery—the gold rush was already well known across the nation. But the details Sutter revealed demonstrate much about who he was as a man as well as the importance of the California gold rush in the history of the state, the region, and the nation.

Sutter had chosen the then-remote area near the confluence of the American and Sacramento Rivers as his land grant some seven years earlier, despite having the chance to acquire land closer to the coast. However, being at a distance from the centers of power suited Sutter well, as he wished to have complete control over the development of his land grant as well as the people residing on it. In Sutter's vision, what was wilderness at the time would become a profitable operation, producing cowhides, beef, horses, and lumber for the slowly growing cities of Monterey and Yerba Buena on the coast. Development had been slower than Sutter anticipated, though, and Sutter's Fort was not yet self-sufficient. As a result, he was often seeking credit from suppliers on the coast to keep his operation functioning, something with which he had quite a bit of experience. Sutter had additional reasons for apprehension about what the future might bring in late 1847 and early 1848, as the United States was still at war with Mexico. Although California was still technically Mexican territory, it was by that time under the control of the United States, and a permanent change in government was almost inevitable. Sutter's authority in the region was largely based upon the fact that the Mexican government in Alta California was weak, and his grant was far enough from the Mexican territorial capitol at Monterey that he had unrestrained control over his land (Brands, 17–18).

In late 1847, Sutter had entered a partnership with James W. Marshall to build a sawmill on the South Fork of the American River. Marshall was a mechanic from New Jersey who, like Sutter, had gradually made his way west. Like Sutter, he had briefly settled in the Oregon Territory, but, disliking the weather, moved farther south into California. Men like Marshall who had extensive experience with tools and construction were in high demand in the West, and he had no problem finding work with Sutter. The main portion of Sutter's 50,000-acre land grant was near the present city of Sacramento, California, but he also had an additional grant in the Coloma Valley, which was in the foothills of the Sierra Nevada. Being close to the mountains and on a stream made a perfect location for a sawmill that would provide Sutter's Fort and the surrounding area with the wood needed for construction, and Sutter and Marshall had agreed to share equally in the lumber that the mill produced.

By January, the workers building the mill were digging out the millrace that was to bring the water from the river into the sawmill, turning the wheel that would power the operation. On January 24, 1848, as the water flowed through the millrace, Marshall noticed flakes of a gleaming yellow metal left behind. As the flowing water would have washed away any dirt or lighter minerals, it was clear to Marshall that the metal left behind was gold. Quickly, Marshall collected the flakes and, together with a number of his workers, performed several tests to verify the identity of the metal. Convinced that it was gold he possessed, four days later Marshall embarked on the forty-five mile trip to from Coloma to Sutter's Fort to discuss this development with his business partner.

As Sutter enters into his description of Marshall's arrival at Sutter's Fort, it is interesting that he veers into what others thought of his decision to settle on the Sacramento River rather than nearer to the coast. It appears that he is using the discovery of gold on his property to justify his decision and make his detractors look like fools, which is ironic considering the fact that Sutter profited very little from the discovery. In Sutter's account, when Marshall does arrive, he appears to have a full sense of the significance of the discovery, as he asked to discuss the matter in "a place where we should not be disturbed, and where no listeners could come and hear what we had to say." Marshall asks Sutter to lock the door, and Sutter portrays himself as somewhat incompetent when he forgets to lock the door and his clerk comes into the room just as Marshall is removing the gold from his pocket.

After Marshall shows Sutter the gold, Sutter does exactly what Marshall did at the mill, chemically testing the metal to ensure that it actually was gold and reading up on the material to determine its quality. Satisfied that this was, indeed, high-quality gold, Marshall returned to Coloma, and Sutter left to join him the next morning. Sutter, too, was well aware of the consequences of the discovery, and he became determined to keep the secret for as long as possible. Although Sutter asks the workers at the mill to keep the discovery secret, he states that he knew that it would be nearly impossible to prevent the workers from talking. After the visit, Sutter explained that "On my way home, instead of feeling happy and contented, I was very unhappy, and could not see that it would benefit me much, and I was perfectly right in thinking so; as it came just precisely as I expected." The workers at the mill were well acquainted with the workers at Sutter's Fort, so Sutter concludes that it was inevitable that word would escape. At the same time, Sutter takes great pride in describing the ring that he had made with the first gold taken from the millrace, which he stated he did very soon after, so Sutter himself could have been responsible for spreading news of the discovery. Rather than seeking a way to profit from the discovery personally, Sutter laments the fact that he could see no way to profit, as it did not fit with his plans to build a flour mill and continue his other operations at Sutter's Fort. Rather than seizing the opportunity to profit from gold before the world rushed in, Sutter remains steadfast in his own operations, "as it was uncertain how it would pay and would probably be only for a government. So I thought it more prudent to stick to the plow, notwithstanding I did know that the country was rich in gold, and other minerals." In fact, finding no way to participate in the gold rush itself, Sutter's other operations suffered as his workers left his employ in droves, looking instead to enrich themselves by being among the first in the gold fields.

Interestingly, Sutter mentions in passing Sam Brannan of Mormon Island, who he said placed a tax on his people to mine there. What he does not mention is that Brannan was also a merchant who ran a store at Sutter's Fort. Perhaps if Sutter had possessed the business acumen of his hero John Jacob Astor, he might have followed Brannan's example. As soon as he learned of the discovery, Brannan bought up all of the mining supplies he could, took a trip to San Francisco, and did everything he could to spread the word of the gold strike. As a result, Brannan became the first millionaire in California, not through joining the rush to the gold fields, but by realizing that he was in the right place at the right time to profit from it. However, Sutter continues to complain about the discovery of gold ruining his dream of setting up his private kingdom: "What a great misfortune was this sudden gold discovery for me! It has just broken up and ruined my hard, restless, and industrious labors, connected with many dangers of life, as I had many narrow escapes before I became properly established." Narrow escapes certainly characterized Sutter's life, though his self-pity was meant to disguise the fact that the narrow escapes were too often from circumstances of his own making.

As the gold rush progressed, Sutter focused on keeping what he had. But the vast majority of those who worked for him, with the exception of American Indian workers who were largely chased away from the gold fields, led the throngs that would come to California from all over the United States and the rest of the world to seek their fortunes. Many of the early miners were successful, as there was a significant portion of gold that could be found in much the same way that Marshall had. Placer gold—gold that is on the surface of the earth rather than underground—was still relatively abundant, and miners quickly descended on the region's streams hoping to follow Marshall's example. Governmental jurisdiction of the land was lax because of the gold fields' distance from the coast and because the Treaty of Guadalupe Hidalgo did not go into effect until July 4, 1848. The absence of effective government restrictions meant that there were no rules and no taxes. Small impresarios like Sutter could no longer hold sway over their land grants, as the miners largely made up their own laws to govern themselves in the mining camps.

As much as Sutter had sought to delay the spreading of the news, those like Brannan, who saw opportunity in the influx of immigrants that was sure to follow, ensured that the word would get out. The first outsiders to seek their fortunes began to arrive during the summer of 1848. News had spread to the neighboring Oregon Territory, where many Americans had already migrated. By the end of the year, miners were appearing from Hawaii, Mexico, and South America, and the first settlers from the eastern United States were beginning to arrive. But those numbers would snowball during 1849, when tens of thousands flocked to the California territory. Most came on the overland route via the California Trail, although those with some means could purchase a ticket to come by ship and sail either around the cape at the southern tip of South America or by the Panama shortcut (the Panama Canal would not be built for another sixty-five years).

Mining became more difficult as the "forty-niners" arrived. Competition over claims in the gold fields was intense, and the prices that miners paid to merchants like Brannan for necessary supplies were often exorbitant. It was said that just to survive, a miner in 1849 or 1850 had to mine one ounce of gold every day. Although those who arrived came looking for easy wealth, mining whatever gold was available was extremely difficult work. Success could still be found during those first few years, but after 1853, the amount of placer gold that was mined began to decrease while the number of miners continued to increase.

It is impossible to separate the history of the gold rush from the story of the rapid population growth in California. Although many of the miners returned home disappointed and destitute, many others decided to stay in the region, which became a state on September 9, 1850. Ironically, it was those very miners who saw the potential of the region as agricultural land who realized many of Sutter's dreams, albeit on a much smaller scale.

Like Sutter's own life, the fate of California was determined by a number of events that seemingly overwhelmed the area. The gold rush, clearly, brought huge numbers of people and made the dream of Manifest Destiny a reality. Only nine days after Marshall's discovery of gold, the Treaty of Guadalupe Hidalgo was signed, which, when ratified by the US Senate, would make California a US territory. The timing of the discovery of gold, combined with the transfer of California from Mexico to the United States, made the fate of the region a national issue, since Congress had been debating for decades whether new states and territories would be admitted into the union as slave or free. The rapid increase in the population of California meant that quick statehood would be a necessity. California was ultimately admitted as a free state, but only as a part of the Compromise of 1850, which allowed for a popular vote on slavery in other parts of the territory gained from Mexico, the continuation of slavery in Washington, DC, and, most importantly to Southerners, the passage of a new Fugitive Slave Act, which stated that Southern slave owners could cross into the nonslave states and territories to capture escaped slaves.

Sutter, however, remained focused not on the transformative impact that the discovery of gold on his land had on the region, but rather on his own personal misfortune that was caused by his poor business decisions. His concluding remarks continue his theme of feeling personally ruined by the discovery of gold. "By this sudden discovery of the gold, all my great plans were destroyed. Had I succeeded for a few years before the gold was discovered, I would have been the richest citizen on the Pacific shore; but it had to be different. Instead of being rich, I am ruined."

Essential Themes

The discovery of gold on John Sutter's land in 1848 had dramatic consequences for many different populations within California. For miners, the impact was felt economically, and for a few of them it was a time of incredible profit and good fortune. For others, it was a fool's errand, and they returned home destitute and in disgrace. Furthermore, for many of California's American Indians, Sutter's discovery was the beginning of the end of their culture. As happened in other regions where Euro-American settlers arrived in large numbers, disease spread rapidly, decimating many communities. The dependency some tribes had on Euro-American trade meant that with the increased prices of those trade goods, many Indians slipped into poverty or even died of starvation. The justice of the gold fields did not include justice for the Indians, who were sometimes killed for their land. Those who remained had their land and their cultures invaded by the flood of Euro-Americans.

The gold rush that resulted from the discovery also greatly diversified the California population. Mexicans and American Indians constituted the majority of native inhabitants in the region at the time of the discovery. That would quickly change, however, as immigrants from all over the world flooded in. The Chinese arrived in greater numbers than any other. By 1850, there were five hundred Chinese in California, and by 1855 the number of Chinese who had made the trip across the Pacific to the "Gold Mountain" reached twenty thousand, over twice the entire population of the region seven years earlier. San Francisco quickly became the center of Chinese American culture, and although many other cities in California developed Chinatowns, San Francisco's remained dominant and iconic. Chinese miners, like Indians, were persecuted and many had their claims stolen by Euro-American miners. However, the Chinese soon earned a reputation for making profitable claims that other miners had abandoned. After the gold rush, discrimination increased, and by 1882, the United States passed the Chinese Exclusion Act, which was the first immigration law restricting the entry of one particular group based on ethnicity.

Finally, the discovery had a dramatic impact on the landscape. Once the placer gold began to run out in 1853, more destructive means were employed to extract gold from beneath the surface. Hydraulic mining decimated entire hillsides by using torrents of water to find the gold hiding underneath. Chemicals such as arsenic, cyanide, and mercury—used to extract the gold from the materials in which it was embedded—poisoned the land and water. The burgeoning population cut down huge stands of timber to fuel the growth of their towns. In the end, the discovery of gold resulted in the creation of a new California, but—as Sutter would have pointed out—at the expense of destroying the old California.

Steven L. Danver, PhD

Bibliography

Brands, H. W. *The Age of Gold: The California Gold Rush and the New American Dream*. Rev. ed. New York: Random, 2002. Print.

Holliday, J. S. *The World Rushed In: The California Gold Rush Experience*. New York: Simon, 1981. Print.

---. *Rush for Riches: Gold Fever and the Making of California*. Berkeley: U of California P, 1999. Print.

Hurtado, Albert L. *John Sutter: A Life on the North American Frontier*. Norman: U of Oklahoma P, 2006. Print.

Osborne, Thomas J. *Pacific Eldorado: A History of Greater California*. New York: Wiley-Blackwell, 2013. Print.

Starr, Kevin. *Americans and the California Dream, 1850–1915*. New York: Oxford UP, 1986. Print.

Additional Readings

Dillon, Richard. *Fool's Gold: The Decline and Fall of Captain John Sutter of California*. Sanger, CA: Write Thought, 2012. Print.

Owens, Kenneth N., ed. *John Sutter and a Wider West*. Rev. ed. Lincoln: U of Nebraska P, 2002. Print.

---. *Riches for All: The California Gold Rush and the World*. Lincoln: U of Nebraska P, 2002. Print.

Trafzer, Clifford E. and Joel R. Hyer, eds. *Exterminate Them! Written Accounts of the Murder, Rape, and Slavery of Native Americans during the California Gold Rush, 1848–1868*. East Lansing: Michigan State UP, 1999. Print.

Vaught, David. *After the Gold Rush: Tarnished Dreams in the Sacramento Valley*. Baltimore: Johns Hopkins UP, 2007. Print.

LESSON PLAN: **Gold Rush in California**

Students analyze John A. Sutter's narrative "The Discovery of Gold in California" and compare his fate to the fates of Mexican American citizens of California in the 1850s.

Learning Objectives

Identify the importance of Sutter's narrative; read Sutter's words imaginatively; challenge historical inevitability; compare perspectives Sutter and Pablo de la Guerra.

Materials: John A. Sutter, "The Discovery of Gold in California" (1857); Pablo de la Guerra, "On Seizing Land from Native Californians" (1855).

Overview Questions

Why does Sutter's narrative impact all other gold rush histories? How might Sutter's prose style affect his readers' acceptance of his conclusions? What evidence does Sutter provide that suggests his conclusions about his ultimate fate might be right? How did the discovery gold have a similar impact on Sutter and Mexican American citizens?

Step 1: Comprehension Questions

What literal details does Sutter supply about the discovery of gold in 1848? What is the value of his reporting?

- **Activity:** Direct students to use details in the opening paragraphs to reconstruct what happened in January 1848. Discuss why Sutter's description is central to an understanding of the discovery of gold in the United States. Have students suggest what other kinds of competing narratives would support or refute the details Sutter offers.

Step 2: Comprehension Questions

What is the tone of this passage? Does the tone reinforce or negate Sutter's point of view and conclusions? Why?

- **Activity:** Have students characterize Sutter's narrative tone and cite examples to support their judgments. Discuss what the tone suggests about Sutter and whether or not it helps validate his conclusions about his fate. Discuss how a different tone might have affected his argument.

Step 3: Context Questions

What in Sutter's narrative suggests that alternative events could have made him "the richest citizen on the Pacific shore"? Was Sutter's fate inevitable once gold was discovered?

- **Activity:** Have students list Sutter's other achievements besides discovering gold. Discuss whether or not Sutter would have had success without the discovery of gold. Challenge students to debate whether or not Sutter could have altered his ultimate fate after gold was discovered.

Step 4: Exploration Questions

What in Sutter's account suggests he would support aspects of Pablo de la Guerra's speech "On Seizing Land from Native Californians"? How might that suggestion affect understandings of de la Guerra's speech?

- **Activity:** Have students identify the passage in Sutter's narrative that suggests he might sympathize with de la Guerra. Discuss how the passage might broaden and redefine de la Guerra's plea. Have students compare Sutter's California fate to that of Mexican American citizens.

Step 5: Response Paper

Word length and additional requirements set by Instructor. Students answer the research question in the *Overview Questions*. Students state a thesis and use as evidence passages from the primary source document as well as support from supplemental materials assigned in the lesson.

Supplemental Historical Documents

HISTORICAL DOCUMENT

Present at the Beginning of the Gold Rush

Date: 1850
Author: Buffum, Edward Gould
Genre: journal

We had at last reached the "mines," although a very different portion of them than that for which we started. We turned out our tired horses, and immediately set forth on an exploring expedition. As my clothing was all dirty and wet, I concluded to indulge in the luxury of a new shirt, and going down to the river found a shrewd Yankee in a tent surrounded by a party of naked Indians, and exposing for sale jerked beef at a dollar a pound, flour at a dollar and a half do., and for a coarse striped shirt which I picked up with the intention of purchasing, he coolly asked me the moderate price of sixteen dollars! I looked at my dirty shirt, then at the clean new one I held in my hand, and finally at my little gold bag, not yet replenished by digging, and concluded to postpone my purchase until I had struck my pick and crowbar into the bowels of the earth, and extracted therefrom at least a sufficiency to purchase a shirt.

The diggings on Yuba River had at that time been discovered only about three months, and were confined entirely to the "bars," as they are called, extending nearly a mile each way from where the road strikes the river, on both its banks. The principal diggings were then called the "upper" and the "lower diggings," each about half a mile above and below the road. We started for the upper diggings to "see the elephant," and winding through the hills, for it was impossible to travel all the way on the river's bank, struck the principal bar then wrought on the river. This has since been called Foster's Bar, after an American who was then keeping a store there, and who had a claim on a large portion of the bar. Upon reaching the bar, a curious scene presented itself. About one hundred men, in miner's costume, were at work, performing the various portions of the labour necessary in digging the earth and working a rocking machine. The apparatus then used upon the Yuba River, and which has always been the favourite assistant of the gold-digger, was the common rocker or cradle, constructed in the simplest manner. It consists of nothing more than a wooden box or hollowed log, two sides and one end of which are closed, while the other end is left open. At the end which is closed and called the "mouth" of the machine, a sieve, usually made of a plate of sheet iron, or a piece of raw hide, perforated with holes about half an inch in diameter, is rested upon the sides.

A number of "bars" or "rifflers," which are little pieces of board from one to two inches in height, are nailed to the bottom, and extend laterally across it. Of these, there are three or four in the machine, and one at the "tail," as it is called, i. e. the end where the dirt is washed out. This, with a pair of rockers like those of a child's cradle, and a handle to rock it with, complete the description of the machine, which being placed with the rockers upon two logs, and the "mouth" elevated at a slight angle above the tail, is ready for operation. Modified and improved as this may be, and as in fact it already has been, so long as manual labour is employed for washing gold, the "cradle" is the best agent to use for that purpose. The manner of procuring and washing the golden earth was this. The loose stones and surface earth being removed from any portion of the bar, a hole from four to six feet square was opened, and the dirt extracted there from was thrown upon a raw hide placed at the side of the machine.

One man shovelled the dirt into the sieve, another dipped up water and threw it on, and a third rocked the "cradle." The earth, thrown upon the sieve, is washed through with the water, while the stones and gravel are retained and thrown off. The continued motion of the machine, and the constant stream of water pouring through it, washes the earth over the various bars or rifflers to the "tail," where it runs out, while the gold, being of greater specific gravity, sinks to the bottom, and is prevented from escaping by the rifflers. When a certain amount of earth has been thus washed (usually about sixty pans full are called "a washing"), the gold, mixed with a heavy black sand, which is always found mingled with gold in California, is taken out and washed in a tin pan, until nearly all the sand is washed away. It is then put into a cup or pan, and when the day's labour is over is dried before the fire, and the sand remaining carefully blown out. This is a simple explanation of the process of gold-washing in the placers of California.

At present, however, instead of dipping and pouring on water by hand, it is usually led on by a hose or forced by a pump, thereby giving a better and more constant stream, and saving the labour of one man. The excavation is continued until the solid rock is struck, or the water rushing in renders it impossible to obtain any more earth, when a new place is opened. We found the gold on the Yuba in exceedingly fine particles, and it has always been considered of a very superior quality. We inquired of the washers as to their success, and they, seeing we were "green horns," and thinking we might possibly interfere with them, gave us either evasive answers, or in some cases told us direct lies. We understood from them that they were making about twenty dollars per day, while I afterwards learned, from the most positive testimony of two men, who were at work there at the time, that one hundred dollars a man was not below the average estimate of a day's labour.

On this visit to Foster's Bar I made my first essay in gold-digging. I scraped up with my hand my tin cup full of earth, and washed it in the river. How eagerly I strained my eyes as the earth was washing out, and the bottom of the cup was coming in view! and how delighted, when, on reaching the bottom, I discerned about twenty little golden particles sparkling in the sun's rays, and worth probably about fifty cents. I wrapped them carefully in a piece of paper, and preserved them for a long time,—but, like much more gold in larger quantities, which it has since been my lot to possess, it has escaped my grasp, and where it now is Heaven only knows.

The labour on Yuba River appeared very severe, the excavations being sometimes made to a depth of twelve feet before the soil containing the gold, which was a gravelly clay, was reached. We had not brought our tools with us, intending, if our expedition in the mountains had succeeded, that one of our party should return for our remaining stock of provisions and tools. We had no facilities for constructing a machine, and no money to buy one (two hundred dollars being the price for which a mere hollowed pine log was offered us), and besides, all the bars upon which men were then engaged in labour were "claimed," a claim at that time being considered good when the claimant had cleared off the top soil from any portion of the bar. We returned to our camp, and talked over our prospects, in a quandary what to do. Little did we then dream that, in less than six months, the Yuba River, then only explored some three miles above where we were, would be successfully wrought for forty miles above us, and that thousands would find their fortunes upon it.

We concluded to return to the Embarcadero, and take a new start. Accordingly, next morning we packed up and set off, leaving at work upon the river about two hundred men. Having retraced our steps, we arrived at Sutter's Fort in safety on the evening of November 30th, just in time to find the member of our party whom we had left behind, packing all our remaining provisions and tools into a cart, ready to start for the "dry diggings" on the following morning.

The history of John A. Sutter, and his remarkable settlement on the banks of the Sacramento, has been one of interest since California first began to attract attention. Captain Sutter is by birth a Swiss, and was formerly an officer in the French army. He emigrated to the United States, became a naturalized citizen, and resided in Missouri several years. In the year 1839 he emigrated to the then wilderness of California, where he obtained a large grant of land, to the extent of about eleven leagues, bordering on the Sacramento River, and made a settlement directly in the heart of an Indian country, among tribes of hostile savages. For a long time he suffered continual attacks and depredations from the Indians, but finally succeeded, by kind treatment and good offices, in reducing them to subjection, and persuading them to come into his settlement, which he called New Helvetia.

With their labour he built a large fort of adobes or sunburnt bricks, brought a party of his Indians under military discipline, and established a regular garrison. His wheat-fields were very extensive, and his cattle soon numbered five thousand, the whole labour being performed by Indians. These he paid with a species of money made of tin, which was stamped with dots, indicating the number of days' labour for which each one was given; and they were returned to him in exchange for cotton cloth, at a dollar a yard, and trinkets and sweetmeats at corresponding prices. The discovery of the gold mines of California has, however, added more to Sutter's fame than did his bold settlement in the wilderness. This has introduced him to the world almost as a man of gold, and connected his name for ever with the most prized metal upon earth. He is quite "a gentleman of the old school," his manners being very cordial and prepossessing.

Sutter's Fort is a large parallelogram, of adobe walls, five hundred feet long by one hundred and fifty broad. Port-holes are bored through the walls, and at its corners are bastions, on which cannon are mounted. But when I arrived there its hostile appearance was entirely forgotten in the busy scenes of trade which it exhibited. The interior of the fort, which had been used by Sutter for granaries and storehouses, was rented to merchants, the whole at the annual sum of sixty thousand dollars, and was converted into stores, where every description of goods was to be purchased at gold-mine prices. Flour was selling at $60 per barrel, pork at $150 per barrel, sugar at 25 cents per pound, and clothing at the most enormous and unreasonable rates. The principal trading establishment at this time was that of Samuel Brannan Co. Mr. Brannan informed me, that since the discovery of the mines, over seventy-five thousand dollars in gold dust had been received by them. Sutter's Fort is in latitude 35° 33' 45" N., and longitude 121° 40' 05" W.

With all our worldly gear packed in an ox-wagon, we left Sutter's Fort on the morning of the 1st of December, and travelling about seven miles on the road, encamped in a beautiful grove of evergreen oak, to give the cattle an opportunity to lay in a sufficient supply of grass and acorns, preparatory to a long march. As we were to remain here during the day, we improved the opportunity by taking our dirty clothing, of which by that time we had accumulated a considerable quantity, down to the banks of the American Fork, distant about one mile from camp, for the purpose of washing. While we were employed in this laborious but useful occupation, Higgins called my attention to the salmon which were working up the river over a little rapid opposite us. Some sport suggested itself; and more anxious for this than labour, we dropped our half-washed shirts, and started back to camp for our rifles, which we soon procured, and brought down to the river. In making their way over the bar, the backs of the salmon were exposed some two inches above water; and the instant one appeared, a well-directed rifle-ball perforated his spine. The result was that before dark Higgins and myself carried into camp thirty-five splendid salmon, procured by this novel mode of sport. We luxuriated on them, and gave what we could not eat for supper and breakfast to some lazy Indians, who had been employed the whole day in spearing some half dozen each. There is every probability that the salmon fishery will yet prove a highly lucrative business in California.

LESSON PLAN: **A Credible Eyewitness**

Students analyze Edward Gould Buffum's 1848 journal entries, which record his presence at the beginning of the gold rush, and contrast his judgment of John A. Sutter's fate with Sutter's own judgment of it.

Learning Objectives

Identify Buffum's purpose in writing; interrogate historical data; analyze the potential effect of Buffum's words on his contemporaries; compare and contrast the views of Buffum and Sutter.

Materials: Edward Gould Buffum, *Six Months in the Gold Mines* (1850), excerpt from Chapter III; John A. Sutter, "The Discovery of Gold in California" (*Hutchings' California Magazine*, November 1857).

Overview Questions

How might Buffum's dual role in the creation of his narrative have affected his insights? How can today's readers judge the real value of money in the 1850s? What details does Buffum supply that might encourage others to go to California? How does Buffum's attitude about Sutter's role in the gold rush compare with Sutter's view?

Step 1: Comprehension Questions

How is Buffum's experience as a journalist evident in his narrative? Buffum describes his own gold-mining efforts. How does this impact his reporting?

- **Activity:** Have students read aloud passages that show Buffum's skill as a journalist. Have students discuss how his descriptions could be collaborated through other sources. Next, have students read aloud Buffum's first-person passages. Discuss why these harm or help the narrative.

Step 2: Comprehension Questions

Why does reading Buffum's narrative require clear understanding of the value of money in 1848? What 1850s' sources and current modern-day sources would help today's readers achieve that understanding?

- **Activity:** Discuss how to estimate the real value of dollar amounts that Buffum cites. Direct some students to use other 1850s' primary sources to find measures of a dollar's value. Have other students use modern-day secondary sources. Compare and discuss the results.

Step 3: Context Questions

What information does Buffum supply that would make a gold rush adventure appealing to his contemporaries? What in his text would soften the appeal?

- **Activity:** Have students create lists of Buffum's pros and cons of searching for gold, both stated and implied. Have students cite specific details in this passage that probably sent others to California but not to find gold.

Step 4: Exploration Questions

What judgments does Buffum make about Sutter's businesses, gold-rush role, and successes? What is Sutter's opinion of the discovery that made him famous?

- **Activity:** Have students take notes as they reread Buffum's comments on Sutter's activities. Next, have them take notes as they read Sutter's description of the effects of the gold rush on his businesses. Have students discuss the factors that led to the differences in their perceptions.

Step 5: Response Paper

Word length and additional requirements set by Instructor. Students answer the research question in the *Overview Questions*. Students state a thesis and use as evidence passages from the primary source document as well as support from supplemental materials assigned in the lesson.

HISTORICAL DOCUMENT

Regarding Oregon Statehood

Date: 1857
Author: Curry, George L.
Genre: speech

Fellow Citizens of the Council and House of Representatives

As in all probability you constitute the last Legislative Assembly that will convene under our present form of government, I have deemed it appropriate if not in the line of my official duty, to address you upon an occasion which would seem to invite an expression of thought upon the past and present of our history, and to suggest a consideration of matters touching the interests of the Territory, as well as the welfare and prosperity of the State which is soon to be inducted into power.

When the history of Oregon comes to be written the mind of the historian will be impressed by the earnestness and sincerity of character—the unobtrusive, unostentatious conduct of those who formed its population from the first reclaiming of the wilderness—the pioneer epoch—to the more refined advancement into social and political existence. Another generation, in the realization of the ease, comfort and affluence, and the various enjoyments of a higher civilization, which will have resulted from ceaseless industry and undiscouraged enterprise, may accord the need of praise to the unwearied toil and patient suffering of those who tracked the wilderness and subdued it to the wants of man. Our pioneer settlers possessed integrity of character. They were energetic and diligent, warm-hearted and strong-willed. Difficulties and [reverses] did not dishearten them, dangers could not. These attributes and labor constituted their only capital and with them they achieved success. They were co-laborers in the service of utility; the pinchings of poverty and their daily privations only made them be more apt and efficient workmen. They accomplished a purpose with every effort. They congregate to reward a bounty for wolf-scalps, and separate after having inaugurated the first republican government on the shores of the Northern Pacific—the polity of which has received the unqualified commendation of the first statesmen of the Union. The only instance of true and successful "squatter sovereignty" in the history of our Country.

The Territorial system of government may be regarded as somewhat under the federal Constitution, in its definition of the enjoyment of the full rights of citizenship. It is an imperfect and unsatisfactory form of government, and may continue to be a fruitful source of trouble and discontent. It would seem just and politic, having full faith in the capacity of the people for self government, that the citizens of the Territories should no longer be debarred the right, which no Constitutional power prohibits, to elect their own executive and judicial officers. Such an amendment of the system would free it from its most objectionable feature—that vestige of monarchical custom which should find no practice, or toleration, in a confederation of republican States, where the intelligence of the people is the basis of the government.

The provisional government which had been instituted by the mixed population of Oregon, after an existence of nearly six years, having admirably achieved its purpose, gave place to the jurisdiction f the United States, in our present Territorial system, on the 3rd day of March, A.D. 1849. In a few months a more satisfactory change will have transpired in the assumption of the powers and authority of a sovereign State. It is a circumstance especially gratifying and congratulatory that, while other Territories have been afflicted with turbulence and desperate feuds, in this effort to perfect their form of government, Oregon has accomplished it with dignity, determining the same questions and causes of unhappiness, without the [disruption] of social obligation, the violation of peace, or the infringement of her honor. This in the main is owing to the fact that we have been let alone by outside pseudo-reformers and philanthropists, that we have not been cursed by the presence of political advocators and emissaries of fanaticism to excite indecent passion, prostitute the public good, and make the blessings of our fathers a scorn.

The people of the Territories are fully competent to manage their own political concerns. They know best their own interests and necessities and least of all do they require foreign influences to educate them as to their political rights and duties. In the peaceful pursuit of agricultural life the settler seeks to obtain a comfortable subsistence. Nature is his daily companion, and the sentiments she inspires elevate his mind and pacify his heart. Is he not to be trusted in the exercise of his prerogatives! Vice does not flourish where agriculture has made her home. The Territories, as the common property of the nation, should be regarded as neutral ground, rather than as arenas for fanatical strife. Life has a better and higher purpose, and the nation a nobler mission than is involved in an interminable crusade.

The Constitution, which has been adopted with such a feeling of unanimity, reflects credit upon those who framed it and our citizens have exhibited their excellent judgment in approving it as the fundamental law. It is liberal in its provisions, and its spirit is in harmony with the progressive and improving impulse of the age. It inculcates the principles of economy in the administration of the government, which it is to be hoped may be always rigidly observed and maintained, for extravagance has characterized the times and should be guarded against by every prudent means. There is nothing that will so fetter the uselessness of the State and impair its healthful vitality. It is an instrument that should be patiently submitted to the test of time, and careful practice and construction, before any encouragement is given to any change whatever.

Oregon presents herself for admission into the Confederation of States in no attitude. No indecent haste impairs the undertaking. Time has matured the event. Her Constitution compares favorably with those of other states. She has adjusted creditably, permanently and satisfactorily all subjects involving differences of opinion. She has evaded no issue, or responsibility, however delicate or exciting. She understands herself and can be readily comprehended by all. Her manifold interests, in their daily increasing magnitude and importance, demand, and inspire the hope, that there may be no hesitation, or delay, in the acknowledgement of her sovereignty.

You are doubtless aware that Dr. John Evans, a gentleman of high scientific attainments has been engaged for several years, under direction of the general government, in making a geological reconnaissance of this and Washington Territory. With the character of his explorations, and the zeal and energy with which they have been conducted, you are likewise familiar. The publications of his report, which is now complete, ought to be a matter of considerable interest, especially to the two Territories, for we may confidently calculate that he has collected much valuable information which will be of importance to the growing interests of this section of the Union. It is desirable that the fruit of his investigation should be made known to the world. I have no doubt that the passage of a joint resolution, by your respective bodies, instructing our delegate to request Congress to make the necessary appropriation for the early publication of the work might be of service in accomplishing that and The Commissioner of the General Law Office estimates the requisite amount for this purpose at $21,400.00. Consider the labors of Dr. Evans "as eminently useful in a scientific point of view as well as subserving the interests of the Pacific coast, by indicating the localities of the Country possessing mineral and agricultural wealth." He correctly observes—

"Either what has been done in the way of exploration and development of coal deposits, under appropriation by Congress, is to go for nothing and remain useless, or be brought to light in proper form, as proposed by further appropriation, to close the business and make the results available. The effect of the . . . measure will be to open up new sources of trade to active industry in the extraction and sale of coal on the Pacific, thereby furnishing the material for propulsion, essential in our rapidly growing steam commerce on the Pacific, at cheap rates, instead of the enormous cost of the article imported from the east."

Our Indian relations remain in an unsatisfactory state. As demand has been made for the surrender of the murderers of Agent Bolen and Wright, and other Indians guilty of similar outrages, although the Superintendent of Indian Affairs has signified to the commanding officer of this military department, the justice and necessity of such an act. Notwithstanding the uncertain affairs no apprehensions need be entertained of hostile demonstrations on the part of the Indians west of the Cascade Mountains so long as the government; by an adequate military force and ample appropriation, maintains its present policy of keeping and subsisting them upon reservations.

The abrogation of the treaties with the Indians east of the Cascades, or rather the failure of the Senate to ratify them, has been regarded as a sufficient cause to justify the closing of the large extent of country beyond the Dalles of the Columbia against settlement, or occupation by the whites. I shall not now undertake to oppose the policy of the measure, however questionable it may be, but I have to observe that the section of the Territory allotted to has been opened to settlement by the positive enactment of Congress. The ratification of the treaties with the Indians west of the Cascades, it should be borne in mind, is only of comparatively recent occurrence. Indeed the first treaties were rejected. Because of this no authority military or other, attempted the assumption and exercise of a power doubtful, at least. When the jurisdiction of the United States was extended over this Country, and its authority established, through executive and judicial officers, it was, it is presumed, for the purpose of protecting its citizens in the enjoyment of their rights and interests and afterwards, in order to foster those interests and increase the population, liberal grants of land were made to those already occupying portions of the public domain, and others were invited to become settlers upon it by virtue of the provisions of the same law and receive a similar gratuity. Wherever the settler located his right he held independent of the possessing rights of the Indians, which was unextinguished, and the "intercourse law," which was quite as applicable as now. It was not his business to inquire who owned the land. He paid for it by his labor to a proprietor powerful enough to guarantee his patent. The expiration of certain provisions of the land law does not affect the inherent principle involved in the subject.

Large sections of the country from which the whites have been thus excluded are well adapted for purposes of pasturage, being covered with highly nutritious grasses. Our citizens had been regarding its occupation as highly advantageous for their rapidly augmenting herds of cattle and other stock.

Our present highly capable Superintendent of Indian Affairs is wholly engaged in the efficient discharge of the difficult duties of his responsible position. An increase of jurisdiction has made his labours truly Herculean. From the forty second to the forty ninth parallel of north latitude and from the ocean to the Rocky Mountains forms now but one Superintendency. This district of country is much too extensive for any one Superintendent, be he ever so efficient. It will be impossible to give entire and complete satisfaction. There should be two, at least, if not three such officers for a field of service so extended and important. I would respectfully suggest the expediency of your memorializing Congress upon the necessity of authorizing additional Superintendents so as the better to insure the prompt discharge of every responsibility pertaining to this important branch of the public service. . . .

LESSON PLAN: **Oregon Statehood**

Students analyze Governor George L. Curry's speech regarding Oregon statehood and compare its content and viewpoint to Pablo de la Guerra's speech on early California challenges.

Learning Objectives

Appreciate historical perspective in Curry's speech; interrogate historical data to identify broad concerns that influenced Oregon's statehood; draw comparisons between Oregon and American exceptionalism; compare and contrast Curry's and de la Guerra's speeches.

Materials: George L. Curry, "Regarding Oregon Statehood" (1857); Pablo de la Guerra, "On Seizing Land from Native Californians" (1855).

Overview Questions

What information in Curry's speech captures the transitory moment in Oregon history? How do the national debates of the mid-nineteenth century resonate in his speech? What special qualities does Curry see in Oregon and its people? How and why do the tone and judgments in the speeches of Curry and de la Guerra differ?

Step 1: Comprehension Questions

What was the context of Curry's speech? What secondary sources would clarify the context?

- **Activity:** Have students read aloud passages that describe Oregon's evolving territorial status. Next, have students use details in the speech to discuss the chain of events that led to that status. Help students identify secondary sources that could clarify the speech's context.

Step 2: Comprehension Questions

What are the "arenas for fanatical strife" that Curry refers to in the fifth paragraph? How does Curry suggest that Oregon is dealing with them?

- **Activity:** Have students review major issues that America faced in the first half of the nineteenth century. Ask students to identify references to those issues within the speech. Discuss Curry's opinion about how the new constitution deals with them.

Step 3: Context Questions

How does Curry portray Oregonians? How do the qualities he admires compare to twenty-first century America's sense of self?

- **Activity:** Have students list phrases that Curry uses to describe early Oregonians. Ask students to identify and discuss the reasons why Curry sees special qualities in his fellow citizens. Discuss how these qualities and reasons compare to how many Americans see the country today.

Step 4: Exploration Questions

What goals motivated Curry and de la Guerra as they addressed their legislative bodies? How might these differing speeches capture both the promises and the challenges of a new, growing country?

- **Activity:** Ask students to first review the purpose, content, and tone of de la Guerra's speech. Have them discuss Curry's speech in the same manner. Next, ask students to draw conclusions about how the speeches together might define the complexity of America.

Step 5: Response Paper

Word length and additional requirements set by Instructor. Students answer the research question in the *Overview Questions*. Students state a thesis and use as evidence passages from the primary source document as well as support from supplemental materials assigned in the lesson.

HISTORICAL DOCUMENT

Compelled to Sell, Little by Little

Date: 1859
Author: Pico, Antonio Maria
Genre: petition

We, the undersigned, residents of the state of California, and some of us citizens of the United States, previously citizens of the Republic of Mexico, respectfully say: That during the war between the United States and Mexico the officers of the United States, as commandants of the land and sea forces, on several occasions offered and promised in the most solemn manner to the inhabitants of California, protection and security of their persons and their property and the annexation of the said state of California to the American Union, impressing upon them the great advantages to be derived from their being citizens of the United States, as was promised them. That, in consequence of such promises and representations, very few of the inhabitants of California opposed the invasion; some of them welcomed the invaders with open arms; a great number of them acclaimed the new order with joy, giving a warm reception to their guests, for those inhabitants had maintained very feeble relations with the government of Mexico and had looked with envy upon the development, greatness, prosperity, and glory of the great northern republic, to which they were bound for reasons of commercial and personal interests, and also because its principles of freedom had won their friendliness.

When peace was established between the two nations by the Treaty of Guadalupe Hidalgo, they joined in the general rejoicing with their new American fellow countrymen, even though some—a very few indeed—decided to remain in California as Mexican citizens, in conformity with the literal interpretation of that solemn instrument; they immediately assumed the position of American citizens that was offered them, and since then have conducted themselves with zeal and faithfulness and with no less loyalty than those whose great fortune it was to be born under the flag of the North American republic—believing, thus, that all their rights were insured in the treaty, which declares that their property shall be inviolably protected and insured; seeing the realization of the promises made to them by United States officials; trusting and hoping to participate in the prosperity and happiness of the great nation of which they now had come to be an integral part, and in which, if it was true that they now found the value of their possessions increased, that was also to be considered compensation for their sufferings and privations. . . .

They heard with dismay of the appointment, by Act of Congress, of a Commission with the right to examine all titles and confirm or disapprove them, as their judgment considered equitable. Though this honorable body has doubtless had the best interests of the state at heart, still it has brought about the most disastrous effects upon those who have the honor to subscribe their names to this petition, for, even though all landholders possessing titles under the Spanish or Mexican governments were not forced by the letter of the law to present them before the Commission for confirmation, nevertheless all those titles were at once considered doubtful, their origin questionable, and, as a result, worthless for confirmation by the Commission; all landholders were thus compelled de facto to submit their titles to the Commission for confirmation, under the alternative that, if they were not submitted, the lands would be considered public property.

The undersigned, ignorant then, of the forms and proceedings of an American court of justice, were obliged to engage the services of American lawyers to present their claims, paying them enormous fees. Not having other means with which to meet those expenses but their lands, they were compelled to give up part of their property, in many cases as much as a fourth of it, and in other cases even more.

The discovery of gold attracted an immense number of immigrants to this country, and, when they perceived that the titles of the old inhabitants were considered doubtful and their validity questionable, they spread themselves over the land as though it were public property, taking possession of the improvements made by the inhabitants, many times seizing even their houses (where they had lived for many years with their families), taking and killing the cattle and destroying their crops; so that those who before had owned great numbers of cattle that could have been counted by the thousands, now found themselves without any, and the men who were the owners of many leagues of land now were deprived of the peaceful possession of even one acre.

The expenses of the new state government were great, and the money to pay for these was only to be derived from the tax on property, and there was little property in this new state but the above-mentioned lands. Onerous taxes were levied by new laws, and if these were not paid, the property was put up for sale. Deprived as they were of the use of their lands, from which they had now no lucrative returns, the owners were compelled to mortgage them in order to assume the payment of taxes already due and constantly increasing. With such mortgages upon property greatly depreciated (because of its uncertain status), without crops or rents, the owners of those lands were not able to borrow money except at usurious rates of interest. The usual interest rate at that time was high, but with such securities it was exorbitant; and so they were forced either to sell or lose their lands; in fact, they were forced to borrow money even for the purchase of the bare necessities of life. Hoping that the Land Commission would take quick action in the revision of titles and thus relieve them from the state of penury in which they found themselves, they mortgaged their lands, paying compound interest at the rate of from three to ten percent a month. The long-awaited relief would not arrive; action from the Commission was greatly delayed; and, even after the Commission would pronounce judgment on the titles, it was still necessary to pass through a rigorous ordeal in the District Court; and some cases are, even now, pending before the Supreme Court of the nation. And in spite of the final confirmation, too long a delay was experienced (in many cases it is still being experienced), awaiting the surveys to be made by the United States Surveyor-General . . . Congress overlooked making the necessary appropriations to that end, and the people were then obliged to face new taxes to pay for the surveys, or else wait even longer while undergoing the continued and exhausting demands of high and usurious taxes. Many persons assumed the payment of the surveyors and this act was cause for objection from Washington, the work of those surveyors rejected, and the patents refused, for the very reason that they themselves had paid for the surveys. More than 800 petitions were presented to the Land Commission, and already 10 years of delays have elapsed and only some 50 patents have been granted.

The petitioners, finding themselves unable to face such payments because of the rates of interest, taxes, and litigation expenses, as well as having to maintain their families, were compelled to sell, little by little, the greater part of their old possessions. Some, who at one time had been the richest landholders, today find themselves without a foot of ground, living as objects of charity—and even in sight of the many leagues of land which, with many a thousand head of cattle, they once had called their own; and those of us who, by means of strict economy and immense sacrifices, have been able to preserve a small portion of our property, have heard to our great dismay that new legal projects are being planned to keep us still longer in suspense, consuming, to the last iota, the property left us by our ancestors. Moreover, we see with deep pain that efforts are being made to induce those honorable bodies to pass laws authorizing bills of review, and other illegal proceedings, with a view to prolonging still further the litigation of our claims.

LESSON PLAN: "Land They Once Had Called Their Own"

Students analyze a petition to Congress from Antonio María Pico and other California residents and compare its reality to the promise of the Treaty of Guadalupe Hidalgo.

Learning Objectives

Reconstruct the literal meaning of the petition; read the petition imaginatively; challenge arguments of historical inevitability; consider long-term perspectives of the settlement of the Mexican-American war.

Materials: Antonio María Pico, et al, "Compelled to Sell, Little By Little" (1859); Treaty of Guadalupe Hidalgo (1848).

Overview Questions

How does the petition describe the attrition of land-ownership rights of California residents? How do the petitioners employ tone as a tool in their appeal? What does the document suggest will be the outcome of the petitioners' attempts to protect their land rights? How does the petition reflect California's selective enforcement of the Treaty of Guadalupe Hidalgo?

Step 1: Comprehension Questions

What actions does the petition suggest were being used to strip landowners of their rights? How did these actions specifically affect landowners?

- **Activity:** Have students list actions and events that the petitioners argue have deprived them of their land. Discuss why such things as title problems, mortgages, tax rates, surveying time, and lost rents could contribute to owners' loss of their lands.

Step 2: Comprehension Questions

What best describes the tone of the petition? What motives probably drove the petitioners tone?

- **Activity:** Select a student to read aloud the first paragraphs. Have students characterize the tone employed in those paragraphs. Have students identify any later phrases or paragraphs that veer from that tone. Discuss why that tone was used and whether or not it might have been effective.

Step 3: Context Questions

What passages hint at the ultimate fate of Mexican-American landowners in California? How might a different fate have affected Mexican-American history in California?

- **Activity:** Have students identify passages that suggest whether or not the petitioners were going to prevail in their appeal. Discuss how the success of this petition may have altered the history of Mexican-American citizens of California.

Step 4: Exploration Questions

What does the petition say about the Treaty of Guadalupe Hidalgo? What justifies petitioners' claims that their rights under the treaty were being denied?

- **Activity:** Have students identify the petition's direct and indirect references to the treaty. Ask students which treaty articles support the petitioners' claims. Challenge students to use these primary sources plus secondary sources to mount an argument for the petitioners based on the treaty.

Step 5: Response Paper

Word length and additional requirements set by Instructor. Students answer the research question in the *Overview Questions.* Students state a thesis and use as evidence passages from the primary source document as well as support from supplemental materials assigned in the lesson.

The Spirit of Reform

In the tumultuous, exuberant years that followed the American Revolution, citizens of the new nation saw opportunities for expansion and change of many kinds. For some it was a broadening of their physical horizons—the opportunity to move into new land. For others, it was an expansion of thought and spirituality, a chance to reshape social relationships and address inequality in the name of progress. The Industrial Revolution changed the nature of labor, creating opportunities for employment that had never existed before, but also setting up conflicts between owners and workers who united to combat unsafe and exploitative conditions.

Of primary social concern during this time was the institution of slavery. The abolitionist cause, which sought to end slavery, developed into a robust movement, particularly in the North, where slavery had been outlawed since the early nineteenth century and the economy did not depend on enslaved agricultural labor. Political developments such as the Fugitive Slave Law of 1850 galvanized opposition in the North, as it was enforced there. Some groups worried that if proslavery elements gained political dominance, they could extend slavery to white people as well.

As a consequence of the organized protest against slavery, however, other social institutions and roles became subject to reconsideration. Social reform was one of the few areas of public discourse where it was considered appropriate for women to have a role, and so they were very well represented in many reform movements. Women who had initially gained a public voice in protest against slavery then began arguing against the widely accepted inferiority of their gender. The language of slavery crept into labor disputes, and a widespread national dialogue began about the proper role of education in fitting citizens of every type and gender for the highest service to the nation.

Reformers were as varied in their arguments as in their causes. Early discussions of women's rights tended to affirm traditionally separate roles for men and women, while arguing for increased opportunities for the education of women, primarily as a way to influence the next generation. As the nineteenth century progressed, however, women began to question the assumption that they were physically and intellectually inferior, ultimately arguing for full equality and the vote.

Another strong reform movement focused on the dangers of alcohol. The temperance movement taught that most social ills were the result of drunkenness and that the consumption of alcohol was not only bad for the physical body, but for the soul. Though the focus of the temperance movement may seem narrow, it became an avenue to argue for all types of social and economic reform.

As social reform movements gained momentum, some argued that it was the right of just people to oppose injustice in government, and even to resist it with force. From Henry David Thoreau's refusal to pay tax to John Brown's attempt to begin a war to free the slaves, radical thinkers increasingly argued against traditional institutions, be they religious, governmental, or ideological, and for the primacy of individual freedom and self-expression.

Bethany Groff

"Observations on the Real Rights of Women"

Date: 1818
Author: Crocker, Hannah Mather
Genre: essay

"They may form good judgement, but it would be improper, and physically very incorrect, for the female character to claim the statesman's birth or ascend the rostrum to gain the loud applause of men."

Summary Overview

Hannah Mather Crocker's essay, "Observations on the Real Rights of Women," is an early example of feminist thought in the post-Revolutionary or early national period of America. It was the first book-length essay devoted to women's rights that had been written by an American woman. In the essay, Crocker argues strongly for women's education as a means to women's equality. The tone of the work, however, in stark contrast to the more radical arguments presented by British women such as Mary Wollstonecraft or Frances Wright. Crocker instead takes a nonconfrontational and modest tone, seen through a Christian lens, as there was a post-Revolutionary backlash against some of the more strident advocates for women's rights at the time. As a result, Crocker's contribution to feminist thought, often referred to as "proto-feminist" thought, has been neglected, although recently rediscovered by historians as an important female voice in the first two decades of the nineteenth century. She is rightly considered a founding mother of the American Revolution by some.

Defining Moment

Hannah Mather Crocker was writing in the post-Revolutionary, or early national, period of American history. It was a time when a young country was beginning to formalize its institutions, its politics, and its social opinions. The American Revolution was over, and now the challenge of building and expanding a new country was beginning. The Age of Enlightenment, or Reason, that had led to revolutionary ideals of liberty and equality also helped to move forward the issue of women's rights. Discourse into women's rights had begun as early as the fifteenth century, and the debates that followed were known as the *querelles des femmes*, or the Woman Question. By the early nineteenth century, there had been a backlash against the more radical of these arguments for women's rights, exemplified by Mary Wollstonecraft's *A Vindication of the Rights of Women*. Even though she was British, Wollstonecraft had a great impact in America and her essay, published in 1792, spurred a flurry of debate on women's rights in the new country. Bear in mind that as with the discussion of equality for men, race was still not a consideration, and therefore the women's rights discussed were restricted to white women's rights.

As Crocker was writing in 1818, she was living in a unique time period. She had lived through the American Revolution and therefore had seen first-hand how American women had participated in this war and had helped win independence for America. As an educated woman, she knew that women were capable of learning and could be educated just the same as men. But she also knew that there was backlash against women's rights and that if she was to be effective in her own messaging about women's rights, she had to be more subtle than Wollstonecraft.

Her discussion about women's rights therefore revolved around the concept of separate spheres: that women had control of the domestic sphere while men had control over the public sphere. They were equal, but different, and women could influence men best by persuading them with reason. They had the potential of being men's intellectual equals, but they should not use these gifts to usurp men's rightful leadership roles in politics or religion. Thus, she was presenting an argument for women's equality in a submissive and non-confrontational way, and she was assuring her audience that women could fulfill their domestic role, while at the same time being the intellectual and moral equal of men. It was for this reason that many who read her essay outside of her own time period did not consider her as an early feminist writer.

Author Biography

Hannah Mather was born in Boston, Massachusetts, on June 27, 1752. She came from an illustrious early American family, and her grandfather, Cotton Mather, was a prominent Puritan minister and writer. She came of age during the Revolutionary War, and she actively participated by smuggling war plans to Joseph Warren, a revolutionary commander and high-ranking freemason. She married Reverend John Crocker, who was a Harvard graduate and captain in the revolutionary militia, in 1779. By the time her husband died in 1797, the couple had produced ten children between 1780 and 1795.

Hannah Crocker was well-educated, no doubt because of the Mather family's strong interest in learning. She was considered a Boston Bluestocking, or a woman who had a strong taste for learning. A member of high social standing in Boston, her maternal uncle, Thomas Hutchinson was also colonial governor of Massachusetts. Crocker had a long history of involvement in Freemasonry and actually set up a rare women's-only lodge, known as St. Ann's Lodge. Freemasonry was a radical intellectual movement that emerged from the Protestant Reformation and was a secret fraternity, almost exclusively of men. Through her involvement with St. Ann's, she was a keen advocate of women's education and wanted to teach illiterate women so that they would be more respected and better treated by their husbands. She was clear that the lodge was set up for friendship and for the pursuit of learning, especially in science and literature.

Crocker did not begin her writing career until after her children were grown. In 1810, she took on the pseudonym of "Aurelia Prudencia Americana" and defended freemasonry from its growing critics in a series of newspaper letters, especially regarding its treatment of women. It was here that she first made plain her argument for women's rights through education. Putting her beliefs about women's education into action again, she established the School of Industry for poor girls in Boston's northern district in 1813. In 1818, she published her main essay in support of women's rights and education, "Observations on the Real Rights of Women." She continued to write and had a keen interest in preserving history, although much of her work remains unpublished and difficult to access for modern readers. Her final project was a personal memoir and narrative history of Boston (*Reminiscences and Traditions of Boston*), but she died before she could complete the work. She died on July 11, 1829, and is buried in the Mather family tomb at Copp's Hill Burying Ground in Boston.

HISTORICAL DOCUMENT

It must be the appropriate duty and privilege of females to convince by reason and persuasion. It must be their peculiar province to sooth the turbulent passions of men, when almost sinking in the sea of care, without even an anchor of hope to support them. Under such circumstances women should display their talents by taking the helm, and steer them safe to the haven of rest and peace, and that should be their own happy mansion, where they may always retire and find safe asylum from the rigid cares of business. It is women's peculiar right to keep calm and serene under every circumstance in life, as it is undoubtedly her appropriate duty, to sooth and alleviate the anxious cares of man, and her friendly and sympathetic breast should be found the best solace for him, as she has an equal right to partake with him the cares, as well as the pleasures of life.

It was evidently the design of heaven by the mode of our first formation, that they should walk side by side as mutual supports in all times of trial. There can be no doubt, that, in most cases, their judgement may be equal with the other sex; perhaps even on the subject of law, politics, or religion, they may form good judgement, but it would be improper, and physically very incorrect, for the female character to claim the statesman's birth or ascend the rostrum to gain the loud applause of men, although their powers of industry may be equal to the task. . . .

From the local circumstances and the domestic cares of which most females are involved, it cannot be expected they should make so great improvement in science and literature, as those whose whole life has been devoted to their studies. It must not be expected that the reputable mechanic will rival the man of letters and science, neither would it well suit the female frame or character to boast of her knowledge in mechanism or her skill in the manly art of slaughtering fellow-men It is woman's appropriate duty and peculiar privilege to cultivate the olive branches around her table. It is for her to implant in the juvenile breast the first seed of virtue, the love of God, and their country, with all the other virtues that shall prepare them to shine as statesmen, soldiers, philosophers, and Christians. Some of our first worthies have boasted that they imbibed their heroic principles with their mother's milk; and by precept and example were first taught the love of virtue, religion, and their country. Surely they should have a right to share with them the laurel, but not the right of conquest; for that must be man's prerogative, and woman is to rejoice in his conquest. There may be a few groveling minds who think women should not aspire to any further knowledge that to obtain enough of the cynical art to enable them to compound a good pudding, pie, or cake for her lord and master to discompound. Others, of a still weaker class, may say it is enough for women scientifically to arrange the spinning wheel and distaff, and exercise her extensive capacity in knitting and sewing, since the fall and restoration of woman these employments have been the appropriate duties of the female sex. The art of dress, which in some measure produced the art of industry, did not commence till sin, folly and shame introduced the first invention of dress which ought to check the modest female from every species of wantonness and extravagance in dress; cultivate the mind and trifling in dress will soon appear in its true colors.

To those who appear unfriendly to female literature let me say, in behalf of the sex, they claim no right to infringe on any domestic economy; but those ladies who continue in a state of celibacy, and find pleasure in literacy researches, have a right to indulge the propensity and solace themselves with the feast of reason and knowledge; also those ladies who in youth have laid up a treasure of literacy and scientific information, have a right to improve further literary researches, after they have truthfully discharged their domestic duties. . . .

Women have an equal right, with the other sex, to form societies for promoting religious, charitable and benevolent purposes. Every association formed for benevolence, must have a tendency to make man mild, and sociable to man; an institution formed for historical and literary researches, would have a happy effect on the mind and manners of the youth of both sexes. As the circulating libraries are often resorted to after novel by both sexes for want of judgement to select works of more merit, the study of history would strengthen their memory and improve the mind, whereas novels have a tendency to vitiate the mind and morals of the youth of each sex before they are ripe for more valuable acquisitions. Much abstruse study or metaphysical reasoning seldom agrees with the natural vivacity or the slender frame of many females, therefore the moral and physical distinction of the sex must be allowed; if the powers of the mind are fully equal, they must still estimate the rights of men, and own it their prerogative exclusively to content for public honors and preferment, either in church or state, and females may console themselves and feel happy, that by the moral distinction of the sexes they are called to move in a sphere of life remote from those masculine contentions, although they hold equal right with them of studying every branch of science, even jurisprudence.

But it would be morally wrong and physically imprudent for any woman to attempt pleading at the bar of justice as no law can give her the right of deviating from the strictest rules of rectitude and decorum. No servile dependence on men can be recommended under the Christian system, for that abolished the law of slavery, and left only a claim on their friendship; as the author of their nature originally intended, they should be the protectors of female innocence, and not the fatal destroyers of their peace and happiness. They aim no right at the gambling table, and to the moral sensibility of females how disgusting must be the horse-race, the bull-bate, and the cock-fight. These are barbarous scenes, not suited to the delicacy of females.

It must be woman's prerogative to shine in the domestic circle, and her appropriate duty to teach and regulate the opening mind of her little flock, and teach their juvenile ideas how to shoot forth into well improved sentiments. It is most undoubtedly the duty and privilege of woman to regulate her garrison with such good order and propriety, that the generalization of her affection, shall never have reason to seek other quarters for well disciplined and regulated troops, and there must not a murmur or beat be heard throughout the garrison, except that of the heart vibrating with mutual affection, reciprocally soft. The rights of woman displayed on such a plan, might perhaps draw the other sex from the nocturnal ramble to the more endearing scenes of domestic peace and harmony. The woman, who can gain such a victory, as to secure the undivided affection of her generalissimo, must have the exclusive right to shine unrivalled in her garrison. . . .

By the mutual virtue, energy and fortitude of the sexes, the freedom and independence of the United States were attained and secured. The same virtue, energy and fortitude, must be called into continual exercise, as long as we continue a free, federal, independent nation. The culture and improvement of the female understanding will strengthen the mental faculties and give vigor to their councils, which will give a weight to any argument used for their mutual defense and safety. No nation or republic ever fell prey to despotism, till by indolence and dissipation it neglected the arts and sciences, and the love of literature. They then became effeminate and degraded; and by then the female character was degraded. As long as the German women were free and honored by the men, it acted as a stimulus to their ambition. On the value and integrity of both sexes their success and independence very much depended.

GLOSSARY

abstruse: obscure; difficult to understand

bull-bate: bull-baiting was the practice of tying a bull to an iron stake so that it could only move in a limited area, while dogs tried to immobilize the bull by attacking it

despotism: tyranny; absolute power or control

discompound: to separate into parts

dissipation: debauchery, excessive indulgence

distaff: a tool used in spinning that holds the unspun thread

indolence: habitual laziness; sloth

jurisprudence: study or philosophy of law

rostrum: a lectern, pulpit or dais for a lecturer

vitiate: spoil or impair the quality of something

wantonness: lack of restraint or control; not being in accord with moral standards

worthies: eminent or notable people

Document Analysis

Hannah Mather Crocker was a woman who was a product of her time and her social standing. Writing during the early national period, her opinions reflected this. Although her essay on the rights of women has been dismissed by some as a conservative rebuke of the more radical proponents of women's rights, it is better to try to understand her writing in a more nuanced way. She knew she had to craft her message of women's equality carefully, or it would be easily dismissed as too radical, as Mary Wollstonecraft before her had been. Therefore, her essay has an intentionally non-confrontational tone. In the first two decades of the nineteenth century when Crocker was writing, there had been backlash surrounding the discussion of women's rights. The issue of women's rights had been raised along with republican virtues of freedom, liberty, and equality, and there were many who were discussing the issues, especially after Mary Wollstonecraft had published *A Vindication of the Rights of Women* in 1792. It was into this atmosphere that Crocker began her own discussion of women's rights. Her title of "Observations on the Real Rights of Women" indicated the fact that she would discuss women's rights from a more pragmatic perspective than others had, particularly the more radical Wollstonecraft. Again, it is worth remembering that women's rights, at least to Crocker, meant middle- to upper-class white women's rights.

Crocker believed that women and men had equal abilities to reason, but in reality they operated in separate spheres. Her strong Christian beliefs supported this distinction. Women were to be active in the domestic sphere, while men had leadership in the public sphere, which included politics and business. Interestingly, her own foray into published writing brought this distinction into conflict in her own life, and at times, in her writings as well. Her rhetorical strategy was on occasion nuanced to argue against this very theory, but her more radical thoughts were only brought out after she had made the reader comfortable by providing a conservative and traditional backdrop to her thesis. It is also important to note that Crocker was from an illustrious Puritan family and therefore also had a strong religious understanding of the world. Her writing refers to Christian concepts quite readily, as this was her world view, as well as that of many others during the time period.

The vast majority of the excerpt of this essay comes from the second chapter of her work, where Crocker explains how women have been restored to equality as a result of Christianity. The excerpt begins with a discussion of how best women can exert influence in society. She feels this can best be accomplished by persuading men using intellect, or reason. This can be done, according to Crocker, within the confines of the home and family, which correlates to her belief in separate spheres and distinct roles for men and women. She here states that women's role is to "sooth the turbulent passions of men," by creating a safe haven for them to retreat into in the form of a stable and caring home and family life. Here they can get away from the "rigid cares of business" and find peace and security. The responsibility for creating this idyllic home life rests squarely with women, and Crocker feels that is it women's role to keep "calm and serene." This can be seen to be a very traditional view and one with which few conservatives, especially men, could argue. Here she is actively employing the tactic of first promoting something traditional that would serve to distract some readers from her more radical conclusions at a later point.

Crocker then states that men and women need to be partners through the good times and the bad times and need to support each other. She next explicitly states her core belief: that women can be equal to men when it comes to judgement and reason, and even when it comes to such traditionally male subjects as "law, politics or religion." Again, she tempers this somewhat radical view though. She states that even though women may be capable of doing it, they should not try to be politicians or orators, as it would be "physically incorrect." Women should not enter the public realms of politics or civil society. Here, her opinion of men's and women's differences when it comes to their physical attributes and competencies is made apparent to the reader. Women and men are equal, but different. Women's influence in the public sphere should be restricted to an advisory role, using their intellect to guide any advice given.

Crocker then goes on to explain further the roles and capacities of women. She explains that the expectations of women when it comes to intellectual pursuits should be tempered, as they have to also take care of the household and children. She may be referring to her own life here, as she did not begin to publish her writing until after her ten children were grown. To provide an example that her reader can better grasp, she explains that a mechanic would obviously not be as learned as a man who had spent his entire life studying.

Just like the mechanic, Crocker makes the comparison now to women, who would not be able to boast of their talents in mechanics or warfare. Instead, women are best-suited to keep the peace ("cultivate the olive branches") within the family, and more particularly, to prepare her children for successful futures by educating them. Although the gender of the children is not stated explicitly, it is through the future careers she gives for these children as "statesmen, soldiers, philosophers," that it seems clear her focus here is on sons and not necessarily on daughters.

Crocker follows the tenets of what has come to be known as "republican motherhood." Under this belief, women had a powerful role in the moral development of their children in order to raise better and more virtuous republican citizens. This in turn would ensure the success of the country in the future. It was in a sense a mother's civic duty to educate her children. Crocker explains that this is to instill in them a love of "virtue, religion and their country." She further states that many notable people (again, she does not state the gender of these people, but it can be inferred she is referring solely to men) were taught "their heroic principles" from the very beginning of their lives by their mothers. At this point, Crocker states her belief that mothers should also be recognized ("share with them the laurel") for their contributions, albeit not publicly. She is clear that it is the man who has the "right of conquest" and women should simply "rejoice" in their success.

After seeming to focus only on a male son's education, Crocker now deftly turns her attention to those people who do not believe women should be educated. Here she makes her opinions of such people clear when she refers to "a few groveling minds" who do not think women should be educated beyond certain domestic chores such as cooking, sewing, knitting or spinning. She also issues a warning to women not to indulge too much in the "art of dress." In other words, Crocker urges women to cultivate their minds and not pay too much attention to their wardrobe, which she views as a frivolous pursuit. In a sense, Crocker believes that if women are to be taken seriously by men, then they must concentrate on serious intellectual pursuits.

Crocker goes on to talk about women who have taken the time to further their studies in education and literature. She defends their right to continue their studies and moreover also defends their right to contribute, presumably publicly through publishing their findings, to furthering knowledge and research. But again, she tempers this with the proviso that they should only do so after they have completed all of their "domestic duties."

As a woman who was very familiar with Freemasonry and its rituals, it is not surprising that Crocker would advocate for women to have the right to organize and promote benevolent societies. She had herself founded one when she set up St. Ann's Lodge, which was established on the principles of masonry. She does not explicitly reference masonic societies here, but rather any society that would promote "religious, charitable and benevolent purposes." She uses as an example a society that would promote research into history and literature, saying that it would be beneficial to both young men and young women. In advocating that women found such societies, however, Crocker was pushing the boundaries of the separate spheres concept, as this would push women more into the public realm that she generally reserved solely for men. It is in these kinds of subtle ways that Crocker at times reverses her position on separate spheres in a rhetorical strategy designed to advocate for women's greater role in society, while appearing at the same time to endorse men's sole ownership of this realm.

Her bias against fictional novels next becomes apparent when she states that reading them could corrupt the minds and the morality of youth of both sexes. Instead, she promotes the reading of history to "strengthen their memory and improve the mind." In fact, Crocker goes further when she says that higher learning that includes such things as metaphysics, or a type of philosophy that aims to understand the world as a whole, does not often agree with women because they are naturally cheerful and are not as physically robust as men. But she insists that women are equally capable of such learning in every type of science and even law.

Again here, she falls back on the distinction between men and women. She makes it clear that women can study law, but they should not practice law, as it would not be proper for a woman to do so under the societal rules of the day, which stated that women should not speak in public. She then discusses the relationship between men and women and how it should operate, presumably within the confines of marriage, although she is not explicit on this point. Crocker is clear that because of her Christian beliefs, the relationship between men and women should never resemble slavery, and women should not have a "servile dependence on men." Their relationship should rather resemble a friendship, as God intended. Here Crocker suggests how men should properly act within such a relationship. They should protect the innocence of women and not make them unhappy. Crocker then states that women would not want to share the leisure interests of men, especially those that involved gambling, horseracing, or the more extreme and "barbarous" pastimes of cock-fighting or bull-baiting. She felt that these were not suitable activities for women who were too delicate. No doubt this distaste for such activities again stemmed from Crocker's strong religious views.

After discussing that women are to be equal to men within relationships, Crocker goes on to explain how women could actually dominate the domestic sphere. She uses a variety of military terms here, which although at first blush seems odd when discussing the household and family but makes some sense when one considers she was married to a Revolutionary War captain and was raising at least part of her family during this same war. She opens by stating that women have the "prerogative to shine" in the home. The term *prerogative* could in fact refer to a king or queen's right to make executive decisions apart from traditional and established laws. In this way, she infers that women can have more, or at least as much, control over the family as men. This is a somewhat radical viewpoint. Christian tradition held at the time that the man was at the head of the household. So here again we see that Crocker at first reading seems traditional, and yet in a deeper reading has a more nonconventional point to make to her readers.

Crocker then speaks to women's roles and responsibilities within the family unit. The first is to educate their children by continually improving their thoughts and minds as they grow. She refers to a woman's children as "her garrison," which is interesting considering a garrison is a military unit that is stationed in a town to defend it. This therefore equates the family with a protective force. Crocker gives women the responsibility of keeping the family unit running smoothly ("good order") and with good and proper morals ("propriety"). By keeping such a calm, ordered, and peaceful home, there is less chance that her husband would stray and ultimately seek such a peaceful atmosphere elsewhere. In short, Crocker is giving a lesson on how to keep a husband satisfied and faithful. She explains that the home must be serene and that no sound be heard with the exception of the "heart vibrating with mutual affection, reciprocally soft." Here again, Crocker evokes a scene of blissful family harmony. She reinforces that such behavior will perhaps keep men from their "nocturnal ramble" and they will instead want to remain at home. If women can attain "such a victory"—note the military terminology, as if this family setting is akin to some sort of battleground or warfare—she will also win the "undivided affection" of her "generalissimo." The term *generalissimo* of course refers to her husband, and here Crocker seems to return the man to his traditional place at the head of the household. However, remember that Crocker used the term *prerogative* earlier, which would presume a woman was able to overrule a man in certain household and family matters. She ends by assuring women that if they are successful in creating this perfect family life, they will have the "exclusive right to shine" without any rival within her family.

The final excerpt from Crocker's essay comes from the fourth chapter of her work, where Crocker compares current women's character and writings to previous examples from history. It is here she is at her most radical. She refers to the historical works of Mercy Otis Warren as well as the life of Martha Washington as but two examples earlier in the chapter. She takes this as a jumping off point to discuss how important women's rights and education are to the future of the republic. Her point here is that both sexes fought for the independence of America, demonstrating "mutual virtue, energy and fortitude." She insists that these same attributes must be continued into the future for the country to thrive. She explains that the continued education of women will allow them to have stronger "mental faculties" and thereby be better advisors. Her warning is that if America were to neglect learning such as arts, sciences, and literature, it would risk falling into tyranny. Tyranny in turn leads a country to become "effeminate and degraded," which can degrade women's characters. She ends with an historical example of "German women" who were independent and venerated by their men, which led to their success as a nation. Crocker is clear then that only by having strong, independent, and equal women will America meet its national ambitions.

Essential Themes

Hannah Mather Crocker's work follows on from other authors who advocated women's rights through education, such as Judith Sargent Murray's writing in *The Gleaner*. She was also writing after Mary Wollstonecraft's more radical and secular *A Vindication of the*

Rights of Women was popularized in America after 1792. The backlash that occurred against women's rights was spurred on by the publication of *Memoirs of the Author of A Vindication of the Rights of Woman* in 1798, written by Wollstonecraft's husband, William Godwin, and published after her death. Since this work exposed the fact that Wollstonecraft had had a child out of wedlock as well as having other sexual affairs, Wollstonecraft became a scandalous and polarizing figure.

Crocker, as a religious Christian Puritan woman, was appropriately scandalized by Wollstonecraft's personal life, but she had the courage to support Wollstonecraft's main tenets that woman were capable of intellectual equality with men and should be educated as such. Given this backlash against women's rights in the post-Revolutionary period, Crocker needed to present her views in a less radical tone. As well, she was strongly influenced by her Christian religion, and she was therefore inclined to believe that men and women operated mainly within separate spheres of society. Many took her views as a far more conservative response than other writers, and therefore some of her feminist descendants have dismissed her work.

Instead, this more subtle argument for women's rights and intellectual equality with men is now viewed as a "proto-feminist" work. Her belief in, yet at the same time subtle questioning of, separate spheres of influence, was rhetorical strategy at its best. As well, her belief that women could and should act as persuasive influences over men's activities in the public realm through reason was her way of advocating for women's voice in politics. It was certainly not what the suffragists envisioned with giving the vote to women, but for her time period, Crocker believed this to be a step forward for women.

Although Crocker was considered one of America's leading political theorists regarding women's education and rights during the first two decades of the nineteenth century, she did not have tremendous long-term influence beyond this time period. Some of this may be due to the fact that much of her work remains unpublished, and her work was therefore difficult to access. Regardless, many writers who followed her dismissed her intellect and advocacy of women's rights through a rather select and cursory reading of her works. She was considered too conservative and, in effect, not feminist enough. It was not until women's history became a more professional branch of history that a new generation of female historians began to re-evaluate Crocker's writings. As more of her work is now being published, Crocker is finding herself restored to being an important voice of change for women in America.

Lee Tunstall, PhD

Bibliography

Botting, Ellen Hunt, and Houser, Sarah L. "'Drawing the Line of Equality': Hannah Mather Crocker on Women's Rights." *American Political Science Review* 100.2 (2006): 265–78. Print.

Copeland, Mary. "The Reverend, the Bluestocking, and Freemasons Behaving Badly: An Exploration and Close Reading of 'A Series of Letters on Freemasonry' by 'a Lady of Boston.'" *Journal for Research into Freemasonry and Fraternalism* 2.1 (2011): 144–57. Print.

Crocker, Hannah Mather. *Observations on the Real Rights of Women, with Their Appropriate Duties, Agreeable to Scripture, Reason and Common Sense.* Eds. Leon Stein and Annette K. Baxter. New York: Arno, 1974. Print.

Zagarri, Rosemarie. *Revolutionary Backlash: Women and Politics in the Early American Republic*. Philadelphia: U of Pennsylvania P, 2007. Print.

Additional Reading

Botting, Ellen Hunt and Carey, Christine. "Wollstonecraft's Philosophical Impact in Nineteenth-Century American Women's Rights Advocates." *American Journal of Political Science* 48 (2004): 707–22. Print.

Crocker, Hannah Mather. *Observations on the Real Rights of Women* and other writings. Lincoln: U of Nebraska P, 2011. Print.

Crocker, Hannah Mather. *Reminiscences and Traditions of Boston*. Eds. Eileen Hunt Botting and Sarah L. Houser. Boston: New England Historic Genealogical Society, 2011. Print.

Crocker, Hannah Mather. *A Series of Letters on Freemasonry.* Boston: John Eliot, 1815. Print.

Kidd, Karen. *Haunted Chambers: The Lives of Early Women Freemasons*. New Orleans: Cornerstone, 2009. Print.

Wollstonecraft, Mary. *A Vindication of the Rights of Women*. Ed. Miriam Brody. New York: Penguin, 2004. Print.

LESSON PLAN: **Women's Rights in the New Republic**

Students analyze Hannah Mather Crocker's assessment of women's roles and rights in the new republic.

Learning Objectives

Explain the influence of Revolutionary ideas on women's rights and roles; compare and contrast the ideas of Crocker and de Gouges on women's rights and roles; analyze their perspectives on women's rights and roles; draw comparisons across eras and regions to define enduring issues.

Materials: Hannah Mather Crocker, "Observations on the Real Rights of Women" (1818); Olympe de Gouges, "Declaration of the Rights of Woman" (1791).

Overview Questions

How did Revolutionary ideas influence women's rights and roles? Do Crocker and de Gouges share similar ideas about women's rights and roles? Why or why not? How are their perspectives alike and different? How does the Revolutionary experience in both the United States and France define the rights and roles of women during this time period?

Step 1: Comprehension Questions

In what ways did Revolutionary ideas about education and religion influence women's rights and roles in that time period? In what ways have women's rights and roles changed? Are there any factors today that influence the roles of women?

- **Activity:** Select students to read aloud key passages from both selections; discuss with students how women's rights and roles have changed; then ask them to write in their own words how women's rights and roles are linked to democracy.

Step 2: Comprehension Questions

In what ways are Crocker's and de Gouges's ideas about women similar? In what ways are their ideas different? What kinds of references to each make to support their arguments?

- **Activity:** Ask students to each make a list of the duties of women and references that Crocker addresses and to compare them to the declarations and references made by de Gouges; then ask them to write a summary of their findings.

Step 3: Context Questions

How are the perspectives of Crocker and de Gouges a reflection of the revolutions in each of their countries? In what context was each piece written?

- **Activity:** Instruct students to compare the time periods in which the American and French revolutions occurred; then have them discuss in small groups how the ideas expressed in each document are similar and different to the ideals of each revolution.

Step 4: Exploration Questions

How does the Revolutionary experience in both the United States and France define the rights and roles of women? Do you agree with their observations and expressions? Why or why not?

- **Activity:** Ask students to discuss in small groups how each woman's writings are a reflection of their experiences with democracy; then have students write a multi-paragraph essay that explains why they agree or disagree with the writers' observations and expressions.

Step 5: Response Paper

Word length and additional requirements set by Instructor. Students answer the research question in the *Overview Questions*. Students state a thesis and use as evidence passages from the primary source document as well as support from supplemental materials assigned in the lesson.

A Plan for Improving Female Education

Date: 1819
Author: Willard, Emma Hart
Genre: political tract

"The object of this Address, is to convince the public, that a reform, with respect to female education, is necessary; that it cannot be effected by individual exertion, but that it requires the aid of the legislature."

Summary Overview

One of the earliest advocates for women's higher education in the United States, Emma Hart Willard in 1819 published *A Plan for Improving Female Education*, both a call for reform and a blueprint for establishing a publically funded women's seminary that would feature a more challenging curriculum and adhere to the high standards already expected of men's colleges. She sent her plan to government leaders and representatives in the hope of gaining their support. Although she was ultimately unable to obtain the necessary governmental support or public funding, Willard established a school for women, the Troy Female Seminary, in 1821 with the support of prominent residents of Troy, New York. Her innovative plan, which became known as the Troy Plan, inspired many other educational reformers and was used to establish more than two hundred similar institutions for girls and women in the United States.

Defining Moment

In the decades following the American Revolution, the United States began to lose some of its more radical republican ideals as its leaders worked to stabilize and formalize the new country's institutions, political processes, and values. As a result, there was some backlash against the concepts of women's rights and women's education during this period. It was in this complex post-revolutionary era that Willard made a name for herself as a trailblazer for girls' and women's higher education. Willard not only advocated for the reform of women's education but also established a seminary, or school, for young women. She was an active teacher and educational administrator throughout her life and was also the author of many foundational textbooks.

As a reformer, Willard focused on the right of women to a proper and advanced education similar to that available to men. She felt that many of the private schools for young women then in operation had less-than-ambitious curricula and was concerned that there were no regulations governing teachers at these schools. To address these problems, Willard proposed that the government regulate a new type of female seminary that would be established using public funds. Teachers would therefore be accountable to the government, and the overall quality of the education girls and women received would increase. Furthermore, Willard believed that improving women's education would be beneficial to the United States and lead to its continued prosperity and success. At the time, mothers were responsible for the earliest education of their children, and Willard believed that an educated and virtuous mother would raise an educated and virtuous child. As such, she argued that educating the mothers of the next generation of Americans would be a prudent use of public funds.

What made Willard different from many other reformers of her time was her development of a workable plan for a model female seminary. She carefully considered the school's ideal organizational structure and determined what types of courses should be offered, producing a logical, clear, and concise plan. Willard lobbied government representatives and other American leaders in order to garner support for the plan, a strategy rarely used by women at the time. But even as she was committed to reaching her goal, she knew that she had to take a cautious approach and avoid making any radical propositions that would alienate the very men who had the power to make her dream a reality. It should especially be noted that while Willard was a champion for women's education, she was not advocating on behalf of all American women—the Troy Female Seminary would cater only to white women from the upper class.

Author Biography

Emma Hart was born in Berlin, Connecticut, in 1787, the sixteenth of Samuel and Lydia Hart's seventeen children. Her father believed in educating his daughters, and so when Emma showed promise, her family supported her intellectual endeavors. She became a teacher by the time she was seventeen and in 1807 opened a school for girls in Middlebury, Vermont. It was there that she met local physician and widower John Willard, whom she married in 1809. Her husband had four children of his own, and the couple had their only son together, John, in 1810. Willard's husband soon encountered financial problems, and to help contribute to her family's income, Willard opened a school for young women in her home in 1814.

At this time, schools were often privately operated, and teachers such as Willard typically charged their students tuition. Although Willard personally benefited from this practice, she identified a problem with this model. As there were no relevant regulations, anyone who wanted to could set up a school for girls and young women, and they often did. Willard soon devised a plan in which seminaries for young women would be funded and regulated by government. She published her plan in the 1819 pamphlet *An Address to the Public; Particularly to the Members of the Legislature of New-York, Proposing a Plan for Improving Female Education*. Willard sent a copy to each New York state legislator as well as to various congressmen, judges, and even past and current presidents. When the governor of New York, DeWitt Clinton, invited her to move to New York to pursue her ideas, she readily agreed and moved her family. She first opened a school in Waterford, New York, but the promised funding did not materialize.

After this false start, Willard was approached by prominent citizens of Troy, New York, and promised four thousand dollars in funds to endow a new seminary for girls. In 1821, ninety girls enrolled in the new Troy Female Seminary. Willard spent the next years managing the school and writing textbooks. Her husband died in 1825, and although she remarried in 1839, the marriage lasted less than a year, as her new husband was abusive. Willard retired in 1838 and left the administration of the school to her son and daughter-in-law. In her retirement, Willard traveled, lectured, and wrote. In the 1840s, she was named a superintendent of public schools in Kensington, Connecticut. She died in 1870, and her lasting legacy, the Troy Female Seminary, was renamed in her honor in 1895.

HISTORICAL DOCUMENT

The object of this Address, is to convince the public, that a reform, with respect to female education, is necessary; that it cannot be effected by individual exertion, but that it requires the aid of the legislature; and further, by shewing the justice, the policy, and the magnanimity of such an undertaking, to persuade that body to endow a seminary for females, as the commencement of such reformation.

The idea of a college for males will naturally be associated with that of a seminary, instituted and endowed by the public; and the absurdity of sending ladies to college, may, at first thought, strike every one to whom this subject shall be proposed. I therefore hasten to observe, that the seminary here recommended, will be as different from those appropriated to the other sex, as the female character and duties are from the male. . . .

If the improvement of the American female character, and that alone, could be effected by public liberality, employed in giving better means of instruction; such improvement of one half of society, and that half, which barbarous and despotic nations have ever degraded, would of itself be an object, worthy of the most liberal government on earth; but if the female character be raised, it must inevitably raise that of the other sex: and thus does the plan proposed, offer, as the object of legislative bounty, to elevate the whole character of the community.

As evidence that this statement does not exaggerate the female influence in society, our sex need but be considered, in the single relation of mothers. In this character, we have the charge of the whole mass of individuals, who are to compose the succeeding generation; during that period of youth, when the pliant mind takes any direction, to which it is steadily guided by a forming hand. How important a power is given by this charge! yet, little do too many of my sex know how, either to appreciate or improve it. Unprovided with the means of acquiring that knowledge, which flows liberally to the other sex—having our time of education devoted to frivolous acquirements, how should we understand the nature of the mind, so as to be aware of the importance of those early impressions, which we make upon the minds of our children?—or how should we be able to form enlarged and correct views, either of the character, to which we ought to mould them, or of the means most proper to form them aright? . . .

Civilized nations have long since been convinced that education, as it respects males, will not, like trade, regulate itself; and hence, they have made it a prime object to provide that sex with everything requisite to facilitate their progress in learning: but female education has been left to the mercy of private adventurers; and the consequence has been to our sex, the same, as it would have been to the other, had legislatures left their accommodations, and means of instruction, to chance also.

Education cannot prosper in any community, unless, from the ordinary motives which actuate the human mind, the best and most cultivated talents of that community, can be brought into exercise in that way. Male education flourishes, because, from the guardian care of legislatures, the presidencies and professorships of our colleges are some of the highest objects to which the eye of ambition is directed. Not so with female institutions. Preceptresses of these, are dependent on their pupils for support, and are consequently liable to become the victims of their caprice. In such a situation, it is not more desirable to be a preceptress, than it would be, to be a parent, invested with the care of children, and responsible for their behaviour, but yet, depending on them for subsistence, and destitute of power to enforce their obedience.

Feminine delicacy requires, that girls should be educated chiefly by their own sex. This is apparent from considerations, that regard their health and conveniences, the propriety of their dress and manners, and their domestic accomplishments. . . .

It is the duty of a government, to do all in its power to promote the present and future prosperity of the nation, over which it is placed. This prosperity will depend on the character of its citizens. The characters of these will be formed by their mothers; and it is through the mothers, that the government can control the characters of its future citizens, to form them such as will ensure their country's prosperity. If this is the case, then it is the duty of our present legislators to begin now, to form the characters of the next generation, by controling that of the females, who are to be their mothers, while it is yet with them a season of improvement.

But should the conclusion be almost admitted, that our sex too are the legitimate children of the legislature; and, that it is their duty to afford us a share of their paternal bounty; the phantom of a college-learned lady, would be ready to rise up, and destroy every good resolution, which the admission of this truth would naturally produce in our favour.

To shew that it is not a masculine education which is here recommended, and to afford a definite view of the manner in which a female institution might possess the respectability, permanency, and uniformity of operation of those appropriated to males; and yet differ from them, so as to be adapted to that difference of character and duties, to which the softer sex should be formed, is the object of the following imperfect

SKETCH OF A FEMALE SEMINARY.

From considering the deficiencies in boarding schools, much may be learned, with regard to what would be needed, for the prosperity and usefulness of a public seminary for females.

I. There would be needed a building, with commodious rooms for lodging and recitation, apartments for the reception of apparatus, and for the accommodation of the domestic department.

II. A library, containing books on the various subjects in which the pupils were to receive instruction; musical instruments, some good paintings, to form the taste and serve as models for the execution of those who were to be instructed in that art; maps, globes, and a small collection of philosophical apparatus.

III. A judicious board of trust, competent and desirous to promote its interests, would in a female, as in a male literary institution, be the corner stone of its prosperity. On this board it would depend to provide,

IV. Suitable instruction. This article may be subdivided under four heads.

1. Religious and Moral.
2. Literary.
3. Domestic.
4. Ornamental.

1. Religious and Moral. A regular attention to religious duties would, of course be required of the pupils by the laws of the institution. The trustees would be careful to appoint no instructors, who would not teach religion and morality, both by their example, and by leading the minds of the pupils to perceive, that these constitute the true end of all education. It would be desirable, that the young ladies should spend a part of their Sabbaths in hearing discourses relative to the peculiar duties of their sex. The evidences of Christianity, and moral philosophy, would constitute a part of their studies.

2. Literary Instruction. To make an exact enumeration of the branches of literature, which might be taught, would be impossible, unless the time of the pupils' continuance at the seminary, and the requisites for entrance, were previously fixed. Such an enumeration would be tedious, nor do I conceive that it would be at all promotive of my object. The difficulty complained of, is not, that we are at a loss what sciences we ought to learn, but that we have not proper advantages to learn any. Many writers have given us excellent advice with regard to what we should be taught, but no legislature has provided us the means of instruction. Not however, to pass lightly over this fundamental part of education, I will mention one or two of the less obvious branches of science, which, I conceive should engage the youthful attention of my sex.

It is highly important, that females should be conversant with those studies, which will lead them to understand the operations of the human mind. The chief use to which the philosophy of the mind can be applied, is to regulate education by its rules. The ductile mind of the child is intrusted to the mother: and she ought to have every possible assistance, in acquiring a knowledge of this noble material, on which it is her business to operate, that she may best understand how to mould it to its most excellent form.

Natural philosophy has not often been taught to our sex. Yet why should we be kept in ignorance of the great machinery of nature, and left to the vulgar notion, that nothing is curious but what deviates from her common course? If mothers were acquainted with this science, they would communicate very many of its principles to their children in early youth. From the bursting of an egg buried in the fire, I have heard an intelligent mother, lead her prattling inquirer, to understand the cause of the earthquake. But how often does the mother, from ignorance on this subject, give her child the most erroneous and contracted views of the causes of natural phenomena; views, which, though he may afterwards learn to be false, are yet, from the laws of association, ever ready to return, unless the active powers of the mind are continually upon the alert to keep them out. A knowledge of natural philosophy is calculated to heighten the moral taste, by bringing to view the majesty and beauty of order and design; and to enliven piety, by enabling the mind more clearly to perceive, throughout the manifold works of God, that wisdom, in which he hath made them all. In some of the sciences proper for our sex, the books, written for the other, would need alteration; because, in some they presuppose more knowledge than female pupils would possess; in others, they have parts not particularly interesting to our sex, and omit subjects immediately relating to their pursuits. There would likewise be needed, for a female seminary, some works, which I believe are no where extant, such as a systematic treatise on housewifery.

3. Domestic Instruction should be considered important in a female seminary. It is the duty of our sex to regulate

the internal concerns of every family; and unless they be properly qualified to discharge this duty, whatever may be their literary or ornamental attainments, they cannot be expected to make either good wives, good mothers, or good mistresses of families: and if they are none of these, they must be bad members of society; for it is by promoting or destroying the comfort and prosperity of their own families, that females serve or injure the community. To superintend the domestic department, there should be a respectable lady, experienced in the best methods of housewifery, and acquainted with propriety of dress and manners. Under her tuition the pupils ought to be placed for a certain length of time every morning. A spirit of neatness and order should here be treated as a virtue, and the contrary, if excessive and incorrigible, be punished with expulsion. There might be a gradation of employment in the domestic department, according to the length of time the pupils had remained at the institution. The older scholars might then assist the superintendent in instructing the younger, and the whole be so arranged, that each pupil might have advantages to become a good domestic manager by the time she has completed her studies.

This plan would afford a healthy exercise. It would prevent that estrangement from domestic duties, which would be likely to take place in a length of time devoted to study, with those, to whom they were previously familiar; and would accustom those to them, who, from ignorance, might otherwise put at hazard their own happiness, and the prosperity of their families.

GLOSSARY

actuate: to motivate into action

caprice: whim; sudden or unpredictable action

commodious: spacious

ductile: easily led or influenced

enumeration: count or list

gradation: a series of stages

judicious: prudent; sensible

magnanimity: generosity of mind and heart

manifold: multiple; many and varied

pliant: easily influenced

preceptress: a female principal or teacher

promotive: tending or serving to promote

seminary: a school of higher education, especially for girls; also a theological school for the training of the clergy

Document Analysis

Willard was one of the most prominent advocates for women's higher education in the post-revolutionary, or early national, period of American history. Her pamphlet *An Address to the Public; Particularly to the Members of the Legislature of New-York, Proposing a Plan for Improving Female Education*, better known as *A Plan for Improving Female Education*, lays out both an argument for publicly funding young women's higher education and a blueprint for a seminary that would provide female students with a more advanced academic curriculum. In essence, Willard wanted young women to have the same opportunities for educational advancement as young men had in American colleges, albeit with some gender-based modifications. She takes a logical, formal approach in building her argument but also tailors it to her audience, which in this case is composed of male legislators and other politicians. She assures her male readers that educated women will not move into the public sphere and interfere with male-dominated political processes and civic institutions. Instead she adopts an argument based on the ideal that has come to be known as republican motherhood, claiming that women must be educated so that they are able to educate their children, who will become the United States' next generation of civic leaders. Willard's writing also displays the influence of the so-called cult of true womanhood, or cult of domesticity, a similar philosophy that was emerging in the United States at the time. This belief held that there were two separate spheres of society: the domestic sphere, where women held primary responsibility, and the public sphere, where men dominated and were charged with governance of the country.

As many men would have found a radical argument in favor of women's education off-putting, Willard needed to be careful not to alienate the very people she was trying to convince. These men had the authority to divert funds and make her plan a reality, and so she had to develop a strategic approach and argument that could persuade them of the worthiness of her plan while putting them at ease. Willard begins by simply stating her objective: to convince the New York legislature to fund a seminary for women. She felt this would be an excellent first step in a greater reform movement.

Her first line of argument is to explain the nature of this new school. She mentions the "absurdity of sending ladies to college" and assures the reader that a women's seminary will be necessarily distinct from a male college, just as men and women are different in "character and duties." She moves from this assurance into an explanation of the ways in which her plan will benefit men, cleverly appealing to her readers' self-interest. She explains that even if her plan only improves "the American female character" by providing women with a better education, that alone would be a worthy goal. She then states that improving the character of women would also improve that of men, thereby elevating "the whole character of the community." Here, Willard is establishing the foundation of her argument that a reformed and therefore better women's education system will benefit the United States in general.

Willard goes on to reinforce this argument by addressing those who may not believe her previous point that the betterment of women will raise the character of the community. She points to mothers as her key example and begins by explaining the importance of the mother's role in raising children. Children's minds are "pliant" and can be easily guided, but mothers need the knowledge necessary to mold these young minds. She notes that it is difficult for women to acquire this knowledge and states it is far easier for men to obtain. Willard also notes that women's education as it stands is too often devoted to "frivolous acquirements," as opposed to the "enlarged and correct views" of educated men. She explains that women need to understand the "nature of the mind" in order to shape it appropriately. Again, this line of argument is in keeping with the philosophy of republican motherhood, in which women's civic duty to the new republic is to prepare the next generation of Americans help the country develop and improve.

The next excerpted section features Willard's discussion of problems and deficiencies in women's education that her plan is intended to solve or eliminate. Willard begins this section by explaining why regulation of education by government is desirable. She contrasts education with trade, which she feels can regulate itself, while education cannot. Governments have provided this regulation to men's educational institutions but not to women's. In fact, Willard notes that women's education has been left to "the mercy of private adventurers" and therefore has no common curricula or standards. Willard explains that in effect, female education has been left "to chance."

Willard's strong belief that the government should have "guardian care" of education stems from her belief that this will improve the quality of the education itself. She states that the positions of president or professor of a male college are considered positions of note "to which the eye of ambition is directed." In contrast, "preceptresses" are often paid by and thus dependent on their students, which makes disciplining students difficult. To emphasize this point further, Willard provides the analogy of a parent who must care for his or her children but is also dependent on them to survive. In such a case, it would be difficult for the parent to exert any type of discipline over the children.

Next, Willard assures her readers that girls should be educated "chiefly" by women. Her use of the word *chiefly* is interesting, as her own sister studied under a man, and she did understand that sometimes young women needed a higher level of education that could only be gained by studying with a male instructor who had been granted educational opportunities that female teachers had not. But primarily, for the sake of "propriety," women should be their instructors. This again reinforces the philosophy of the separate spheres and provides an example of the separation of the sexes in the new republic. Before this time, the United States had been a predominantly agrarian society in which men and women worked alongside each other in the fields and in the home. As the new country developed and industrialized, men began working outside of the home more often. As a result of this, work life and home life became separate and gendered.

After discussing the deficiencies of the current model of women's education, Willard then logically turns to her thoughts on how education should be regulated and why. She again addresses her readers as government representatives who are charged with the betterment of society both in the present and in the future. Willard first equates character with the success, or "prosperity," of a nation and reiterates her point that mothers are responsible for forming character. She goes on to make a clever circular argument. If mothers control character development, then the "government can control the characters of its future citizens" through mothers. Logically, then, the government should take on the responsibility of educating young women (future mothers) to ensure the country's future success. The United States' leaders could in this way control the formation of the characters of their future citizens by controlling the educational development of the future citizens' mothers. Willard thus promotes her plan by strategically appealing to men who are responsible for the success of a young country. She reinforces her strategy by saying that it is the "duty" of legislators to support the development of the next generations of Americans, implying that they have little choice but to follow her plan.

After making this strong and logical point in favor of education for women, Willard takes care to deflect anticipated concerns of male legislators, who may worry that they will simply be providing resources to create a "college-learned lady." Aware that many men would view such a woman as radical and quite possibly a threat to society, she therefore emphasizes that she is advocating "not a masculine education" but an education that is similar yet different. Willard demands the "respectability, permanency, and uniformity" of a men's educational institution but notes that her proposed seminary must be adapted to take into account the "difference of character and duties" of men and women.

Up until this section of her plan, Willard has concentrated on providing a logical and clear argument for the need to reform women's education and allow girls and young women to study more substantial subjects, similar to the curricula for men at the time. She has also argued for public funding and government regulation of women's education. In the next section, Willard becomes an architect of her own vision and provides a blueprint or sketch of what a model women's seminary might look like. By providing concrete details, Willard gives the legislators a clear idea of where the public's money would go and tries to allay any fears that her seminary is actually a women's college in disguise. She refers to her sketch as "imperfect" in an attempt to show both humility and submissiveness to her male readers.

Willard proposes four elements essential to the operation of the ideal women's seminary: a building, a library, a governance structure, and a core educational program. The school building would need to include student lodgings, lecture rooms, and an area in which the domestic department could operate. A particularly important room is the library, which Willard notes should include not only books but also maps, globes, paintings, and musical instruments. A "competent" and "judicious board of trust" would handle the overall operation of the seminary and develop an appropriate and challenging curriculum.

Willard emphasizes the importance of the curriculum to the success of the ideal seminary. She wanted girls and young women to study topics similar to those studied by their male counterparts, but she also understood that because women lived in a separate sphere, they must study subjects distinct from men as well. As such, she explains that the curriculum should be separated into four primary areas of instruction: religious and moral, literary, domestic, and ornamental. This excerpt does not discuss the ornamental courses, but Willard proposes they include such topics as drawing, painting, music, dancing, and penmanship.

As the post-revolutionary United States was deeply Christian, it is no surprise that Willard wanted her female students to be well versed in religious and moral subjects. This would help build the all-important "character" that Willard wanted her students, who in her mind were all future mothers, to instill in their children. This component of the curriculum was so important that Willard proposes it be considered mandatory "by the laws of the institution."

The second component of the curriculum is "literary instruction," which according to Willard should encompass far more than merely literature. Willard is not concerned with detailing the subjects that should be covered in this department; rather, she is more concerned that girls and young women be granted the opportunity to study such topics. She mentions that she can find many people to advise the school regarding the courses that should be offered, but her real concern is that the government provide "the means of instruction" through both public funds and regulation. After reinforcing her key point once again, Willard goes on to detail "one or two of the less obvious branches of science" that might appeal to her students.

Here, Willard returns yet again to her favorite point. In order to fulfill the goal of educating character-building mothers, the ideal women's seminary must include the study or philosophy of the human mind in its curriculum. A mother educated in these areas could use her knowledge to help mold her child's mind and character. Willard's second suggested subject is "natural philosophy," or natural science. She opens by noting that this topic is not commonly taught to women, but she argues that it should be. Appropriately, she cites the example of a mother educating her child about nature. If educated, the mother can impart the correct knowledge, while if she is unaware of the laws of nature, she can implant erroneous information into the mind of her child that will need to be corrected later. Willard also mentions additional benefits of studying natural science, arguing that it will "heighten the moral taste" and "enliven piety" by providing a better understanding of the majesty of nature, of which God was believed to be the ultimate architect. She expresses her opinion that current textbooks would need to be altered, as some would be too advanced, some would have sections that would not interest girls and young women, and still others would need to include more appropriate subjects. She also felt that a new textbook on "housewifery" was needed. As Willard went on to become a textbook author of some note, she clearly took this observation seriously.

The next section details Willard's thoughts on domestic instruction. As women were expected to marry and have children, Willard sought to prepare her students to manage happy, well-organized, and well-mannered homes and families. This emphasis is representative of the separation of work and home that was becoming typical in the United States at the time. For Willard, women who were not "good wives, good mothers, or good mistresses of families" were simply "bad members of society." Worse, they would ultimately be responsible for injuring their communities.

Willard envisions the seminary's domestic department operating under the supervision of a "respectable lady" who knows how to dress modestly and is "experienced in the best methods of housewifery." The students would spend a portion of each morning with her, and any students who could not grasp the "spirit of neatness and order" would be expelled. Willard also notes that the senior students should tutor the younger ones and thus learn how to supervise and manage a household. She explains that emphasizing domestic education would prevent her students from becoming disconnected from their household duties, which could occur if they became too engrossed in their academic studies. She reassures her male readers that educating women will not cause them to abandon their domestic duties and their families; rather, education will prepare young women to be better wives and mothers. This point further reinforces Willard's key argument that by educating women, the government of the United States would strengthen the country's future.

Essential Themes

Willard's life was spent in the pursuit of furthering women's higher education by lobbying the government to fund and regulate it. While never successful in her dream of establishing a publicly funded seminary for women, she did found the privately funded Troy Female Seminary. Troy was incredibly successful, and Willard's *Plan for Improving Female Education* became a foundational document for women's education in the United States and abroad. Her school educated some of the leading female minds of the period, including Elizabeth Cady Stanton, who fought for women's suffrage, or right to vote, throughout the latter half of the nineteenth century. By 1871, Troy's fiftieth anniversary, more than one hundred of the school's alumnae had gone on to administer or establish their own schools. Renamed the Emma Willard School in 1895, the school continues to operate as a private independent school for girls and counts as its alumnae many prominent American women, including a number of successful business leaders, scientists, activists, and politicians.

Willard's argument that the education of women is beneficial to society has continued to resonate with activists in the nearly two centuries since the publication of her pamphlet, fueling the continuing struggle for equal opportunities in higher education. Her goal of educating better mothers in order to raise better citizens, however, has lost its relevance. Within her time period, Willard made the argument that she felt would be accepted by the male legislators who could make the changes she desired. By avoiding even the suspicion of being a radical, Willard was able to navigate within male power structures and be seen as a conservative, nonthreatening woman. Perhaps it was the same strategy that led her to disapprove publicly of the activism surrounding the women's suffrage movement and the antislavery movement later in her life.

By the end of her life, Willard had amassed a lasting legacy of female graduates and teachers, created a challenging curriculum, and laid the groundwork for publicly funded education for women. She had written some of the period's most popular and enduring textbooks on the subjects of world and American history as well as geography. She stayed in touch with many of her graduates and traveled and lectured widely. A constant voice for women's higher education in the nineteenth century, Willard changed both the way women learned and American society itself.

Lee Tunstall, PhD

Bibliography

Beadie, Nancy. "Emma Willard's Idea Put to the Test: The Consequences of State Support of Female Education in New York, 1819–67." *History of Education Quarterly* 33.4 (1993): 543–62. Print.

Campbell, Karlyn Kohrs. *Women Public Speakers in the United States, 1800–1925: A Bio-Critical Sourcebook*. Westport: Greenwood, 1993. Print.

De Simone, Debra. "Troy Female Seminary." *Historical Dictionary of Women's Education in the United States*. Ed. Linda Eisenmann. Westport: Greenwood, 1998. 435–36. Print.

"Emma Hart Willard." *The History of Women and Education*. National Women's History Museum, n.d. Web. 19 Mar. 2013.

Mulvihill, Thalia M. "Willard, Emma Hart." *Historical Dictionary of Women's Education in the United States*. Ed. Linda Eisenmann. Westport: Greenwood, 1998. 465–67. Print.

Willard, Emma Hart. *An Address to the Public; Particularly to the Members of the Legislature of New-York, Proposing a Plan for Improving Female Education*. Middlebury: Copeland, 1819. Print.

Additional Reading

Badilescu, Simona. "Sisters in Mind—Early Networking for the Advancement of Women's Education: Emma Willard's French Connection." *Vitae Scholasticae* 22.1 (2005): 135–48. Print.

Fishburn, Eleanor, and Mildred Fenner. "Emma Willard and Her Plan for Improving Female Education." *National Educational Association Journal* 30.6 (1941): 177–78. Print.

Lutz, Alma. *Emma Willard: Daughter of Democracy*. Boston: Houghton, 1929. Print.

---. *Emma Willard: Pioneer Educator of American Women*. Boston: Beacon, 1964. Print.

Reddick, Robert Nelson. "History, Myth, and the Politics of Educational Reform." *Educational Theory* 54.1 (2004): 73–87. Print.

Scott, Anne Firor. "The Ever-Widening Circle: The Diffusion of Feminist Values from the Troy Female Seminary, 1822–1872." *History of Education Quarterly* 19 (1979): 3–25. Print.

LESSON PLAN: **Women and Education**

Students analyze Emma Willard's work on women, education, and the need for a women's seminary in the early republic.

Learning Objectives

Describe the values and hopes that advocates for women's education shared; compare and contrast the motives of Willard and Wright as well as those of their audience; explain how perspectives on women's education were similar and different; formulate examples of historical contingency to show how different choices could have led to different consequences.

Materials: Emma Hart Willard, *A Plan for Improving Female Education (1819)*; Frances Wright, "Letter XXIII: Condition of Women" (1820).

Overview Questions

How are Willard's and Wright's values and hopes for women's education similar and different? Compare their motives. Did they write for the same audience? Why or why not? How are their perspectives similar and different? How might ideas on women's education have changed if the American Revolution had never happened or if it had happened at a later time?

Step 1: Comprehension Questions

How are Willard's and Wright's values and hopes for women's education similar? How are they different? Explain.

- **Activity:** Select students to read aloud key passages in both selections. Ask students to underline phrases that convey each writer's values and hopes for women's education, then discuss as a class how they are similar and different.

Step 2: Comprehension Questions

Compare the motives of Willard and Wright. What prompted them to express their ideas? Who were their audiences?

- **Activity:** Have each student write a summary that compares the motives of Willard and Wright. Ask students to compare the audiences each addresses and explain how these audiences affected their writing styles.

Step 3: Context Questions

How are the perspectives of Willard and Wright similar and different? How do their experiences affect their perspectives? Why does Willard advocate government support and the need for a female seminary?

- **Activity:** Ask students to work with a partner to compare the perspectives of Willard and Wright by making a T-chart and locating specific passages that illustrate their viewpoints. Invite students to share their findings and to explain how each writer's experiences affected her perspective.

Step 4: Exploration Questions

How might ideas on women's education have changed if the American Revolution had never happened or if it had happened at a later time? Explain.

- **Activity:** Instruct students to write an outline for an essay that addresses how ideas on women's education might have been different had the American Revolution happened at a later time or not at all. Discuss the factors that led to the movement in support of women's education in the United States.

Step 5: Response Paper

Word length and additional requirements set by Instructor. Students answer the research question in the *Overview Questions*. Students state a thesis and use as evidence passages from the primary source document as well as support from supplemental materials assigned in the lesson.

Condition of Women

Date: 1821
Author: Wright, Frances
Genre: letter; memoir

"Perhaps the condition of women affords, in all countries, the best criterion by which to judge of the character of men."

Summary Overview

Frances "Fanny" Wright was a radical thinker, writer, and orator in the early part of the nineteenth century, active in both America and Great Britain. Scottish by birth, she was an early admirer of the young American Republic and travelled often on both sides of the Atlantic throughout her life. She was particularly engaged in the struggle for women's rights, especially women's education, as well as being an early antislavery activist. During her first trip to America, where she stayed from 1818 to 1820, she wrote many letters home that she reworked into her first publication, *Views of Society and Manners in America*, in 1821, which became a bestseller in America. This work included an important letter on her views of the condition of American women during this time period. She was seen by the feminists who followed her (such as Elizabeth Cady Stanton) as an important influence and early activist for women's rights.

Defining Moment

The post-Revolutionary, or early national, period in American history was a time when a young country was attempting to navigate new political processes, institutions, and beliefs. As is often the case in the time period after revolutions, the more radical views were being tempered as the new country tried to stabilize and find its place in the world. The discussions about women's rights that began during the American Revolution had been scaled back, and a certain backlash occurred in the early part of the nineteenth century.

When Frances Wright came to America she was immediately struck by its egalitarian nature, with the exception of the continued practice of slavery. She not only became a strong women's rights advocate, she was also an early abolitionist. Both of these movements did not really gain momentum until the 1830s and 1840s, so Wright was a trailblazer in both of these causes. She was also one of the first women to speak in public, in particular to audiences of both sexes. She was seen as a radical to many conservatives and a successor to Mary Wollstonecraft, who had written A *Vindication of the Rights of Women* in 1792. Wollstonecraft in particular was viewed as a radical, especially after her husband, William Godwin, had published a scandalous memoir after her death admitting she had had numerous affairs and had given birth to a child out of wedlock. Wright's own life was equally scandalous, as she herself believed in free love and sanctioned interracial relationships. She became a polarizing figure with some supporters hailing her as one of the most important minds of her time, while her opponents took great joy in referring to her as the "Red Harlot of Infidelity" or the "Whore of Babylon."

Her first publication, *Views of Society and Manners in America* was released in 1821, and it became an immediate bestseller. As it was extremely complimentary to America and Americans, she was soon catapulted into the public eye, and Wright discovered she enjoyed a certain celebrity and some notoriety. Letter number twenty-three was titled "On the Condition of Women" and was her first foray into writing about women's rights, a topic she was to become passionate about in later years. Her view of American women was that they were well respected by men and had good access to education, and this provided an excellent basis for the new country to thrive.

When she published this work, she was still a young woman of twenty-six and was only beginning to formulate her ideas. The letter is more an observation on women in America than it is a radical call to action, and yet Wright still sees in this new country a stark difference between how women are treated there than they are in Britain.

Author Biography

Throughout her turbulent life, Frances Wright was a passionate and outspoken advocate for women's education, women's rights, changes to marriage laws, and even birth control. Frances, or "Fanny" as she was also known, was born in Dundee, Scotland, on September 6, 1795. Her parents died within months of each other when she was two, so she and her sister, Camilla, were sent to their maternal grandfather and aunt to be raised. At age eighteen, she left to live with her great-uncle, James Milne, who held the chair of moral philosophy at Glasgow University. In this household, Wright developed her radical philosophy and learned to question conventional ideas. After reading a history of the American Revolution, Wright believed America to be a republican utopia that was based on progressive ideals.

In 1818, she and Camilla travelled to America and toured many of the Northern states. They avoided the south, where slavery was more prevalent, until the end of her trip, and Wright found herself appalled at this practice. Her letters from this American trip were published as *Views of Society and Manners in America in 1821* and transformed her into a person of public note. She was soon busy cultivating relationships with learned men such as the Marquis de Lafayette, with whom she travelled to America again in 1824, and Robert Owen and his son, Robert Dale Owen. The Owens had founded a socialist community in New Harmony, Indiana, that sparked Wright's own idea for a cooperative community. Using some of her inheritance, she established Nashoba (Chickasaw for "wolf") near Memphis, Tennessee, in 1825. Here on two thousand acres, she bought slaves and then gave them the opportunity to work the land to make enough money to buy their freedom. The community was eventually a failure, and Wright freed the remaining slaves and transported them to Haiti, which was the first black-led, independent republic. By 1829, Wright was lecturing in New York and was involved in the workingmen's movement, which advocated for better working conditions and free public education for workers.

Although she was opposed to marriage as an institution (she felt it oppressed women), she married a French doctor, Guillaume P. D'Arusmont, in 1831. They moved to France and Wright gave birth to a daughter, Frances Sylva, the following year. She moved back to America in 1835, to Cincinnati, where she began to give public lectures again. She travelled back and forth from France to America numerous times during this period of her life. By 1851, she had divorced D'Arusmont and was in conflict with him over finances and access to Sylva. She died on December 13, 1852, after having fallen on ice and broken her hip earlier that year.

HISTORICAL DOCUMENT

In the education of women, New England seems hitherto to have been peculiarly liberal. The ladies of the eastern states are frequently possessed of the most solid acquirements, the modern and even the dead languages, and a wide scope of reading; the consequence is that their manners have the character of being more composed than those of my gay young friends in this quarter. I have already stated, in one of my earlier letters, that the public attention is now everywhere turned to the improvement of female education. In some states, colleges for girls are established under the eye of the legislature, in which are taught all those important branches of knowledge that your friend Dr. Rush conceived to be so requisite.

In other countries it may seem of little consequence to inculcate upon the female mind "the principle of government, and the obligation of patriotism," but it was wisely forseen by that venerable apostle of liberty that in a country where a mother is charged with the formation of an infant mind that is to be called in future to judge of the laws and support the liberties of a republic, the mother herself should well understand those laws and estimate those liberties. Personal accomplishments and the more ornamental branches of knowledge should certainly in America be made subordinate to solid information. This is perfectly the case with respect to the men; as yet the women have been educated too much after the European manner. French, Italian, dancing, drawing engage the hours of the one sex (and this but too commonly in a lax and careless way), while the more appropriate studies of the other are philosophy, history, political economy, and the exact sciences. It follows, consequently, that after the spirits of youth have somewhat subsided, the two sexes have less in common in their pursuits and turn of thinking than is desirable. A woman of a powerful intellect will of course seize upon the new topics presented to her by the conversation of her husband. The less vigorous or the more thoughtless mind is not easily brought to forego trifling pursuits for those which occupy the stronger reason of its companion.

I must remark that in no particular is the liberal philosophy of the Americans more honorably evinced than in the place which is awarded to women. The prejudices still to be found in Europe, though now indeed somewhat antiquated, which would confine the female liberty to romances, poetry, and belles-lettres, and female conversation to the last new publication, new bonnet, and pas seul, are entirely unknown here. The women are assuming their place as thinking beings, not in despite of the men, but chiefly in consequence of their enlarged views and exertions as fathers and legislators.

I may seem to be swerving a little from my subject, but as I have adverted to the place accorded to women in one particular, I may as well now reply to your question regarding their general condition. It strikes me that it would be impossible for women to stand in higher estimation than they do here. The deference that is paid to them at all times and in all places has often occasioned me as much surprise as pleasure

In domestic life there is a tenderness on the part of the husband to his weaker helpmate, and this in all situations of life that I believe in no country is surpassed and in few equaled. No cavaliere servente of a lady of fashion, no sighing lover, who has just penned a sonnet to his "mistress's eyebrow," ever rendered more delicate attentions to the idol of his fancy that I have seen rendered by an American farmer or mechanic, not to say gentleman, to the companion of his life. The wife and daughters of labouring citizen are always found neatly dressed and occupied at home in household concerns; no field labour is ever imposed upon a woman, and I believe that it would outrage the feelings of an American, whatever be his station, should he see her engaged in any toil seemingly unsuited to her strength. In travelling, I have myself often met with a refinement of civility from men, whose exterior promised only the roughness of the mechanic or working farmer, that I should only have looked for from the polished gentleman.

Perhaps the condition of women affords, in all countries, the best criterion by which to judge of the character of men. Where we find the weaker sex burdened with hard labour, we may ascribe to the stronger something of the savage, and where we see the former deprived of free agency, we shall find in the latter much of the sensualist. I know not a circumstance which more clearly marks in England the retrograde movement of the national morals than the shackles now forged for the rising generation of women. Perhaps these are as yet more exclusively laid upon what are termed the highest class, but I apprehend that thousands of our countrywomen in the middle ranks, whose mothers, or certainly whose grandmothers, could ride unattended from the Land's End to the border and walk abroad alone or with an unmarried friend of the other sex armed with all the unsuspecting virtue of Eve before her fall—I apprehend that the children and grandchildren of these matrons are now condemned to walk in leading strings from the cradle to the altar, if not to the grave, taught to see in the other sex a race of seducers rather than protectors and of masters rather than companions. Alas for the morals of a country when female dignity is confounded with helplessness and the guardianship of a woman's virtue transferred from herself to others! If any should doubt the effect produced by the infringement of female liberty upon the female mind, let them consider the dress of the present generation of English women. This will sufficiently settle the question without refrence to the pages of the daily journals. Of the two extremes it is better to see a woman, as in Scotland, bent over the glebe, mingling the sweat of her brow with that of her churlish husband or more churlish son, than to see her gradually sinking into the childish dependence of a Spanish donna.

The liberty here enjoyed by the young women often occasions some surprise to foreigners, who, contrasting it with the constraint imposed on the female youth of Paris or London, are at a loss to reconcile the freedom of the national manners with the purity of the national morals; but confidence and innocence are twin sisters, and should the American women ever resign the guardianship of their own virtue, the lawyers of these democracies will probably find as good occupation in prosecuting suits for divorce as those of any of the monarchies of Europe.

I often lament that in the rearing of women so little attention should be commonly paid to the exercise of the bodily organs; to invigorate the body is to invigorate the mind, and Heaven knows that the weaker sex have much cause to be rendered strong in both. In the happiest country their condition is sufficiently hard. Have they talents? It is difficult to turn them to account. Ambition? The road to honorable distinction is shut against them. A vigorous intellect? It is broken down by sufferings, bodily and mental. The lords of creation receive innumerable, incalculable advantages from the hand of nature, and it must be admitted that they everywhere take sufficient care to foster the advantages with which they are endowed. There is something so flattering to human vanity in the consciousness of superiority that it is little surprising if men husband with jealousy that which nature has enabled them to usurp over the daughters of Eve. Love of power more frequently originates in vanity than pride (two qualities, by the way, which are often confounded) and is, consequently, yet more peculiarly the sin of little than of great minds.

Now an overwhelming proportion of human minds appertains to the former class and must be content to soothe their self-love by considering the weakness of others rather than their own strength. You will say this is severe; is it not true? In what consists the greatness of a despot? In his own intrinsic merits? No, in the degradation of the multitude who surround him. What feeds the vanity of a patrician? The consciousness of any virtue that he inherits with his blood? The list of his senseless progenitors would probably soon cease to command his respect if it did not enable him to command that of his fellow creatures. "But what," I hear you ask, "has this to do with the condition of women? Do you mean to compare men collectively to the despot and the patrician?" Why not? The vanity of the despot and the patrician is fed by the folly of their fellow men, and so is that of their sex collectively soothed by the dependence of women: it pleases them better to find in their companion a fragile vine clinging to their firm trunk for support, than a vigorous tree with whose branches they may mingle theirs. I believe they sometimes repent of their choice when the vine has weighed the oak to the ground. It is difficult, in walking through the world, not to laugh at the consequences which, sooner or later, overtake men's follies, but when these are vested upon women I feel more disposed to sigh. Born to endure the worst afflictions of fortune, they are enervated in soul and body lest the storm should not visit them sufficiently rudely. Instead of essaying to the counteract the unequal law of nature, it seems the object of man to visit it upon his weaker helpmate more harshly. It is well, however, that his folly recoils upon his own head, and that the fate of the sexes is so entwined that the dignity of the one must rise or fall with that of the other.

In America much certainly is done to ameliorate the condition of women, and as their education shall become, more and more, the concern of the state, their character may aspire in each succeeding generation to a higher standard. The republic, I am persuaded, will be amply repaid for any trouble or expense that may be thus bestowed. In her struggles for liberty much of her virtue emanated from the wives and daughters of her senators and soldiers, and to preserve to her sons the energy of freemen and patriots she must strengthen that energy to her daughters.

To invigorate the character, however, it is not sufficient to cultivate the mind. The body also must be trained to wholesome exercise, and the nerves braced to bear those extremes of climate which here threaten to enervate the more weakly frame. It is the union of bodily and mental vigor in the male population of America which imparts to it that peculiar energy of character which in its first infancy drew forth so splendid a panegyric from the British orator: "What in the world is equal to it?" exclaimed Mr. Burke. "Whilst we follow them (the colonists) among the tumbling mountains of ice, and behold them penetrating into the deepest frozen recesses of Hudson's Bay and Davis' Straits, whilst we are looking for them beneath the Arctic Circle, we hear that they have pierced into the opposite region of polar cold, that they are at the antipodes, and engaged under the frozen serpent of the South. Falkland Island, which seemed too remote and romantic an object for the grasp of national ambition, is but a stage and resting place in the progress of their victorious industry; nor is the equinoctial heat more discouraging to them than the accumulated winter of both the poles. We know that while some of them draw a line and strike the harpoon on the coast of Africa, others run the longitude, and pursue their gigantic game along the coast of Brazil. No sea but what is vexed by their fisheries; no climate that is not witness to their toils."

Now, though it is by no means requisite that the American women should emulate the men in the pursuit of the whale, the felling of the forest, or the shooting of wild turkeys, they might, with advantage, be taught in early youth to excel in the race, to hit a mark, to swim, and in short to use every exercise which could impart vigor to their frames and independence to their minds. But I have dwelt enough upon this subject, and you will, perhaps, apprehend that I am about to subjoin a Utopian plan of national education: no, I leave this to the republic herself, and, wishing all success to her endeavours, I bid your farewell.

GLOSSARY

adverted: to call attention; refer

ameliorate: improve

appertains: concerns; relates to

cavaliere servente: lover and/or escort of higher social standing, especially of a married woman in the eighteenth century and often known to and approved of by the woman's husband

equinoctial: relating to either or both equinoxes

enervated: weakened; deprived of strength

glebe: archaic term referring to earth or land; more specifically land providing income to an English parish church or office holder

inculcate: to instill or teach an idea or attitude by persistent repetition

panegyric: formal or elaborate praise, often in the form of a speech or writing

pas seul: a solo dance

patrician: a person of breeding; an aristocrat or noble

subjoin: to append something; add at the end

Document Analysis

In 1818, a young Scottish woman and her sister travelled to America to see first-hand what the new country had to offer and how it differed from Great Britain. Fanny and Camilla Wright arrived in New York in September and stayed until May of 1820. Throughout this time, Fanny Wright wrote letters to an older friend, Mrs. Rabina Craig Millar, detailing their trip and their adventures as well as expressing opinions about aspects of the new country. In her twenty-third letter, she turned her attention to the condition of women in America. She was impressed by the fact that women in America had more access to education than women in her home country and that this practice was extremely beneficial to the new country. Her writing style in these letters was quite secular in tone, which differed somewhat from the more Christian references and allusions that many women writers of the day employed. In fact, her letters were more like a running narrative of her experiences, with colorful descriptions of the people and places she visited. Interspersed with this, Wright also made astute observations of society and in particular how Americans were trying to live out their revolutionary ideals of liberty and freedom for all.

During her tour of New England, she was very impressed with the high level of education of women. She mentioned that they were adept in languages, both those that were no longer widely spoken ("dead"), such as Latin, and "modern" languages, such as French or Italian. She feels that their "wide scope of reading" had matured them more than her own "gay young" friends. "Gay" here is used in its traditional definition of being happy and carefree. She alludes to colleges being established for women, some of them sanctioned by the state governments. She also mentions that there is a widespread discussion on improving the education of women in America, and indeed there was a movement to establish academies and seminaries to provide secondary education for women. Bear in mind that this was restricted to white women, and that black and American Indian women were not included in this educational movement. Wright also refers to Mrs. Millar's friend Dr. Rush. This no doubt refers to Benjamin Rush, a Founding Father, who was an esteemed medical doctor and a strong advocate of women's education.

Wright then explains exactly why women's education is so important, especially to America. In particular, women needed to understand government and patriotism, as it is the mother who is in charge of the early education of her children. This argument became known as "republican motherhood"; this meant that for the new republic to be secure, future generations of its citizens needed to be taught a strong sense of civic duty. Mothers were seen as the best people to accomplish this task. Additionally, Wright felt that women's education should not follow the European tradition where women are taught more "ornamental branches" of learning that included drawing and dancing. America demanded that women be taught more "solid information." Then Wright offers another more practical and personal reason for women's education. If women are not educated in the same subjects and to the same level as men, they will be ill suited as companions in marriage and not able to engage in significant conversations with their husbands.

Wright is also impressed with the standing in society that American women hold and believes that this is because of their higher level of education. This is in contrast to European women, who are confined to the study of literature and their conversation restricted to the newest fashion styles, dance ("pas seul"), or publication. She sees women as "assuming their place as thinking beings" and that men, in their roles as fathers and politicians, have helped facilitate this. She continues in this vein as she responds directly to Mrs. Millar's question, no doubt sent to her in an earlier letter, about the general condition of American women. Wright is effusive in her praise, saying that she feels that in no other country could they be held in "higher estimation" than in America. She feels they are respected "at all times and in all places."

Wright then turns her attention to the domestic life of American women. Here she does touch on class and makes the differentiation between the "farmer or mechanic" and the "gentleman," but she also feels both classes are as affectionate and caring towards the women in their lives as the other. Indeed, Wright feels that even a "cavaliere servente" or a lover could not be more attentive than American men. Again, Wright feels that women are extremely well treated and respected within marriages in America. She does, however, use the traditional rhetorical point that women are physically weaker than men and that their activities are in a separate sphere to those of men. Where women are busy with "household concerns," men are out labouring in the field. Wright is clear that American men believe that this type of heavy labour is not suited to women's weaker strength and they would be offended if women were to undertake it. In this way, Wright clearly believes that men and women are equal, but different.

Wright then makes a key point that how a country treats its women is perhaps the best way to judge its men. In order to better demonstrate this difference between American and European women and to give further weight to her argument, she gives examples. She states that where women are laborers, men are less developed and more like savages, and where women do not have freedom to act independently, men are more likely to be "sensualists," or those who are addicted to or obsessed with sensual pleasures.

Wright then turns to the regressive attitudes toward women's morals that she feels is present in England. She explains that women in England have lost considerable independence and that where they were once able to travel without a companion or even with an unmarried male friend without their virtue being questioned, this new generation of British women would find that impossible. They are more dependent on men throughout their entire lives, from the cradle to the altar to the grave, and they do not have control over their own virtue anymore; rather it is men who are charged with safeguarding it for them. Wright again uses as an example women's impractical preoccupation with fashion as keeping their minds diverted from more important learning. When she was at Nashoba, Wright actually designed her own practical outfit for women, including bodices, ankle-length pantaloons, and a dress cut above the knee. Other prominent feminists later adopted it, including Elizabeth Cady Stanton, Amelia Bloomer, and Susan B. Anthony. As a way to drive this point home, Wright states that she would rather see women as they are in Scotland, working side by side with their boorish husband and rude son in hard manual labour, than see them dependent on men as a child would be.

After discussing the restrictions on European women, Wright contrasts this with the "liberty here enjoyed" by American women. She feels it may be confusing to some people to try and understand how American women can enjoy such freedoms, while at the same time retaining their virtue and moral purity. She believes that it is because of their confidence and the fact that they are innocent of any other way of being. Wright ends with a warning that if American women ever give up safeguarding their own virtue, divorce rates will go up.

Wright changes her focus now from the intellectual education of women to their physical health. She is a strong advocate for physical exercise for women as a means to increase their intellectual capacity ("to invigorate the body is to invigorate the mind"). This was a radical idea at the time, and not one commonly proposed. In this, Wright predated Catharine Beecher's 1841 proposal for daily physical education for women, made up of calisthenics set to music. She then goes on to explain that even though women in America have an extremely strong position in society, they are also held back from reaching their true potential. It is difficult for women to realize their talents, they cannot demand public honors if they have personal ambition, and even if they are strongly intellectual, their bodies and their mental health often let them down. Here, Wright seems to take issue with men's natural advantages due to the simple fact they are physically superior to women. And she feels that men lord this over women and actually enjoy this power over women ("the daughters of Eve"). Wright then equates this "love of power" with men's vanity, rather than pride, and that this thought process is the product of "little than of great minds."

In the next paragraph, Wright's tone becomes more radical and it is here that her future role as an orator and speaker is foreshadowed. She begins by considering that men "soothe their self-love" by keeping women subservient rather than focusing on their own strength. She appears to realize that this may be a radical thought and asks the question of Mrs. Millar, and all readers, if this is not too severe an opinion. Her use of questions in this paragraph is an effective rhetorical strategy: it breaks up the narrative and makes the reader think more intently on the subject at hand. She follows this up by asking the reader to consider what makes a tyrant, or despot, great, and she answers the question with the fact that he keeps those around him in an inferior position. She moves next to the patrician, or nobleman, and asks what keeps him conceited, and lands on the simple fact of his bloodline. Next, Wright proposes what she assumes is a radical question: "Do you mean to compare men collectively to the despot and the patrician?" This gives her the opening to expand on her main point that men prefer dependent women ("a fragile vine") to an equal ("a vigorous tree"). Wright then takes this argument to its natural conclusion. She pointedly states that many men may feel this was ill thought through when such dependent women create too many problems and stresses for men to bear. She is equally piercing when she states that instead of helping to raise women up "to counteract the unequal law of nature," men simply treat women even worse. Returning to the metaphor of the vine and the tree, Wright ends this section by reminding her reader that both men's and women's fates are "entwined." If a woman's dignity is degraded, then so is a man's.

Wright returns to the subject of women's education in America after this diatribe on men's failings. Again, she states that it is in the best interests of the country to educate women. She also believes that this education will soon become the responsibility of the government to execute, which at the time was only just beginning. Many of the female academies and schools were privately run. This new public education system will be worth "any trouble or expense" that it would cost to establish. In fact, publicly funded elementary schools were not in place across the country until 1870. To reinforce this point, Wright reminds her reader that it was "wives and daughters" who played a great role in the revolutionary war, and to ensure liberty is upheld in America in the future, women's rights should be strengthened.

Wright then turns her attention to the relationship between character, intellect, and physical health. Character, according to Wright, is built not only through the mind, but also through a healthy body. She makes the point that this is particularly true for American women, as the climate is much more extreme than that of Europe and is therefore harsher on them. She changes her strategy and begins to praise American men as examples of how "the union of bodily and mental vigor" created such an energetic character.

She then quotes extensively from Edmund Burke's "Speech on Conciliation with America," which he gave in 1775 in the British House of Commons, in an attempt to further explain and give examples of this unique American character. Burke was a prominent British-Irish politician during the American Revolution, and he was a proponent of trying to appease the then still British colonies to keep them under British rule. At first glance, this seems an odd choice for the radical Wright to quote, given Burke's conservative nature and respect for the past and for traditions. Although his conservative reputation was earned from his strong opposition to the French Revolution, Burke did in fact champion many liberal causes, and so his worldview was actually far more complex than it first appeared. The excerpt she chose to quote in full was one where Burke was explaining America's success in commerce, in particular whaling, and how the American character led to this success. He talks of their ability to traverse the world and suffer through the various changes in weather and landscape, such as "deepest frozen recesses of Hudson's Bay" and the "equinoctial heat." The Americans successfully pursue the whales they are fishing from Africa to Brazil and to both poles. To Burke, this was an extraordinary example of the American male's character and therefore his industry as well.

Wright admits to her correspondent Millar that she does not believe that American women should join American men in such harsh activities, to which she adds the examples of forestry and hunting. She does, however, encourage women to participate in more physical pursuits such as swimming, archery, or running. She again states that taking part in such activities will create both a healthy mind and a healthy body, which in turn will lead women ultimately to find their independence, as opposed to dependence upon men.

To end her letter, Wright teases Millar with the thought that through this line of argument, Millar might think Wright is about to embark on a discussion of the need for a plan for national public education. She refers to such as plan as "Utopian," insinuating that it was the ideal and ultimate form of educational system America could create. However, she admits that this is not her role, and instead she leaves it to Americans and their republic to develop this plan. She does, however, end with a wish that America is successful in this venture, which in fact it was, albeit not in Wright's lifetime.

Essential Themes

Frances Wright believed strongly in women's right to an education and women's equal rights with men. As she travelled the new country of America, she saw the stark differences between opportunities for women to be educated in this new world and the stagnation and despair of some women's lives in England. Wright felt that America was a better country because it took care to educate its women, who in turn would be able to educate their children and thereby raise better future citizens.

Wright was a young woman at the time of writing this piece, and her ideas about women's rights evolved and became even more radical as she matured. She lectured publicly—a rarity for a woman of this time period—and was interested in such other free-thinking topics as abolition, better working conditions for the working class, and sexual equality for women. Her interests in gender, race, and class placed her far ahead of her time, and she was seen as a radical to many and as a successor to Mary Wollstonecraft. She was most definitely a polarizing figure with many seeing her as a shining light of liberalism, while others viewed her as a danger to the fabric of society.

After the publication of *Views of Society and Manners in America*, she became a popular figure in America, especially through her lecture tours. Although she lost this celebrity in later years when she spent time in France, she was considered an important influence by such early American feminists as Elizabeth Cady Stanton, who owned many of her books and put Wright's portrait in one of her own books. Other early feminists, such as Susan B. Anthony, Lucretia Mott, and Ernestine Rose, all named her as an inspiration for their own work in women's rights. Walt Whitman and John Stuart Mill were considered admirers as well. Mill considered her to be one of the most important women of her time.

Wright's place in women's history has continued to be debated over the years. There are some who dismiss her completely as a failure and negative example, while others see in her an early example of a courageous woman who spoke out about her radical ideas in a public setting. In this she set the stage for many abolitionist and suffragist women who spoke to mixed audiences beginning in the 1830s. Perhaps Wright is best remembered as a prime example of Professor Laurel Thatcher Ulrich's now-famous slogan, "well-behaved women seldom make history."

Lee Tunstall, PhD

Bibliography

Bederman, Gail. "Revisiting Nashoba: Slavery, Utopia, and Frances Wright in America, 1818–1826." *American Literary History* 17.3 (2005): 438–59. Print.

Browne, Stephen H. *Edmund Burke and the Discourse of Virtue*. Tuscaloosa: U of Alabama P, 1993. Print.

Kissel, Susan S. *In Common Cause: The "Conservative" Frances Trollope and the "Radical" Frances Wright*. Bowling Green: Bowling Green State UP, 1993. Print.

Morris, Celia. *Fanny Wright: Rebel in America*. Urbana: U of Illinois P, 1992. Print.

Perkins, Alice J. G., and Theresa Wolfson. *Frances Wright, Free Enquirer: The Study of a Temperament*. Philadelphia: Porcupine, 1972. Print.

Voss, Cary R. W., and Robert C. Rowland. "Pre-Inception Rhetoric in the Creation of a Social Movement: The Case of Frances Wright." *Communication Studies* 51.1 (2000): 1–14. Print.

Wright, Frances. *Views of Society and Manners in America (A Travel Memoir)*. 1821. Cambridge: Harvard UP, 1963. Print.

Additional Reading

Bartlett, Elizabeth Ann. *Liberty, Equality, Sorority: The Origins and Interpretation of American Feminist Thought: Frances Wright, Sarah Grimke, and Margaret Fuller*. Brooklyn: Carlson, 1994. Print.

Connors, Robert J. "Frances Wright: First Female Civic Rhetor in America." *College English* 62.1 (1999): 30–57. Print.

D'Arusmont, Frances Wright. *Life, Letters, and Lectures 1834–1844*. New York: Arno, 1972. Print.

Frost, Elizabeth, and Kathryn Cullen-Dupont. *Women's Suffrage in America: An Eyewitness History*. New York: Facts on File, 1992. Print.

Ginzberg, Lori D. "'The Hearts of Your Readers Will Shudder': Fanny Wright, Infidelity, and American Freethought." *American Quarterly* 46.2 (1994): 195–226. Print.

Wollstonecraft, Mary. *A Vindication of the Rights of Women*. Ed. Miriam Brody. New York: Penguin, 2004. Print.

Wright, Frances. *A Plan for the Gradual Abolition of Slavery in the United States without Danger of Loss to the Citizens of the South*. Baltimore: Lundy, 1825. Print.

---. *Course of Popular Lectures, as Delivered by Frances Wright*. New York: Matsell, 1829. Print.

LESSON PLAN: **The Impact of Education on the Rights of Women**

Students analyze Frances Wright's commentary on women and education in the early republic and in Great Britain.

Learning Objectives

Explain how customs and ideas influenced women's rights in the United States; explain the effect of women's education abroad on women's education in the United States; describe women's and men's rights and roles in and within regions of the United States; analyze how perspectives on women's rights and education set a precedent.

Materials: Frances Wright, "Condition of Women" (1821); Hannah Mather Crocker, "Observations on the Real Rights of Women" (1818).

Overview Questions

How have customs and ideas in other countries influenced women's aspirations and achievements in the new republic? What effect has women's education in other countries had on women's education in the United States? How are women's roles similar to and different from those of men in and within other regions of the United States? How do the writers' perspectives on women's rights and education help to set a precedent for women's rights and reforms in the United States?

Step 1: Comprehension Questions

How have customs and ideas in other countries influenced women's aspirations and achievements in the new republic?

- **Activity:** Have students work in small groups; ask them to read both selections and highlight the customs and ideas that both writers address; instruct them to prepare a brief oral presentation on how these customs and ideas influenced women's education in the new republic.

Step 2: Comprehension Questions

What effect has women's education in other countries had on women's education in the United States?

- **Activity:** Discuss how women's education in Europe affected women's education in the United States; then ask students to each write to compare and contrast women's rights in the United States and abroad as expressed by both writers.

Step 3: Context Questions

How are women's roles similar and different from those of men in and within regions of the United States?

- **Activity:** Instruct students to work in small groups to make a list of the roles that men and women have, as defined by both writers; have groups share their lists with the class and discuss how those roles have changed.

Step 4: Exploration Questions

How do the writers' perspectives on women's rights and education help to set a precedent for women's rights and reforms in the United States?

- **Activity:** Ask students to write a thesis statement about how the writers' perspectives on women's rights and education helped to set a precedent for women's rights and reform in the United States.

Step 5: Response Paper

Word length and additional requirements set by Instructor. Students answer the research question in the *Overview Questions*. Students state a thesis and use as evidence passages from the primary source document as well as support from supplemental materials assigned in the lesson.

The Nature and Occasions of Intemperance

Date: 1828
Author: Beecher, Lyman
Genre: political sermon; sermon

"Intemperance is the sin of our land, and, with our boundless prosperity, is coming in upon us like a flood."

Summary Overview

In the opening decades of the nineteenth century in the United States, the Second Great Awakening was a Protestant revival movement that saw an increase in agitation for conservative Christian moral and social reforms, one of which was the ban of alcoholic beverages. Believing alcohol to be the root of many social and moral problems, these early reformers would give rise to the prohibition movement later in the century and, ultimately, to the passing of the Eighteenth Amendment to the United States Constitution in 1919, which made the production, sale, and consumption of alcohol illegal.

A prominent leader in the Second Great Awakening, Congregationalist minister Lyman Beecher was active in efforts to ban alcohol in the early nineteenth century. Drawing from his experience as a clergyman and a moral reformer, Beecher used his sermons to extol the virtues of temperance to those who came to hear him speak. For Beecher, the key to a happy, healthy, fulfilling life was religion, not alcohol.

Defining Moment

The tumultuous opening decades of the nineteenth century in America gave rise to the Second Great Awakening, a Protestant religious movement that emphasized salvation for all. Led in large part by Methodist and Baptist churches, the movement was known for its elaborate and well-attended religious revivals at which well-known preachers would give stirring sermons aimed at the conversion of souls. One of the target areas for the movement was the so-called burned-over district of present-day upstate New York. In the early years of the nineteenth century, this area was considered to be frontier land in need of religious renewal, and it was so popular a destination for revivals and camp meetings that opportunities for new religious converts were ultimately considered to have "burned" out.

The Second Great Awakening was also a period in which ardent Christians in America took up social causes such as abolition, women's rights, and temperance. In a period of moral reform, it became abundantly clear to reformers that society's ills were in large part due to the prevalence of alcohol consumption. Men in particular were the focus of this movement. Once part of a domestic economy in which men and women worked together in the home, men increasingly had to leave their families during the day for work as American industries grew. Reformers targeted these men, who they believed had turned away from the morality of the home and toward the corruption of secular, industrialized society. Those who advocated for temperance viewed alcohol, usually indulged in outside of the home, as a further division between men and their families.

The Reverend Lyman Beecher, a strong advocate for moral improvement, was among the temperance reformers. For Beecher, alcohol not only took men away from their families but also distracted them from God. Beecher believed that men mistook the sensations that they experienced under the influence of alcohol for those granted naturally by God; one of his primary concerns was that alcohol would push individuals farther away from salvation in the life to come.

Author Biography

Lyman Beecher was born on October 12, 1775, in New Haven, Connecticut. After his mother's death when Beecher was just days old, his father, blacksmith David Beecher, sent him to be raised by his mother's sister and her family in nearby Guilford, Connecticut. Beecher graduated from Yale University in 1797 and subsequently worked as a pastor in Long Island, New York; Litchfield, Connecticut; and Boston, Massachusetts, before taking a position as the president of Lane Theological Seminary in Cincinnati, Ohio, in 1832. Beecher married Roxana Foote in 1799. After her death, he married Harriet Porter in 1817. Between them, Foote and Porter bore Beecher thirteen children, including Harriet Beecher Stowe, Catharine Beecher, and well-known Congregationalist minister Henry Ward Beecher. Lyman Beecher's career-long desire for social reform undoubtedly had an impact on his equally famous and influential children. After his second wife's death in 1835, Beecher married Lydia Beals Johnson, but he had no more children.

In the early nineteenth century, Beecher, newly graduated from college, applied his religious education to secular issues such as intemperance and slavery, which he considered to be immoral and corrupting forces in American society. As a revivalist during the Second Great Awakening, Beecher used his sermons and public role to support his causes while also speaking out against the Catholic and Unitarian churches, which he opposed. For Beecher and his religiously minded contemporaries, religious reform was the best way to remedy the moral turmoil in society. Although Beecher advocated an end to slavery, he believed that the best means to that end was not sudden, radical nationwide abolition but a gradual change, so that the nation would not experience too dramatic of a cultural shift. Beecher returned to the East Coast in the 1850s. He died in Brooklyn on January 10, 1863.

HISTORICAL DOCUMENT

This is a glowing description of the sin of intemperance. None but the pencil of inspiration could have thrown upon the canvass so many and such vivid traits of this complicated evil, in so short a compass. It exhibits its woes and sorrows, contentions and babblings, and wounds and redness of eyes; its smiling deceptions in the beginning, and serpent-bite in the end; the helplessness of its victims, like one cast out upon the deep; the danger of destruction, like that of one who sleeps upon the top of a mast; the unavailing lamentations of the captive, and the giving up of hope and effort. "They have stricken me, and I was not sick; they have beaten me, and I felt it not: when shall I awake? I will seek it yet again"; again be stricken and beaten; again float upon the deep, and sleep upon the mast.

No sin has fewer apologies than intemperance. The suffrage of the world is against it; and yet there is no sin so naked in its character, and whose commencement and progress is indicated by so many signs, concerning which there is among mankind such profound ignorance. All reprobate drunkenness; and yet, not one of the thousands who fall into it, dreams of danger when he enters the way that leads to it.

The soldier, approaching the deadly breach, and seeing rank after rank of those who preceded him swept away, hesitates sometimes, and recoils from death. But men behold the effects upon others, of going in given courses, they see them begin, advance, and end, in confirmed intemperance, and unappalled rush heedlessly upon the same ruin.

A part of this heedlessness arises from the undefined nature of the crime in its early stages, and the ignorance of men, concerning what may be termed the experimental indications of its approach. Theft and falsehood are definite actions. But intemperance is a state of internal sensation, and the indications may exist long, and multiply, and the subject of them not be aware that they are the signs of intemperance. It is not unfrequent, that men become irreclaimable in their habits, without suspicion of danger. Nothing, therefore, seems to be more important, than a description of this broad way, thronged by so many travelers, that the temperate, when they come in sight of it, may know their danger and pass by it and turn away.

What I shall deliver on this subject, has been projected for several years, has been delayed by indisposition, and the pressure of other labors, and is advanced now without personal or local reference

Intemperance is the sin of our land, and, with our boundless prosperity, is coming in upon us like a flood; and if anything shall defeat the hopes of the world, which hang upon our experiment of civil liberty, it is that river of fire, which is rolling through the land, destroying the vital air, and extending around an atmosphere of death.

It is proposed in this and the subsequent discourses, to consider the nature, the occasions, the signs, the evils, and the remedy of intemperance. In this discourse we shall consider

THE NATURE AND OCCASIONS OF INTEMPERANCE

The more common apprehension is that nothing is intemperance, which does not supercede the regular operations of the mental faculties and the bodily organs. However much a man may consume of ardent spirits, if he can command his mind, his utterance, and his bodily members, he is not reputed intemperate. And yet, drinking within these limits, he may be intemperate in respect to inordinate desire, the quantity consumed, the expense incurred, the present effect on his health and temper, and moral sensibilities, and what is more, in respect to the ultimate and inevitable results of bodily and mental imbecility, or sottish drunkenness.

God has made the human body to be sustained by food and sleep, and the mind to be invigorated by effort and the regular healthfulness of the moral system, and the cheering influence of his moral government. And whoever, to sustain the body, or invigorate the mind, or cheer the heart, applies habitually the stimulus of ardent spirits, does violence to the laws of his nature, puts the whole system into disorder, and is intemperate long before the intellect falters, or a muscle is unstrung.

The effect of ardent spirits on the brain, and the members of the body, is among the last effects of intemperance, and the least destructive part of the sin. It is the moral ruin which it works in the soul that gives it the denomination of giant-wickedness. If all who are intemperate, drank to insensibility, and on awaking, could arise from the debauch with intellect and heart uninjured, it would strip the crime of its most appalling evils. But among the woes which the scriptures denounce against crime, one is, "wo unto them that are mighty to drink wine, and men of strength to consume strong drink." These are captains in the bands of intemperance, and will drink two generations of youths into the grave, before they go to lie down by their side. The Lord deliver us from strong-headed men, who can move the tongue when all are mute around them, and keep the eye open when all around them sleep, and can walk from the scene of riot, while their companions must be aided or wait until the morning.

It is a matter of undoubted certainty, that habitual tippling is worse than periodical drunkenness. The poor Indian, who, once a month, drinks himself *dead* all but simple breathing, will out-live for years the man who drinks little and often, and is not, perhaps, suspected of intemperance. The use of ardent spirits daily, as ministering to cheerfulness, or bodily vigor, ought to be regarded as intemperance. No person, probably, ever did, or ever will, receive ardent spirits into his system once a day, and fortify his constitution against its deleterious effects, or exercise such discretion and self government, as that the quantity will not be increased, and bodily infirmities and mental imbecility be the result, and, in more than half the instances, inebriation. Nature may hold out long against this sapping and mining of the constitution, which daily tippling is carrying on; but, first or last, this foe of life will bring to the assault enemies of its own formation, before whose power the feeble and the mighty will be alike unable to stand.

All such occasional exhilaration of the spirits by intoxicating liquors, as produces levity and foolish jesting, and the loud laugh, is intemperance, whether we regard those precepts which require us to be sober-minded, or the effect which such exhilaration and lightness has upon the cause of Christ, when witnessed in professors of religion. The cheerfulness of health, and excitement of industry, and social intercourse, is all which nature demands, or health or purity permits.

A resort to ardent spirits as a means of invigorating the intellect, or of pleasurable sensation, is also intemperance. It is a distraint upon nature, to extort, in a short time, those results of mind and feeling, which in her own unimpelled course would flow with less impetuosity, but in a more equable and healthful current. The mind has its limits of intellectual application, and the heart its limits of feeling, and the nervous system of healthful exhilaration; and whatever you gain through stimulus, by way of anticipation, is only so much intellectual and vital power cut off at the latter end of life. It is this occult intemperance, of daily drinking, which generates a host of bodily infirmities and diseases: loss of appetite—nausea at the stomach—disordered bile—obstructions of the liver—jaundice—hoarseness of voice—coughs—consumptions—rheumatic pains—epilepsy—gout—colic—palsy—apoplexy—insanity—are the body-guards which attend intemperance, in the form of tippling, and where the odious name of drunkenness may perhaps be never applied.

A multitude of persons, who are not accounted drunkards, create disease, and shorten their days, by what they denominate a "prudent use of ardent spirits." Let it therefore be engraven upon the heart of every man, THAT THE DAILY USE OF ARDENT SPIRITS, IN ANY FORM, OR IN ANY DEGREE, IS INTEMPERANCE. Its effects are certain, and deeply injurious, though its results may be slow, and never be ascribed to the real cause. It is a war upon the human constitution, carried on ostensibly by an auxiliary, but which never fails to subtract more vital power than it imparts. Like the letting out of waters by little and little, the breach widens, till life itself is poured out. If all diseases which terminate in death, could speak out at the grave, or tell their origin upon the coffin-lid, we should witness the most appalling unexpected disclosures. Happy the man, who so avoids the appearance of evil, as not to shorten his days by what he may call the prudent use of ardent spirits. . . .

THERE IS NO NUTRITION IN ARDENT SPIRIT. ALL THAT IT DOES IS, TO CONCENTRATE THE STRENGTH OF THE SYSTEM FOR THE TIME, BEYOND ITS CAPACITY FOR REGULAR EXERTION. It is borrowing strength for an occasion, which will be needed for futurity, without any provision for payment, and with the certainty of ultimate bankruptcy.

The early settlers of New-England endured more hardship, and performed more labor, and carried through life more health and vigor, than appertains to the existing generation of laboring men. And they did it without the use of ardent spirits.

Let two men, of equal age and firmness of constitution, labor together through the summer, the one with and the other without the excitement of ardent spirits, and the latter will come out at the end with unimpaired vigor, while the other will be comparatively exhausted. Ships navigated as some now are without the habitual use of ardent spirits—and manufacturing establishments carried on without—and extended agricultural operations—all move on with better industry, more peace, more health, and a better income to the employers and the employed. The workmen are cheerful and vigorous, friendly and industrious, and their families are thrifty, well fed, well clothed and instructed; and instead of distress and poverty, and disappointment and contention—they are cheered with the full flow of social affection, and often by the sustaining power of religion.

But where ardent spirit is received as a daily auxiliary to labor, it is commonly taken at stated times—the habit soon creates a vacancy in the stomach, which indicates at length the hour of the day with as much accuracy as a clock. It will be taken besides, frequently, at other times, which will accelerate the destruction of nature's healthful tone, create artificial debility, and the necessity of artificial excitement to remove it; and when so much has been consumed as the economy of the employer can allow, the growing demand will be supplied by the evening and morning dram, from the wages of labor—until the appetite has become insatiable, and the habit of intemperance nearly universal—until the nervous excitability has obliterated the social sensibilities, and turned the family into a scene of babbling and wo—until voracious appetite has eaten up the children's bread, and abandoned them to ignorance and crime—until conscience has become callous, and fidelity and industry have disappeared, except as the result of eye service; and wanton wastefulness and contention, and reckless wretchedness characterize the establishment.

GLOSSARY

ardent spirits: strong distilled alcohol such as brandy, rum, or whiskey

distraint: compulsion or seizure by means of distress

intemperance: lack of moderation, especially when drinking alcohol

sottish: stupid or foolish

tippling: frequent or continuous drinking of alcohol in relatively small amounts

Document Analysis

Lyman Beecher's "The Nature and Occasions of Intemperance" is the introductory sermon in a series of six sermons in which Beecher outlines the sins and individual and social repercussions of intemperance. Although Beecher was concerned about alcohol consumption in America from the perspective of a social activist, his claims about intemperance are largely rooted in morality and religion. His approach, therefore, is one that condemns alcohol for its negative impact on society while considering the long-term effects of intemperance on one's soul. In the early nineteenth century in America, the divisions between church and state had been drawn with the disestablishment of state churches, but in reality, the nation was still very much fixed in Protestant Christian beliefs and practices. For Beecher to consider temperance from the perspective of an activist and clergyman would therefore have been not just socially permissible but widely accepted.

As the introductory statement for Beecher's longer series of grievances about intemperance and its increasingly concerning effects on American society and life, this initial sermon in many ways merely sets the stage for the author's much broader arguments about the signs and evils of intemperance and his proposed remedies for them. Beecher's forceful language and vivid imagery would have been particularly interesting to audiences listening to his sermons before they were published. The image that Beecher presents of soldiers marching blindly to a certain death in battle is a good example of this. Although not all those in his audience would have been on the brink of alcoholism, many Americans were familiar with war imagery, as it had been just decades since the Revolutionary War and the War of 1812. According to Beecher's analogy, those individuals who chose to drink were likewise heedlessly entering into what would ultimately be a losing battle leading to death, despite the sad examples of those who had met a similar demise before them.

When Beecher composed this sermon and presented it in the 1820s, the idea of temperance was not a new one. From the time of the Revolution through the Civil War, social and religious reformers responded to crises in the nation by attempting to eliminate what they saw as the sins for which the country was being punished, particularly slavery and intemperance. These two "evils" were especially emphasized, as they were both considered to be the source of many other social and domestic problems. In the case of slavery, tensions existed between Christians who were in support of slavery and those who were against it. This raised questions about whether or not God intended for slavery to be part of American life and if Christian morality could possibly be used to support proslavery arguments. In the case of intemperance, reformers like Beecher connected excessive alcohol consumption to poor health, the breakdown of family units, violence, reduced productivity, and, ultimately, the risk of not being able to attain salvation upon one's death. For these reformers, religion and social tensions were inextricably linked, and all of one's actions in life translated to one's state after death.

In his sermons on intemperance, Beecher is expressly dumbfounded by the public, and therefore obvious, trouble that intemperance causes. For Beecher, the problem is not just the impact of alcohol on the individual but the social influence that intemperance has on those who are in contact with the intemperate. It is most concerning to him that the destructive actions of "sottish" drinkers do not stop others from going down the same path to self- and social degradation. Beecher is concerned that despite the many social ills caused by intemperance, including selfishness, wastefulness, poverty, and illness, the consumption of alcohol continued to grow in America as the nineteenth century progressed.

For Beecher to note health issues surrounding the temperance cause is to put his observations into dialogue with the many wellness movements of the era. It was during these same decades that Sylvester Graham introduced the graham cracker, a food made with whole grains instead of bolted flour (a type of whole-wheat flour from which the majority of bran has been removed), along with a strict diet that eliminated meat and alcohol in order to purify one's body and mind. Graham's efforts would lead to continued dietary movements later in the century by Seventh-Day Adventists Ellen G. White and John Harvey Kellogg, both of whom advocated temperate, vegetarian diets for physical and spiritual well-being at their Battle Creek Sanitarium in Michigan. Beecher's observations about intemperance in relation to the overall condition of the body are therefore very much in tune with the contemporary wellness movements of his day.

Although Beecher was concerned for the condition of the body due to intemperance, his fears were not merely about the impact of alcohol on one's health. For Beecher, and other religious reformers like him, the body was a creation of God, to be "sustained by food and sleep," not by alcohol or other artificial means. Beecher also warns against intemperance as a means for alleviating of pain or generating happiness. As a clergyman heavily steeped in Christian doctrine and practice, Beecher argues that the only true paths to peace and joy are those that lead to and are created by God, not the artificial ones shaped by drunkenness. According to Beecher, drink is not only an unnatural way to evoke emotions but also a sinful one. For a religious revivalist like Beecher, salvation was the ultimate goal of conversion experience, and a happy position in the life to come. Therefore, Beecher suggests that it is not just one's temporal comfort that is at stake when one is intemperate but the condition of one's very soul.

As Beecher reiterates throughout his sermons on the subject, the term *intemperance* in the nineteenth century came to encompass much more than simply excess in drink. Intemperance, for Beecher, extended beyond drinking too much alcohol to include excessive poor judgment, increased poverty due to men spending their earnings on alcohol rather than their responsibilities at home, and more and more instances of poor physical and mental health. In talking about intemperance in this way Beecher reiterates the negative effects of alcohol consumption on many aspects of American life.

The author, and later activists like those from the American Society for the Promotion of Temperance (1826) and the Women's Christian Temperance Union (1873), used this emphasis on the totality of social reform achieved through temperance as their platform into the early years of the twentieth century. It is important to note here that the initial reforms for alcohol consumption were at first aimed at abstinence, not the total exclusion of alcohol. However, as time went on, reformers increasingly argued for the complete elimination of alcohol consumption as a model for social reform.

According to these advocates for temperance, one's awareness of alcohol consumption could be heightened simply by agreeing to abstain from using alcohol for anything other than medicinal purposes. "Ardent spirits" were dangerous because one did not start out drinking with the intention of becoming a regular drunkard. As an example, Beecher points to an "Indian" whom he notes as being occasionally intoxicated to the point of oblivion. While he certainly did not consider this to be acceptable, Beecher suggests that it would be far worse for one to consume alcohol in smaller amounts but constantly and daily, with equally destructive, though perhaps not as immediately noticeable, effects. This alludes not only to historical criticisms of colonists for introducing alcohol to American Indians but also to the implication that alcohol is in some ways a rather sneaky vice. Beecher suggests that it is only over time that one truly begins to notice the effects of regular alcohol consumption on one's physical body and life, and by the time that awareness of the problem of intemperance sets in, it is too late for one to do much about it.

In summary, Lyman Beecher as clergyman, revivalist, and social activist argues in "The Nature and Occasions of Intemperance" that alcohol is dangerous because it mimics the natural state of man granted to him by God, and it is therefore not healthy either for one's physical body or for one's prospects of salvation. During the profoundly religious period of the Second Great Awakening, Beecher offered religion as the alternative to alcohol consumption for endowing one's life with cheerfulness and providing comfort during difficult times.

Beecher argues that those who are intemperate are neither useful nor productive—truly a problem in an increasingly industrialized and urbanized society. In order for a more productive and moral society to emerge, in which the family would come first, he believed, alcohol would ultimately need to be eliminated, as it was the source of many social ills. In order to appeal to his audience of what would presumably have been fellow believers Beecher anchors his argument in strong support of the use of one's faith, not alcohol, to get through life in order that one's soul might be saved upon death. These are all themes that continued to be played out by temperance reformers through the later decades of the nineteenth century and into the twentieth, until the successful passage of the Eighteenth Amendment to the Constitution in 1919, which forbade the legal production, sale, and consumption of alcohol in the United States until its repeal in 1933.

Essential Themes

The temperance movement extended from the United States into Europe as the decades of the nineteenth century progressed. Lyman Beecher's religious view of temperance was not unique. Many others, from Elizabeth Cady Stanton to Herbert Hoover, found intemperance to be one of the central social and moral problems in nineteenth- and early twentieth-century America. This was a period in American history marked by great social and religious change; from the revivals of the Second Great Awakening to the rise of sects and new religions midcentury to the Gilded Age and subsequent Progressive Era and Social Gospel movement, Americans were looking for outlets for their awe and frustration in a country increasingly influenced by immigration, industrialization, urbanization, capitalism, advances in transportation, slavery, and the devastating effects of the Civil War and World War I.

Temperance, despite its widespread influence, was by no means embraced by all Americans. In particular, those who made and sold alcohol were not pleased by the limitations suggested by temperance reformers. While the passing of the Eighteenth Amendment in the early twentieth century curbed the open production and consumption of alcohol, it was illegally served to patrons in speakeasies, secret rooms in buildings all over the country. Such establishments were often associated with those involved in organized crime, which further supported Beecher's theories that the consumption of alcohol was connected to many negative activities in American life.

Emily Bailey, MA

Bibliography

Beecher, Lyman. *Six Sermons on the Nature, Occasions, Signs, Evils, and Remedy of Intemperance*. New York: Amer. Tract Soc., 1827. Print.

Beecher, Lyman, and Harriet Beecher Stowe. *The American Woman's Home; or, Principles of Domestic Science: Being a Guide to the Formation and Maintenance of Economical, Healthful, Beautiful, and Christian Homes*. Boston: Brown, 1869. Print.

Clark, Norman H. *Deliver Us from Evil: An Interpretation of American Prohibition*. New York: Norton, 1976. Print.

Dorsey, Bruce. *Reforming Men and Women: Gender in the Antebellum City*. Ithaca: Cornell UP, 2002. Print.

Henry, Stuart. *Unvanquished Puritan: A Portrait of Lyman Beecher*. Grand Rapids: Eerdmans, 1973. Print.

Williams, Susan. *Food in the United States, 1820s–1890*. Westport: Greenwood, 2006. Print.

Additional Reading

Bordin, Ruth. *Frances Willard: A Biography.* Chapel Hill: U of North Carolina P, 1986. Print.

Hamm, Richard F. *Shaping the Eighteenth Amendment: Temperance Reform, Legal Culture, and the Polity, 1880–1920*. Chapel Hill: U of North Carolina P, 1995. Print.

Mattingly, Carol. *Well-Tempered Women: Nineteenth-Century Temperance Rhetoric*. Carbondale: Southern Illinois UP, 2000. Print.

Wacker, Grant. *Religion in Nineteenth Century America*. New York: Oxford UP, 2000. Print.

Willard, Frances E. *Women and Temperance; or, The Work and Workers of the Women's Christian Temperance Union*. Hartford: Park, 1883. Print.

LESSON PLAN: **Intemperance**

Students analyze Lyman Beecher's sermon on the dangers and harmful effects of intemperance.

Learning Objectives

Describe the causes and effects of intemperance; explain how intemperance was an important issue during the Second Great Awakening; compare and contrast enduring issues; distinguish between unsupported expressions of opinion and informed hypotheses grounded in evidence.

Materials: Lyman Beecher, "The Nature and Occasions of Intemperance" (1828)

Overview Questions

What are the causes and effects of intemperance, according to Beecher's sermon? What ideas does Beecher raise that reflect those of the Second Great Awakening? To what does Beecher compare intemperance, and why does he make this comparison? What evidence does Beecher use to support his opinion, point of view, and purpose?

Step 1: Comprehension Questions

According to Beecher, what has caused intemperance? Why does he think it is a problem? How does he use these causes and effects to craft his argument?

- **Activity:** have students work in small groups to read the selection and then to make a list of the causes and effects of intemperance that Beecher raises, using a graphic organizer if desired; invite groups to share their lists and to use a basis for a class discussion

Step 2: Comprehension Questions

What ideas does Beecher raise that reflect those of the Second Great Awakening? Are they similar or different?

- **Activity:** ask students to review the ideas of the Second Great Awakening and then to write a multi-paragraph essay that compare Beecher's ideas with those that were central to the Second Great Awakening

Step 3: Context Questions

To what does Beecher compare intemperance, and why does he make this comparison? Is it effective to his overall argument?

- **Activity:** assign students to read select key passages and then identify as a class to what Beecher compares intemperance; then divide the class into two sides to hold a debate, with each side defending or refuting whether Beecher's comparison is effective to his overall argument

Step 4: Exploration Questions

What is Beecher's greatest fear? What evidence does he cite to support his opinion and point of view? Does his evidence support his motive or purpose?

- **Activity:** instruct students to work with a partner and highlight the references that Beecher makes as well as the evidence that he uses; then ask them to each write a response in support of or against Beecher's use of evidence in his argument; remind students to address and explain whether the evidence he uses supports his motive or purpose

Step 5: Response Paper

Word length and additional requirements set by Instructor. Students answer the research question in the *Overview Questions*. Students state a thesis and use as evidence passages from the primary source document as well as support from supplemental materials assigned in the lesson.

■ Address Delivered before the General Trades' Union of the City of New York

Date: December 2, 1833
Author Name: Moore, Ely
Genre: address; political tract; speech

"Wherever man exists . . . this principle of his nature, selfishness, will appear, operating either for evil or for good. To curb it sufficiently by legislative enactments is impossible. Much can *be done, however, towards restraining it within proper limits, by unity of purpose, and concert of action, on the part of the* producing classes."

Summary Overview

Ely Moore's December 1833 speech to the assembled members of the newly formed General Trades' Union marked the beginning of a powerful and innovative labor movement in the United States. Instead of representing the practitioners of a single trade, as the guild system traditionally had, the General Trades' Union sought to represent the entire working class of American society. In his groundbreaking address, Moore elucidates several points that came to be central to the philosophy of labor organizing in subsequent generations.

Moore explains that the true nature of humans is not to be good or evil but to be selfish and self-interested. As such, people will always try to exploit one another. It is therefore necessary for the working class to protect its interests from the competing interests of the merchant and investing classes. Moore similarly encourages the members of the General Trades' Union to take pride in their status as members of the working class. The efforts of common laborers undergird all great technological and artistic achievements, he argues, so the working class is extremely important to the maintenance of a civilized society. Moore closes his speech by asking the workers to consider the great potential a free society such as the United States holds for them, giving examples of those who have risen from working-class obscurity to fame and telling his audience to make the most of the nation's many opportunities.

Defining Moment

As one of the major American ports, New York City has always exerted a strong influence over the economy of the United States. The city has long attracted members of the merchant class intent on making their fortunes through the lucrative intercontinental import trade, which in the city's early years was centered on sugar, rum, and slaves. At the same time, New York had a strong manufacturing class, as the city's merchants depended on a massive retinue of shipwrights, sailmakers, rope weavers, coopers, and other workers to keep their fleets outfitted. As the city grew in the decades leading up to the Revolutionary War, manufacturers flourished, serving the increasingly large home market. During the war, the importation of goods became difficult, and the country as a whole began to rely more on domestic production.

The decades between the end of the Revolutionary War and 1833, when Moore delivered his famous address to the General Trades' Union, prepared the workers of the city to hear Moore's prolabor message. Slavery was partially banned in the state of New York in 1799, marking the end of what had been one of the city's main mercantile businesses and shifting the balance of power toward manufacturers and away from merchants. The city's population swelled significantly, with many of the city's new residents arriving from Europe.

This spike in immigration to New York was primarily caused by a paradigm shift in the global economy, a complex set of technological changes that are collectively referred to as the Industrial Revolution. These changes included the development of steam power, the introduction of interchangeable mechanical parts, and the building of large-scale factories to replace small-scale craft enterprises. With goods able to be produced more efficiently in centralized factories, many rural people lost their ability to make a living. As a result, there was a massive wave of urbanization as workers moved from the countryside to the cities in which industrial manufacturing took place. The newly formed United States, with its vast natural resources and promise of personal freedoms, attracted a significant percentage of the displaced population of Europe.

In the United States and other parts of the rapidly industrializing world of the early nineteenth century, workers sought a means of expressing their interests and concerns. Developments in American politics in the late 1820s and early 1830s fueled this interest in laying out an agenda for defending workers' rights. Property requirements for voting had largely been dropped in the decades after the Revolutionary War, allowing nearly all white male citizens to vote in elections, and the rise of Jacksonian democracy resulted in an increased popular expectation that the common people should have a voice in running society.

The first wave of what can be called modern American labor organizing began in this period. Labor unions developed in the United States' more industrialized northeastern cities, notably Philadelphia, Boston, and New York. They were primarily interested in increasing pay for untenured journeymen in trades such as carpentry, but also petitioned to improve working conditions and decrease the number of hours in the work day. Although these early associations were small and short lived, they represented the beginning of the American labor movement.

Author Biography

Ely Moore was born on July 4, 1798, near the town of Belvidere, New Jersey. After finishing his secondary education, he moved to New York City to pursue a medical degree. However, he showed little interest in practicing medicine professionally and instead obtained work as a printer. From there, he moved into journalism, proving to be a talented writer and editor. He also demonstrated a keen interest in advocating for the rights of workers. These talents and interests led Moore to become the chief editor of the *National Trades Union*, a New York labor newspaper. He was elected president of the Typographers' Union in 1832.

Moore eventually gained a strong city-wide reputation as a formidable debater, orator, and defender of working-class interests. Because of his commitment to the labor cause, Moore was chosen by his peers as the first president of the General Trades' Union in August of 1833, the year it was formed. The General Trades' Union was part of a new wave of groundbreaking labor organizations that sought to achieve higher wages for journeymen and represent the interests of all working-class people in New York.

On December 2, 1833, at the Chatham Street Chapel, Moore delivered his most famous speech. The oration, known as "Address Delivered before the General Trades' Union of the City of New York," lays out a philosophy of working-class solidarity against exploitation by the wealthy that would come to define the American labor movement. As a result of this speech, which was later made available in printed form, Moore's reputation spread beyond New York, and he came to be perceived as an important regional leader. Moore used his local political clout to run for national political office. In 1834, he ran for Congress on the Jacksonian ticket and won. He served two terms in the House of Representatives, advocating for the common people of New York and helping to define the emerging Democratic Party. Many scholars consider Moore to have been the first explicitly prolabor member of Congress in American history.

During his last term in Congress, Moore returned to the newspaper industry, becoming editor of the prestigious *New York Evening Post*. After leaving Congress, Moore was appointed president of the Board of Trade and surveyor of the port of New York City, two posts that afforded him a good deal of control over commerce in what was becoming one of the world's most important commercial hubs. In 1845, US president James K. Polk appointed Moore US marshal for southern New

York, giving him command over one of the most politically sensitive jurisdictions in the country. During this time, Moore also became the owner and proprietor of the *Warren Journal* in his hometown of Belvidere.

In 1853, Moore became the agent in charge of the American Indian tribes in Kansas, including the Miami nation. Along with this appointment, Moore was given the rank of colonel. Two years later, he was appointed register of the United States Land Office and settled on a farm near the small town of Lecompton, Kansas. Moore died on January 7, 1860, and was buried on his farm.

HISTORICAL DOCUMENT

Fellow Mechanics,

We have assembled, on the present occasion, for the purpose of publicly proclaiming the motives which induced us to organize a General Union of the various trades and arts in this city and its vicinity, as well as to defend the course, and to vindicate the measures we design to pursue. This is required of us by a due regard to the opinions of our fellow men.

We conceive it, then, to be a *truth*, enforced and illustrated by the concurrent testimony of history and daily observation, that man is disposed to avail himself of the possessions and services of his fellow man, without rendering an equivalent, and to prefer claims to that which of right belongs to another. This may be considered a hard saying; but we have only to turn our eyes inward, and examine ourselves, in order to admit, to the full extent, the truth of the proposition, that man, by nature, is selfish and aristocratic. *Self-love* is constitutional with man, and is displayed in every stage, and in all the diversities of life; in youth, and in manhood, in prosperity and in adversity. It not only discovers itself in the strifes and contentions of states and empires, but in the smallest fraternities—in the factory and the workshop—in the village school and the family circle. In fact, wherever society exists, however small the number, or rude the members, you will find *self-love* stimulating to a contest for power and dominion. This prevailing disposition of the human heart, so far from being an evil in itself, is one of the elements of life, and essential to the welfare of society. The *selfish* generate the *social* feelings. It is only pernicious in its tendency and operation, therefore, when it passes its true and natural bounds, and urges man to encroach upon the rights and immunities of man.

In order to mitigate the evils that ever flow from inordinate desire and unrestricted selfishness; to restrain and chastise unlawful ambition; to protect the weak against the strong, and to establish an equilibrium of power among nations and individuals, conventional compacts were formed. These confederative associations have never been fully able to stay the march of intolerance, of mercenary ambition, or of political despotism. Even in this fair land of freedom, where liberty and equality are guaranteed to all, and where our written constitutions have so wisely provided limitations to power, and securities for rights, the *twin fiends, intolerance* and *aristocracy*, presume to rear their hateful crests! But we have no cause to marvel at this. Wherever man exists, under whatever form of government, or whatever be the structure or organization of society, this principle of his nature, selfishness, will appear, operating either for evil or for good. To curb it sufficiently by legislative enactments is impossible. Much *can* be done, however, towards restraining it within proper limits, by unity of purpose, and concert of action, on the part of the *producing classes*. To contribute toward the achievement of this great end, is one of the objects of the "General Trades' Union." Wealth, we all know, constitutes the aristocracy of this country. Happily no distinctions are known among us save what wealth and worth confer. No legal barriers are erected to protect exclusive privileges, or unmerited rank. The law of primogeniture forms no part of American jurisprudence; and our revolution has converted all feudal tenures into allodial rights. The greatest danger, therefore, which threatens the stability of our government, and the liberty of the people, is an undue accumulation and distribution of wealth. And I do conceive, that *real danger* is to be apprehended from this source, notwithstanding that tendency to distribution which naturally grows out of the character of our statutes of conveyance, of inheritance, and descent of property; but, by securing to the producing classes a fair, certain, and equitable compensation for their toil and skill, we insure a more just and equal distribution of wealth than can ever be effected by statutory law. . . .

I am aware, that the charge of "illegal combination" is raised against us. The cry is as senseless, as 'tis stale and unprofitable. Why, I would inquire, have not journeymen the same right to ask their own price for their own property, or services, that employers have? or that merchants, physicians, and lawyers have? Is that equal justice, which makes it an offence for journeymen to combine for the purpose of maintaining their present prices, or raising their wages, while employers may combine with impunity for the purpose of lowering them? I admit that such is the common law. All will agree, however, that it is neither wise, just, nor politic, and that it is directly opposed to the spirit and genius of our free institutions, and ought, therefore, to be abrogated.

It is further alleged, that the "General Trades' Union" is calculated to encourage *strikes* and *turn-outs*. Now, the truth lies in the converse. Our constitution sets forth, that "Each trade or art may represent to the Convention, through their delegates, their grievances, who shall take cognizance thereof, and decide upon the same." And further, that "No trade or art shall strike for higher wages than they at present receive, without the sanction of the Convention." True, if the Convention shall, after due deliberation, decide that the members of any trade or art there represented are aggrieved, and that their demands are warrantable, then the Convention is pledged to sustain the members of such trade or art to the uttermost. Hence, employers will discover, that it is idle, altogether idle, to prolong a contest with journeymen, when they are backed by the Convention. And journeymen will perceive, that in order to obtain assistance from the Convention, in the event of a *strike*, or *turn-out*, that their claims must be founded in justice, and all their measures be so taken as not to invade the rights, or sacrifice the welfare, of employers. So far, then, from the Union encouraging strikes or turn-outs, it is destined, we conceive, to allay the jealousies, and abate the asperities, which now unhappily exist between employers and the employed.

We all know, that whenever journeymen stand out for higher wages, that the public are sufferers, as well as the parties more immediately concerned. The Trades' Union, we conceive, will have a tendency to correct this evil.

Again; it is alleged, that it is setting a dangerous precedent for journeymen to combine for the purpose of coercing a compliance with their terms. It may, indeed, be dangerous to aristocracy—dangerous to monopoly—dangerous to oppression—but not to the general good, or the public tranquillity. Internal danger to a state is not to be apprehended from a general effort on the part of the people to improve and exalt their condition, but from an alliance of the crafty, designing, and intriguing few. What! tell us, in this enlightened age, that the welfare of the people will be endangered by a voluntary act of the people themselves? That the people will wantonly seek their own destruction? That the safety of the state will be plotted against by three fourths of the members comprising the state! O how worthless, how poor and pitiful, are all such arguments and objections!

Members of the "General Trades' Union!" permit me, at this time, and before I leave this part of my subject, to caution you against the wiles and perfidy of those individuals, who will approach you as friends, but who, in reality and in truth, are your secret enemies. You will know them by this sign: an attempt to excite your jealousy against certain individuals, who, peradventure, may stand somewhat conspicuous among you; by insinuations that these men have ulterior designs to accomplish; that political ambition lies at the root of the whole matter, and all that. This will be done, recollect, not so much to injure the individuals against whom the insinuations are ostensibly directed. as to abuse you, by impairing your confidence in the "Union." It is the heart of the Union at which these assassins aim the stroke! 'Tis the Union! your political safeguard, that they would prostrate! 'Tis the Union! the citadel of your hopes, that they would sack and destroy!! I entreat you, therefore, to shun such counselors as you would the pestilence. Remember the tragedy in the garden of Eden, and hold no communion with the adversary. But why caution you thus, when your own good sense would so readily teach you, that the very attempt to deceive you was an insult to your understandings? Because, did they not presume upon your ignorance and credulity, they would never attempt to alienate your affections from the Union. Remember, then, fellow mechanics, that the man who attempts to seduce you from your duty .to yourselves, to your families, and your brother mechanics, by misrepresenting the objects of the Union, offers you not only an insult, but an *injury*! Remember! that those defamers would exult at your misfortunes—would "laugh at your calamity, and mock when your fear cometh." Aye, would trample down your liberties, and rejoice at beholding—

"The seal of bondage on your brows—
Its badge upon your breasts!"

You will not regard it as ill-timed, nor irrelevant to the present occasion, my friends, should I invite your attention for a moment to the important bearing which the useful arts have upon the welfare of society. In order to estimate their importance correctly, it is necessary to contemplate the condition of man as we find him in a state of nature, where the arts are unknown, and where the lights of civilization have never dawned upon his path. Wherever man is thus situated, we find him a creature of blind impulse, of passion, and of instinct—of groveling hopes, and of low desires; and his wants, like those of the brute, supplied only by the spontaneous productions of nature—his only covering, a scanty supply of hair—his food, the acorn and the loathsome insect—the cavern his dwelling, the earth his couch, and the rock his pillow! The superiority of man's condition, therefore, over that of other animals, is attributable solely to the influence of the mechanic arts. Without their aid, the native powers of his mind, however great, could never have been developed; and the physical sciences, which he has been enabled to master, in a state of civilization, would have still been numbered among the secrets of nature. What progress, for example, could he have made in the science of astronomy, without the aid of the telescope? In chemistry, without the retort and receiver? In anatomy and surgery, without the knife and the tourniquet? In agriculture, without the hoe and the mattock, the spade and the plough, the scythe and the pruning hook?

Contrast *civilized*, with *savage* man. Compare, for example, the Boschmen of Southern Africa, whose chief supply of food consists of the locust and the ant; or the Esquimaux, who feast and fatten upon train oil and seals' blubber, with the inhabitants of those countries where the useful arts are known and cultivated, and you will be enabled to estimate more correctly their influence upon the welfare of man. The condition of the Esquimaux, although wretched and degraded, is far preferable to that of the Bosjesman. Physiologists tell us, that their physical structures and capacities are about the same. The comparative elevation, therefore, of the one, is ascribable, directly, to the fact of the arts having been partially introduced among them. The Esquimaux has been taught to construct the boat, to string the bow, and to fashion the spear. But the Boschmen are utterly ignorant of the arts, and, consequently, strangers to civilization and improvement; their moral and intellectual features, therefore, have been the same, through the succession of ages, and the lapse of centuries! No improvement—no melioration in their condition has taken place; but, through the transition of generations, sires and sons have lived and died alike degraded!

GLOSSARY

allodial rights: the rights to own property directly rather than through an intermediary such as a lord or king

journeyman: a worker who has completed an apprenticeship but is not yet a master of a trade

law of primogeniture: a legal principle under which the oldest son inherits his parents' property

mechanics: people who make a living by manufacturing products or working with their hands rather than through trade in premade goods

turn-outs: strikes in which striking workers compel other laborers to leave their work spontaneously to show solidarity for the cause

Document Analysis

Moore begins his famous speech to the members of the General Trades' Union by referring to them as his "fellow mechanics." In the early nineteenth century, this term referred to all people who made their livings through manufacturing or repairing goods. Moore uses this broad term to signify that the new movement is meant to include all members of the working class. In addition, by addressing his audience as fellow mechanics, Moore imbues his speech with historical resonance that was particularly relevant to the workers of New York. During the Revolutionary War, mechanics asserted their power over the merchant class, which had until then almost completely dominated New York City politics. In that earlier era, workers from various trades came together to discuss the important issues of the day, namely independence from Great Britain and the impending war. The actions of the Revolutionary War–era mechanics groups sowed the seeds for later campaigns for workers' rights, and early nineteenth-century organizations such as the General Trades' Union were the first fruits of the modern labor movement.

Moore goes on to state why the workers have come together for the meeting. He explains that their purpose is to disclose fully why practitioners of various trades have chosen to form a single union rather than rely on their traditionally separate guilds. The workers, Moore says, owe other people around the city and indeed around the world an explanation of why they are engaging in this new form of multitrade organizing.

The main reason they have chosen to organize in such a manner, he explains, has to do with the innate human tendency to be greedy. Moore contends that history and common sense show that people are always inclined to take possession of the material goods and labor of others without giving them due compensation. Greed, in Moore's opinion, is natural in humans because all humans have what he describes as an inborn self-love. This leads to an ever-present willingness to do what benefits the individual rather than what is morally right. In every known society, people struggle for power over one another to satisfy this natural greed and selfishness.

Moore's view of human beings as inherently selfish is a radical departure from the prevailing thought of his day. Traditionally, the debate over innate human character was presented in terms of good and evil, with some theologians arguing that humans are born good and others claiming that they are born sinners because of the fall of Adam and Eve in the Garden of Eden. Moore refuses to engage in this sort of discussion, stating that selfish motivations have historically led people to do both good and evil, but that at root they were motivated by an inborn self-love rather than any other sensibility.

This inherent selfishness and its propensity to create conflict are, he explains, the reason that people enter into compacts. Laws to govern a nation and treaties between nations, in Moore's view, exist to prevent the strong from doing harm to the weak and to preserve some sense of stability so that people can prevent "intolerance, of mercenary ambition, or of political despotism." These restrictions have never been perfect, Moore admits, but they represent the sincere efforts of humankind to achieve equality and safety.

He then expresses the perhaps most important part of his vision, a desire for the "producing classes" to come together in American society as they have in the General Trades' Union. Law alone will never fully stop selfish individuals from creating intolerable conditions for workers; rather, labor organizing represents the best chance to curb the influence of greed. It would be possible and advisable, Moore asserts, for the working people of the country to act together for the betterment of the overall society.

Moore next explains that there is no real aristocracy in the United States except for that created by wealth. The country does not have laws to protect unearned status. Inheritance does not necessarily pass from father to eldest son, as was the case during Europe's feudal period, and common people are free to own property. The main threat to American government, Moore contends, is the excess accumulation of wealth by a minority of citizens. Distributing the wealth more evenly will help counter this threat, and the best way to do this is to ensure that workers receive an honest wage for their labors.

Moore acknowledges that the decision to form the General Trades' Union will be controversial in some circles and that many people in the United States may even consider such a move to be a violation of US law. He defends the members of the union, arguing that it is absurd to say that they are breaking the law. Doctors, merchants, and lawyers organize to fix prices for their services, and factory owners regularly organize to set wages as low as possible. Working-class people, Moore argues, just want the chance to do the same thing. As he sees it, they certainly have the same right to determine a fair level of compensation for their labor, since the law grants equal rights to every citizen regardless of profession. Those who study labor history identify Moore's assertion as an early expression of the right of laborers to determine their pay on a mass scale, a hallmark of the labor movement that developed among later generations of American workers.

Moore then responds to allegations that the General Trades' Union seeks to cause strikes. He explains that this is actually the opposite of the truth. The rules of the General Trades' Union state that no trade may call a strike or a turn-out unless it is approved by the entire council. This policy will bring an end to the small, scattered strikes that had previously occurred. In Moore's view, this will lead to greater labor stability and reduce the amount of disruption caused by individual workshops or trades going on strike without consulting their peers in other lines of work. He acknowledges that strikes are actually bad for the public as well as for merchants and factory owners, as they represent lost productivity and wages. Under the new system, he contends, strikes will be much shorter because employers will be dealing with the entire General Trades' Union and not just a small contingent of workers. Furthermore, the collective power of the union will help win reforms quickly and thus negate the need for painful, ongoing work stoppages. This idea that the collective power of workers can help shore up, rather than disrupt, social well-being was new and radical and has greatly influenced the rhetoric of labor organizing since Moore's day.

He next responds to the claim that allowing common laborers to organize will set "a dangerous precedent." It will be dangerous, he states, for some special interests in society, such as the upper class and those who hope to preserve unfair monopolies. However, it will pose no threat to society as a whole. Laborers make up the majority of the nation's population, Moore notes, and he rhetorically asks how a democracy can be put at risk by its majority being better organized. He dismisses the possibility of such a threat as nonsensical.

The next theme that Moore touches upon is the threat posed to the union by saboteurs. He admonishes his fellow workers to be wary of people who seek to create jealousies and factions within the labor movement and states that such individuals will try to undermine workers' confidence in the General Trades' Union. Comparing them to "assassins" and the serpent in the Garden of Eden, Moore declares that such saboteurs are motivated by personal greed and ambition. He advises his fellows to treat any attempt to dissuade them from unionizing as an insult and an injury and to avoid those who seek to undermine the union while claiming to be friends of the working class. He underscores his reference to the Garden of Eden with dire biblical references to impending calamity for those who fail to take this warning seriously.

After this stern warning, Moore turns to a far more philosophical line of reasoning for supporting labor rights. First, he argues that it is, in fact, the material culture created by the crafts of the assembled workers that makes society civilized. In an argument that displays the racial prejudices of his time, Moore contrasts the culture of the Bushmen of South Africa, whom he describes as having very little material culture, with that of the Eskimo, who seem to have more material culture. He concludes that the Eskimo are relatively more advanced because they have more knowledge of the manufacturing arts than the Bushmen. After mentioning some theories about why the material cultures of the two societies differ, he again declares that it is knowledge of the material arts that distinguishes civilized people from savages. As the material arts are crucial to civilization, those who practice these arts should certainly be granted the same rights as those who merely sell or purchase the products of their work.

Essential Themes

Moore's analysis of the purpose of the General Trades' Union is quite practical and neatly lays the groundwork for an equally radical idea. He frankly states that those who make things naturally need to protect their interests against those who buy and sell things, since it is in humankind's very nature to exploit others for personal gain. As Moore explains, the aristocracy of the United States is determined by wealth, and it is up to organized labor to ensure that wealth is not concentrated in the hands of the few, but shared by the majority of people. Many scholars identify this element of Moore's famous speech as one of the earliest clear examples of a modern expression of class interest.

In addition to addressing his immediate audience of workers, Moore spends a significant portion of his speech responding to the union's critics, particularly those who assert that the creation of a multitrade union is illegal. Throughout this section, he focuses on the idea of equality, arguing that the owner and merchant classes coordinate to determine wages paid or fees charged for goods and concluding that it is therefore not illegal for workers to set the cost of their labor using the same tactic. Moore also tackles the allegation that a large union would be dangerous to social stability, arguing that it will actually ensure better social stability by decreasing the length and frequency of strikes, thus preventing prolonged work stoppages. This point likely appealed to both his immediate audience of workers, who would go without pay for the duration of a strike, and the union's critics, who were more concerned with the disruption of production.

Interestingly, the majority of Moore's speech has to do not with the practicalities of creating a large labor union, but with the need for workers to take pride in their working-class status. Working-class pride was a new concept, as many people in Moore's day considered common laborers to be the basest and least worthwhile members of society. Moore goes to great lengths to point out that the efforts of laborers are what make American society civilized and that all technological and artistic innovation ultimately rests on their efforts. He further asserts that the United States, as a free society, is the perfect place for the flourishing of great ideas and notes that members of the working class can and historically have become leaders in many important fields. This latter point is an early and powerful expression of what later generations would call the American dream, the great and enduring belief that the United States is a land of opportunity for all who are willing to work hard.

Adam Berger, PhD

Bibliography

Berlin, Ira, and Leslie Harris. *Slavery in New York*. New York: New, 2005. Print.

Bugg, James. *Jacksonian Democracy: Myth or Reality?* New York: Holt, 1962. Print.

Greenberg, Joshua. *Advocating the Man: Masculinity, Organized Labor, and the Household in New York, 1800–1840*. New York: Columbia UP, 2008. Print.

Hugins, Walter. "Ely Moore: The Case History of a Jacksonian Labor Leader." *Political Science Quarterly* 65 (1950): 105–25. Print.

Mark, Irving, and Eugene Schwaab. *The Faith of Our Fathers: An Anthology Expressing the Aspirations of the American Common Man, 1790–1860*. New York: Knopf, 1952. Print.

Pease, Otis. *The Progressive Years: The Spirit and Achievement of American Reform*. New York: Braziller, 1962. Print.

Stearns, Peter. *The Industrial Revolution in World History*. Boulder: Westview, 1998. Print.

Zahler, Helene. *Eastern Workingmen and National Land Policy, 1829–1862*. New York: Columbia UP, 1941. Print.

Additional Reading

Ashton, T. S. *The Industrial Revolution, 1760–1830*. Oxford: Oxford UP, 1997. Print.

Commons, John. *History of Labour in the United States*. New York: Macmillan, 1918. Print.

Perlman, Selig. *A History of Trade Unionism in the United States*. New York: Macmillan, 1922. Print.

Pessen, Edward. *Most Uncommon Jacksonians: The Radical Leaders of the Early Labor Movement*. Albany: State U of New York P, 1967. Print.

Wilentz, Sean. *Chants Democratic: New York City and the Rise of the Working Class, 1788–1850*. Oxford: Oxford UP, 1984. Print.

LESSON PLAN: **The General Trades' Union**

Students analyze a speech by Ely Moore delivered to New York mechanics to consider labor and economic inequality during Andrew Jackson's presidency.

Learning Objectives

Compare and contrast differing ideas about trade unions and laborers; analyze how economic growth affected wage earners and income distribution; consider the multiple causes that contributed to the formation of the Democratic Party.

Materials: Ely Moore, "Address Delivered Before the General Trades' Union of the City of New York" (1833).

Overview Questions

Why does Moore think trade unions are necessary and beneficial? What evils does he hope unions will mitigate? What is Moore's opinion of his fellow man, and how does this view inform his argument? In what ways does his speech reflect the spirit of Jacksonian democracy and the interests of the common man?

Step 1: Comprehension Questions

What was the General Trades' Union? What did it hope to accomplish? According to Moore, who might have opposed the union, and why?

- **Activity:** Have students review the speech and state in their own words the objectives of the union. Ask students to summarize the arguments made against the union and explain why, according to Moore, these arguments are unsound.

Step 2: Comprehension Questions

What truth does Moore observe among men? What does this suggest about his views of humanity? How does he propose to curb these innate aspects of humankind?

- **Activity:** Read aloud the first sentence in paragraph two, which begins, "We conceive it, then, to be a *truth*." Ask students to restate the sentence in their own words. Have students review the first two paragraphs and discuss why Moore thinks trade unions will limit the evils he observes.

Step 3: Context Questions

What does Moore's speech suggest about wages during this time? How does he contrast wage-earning workers to the moneyed aristocracy? How does he propose to address economic inequality?

- **Activity:** Pair students to make a two-column chart titled "workers" and "aristocracy," and fill in the chart with Moore's description of each. Have students use their charts to discuss why Moore thought the General Trades' Union would reduce the gap between these groups.

Step 4: Historical Connections Questions

How do Moore's views of laborers reflect the principles of Jacksonian democracy? What arguments might anti-Jacksonian leaders have leveraged against Moore and the General Trades' Union, and why?

- **Activity:** Divide students into two groups, one supporting Moore's policies and the other opposed to them. Host a debate in which each side argues for or against the activities of the union, citing passages for support.

Step 5: Response Paper

Word length and additional requirements set by Instructor. Students answer the research question in the *Overview Questions*. Students state a thesis and use as evidence passages from the primary source document as well as support from supplemental materials assigned in the lesson.

■ Lowell Mill Girls

Date: 1898; 1836
Author: Robinson, Harriet H.
Genre: memoir; report

"In those days there was no need of advocating the doctrine of the proper relation between employer and employed. Help was too valuable to be ill treated."

Summary Overview

The middle of the first half of the nineteenth century saw the boom of the cotton industry in New England, spurring the creation of vast mill buildings in towns such as Manchester, New Hampshire; Biddeford, Maine; and Lawrence and Lowell, Massachusetts. The mills created hundreds of jobs, particularly for young women for whom employment options were severely limited. Harriet H. Robinson wrote a memoir entitled *Loom and Spindle; or, Life among the Early Mill Girls* (1898), an indispensable piece for research into the women and girls who worked within the mills; the second piece below is an excerpt of that book and was likely written in 1836. The first excerpt below comes from Robinson's essay "Early Factory Labor in New England," published in an 1883 Massachusetts Bureau of Statistics of Labor report. Robinson herself was a Lowell mill girl who began her career at a young age. As she grew, so too did the industry, but unfortunately, the changes that came were not for the better. Robinson and those like her found themselves working harder for fewer wages and, as a result, tried push for reform. Her memoirs provide a frank narrative of her plight and that of other mill girls and description of all those who chose not to back down.

Defining Moment

This excerpt of Harriet H. Robinson's writing, while providing historical background initially, is an impassioned attempt to show how it came to pass that she and others within the mills decided to "turn out," or strike. Simply put, the mill owners were taking advantage of them, lowering wages and increasing work for higher profits. As Robinson states aptly, "Help was too valuable to be ill-treated"; the girls and women employed by the mills exerted themselves day in and day out, starting at dawn and ending fourteen hours later, with two breaks in between for meals. Initially, as she mentions, the cost of bed and board ($1.50) was partially subsidized by the employer; this certainly would have been an excellent incentive for those thinking of factory work. However, this fee eventually became payable by the employee alone, along with an overall reduction in wages, and of course, this change in compensation did not come with a reduction of expected output.

Many historians, as well as contemporaries, utilized a comparison of the mill workers with their cotton "counterparts" in the South: the slaves. Robinson, in fact, recounts a song sung during turnouts that included the repeated line, "I will not be a slave." Slave owners treated their human property however they saw fit, but the mill workers were not considered property; they were *help*. They were employees who therefore should have been treated properly. It is vital to remember that, at this stage of American history, in the 1830s and 1840s, the country had not yet been inundated with the influx of immigrants from eastern and southern Europe. Harriet H. Robinson was working, predominantly, in the years preceding the first wave of Irish immigration, which was spurred by the famine in Ireland during the late 1840s. For the most part, the employee pool in her time was made up of native-born Anglo-American women. In her memoir, Robinson writes, "Before 1840, the foreign element in the factory population was almost an unknown quantity" (*Loom* 12). The mill workers were proud of their work, proud to help earn their livelihood and that of their families, and were not prepared to be basely treated, especially considering the amount of labor they provided at the rate of pay offered and hours endured.

Author Biography

Harriet Jane Hanson Robinson was born on February 8, 1825, in Boston, Massachusetts, to William and Harriet Browne Hanson. Robinson, one of four children, lost her father in 1831. As recounted in her book, an affluent neighbor offered to adopt her, thereby easing, if only slightly, the family's financial obligations, a proposal her mother refused, preferring to keep all the children with her. Her mother was soon helped by friends of her late husband who assisted her in the opening of a small shop, where she sold confectionary and other small goods, but it did not garner a healthy income for the family.

In *Loom and Spindle*, Robinson writes that the family's move to Lowell had been suggested and facilitated by her widowed maternal aunt, who worked there as a boardinghouse matron. It was there, at the age of ten, that Robinson started working in a Lowell mill, the Tremont Corporation, as a doffer, changing out empty bobbins for full ones in the spinning room. While she doffed, her mother kept a boardinghouse for young men, and it was during this time that young Robinson, a future suffragist, took to joining them in games such as checkers, which helped inspire her belief in the equality of the sexes.

While still in her mid-teens, Robinson added to her role as a mill girl by becoming a writer for the *Lowell Offering*, a magazine for the workers; topics included childhood stories, their work and experience in the mills, and poems. As historian William Moran relates in his book *Belles of New England: The Women of the Textile Mills and the Families whose Wealth They Wove*, the magazine's initial bright start began to wane within a few years, receiving criticism that writers were too sympathetic to the mill owners and that the publication voiced the workers' concerns too little. The *Lowell Offering* ended in 1845.

Robinson's rich life, as a mill girl and writer, eventually included that of wife, mother of four, abolitionist, and suffragist, fighting valiantly for equality for women. She died at the age of eighty-six, on December 22, 1911, in Malden, Massachusetts, a suburb close to the city of her birth.

HISTORICAL DOCUMENT

Early Factory Labor in New England

In 1832, Lowell was little more than a factory village. Five "corporations" were started, and the cotton mills belonging to them were building. Help was in great demand and stories were told all over the country of the new factory place, and the high wages that were offered to all classes of work-people; stories that reached the ears of mechanics' and farmers' sons and gave new life to lonely and dependent women in distant towns and farm-houses. . . . Troops of young girls came from different parts of New England, and from Canada, and men were employed to collect them at so much a head, and deliver them at the factories. . . .

At the time the Lowell cotton mills were started the caste of the factory girl was the lowest among the employments of women. In England and in France, particularly, great injustice had been done to her real character. She was represented as subjected to influences that must destroy her purity and self-respect. In the eyes of her overseer she was but a brute, a slave, to be beaten, pinched and pushed about. It was to overcome this prejudice that such high wages had been offered to women that they might be induced to become mill-girls, in spite of the opprobrium that still clung to this degrading occupation. . . .

The early mill-girls were of different ages. Some were not over ten years old; a few were in middle life, but the majority were between the ages of sixteen and twenty-five. The very young girls were called "doffers." They "doffed," or took off, the full bobbins from the spinning-frames, and replaced them with empty ones. These mites worked about fifteen minutes every hour and the rest of the time was their own. When the overseer was kind they were allowed to read, knit, or go outside the mill-yard to play. They were paid two dollars a week. The working hours of all the girls extended from five o'clock in the morning until seven in the evening, with one half-hour each, for breakfast and dinner. Even the doffers were forced to be on duty nearly fourteen hours a day. This was the greatest hardship in the lives of these children. Several years later a ten-hour law was passed, but not until long after some of these little doffers were old enough to appear before the legislative committee on the subject, and plead, by their presence, for a reduction of the hours of labor.

Those of the mill-girls who had homes generally worked from eight to ten months in the year; the rest of the time was spent with parents or friends. A few taught school during the summer months. Their life in the factory was made pleasant to them. In those days there was no need of advocating the doctrine of the proper relation between employer and employed. *Help was too valuable to be ill-treated*. . . .

The most prevailing incentive to labor was to secure the means of education for some *male* member of the family. To make a *gentleman* of a brother or a son, to give him a college education, was the dominant thought in the minds of a great many of the better class of mill-girls. I have known more than one to give every cent of her wages, month after month, to her brother, that he might get the education necessary to enter some profession. I have known a mother to work years in this way for her boy. I have known women to educate young men by their earnings, who were not sons or relatives. There are many men now living who were helped to an education by the wages of the early mill-girls. . . .

It is well to digress here a little, and speak of the influence the possession of money had on the characters of some of these women. We can hardly realize what a change the cotton factory made in the status of the working women. Hitherto woman had always been a money *saving* rather than a money earning, member of the community. Her labor could command but small return. If she worked out as servant, or "help," her wages were from 50 cents to $1.00 a week; or, if she went from house to house by the day to spin and weave, or do tailoress work, she could get but 75 cents a week and her meals. As teacher, her services were not in demand, and the arts, the professions, and even the trades and industries, were nearly all closed to her.

As late as 1840 there were only seven vocations outside the home into which the women of New England had entered. At this time woman had no property rights. A widow could be left without her share of her husband's (or the family) property, an "incumbrance" to his estate. A father could make his will without reference to his daughter's share of the inheritance. He usually left her a home on the farm as long as she remained single. A woman was not supposed to be capable of spending her own, or of using other people's money. In Massachusetts, before 1840, a woman could not, legally, be treasurer of her own sewing society, unless some man were responsible for her.

The law took no cognizance of woman as a money-spender. She was a ward, an appendage, a relict. Thus it happened, that if a woman did not choose to marry, or, when left a widow, to remarry, she had no choice but to enter one of the few employments open to her, or to become a burden on the charity of some relative. . . .

***

Loom and Spindle; or, Life among the Early Mill Girls

One of the first strikes of cotton-factory operatives that ever took place in this country was that in Lowell, in October, 1836. When it was announced that the wages were to be cut down, great indignation was felt, and it was decided to strike, *en masse*. This was done. The mills were shut down, and the girls went in procession from their several corporations to the "grove" on Chapel Hill, and listened to "incendiary" speeches from early labor reformers.

One of the girls stood on a pump, and gave vent to the feelings of her companions in a neat speech, declaring that it was their duty to resist all attempts at cutting down the wages. This was the first time a woman had spoken in public in Lowell, and the event caused surprise and consternation among her audience.

Cutting down the wages was not their only grievance, nor the only cause of this strike. Hitherto the corporations had paid twenty-five cents a week towards the board of each operative, and now it was their purpose to have the girls pay the sum; and this, in addition to the cut in the wages, would make a difference of at least one dollar a week. It was estimated that as many as twelve or fifteen hundred girls turned out, and walked in procession through the streets. They had neither flags nor music, but sang songs, a favorite (but rather inappropriate) one being a parody on "I won't be a nun."

"Oh! isn't it a pity, such a pretty girl as I—
Should be sent to the factory to pine away and die?
Oh ! I cannot be a slave,
I will not be a slave,
For I'm so fond of liberty
That I cannot be a slave."

My own recollection of this first strike (or "turn out" as it was called) is very vivid. I worked in a lower room, where I had heard the proposed strike fully, if not vehemently, discussed; I had been an ardent listener to what was said against this attempt at "oppression" on the part of the corporation, and naturally I took sides with the strikers. When the day came on which the girls were to turn out, those in the upper rooms started first, and so many of them left that our mill was at once shut down. Then, when the girls in my room stood irresolute, uncertain what to do, asking each other, "Would you? " or "Shall we turn out?" and not one of them having the courage to lead off, I, who began to think they would not go out, after all their talk, became impatient, and started on ahead, saying, with childish bravado, "I don't care what you do, *I* am going to turn out, whether anyone else does or not;" and I marched out, and was followed by the others.

As I looked back at the long line that followed me, I was more proud than I have ever been since at any success I may have achieved, and more proud than I shall ever be again until my own beloved State gives to its women citizens the right of suffrage.

The agent of the corporation where I then worked took some small revenges on the supposed ringleaders; on the principle of sending the weaker to the wall, my mother was turned away from her boarding-house, that functionary saying, "Mrs. Hanson, you could not prevent the older girls from turning out, but your daughter is a child, and *her* you could control."

It is hardly necessary to say that so far as results were concerned this strike did no good. The dissatisfaction of the operatives subsided, or burned itself out, and though the authorities did not accede to their demands, the majority returned to their work, and the corporation went on cutting down the wages.

And after a time, as the wages became more and more reduced, the best portion of the girls left and went to their homes, or to the other employments that were fast opening to women, until there were very few of the old guard left; and thus the *status* of the factory population of New England gradually became what we know it to be to-day.

GLOSSARY

bravado: audacity, daring, boldness

en masse: as a group, all together

incendiary: aggressive, stirring, rousing

incumbrance (encumbrance): burden, impediment, strain

irresolute: indecisive, unsure

Lowell: a city in Massachusetts, approximately twenty-five miles north of Boston, named for industrialist Francis Cabot Lowell

old guard: workers native to the New England area

Document Analysis

The wide, towering red brick buildings in Lowell, Massachusetts, are silent now. While some house historical societies, offices, museums, and apartments, the rest, like those in other former mill cities throughout New England, stand as hushed reminders to an era of bustle and noise, back when the buildings reverberated with the din of heavy machinery and the voices of hundreds of workers. Lowell began as an ideal planned city, combining the mill buildings and company boardinghouses with plenty of greenery; the location of the city was strategic, as the mill could operate by harnessing the waterpower of the nearby Merrimack River.

Mill Beginnings

This system of mills was inspired by those functioning within Great Britain, such as in Manchester, England, in the early nineteenth century. These were viewed by Francis Cabot Lowell and one of his associates, Nathan Appleton. While Lowell and Appleton admired the mills and their place within the English textile industry, they were shocked and astounded by the treatment of the workers therein. They were determined to bring the English mill idea to New England, but with a completely different ethos for dealing with their employees. *Their* employees would be cared for and without the stigma attached to the factory girls of England. Robinson devotes time to this phase in the history of the Lowell mills: "'The Lowell factory system' went into operation, a practice which included the then new idea, that corporations should have souls, and should exercise a paternal influence over the lives of their operatives" (*Loom* 7). Clearly, what Lowell and Appleton saw had an effect, and they were determined not to follow England's example. As Robinson notes in the first excerpt above,

> The factory girl was the lowest among the employments of women. . . . [In Europe] great injustice had been done to her real character. She was represented as subjected to influences that must destroy her purity and self-respect. In the eyes of her overseer she was but a brute, a slave, to be beaten, pinched and pushed about. ("Early" 381)

Lowell and his initial counterparts sought to make their operatives' position one of esteem, an employ of which to be proud. The paternal influence remarked upon earlier in *Loom and Spindle* was to be incorporated into the mills and boardinghouses; the corporations would help their help. Sandra Adickes, in her work "Mind among the Spindles," relates that careful attention was paid to the boardinghouses; they were installed with "resident chaperones" who upheld the girls' "standards of moral conduct" and enforced "mandatory Sunday church attendance" (280). Robinson's memoir verifies this part of boardinghouse living: "The mill-girls went regularly to meeting and 'Sabbath school;' and every Sunday the streets of Lowell were alive with neatly dressed young women, going or returning therefrom" (*Loom* 79). The houses themselves, as remembered by Robinson, were homey and attractive and even admired by such illustrious persons as English author Charles Dickens; she quotes him as saying, "'There is a piano in a great many of the boarding-houses, and nearly all the young ladies subscribe to circulating libraries'" (90). Given his reputation for wanting better working and living conditions for the working man, woman, and child, the Lowell mills could not have wished for a better endorsement.

The Mill Girls

The first generation of this workforce was predominantly from New England and was relatively young. Robinson states that the average worker was in her mid-teens to mid-twenties, but it was not unusual for a younger girl to be found among the other workers. Historian Thomas Dublin, in his article "Women, Work, and Protest," reveals the following statistics for Lowell's Hamilton Company around the time of Robinson's introduction to mill work: "more than 85 per cent of those employed in July 1836 were women and that over 96 percent were native-born" (106). Robinson was among the youngest workers, the doffers, when her mill career began. In "Early Factory Labor," Robinson writes of what a girl could expect in such a position: "The very young girls were called 'doffers.' They 'doffed,' or took off, the full bobbins from the spinning-frames, and replaced them with empty ones. These mites worked about fifteen minutes every hour and the rest of the time was their own. When the overseer was kind they were allowed to read, knit, or go outside the mill-yard to play" (382). Despite working a quarter of every hour, the doffers were still required to be "on duty" for the full day; this was continued until a law was passed in Massachusetts in 1842 attempting to limit a child's working hours. Of course, it is really left to history as to how faithfully this law was regularly enforced by a company desperate for profits or by a family desperate for income. The workforce did contain men, but as documented in "The Family and Industrial Discipline in Ante-Bellum New England" by Barbara Tucker, this segment of employees consisted of higher-paying skilled or managerial positions such as overseer. Dublin notes that while the mill girls worked primarily in the weaving and spinning rooms, male employees typically served in other roles such as pickers, carders, or mechanics.

To many of the girls making their way through the factory gates every morning, their position held much promise and pride, both to them and their families in many ways. William Moran quotes Ann Swett Appleton, a mill worker from New Hampshire, as having written, "The thought that I am living on no one is a happy one, indeed" (4). Despite the fourteen-hour days for six days out of the week, mill work could be seen as liberating as compared to domestic service. Historian Sandra Adickes writes that the work in a factory garnered higher pay when compared with other employment opportunities for women. Live-in work in domestic service, depending on the employer, included the requirement to be "on-call" at any or all hours.

The average age of the mill girls is intriguing; they were young and still under the typical marital age, allowing ample time to settle down. Young workers, in general, did not seek to make their positions within the mill lifelong endeavors; this is a topic a number of historians have touched upon, as does Robinson herself. The motives bringing in the workers were varied but not attached with indefinite participation. Some, as mentioned in the excerpt above, labored to finance a brother's education; Robinson terms this "the most prevailing incentive" ("Early" 387). Mortgages for the family home or farm were another motivation for their earnings. Sarah G. Bagley, another mill worker, writer, and suffragist like Robinson, used her wages to put a down payment on a piece of land for her family in 1840. Bagley's ability to do this, as outlined by Helena Wright in her article "Sarah G. Bagley: A Biographical Note," demonstrates that the earning power of female workers like Bagley was "not as insignificant as has been generally supposed of many mill women" (406–7). Others sought to earn their dowry before marriage.

Even if they did not seek to labor for their brother's education or to secure payment for their family's home, some early mill girls saved to fund their own education or to save money before marrying. These early mill girls, like Ann Swett Appleton, Sarah G. Bagley, and Harriet Robinson, saw their position as operatives as temporary, not a lifelong occupation. Their time within the vast buildings, before they moved on to higher education, marriage, or perhaps another vocation, served to heightened their own self-importance, as well as providing for themselves. Were it not for these opportunities, many of these girls would have been left "to become a burden on the charity of some relative," as Robinson notes ("Early" 388).

Turnouts

The idyllic vision of the mills and their operatives did not last long, and soon changes were brought that faded the luster from Lowell and its sister cities. Years passed, and overproduction led to a fall in the price allotted to the finished product. This then led to wage cuts and an increase in expected output. Robinson points out that this instigated the first strike, as related above, in October 1836. Despite her young age of eleven, she, too, took part, later recalling, "As I looked back at the long line that followed me, I was more proud than I have ever been since at any success I may have achieved, and more proud than I shall ever be again until my own beloved State gives to its women citizens the right of suffrage" (*Loom* 85). Although this initial strike was not successful, it did not stop the mill workers from taking action again and again. Historian Thomas Dublin cites further attempts between the years 1834 and 1848, both to maintain pay and to demand more reasonable hours.

Although wishing to recapture a better income was, indeed, a fundamental part of turning out, Dublin stresses something more formed a part of the drive to strike, a feeling alluded to by Robinson in the excerpt. He writes that "the wage cuts undermined the sense of dignity and social equality which was an important element in their Yankee heritage" and that such cuts were considered "an attack on their economic independence" (Dublin 108). This again brings to mind the refrain of the song sung by strikers in which they declare they will not be slaves. The mill operatives were not going to labor fourteen hours a day for a pittance of a wage. Earning their own income freed their families from having to support them and freed charities from offering them assistance, not to mention the added incentive of helping a brother through school or purchasing the family home, as Sarah G. Bagley did. These women knew they deserved better than how the mills chose to treat them, having strayed from the original vision held by Francis Cabot Lowell, Nathan Appleton, and their associates.

Although she mentions it only briefly, Robinson does allude to the dire consequences the mill girls faced for striking. Robinson calls the actions of the company agent against the strike's organizers "some small revenges," yet goes on to say that her mother "was turned away from her boarding-house" for not having prevented her from participating in the strike (*Loom* 85). Recalling what Robinson relates earlier in her memoir, this suggests that her mother, who was struggling to support four children on her own, lost her best employment. As William Moran notes in *The Belles of New England*, terminating striking workers was not uncommon, and later on, the corporations "blacklisted" known agitators, preventing them from gaining employment at other mills in the city. It is obvious from her own account that Robinson was not one of those unfortunates who were blacklisted, as she says elsewhere in her memoir that she continued her factory work into her twenties, when she received an "honorable discharge" and married (73).

As the years brought more wage reductions and consequently more strikes, the young women of New England moved away from mill work, their places taken by different waves of immigrants: first the Irish and French Canadians, before the boats brought those from eastern and southern Europe. "Thus," as Robinson notes, "the status of the factory population of New England gradually became what we know it to be to-day" (*Loom* 85).

Essential Themes

Throughout Robinson's essay "Early Factory Labor in New England," and even more so within the length of her book, *Loom and Spindle*, there reads inherent pride in the work performed in the mills. The early days of the mills helped to promote this feeling. Moran writes that Maine's Bates Mills boasted that "their bedspreads were 'Loomed to be Heirloomed'" (6). The New England mills produced materials that were made into the uniforms worn by Civil War soldiers, as well as those serving in the World Wars. It is no wonder these women held such pride in their participation within the industry.

This pride played into their distress at the changes wrought within the mills. Earning their own income and thereby able to contribute to their families or to gain their independence, allowed these women to recognize a new and dynamic level of self-worth. In legal terms, as recalled by Robinson, a woman "was a ward, an appendage, a relict." Mill employment had shown these young women a glimpse of more freedom within their restricted lives. The lowered wages and increased production degraded them, setting the stage for the later women's and labor movements and for the corporations' replacement of the increasingly dissatisfied mill girls with foreign immigrant laborers, whom they could exploit more readily.

Jennifer L. Henderson Crane

Bibliography

Adickes, Sandra. "Mind among the Spindles: An Examination of Some of the Journals, Newspapers, and Memoirs of the Lowell Female Operatives." *Women's Studies* 1.3 (1973): 279–87. Print.

Dublin, Thomas. "Women, Work, and Protest in the Early Lowell Mills: 'The Oppressing Hand of Avarice Would Enslave US.'" *Labor History* 16.1 (1975): 99–116. Print.

Farfield, Roy P. "Labor Conditions at the Old York: 1831–1900." *New England Quarterly* 30.2 (1957): 166–80. Print.

Gersuny, Carl. "Industrial Causalities in Lowell, 1890–1905." *Labor History* 20.3 (1979): 435–42. Print.

Moran, William. *The Belles of New England: The Women of the Textile Mills and the Families Whose Wealth They Wove*. New York: St. Martin's, 2004. Print.

Robinson, Harriet J. Hanson. "Early Factory Labor in New England." *Fourteenth Annual Report of the Bureau of Statistics of Labor*. Boston: Wright, 1883. 337–401. Print.

---. *Loom and Spindle; or, Life among the Early Mill Girls*. New York: Crowell, 1898. Print.

Schlereth, Thomas J. *Victorian American: Transformations in Everyday Life*. New York: Harper, 1991. Print.

Tucker, Barbara M. "The Family and Industrial Discipline in Ante-Bellum New England." *Labor History* 21.1 (1979): 55–74. Print.

Weiss, Jane. "'In the Mills, We Are Not So Far from God and Nature': Industrialization and Spirituality in Nineteenth-Century New England." *Journal for the Study of Religion, Nature & Culture* 5.1 (2011): 82–100. Print.

Wolfe, Allis Rosenberg, and H. E. Back, eds. "Letters of a Lowell Girl and Friends, 1845–1846." *Labor History* 17.1 (1976): 96–102. Print.

Wright, Helena. "Sarah G. Bagley: A Biographical Note." *Labor History* 20.3 (1979): 398–413. Print.

Additional Reading

American Textile History Museum. American Textile History Museum, n.d. Web. 15 Mar. 2013.

Eisler, Benita, ed. The Lowell Offering: *Writings by New England Mill Women (1840–1845)*. New York: Norton, 1998. Print.

Flather, Roger. *The Boss' Son: Remembering the Boott Mills in Lowell, Massachusetts, 1937–1954*. Bloomington: AuthorHouse, 2011. Print.

Gross, Laurence F. *The Course of Industrial Decline: The Boott Cotton Mills of Lowell, Massachusetts, 1835–1955*. Baltimore: Johns Hopkins UP, 2000. Print.

"Lowell: History & Culture." *National Park Service*. National Park Service, US Dept. of the Interior, 9 Mar. 2013. Web. 15 Mar. 2013.

"Lowell History Chronology." *Lowell Historical Society*. Lowell Historical Society, 2012. Web. 15 Mar. 2013.

LESSON PLAN: **Strike!**

Students analyze two essays by mill worker Harriet H. Robinson to consider women's labor and the factory system in the antebellum period.

Learning Objectives

Interrogate historical information about women's occupations and social status in antebellum America; analyze how industrialization affected women's roles; consider multiple perspectives of the factory system and the rise of the labor movement.

Materials: Harriet H. Robinson, "Early Factory Labor in New England" (1885); Harriet H. Robinson, *Loom and Spindle; or, Life among the Early Mill Girls* (1898).

Overview Questions

What does Robinson's essay suggest about life for mill workers in Lowell, Massachusetts? How did the mill workers fight for labor reforms? How did the factory system impact women's opportunities and status in the antebellum period? How might accounts like Robinson's have impacted nineteenth-century movements for labor reform and women's rights?

Step 1: Comprehension Questions

Who worked in the Lowell mills? What did they do at the mills? What were their working conditions like?

- **Activity:** Call on students to locate passages depicting the Lowell mill girls and their working conditions. Have students describe in their own words what it might have been like to work in the mills.

Step 2: Context Questions

In what ways were women's options and opportunities limited in the early nineteenth century? According to Robinson, how did the factory system impact or change these possibilities?

- **Activity:** Have students review paragraphs 6 and 7 and list the limitations Robinson describes. Have students discuss how working outside the home and for wages affected women's opportunities. Ask students what limitations they think persisted for girls at the mills.

Step 3: Context Questions

Why did the mill workers go on strike in 1836? What were the effects of the strike, both on Robinson and on other workers? What does Robinson's essay suggest about the potential for strikes to reform factory conditions?

- **Activity:** Pair students to make a two-column chart listing the causes and effects of the strike. Have students use their charts to discuss the impacts the strike did—and did not—have on factory conditions, citing passages to support their claims.

Step 4: Historical Connections Questions

Robinson's memoir was published in 1898. Based on her account, how did the factory system change between 1832 and the 1890s? What additional reforms does Robinson suggest still need to be made?

- **Activity:** Have students read aloud the final paragraph and draw inferences about how the factory system changed from 1832 to Robinson's present. Have students brainstorm what additional changes to industry and women's labor Robinson was likely to see throughout her lifetime.

Step 5: Response Paper

Word length and additional requirements set by Instructor. Students answer the research question in the *Overview Questions*. Students state a thesis and use as evidence passages from the primary source document as well as support from supplemental materials assigned in the lesson.

The Sphere of Woman and Man as Moral Beings the Same

Date: August 28, 1837
Author: Grimké, Angelina
Genre: letter

"Now, if I understand the real state of the case, woman's rights are not the gifts of man—no! Nor the gifts of God. His gifts to her may be recalled at his good pleasure—but her rights are an integral part of her moral being; they cannot be withdrawn; they must live with her forever."

Summary Overview

Angelina Grimké was an early American activist and writer. Her two main concerns were women's rights and the abolition of slavery. She and her elder sister, Sarah Grimké, wrote and spoke passionately on both of these topics, but they are best known for a speaking tour against slavery they undertook in 1837–38. This was a particularly unique occurrence, as it was highly unusual for women to speak publicly at the time, especially to a mixed audience of women and men. Angelina Grimké's speaking tour culminated with an address to the Massachusetts legislature, the first given by a woman to a legislative body in the United States. During the same time period, she became involved in a public debate through a series of published letters to Catherine Beecher, who disagreed both with her views on slavery and on women's rights. In these letters, Grimké made clear her belief in the equality of American women, views which she clearly shared with her sister Sarah, who had published her own *Letters on the Equality of the Sexes* around the same time.

Defining Moment

The antebellum period of American history saw the young country trying to come to terms with a number of important social issues, including slavery and women's rights. With the rapid expansion of the cotton industry in the Southern states, slavery also expanded rapidly. A plantation culture emerged in the South, which contrasted sharply with the culture of the North, where slavery was on the decline. Thus began the separation of ideologies and economies that ultimately fuelled the Civil War between the North and the South. The abolitionist, or antislavery movement, began in the North. Several prominent abolitionists were Quakers, whose faith was known for its emphasis on peace, simplicity, and spiritual equality for all.

Many women were drawn to the antislavery movement, as they increasingly saw parallels between the enslavement of African Americans and the treatment of women (more particularly, white women) in American society at the time. Women's proper place within the antislavery movement, and therefore within the broader public life of America, soon became a point of discussion. The related concepts of the cult of true womanhood, which advocated a division of society into separate spheres for men and women, and of republican motherhood, which promoted women's education only in order to further the education of future civic leaders (male) and their mothers, helped constrain women's roles in society. Societal norms pressured women to stay within the private sphere—the domestic world of the family home—and to eschew the public sphere of politics and business, which was traditionally left to men. Within the antislavery movement, however, women were increasingly involved as organizers and speakers, which exposed them more and more to the public sphere. The revolutionary ideals of freedom and liberty were soon seen by many as only available to a certain class of American society: those who were white and male.

The years 1837 and 1838 were highlights in the lives and public careers of Angelina Grimké and her sister Sarah Grimké. By speaking to mixed audiences of men and women, the two sisters helped spark a debate on women's roles, rights, and equality in America. When Catharine Beecher took issue with Angelina Grimké on women's proper place in society, Grimké saw this as an opportunity to engage Beecher in a public debate on women's rights as well as abolitionism, another issue on which the two women disagreed. Catharine Beecher was the elder sister of Harriet Beecher Stowe, the author of *Uncle Tom's Cabin*, a seminal antislavery novel. Grimké published her letters in the abolitionist newspapers *The Liberator* and *The Emancipator*, and they were then were reprinted in book form.

Author Biography

Angelina Grimké Weld was born on February 20, 1805, to John Grimké and Mary Smith Grimké. She was the sixth of fourteen children born into a traditional, upper-class Southern family that lived in Charleston, South Carolina, and were members of the Episcopal Church. While her father was a slave owner his entire life, Grimké and her elder sister Sarah both became enthusiastic antislavery advocates. Growing up in a slave-owning household, the two girls were exposed to its many inequities and cruelties first hand, which influenced their future abolitionist views. The two sisters, although separated in age by more than twelve years, were extremely close, and Sarah even successfully petitioned her parents to be Grimké's godmother. Sarah took on a maternal role for her younger sister, to the point which Grimké often called her "mother." It was Sarah who, in 1827, introduced Grimké to the Quaker religion, which included many leading abolitionists among its members. Grimké had left the Episcopal Church to convert to Presbyterianism, but became a Quaker like her sister and, in 1829, moved to Philadelphia to live with her.

Grimké's views on abolition began to solidify during this time. In response to William Lloyd Garrison's formation of the American Anti-Slavery Society (AASS) in 1833, she wrote Garrison an impassioned letter, which he then published in his abolitionist newspaper, the *Liberator*, without her permission. This catapulted Grimké and, by extension, her sister Sarah, into the public spotlight. As the Philadelphia Quakers disapproved of the Grimkés' new public roles, the two sisters moved to Providence, Rhode Island, where the Quakers were more liberal about the public activities of women. In 1836, Grimké wrote an abolitionist pamphlet, *An Appeal to the Christian Women of the Southern States*; the following year, she and Sarah undertook a highly successful speaking tour of the northeast states as the first female agents of AASS. During the tour, Grimké discovered she was a powerful and persuasive orator—both impassioned and persuasive. She spoke to mixed gender audiences, which was frowned upon at the time. In 1837, she became the first woman to speak before a legislative body in the United States when she spoke to the Massachusetts legislature.

Grimké married a fellow abolitionist leader and author, Theodore Weld, in 1838. After one of her speeches ended in violence later that year, her career as a lecturer virtually ended. Over the next decades, Grimké and Weld, along with her sister, earned a modest living as teachers. They all strongly supported the Union during the Civil War, although Grimké had hoped violence could be avoided in ending slavery. She died on October 26, 1879, after having been paralyzed for some years due to strokes.

HISTORICAL DOCUMENT

DEAR FRIEND: I come now to that part of thy book, which is, of all others, the most important to the women of this country; thy 'general views in relation to the place woman is appointed to fill by the dispensations of heaven.'I shall quote paragraphs from thy book, offer my objections to them, and then throw before thee my own views.

Thou sayest, 'Heaven has appointed to one sex the *superior*, and to the other the *subordinate* station, and this without any reference to the character or conduct of either.' This is an assertion without proof. Thou further sayest, that 'it was designed that the mode of gaining influence and exercising power should be *altogether different and peculiar*.' Does the Bible teach this? 'Peace on earth, and good will to men, is the character of all the rights and privileges, the influence and the power of *woman*.' Indeed! Did our Holy Redeemer preach the doctrines of *peace to our sex only*? 'A *man* may act on Society by the collision of intellect, in public debate; *he* may urge his measures by a sense of shame, by fear and by personal interest; *he* may coerce by the combination of public sentiment; *he* may drive by physical force, and *he* does *not* overstep the boundaries of his sphere.' Did Jesus, then, give a different rule of action to men and women? Did he tell his disciples, when he sent them out to preach the gospel, that man might appeal to the fear, and shame, and interest of those he addressed, and coerce by public sentiment, and drive by physical force? "But (that) all the power and all the conquests that are lawful to *woman* are those only which appeal to the kindly, generous, peaceful and benevolent principles? If so, I should come to a very different conclusion from the one at which thou hast arrived: I should suppose that *woman was the superior*, and *man the subordinate being*, inasmuch as moral power is immeasurably superior to 'physical force.'

'Woman is to win everything by peace and love; by making *herself* so much respected, &c. that to yield to *her* opinions, and to gratify *her* wishes, will be the free-will offering of the heart.' This principle may do as the rule of action to the fashionable belle, whose idol is *herself*; whose every attitude and smile are designed to win the admiration of others to *herself*; and who enjoys, with exquisite delight, the double-refined incense of flattery which is offered to her vanity, by yielding to *her* opinions, and gratifying *her* wishes, because they are *hers*. But to the humble Christian, who feels that it is *truth* which she seeks to recommend to others, *truth* which she wants them to esteem and love, and not herself, this subtle principle must be rejected with holy indignation. Suppose she could win thousands to her opinions, and govern them by her wishes, how much nearer would they be to Jesus Christ, if she presents no higher motive, and points to no higher leader?

'But this is all to be accomplished in the domestic circle.' Indeed! 'Who made thee a ruler and a judge over all?' I read in the Bible, that Miriam and Deborah, and Huldah, were called to fill *public stations* in Church and State. I find Anna, the prophetess, speaking in the temple 'unto all them that looked for redemption in Jerusalem.' During his ministry on earth, I see women following him from town to town, in the most public manner; I hear the woman of Samaria, on her return to the city, telling the *men* to come and see a man who had told her all things that ever she did. I see them even standing on Mount Calvary, around his cross, in the most exposed situation; but He never *rebuked* them; He never told them it was unbecoming *their sphere in life* to mingle in the crowds which followed his footsteps. . . .

I find, too, that Philip had four daughters which did *prophesy*; and what is still more convincing, I read in the xi. of I. Corinthians, some particular directions from the Apostle Paul, as to *how* women were to pray and prophesy in the assemblies of the people—*not* in the domestic circle. On examination, too, it appears that the very same word, *Diakonos*, which, when applied to Phoebe, Romans xvi. 1, is translated *servant*, when applied to Tychicus, Ephesians vi. 21, is rendered *minister*. Ecclesiastical History informs us, that this same Phoebe was preeminently useful, as a minister in the Church, and that female ministers suffered martyrdom in the first ages of Christianity. And what, I ask, does the Apostle mean when he says in Phillipians iv. 3. 'Help those women who labored with me in the gospel'? Did these holy women of old perform all their gospel labors in 'the domestic and social circle'? I trow not.

Thou sayest, 'the moment woman begins to feel the promptings of ambition, or the thirst for power, her aegis of defence is gone.' Can man, then, retain when he indulges these guilty passions? Is it woman only who suffers this loss?

'All the generous promptings of chivalry, all the poetry or romantic gallantry depend upon woman's retaining her place as *dependent* and *defenceless*, and making no claims, and maintaining no rights, but what are the gifts of honor, rectitude and love.'

I cannot refrain from pronouncing this sentiment as beneath the dignity of any woman who names the name of Christ. No woman, who understands her dignity as a moral, intellectual, and accountable being, cares aught for any attention or any protection, 'vouchsafed by the promptings of chivalry, and the poetry of romantic gallantry'? Such a one loathes such littleness, and turns with disgust from all such silly insipidities. Her noble nature is insulted by such paltry sickening adulation, and she will not stoop to drink the foul waters of so turbid a stream. If all this sinful foolery is to be withdrawn from our sex, with all my heart I say, *the sooner the better*. Yea, I say more, no woman who lives up to the true glory of her womanhood, will ever be treated with such *practical contempt*. Every man, when in the presence of true moral greatness, 'will find an influence thrown around him,' which will utterly forbid the exercise of 'the poetry of romantic gallantry.'

What dost thou mean by woman's retaining her place as defenceless and dependent? Did our Heavenly Father furnish man with any offensive or defensive weapons? Was *he* created any less defenceless than *she* was? Are they not equally defenceless, equally dependent on Him? What did Jesus say to his disciples, when he commissioned them to preach the gospel?—'Behold, I send you forth as SHEEP in the midst of wolves; be ye wise as serpents, and *harmless as doves*.' What more could he have said to women?

Again, she must 'make no claims, and maintain no rights, but what are the gifts of honor, rectitude and love.' From whom does woman receive her *rights*? From God, or from man? What dost thou mean by saying, her rights are the *gifts* of honor, rectitude, and love? One would really suppose that man, as her lord and master, was the gracious giver of her rights, and that these rights were bestowed upon her by 'the promptings of chivalry, and the poetry of romantic gallantry,'—out of the abundance of his honor, rectitude and love. Now, if I understand the real state of the case, woman's rights are not the gifts of man—no! Nor the *gifts* of God. His gifts to her may be recalled at his good pleasure—but her *rights* are an integral part of her moral being; they cannot be withdrawn; they must live with her forever. Her rights lie at the foundation of all her duties; and, so long as the divine commands are binding upon her, so long must her rights continue.

'A woman may seek the aid of co-operation and combination among her own sex, to assist her in her appropriate offices of piety, charity,' &c. *Appropriate* offices! Ah! Here is the great difficulty. What are they? Who can point them out? Who has ever attempted to draw a line of separation between the duties of men and women, as *moral* beings, without committing the grossest inconsistencies on the one hand, or running into the most arrant absurdities or the other? . . .

According to what thou sayest, the women of this country are not to be governed by principles of duty, but by the effect their petitions produce on the members of Congress, and by the opinions of these men. If they deem them 'obtrusive, indecorous and unwise,' they must not be sent. If *thou* canst consent to exchange the precepts of the Bible, for the opinions of *such a body of men* as now sit on the destinies of this nation, I cannot. What is this but *obeying man* rather than God, and seeking the *praise of man* rather than of God? As to our petitions increasing the evils of slavery, this is merely an opinion, the correctness or incorrectness of which remains to be proved. When I hear Senator Preston of South Carolina, saying, that 'he regarded the concerted movement upon the District of Columbia as an attempt to storm the gates of the citadel—as throwing the bridge over the moat'—and declaring that 'the South must resist the danger in its inception, or it would *soon become irresistible*'—I feel confident that petitions will effect the work of emancipation, *thy* opinion to the contrary notwithstanding. . . .

Another objection to woman's petitions is, that they may 'tend to bring females, as petitioners and partisans, into every political measure that may tend to injure and oppress their sex.' As to their ever becoming partisans,

i. e. sacrificing principles to power or interest, I reprobate this under all circumstances, and in *both* sexes. But I trust my sisters may always be permitted to *petition* for a redress of grievances. Why not? The right of petition is the only political right that women have: why not let them exercise it whenever they are aggrieved? Our fathers waged a bloody conflict with England, because *they* were taxed without being represented. This is just what unmarried women of property now are. *They* were not willing to be governed by laws which *they* had no voice in making; but this is the way in which women are governed in this Republic. If, then, *we* are taxed without being represented, and governed by laws *we* have no voice in framing, then, surely, we ought to be permitted at least to remonstrate against 'every political measure that may tend to injure and oppress our sex in various parts of the nation, and under the various public measures that may hereafter be enforced.' Why not? Art thou afraid to trust the women of this country with discretionary power as to petitioning? Is there not sound principle and common sense enough among them, to regulate the exercise of this right? I believe they will always use it wisely. I am not afraid to trust my sisters—not I.

Thou sayest, 'In this country, petitions to Congress, in reference to official duties of legislators, seem, IN ALL CASES, to fall entirely without the sphere of female duty. Men are the proper persons to make appeals to the rulers whom they appoint,' &c. Here I entirely dissent from thee. The fact that women are denied the right of voting for members of Congress is but a poor reason why they should also be deprived of the right of petition. If their numbers are counted to swell the number of Representatives in our State and National Legislatures, the *very least* that can be done is to give them the right of petition in all cases whatsoever and without any abridgement. If not, they are mere slaves, known only through their masters.

In my next, I shall throw out my own views with regard to 'the appropriate sphere of woman'—and for the present subscribe myself,

Thy Friend,

A. E. GRIMKÉ.

GLOSSARY

aegis: protection; support

arrant: flagrant; utter

dispensations: commands or promises that govern human affairs; orders; arrangements

Holy Redeemer: Jesus Christ

indecorous: improper; indecent

martyrdom: suffering and death of someone who holds strongly to a belief, principle or cause, usually religious

precepts: commandments; directions given as a rule relating to conduct

remonstrate: plead in protest

reprobate: condemn; disapprove of

trow: believe; think

turbid: muddy or opaque

Document Analysis

The letter under study here is one of a number of letters that Angelina Grimké wrote in response to Catharine Beecher's *Essay on Slavery and Abolitionism, with Reference to the Duty of American Females*, which was published in 1837 and was directly addressed to Grimké. Grimké had once considered studying at Catharine Beecher's academy for women in Hartford, Connecticut, but eventually decided against it. Still, she held Beecher in high esteem as a woman who had advanced women's educational opportunities. When Beecher published her essay, Grimké, encouraged by her future husband Theodore Weld, decided to respond in a series of letters published in abolitionist newspapers. Her letters were each focused on one topic of rebuttal to Beecher's essay. Her overall rhetorical style was to quote Beecher's arguments, and then refute them point by point. In this letter, she targets Beecher's argument that the limiting of women's proper roles to the private sphere is divinely ordained. Grimké's counterargument also leads her to the topic of women petitioning government officials. Women's suffrage was still almost a century away, and so petitioning elected officials was one of the few ways women could make their political opinions publicly known at this time.

The difference in Grimké and Beecher's views on women's rights stemmed from their differences on how to solve the problem of slavery. Even among abolitionists there were divisions during the 1830s between the more conservative and respectable American Colonization Society (ACS) and the more radically egalitarian American Anti-Slavery Society (AASS). The ACS believed that black people and white people could never live together in a multiracial country, and therefore the best way to end slavery would be for black people to gradually gain freedom and then emigrate to Africa. The AASS believed that slavery should be immediately ended and all freed slaves should be at liberty to make their own choices as to where to live and how to make a living. Beecher leaned more towards the ACS stance, while Grimké was strongly in the AASS camp, which meant yet another source of contention between the two women.

Grimké herself is clear on her rhetorical format for this letter and states it in the salutation. She will first quote from Beecher's essay, then offer her "objections" to each point, and finally present her own ideas about the topic. This was an extremely effective way to refute Beecher's arguments point by point, and Grimké's letters were seen by her contemporaries as a thorough rhetorical victory for her.

Grimké begins by questioning Beecher's assertion that there is one sex that is superior and one that is inferior, and that this system was established by "Heaven" or God. Grimké's religious beliefs as a Quaker, particularly the belief in the spiritual equality of all persons, prompt her to take immediate issue with this statement. She dismisses it curtly as "an assertion without proof." She then confronts Beecher's further explanation that there is a difference in how men and women gain influence and exercise power. Women, in Beecher's opinion, do this peacefully. Grimké is offended by Beecher's idea that God preached the concept of peace only to women, while leaving men to use fear, shame, and physical force to influence others. She makes her point more forcefully by framing it in the form of a question, asking if Jesus had given two distinct "rule[s] of action" to men and to women. She ends this paragraph by turning Beecher's point against her by saying that if she believed this to be the case, then it must be women, and not men, who should be considered the superior sex, by virtue of the fact that "moral power" outweighs mere "physical force."

Grimké then moves on to Beecher's point that women should "win everything by peace and love," and that this should be women's preferred method of winning influence over others. Grimké considers this influence to be hollow if it only reinforces the personality and views of the individual woman, and that it therefore borders on vanity. Rather, Grimké feels that women should aim to find and share the truth, which she defines as being "nearer . . . to Jesus Christ," and not just their own views and opinions. This is especially true if a woman is able to influence and govern thousands. Without a "higher motive" or "higher leader" than herself, she will not lead her followers to the truth.

The next paragraph addresses the issue of separate spheres for women and men, and women's relegation to the domestic sphere. Grimké's next letter to Beecher develops her argument on this point more fully, but in this letter she refutes completely the fact that women have no public role. She supports her argument by citing the Bible, stating that four women of the Bible (Miriam, Deborah, Huldah, and Anna) had public roles. She also makes the point that women were present at Christ's crucifixion at Mount Cavalry in a "most exposed situation," but that Christ himself never told them it was wrong to leave their domestic sphere to do this. By referring back to the Bible itself, Grimké is able to supersede Beecher's argument, which is informed only through the lens of the current American societal norms.

Seeing that her line of argument holds weight, Grimké stays with it. She cites that Philip had four daughters "which did *prophesy*" and then even cites even more concrete passages from the Bible to support her argument. She explains that women were told "*how* . . . to pray and prophesy in the assemblies of the people," which clearly meant they did so in the public sphere. She also points to the fact that another woman mentioned in the Bible, Phoebe, was called a *Diakonos*, which can translate into "minister," and which again is a highly public role.

Beecher's point that women can be easily corrupted if allowed to become ambitious and powerful is easily and quickly refuted by Grimké, who reframes the point by posing a question. She asks if women are at risk of such corruption, are not men at the same risk?

Grimké saves some of her most contemptuous rebuttals for Beecher's discussion on chivalry and women's dependence on it as defenseless creatures. She does not hold back here, saying that Beecher's argument is quite simply "beneath the dignity of any woman who names the name of Christ." In essence, Grimké is insulted that Beecher views women as "defenceless" and in need of men's protection. Grimké's view of women is that they are "moral, intellectual, and accountable being[s]," and as such would be "insulted by such paltry sickening adulation." This is strong language, and no doubt made a serious impression on her readers. Grimké moves to her favorite rhetorical method of asking if being defenseless does not apply equally to men and to women: "Was *he* created any less defenceless than *she* was?" She then again uses a rhetorical question to wonder if both men and women are not equally dependent on God.

When Beecher turns explicitly to the question of women's rights, and how women are to receive these rights, Grimké again disputes her logic. To Beecher, women have no rights and can make no claims, except those that are gifted to her in the form of "honor, rectitude and love." For Grimké, this passage makes little sense. It is a given fact to Grimké that women have rights, and they are an inherent part of her moral being. To Grimké, rights are not given out differently to men and to women. Instead, they are universal—in essence, she is talking here about the concept of universal human rights. In fact, Grimké seems not to even understand Beecher's point, when she asks plainly: "What dost thou mean by saying, her rights are the gifts of honor, rectitude, and love?" Grimké believes rights cannot be given by man or God, and that they cannot be taken away, as can a gift. Rather, "they must live with her forever," because they are an inherent part of each person.

Next, Grimké quickly dispenses with Beecher's discussion of "appropriate offices" for, or moral duties of, women. Beecher states that women can seek help and support from other women when working in organizations dedicated to charity and piety. Grimké believes there are no appropriate offices designated as being solely for women. She asks Beecher for details of such offices and who decides what those offices should be. Again, to Grimké, there is no difference between men and women when it comes to their positions as "moral beings."

Beecher also expressed serious misgivings about women petitioning elected officials. She does not believe women should become involved in sending such requests for political change, especially if men consider the requests to be "obtrusive, indecorous and unwise." Grimké does not believe that men should be the judges of the content of such petitions; rather, she believes that God should be. Grimké's clever use of appealing directly to God and bypassing men is designed once again to counter Beecher's argument. Grimké then gives an example of a Southern senator expressing his concern that these petitions should be stopped before they gain momentum, as they are highly effective and could lead to the end of slavery in time. Grimké wholeheartedly agrees with the senator on the petitions' effectiveness, as much as Beecher may not.

Beecher's next point is that if women are allowed to petition, it could lead to their corruption due to partisanship and power. Grimké again falls back on her tried and true method of applying the argument that such partisanship should be avoided equally by men; "in all circumstances, and in *both* sexes." Grimké is adamant that women should be allowed to petition their government about their own grievances, whatever they may be. In this, she clearly states that it is the only "political right" that women have, as they cannot vote, let alone run for election themselves. Grimké then reaches back to one of the key reasons for the American Revolution: taxation without representation. She makes the comparison that unmarried women with property face the same reality, and that therefore, the injustice is the same. What is worse is that women also do not have a say in crafting the laws that they are forced to live under. At the very least then, they should be allowed to complain about these laws. Grimké then directly confronts Beecher's trust in and loyalty to other American women. She asks Beecher why she should not trust her sisters with the right to petition. She then follows that up with her own statement of strong belief that other women will use "common sense" and that they "will always use it wisely." Her final sentence issues a challenge to Beecher to trust women with the right to petition: "I am not afraid to trust my sisters—not I."

Grimké concludes by disagreeing with Beecher on her point that women should not be allowed to petition legislators that they have not themselves elected, and that such behavior falls outside of their domestic sphere. Grimké counters that is a "poor reason" for disallowing women to petition, and that it is particularly unfair as their numbers are counted towards the numbers of representatives allowed to be elected in state and federal electoral divisions. Again, it is with her final sentence that Grimké brings home her point with emotion: "If not, they [women] are mere slaves, known only through their masters." Since both women were abolitionists, this assertion is particularly cutting.

Essential Themes

Angelina Grimké's response to Catharine Beecher, especially on the topic of women's rights, set the tone for American feminism that would eventually flourish later in the nineteenth century and well into the twentieth. Grimké's perspective that women were equals in the eyes of God as moral beings and therefore should also be equal in the world he created, may have stemmed from her Quaker beliefs, but it was reinforced by her own experiences in life. By speaking publicly on a contentious social issue such as slavery, Grimké put herself squarely in the middle of the debate about the proper roles and rights of women in society.

In defending and advocating for equal rights for women, Grimké was following in the pioneering footsteps of women such as Frances Wright and Britain's Mary Wollstonecraft. She was also influencing, and influenced by, her own sister, Sarah, who was writing on the subject at the same time. By publicly declaring her position that there should be no separate spheres for the sexes, she came out in direct opposition to another woman. To demand for women the right to petition their elected representatives, and to then to compare it to the revolutionary ideals of taxation without representation and then slavery itself, she was clearly writing to provoke thought and heighten emotion.

Many in the abolitionist movement were worried about the encroachment of women's rights into their own movement. Many others outside of the movement were offended that the sisters spoke in public, and that they spoke and wrote about women's rights. The two were controversial figures, but Angelina and Sarah Grimké were only publicly active for a short period of time in the late 1830s. After that, they virtually retired from public life. But their ideas and influence continued, and were taken up by a new generation of American feminists decades later. The ideas they espoused were further explained and articulated by Margaret Fuller in *Woman in the Nineteenth Century* in 1845 and by activists Lucretia Mott and Elizabeth Cady Stanton at the Seneca Falls Convention on women's rights in 1848. To many, the Grimké sisters appeared ahead of their time. It was fitting that they lived long enough to see the end of slavery, and also to witness a new generation of women's right activists who were determined to ensure that women not only had the right to petition their legislators, but had the right to both elect and become legislators as well.

Lee Tunstall, PhD

Bibliography

Beecher, Catharine E. *An Essay on Slavery and Abolitionism, with Reference to the Duty of American Females.* 2nd ed. Philadelphia; Boston: Perkins, 1837. *Electronic Text Center, University of Virginia Library.* Web. 14 April 2011.

Berkin, Carol. "Angelina and Sarah Grimke: Abolitionist Sisters." *Gilder Lehrman Institute of American History.* Gilder Lehrman Institute of American History, 2009–2013. Web. 15 April 2013.

Birney, Catherine H. *The Grimké Sisters: Sarah and Angelina Grimké, the First American Women Advocates of Abolition and Woman's Rights.* 1885. New York: Haskell, 1970. Print.

Browne, Stephen H. *Angelina Grimké: Rhetoric, Identity, and the Radical Imagination.* East Lansing: Michigan State UP, 1999. Print.

Grimké, Angelina E. *Letters to Catherine E. Beecher [Excerpts]: Electronic Edition.* 1838. Web. Charlottesville: Railton; IATH; Electronic Text Center, 1998. Web. 11 Apr. 2013.

Lerner, Gerda. *The Grimké Sisters from South Carolina: Pioneers for Woman's Rights and Abolition.* New York: Oxford UP, 1998. Print.

Additional Reading

Ceplair, Larry. *The Public Years of Sarah and Angelina Grimké: Selected Writings.* New York: Columbia UP, 1989. Print.

Durso, Pamela R. *The Power of Woman: The Life and Writings of Sarah Moore Grimké.* Macon: Mercer UP, 2003. Print.

Gold, Ellen Reid. "The Grimké Sisters and the Emergence of the Women's Rights Movement." *Southern Speech Communication Journal* 46.4 (1981): 341–60. Print.

Grimké, Angelina. *Appeal to the Christian Women of the Southern States.* New York: American Anti-Slavery Society, 1836. Print.

Grimké, Sarah. *The Feminist Thought of Sarah Grimké. Edited by Gerda Lerner.* New York: Oxford UP, 1998. Print.

Japp, Phyllis M. "Esther or Isaiah?: The Abolitionist-Feminist Rhetoric of Angelina Grimké," *Quarterly Journal of Speech* 71.3 (1985): 335–48. Print.

Lumpkin, Katharine Du Pre. *The Emancipation of Angelina Grimké.* Chapel Hill: U of North Carolina P, 1974. Print.

Portnoy, Alisse. *Their Right to Speak: Women's Activism in the Indian and Slave Debates.* Cambridge: Harvard UP, 2005. Print.

LESSON PLAN: **A Case for Women's Rights**

Students analyze a letter from Angelina Grimké to Catharine Beecher to consider the arguments of women reformers during the antebellum period.

Learning Objectives

Consider multiple perspectives of women's political roles; compare and contrast different approaches to the women's and abolition movements; hypothesize the influence of Grimké's arguments on twentieth century feminism.

Materials: Angelina Grimké, "The Sphere of Woman and Man as Moral Beings the Same," (1837).

Overview Questions

Why does Grimké disagree with Beecher about gender inequality? Why does she think women should be involved in the abolition movement? How does she think women can bring about reform? How might her arguments have compelled later feminists to argue for women's political participation?

Step 1: Comprehension Questions

Why does Grimké think men and women are "beings the same"? What are her arguments for the equality of the sexes?

- **Activity:** Pair students to make a two-column chart comparing and contrasting the arguments of Beecher and Grimké. Have students use their charts to write a paragraph explaining why Grimké believes in equality between men and women.

Step 2: Comprehension Questions

In what ways does Grimke draw upon the Bible to support her arguments? How might her religious beliefs have strengthened her commitments to the women's movement?

- **Activity:** Have each student select a passage in which Grimké uses the Bible for support. Call on students to read aloud their passage, restate it in their own words, and explain how Grimké uses it to advance her views.

Step 3: Context Questions

Beecher argued that women should not participate in the abolition movement. Why does Grimké disagree? How does she think women can advance the abolitionist cause?

- **Activity:** Have students review the last four paragraphs of the letter and consider the reasons Grimké thinks women should be involved in politics. Discuss what Grimké means by "the right to petition." Ask students how women might have exercised this right and the benefits and drawbacks to this form of political participation.

Step 4: Historical Connections Questions

How might Grimké's writings have influenced later feminists in the nineteenth and twentieth centuries? What further gains have women made since this time? How might early reformers like Grimké have contributed to these advancements?

- **Activity:** Discuss the various political gains women have made since Grimké's time, such as the right to vote and to serve as politicians. Have students select a gain made in the twentieth century and imagine how Grimké would have viewed the change. Have students write a paragraph from Grimké's perspective supporting the reform.

Step 5: Response Paper

Word length and additional requirements set by Instructor. Students answer the research question in the *Overview Questions.* Students state a thesis and use as evidence passages from the primary source document as well as support from the secondary historical document/s assigned in the lesson.

Self-Reliance

Date: 1841
Author: Emerson, Ralph Waldo
Genre: essay

"Trust thyself: every heart vibrates to that iron string. Accept the place the divine providence has found for you, the society of your contemporaries, the connection of events. Great men have always done so, and confided themselves childlike to the genius of their age."

Summary Overview

Ralph Waldo Emerson is perhaps the best-known early American philosopher. His system of beliefs—which came to be known as transcendentalism—emphasized the universality of the divine, the appreciation of nature as a manifestation of that divinity, and the importance of creativity as a means of worship. *Self-Reliance*, published in 1841, brought together some of the ideas Emerson had expressed in the years since he began his career as a secular public lecturer in 1833.

In a sense, *Self-Reliance* was a response to his critics, who considered him eccentric or even dangerously heretical. At a more basic level, it was an expression in one of his core beliefs—that spontaneous, free, and creative self-expression is actually a form of worshipping the universal divine. It was intended by the author to be a passionate defense of the basic human right of people to develop and express their own beliefs, free from external coercion, and an indictment of institutions that discourage this freedom.

Defining Moment

Ralph Waldo Emerson, who had such a profound impact on American intellectual history, has always been regarded as a radical and a maverick, breaking with the conventions of his day to develop transcendentalism, a school of thought unlike any other known previously in the United States. Although there is no doubt that he was a great innovator, Emerson was also a product of his times. It is important to understand some of the ways Emerson's thinking was shaped by his environment, and why the intellectuals of his day were so receptive to his ideas.

Emerson came from a long line of Unitarians, proponents of a theology that emphasized the singularity of God, rather than the Trinitarian view favored by the Catholic Church and the Church of England. Unitarianism first began as a theological movement in the seventeenth century. It gained more widespread appeal in post-Enlightenment England in the late eighteenth century and became a respected form of worship in the newly formed United States in the early nineteenth century. Unitarian thinkers questioned many of the supernatural beliefs of other branches of Christianity, including the divine origin of scripture and the virgin birth of Jesus. It emphasized the importance of a personal relationship with God and deemphasized the importance of ritual and clerical hierarchy.

Unitarianism in the United States mainly developed in New England, especially in Boston. As the son of the minister of Boston's First Church, a leading Unitarian institution, Emerson grew up at the very epicenter of nineteenth-century American Unitarianism. The philosophy he developed—transcendentalism, with its emphasis on the divine as an all-pervasive force knowable through subjective appreciation of natural beauty—can in a very real way be read as a continuation of the Unitarian move away from the more mainstream belief in the supernatural and unknowable nature of God.

At the same time, political changes were unfolding in America that made the nation particularly receptive to Emerson's philosophy. The elimination of severe property requirements for voters greatly expanded suffrage among adult men. As a result, there was an increasing emphasis on the power of the so-called common man. The 1820s and 1830s came to be known as the Jacksonian Era, after Andrew Jackson, president of the United States from 1829–1837.

The Jacksonian Era was actually a wider shift in political sentiment than the election of a single president, celebrating individual freedom and a potential for fresh beginnings on the American frontier. Although Emerson was based in New England, far from the great western frontier itself, he drew attention to the importance of furthering intellectual frontiers, and defending individual freedom. Just as pioneer fever was sweeping the nation, Emerson came on the scene with his groundbreaking transcendental philosophy.

Author Biography

Ralph Waldo Emerson was born in Boston, Massachusetts, on May 25, 1803. He was the fourth child of William Emerson and Ruth Haskins Emerson. William Emerson was the Unitarian minister of Boston's First Church, well respected but never wealthy, and his mother also enjoyed a reputation for her deep sense of piety.

William Emerson died in 1811, when Emerson was eight years old. Ruth opened a boarding house to support her children, and the family continued to receive material and emotional support from their relatives. His paternal aunt, Mary Moody Emerson, was particularly devoted to young Emerson , and her love of written correspondence and journaling sparked his lifelong interest in writing.

Emerson began school the year after his father died, at the age of nine. He first attended Boston Public Latin School before moving on to Harvard College when he was fourteen. Although he was considered a precocious and intelligent boy, he never did particularly well in school, because he only applied himself to those subjects that interested him.

In 1821, Emerson dabbled in an educational career after graduating from Harvard, but teaching did not suit him. He returned to Harvard to pursue a degree in divinity. In 1829, he began work as the Unitarian minister at Boston's Second Church. This career path came naturally to him, not only because he was following in his father's footsteps, but also because he had gained some amount of celebrity for delivering powerful sermons as a university student.

In September of 1829, he married Ellen Tucker, the daughter of a Boston merchant, but Ellen died of tuberculosis in February of 1831, less than a year and a half after their marriage. This tragic turn greatly affected Emerson and inflamed his already smoldering doubts about the presence of a divine being as described in the Bible. In the year that followed, he became vocal about his inability to continue performing the ritual duties of his clerical office, for which he was soundly chastised by his beloved and firmly pious aunt. He finally quit his position at Boston's Second Church in October of 1832.

In a mood of frustration and despair, Emerson sold his house and went to Europe. He worked his way through Italy, France, and Great Britain, developing a love for philosophy, botany, and zoology. In Britain, he became friends with several of the literary notables of the day, including essayist Thomas Carlyle and the poets Samuel Taylor Coleridge and William Wordsworth.

When Emerson returned to the United States in the autumn of 1833, he began giving lectures on the life sciences and literature, and quickly gained a reputation as a strong and interesting public speaker. He remarried, to a woman named Lydia Jackson, and moved to Concord, Massachusetts. In the years that followed, Emerson's lectures became more philosophical in nature, incorporating many of the ideas he had encountered in Europe, especially the idealism of the German philosopher Immanuel Kant.

Kant's idealism, which itself was influenced by Plato and mystical Hinduism, held that the human world was fundamentally shaped by human ideas, rather than innate order or divine intention. By 1836, Emerson was primarily engaged in lecturing about a new American philosophy, called transcendentalism, that was opposed to organized religion; it supported the subjective rather than objective appreciation of art, freedom in creative expression, and a belief in the natural divinity of all things.

In 1836, supporters of this new philosophy formed an organization called the Transcendental Club in Cambridge, Massachusetts. Four years later, the club began its regular publication, called the *Dial*. Transcendentalism was destined to have a powerful impact on American social thought in the decades that followed, and is seen by many historians as sparking an intellectual and artistic renaissance in pre–Civil War America.

For the rest of his long life, Emerson worked as a touring lecturer, mainly in New England, but also in California, Europe, and Egypt. He remained friends with a myriad of the most notable scholars and activists of his day, including Walt Whitman, Henry David Thoreau, and Margaret Fuller. Emerson died of pneumonia on April 27, 1882, and was buried in Concord, Massachusetts. He is widely remembered as America's most prominent early philosopher.

HISTORICAL DOCUMENT

I read the other day some verses written by an eminent painter which were original and not conventional. The soul always hears an admonition in such lines, let the subject be what it may. The sentiment they instill is of more value than any thought they may contain. To believe your own thought, to believe that what is true for you in your private heart is true for all men,—that is genius. Speak your latent conviction, and it shall be the universal sense; for the inmost in due time becomes the outmost,—and our first thought is rendered back to us by the trumpets of the Last Judgment. Familiar as the voice of the mind is to each, the highest merit we ascribe to Moses, Plato, and Milton is, that they set at naught books and traditions, and spoke not what men but what they thought. A man should learn to detect and watch that gleam of light which flashes across his mind from within, more than the lustre of the firmament of bards and sages. Yet he dismisses without notice his thought, because it is his. In every work of genius we recognize our own rejected thoughts: they come back to us with a certain alienated majesty. Great works of art have no more affecting lesson for us than this. They teach us to abide by our spontaneous impression with good-humored inflexibility then most when the whole cry of voices is on the other side. Else, to-morrow a stranger will say with masterly good sense precisely what we have thought and felt all the time, and we shall be forced to take with shame our own opinion from another.

There is a time in every man's education when he arrives at the conviction that envy is ignorance; that imitation is suicide; that he must take himself for better, for worse, as his portion; that though the wide universe is full of good, no kernel of nourishing corn can come to him but through his toil bestowed on that plot of ground which is given to him to till. The power which resides in him is new in nature, and none but he knows what that is which he can do, nor does he know until he has tried. Not for nothing one face, one character, one fact, makes much impression on him, and another none. This sculpture in the memory is not without preestablished harmony. The eye was placed where one ray should fall, that it might testify of that particular ray. We but half express ourselves, and are ashamed of that divine idea which each of us represents. It may be safely trusted as proportionate and of good issues, so it be faithfully imparted, but God will not have his work made manifest by cowards. A man is relieved and gay when he has put his heart into his work and done his best; but what he has said or done otherwise, shall give him no peace. It is a deliverance which does not deliver. In the attempt his genius deserts him; no muse befriends; no invention, no hope.

Trust thyself: every heart vibrates to that iron string. Accept the place the divine providence has found for you, the society of your contemporaries, the connection of events. Great men have always done so, and confided themselves childlike to the genius of their age, betraying their perception that the absolutely trustworthy was seated at their heart, working through their hands, predominating in all their being. And we are now men, and must accept in the highest mind the same transcendent destiny; and not minors and invalids in a protected corner, not cowards fleeing before a revolution, but guides, redeemers, and benefactors, obeying the Almighty effort, and advancing on Chaos and the Dark.

What pretty oracles nature yields us on this text, in the face and behaviour of children, babes, and even brutes! That divided and rebel mind that distrust of a sentiment because our arithmetic has computed the strength and means opposed to our purpose, these have not. Their mind being whole, their eye is as yet unconquered, and when we look in their faces, we are disconcerted. Infancy conforms to nobody: all conform to it, so that one babe commonly makes four or five out of the adults who prattle and play to it. So God has armed youth and puberty and manhood no less with its own piquancy and charm, and made it enviable and gracious and its claims not to be put by, if it will stand by itself. Do not think the youth has no force, because he cannot speak to you and me. Hark! in the next room his voice is sufficiently clear and emphatic. It seems he knows how to speak to his contemporaries. Bashful or bold, then, he will know how to make us seniors very unnecessary.

The nonchalance of boys who are sure of a dinner, and would disdain as much as a lord to do or say aught to conciliate one, is the healthy attitude of human nature. A boy is in the parlour what the pit is in the playhouse; independent, irresponsible, looking out from his corner on such people and facts as pass by, he tries and sentences them on their merits, in the swift, summary way of boys, as good, bad, interesting, silly, eloquent, troublesome. He cumbers himself never about consequences, about interests: he gives an independent, genuine verdict. You must court him: he does not court you. But the man is, as it were, clapped into jail by his consciousness. As soon as he has once acted or spoken with eclat, he is a committed person, watched by the sympathy or the hatred of hundreds, whose affections must now enter into his account. There is no Lethe for this. Ah, that he could pass again into his neutrality! Who can thus avoid all pledges, and having observed, observe again from the same unaffected, unbiased, unbribable, unaffrighted innocence, must always be formidable. He would utter opinions on all passing affairs, which being seen to be not private, but necessary, would sink like darts into the ear of men, and put them in fear.

These are the voices which we hear in solitude, but they grow faint and inaudible as we enter into the world. Society everywhere is in conspiracy against the manhood of every one of its members. Society is a joint-stock company, in which the members agree, for the better securing of his bread to each shareholder, to surrender the liberty and culture of the eater. The virtue in most request is conformity. Self-reliance is its aversion. It loves not realities and creators, but names and customs.

Whoso would be a man must be a nonconformist. He who would gather immortal palms must not be hindered by the name of goodness, but must explore if it be goodness. Nothing is at last sacred but the integrity of your own mind. Absolve you to yourself, and you shall have the suffrage of the world. I remember an answer which when quite young I was prompted to make to a valued adviser, who was wont to importune me with the dear old doctrines of the church. On my saying, What have I to do with the sacredness of traditions, if I live wholly from within? my friend suggested,—"But these impulses may be from below, not from above." I replied, "They do not seem to me to be such; but if I am the Devil's child, I will live then from the Devil." No law can be sacred to me but that of my nature. Good and bad are but names very readily transferable to that or this; the only right is what is after my constitution, the only wrong what is against it. A man is to carry himself in the presence of all opposition, as if every thing were titular and ephemeral but he. I am ashamed to think how easily we capitulate to badges and names, to large societies and dead institutions. Every decent and well-spoken individual affects and sways me more than is right. I ought to go upright and vital, and speak the rude truth in all ways. If malice and vanity wear the coat of philanthropy, shall that pass? If an angry bigot assumes this bountiful cause of Abolition, and comes to me with his last news from Barbadoes, why should I not say to him, 'Go love thy infant; love thy wood-chopper: be good-natured and modest: have that grace; and never varnish your hard, uncharitable ambition with this incredible tenderness for black folk a thousand miles off. Thy love afar is spite at home.' Rough and graceless would be such greeting, but truth is handsomer than the affectation of love. Your goodness must have some edge to it,—else it is none. The doctrine of hatred must be preached as the counteraction of the doctrine of love when that pules and whines. I shun father and mother and wife and brother, when my genius calls me. I would write on the lintels of the door-post, *Whim*. I hope it is somewhat better than whim at last, but we cannot spend the day in explanation. Expect me not to show cause why I seek or why I exclude company. Then, again, do not tell me, as a good man did to-day, of my obligation to put all poor men in good situations. Are they *my* poor? I tell thee, thou foolish philanthropist, that I grudge the dollar, the dime, the cent, I give to such men as do not belong to me and to whom I do not belong. There is a class of persons to whom by all spiritual affinity I am bought and sold; for them I will go to prison, if need be; but your miscellaneous popular charities; the education at college of fools; the building of meeting-houses to the vain end to which many now stand; alms to sots; and the thousand fold Relief Societies;—though I confess with shame I sometimes succumb and give the dollar, it is a wicked dollar which by and by I shall have the manhood to withhold.

Virtues are, in the popular estimate, rather the exception than the rule. There is the man *and* his virtues. Men do what is called a good action, as some piece of courage or charity, much as they would pay a fine in expiation of daily non-appearance on parade. Their works are done as an apology or extenuation of their living in the world,—as invalids and the insane pay a high board. Their virtues are penances. I do not wish to expiate, but to live. My life is for itself and not for a spectacle. I much prefer that it should be of a lower strain, so it be genuine and equal, than that it should be glittering and unsteady. I wish it to be sound and sweet, and not to need diet and bleeding. I ask primary evidence that you are a man, and refuse this appeal from the man to his actions. I know that for myself it makes no difference whether I do or forbear those actions which are reckoned excellent. I cannot consent to pay for a privilege where I have intrinsic right. Few and mean as my gifts may be, I actually am, and do not need for my own assurance or the assurance of my fellows any secondary testimony.

What I must do is all that concerns me, not what the people think. This rule, equally arduous in actual and in intellectual life, may serve for the whole distinction between greatness and meanness. It is the harder, because you will always find those who think they know what is your duty better than you know it. It is easy in the world to live after the world's opinion; it is easy in solitude to live after our own; but the great man is he who in the midst of the crowd keeps with perfect sweetness the independence of solitude.

GLOSSARY

cumber: to hinder or burden

Divine Providence: Christian concept meaning God's will or participation in the world

éclat: with striking effect or glory

extenuation: excuse or justification

Lethe: a river of the underworld, or Hades, in Greek mythology; those that drink of its waters were believed to forget everything they knew

meanness: poor quality or low value

Document Analysis

Ralph Waldo Emerson's *Self-Reliance* is an amalgamation of thoughts and insights from speeches he had given over the years. A meandering and at times redundant document, it expresses the loosely related set of beliefs that came to be known as the philosophy of transcendentalism. In particular, it presents arguments in favor of casting off the limitations of social conformity and living according to one's own character and sincere beliefs. In Emerson's view, doing so is not only the path to achieving greatness, but is the best way to get in touch with the divine energy which informs all of nature. *Self-Reliance* is a critique of contemporary intellectual trends as well, as the author feels that many of the movements current in his time were blocking people from the greater goal of living according to their natural characters.

Emerson begins *Self-Reliance* by relating that he recently read an unconventional commentary by a famous painter, and that this called to mind an important truth.

He explains that he was reminded that true genius comes from the bold assertion of sincere beliefs in a way that transcends the content of the expressed words themselves. He gives the examples of Moses, John Milton, and Plato as great thinkers, saying that they came to be highly regarded not because they expressed widely known and accepted truths, but because they were brave enough to state what they actually thought, regardless of established social conventions.

People everywhere have the ability to independently come to the same brilliant conclusions as the so-called great thinkers. They shy away from expressing such ideas, however, because they assume that they are not worthy of such a task. That, Emerson explains, is why it is so common to have a glimmer of recognition when reading works of acknowledged genius, since they reflect thoughts that many have had, but were not bold enough to fully develop or state in an explicit manner.

Emerson goes on to describe that there comes a point in the intellectual maturation process when one realizes that there is no point in being envious of others. Attempting to copy the achievements of other people is a fundamentally flawed tactic for gaining success, since it goes against one's own unique personal nature. Instead, it is prudent for people to accept the good and bad points of their own nature and use that knowledge as the basis for self-expression. Since all people are different, each personality is a new creative force in the world; it is therefore an affront to God to ignore the potential for iconoclastic self-expression. Doing sincere and exuberant work while aware of that uniqueness is the greatest way to achieve happiness and give praise to the divine creator.

The best course of action is for all people to accept who they are and where they find themselves, both geographically and socially. Then, they should trust in the divine force that arranged things in such a manner to look after them as they do their work and, most importantly, trust in themselves. That, Emerson argues, is what all great thinkers in history have done. God has a plan, and each person will play a role in it, so there is no need to hide from it or be afraid of it as it unfolds.

Nature provides many examples of the power provided by not second-guessing one's own abilities. It is seen, Emerson contends, in babies, who simply act as they want without consideration of social constrictions. He says that interacting with babies disrupts the typical process of self-doubt, as evidenced by people lapsing into cheerful baby talk at the sight of an infant, which would be highly embarrassing in other contexts. Emerson also believes that this power to resist conformity is also seen in children. He gives the example of boys, who have an ability to unhesitatingly judge others as they see them, and to voice these opinions without shame. Adults have forgotten that ability, and there is no elixir of forgetfulness to help unlearn our inhibitions and take us back to that more innocent state.

Emerson then says that society itself is antithetical to the free development of its members. It prevents people from growing beyond their self-doubts to a true adulthood of self-acceptance. As he says, "whoso would be a man must be a nonconformist" and ignore the strictures imposed by the social contract to revel in his own freedom of expression. That, he explains, is the ultimate goal of self-reliance—to rid oneself of the inhibitions of conventional thinking to reach real emotional maturity.

He then takes the highly controversial position of admonishing the reader that "nothing is at last sacred but the integrity of your own mind," a sentiment that would certainly have been perceived as dangerously heretical by most people of his day. He furthers this snub of orthodoxy by saying that a friend challenged him on this point, asking him to consider that his instincts might be from the devil rather than God. In what would be construed as blasphemy by nearly all Christians of his time, Emerson rhetorically retorted that he did not think this was the case, but "if I am the Devil's child, I will live then from the Devil."

Emerson justifies his highly unorthodox position by stating that good and evil are merely labels, used by society to mask people's true nature and intentions. He gives examples of a bigot who takes up the cause of abolition for people in other countries, but acts with intolerance at home. Such a man, he states, is not to be praised for his theoretical stand against slavery, for his actual behavior has not changed at all. Emerson also lashes out against impersonal acts of charity—such as giving money to anonymous relief organizations—as an ultimately hollow way for people to appear virtuous to one another. He endorses a more sincere and genuine approach to helping fellow human beings, one that shows people as intrinsically virtuous, rather than merely appearing virtuous through meaningless actions.

Taking the easy path of conformity weakens a person. Those who follow the forms of religious rituals, even if they do not really believe them, use their time in a wasteful manner. People who adhere to religious orthodoxy are not worth speaking with, because they cannot ever take a novel position on the subject of faith. Emerson compares those who cling to social norms to people blinded by tying a handkerchief around their eyes, they are willingly blinding themselves to the complex beauty of the world.

However, it is very difficult to go against social norms. There is strong pressure to conform, and those who do not are exposed to the displeasure and scorn of their peers. Moreover, people expect one another to act consistently. It becomes challenging for a person to take on new ideas or modes of expression without making friends suspicious and confused.

Emerson describes the drive to maintain consistency in order to appease social norms as "foolish" and "the hobgoblin of little minds." People should be free to speak their minds each day, and not be afraid that it might go against something they might have said on another day. He also argues that being misunderstood is no shame. Some of the greatest scientific innovators, including Copernicus, Galileo, and Pythagoras, were not understood in their lives; nor were the great religious and philosophical leaders, such as Martin Luther, Jesus, and Socrates.

The most important reason to not be too concerned with conformity is the fact that nobody can truly deny the force of their own character. To be honest and forthright is the best approach, for living in a sincere manner will allow a person to accomplish that which they are truly able to in this lifetime. Emerson compares the movements of a sincerely lived life to the course of a ship. Although it is continuously making tacks and adjustments, its movements cumulatively show its overall course. Emerson then states that all institutions are actually the long-term legacies of individuals living sincere lives. For example, Christianity is the legacy of the sincere life lived by Jesus, and the Reformation was the legacy of Martin Luther's force of character. People should therefore understand the power that a single person has to help shape the world and be confident and proud to express their sincere thoughts.

The key to being fully human, in Emerson's view, is to embrace what he calls spontaneity or instinct. It is possible to use this unconquerable force to live an independent life. Guiding daily actions by reference to these forces is living according to the character of one's own soul, and this individual soul is connected to and reflective of the divine spirit.

Adults, unlike children, have learned the demeaning habit of expressing their beliefs by referring to well-known and accepted thinkers; instead of stating their opinions, they cloak them in the opinions of respected scholars and leaders. Emerson says it is unnecessary to live by constant reference to the past. He gives the poetic example of roses—they are growing now, and are beautiful in their own right, without reference to past roses.

Emerson's next theme is among the most radical of this eminently unorthodox piece. He puts forth the mystical idea that all existence is actually the manifestation of one underlying force, which he names "the ONE" or the "Supreme Cause." God, in this view, does not exist wholly outside of humans, but within them as well, as in all aspects of the natural order. Living a life of self-reliance, rather than following social norms of right and wrong, Emerson goes on to explain, requires a person to be somewhat godlike. Such socially unencumbered people have confidence in their own abilities to judge the best courses of action.

Part of Emerson's philosophy, and an important aspect of *Self-Reliance*, is the romanticizing of rural life as producing more sincere and stronger people than urban life. He says there are countless young men from New York or Boston who have brilliant university careers, but consider themselves failures if they do not hold important offices one year after graduating. He contrasts these "city dolls" with their hardier counterparts from Vermont or New Hampshire who make their livings as they can, by farming, running a team, peddling, teaching school, working at a newspaper, or being a congressman, and simply take each step in life as it comes. The latter type of person—through the types of challenges natural to life in a more rural setting, Emerson believes—is better able to tap into their own inner strengths.

Emerson is critical of mainstream religion as antithetical to true self-reliance. Most people's prayers, for example, seek to compel some external supernatural force to intervene on their own behalf for the achievement of selfish goals. Emerson calls such prayers "vicious," especially if they are focused on material gain. Instead, he endorses a kind of prayer that meditates on the divine goodness behind mundane realities. These "true prayers" seek to bring the individual into a conscious atonement with God; this allows the better understanding of human nature as part of the greater natural order, and therefore as a manifestation of the divine creator.

Self-Reliance is also against the idea of religious denominations, or creeds, as the author calls them. First of all, they limit people's perception of the divine, as those of a specific creed think that they have to adhere to the established principles that comprise it. This clouds the perception of new things. Second, denominations unnaturally segregate people, emphasizing their differences and keeping them apart from those of other denominations.

Emerson also takes aim at the current trend of American people going traveling to destinations such as England, Greece, Italy, and Egypt. This is an unusual target for criticism, since he himself was clearly transformed by his travels, which took him to the very destinations that he names as popular among the American intellectual masses. He goes on to explain, however, that it is not travel itself that bothers him, but travel as entertainment. Those people who engage in a journey for such trivial purposes, he contends, are likely to be interested in imitating what has already been done in the world of art and philosophy, instead of being open to the experiences that will allow them to develop their own ideas. The popularity of travel as entertainment, Emerson believes, is a symptom of the intellectual restlessness of the day. It shows that people are not content in their own lives and worlds, but are hungry to experience cultures that they perceive to be categorically different and more authentic.

Emerson segues from this discussion of authentic versus inauthentic culture into a controversial commentary about the nature of human culture. Contradicting the accepted truth of his day that human culture progressed from primitive to advanced or modern, Emerson declares that "society never advances." Instead, he says, it shifts and morphs, but does not categorically change. As it gains some attributes, it loses others.

He gives a series of examples to demonstrate his point. In one, he says that although the aborigine from New Zealand lacks the clothing and material trappings of the American, he has a strength of body and robustness of health that the American has lost. Technology has allowed for some conveniences, but it also has resulted in unintended social harms that, on balance, render it a neutral force in providing better lives for people. Although this point could be seen as a romanticizing of traditional cultures, it is more fair to say that it is an insistence on the equality of all people.

This conclusion is underscored in Emerson's next line of reasoning, in which he contends that people are not now any different than people were in the past. The intellectual and religious leaders of the past are not any different, deep down, than modern people. What those who achieved greatness have in common is their ability to think for themselves and act according to their own consciences, and this is exactly the track to greatness available for people in the present age.

The last thought in *Self-Reliance* is a criticism of blind materialism. Emerson explains that people have a tendency to ignore who they are, and instead focus on what they have. Due to a fear of losing their material wealth, people construct governments to protect them, and these governments insist on a level of social conformity that is akin to slavery. The way to break free of the conceptual chains of this conformity is for people to be themselves, no matter what good or bad fortune befalls them.

Essential Themes

Between 1833 and 1841, Ralph Waldo Emerson worked as a traveling lecturer in the northeastern United States. Around 1836, he began to primarily speak about transcendentalism. This school of thought was inspired by a number of philosophies and systems of belief, including his own Unitarian tradition, German idealism as expressed by Immanuel Kant, the insights of Plato, and the revelations of mystical Hinduism.

Self-Reliance is widely considered to be the fullest expression of his transcendentalist philosophy. It is florid in tone, prone to digression, and repeats several key refrains. In sum, it is structured more like a speech than a written work, and may be difficult for modern readers to digest. Moreover, its conclusions may seem less profound new truths than statements of common sense to present-day readers, but that is precisely because of the massive effect it had on American culture.

The chief point of *Self-Reliance*, voiced repeatedly throughout the piece, is the importance of free self-expression. There is strong social pressure to conform, to resist saying anything unorthodox, and to maintain consistent philosophical positions in order to meet the expectations of others. However, Emerson dramatically declared, individuals should trust in their own insights and creative powers. All great human achievements, the author argues, have been made by those people able to come up with new and unique insights.

Emerson glorified, and indeed deified, the individual. He saw true individuality as both the source of all genius as well as the best way to worship the divine power which—he controversially argued—is the true and unifying nature of all things. This view that the divine is not an external, supernatural power, but instead is a natural phenomenon that exists in all aspects of nature, including the human individual, did much to chip away at the monopoly on faith enjoyed by the Christian church in nineteenth century society. Transcendentalism can be seen as an early form of both American deism and of cultural humanism.

In *Self-Reliance*, Emerson also challenged the popularly held belief that the urban and the modern is always superior to the rural and traditional. He spoke disparagingly of the weakness of character of young men born in Boston and New York, contrasting them with the heartiness of their counterparts in Vermont and New Hampshire. He also gave examples of how culture does not progress as it changes from primitive to contemporary, but argued that present-day or civilized people have lost some of the strengths of their tribal counterparts while gaining certain material comforts.

The key themes of *Self-Reliance* inspired and were echoed by some of the most influential writers in nineteenth-century America. Chief among those touched by Emerson's philosophy were Henry David Thoreau and Walt Whitman, who helped to shape the literary scene in the United States. As a key expression of Emerson's transcendentalist ideas, *Self-Reliance* transmitted the author's insights to his contemporary audience, challenging many widely held beliefs and ushering in a new age of American creative achievement.

Adam Berger, PhD

Bibliography

Buell, Lawrence. *Emerson*. Cambridge: Belknap, 2003. Print.

Carpenter, Frederick. *Emerson Handbook*. New York: Hendricks, 1953. Print.

Cole, Phyllis. *Mary Moody Emerson and the Origins of Transcendentalism: A Family History*. Oxford: Oxford UP, 1998. Print.

Garnett, Richard. *Life of Ralph Waldo Emerson*. London: Scott, 1888. Print.

MacLear, J. F. *Church and State in the Modern Age: A Documentary History*. Oxford: Oxford UP, 1995. Print.

Myerson, Joel. *Ralph Waldo Emerson: A Descriptive Biography*. Pittsburg: U of Pittsburg P, 1982. Print.

Van Cramphout, Gustav. *Emerson's Ethics*. Colombia: U of Missouri P, 1999. Print.

Additional Readings

Cayton, Mary. *Emerson's Emergence: Self and Society in the Transformation of New England, 1800–1845*. Chapel Hill: U of North Carolina P, 1998. Print.

Smith, Harmon. *My Friend, My Friend: The Story of Thoreau's Relationship with Emerson*. Amherst: U of Massachusetts P, 1999. Print.

Trent, William. *A History of American Literature, 1607–1865*. New York: Appleton, 1920. Print.

Versluis, Arthur. *The Esoteric Origins of the American Renaissance*. Oxford: Oxford UP, 2001. Print.

Whicher, George. *The Transcendentalist Revolt against Materialism*. Lexington: Heath, 1949. Print.

LESSON PLAN: **Solitude and Independence**

Students analyze an essay by Ralph Waldo Emerson to consider the views of the individual and society put forth by a major transcendentalist thinker.

Learning Objectives

Examine the influence of transcendentalist ideas on American culture; consider multiple perspectives of people in the past regarding society and social movements; compare and contrast differing sets of ideas about the individual's place in society.

Materials: Ralph Waldo Emerson, *Self-Reliance* (1841).

Overview Questions

What central transcendentalist beliefs does Emerson's essay express? What is his view of the individual and of society? Why does he consider "self-reliance" a primary virtue? In what ways does this principle endure, and in what ways has it changed over time?

Step 1: Comprehension Questions

What does Emerson consider "genius"? What qualities and actions make men "great"?

- **Activity:** Create a concept web on the board with the word "genius" at the center. Call on students to fill in the web with the qualities Emerson associates with genius. Have students use the web to write a short paragraph explaining what characteristics Emerson elevates in humankind, and why.

Step 2: Context Questions

What is Emerson's view of society? How does he think American society has gone wrong? How would he like to see people behave instead?

- **Activity:** Have students read aloud paragraph six and discuss Emerson's critique of society. Have students draw inferences about what kind of ideal society Emerson would like to see, citing passages to support their claims.

Step 3: Context Questions

What is Emerson's view of the individual? Why does he elevate individuality above community? What does he think people must do in order to live well? What qualities keep people from achieving this?

- **Activity:** Pair students to select a sentence or short passage in which Emerson discusses the virtues of the individual. Ask students to restate the passage in their own words and discuss why Emerson views the individual in such terms. Call on pairs to share their findings with the class.

Step 4: Explorations Questions

What are the possibilities and limitations made possible by the transcendentalist elevation of the solitary individual? How might this view of the individual change in the decades leading up to the Civil War?

- **Activity:** Read aloud the final sentence of the essay and ask students to consider the "perfect sweetness" Emerson describes. Have students discuss the benefits and drawbacks to such independence. Ask students whether they think Emerson's ideas still persist or whether the elevation of the individual has waned over time.

Step 5: Response Paper

Word length and additional requirements set by Instructor. Students answer the research question in the *Overview Questions*. Students state a thesis and use as evidence passages from the primary source document as well as support from supplemental materials assigned in the lesson.

The Great Lawsuit: Man versus Men, Woman versus Women

Date: July 1843
Author: Fuller, Margaret
Genre: essay; political tract

"Male and female represent the two sides of the great radical dualism. But, in fact, they are perpetually passing into one another. . . . There is no wholly masculine man, no purely feminine woman."

Summary Overview

Margaret Fuller is known as one of the first feminist thinkers in America, if not the first. She strongly advocated for women's rights to both education and employment. She published her thoughts in a serialized essay that appeared in July 1843 in the *Dial*, a magazine that she cofounded with Ralph Waldo Emerson and edited from 1840 to 1842. In the essay, entitled "The Great Lawsuit: Man versus Men, Woman versus Women," she states that there should not be separate spheres in society for women and men and that each woman and each man actually has characteristics of both genders within them. This essay was expanded by Fuller in 1845 and was published as *Woman in the Nineteenth Century*. It has become known as a foundational document of American feminism and, along with Fuller's other works, has been cited as a source of inspiration for early American feminist activists such as Susan B. Anthony and Elizabeth Cady Stanton.

Defining Moment

In the early nineteenth century, the antebellum United States was beginning to see that the revolutionary ideals it had fought so hard attain were beginning to fray. Slavery was increasingly seen by many as a prime example that liberty and freedom were not, indeed, for all men. The abolitionist movement also provided an impetus for American women to take a good look at their own status and position in society. Indeed, many abolitionists, such as Angelina and Sarah Grimke, were also early advocates for women's rights.

Margaret Fuller was influenced by the abolitionist movement, but mainly through her involvement in the transcendentalist movement, whose members were also active in social reform movements. Transcendentalism was closely linked to Ralph Waldo Emerson, whom Fuller befriended after hearing him speak. The philosophy had as one of its main tenets the cultivation of the individual. To Fuller, the individual soul was without gender, and so this philosophy applied equally to women and men. Fuller was also influenced by European romanticism, which was particularly strong in the arts and literature. This intellectual movement was in part a reaction to the Enlightenment and its commitment to the scientific rationalization of nature. The romantics advocated strong emotions and embraced classical history and literature.

Fuller was certainly aware of the issues facing nineteenth-century American women, as she herself had to overcome many of them. A highly educated woman who made her own living by writing and teaching, she was the exception and not the norm in American society. She believed that other women should have the same opportunities that she had, and it was for this reason she wrote on the topic of women's rights and women's ability to be equal to men. This was a radical theory at the time for many in the United States who had embraced the ideals of separate spheres for the two sexes: domestic or private for women and political or public for men. Most female writers also embraced the notion of "republican motherhood," which held that American women should be educated in order to provide a better early education for boys who would one day take their place as leaders of the country and girls who would repeat the cycle and become mothers to boys themselves. Fuller's call for women's rights was like an American echo of Mary Wollstonecraft's *A Vindication of the Rights of Woman*, which caused some controversy when it was published in 1792. Although America's attention was soon focused on abolition during the years of the Civil War, Fuller's work set the tone for many early American feminist activists whose work began in earnest after the war was over.

Author Biography

Sarah Margaret Fuller was born on May 23, 1810, to her parents Timothy Fuller and Margaret Crane Fuller in Cambridgeport, Massachusetts. She was their first child, followed over the years by two sisters and six brothers, although one sister and one brother died while in infancy. Margaret was provided the finest of educations by her father, who saw that she was keen and able to learn. She attended various schools in the Cambridge area, including the prestigious Port School in Cambridgeport, which prepared young boys for Harvard but also allowed girls to attend. By sixteen, she had left school and started a self-study program designed with the help of her father, and by 1833, she was tutoring her own siblings, which she found somewhat exhausting. She would have to continue teaching, though, as her father died suddenly of cholera in 1835. She began to teach at schools and publish literary criticism.

Fuller was surrounded by fellow intellectuals in the Harvard University area, and it was here that she heard Ralph Waldo Emerson speak on transcendentalism, a new philosophy that was emerging in America at the time. Hearing his talk inspired her to join the Transcendental Club. In 1839, she began holding "conversations" for women intellectuals and activists in her home. It was during this time that she began to be viewed as a leader in the transcendentalist movement. In 1839, she translated a book about the German writer Johann Wolfgang von Goethe. She then cofounded the transcendentalist magazine the *Dial* with Emerson and, between 1840 and 1842, served as its editor. After stepping down as editor, she continued to contribute to the *Dial* and published her landmark essay, "The Great Lawsuit: Man versus Men, Woman versus Women," in July 1843. Fuller expanded "The Great Lawsuit" and published it separately under the title *Woman in the Nineteenth Century* in 1845. Throughout this time, she earned the reputation of being the most well-read person, male or female, in New England and became the first woman who was allowed to use Harvard Library as a researcher.

At the end of 1844, Fuller left her family and friends in Massachusetts and moved to New York to join the *New York Tribune* as its literary critic. In 1846, the newspaper sent her to Europe as its first female foreign correspondent. While traveling in Italy, she met Marquis Giovanni Angelo Ossoli and joined him in the Republican fight for independence in Rome. On September 5, 1848, Fuller gave birth to Ossoli's son, Angelo Eugene Philip "Nino" Ossoli, out of wedlock. In April 1849, she left her son with a nurse and returned to Rome, where she ran a hospital and provided supplies to Ossoli's group of fighters. Upon the Republican defeat in July 1849, Fuller fled with Ossoli and their son to Florence. While there, she wrote a history of the Italian revolution, but she wanted to publish it in the United States and decided to move back. She and her family had almost completed their transatlantic journey when they perished in a shipwreck off Fire Island near New York City on July 19, 1850.

HISTORICAL DOCUMENT

There are two aspects of woman's nature, expressed by the ancients as Muse and Minerva. It is the former to which the writer in the *Pathfinder* looks. It is the latter which Wordsworth has in mind, when he says,

> With a placid brow,
> Which woman ne'er should forfeit, keep thy vow.

The especial genius of woman I believe to be electrical in movement, intuitive in function, spiritual in tendency. She is great, not so easily in classification, or re-creation, as in an instinctive seizure of causes, and a simple breathing out of what she receives that has the singleness of life, rather than the selecting or energizing of art.

More native to her is it to be the living model of the artist, than to set apart from herself any one form in objective reality; more native to inspire and receive the poem than to create it. In so far as soul is in her completely developed, all soul is the same; but as far as it is modified in her as woman, it flows, it breathes, it sings, rather than deposits soil, or finishes work, and that which is especially feminine flushes in blossom the face of earth, and pervades like air and water all this seeming solid globe, daily renewing and purifying its life. Such may be the especially feminine element, spoken of as Femality. But it is no more the order of nature that it should be incarnated pure in any form, than that the masculine energy should exist unmingled with it in any form.

Male and female represent the two sides of the great radical dualism. But, in fact, they are perpetually passing into one another. Fluid hardens to solid, solid rushes to fluid. There is no wholly masculine man, no purely feminine woman.

History jeers at the attempts of physiologists to bind great original laws by the forms which flow from them. They make a rule; they say from observation what can and cannot be. In vain! Nature provides exceptions to every rule. She sends women to battle, and sets Hercules spinning; she enables women to bear immense burdens, cold, and frost; she enables the man, who feels maternal love, to nourish his infant like a mother. Of late she plays still gayer pranks. Not only she deprives organizations, but organs, of a necessary end. She enables people to read with the top of the head, and see with the pit of the stomach. Presently she will make a female Newton, and a male Syren.

Man partakes of the feminine in the Apollo, woman of the Masculine as Minerva.

Let us be wise and not impede the soul. Let her work as she will. Let us have one creative energy, one incessant revelation. Let it take what form it will, and let us not bind it by the past to man or woman, black or white. Jove sprang from Rhea, Pallas from Jove. So let it be.

If it has been the tendency of the past remarks to call woman rather to the Minerva side,—if I, unlike the more generous writer, have spoken from society no less than the soul,—let it be pardoned. It is love that has caused this, love for many incarcerated souls, that might be freed could the idea of religious self-dependence be established in them, could the weakening habit of dependence on others be broken up.

Every relation, every gradation of nature, is incalculably precious, but only to the soul which is poised upon itself, and to whom no loss, no change, can bring dull discord, for it is in harmony with the central soul.

If any individual live too much in relations, so that he becomes a stranger to the resources of his own nature, he falls after a while into a distraction, or imbecility, from which he can only be cured by a time of isolation, which gives the renovating fountains time to rise up. With a society it is the same. Many minds, deprived of the traditionary or instinctive means of passing a cheerful existence, must find help in self-impulse or perish. It is therefore that while any elevation, in the view of union, is to be hailed with joy, we shall not decline celibacy as the great fact of the time. It is one from which no vow, no arrangement, can at present save a thinking mind. For now the rowers are pausing on their oars, they wait a change before they can pull together. All tends to illustrate the thought of a wise contemporary. Union is only possible to those who are units. To be fit for relations in time, souls, whether of man or woman, must be able to do without them in the spirit.

It is therefore that I would have woman lay aside all thought, such as she habitually cherishes, of being taught and led by men. I would have her, like the Indian girl, dedicate herself to the Sun, the Sun of Truth, and go nowhere if his beams did not make clear the path. I would have her free from compromise, from complaisance, from helplessness, because I would have her good enough and strong enough to love one and all beings, from the fulness, not the poverty of being.

Men, as at present instructed, will not help this work, because they also are under the slavery of habit. I have seen with delight their poetic impulses. A sister is the fairest ideal, and how nobly Wordsworth, and even Byron, have written of a sister.

There is no sweeter sight than to see a father with his little daughter. Very vulgar men become refined to the eye when leading a little girl by the hand. At that moment the right relation between the sexes seems established, and you feel as if the man would aid in the noblest purpose, if you ask him in behalf of his little daughter. Once two fine figures stood before me, thus. The father of very intellectual aspect, his falcon eye softened by affection as he looked down on his fair child, she the image of himself, only more graceful and brilliant in expression. I was reminded of Southey's Kehama, when lo, the dream was rudely broken. They were talking of education, and he said.

"I shall not have Maria brought too forward. If she knows too much, she will never find a husband; superior women hardly ever can."

"Surely," said his wife, with a blush, "you wish Maria to be as good and wise as she can, whether it will help her to marriage or not."

"No," he persisted, "I want her to have a sphere and a home, and some one to protect her when I am gone."

It was a trifling incident, but made a deep impression. I felt that the holiest relations fail to instruct the unprepared and perverted mind. If this man, indeed, would have looked at it on the other side, he was the last that would have been willing to have been taken himself for the home and protection he could give, but would have been much more likely to repeat the tale of Alcibiades with his phials.

But men do not look at both sides, and women must leave off asking them and being influenced by them, but retire within themselves, and explore the groundwork of being till they find their peculiar secret. Then when they come forth again, renovated and baptized, they will know how to turn all dross to gold, and will be rich and free though they live in a hut, tranquil, if in a crowd. Then their sweet singing shall not be from passionate impulse, but the lyrical overflow of a divine rapture, and a new music shall be elucidated from this many-chorded world.

Grant her then for a while the armor and the javelin. Let her put from her the press of other minds and meditate in virgin loneliness. The same idea shall reappear in due time as Muse, or Ceres, the all-kindly, patient Earth-Spirit.

I tire every one with my Goethean illustrations. But it cannot be helped.

Goethe, the great mind which gave itself absolutely to the leadings of truth, and let rise through him the waves which are still advancing through the century, was its intellectual prophet. Those who know him, see, daily, his thought fulfilled more and more, and they must speak of it, till his name weary and even nauseate, as all great names have in their time. And I cannot spare the reader, if such there be, his wonderful sight as to the prospects and wants of women.

As his Wilhelm grows in life and advances in wisdom, he becomes acquainted with women of more and more character, rising from Mariana to Macaria.

Macaria, bound with the heavenly bodies in fixed revolutions, the centre of all relations, herself unrelated, expresses the Minerva side. Mignon, the electrical, inspired lyrical nature.

All these women, though we see them in relations, we can think of as unrelated. They all are very individual, yet seem nowhere restrained. They satisfy for the present, yet arouse an infinite expectation.

The economist Theresa, the benevolent Natalia, the fair Saint, have chosen a path, but their thoughts are not narrowed to it. The functions of life to them are not ends, but suggestions.

Thus to them all things are important, because none is necessary. Their different characters have fair play, and each is beautiful in its minute indications, for nothing is enforced or conventional, but everything, however slight, grows from the essential life of the being.

Mignon and Theresa wear male attire when they like, and it is graceful for them to do so, while Macaria is confined to her arm chair behind the green curtain, and the Fair Saint could not bear a speck of dust on her robe.

All things are in their places in this little world because all is natural and free, just as "there "is room for everything out of doors." Yet all is rounded in by natural harmony which will always arise where Truth and Love are sought in the light of freedom.

Goethe's book bodes an era of freedom like its own, of "extraordinary generous seeking," and new revelations. New individualities shall be developed in the actual world, which shall advance upon it as gently as the figures come out upon his canvass.

A profound thinker has said "no married woman can represent the female world, for she belongs to her husband. The idea of woman must be represented by a virgin."

But that is the very fault of marriage, and of the present relation between the sexes, that the woman does belong to the man, instead of forming a whole with him. Were it otherwise there would be no such limitation to the thought.

Woman, self-centred, would never be absorbed by any relation; it would be only an experience to her as to man. It is a vulgar error that love, a love to woman is her whole existence; she also is born for Truth and Love in their universal energy. Would she but assume her inheritance, Mary would not be the only Virgin Mother. Not Manzoni alone would celebrate in his wife the virgin mind with the maternal wisdom and conjugal affections. The soul is ever young, ever virgin.

And will not she soon appear? The woman who shall vindicate their birthright for all women; who shall teach them what to claim, and how to use what they obtain? Shall not her name be for her era Victoria, for her country and her life Virginia? Yet predictions are rash; she herself must teach us to give her the fitting name.

GLOSSARY

bodes: predicts; indicates

complaisance: deference to others' wishes; amiability

dross: waste or foreign matter

dualism: a state consisting of two parts

elucidated: explained; clarified

Femality: coinage by two articles that appeared in the New York *Pathfinder*, which Fuller uses in her essay to mean "women's special element"

gradation: step, degree, or stage in a series that changes gradually

incarnated: personified; embodied in human form

Minerva: Roman goddess of wisdom

Muse: ancient goddess who embodied the arts

***Pathfinder*:** New York weekly newspaper run by journalist Parke Godwin that lasted only three months in 1843

physiologists: those who study the functioning of organisms

placid: calm; peaceful

Document Analysis

Margaret Fuller was one of the first proponents of women's rights in the United States, advocating for full equality between men and women. In 1843, she wrote one of the first feminist tracts in United States history when she penned "The Great Lawsuit: Man versus Men, Woman versus Women." This essay appeared in the *Dial*, a transcendentalist magazine that she had cofounded and then edited for two years between 1840 and 1842. The essay's main point is that men and women are equal and should have equal opportunities to develop to their full potential, especially in a spiritual way. She dismissed the concept of separate spheres for women and men that was the current wisdom in America at the time. She also believed that both men and women had characteristics of the other sex within them. Given her intense and classical education, Fuller's work was meant to be read by others as educated as she was. She uses a complex rhetorical style, with many voices and a somewhat disjointed and wandering style that is reminiscent of one of her favorite authors, Johann Wolfgang von Goethe. Within this essay, allegories and allusions to classical works and personalities are common, which was in keeping with the romantic style that was prevalent at the time. Fuller's writing style made her work less accessible to the general public, but it nonetheless set the stage for both her follow-up work, *Woman in the Nineteenth Century*, and the feminist movement that emerged later in the nineteenth century.

The excerpt chosen here is the latter part and ending of Fuller's essay. In previous sections, she discusses aspects of abolition and differing types of marriages, among other issues. She begins this section by explaining what she views as the "two aspects of women's nature," Minerva and Muse. Fuller uses Minerva, the Roman goddess of wisdom, to represent the wisdom and intellect of women and Muse to refer to women's more spiritual and intuitive side, as personified by the ancient muses of Greece and Rome. Fuller thinks that women's Muse side has been overemphasized and that women can achieve more harmony and autonomy if they also concentrate on developing their Minerva side. Fuller's essay also demonstrates her wide reading, as she mentions a recent article in the New York *Pathfinder*, a weekly magazine. Fuller feels that the author of the article is referring to the Muse side of women, while the Minerva, or intellectual, side is portrayed more by quoted words of the poet William Wordsworth. Not content with only classical allusions to Minerva and the Muse, Fuller refers to these more current writings to further her point.

She then goes on to explain more fully the Muse side of women. In this, she celebrates women's intuitive, spiritual, and "electrical" sides. She represents women as aligned more fully with the natural rhythms of nature and as a source of inspiration for art, rather than the interpreter of art, the artist. The Muse is women's more natural role, and represents this "especially feminine element, spoken of as Femality"—another reference to the New York *Pathfinder*, which had published two articles on the subject. As soon as she has made this point, however, she makes the next point that this feminine element is not the unique domain of women alone, and it is not necessarily natural that it should be "incarnated pure"; rather, she asserts, "masculine energy" can also be combined with this feminine element.

Here, Fuller begins to make her case that masculine and feminine are not completely separate and exclusive. Rather, they ebb and flow into each other, and just as women can have masculine attributes, so too can men employ feminine characteristics. This is Fuller's expression of the "great radical dualism" that exists between male and female. She then chides "physiologists" who try and reinforce the supposedly separate and exclusive characteristics of men and women by scientific methods. Such criticism betrays her leanings toward romanticism, which opposes some of the more scientific rationalizations that were widespread during the Enlightenment in the seventeenth and eighteenth centuries. She insists that "nature provides exceptions to every rule." Fuller then turns to history for examples of women who have acted with more masculine actions, such as participating in wars, and of men who exhibit a more feminine side, such as a man who shows "maternal love" for a child. She also cites classical mythology with her reference to Hercules, a hero known for his masculine strength, and his penchant for spinning, a particular female occupation. She goes even further by predicting that soon there will be a female scientist capable of great breakthroughs, along the lines of Isaac Newton, who had discovered the law of gravity. She gives another example, predicting that a man may soon become a "Syren," or siren, a mythical female sea nymph who called to sailors and was blamed for causing them to shipwreck on the coast. Fuller's view is that this fluidity of gender identity was accepted by the ancients: "Man partakes of the feminine in the Apollo, woman of the Masculine as Minerva."

Fuller then calls for action to allow the soul to develop in the absence of gender, which is a key element of transcendentalism. Every individual has access to the "Oversoul," which has no gender or race. Fuller makes references to the classical Greek and Roman mythology when she mentions Jove's birth by his mother, Rhea, and the birth of Jove's daughter, Pallas (Athena; equated with Minerva), who sprang forth from his head fully grown and armed for combat. Jove, or Jupiter, was king of the Roman gods and was known as Zeus to the ancient Greeks. Fuller's reference to a child born of a male helps again to reinforce her argument for gender fluidity.

Fuller next explains her views on relationships and how people are best prepared to enter into them. In Fuller's perspective, men and women need to give themselves time apart and alone to develop their own utmost potentials. In essence, people must get to know themselves first before they can enter into any kind of union with another. In fact, she states this plainly when she says, "Union is only possible to those who are units." She wants people, especially women, to take time to develop their own thoughts and opinions and above all to cultivate independence and autonomy over dependence on another person. She mentions the "Indian girl," which is a reference to a story she told earlier in the essay. A young American Indian woman had made the decision not to marry, told her tribe that she was betrothed to the sun, and led a solitary and independent life "sustained by her own exertions."

Fuller is clear that men will probably not help with this kind of personal development for women, because they "are under the slavery of habit." To illustrate her point, she first sets the scene with a father and his daughter. Fuller felt men have the same capacity for "maternal love" as women do; she also had her own experience with a father who pushed her to develop her intellect, and she may have been drawing on her own personal experience throughout this segment. Although she has already posited that men cannot or will not assist in women's self-development, she then states that if men could ever be convinced to help, it would be the result of a man having a daughter. Here she also casually alludes to an epic poem by Robert Southey called *The Curse of Kehama*, which he wrote in 1810. Southey cited his inability to sleep at a boarding school as his inspiration for this poem, which Fuller refers to when she states, "When lo, the dream was rudely broken."

She changes her rhetorical style here and moves into a direct dialogue conversation between a husband and wife about the future of their daughter. The husband makes the point quite clearly that he does not want his daughter too educated ("brought too forward") because "superior women" have trouble finding husbands. His wife responds in defense of educating their daughter, as he should want this regardless of whether or not she eventually marries. In response to this, he invokes the separate-spheres argument, saying that he wants her to have a "sphere and a home" while also having someone to protect her after he dies, thus rather obviously making the assumption that she will not be able to protect herself.

Fuller relates that this exchange left a "deep impression" on her. She notes that this man, if he were looking at the other side of the argument and placing himself in the role of potential husband and not father, may have viewed things differently and allowed his daughter to pursue her education. Again she invokes a classical reference when she says that the father would have been "much more likely to repeat the tale of Alcibiades," who was a Greek general who stole "phials," or cups, made of gold and silver from his friend Anytus during a dinner. Although Anytus's other guests criticized him for allowing Alcibiades to treat him with such contempt, Anytus loved Alcibiades so much that he forgave him.

It was clear to Fuller that because men do not "look at both sides," women cannot rely on them to enable their intellectual development. She urges women instead to "retire within themselves" and go on a voyage of self-discovery. She believes this will be as a rebirth for them, and they will be ready to go forth into the world and express a new and unique creativity. They will be able to turn "dross to gold" and will be "rich and free" from this experience. In essence, she is saying that the world will be a better place for all if women do this.

She reinforces her argument by saying that women should be granted "the armor and the javelin" in order to protect themselves from the outside world. Such protection would also shield them from the "press of other minds" so that women could be left alone to "meditate in virgin loneliness." Fuller felt that women need to do this before they marry, if they marry at all. She then tries to align this behavior, which is somewhat unorthodox, at least for America in the nineteenth century, with a most natural state. She is sure that this idea will reappear, as it has in the past when personified by Muse, or Ceres, who is the Roman goddess of the harvest (the "Earth-Spirit").

At this point, Fuller veers into territory that is somewhat familiar, at least to her. She illustrates her point this time using a work by Goethe, whom she considered one of the great minds of his time.. Goethe was a German writer, scientist, politician who lived between 1749 and 1832, so his death was a fairly recent event when Fuller was writing. He was one of the earliest writers of the romantic period, which influenced the American transcendentalists to a great degree. Fuller had published her translation of *Eckermann's Conversations with Goethe* in 1839, and she was quite conversant in his life and his writings, some of which she had translated into English.

Fuller was aware that many knew of her admiration for Goethe, and she states she knows that she may "tire" her readers with her "Goethean illustrations." She chooses one of Goethe's masterpieces, *Wilhelm Meister's Apprenticeship*, as her example. Originally published in German in 1795–96, the novel was translated into English in 1824. Fuller finds the book's female characters compelling because they are strong and self-developed. It is for this reason that, even if Goethe's name may "nauseate" the reader, she feels it is vital to delve into his writing to bolster her own argument.

Wilhelm Meister's Apprenticeship follows the protagonist, Wilhelm, as he progresses through his life. There are numerous female characters in Goethe's novel, the first being Mariana, an actress with whom Wilhelm falls in love but whom he eventually leaves when he finds out she is seeing another man. Fuller feels that with each female character Wilhelm meets, he encounters women "of more and more character"—in other words, women who are more self-realized or self-actualized than the last. She views Mariana as the least well-developed character and Macaria as the most fully developed. To Fuller, Macaria represents the Minerva, or intellectual, side of women. Another female character, Mignon, represents the Muse side of women, or the intuitive and emotional side. Mignon is an abused young woman who was part of an acrobatic troupe, which she left to accompany Wilhelm on his travels.

Fuller is intrigued that Goethe presents these women as fully formed individuals, and so they appear to her as "unrelated." They do have relationships with people and exist within them, but they are not dependent on or "restrained" by a man. She mentions three other of Goethe's characters: Theresa, Natalia, and Natalia's aunt, the "Fair Saint." Theresa is an excellent "economist," which in this case means the keeper of a household and its accounts. At the end of the book, Wilhelm actually marries Natalia, who saved him from bandits earlier in the book.

Fuller is impressed that each of these female characters is not bound by their chosen paths in life. They are free to develop as they will, as nothing is "enforced or conventional." She notes that Mignon and Theresa wear male clothing, which is hardly conventional, but she considers it "graceful." On the other hand, Macaria does not move from a chair, and the Fair Saint has a phobia about dust appearing on her clothing. Each of these women has different thoughts, different opinions, and different ideas of how to live her life. Fuller views this as being "natural and free," allowing for the harmony of nature to arise because the women have followed paths of "Truth and Love," which have led to their freedom. For Fuller, Goethe's women act as role models for how American women could find their own freedom, especially when she states that "new individualities shall be developed in the actual world."

Leaving Goethe, Fuller turns her attention again to the topic of marriage, which she discussed earlier in her essay at some length. Here she quotes an anonymous "profound thinker" as saying that a married woman cannot represent the concept of "woman," as she is not an individual herself but rather property of her husband; therefore, only a single and virginal woman can represent women conceptually. Of course, Fuller disagrees with this representation, although she herself was single at the time she was writing this essay. Fuller believes that it is this concept of a husband owning a wife that is the "very fault of marriage." Instead, she argues that a marriage should be the union of two autonomous individuals who come together to form a whole.

Fuller reinforces this by stating that a self-developed, or "self-centred," woman would not live her life through the lens of a relationship, in this case a marriage. She would not let herself and her identity be subsumed by another, in this case her husband. Fuller views it as a "vulgar error" that people could view women through this lens only. Women have more ability and capacity to show "Truth and Love in their universal energy." This refers back to the theme of a more spiritual soul that exists without gender. To make her point even clearer, Fuller suggests that if women claim for themselves this self-development and autonomy, they could be at once both virgins and mothers, like the Virgin Mary. Fuller previously quoted in this essay a dedication of the tragedy *Adelchi* by Italian poet

Alessandro Manzoni, published in 1822. In this dedication, Manzoni refers to his wife as having a "conjugal affections and maternal wisdom" while at the same time preserving "a virgin mind."

Fuller concludes by wondering aloud when such a woman will appear to act as a role model for others to follow this path. She suggests two names for such a woman, the first being Victoria, which has the dual significance of meaning a triumphant and powerful woman and being the name of the new British queen, who ascended to the throne in 1837. The other name she suggests is Virginia, which may refer back to her discussion of the virgin mind. In the end, she decides she cannot predict a name, as she feels that this woman "must teach us to give her the fitting name."

Essential Themes

Margaret Fuller was a pioneer in American feminist thought. While others were advocating solely for women's education, and therefore remaining within the accepted social roles of the time, Fuller was adamant that women should settle for nothing less than full equality with men. Her belief that women needed to become self-realized and develop fully within themselves was a departure from the norms of the time. Most women writers respected the concept of separate spheres for men and women that had developed through the so-called cult of true womanhood or cult of domesticity, which idealized women's role in the domestic or private sphere. Fuller did not believe this, ascribing instead to American transcendentalist beliefs that each person could have a direct relationship with God, as well as with nature, and should aspire to cultivate their own soul. To Fuller, this translated to a soul without a sex, and so each individual person, male or female, was capable of the same level of self-discovery and spiritual development.

From this egalitarian starting point, it easily follows that women should have equal access to education and to employment. Fuller believed that each woman should be allowed to live her life without dependence on a husband. She also believed strongly that women have an intellectual side, represented by Minerva, and a more intuitive, natural, and emotional side, represented by Muse, and that cultivating the Minerva side would balance the Muse side. Further, she believed that both men and women have elements of each of these sides to their personality, so that there is no one who is purely male or purely female in existence. Fuller regarded masculinity and femininity as fluid concepts that each gender employs and enjoys from time to time. In this, Fuller was less like her contemporaries and more like her counterparts in the twentieth century, who fought for the vote early in the century and for equal rights in the 1960s and 1970s. Indeed, she and her work were only rediscovered when women's history became an accepted branch of history. She was a woman ahead of her time. As a result, and because of her highly erudite writing style that references many classical and literary works, her writing was not as popular as that of other writers of the day. The reaction to this essay was quite favorable within her circle of transcendentalist friends, which included Ralph Waldo Emerson, but she wanted it to have a wider audience. She expanded it to a book-length work and published it two years later as *Woman in the Nineteenth Century*. The book retains the essay's complex rhetorical style, however, and Fuller recognized that it may still have a limited readership.

Fuller's importance as an American intellectual and feminist writer faded after her premature death in 1850. The Civil War focused American attention squarely on race rather than gender, and American feminists had to wait until the second half of the nineteenth century for their concerns to come to the forefront of public discourse in the United States. When women's rights resurfaced as an issue, many of the activists looked back to Fuller for inspiration. She was in many ways to the United States what Wollstonecraft was to Britain—the first truly feminist voice.

Lee Tunstall, PhD

Bibliography

Capper, Charles. *Margaret Fuller: An American Romantic Life*. Vol 2. Oxford: Oxford UP, 2007. Print.

Goethe, Johann Wolfgang von. *Wilhelm Meister's Apprenticeship*. Trans. R. Dillon Boylan. London: Bell, 1886. Print.

MargaretFuller.org. Unitarian Universalist Women & Religion, 2010. Web. 10 April 2013.

Mehren, Joan von. *Minerva and the Muse: A Life of Margaret Fuller.* Amherst: U of Massachusetts P, 1994. Print.

Murray, Meg McGavran. *Margaret Fuller, Wandering Pilgrim*. Athens: U of Georgia P, 2008. Print.

Myerson, Joel, ed. *Transcendentalism: A Reader*. New York: Oxford UP, 2000. Print.

Steele, Jeffrey. *Transfiguring America: Myth, Ideology, and Mourning in Margaret Fuller's Writing*. Columbia: U of Missouri P, 2001. Print.

Wayne, Tiffany K. *Woman Thinking: Feminism and Transcendentalism in Nineteenth-Century America*. Lanham: Lexington, 2005. Print.

Additional Reading

Bailey, Brigitte Viens, Katheryn P. Wright, and Conrad Edick. *New England in the World: Margaret Fuller and Her Circles*. Durham: U of New Hampshire P, 2013. Print.

Dickenson, Donna. *Margaret Fuller: Writing a Woman's Life*. New York: St. Martin's, 1993. Print.

Gura, Philip F. *American Transcendentalism: A History*. New York: Hill, 2007. Print

Gustafson, Sandra M. "Choosing a Medium: Margaret Fuller and the Forms of Sentiment." *American Quarterly* 47.1 (1995): 34–65. Print.

Marshall, Megan. *Margaret Fuller: A New American Life*. Boston: Houghton, 2013. Print.

Slater, Abby. *In Search of Margaret Fuller.* New York: Delacorte, 1978. Print.

LESSON PLAN: **Women's Nature**

Students analyze an essay by Margaret Fuller to understand the antebellum women's movement and its relationship to transcendental philosophy.

Learning Objectives

Consider the multiple perspectives of early advocates for women's rights; examine the influence of transcendentalism on Fuller's ideas about women and society; hypothesize the influence of the antebellum women's movement on later women's movements.

Materials: Margaret Fuller, "The Great Lawsuit: Man versus Men, Woman versus Women" (1843).

Overview Questions

What similarities and differences does Fuller observe between men and women? According to Fuller, why haven't women achieved full equality? What does she consider "female nature" and how does she think it should be cultivated? How might Fuller's account of masculinity and femininity have influenced other reformers to reconsider gender relations?

Step 1: Comprehension Questions

What is the "radical dualism" that Fuller describes between men and women? Does she think this duality fully exists? Why or why not?

- **Activity:** Have students read aloud paragraph four and describe this dualism in their own words. Have students locate passages in which Fuller upholds or contests this dichotomy, especially in paragraphs five through seven of the excerpt. Ask students to explain how Fuller views gender differences, citing passages in the text.

Step 2: Comprehension Questions

What problems with marriage does Fuller observe? In Fuller's view, why do such problems hinder women's development? What does she think an ideal marriage should be?

- **Activity:** Pair students to locate references to marriage, union, and relations, and list the problems and solutions Fuller proposes. Have students discuss what Fuller thinks marriage should be like and why she finds this ideal lacking in her day. Call on pairs to share their findings with the class.

Step 3: Context Questions

In what ways do Fuller's views of the individual, nature, and the soul reflect transcendentalist ideals? How might her connections to transcendentalism have shaped her views of gender?

- **Activity:** Have students select passages that reveal Fuller's grounding in transcendentalism. Call on students to read the passage aloud, restate it in their own words, and explain how it reflects transcendentalist thinking.

Step 4: Historical Connections Questions

What similarities might exist between Fuller's thinking and the arguments of twentieth-century feminists? How are the concerns of later feminists different from Fuller's? How might Fuller's text have advanced feminist thinking in her own period and beyond?

- **Activity:** Discuss the ways students think Fuller may have influenced later feminists. Have students write a paragraph explaining whether they think Fuller's account of women's nature remains relevant today, citing passages to support their claims.

Step 5: Response Paper

Word length and additional requirements set by Instructor. Students answer the research question in the *Overview Questions.* Students state a thesis and use as evidence passages from the primary source document as well as support from the secondary historical documents assigned in the lesson.

Manifesto of Robert Owen

Date: December 1844
Author: Owen, Robert
Genre: essay

"But thus to rebase, reorganize, reclassify and reconstruct society, it is also necessary that the character of every one . . . should be, from birth, recreated . . . thus gradually, without violence or injustice or misery of any kind, a terrestrial paradise may be formed for all."

Summary Overview

Robert Owen spent his life trying to raise the standard of living for all people. Initially focusing on those who had the greatest need, the poor and working class, he later broadened his goal to that of a global utopia. The technological changes occurring throughout the world gave him hope that the natural educational system he envisioned would begin to take root. In addition, the rational scientific process was becoming more firmly established as a guiding philosophy in the Western world. Owen had great hope that this was the precursor to a full understanding of the role community played within human development, leading to the final transformation of society. In writing his manifesto, Owen offered guidance for transforming the entire world. For America, which had just chosen the expansionist candidate James K. Polk for president, Owen presented a vision that went beyond just annexing the territory west of the Louisiana Purchase; instead, he thought the United States should incorporate all of North and South America.

Defining Moment

At various times in the past, individuals or groups have firmly believed that dramatic changes were about to happen. During the first half of the nineteenth century, change seemed to be in the air. Several religious groups anticipated that the world would end quite soon and made radical preparations for that event. Other new religious and spiritual groups formed, including the growth of the spiritualist movement in the 1840s. Technology was changing the way people saw themselves and the world. Railroads, the telegraph, and photography changed what was considered possible. New and larger telescopes and new ideas in physics, chemistry, geology, and biology were opening new avenues of thought and inquiry, and the biblical story of creation was starting to be more widely questioned. For Owen, as for many others, all of these things were signs that change was imminent. While there were many different theories as to where this change was going, Owen believed that one did not have to wait upon some outside factor to direct the change. Some thirty years prior to writing his manifesto, Owen had developed his understanding of humanity. For him, now was the time to implement the steps necessary to create a positive change for the entire world. Thus, as the "new era in human existence" was about to begin, Owen wanted to ensure that it would be "based on principles of nature" that would create a world of "knowledge, goodness, and happiness."

All of this was possible, in Owen's mind, because rational scientific thought was becoming the primary way to search for answers to the problems confronting humanity. Owen had been a rationalist for decades. He believed that most of the prevailing social structure, including religion, was an impediment to a true understanding of the world. Just as the natural laws were being discovered through the development of the physical sciences and technological developments were being made based on this knowledge, Owen asserted that natural laws of human development had been discovered (by him) and that now was the time to develop human society based on this knowledge. Most of the Western Hemisphere had relatively recently become independent from European domination, so this was the logical place for the transition to begin. The United States was in the process of further expanding its borders and flexing its power. For Owen, it was only a small step from the Monroe Doctrine and President Polk's expansionist policies to the path that Owen set forth in the second of his three papers.

Author Biography

Robert Owen was born May 14, 1771, in the Welsh town of Newtown, the sixth child of Robert Owen and Anne Williams. Owen was bright and was a teacher's assistant for a few years while still in school. Outside school, he avidly studied religion, arriving at the conclusion that a secular worldview was the correct one. When he was about ten, Owen was sent to London to apprentice in a drapery shop. After learning the trade, Owen eventually moved to Manchester, where he established his own business when he was eighteen.

Desiring a larger venue in which to try his innovative ideas, Owen offered his managerial services to the owner of a large textile mill when he was only twenty-one and convinced the owner to pay him a substantial salary and a share of the profits. After three years, having been successful in increasing the mill's profits, Owen left to establish a wholesale operation, which was also a success. While in Manchester, Owen became a member of the Manchester Literary and Philosophical Society, which broadened his exposure to others interested in industrial reform and current philosophical ideas. In addition, he worked with the Manchester Board of Health to improve conditions for workers and helped establish Manchester College.

In 1799, Owen made the decision to leave Manchester and purchase Scotland's largest mill, located in New Lanark. He married the former mill owner's daughter, Caroline Dale, with whom he had seven children who survived infancy. At New Lanark, Owen focused on the conditions of the workers rather than on profits, taking his initial steps toward instituting a rational, secular socialist system. He developed schools and an innovative curriculum for young children instead of working them in his mills. He gained higher output and a superior product from satisfied, skilled workers, earning Owen exceptional profits.

During this time, Owen began to publish his views on human nature, economics, and education, through which he tried to transform the lives of the working poor. In 1825, Owen purchased a town in Indiana and created New Harmony to try out his ideals in a new setting. However, the artificial community failed within just a few years. Returning to Great Britain, Owen continued to write on what came to be called socialism. He started cooperative stores and workers' unions during the late 1820s and early 1830s. Others started communities based on his theories. He focused on education as the key to changing the world, as well as people's lives. Through this educational process, he believed that eventually a cooperative system would replace capitalism. He continued to publicize his ideas until just before his death on November 17, 1858.

HISTORICAL DOCUMENT

MANIFESTO OF ROBERT OWEN,
Or public papers, numbers 1, 2, and 3, addressed to all governments and people who desire to become civilized, to aid in the adoption of measures to lay a solid foundation for the permanent peace of the world, the progressive intelligence, morality, and happiness of all individuals, and to give right direction to the illimitable mechanical, chemical, and other scientific productive power, in order that it may become the slave and servant of humanity, instead of being made, as at present, the tyrant master and cruel oppressor of the most industrious portion of society.

It is evident, from the signs of the times, especially from the illimitable progress and power of new scientific productive power and the rapid increase of real knowledge among the working classes, that a new era in human existence is about to commence, and that the ignorance, division, poverty, wars, crime, and misery, which the system of society hitherto alone in practice has inflicted upon nations and people, is now in due order of nature about to terminate, and to be superseded by another based on principles of nature, which will ever lead to knowledge, goodness, and happiness.

Fortunately for the human race, it has been discovered that the base of all past society, under every variety of form and name, has been a few unchanging errors of inexperienced imagination—errors which have ever destroyed the rational faculties of man, and made the attainment of virtue and happiness by any portion of the human race impossible.

To enable mankind to become civilized, permanently prosperous, virtuous, rational, and progressively happy, these errors of imagination must be at once and forever abandoned. They must be abandoned, because they can never produce, under any change of form or name, aught except ignorance, falsehood, division, wars, contentions, crime and misery.

It is, then, the immediate and highest interest of one and all over the earth that these errors should be made manifest, and their lamentable, unchanging evil effects, laid bare to all nations and people.

This course of action is necessary to accomplish the well being and happiness of man; for these errors are, from the beginning of time, unsupported by a single fact, and are directly opposed by every known fact; and their unchanging influence on humanity is to create and perpetuate falsehood, deceit, moral cowardice, contention, wars, crimes, and misery; and to make man, through every succeeding generation, probably the most irrational animal upon the earth,—a being possessed of all the means of high physical, mental, and moral attainments, and progressive rational enjoyment around him; yet who is, through demonstrable fundamental errors, continually applying these means of permanent and general happiness, to inflict misery on himself and his race.

To those who reflect, it is now evident, that, contrary to the inexperienced imaginations of our ancestors, individual man does not possess the power to create, at his birth, the smallest part of his physical, mental, or moral organization; or afterwards of his sentiments, or opinions, or feelings; or of his conduct, except through his original organization and the subsequent influence upon it of external circumstances; both of which powers have been formed for him, by mysterious means, beyond his knowledge or control.

And yet, hitherto, the population of the world has been governed under institutions based on the very opposite impressions early made on the inexperienced imaginations of men, made before men know how to observe and accurately investigate facts. They imagined that all individuals have been created with an internal independent power to form their own physical, mental, and moral capacity, and, by a supposed will of their own creating, to decide upon their own opinions, and, at their pleasure, change their belief or disbelief in any of them; and in like manner form and change their own feelings, affections, and conduct. In consequence of these erroneous impressions respecting the laws of humanity, certain portions of the human race have made their ignorant and most irrational notions standard of perfectibility. These portions, at various times and places, having accidentally acquired power over their fellows, have made this weaker portion responsible to them, the stronger, for what they should feel, think, and do; and have, through all past ages, endeavored to force them to believe, feel, and act according to their most ignorant and superstitious previously taught fanciful imaginations. These ignorant and superstitious men have assumed also to govern the weaker part physically, mentally, and morally, up to this period, in the most oppressive, unjust, cruel, and irrational manner, in accordance with these fundamental errors, by force and fraud, the only mode of governing which is practicable while these errors are maintained. And to effect this object, they have been compelled to make laws in accordance with those errors, in direct opposition to nature's laws. Now the adoption of nature's laws, when fully comprehended and rightly applied, would insure the rationality of the human race, and their permanent happiness through all succeeding generations.

These, then, are the fundamental errors on which alone, to this period, the characters of men have been formed, and the various governments have been instituted; and hence the universality of the irrational conduct of the human race.

Thence the present heterogeneous mass of error, by which the human character is now formed, and the nations of the earth are now governed.

Thence the irrational classifications, divisions, contests, and wars among all nations, and the strange, incongruous, and immoral institutions, which have been established throughout the world; institutions founded often by well meaning men, with the professed view to produce knowledge, health, riches, unity, justice, charity, and kindness among men; but which institutions have never yet succeeded to produce these blessings in a single instance to any population.

To civilize the human race, to make all permanently prosperous, truly virtuous, rational and happy, these fundamental errors must be now openly abandoned by all governments and people, society must be *rebased* on demonstrably true and unchanging laws of nature. It must be *reorganized* on a knowledge of those laws, and in a spirit of universal charity, which can alone emanate from a knowledge of those laws.

It must be *reclassified* according to age, in accordance with those laws.

It must be *reconstructed* in all its parts, to be in unison with the principles upon which this new order of society is based, that it may form one consistent whole, and at all times and under all circumstances work harmoniously, from the centre, which will be *every where*, to the circumference, which will, in every case, extend from each centre to the uttermost parts of the earth; ultimately forming, among all men, one language, one code of simplified laws, one interest, one currency, one spirit, and one general superior mind, and conduct over the globe.

But thus to *rebase, reorganize, reclassify* and *reconstruct* society, it is also necessary that the character of every one, as soon as practicable, should be, from birth, *recreated* through a new creation and arrangement of superior external circumstances, and a new spirit thereby within it of charity, kindness, and love. Thus, through a correct knowledge of the eternal laws of humanity, and how to apply them to practice, this divine spirit may be made to pervade the whole being in all his feelings, thoughts and conduct, not only to all his fellow men, but, as far as compatible with the happiness of the human race, to all sensitive life upon the earth. And thus gradually, without violence or injustice or misery of any kind, a terrestrial paradise may be formed for all; contention of every kind may be made to cease among men and nations, and sound practical wisdom, united with activity of mind and body, may be made to pervade the human race, and thus insure permanent, high, rational enjoyment to every son of man.

The materials to effect this change over the earth wherever men need to live, now superabound; and it is the interest of all, without one exception, that this change should be *now* made. The means by which it shall be accomplished, in peace and order, although the greatest of all changes which have yet been experienced by the human race, shall be explained, in extended principles and practice, in public papers No. 2 and 3, and subsequent publications.

ROBERT OWEN.
December 16, 1844.

***

P.S. These papers are intended for public documents for the immediate and future benefit of all without exception. They have no reference to party of any description, but are now published with the view to the general, permanent and substantial advantage of every individual; it is therefore requested that the editors of all newspapers and periodicals will give circulation to them at their earliest convenience.

***

Public paper No. 2, addressed to the leading men of all parties in the United States, who possess extensive experience in the general business of society.

You have a country which possesses the power, and contains the most ample means, now to insure a high progressive prosperity to every one within the Union.

Your position, therefore, at this crisis, is one of great interest to yourselves, your country, the world, and to all future ages.

By your union upon new and neutral ground, you may now lay a solid foundation for the most powerful and splendid empire, without war or conquest, that the world has known.

The path is now open and straight before you; it requires only that you should enter it fearlessly and boldly, and to pursue it with moral courage, without turning to the right or the left for any petty or party consideration, come from whatever quarter it may.

To found and sustain a great empire in peace with all the world, and to continue to progress without stay or temporary retrogression, six things are required, all of which you possess, or soon may easily attain. These are, 1st, a strong position upon the globe, with sufficient extent and quality of domain to support, in permanent comfort, a numerous population. 2d. The means to well form the character of the whole of this population. 3d. The means to beneficially occupy or exercise physically and mentally all, at all times, according to age, to produce wealth, and, at the same time, keep them in the best state of physical and mental health. 4th. To secure to all an ample supply, at all times, of those things which experience shall prove to be the best for the permanent well being and happiness of humanity, through every period of the life of each individual. 5th. The means to replace, without disorder of any kind, all the inferior external circumstances of human creation, with others, all useful, beneficial, and highly superior; and lastly, the means of extending a federative union, without limit, over the western hemisphere.

The United States now possess these advantages, or the means to acquire them, to the full extent that can be desired. It is for the leading men of the present day to unite these means, and to combine them into a scientific new arrangement of society, to secure these benefits to themselves, to their country, and to the world.

To proceed aright in this new path, it is necessary to consider what is now the permanent interest of every individual; for the permanent interest of one will be found to be the true interest of all. This interest is to become an independent subject in a powerful, well governed, and respected country; to have all his faculties well cultivated from birth; and to be made physically, mentally, morally, and practically, the best subject, in these respects, that his original organization and the knowledge and means of society will admit; to be surrounded from birth with superior animate and inanimate circumstances only, to the entire exclusion of all that experience has proved to be inferior; to be well and beneficially occupied through life, without over-anxiety for the present or future, or regrets for the past. That there should be in the world the fewest variety of languages, religions, governments, laws, or currencies, or institutions creating prejudices and obstacles to his progress in the attainment of knowledge, or to his traveling into every quarter or district of the world. That all other human beings should be as well trained, educated, and placed as himself; and that he should find himself everywhere surrounded by society, well informed, with superior habits, manners, and conduct; with the pure spirit of charity, confidence, kindness, and love, pervading the heart and mind of every one; each possessing the desire and means to promote, cordially and heartily, the well being, well doing, and permanent happiness of all others. Society has now, for the first time in the life of man, attained the period when these results, to a considerable extent, may be gradually obtained, progressed in, and secured in unceasing growing perfection through all future generations.

The circumstances in which the United States now exist are by far the most favorable for the *commencement* of this great and glorious change in the condition of humanity.

These States possess within themselves land, minerals, materials of every description, mechanical and chemical power, inventive faculties, skill and manual power more than sufficient to commence, with certainty of success, this new, superior, and rational state of human existence.

GLOSSARY

errors of imagination: Owen's term for the ideas that undergirded the structure of society throughout history

federative union: a group formed for the mutual benefit and protection of its members; in this case, the United States

illimitable: unlimited, not being able to be limited

influence upon it of external circumstances: things that happen during life, such as injury or good nutrition, that affect a person's physical or mental abilities

manifesto: a public declaration of principles or intent

original organization: Owen's term for the body and the limitations that people have because of their physical size or mental abilities

superabound: plentiful to an extreme degree

Document Analysis

Robert Owen was a great believer in human ability as guided by rational thought. In his mind, the problems of the world could be overcome through the proper education of all people. The result would be a utopia, with morality and happiness prevailing in each person's life. Increased personal well-being would create harmony among all human organizations, although Owen also thought it would be more rational to have fewer divisions between people by eliminating most languages, religions, nations, and any other factors that have historically divided groups from one another. In order to do this, he believed, the Eastern and Western Hemispheres should unite into one political unit. By sharing in all things, the human race could overcome the "fundamental errors" that had plagued it from antiquity. With the advances that were being made in the early nineteenth century, Owen believed the time was right to undertake this ambitious agenda.

Over a four-day period, Owen submitted three papers for publication. The excerpt contains the entire first paper, about the first two-thirds of the second, and none of the third. The first paper is a general call for the transformation of people and society, while the second deals with the United States and the Western Hemisphere. The third paper addresses the Eastern Hemisphere and Great Britain, with the same goal and virtually the same approach as in the second paper. Owen thought that the steps taken to unify the Eastern Hemisphere would have to be slightly different, given its strong heritages, which would need to be overcome. If changes in the East were not possible, Owen believed the Western Hemisphere could implement the system and be self-sufficient. Ideally, however, the United States and Great Britain would lead their respective hemispheres into the utopian future that Owen envisioned.

The general introduction to all three papers presents an overview of Owen's goals for the near future, as well as a very brief summary of the current situation. It is clear that Owen thought the situation in 1844 was far from ideal. He implies that the world is not civilized by writing that his papers are for "people who desire to become civilized." In addition, he states that technology is the "tyrant master and cruel oppressor of . . . society."

However, he does give hope. If the "governments and people" listen to and act on Owen's propositions, then they will obtain "permanent peace" as well as increase everyone's intelligence, ethics, and happiness. Following the steps he prescribes will ensure technology's shift from tyrant to "slave and servant of humanity." Owen offers the world a chance to become a brilliant success rather than a total failure—if people listen to and act on his advice. He then goes on to outline why this is in the interest of the world at large.

In most of his written works, Owen does not shy away from taking ownership of his ideas, but in this first paper, he does not identify himself as the source of the theories that undergird his discussion. Although any who knew him would recognize his line of thought, by not stating that this theory of human development is one that he has created, he is trying to make it a more universal statement of truth. Thus, when he states that a discovery has been made that identifies the "few unchanging errors of inexperienced imagination" that plague every society, he makes it sound as if this were a fact—which, in his mind, it probably was. Owen's statement on the cause of all societal problems is made in a way that assumes rational thinkers agree with him. The same is true of the solution that he gives: doing away with these "errors of imagination." This, for Owen, would solve all problems. He is correct in saying that the things that have led in the past to "ignorance, falsehood, division, wars, contentions, crime and misery" will continue to do so in the future; however, he is not correct in his implication that his approach was generally understood as the best way to avoid these things.

Having identified the unfortunate outcomes of the past, Owen seeks to have as many people as possible understand what happened in order to do better in the future. Owen continues to argue, without giving specifics, that people live and structure society by accident or chance, rather than by a sound philosophical or scientific understanding. In the fifth paragraph of this first paper, he continues to list the failures of society. He emphasizes the irrationality of expecting the foundation of a flawed society to produce an idyllic result in the future.

It is only in the sixth paragraph that Owen presents a statement of past errors and, implicitly, the correct understanding that should be used in the future. The basic error Owen sees is the societal belief that anyone can be a self-made man. He argues that at birth, a child "does not possess the power to create" anything. The resources for physical development come from the outside, as does the stimulation for intellectual and moral development. The same, he asserts, is true as the child grows. The commonly accepted ideal of the individual who personally develops his own talents and then builds his own success is wrong, according to Owen. The only thing that a person can claim—having been done "by mysterious means"—is the body and mind with which one was born, or accidents that might have occurred. By implication, Owen asserts that the development of the person takes place based on external factors and forces that most would say were outside the control of the individual. Thus, philosophically Owen falls into the school of thought that sees people as innately neither good nor bad but as blank tablets (tabula rasa) upon which life's experiences create the individual's outlook on and understanding of the world. Although Owen saw this understanding of the world and human development as a major breakthrough, he was not the first or the only one to believe that human beings are a reflection of the environment in which they are raised.

Given this understanding of human development, in his manifesto, Owen emphasizes his four *R*s: rebase, reorganize, reclassify, and reconstruct. From his point of view, because people absorb what is around them, he advocates that "society must be *rebased* on demonstrably true and unchanging laws of nature." In Owen's mind, these laws of nature were the things that led to a life and society full of happiness, goodness, harmony, and a plentiful supply of material things. This was the state of being that should exist; thus, in his opinion, the conditions that produce it were the laws of nature. He understood this to be the truth, and with the greater acceptance of rational scientific changes, he believed it was then possible for everyone to understand and accept them as well.

Although he does not spell it out as much in this paper as in some of his other writings, Owen believed that society must be reorganized for the implementation of these "laws of nature." From his time at New Lanark, he understood that education was the key. There, he had implemented an educational process from birth through the teen years. In his ideal society, the educational process would last at least through the twenties, with individuals mixing work and education during the last half of the process. Thus, he believed that society needed to be reorganized so that either babies would be sent to school each day or parents would be trained to begin the educational process at home. The entire educational process would be a positive reinforcing experience, one that took place "in a spirit of universal charity."

Because of his extended educational process, Owen believed in what he called the need to "reclassify" people as they matured. The most obvious aspect of this is the change in the formal educational process as children get older and have a better understanding of the various subjects. His model used five-year cohorts, or groups, so that every five years, the child or young adult would move to a new level with a new educational emphasis. Owen believed that in his utopian society, many fewer hours would be needed to produce the necessary goods. In some of his enterprises, he introduced the eight-hour workday; however, he thought it possible that people might only have to work two hours, thereby leaving the remainder of their time free for the discussion of philosophical ideas and the needs of the society.

It was clear to Owen that society "must be reconstructed in all its parts, to be in unison with the principles." He had no doubt that humanity was up to the task of this total reconstruction. He saw the utopian world as one in which human-created (cultural) differences would disappear, leaving "one language, one code of simplified laws, one interest, one currency, one spirit, and one general superior mind, and conduct over the globe." In order for this to happen, every person "should be, from birth, recreated through a new creation and arrangement of superior external circumstances." This was the world that Owen wanted everyone to create. Unlike others, he did not believe this creation should happen through force; rather, he thought that if people knew it were possible to create "a terrestrial paradise" for everyone, they would gladly make changes in their lives to make it a reality. He was convinced that the necessary ingredients were at hand for this transformation, if people would just accept his ideals and act on them. In the second and third papers, Owen gives the broad proposals to show how this might occur.

The second paper is directed "to the leading men of all parties in the United States." Owen had been to the United States and understood the potential "within the Union." Owen possessed a strong ego and would initiate social experiments without hesitation or doubt. He believed that others should be willing to do the same, including the leaders of the entire country. The opportunity, in Owen's eyes, was for the United States to develop "the most powerful and splendid empire" through the peaceful means of his educational process. For Owen, one key ingredient was to adopt the new lifestyle wholeheartedly. He believed that a person, or society, either lived up to his ideals or failed and fell back into the old ways.

Owen lists six qualities that would be necessary for this social transformation to work with the fewest problems during the transition. He writes, "The United States now possess these advantages, or the means to acquire them." What was required was for the political and social leaders of the country to make the initial decision to move toward the goal of a united Western Hemisphere. Owen saw no problem in moving from the relative freedoms and various constitutional rights American society to a setting where the government would implement strict requirements such as demanding all citizens "exercise physically and mentally all, at all times." However, many of the requirements that Owen lists for the United States were possible because of the relative newness of the countries in the Western Hemisphere. The United States was clearly the power in the hemisphere, even without the twenty-year-old Monroe Doctrine. Owen truly believed in a rational, scientific approach to life and social structure. Thus, for him, it was possible for American leaders to take the assets required and "combine them into a scientific new arrangement of society." The benefits of this social engineering, in Owen's mind, would greatly outweigh any inconveniences.

Examining Owen's argument for these social changes, it was, and is, difficult to disagree with his assertion that people want to be part of a "well governed" country and would want to have their physical and mental attributes "well cultivated from birth" in order to be the best people possible. However, if one accepted Owen's arguments, then one would also be accepting Owen's judgments of what was best. Doing away with "languages, religions, governments, laws, or currencies" in order to simplify interactions with others does follow a rationalistic logic. However, it is Owen's perceptions that dictate what should be kept, not a scientific study of human culture, as he seems to imply in his papers. For a society to have the qualities that Owen lists, including "superior habits, manners, and conduct; with the pure spirit of charity, . . . and love," would be good. He offers all of this and more if the United States is willing to follow his teachings on how to shape the life of each person. He expresses his certainty that the United States and the rest of the hemisphere had the resources to make this a success. However, as in other places where Owen had suggested such a plan, the leaders and the people were not willing to adopt his extreme form of socialism, which included turning all child care over to the state.

In the remainder of the second and in the third paper, Owen continues to assure the reader that the benefits of making these changes, in either hemisphere, are great enough that the people would accept the discomfort that change has always brought. The fact that it would be decades before the system would be fully implemented was always ignored by Owen when he proposed it to various groups. Owen understood many aspects of human nature and the problems that confronted many urban areas during the first half of the nineteenth century. He made important contributions to understanding the educational process and argued that mills could make greater profits by treating their workers well. However, he was overly optimistic as to how rational the average person really was and how large an immediate change they would be willing to make to be part of "this new, superior, and rational state of human existence."

Essential Themes

The dramatic changes that Robert Owen proposed did not come to pass. While the United States and Great Britain were political leaders within their respective hemispheres, they did not use this position to try to implement anything like his proposal. For better or for worse, they continued with the old way of doing things. Thus the heritage of Owen was not a new political and social order. What he contributed were specific aspects of his utopian dream, which were important challenges to the status quo.

Owen's most significant contribution was his emphasis on the importance of education. When he stopped employing children under the age of ten at New Lanark, he was called before a parliamentary committee and questioned as to whether this did not cause the working-class children to become immoral and dangerous. Owen replied that by receiving an education at this age, they actually became better citizens and workers. The policy changes he advocated—universal education and the extension of education beyond the very basics—have become the norm in all developed nations.

A second major contribution that came from his vision for the world was a change how workers were treated. At the beginning of the Industrial Revolution, workers were treated like pieces of machinery that could be easily replaced. Through his example, Owen demonstrated that this was not really the case. Although workers could be replaced, the quality of the work diminished. By caring for their health, helping them learn, and limiting the time spent on the job, productivity actually increased. While the two-hour workday was never achieved, Owen's advocacy of shorter work shifts was gradually accepted, as was the offering of employee benefits such as health insurance and tuition reimbursement.

Philosophically, Owen challenged the idea that people were able to "form their own physical, mental, and moral capacity." He pushed the idea that society played the dominant role in a person's development. He did not believe in the philosophy of "might makes right." Most agreed with him that the world would be a better place if people knew the essential truths and lived by these truths; however, almost everyone rejected the idea that Owen had discovered these essential truths and the proper lifestyle with which to implement them. Thus, while Owen failed to see his global vision implemented, the questions he raised and parts of his plan have been beneficial to society as a whole.

Donald A. Watt, PhD

Bibliography

Gordon, Peter. "Robert Owen (1771–1858)." *Prospects* 24.1/2 (1994): 279–96. PDF file.

Owen, Robert. *Manifesto of Robert Owen*. Washington: Globe Office, 1844. Print.

Additional Reading

Brown, Paul. *Twelve Months in New Harmony.* Philadelphia: Porcupine, 1972. Print.

Claeys, Gregory. *Machinery, Money and the Millennium: The New Moral Economy of Owenite Socialism, 1815–60*. Princeton: Princeton UP, 1987. Print.

Harrison, J. F. C. *Robert Owen and the Owenites in Britain and America*. New York: Routledge, 2010. Print.

Owen, Robert. *A New View of Society and Other Writings*. New York: Dutton, 1927. Print.

---. *Selected Works of Robert Owen*. Ed. Gregory Claeys. London: Pickering, 1993. Print.

Robert Owen and New Lanark: A Man ahead of His Time. New Lanark Trust, n.d. Web. 5 Apr. 2013.

LESSON PLAN: **Making a New Society**

Students analyze a manifesto by Robert Owen to consider utopian movements and social reform in the antebellum period.

Learning Objectives

Consider multiple perspectives of social reformers from the past; analyze the ideals of the major utopian thinkers and their social experiments; examine the influence of utopianism on antebellum society.

Materials: Robert Owen, "Manifesto of Robert Owen" (1844).

Overview Questions

What societal problems does Owen propose to solve in his manifesto? What are the solutions he proposes and why does he think they would be effective? What kind of utopian society does Owen imagine the United States could be? According to Owen, in what ways would the United States have to change for this ideal to be realized?

Step 1: Comprehension Questions

To whom is Owen's manifesto addressed? What does he hope his writing will inspire?

- **Activity:** Have students read aloud the first paragraph and describe Owen's potential audience. Ask students what Owen means by the "desire to become civilized." Have students describe the social vision Owen puts forth in his opening address and make predictions about what kinds of reforms his manifesto will demand.

Step 2: Comprehension Questions

What factors does Owen think most influence individuals? How does this perspective differ from other views of "individual man"? Why does this opinion lead him to advocate for social reforms?

- **Activity:** Have students review paragraphs seven and eight and identify passages in which Owen argues that environment shapes individuals. Contrast this to the emphasis on self-creation that Owen describes as the dominant attitude in American life. Have students review paragraph fifteen and discuss the ways that Owen thought his proposed reforms would reshape people's environments.

Step 3: Context Questions

According to Owen, what mistakes has humanity made? How can these problems be solved? What qualities and characteristics define the better world Owen desires?

- **Activity:** Pair students to make a two-column chart listing the societal flaws Owen describes and his proposed solutions. Have students use their charts to discuss what Owen's "new era" would be like. Ask students how this era would differ from both Owen's period and their own.

Step 4: Explorations Questions

According to Owen's manifesto, what should the United States do to improve society? How would this change the country? What reforms did Owen hope his manifesto would inspire? What are the limitations of his vision?

- **Activity:** Have students write a paragraph responding to Owen's utopian vision. Have them include factors they find desirable as well as any reservations they might have about his new world. Remind students to include passages from the text for support. Call on students to share their responses with the class.

Step 5: Response Paper

Word length and additional requirements set by Instructor. Students answer the research question in the *Overview Questions*. Students state a thesis and use as evidence passages from the primary source document as well as support from the secondary historical document/s assigned in the lesson.

Address to the First Women's Rights Convention, July 19, 1848

Date: July 19, 1848
Author: Stanton, Elizabeth Cady
Genre:address; speech; political tract

"But we are assembled to protest against a form of government existing without the consent of the governed—to declare our right to be free as man is free."

Summary Overview

Elizabeth Cady Stanton was one of the founding mothers of women's rights in America. She was the first American woman to publicly argue for suffrage, or the right to vote, for women. Stanton took a lead role in organizing the first women's rights convention (originally called the Woman's Rights Convention) in her hometown of Seneca Falls, New York, in 1848. It was during this convention that Stanton gave an address that outlined her positions on the rights of women for many years to come. Stanton worked closely with another of the founding mothers of American feminism, Susan B. Anthony, who often delivered speeches that Stanton wrote. Stanton was a leader in the women's rights movement until her death in 1902, establishing and leading organizations that advocated for women's rights. Unfortunately, Stanton did not live to see American women obtain the right to vote in 1920.

Defining Moment

The year 1848 is often referred to as the Year of Revolution, due to the many uprisings demanding democracy that occurred in Europe that year. These revolutions, which did not last the year and did not lead to many lasting changes, included demands for women's rights. American women also took their first tentative steps toward emancipation and equality with men during this year. At this time, only white men in America had the vote. Elizabeth Cady Stanton and four other women—all of whom, except Stanton, were Quakers—organized the first women's rights convention at Seneca Falls, New York, in July of 1848. Stanton authored the Declaration of Sentiments and its accompanying Resolutions to be debated at the convention. Within these documents, she demands suffrage as well as other rights for women: to keep custody of their children after divorce; to sign contracts on their own when married; to keep their own property when married; and, in a nod to Stanton's own marriage vows, the end of women having to obey men. Stanton also demands better educational and career opportunities for women.

Antebellum (pre–Civil War) America had developed defined roles for women and for men into separate spheres: domestic, or private, for women, and public for men. It was considered inappropriate for a woman to speak in public or to actively engage in politics, although some women did disregard these restrictions. The progress of abolitionist politics leading up to the Civil War in 1861 provided women with some limited opportunities for action, and it also raised their awareness to the inequalities and basic lack of liberty faced by much of the American population, be it on the basis of race, class, or sex.

The Seneca Falls convention was a tremendous success, with over three hundred people attending, including forty men. There was some discussion about not allowing men into the convention, but eventually the decision was made to let them participate. Since this was now a mixed gathering, the female organizers felt it inappropriate for a woman to chair the convention, and therefore one of the organizers' husbands acted as chairman. Stanton's own husband did not attend, as he disapproved of her demand for women's suffrage. There is some debate as to whether or not the text of Stanton's keynote address, which was first published in 1870, was a verbatim version of the address she gave at Seneca Falls in 1848 or not, and yet there is no doubt that Stanton's words helped launch the women's movement in America.

Author Biography

Elizabeth Cady was born to Margaret Livingston and Daniel Cady in Johnstown, New York, in 1805. Her father was a prominent lawyer who eventually became a New York Supreme Court judge. Elizabeth was educated at Emma Willard's Troy Female Seminary, which was known for its rigorous academic curriculum for young women. In 1840, she married Henry Brewster Stanton, who was a lawyer like her father; he dedicated his life to the abolition of slavery and so was better known as a politician and activist. In a foreshadowing of her feminist leadership, Stanton refused to include the word "obey" in her wedding vows. The couple spent their honeymoon in London attending the World's Anti-Slavery Convention. Here, Stanton met her future friend, American Quaker and abolitionist Lucretia Mott, and the two found common complaint in not being allowed to actually attend the convention because of their sex.

Over the next years, Stanton began her family, which would include seven children. In 1847, the family moved from Boston to Seneca Falls, New York, which was a smaller, more rural community. Here, Stanton keenly felt the "drudgery" of female domestic life, and the separation of male and female lives into distinct private and public spheres. By 1848, she felt ready to take on the struggle for women's rights. Stanton and Lucretia Mott—along with Martha C. Wright, Jane Hunt, and Mary Ann McClintock—organized the Seneca Falls convention on women's rights on July 19 and 20, 1848. It was Stanton who insisted that a clause on women's suffrage be included in the Declaration of Sentiments that was presented at the convention. This was controversial at the time, but it would lead to the adoption of suffrage as a key demand of the women's rights movement from this point forward.

In the years that followed, the American Civil War pushed the nation's attention to race as opposed to gender, but Stanton continued to organize for women's rights. She became a leader of this movement, along with her lifelong friend Susan B. Anthony, whom she met at the Seneca Falls convention. She led various organizations devoted to women's rights, including the National Woman Suffrage Association (NWSA, 1869–90) and the National American Woman Suffrage Association (1890–92), a merger of NWSA and the American Woman Suffrage Association. Always a prolific writer, in her later years Stanton published widely on women's rights, including *The Woman's Bible* (1895–98), which led to a backlash from the very women she was trying to help. She produced her memoirs in 1898. When Stanton died in 1902, America lost one of its strongest and earliest voices for women's rights.

HISTORICAL DOCUMENT

I should feel exceedingly diffident to appear before you at this time, having never before spoken in public, were I not nerved by a sense of right and duty, did I not feel the time had fully come for the question of woman's wrongs to be laid before the public, did I not believe that woman herself must do this work; for woman alone can understand the height, the depth, the length, and the breadth of her own degradation. Man cannot speak for her, because he has been educated to believe that she differs from him so materially, that he cannot judge of her thoughts, feelings, and opinions by his own. Moral beings can only judge of others by themselves. The moment they assume a different nature for any of their own kind, they utterly fail. . . .

Let us consider . . . man's superiority, intellectually, morally, physically.

Man's intellectual superiority cannot be a question until woman has had a fair trial. When we shall have had our freedom to find out our own sphere, when we shall have had our colleges, our professions, our trades, for a century, a comparison then may be justly instituted. When woman, instead of being taxed to endow colleges where she is forbidden to enter—instead of forming sewing societies to educate "poor, but pious," young men, shall first educate herself, when she shall be just to herself before she is generous to others; improving the talents God has given her, and leaving her neighbor to do the same for himself, we shall not hear so much about this boasted superiority. . . .

God's commands rest upon man as well as woman. It is as much his duty to be kind, self-denying and full of good works, as it is hers. As much his duty to absent himself from scenes of violence as it is hers. . . . The false ideas that prevail with regard to the purity necessary to constitute the perfect character in woman, and that requisite for man, has done an infinite deal of mischief in the world. I would not have woman less pure, but I would have man more so. I would have the same code of morals for both. . . .

Let us now consider man's claim to physical superiority. Methinks I hear some say, surely, you will not contend for equality here. Yes, we must not give an inch, lest you take an ell. We cannot accord to man even this much, and he has no right to claim it until the fact has been fully demonstrated. . . . We cannot say what the woman might be physically, if the girl were allowed all the freedom of the boy in romping, climbing, swimming, playing whoop and ball.

Among some of the Tartar tribes of the present day, women manage a horse, hurl a javelin, hunt wild animals, and fight an enemy as well as a man. The Indian women endure fatigues and carry burdens that some of our fair-faced, soft-handed, moustached young gentlemen would consider quite impossible for them to sustain. . . . it is no uncommon sight in our cities, to see the German immigrant with his hands in his pockets, walking complacently by the side of his wife, whilst she bears the weight of some huge package or piece of furniture upon her head. Physically, as well as intellectually, it is use that produces growth and development. . . .

We have met here today to discuss our rights and wrongs, civil and political, and not, as some have supposed, to go into the detail of social life alone. We do not propose to petition the legislature to make our husbands just, generous, and courteous, to seat every man at the head of a cradle, and to clothe every woman in male attire. None of these points, however important they may be considered by leading men, will be touched in this convention. As to their costume, the gentlemen need feel no fear of our imitating that, for we think it in violation of every principle of taste, beauty, and dignity; notwithstanding all the contempt cast upon our loose, flowing garments, we still admire the graceful folds, and consider our costume far more artistic than theirs. Many of the nobler sex seem to agree with us in this opinion, for the bishops, priests, judges, barristers, and lord mayors of the first nation on the globe, and the Pope of Rome, with his cardinals, too, all wear the loose flowing robes, thus tacitly acknowledging that the male attire is neither dignified nor imposing. No, we shall not molest you in your philosophical experiments with stocks, pants, high-heeled boots, and Russian belts. Yours be the glory to discover, by personal experience, how long the kneepan can resist the terrible strapping down which you impose, in how short time the well-developed muscles of the throat can be reduced to mere threads by the constant pressure of the stock, how high the heel of a boot must be to make a short man tall, and how tight the Russian belt may be drawn and yet have wind enough left to sustain life.

But we are assembled to protest against a form of government existing without the consent of the governed—to declare our right to be free as man is free, to be represented in the government which we are taxed to support, to have such disgraceful laws as give man the power to chastise and imprison his wife, to take the wages which she earns, the property which she inherits, and, in case of separation, the children of her love; laws which make her the mere dependent on his bounty. It is to protest against such unjust laws as these that we are assembled today, and to have them, if possible, forever erased from our statute books, deeming them a shame and a disgrace to a Christian republic in the nineteenth century. We have met

> To uplift woman's fallen divinity
> Upon an even pedestal with man's.

And, strange as it may seem to many, we now demand our right to vote according to the declaration of the government under which we live. This right no one pretends to deny. We need not prove ourselves equal to Daniel Webster to enjoy this privilege, for the ignorant Irishman in the ditch has all the civil rights he has. We need not prove our muscular power equal to this same Irishman to enjoy this privilege, for the most tiny, weak, ill-shaped stripling of twenty-one has all the civil rights of the Irishman. We have no objection to discuss the question of equality, for we feel that the weight of argument lies wholly with us, but we wish the question of equality kept distinct from the question of rights, for the proof of the one does not determine the truth of the other. All white men in this country have the same rights, however they may differ in mind, body, or estate.

The right is ours. The question now is: how shall we get possession of what rightfully belongs to us? We should not feel so sorely grieved if no man who had not attained the full stature of a Webster, Clay, Van Buren, or Gerrit Smith could claim the right of the elective franchise. But to have drunkards, idiots, horse-racing, rum-selling rowdies, ignorant foreigners, and silly boys fully recognized, while we ourselves are thrust out from all the rights that belong to citizens, it is too grossly insulting to the dignity of woman to be longer quietly submitted to. The right is ours. Have it, we must. Use it, we will. The pens, the tongues, the fortunes, the indomitable wills of many women are already pledged to secure this right. The great truth that no just government can be formed without the consent of the governed we shall echo and re-echo in the ears of the unjust judge, until by continual coming we shall weary him. . . .

There seems now to be a kind of moral stagnation in our midst. Philanthropists have done their utmost to rouse the nation to a sense of its sins. War, slavery, drunkenness, licentiousness, gluttony, have been dragged naked before the people, and all their abominations and deformities fully brought to light, yet with idiotic laugh we hug those monsters to our breasts and rush on to destruction. Our churches are multiplying on all sides, our missionary societies, Sunday schools, and prayer meetings and innumerable charitable and reform organizations are all in operation, but still the tide of vice is swelling, and threatens the destruction of everything, and the battlements of righteousness are weak against the raging elements of sin and death. Verily, the world waits the coming of some new element, some purifying power, some spirit of mercy and love. The voice of woman has been silenced in the state, the church, and the home, but man cannot fulfill his destiny alone, he cannot redeem his race unaided. There are deep and tender chords of sympathy and love in the hearts of the downfallen and oppressed that woman can touch more skillfully than man.

The world has never yet seen a truly great and virtuous nation, because in the degradation of woman the very fountains of life are poisoned at their source. It is vain to look for silver and gold from mines of copper and lead. It is the wise mother that has the wise son. So long as your women are slaves you may throw your colleges and churches to the winds. You can't have scholars and saints so long as your mothers are ground to powder between the upper and nether millstone of tyranny and lust. How seldom, now, is a father's pride gratified, his fond hopes realized, in the budding genius of his son! The wife is degraded, made the mere creature of caprice, and the foolish son is heaviness to his heart. Truly are the sins of the fathers visited upon the children to the third and fourth generation. God, in His wisdom, has so linked the whole human family together that any violence done at one end of the chain is felt throughout its length, and here, too, is the law of restoration, as in woman all have fallen, so in her elevation shall the race be recreated.

"Voices" were the visitors and advisers of Joan of Arc. Do not "voices" come to us daily from the haunts of poverty, sorrow, degradation, and despair, already too long unheeded? Now is the time for the women of this country, if they would save our free institutions, to defend the right, to buckle on the armor that can best resist the keenest weapons of the enemy—contempt and ridicule. The same religious enthusiasm that nerved Joan of Arc to her work nerves us to ours. In every generation God calls some men and women for the utterance of truth, a heroic action, and our work today is the fulfilling of what has long since been foretold by the Prophet—Joel 2:28: "And it shall come to pass afterward, that I will pour out my spirit upon all flesh; and your sons and your daughters shall prophesy." We do not expect our path will be strewn with the flowers of popular applause, but over the thorns of bigotry and prejudice will be our way, and on our banners will beat the dark storm clouds of opposition from those who have entrenched themselves behind the stormy bulwarks of custom and authority, and who have fortified their position by every means, holy and unholy. But we will steadfastly abide the result. Unmoved we will bear it aloft. Undauntedly we will unfurl it to the gale, for we know that the storm cannot rend from it a shred, that the electric flash will but more clearly show to us the glorious words inscribed upon it, "Equality of Rights."

GLOSSARY

abide: to comply with; to put up with, tolerate

bulwarks: strong supports or protection

degradation: changing to a less respected state; debasement

diffident: shy; timid; being of a reserved manner

ell: a unit of measurement common until the nineteenth century; originally a cubit.

indomitable: cannot be subdued or overcome; unconquerable

kneepan: kneecap; patella

licentiousness: lacking moral discipline; disregard for accepted rules and customs

methinks: it seems to me

rend: tear; rip into pieces

Russian belts: cinch belts worn by Russian army officers in the nineteenth century. They became fashionable with men trying to make themselves look more broad-shouldered and therefore imposing.

stock: men's formal neckwear; a piece of fine fabric was gathered or pleated into a slightly stiffened band that fastened at the back of the neck.

stripling: an adolescent youth

Tartar: someone who is seen as violent or barbarous; an ethnic group of Turkic or Mongolian origin from Central Asia, who invaded Europe in the Middle Ages

verily: in fact

Document Analysis

It seems difficult to believe that American women have had the right to vote for less than one hundred years, but this is the case. Women received the vote via the Nineteenth Amendment in 1920. But it was Elizabeth Cady Stanton who first raised the cause (also known as suffrage) publicly as something that women should fight for and duly receive. In 1848, when she made her case through an address given at the Woman's Rights Convention at Seneca Falls, the thought of women voting was almost absurd. Even some of her fellow organizers thought so.

Stanton's speech at this convention, said to be the first of her career, was published in 1870. Is this the verbatim text of her speech in 1848? Probably not, but the themes and arguments included in it set the tone of the women's rights movement for decades to come. In her speech, Stanton draws on the liberal philosophy prevalent in the nineteenth century, especially natural rights theory, or the theory that all people (not just white men) are created equal. This new concept of natural rights, part of the secular, liberal philosophy that was becoming popular in mid-century America, was redefining society. It was apparent in the antislavery movement that was coalescing and that would eventually lead to the Civil War. Stanton also often refers back to republican principles in her speech, as the Declaration of Sentiments presented at the convention was based on the Declaration of Independence. She also includes the concept of "republican motherhood," which held that women have a powerful role in the moral development of their children in order to raise better and more virtuous republican citizens. Stanton's audience here, it is important to remember, was restricted to white, educated, Protestant women, and so her demand for rights is also limited to this population group.

The year 1848 was a year of revolution in Europe, and it was therefore a fitting year for an American woman to state the revolutionary idea of women's right to vote. Stanton begins her Seneca Falls speech with appropriate modesty, saying she is "exceedingly diffident" or timid to be speaking and admitting it is her first public speech. At this time period, men and women were restricted to the separate spheres of public and private: men inhabited the public sphere while women were restricted to the private sphere. For this reason, it was uncommon for women to speak in a public setting, although not unknown. As the abolitionist movement grew in popularity, more and more women began speaking in public and sharing their opinions and beliefs in this way. In her speech, Stanton states clearly her reasons for taking this somewhat radical move; she believes that women themselves need to speak up about "woman's wrongs," as they cannot rely on men to do this for them. She further states that men cannot understand "the depth, the length, and the breadth of her [woman's] own degradation." She explains that men's education makes it extremely difficult for them to understand women's concerns, as they are conditioned to believe in being completely and "materially" different from women.

In order to build her case, Stanton addresses the common wisdom of the day that men are superior to women "intellectually, morally, physically." The next three paragraphs are dedicated to refuting this assertion. Stanton discusses men's alleged intellectual superiority, and she makes the logical assertion that women cannot be judged in this regard until they have access to the same educational opportunities that men have. At this point in America's history, women's colleges, or "seminaries" as they were often called, were not as plentiful or as rigorous academically as men's colleges. Stanton herself had been fortunate enough to be educated at the Troy Female Seminary, which had been founded by Emma Willard, an early advocate for women's right to an education. Stanton also objects to women having to pay taxes and at times even raise money through "sewing societies" for men to attend these colleges, when women are banned from these same schools. She states that if women can educate themselves, then "we shall not hear so much about this boasted superiority."

Stanton then turns her attention to morality and takes issue with the different expectations of morality and purity between the sexes. She states that this disconnect has "done a great deal of mischief in the world," and that both sexes should adhere to the same moral codes. She is clear in her belief that men have the inferior moral code, and that they need to improve in this regard to reach the higher level of women. It does not make sense in her mind for women to become "less pure."

Regarding the physical superiority of men, Stanton understands that many may not believe equality could occur between men and women. But even here, she believes there is an argument to be made, and so she makes it. Again, she relies on the point that women have not had the same freedoms to develop their physical strength and abilities as have men. From childhood on, men have had more freedom to play ball, swim, or climb, and so she believes the true physical potential of women has not yet been seen. To further reinforce her case, she cites examples of strong women from other ethnicities and cultures, in particular Tatar, American Indian, and German women. She explains how "Tartar" women hunt, fight, and ride "as well as any man," while American Indian and German immigrant women often carry heavy burdens. Her point here is clear: when it comes to both physical and intellectual development, a woman must be free to achieve her full potential.

Next discussed is clothing, and here Stanton displays a clever use of rhetoric. She assures her audience that the focus of the convention is to discuss civil and political issues and not social issues, and then dedicates the next paragraph to social issues, cleverly including them when she said she would not. By social, she means such things as childcare, changing the behavior and manners of men, and attire. She assures her audience that women have no interest in "imitating" male clothing, as she believes women's "loose, flowing garments" are "far more artistic" than men's clothing. Here, her tone turns slightly sarcastic, as she gives examples of men who choose to dress in a similar fashion to women: barristers and judges, priests and bishops, mayors and even the Pope himself wear flowing robes similar to women's garments. She adds that this must mean that these men see the advantages of female clothing styles and therefore "tacitly" acknowledge that male clothing is "neither dignified nor imposing." Turning her attention more directly to male attire, she focuses in on four particular fashion trends of the time for men: "stocks, pants, high-heeled boots, and Russian belts." Her use of humor here is notable, as she invites men to discover for themselves how uncomfortable these items of clothing can be, all worn for the sake of vanity.

After this statement on clothing, Stanton turns from what is not going to be discussed to the important issues that are. She goes on to list the wrongs against women that need to be righted. Of course, she begins with the right to vote, the most contentious, but most important issue to her. Everything else can be addressed by legislation after women win the vote. Here, Stanton relies on the old republican theme of taxation without representation to make her point. Women pay taxes to be governed, but then have no voice in government. To add insult to injury, this same government has imposed legislation on women that greatly restricts various aspects of their lives. Stanton explains that a man can legally imprison his wife, take control of any property she inherits, take any wages she earns from employment, or if the couple separates, even take her children from her. This then is her agenda for action, and this is what she wants changed. She calls these wrongs against women a "shame and a disgrace to a Christian republic in the nineteenth century."

Although usually speaking from a secular and anticlerical perspective, as Stanton was not an overly religious woman, she was not above referring to Christian principles when it suited her. She speaks next to the ultimate goal of the Seneca Falls convention and refers back to the Original Sin, when Eve fell from grace. She speaks of women's "fallen divinity" and that the convention's goal will be to place women on an even "pedestal" with men. In short, the goal of the Seneca Falls convention was full equality for women.

Stanton then returns to her key demand of women's right to vote. She admits that this demand may sound strange to some people, but makes the controversial argument that women already have the right to vote under the Declaration of Independence, and that no one would deny it. She is careful here to distinguish between rights and equality, and makes the point that proving one's rights does not necessarily guarantee that equality will be the result. Stanton reinforces her point further by providing three examples of men of different classes and ages, all of whom enjoy the right to vote. She begins with Daniel Webster, who was a leading Massachusetts statesman of the time, and then explains that even an "ignorant Irishman in the ditch" enjoys the same rights as Webster does, as does any weak young man aged twenty-one. She concludes that this is the current situation with white men in America; that all can vote, but not all are equally educated, able-bodied, or wealthy. It is interesting to note here that she clearly refers to "white men." This is no doubt a result of her close association with the abolitionist movement, given her husband's status as a leading abolitionist.

The next paragraph begins with a bold, simple statement: "The right is ours." By using this short, simple phrase, Stanton adds impact, especially as this is an address designed to be spoken. Stanton then expands on the concept of having natural rights versus the possession of these rights. Again she uses examples to illustrate her point. In this case, she refers to Daniel Webster again; Henry Clay, another noted statesman of the day from Kentucky; Martin Van Buren, eighth President of the United States; and Gerrit Smith, a well-known abolitionist and a man who would soon take up Stanton's universal suffrage message. Smith was also Stanton's cousin. In these men, Stanton sees honorable male leaders worthy of the vote. She contrasts these men sharply with "drunkards, idiots, horse-racing, run-selling rowdies, ignorant foreigners, and silly boys" who can also vote under present laws. She considers this to be "grossly insulting" to women, and that it must not continue. Stanton repeats her short opening phrase again, adding two other short sentences—"Have it, we must. Use it, we will."—to provide even greater impact. She finishes this line of argument by going back to her point that there can be no "just government" without "the consent of the governed," meaning women. Stanton then explains that the best strategy to obtain the vote is persistence and that women should continue repeating this message to men in government, until they are finally worn down enough to relent.

After stating that women already have the inherent right to vote, Stanton shifts her argument to why women should be given the vote, and what benefits it will have for American society. She paints an ugly picture of the current state of American society ("moral stagnation") in order to show that there is, in fact, a crisis that needs a solution. She concentrates on the sins of the fathers, so to speak, and notes the prevalence of "drunkenness, licentiousness, gluttony," mentioning slavery and war as well. While these sins are multiplying, Americans are busy establishing new churches, charities, and associations, but to no avail. Society continues on its downward path. Here, having taken her audience to the brink of despair, Stanton provides the solution. It is of course women. She positions women as a "purifying power" providing "a spirit of mercy and love." This refers back not only to women as keepers of virtue in the new republic, but now also saviors of it. Again, this is a Christian reference that would have been easily understood by her audience.

Stanton continues along this line of argument, explaining that the current "moral stagnation" of America is due in no small part to the continued "degradation of women." She argues that there can be no "truly great and virtuous nation" when "your women are slaves." Note the use of the word "slave," which would resonate strongly with those holding abolitionist opinions, many of whom attended the convention. This line of argument also refers back to the theme of republican motherhood, which held that women must be educated in order to be able to properly educate and imbue virtue in their children, which in turn will properly prepare the next generation of good republican citizens. Stanton puts it even more bluntly: "It is the wise mother that has the wise son." She again alludes to the Christian concept of redemption when she states that America can be saved by elevating women to an equal position to that of men.

Stanton ends her speech with an example of an exceptional woman from history who was successful in speaking truth to power: Joan of Arc. This French Christian saint from the fifteenth century heard "voices" telling her to take charge of the French army and lead it to victory over the English. She was also a skilled and renowned military leader, known for her military victories and keen strategy. This was exactly the type of woman Stanton needed to inspire her audience to action. Her concluding call to action is for American women to hear the voices of this moral crisis and to "buckle on the armor" to confront what their enemies would surely use against them in their fight for women's rights, in this case "contempt and ridicule." She quotes scripture at this point and then mentions the "thorns of bigotry," which suggests the imagery of the crown of thorns worn by Christ when he was crucified. In this paragraph, she is trying to prepare her audience for the long fight it will take to achieve women's equality. Her use of military terms such as "stormy bulwarks" and "fortified their position" makes it clear she thinks this will be a battle, or perhaps even a long and drawn out siege. She needed to inspire her audience, as it was these women, and some men, who would be the leaders of this new women's rights movement.

Essential Themes

Elizabeth Cady Stanton's bold decision to include the right to vote as a central demand for women's rights and equality was one that had ramifications for the women's movement for many decades to come. Her address at Seneca Falls includes other demands, such as married women's property rights, divorced women's rights to the custody of their children, and better educational and career opportunities for women. These were secondary, however, to the right to vote.

Although the women's movement lagged somewhat after Seneca Falls, as a result of the Civil War and its aftermath, women continued to organize and galvanize throughout the century. Many women were also active in the abolitionist movement, and this experience provided them with the needed organizational skills to take up the cause of women's rights. Stanton's 1848 Seneca Falls address was passed around and used by many other women as a source document as they created their own speeches. The foundational document had a limited audience, however, as it was not published until 1870. By the time the American women's movement became a driving force in society again in the 1890s, Stanton's address was more of a distant echo of inspiration than a current call to action. Stanton was increasingly marginalized from the very movement she helped to create in her later years.

In addition to the abolitionist movement, the women's rights movement was also closely aligned with the temperance movement. The temperance movement believed that drinking alcohol, especially by men, leads to increased crime and many social evils, including those against women. Many women were active in more than one of these nineteenth-century social reform movements, and through them grew skilled in organizing and protesting. A number of Stanton's Quaker friends, such as Lucretia Mott, devoted their lives to reforming American society in this way. The Quaker religion, or the Society of Friends as it is also known, has always acknowledged the spiritual equality of women since its seventeenth-century origins and has allowed them to travel, preach, and publish religious writings. It is no surprise that Stanton's staunch friend and ally Susan B. Anthony was herself a Quaker.

Ironically, it was the Civil War that led to a schism in the early American women's movement. After African American men were given the vote in 1870, the women's movement split into two camps; one focused on moving women's suffrage through local and state legislation, while Stanton and Anthony's group were determined to work for the vote instead at the federal level. The two distinct organizations merged in 1890 to become the National American Woman Suffrage Association (NAWSA). Although Stanton became the founding president of this new organization, she was not enthusiastic about it and immediately left for England after she was elected. She refused to stand for reelection in 1892, effectively retiring from active participation in the movement she helped to found, and instead concentrated on her writing career. Nevertheless, she must always be remembered for her 1848 address at Seneca Falls, and her audacious demand that women be allowed to vote.

Lee Tunstall, PhD

Bibliography

Anderson, Bonnie S. "The Lid Comes Off: International Radical Feminism and the Revolutions of 1848." *NWSA Journal* 10.2 (1998): 1–12. Print.

Davis, Sue. *The Political Thought of Elizabeth Cady Stanton: Women's Rights and the American Political Traditions*. New York: New York UP, 2008. Print.

DuBois, Ellen Carol. *Woman Suffrage and Women's Rights*. New York: New York UP, 1998. Print.

Griffith, Elisabeth. *In Her Own Right: The Life of Elizabeth Cady Stanton*. New York: Oxford UP, 1984. Print.

Sigerman, Harriet. *Elizabeth Cady Stanton: The Right Is Ours*. New York: Oxford UP, 2001. Print.

Stanton, Elizabeth Cady. "Address by Elizabeth Cady Stanton on Woman's Rights: September 1848." *The Elizabeth Cady Stanton and Susan B. Anthony Papers Project*. Rutgers, State University of New Jersey, Aug. 2010. Web. 20 Mar. 2013.

Additional Reading

DuBois, Ellen Carol, ed. *The Elizabeth Cady Stanton–Susan B. Anthony Reader: Correspondence, Writings, Speeches*. Boston: Northeastern UP, 1992. Print.

DuBois, Ellen Carol, and Richard Cándida Smith, eds. *Elizabeth Cady Stanton: Feminist as Thinker*. New York: New York UP, 2007. Print.

Stanton, Elizabeth Cady. *Eighty Years and More; Reminiscences 1815–1897*. 1898. *A Celebration of Women Writers. Penn Libraries*. University of Pennsylvania, n.d. Web. 20 Mar. 2013.

---. *The Woman's Bible: A Classic Feminist Perspective*. 1895–98. Mineola: Dover, 2002. Print.

Stanton, Elizabeth Cady, et al, eds. *History of Woman Suffrage*. 6 vols. 1881–1922. Charleston: Salem: Ayer, 1985. Print.

LESSON PLAN: **Women's Rights**

Students analyze a speech by Elizabeth Cady Stanton to consider the women's rights movement and calls for suffrage in the antebellum period.

Learning Objectives

Analyze the causes and effects of the Seneca Falls Convention; consider the significance of the resolutions produced by the convention; examine the importance of Elizabeth Cady Stanton to the early women's rights movement.

Materials: Elizabeth Cady Stanton, " Address to the First Women's Rights Convention, July 19, 1848"

Overview Questions

Why did Stanton lead a gathering in Seneca Falls, New York, and what did she hope to accomplish? What were the primary concerns of the convention, and why? What case does Stanton make for suffrage? How did her speech rally support for women's rights?

Step 1: Comprehension Questions

Why does Stanton believe a convention necessary? What issues does she maintain are not concerns of the women's movement? What does she say the convention will address instead?

- **Activity:** Have students read aloud paragraph one and discuss the reasons for the convention. Then have students locate passages in which Stanton proclaims the need for suffrage. Ask students why Stanton names issues the convention was not protesting, and how the audience might have responded.

Step 2: Comprehension Questions

What distinction does Stanton make between equality and rights? Why does she call suffrage a right? What case does she make for the vote?

- **Activity:** Read aloud the sentence in paragraph eight of the excerpt that begins, "We have no objection." Ask students to explain the distinction Stanton makes. Have students list the reasons Stanton gives for suffrage and explain why Stanton thought suffrage a right.

Step 3: Context Questions

What problems does Stanton perceive in American society? How does she think suffrage can mitigate these ills? Why does she think the elevation of women will improve the nation?

- **Activity:** Have students review paragraphs ten and eleven and discuss the evils Stanton observes. Ask why Stanton thinks suffrage will solve these problems. Call on students to explain whether they agree with Stanton, reminding them to cite passages to support their claims.

Step 4: Historical Connections Questions

At the convention, Stanton drafted a declaration endorsing suffrage. Why might many, including women, have opposed this declaration? What impact did it have on the movement for women's rights?

- **Activity:** Remind students that women gained suffrage in 1920. Have students write a paragraph considering what they think the impact of the declaration might have been, and how others might have reacted to it. Remind them to cite passages for support.

Step 5: Response Paper

Word length and additional requirements set by Instructor. Students answer the research question in the *Overview Questions*. Students state a thesis and use as evidence passages from the primary source document as well as support from supplemental materials assigned in the lesson.

Resistance to Civil Government

Date: 1849
Author: Thoreau, Henry David
Genre: essay

"I heartily accept the motto, 'That government is best which governs least'; and I should like to see it acted up to more rapidly and systematically."

"Under a government which imprisons any unjustly, the true place for a just man is also in prison."

Summary Overview

On July 23, 1846, during a sojourn to the isolated Walden Pond, Henry David Thoreau walked into Concord, Massachusetts, to get his shoe fixed. He ran into the local law-enforcement official, Sam Staples, who was in charge of collecting taxes. Thoreau owed six years of outstanding poll taxes, which he had chosen not to pay as a way of protesting the fact that slavery remained legal in part of the United States. When Thoreau again refused to pay the tax, restating his opposition to slavery and saying that he was also disgusted by the Mexican-American War, Staples placed him under arrest and put him in jail.

Thoreau was bailed out the following day, against his will, possibly by his aunt. However, the experience left a mark on the author. For the next several years, he delivered spoken addresses about the natural propensity of governments to act in unethical ways, the need for individuals to be vigilant critics of government actions, and, most importantly, the argument that righteous people should not participate in any way in the workings of unrighteous governments. These ideas were published in 1849 under the title "Resistance to Civil Government." In 1866, after Thoreau's death, "Resistance to Civil Government" was republished with a new title, "Civil Disobedience," by which it is better known today.

Defining Moment

Although Henry David Thoreau was clearly a man of great inspiration, acting from a strong sense of iconoclastic creativity, he was also a product of his times. Events on an international, national, and regional scale helped to shape his personal character and the content of his work. Understanding these forces is the key to making sense of Thoreau as a person and an author and appreciating what "Resistance to Civil Government" meant to him.

The Industrial Revolution, which began in the middle of the eighteenth century, had dramatically transformed American and European society by the mid-nineteenth century, when Thoreau did the bulk of his writing. It shifted the base of the economy from agricultural to manufacturing activities and led to a large-scale movement of people from rural to urban settings. While most people of his day had a purely positive view of the Industrial Revolution's impact, Thoreau was more critical in his reactions to it. He was concerned that people were growing out of touch with the power of nature and the ways of life associated with traditional agrarian rural communities, which he considered to be healthier and more authentic than those that came from living in large cities.

He shared these atypical beliefs with another important writer in the region, Ralph Waldo Emerson (1803–82). Beginning around 1836, Emerson gained fame as a touring lecturer in the northeastern United States. He expounded on a loosely congruous set of topics, including the divine character of nature, the importance of individual creativity, and the superiority of rural life to urban life. This general philosophy came to be known as transcendentalism. As a young man, freshly graduated from Harvard and working as a schoolteacher, Thoreau became close friends with Emerson, and he lived with Emerson's family on and off through much of his adult life. Thoreau's inclusion in the circle of philosophers, essayists, and poets who published the transcendentalist journal the *Dial* must be considered one of the great influences on his writing career.

At the same time, Thoreau was more frankly political than many other transcendentalists, and he was always known to be concerned about the key issues of his day. He developed the ideas expressed in "Resistance to Civil Government" after being briefly jailed in 1846 for refusing six years of outstanding poll tax. He claimed he did so as a protest against slavery and the Mexican-American War.

The northeastern states banned slavery in the decades after the Revolutionary War, but it remained a thriving and lucrative institution in the South until the Emancipation Proclamation of 1863. Thoreau's was among an increasing number of Northern voices calling for a federal ban on slavery, and in his later life, he supported controversial antislavery activists such as John Brown, who led slaves in a violent rebellion against proslavery white Southerners.

Thoreau was staunchly against the Mexican-American War, which lasted from 1846 to 1848, from its outset. The war was fundamentally a dispute over where the borders of the two countries should be drawn, especially in Texas. It was opposed by many Americans, particularly in the North. Abolitionists considered the American incursion into Mexico to be a ploy by Southern proslavery activists to expand the area of legalized slavery in the United States. Many others simply felt it was an unnecessary act of aggression, and costly in terms of American lives and resources.

Author Biography

Henry David Thoreau was born as David Henry Thoreau on July 12, 1817. His parents, John Thoreau and Cynthia Dunbar, were of modest financial means, as his father worked as a pencil manufacturer. However, the Thoreau family enjoyed a good reputation for hard work and honesty in their Concord, Massachusetts, community.

Thoreau was a keen student in his early years, and he drew attention to himself for his wit and intellect at Concord Academy. After secondary school, he began his studies at Harvard College, which he attended from 1833 to1837. After graduating from Harvard, he became a schoolteacher at a public school in Concord. He soon found that he did not agree with administering corporal punishment to misbehaving students as directed by his superiors and resigned from his post in protest. In the following years, he worked alongside his brother John in an alternative private school in Concord. His brother died of tetanus after cutting himself shaving, and this tragedy deeply impacted Thoreau.

During this time, Henry David Thoreau, as he was now calling himself, became acquainted with several members of the locally flourishing transcendentalist movement, including the patriarch of the philosophy, Ralph Waldo Emerson. Emerson became convinced of the younger man's literary talent and encouraged him to write essays for the transcendentalist journal the *Dial*. Starting with an initial essay in 1840, Thoreau soon became a favorite contributor to the periodical. Thoreau grew very close to Emerson and lived with his family from 1841 to1843, both in Massachusetts and at Emerson's brother's home on Staten Island, New York. Thoreau became a tutor and caretaker for Emerson's children, as well as a sort of groundskeeper for the Emerson estates.

In 1843, Thoreau returned to his hometown of Concord and took over the family pencil-manufacturing business, which he ran on and off for the rest of his life. However, he continued to take sojourns to pursue his writing and lecturing interests. The most famous of these took place from 1845 to 1847, when he moved to a small cabin on the edge of Walden Pond and built a cabin on land owned by Emerson. This experience, which Thoreau considered a great experiment in simple living away from society, resulted in the celebrated *Walden*, eventually published in 1854.

During his stay at Walden Pond, Thoreau had an altercation with the law when a tax collector demanded that he pay six years of delinquent poll taxes. Thoreau refused, saying that he was opposed to slavery and the Mexican-American War, and was thrown in jail for the night of July 23, 1846. Although he was freed when his aunt paid the taxes without his knowledge, the arrest shaped Thoreau's political opinions, which he expressed in a series of lectures and papers. These thoughts were ultimately published as the essay "Resistance to Civil Government" in 1849.

Thoreau moved back to Concord in the autumn of 1847. He first lived at the Emerson's home but had two subsequent homes of his own in town. For the decade of the 1850s, Thoreau ran his family's pencil-manufacturing business. He occasionally traveled throughout the northeastern United States and Canada to give popular lectures and pursue his passionate interest in the natural history of the region.

Henry David Thoreau died on May 6, 1862, finally succumbing to complications from tuberculosis, which he had contracted decades earlier in college. He is remembered as one of the leading voices in early American literature. As a poet, essayist, and social activist, he gave voice to a philosophical radicalism developing in the New England region in the middle of the nineteenth century. Like his close friend Ralph Waldo Emerson, Thoreau used his prowess as a writer and speaker to challenge the status quo of New England society and encourage new ways of understanding what it meant to be American.

HISTORICAL DOCUMENT

I heartily accept the motto, "That government is best which governs least"; and I should like to see it acted up to more rapidly and systematically. Carried out, it finally amounts to this, which also I believe—"That government is best which governs not at all"; and when men are prepared for it, that will be the kind of government which they will have. Government is at best but an expedient; but most governments are usually, and all governments are sometimes, inexpedient. The objections which have been brought against a standing army, and they are many and weighty, and deserve to prevail, may also at last be brought against a standing government. The standing army is only an arm of the standing government. The government itself, which is only the mode which the people have chosen to execute their will, is equally liable to be abused and perverted before the people can act through it. Witness the present Mexican war, the work of comparatively a few individuals using the standing government as their tool; for in the outset, the people would not have consented to this measure.

This American government—what is it but a tradition, though a recent one, endeavoring to transmit itself unimpaired to posterity, but each instant losing some of its integrity? It has not the vitality and force of a single living man; for a single man can bend it to his will. It is a sort of wooden gun to the people themselves. But it is not the less necessary for this; for the people must have some complicated machinery or other, and hear its din, to satisfy that idea of government which they have. Governments show thus how successfully men can be imposed upon, even impose on themselves, for their own advantage. It is excellent, we must all allow. Yet this government never of itself furthered any enterprise, but by the alacrity with which it got out of its way. It does not keep the country free. It does not settle the West. It does not educate. The character inherent in the American people has done all that has been accomplished; and it would have done somewhat more, if the government had not sometimes got in its way. For government is an expedient, by which men would fain succeed in letting one another alone; and, as has been said, when it is most expedient, the governed are most let alone by it. Trade and commerce, if they were not made of india-rubber, would never manage to bounce over obstacles which legislators are continually putting in their way; and if one were to judge these men wholly by the effects of their actions and not partly by their intentions, they would deserve to be classed and punished with those mischievous persons who put obstructions on the railroads.

But, to speak practically and as a citizen, unlike those who call themselves no-government men, I ask for, not at once no government, but at once a better government. Let every man make known what kind of government would command his respect, and that will be one step toward obtaining it.

After all, the practical reason why, when the power is once in the hands of the people, a majority are permitted, and for a long period continue, to rule is not because they are most likely to be in the right, nor because this seems fairest to the minority, but because they are physically the strongest. But a government in which the majority rule in all cases cannot be based on justice, even as far as men understand it. Can there not be a government in which the majorities do not virtually decide right and wrong, but conscience?—in which majorities decide only those questions to which the rule of expediency is applicable? Must the citizen ever for a moment, or in the least degree, resign his conscience to the legislator? Why has every man a conscience then? I think that we should be men first, and subjects afterward. It is not desirable to cultivate a respect for the law, so much as for the right. The only obligation which I have a right to assume is to do at any time what I think right. . . .

The mass of men serve the state thus, not as men mainly, but as machines, with their bodies. They are the standing army, and the militia, jailers, constables, posse comitatus, etc. In most cases there is no free exercise whatever of the judgment or of the moral sense; but they put themselves on a level with wood and earth and stones; and wooden men can perhaps be manufactured that will serve the purpose as well. Such command no more respect than men of straw or a lump of dirt. They have the same sort of worth only as horses and dogs. Yet such as these even are commonly esteemed good citizens. Others—as most legislators, politicians, lawyers, ministers, and office-holders—serve the state chiefly with their heads; and, as the rarely make any moral distinctions, they are as likely to serve the devil, without intending it, as God. A very few—as heroes, patriots, martyrs, reformers in the great sense, and men—serve the state with their consciences also, and so necessarily resist it for the most part; and they are commonly treated as enemies by it. A wise man will only be useful as a man, and will not submit to be "clay," and "stop a hole to keep the wind away," but leave that office to his dust at least:

> "I am too high-born to be propertied,
> To be a second at control,
> Or useful serving-man and instrument
> To any sovereign state throughout the world."

He who gives himself entirely to his fellow men appears to them useless and selfish; but he who gives himself partially to them in pronounced a benefactor and philanthropist.

How does it become a man to behave toward the American government today? I answer, that he cannot without disgrace be associated with it. I cannot for an instant recognize that political organization as my government which is the slave's government also.

All men recognize the right of revolution; that is, the right to refuse allegiance to, and to resist, the government, when its tyranny or its inefficiency are great and unendurable. But almost all say that such is not the case now. But such was the case, they think, in the Revolution of '75. If one were to tell me that this was a bad government because it taxed certain foreign commodities brought to its ports, it is most probable that I should not make an ado about it, for I can do without them. All machines have their friction; and possibly this does enough good to counter-balance the evil. At any rate, it is a great evil to make a stir about it. But when the friction comes to have its machine, and oppression and robbery are organized, I say, let us not have such a machine any longer. In other words, when a sixth of the population of a nation which has undertaken to be the refuge of liberty are slaves, and a whole country is unjustly overrun and conquered by a foreign army, and subjected to military law, I think that it is not too soon for honest men to rebel and revolutionize. What makes this duty the more urgent is that fact that the country so overrun is not our own, but ours is the invading army. . . .

Practically speaking, the opponents to a reform in Massachusetts are not a hundred thousand politicians at the South, but a hundred thousand merchants and farmers here, who are more interested in commerce and agriculture than they are in humanity, and are not prepared to do justice to the slave and to Mexico, cost what it may. I quarrel not with far-off foes, but with those who, neat at home, co-operate with, and do the bidding of, those far away, and without whom the latter would be harmless. We are accustomed to say, that the mass of men are unprepared; but improvement is slow, because the few are not as materially wiser or better than the many. It is not so important that many should be good as you, as that there be some absolute goodness somewhere; for that will leaven the whole lump. There are thousands who are in opinion opposed to slavery and to the war, who yet in effect do nothing to put an end to them; who, esteeming themselves children of Washington and Franklin, sit down with their hands in their pockets, and say that they know not what to do, and do nothing; who even postpone the question of freedom to the question of free trade, and quietly read the prices-current along with the latest advices from Mexico, after dinner, and, it may be, fall asleep over them both. What is the price-current of an honest man and patriot today? They hesitate, and they regret, and sometimes they petition; but they do nothing in earnest and with effect. They will wait, well disposed, for other to remedy the evil that they may no longer have it to regret. At most, they give up only a cheap vote, and a feeble countenance and Godspeed, to the right, as it goes by them. There are nine hundred and ninety-nine patrons of virtue to one virtuous man. But it is easier to deal with the real possessor of a thing than with the temporary guardian of it.

All voting is a sort of gaming, like checkers or backgammon, with a slight moral tinge to it, a playing with right and wrong, with moral questions; and betting naturally accompanies it. The character of the voters is not staked. I cast my vote, perchance, as I think right; but I am not vitally concerned that that right should prevail. I am willing to leave it to the majority. Its obligation, therefore, never exceeds that of expediency. Even voting for the right is doing nothing for it. It is only expressing to men feebly your desire that it should prevail. A wise man will not leave the right to the mercy of chance, nor wish it to prevail through the power of the majority. There is but little virtue in the action of masses of men. When the majority shall at length vote for the abolition of slavery, it will be because they are indifferent to slavery, or because there is but little slavery left to be abolished by their vote. They will then be the only slaves. Only his vote can hasten the abolition of slavery who asserts his own freedom by his vote. . . .

Under a government which imprisons unjustly, the true place for a just man is also in prison. The proper place today, the only place which Massachusetts has provided for her freer and less desponding spirits, is in her prisons, to be put out and locked out of the State by her own act, as they have already put themselves out by their principles. It is there that the fugitive slave, and the Mexican prisoner on parole, and the Indian come to plead the wrongs of his race, should find them; on that separate, but more free and honorable ground, where the State places those who are not with her, but against her,—the only house in a slave State in which a free man can abide with honor. If any think that their influence would be lost there, and their voices no longer afflict the ear of the State, that they would not be as an enemy within its walls, they do not know by how much truth is stronger than error, nor how much more eloquently and effectively he can combat injustice who has experienced a little in his own person. Cast your whole vote, not a strip of paper merely, but your whole influence. A minority is powerless while it conforms to the majority; it is not even a minority then; but it is irresistible when it clogs by its whole weight. If the alternative is to keep all just men in prison, or give up war and slavery, the State will not hesitate which to choose. If a thousand men were not to pay their tax bills this year that would not be a violent and bloody measure, as it would be to pay them, and enable the State to commit violence and shed innocent blood. This is, in fact, the definition of a peaceable revolution, if any such is possible. If the tax-gatherer, or any other public officer, asks me, as one has done, "But what shall I do?" my answer is, "If you really wish to do anything, resign your office." When the subject has refused allegiance, and the officer has resigned his office, then the revolution is accomplished. But even suppose blood should flow. Is there not a sort of blood shed when the conscience is wounded? Through this wound a man's real manhood and immortality flow out, and he bleeds to an everlasting death. I see this blood flowing now.

GLOSSARY

constable: a local law-enforcement officer similar to a sheriff

expedient: something that serves a purpose or makes a course of action easier

posse comitatus: a local militia force

Revolution of '75: an early nineteenth-century way of referring to the American Revolutionary War, which in fact began in 1775

standing army: a military that exists even in times of peace

Document Analysis

The first line of "Resistance to Civil Disobedience" is clearly its most famous. Specifically, the quoted phrase, "That government is best which governs least," is remembered as most forcefully communicating the point of the essay. The origin of this quote is unclear, however. It is commonly considered to be a phrase coined by Thomas Jefferson, but this has not been documented by historians. It may be the case that the phrase was attributed without evidence to Jefferson in Thoreau's day, just as it is now, and Thoreau believed that he was in fact quoting the author of the Declaration of Independence, even if he was incorrect in this belief.

Whatever the authenticity of this alleged Jefferson quote, Thoreau is clearly using it as a response to his friend Ralph Waldo Emerson. In an 1844 essay entitled "Politics," Emerson stated, "The less government we have the better." Although Thoreau was a more outspoken political activist, the theme of mistrust of government was a staple of transcendentalist philosophy, since government control was antithetical to individual freedom.

In the next several passages, Thoreau states the point even more forcefully, saying, "That government is best which governs not at all." Although he writes the phrase as though as though he is quoting an outside source again, this line is clearly of his own invention. He goes on to explain his position, saying that the whole point of government is that it is supposed to make life easier for its citizens, but in reality it makes life more difficult.

Next, he relates that there is a controversy about governments having standing armies. Many Americans of his day were opposed to such a military institution, preferring that a suitable military be formed to meet challenges as they occurred and disbanded when these challenges passed. Thoreau argues that it is equally unnecessary to have a standing government that continues to exist even in times when it is not required by the people of the nation.

Thoreau couches his main objection to a standing government in the observation that it can be "abused and perverted" by people with special interests. He gives the example of the Mexican-American War, which was largely unpopular, especially in the North. Many abolitionists considered it to be driven by the Southern slaveholding lobby, which sought to create a larger Southern zone in which slavery was legal and thereby increase their power on a national level. According to Thoreau, the Mexican-American War would not have occurred except that "a few individuals using the standing government as their tool" forced it on the American people.

He continues by saying that the American government, a relatively new institution, is changing in character, shifting from merely reflecting the will of the people to imposing its own will on the people. Thoreau passionately exclaims that it is not government that keeps people free, pushes the western frontier, and educates the citizens. These achievements, he argues, must be acknowledged as the achievements of the American people themselves.

He next takes a more economic approach to furthering his argument against government. According to Thoreau, the American government has recently imposed so many complicated regulations on trade that it is a wonder that commerce has continued at all. The author contends that if they were to be judged on the actual impact of their actions rather than their good intentions, the men who drafted the laws concerning trade would be found to be criminally obstructive.

In the following section of the essay, Thoreau significantly tempers the tone of his argument. He steps back from his radically anarchistic position, saying that he knows it is not actually possible for the nation to exist without any government at all. As a responsible citizen, then, what he is truly calling for is for his fellow Americans to demand a better government than the one that is currently developing.

Notably, he is against the idea of a government acting based solely on the will of the majority of its citizens. Such a system, he explains, will not automatically result in a government that makes the right decisions. Such a government will often commit injustices against the minorities within the nation. The only way to prevent a government ruled by majority opinion from becoming a destructive force is for all of the citizens who shape the actions of the government to always listen to their consciences when making decisions that impact their fellow Americans. Law alone, Thoreau, states, will not make people act better toward one another; that can only come from people individually acting according to a well-developed sense of morality.

Thoreau points out that one result of too much blind adherence to the law is unthinking militarism. When men do what they think is expected of them by their government, rather than what they know to be right, they become part of a dehumanizing military machine. Even though the men assembled in a military procession are alive, they may as well be ready to be buried with military ceremony. Thoreau caps off his point by quoting a famous dirge by the poet Charles Wolfe (1791–1823) entitled "The Burial of Sir John Moore after Corruna," which is about the British fighting the French in Spain in 1809. Men who serve out of a sense of duty to the state, whether in the army and navy or as constables or jailers, are of no more actual value, according to Thoreau, than dogs or horses.

Other people serve with their minds rather than with their bodies. Instead of serving in a military capacity, these people act as lawyers and politicians. They are just as likely, in Thoreau's view, to unintentionally do evil, even if they perceive themselves as doing good for the country.

Only rarely do people who truly deserve respect participate in the functioning of the state. Indeed, people who are honest and true to their own sense of morality will soon find that they have a difficult time remaining in office, since many within the government will have disdain for them and consider them enemies of the state. However, these are the true "heroes, patriots," and "martyrs." Thoreau again uses a literary allusion to underscore his point, this time quoting Shakespeare's play *King John*, in which the king's son Lewis proclaims, "I am too high born to be propertied, / To be a secondary at control, / Or useful serving-man and instrument, / To any sovereign state throughout the world."

Thoreau then rhetorically asks how a righteous person should interact with the government. He responds by saying that a decent person should not participate at all in the government, since it is also the government that allows the institution of slavery to continue. Although Americans recognized the right to rebel against the British government during the Revolutionary War, many of Thoreau's readers would not have thought revolution appropriate at this juncture. Thoreau argues that it is worth contemplating revolutionary change because the current government keeps a sixth of its population enslaved and acts like an occupying army toward the rest of its citizens.

In the section of the essay that follows, Thoreau directly responds to the ideas of an English Enlightenment philosopher named William Paley (1743–1805). In several essays that appeared in his 1785 tome *Principles of Moral and Political Philosophy*, Paley put forth the argument that it is God's will that a government be obeyed as long as it is acting in the interest of the overall society. As a utilitarian philosopher, Paley believed that the benefits of a government should be measured by how it benefits the majority of its citizens. Thoreau takes issue with this mode of judging actions, saying that even if the acts of a government are good for the majority of people, they can still be morally wrong if they negatively impact some of the people in the governed society. The examples he gives of this, not surprisingly, are slavery and the Mexican-American War.

The reality is, Thoreau states, that the reason that slavery continues and the Mexican-American War is being fought is not only because the Southern slaveholders are protecting their interests but also because the far larger number of Northern merchants simply do not want to hobble their own incomes by disrupting farming or trade by pressing for emancipation. Even though the majority of people might be against slavery or the war in theoretical terms, they are unwilling to risk their own temporary well-being by taking principled stands against the immoral institutions of slavery and aggressive wars. In Thoreau's view, there are simply far too few real patriots willing to act to make America a true land of freedom.

Thoreau cautions against putting too much faith in the ballot. He compares voting to a kind of gambling or gaming, with voters placing bets on the side they think will win. Although it has some elements of moral judgment, is it a weak substitute, in Thoreau's view, for people actually voicing their opinions about the issues of the day. He even goes so far as to say that voting is actually doing nothing.

Thoreau clarifies that he does not intend this essay to mean that it is the responsibility of every good person to singlehandedly take on all the moral wrongs of the day. Instead, what he means is that decent people must find a way to avoid participating in the immoral acts, directly or indirectly. As he says, he knows many people who would not serve if ordered to fight in Mexico or put down a slave rebellion, yet still willingly pay their taxes, thus sending people in their place to commit these immoral acts. Instead of seeking to dissolve the government, Thoreau advocates that people of conscience dissolve the connections between themselves and an immoral government.

It is not enough, Thoreau continues, for people merely to have opinions on political matters; they must act. He states as fact that there are unjust laws, then asks his audience to think about the best way to proceed in such a context. Should a person follow unfair laws, speak out against them but continue to obey them, or simply break them? For Thoreau, the last option is clearly the right choice.

Not participating in the operation of an unjust government seems to Thoreau to be the strategy that most confounds those within it. This is evidenced, in his opinion, by the state's eagerness to indefinitely jail even a very poor man if he does not pay his taxes to the government. Meanwhile, the government barely does anything to those people who siphon off government funds for private gain, allowing them to remain free.

In a metaphor that he repeats throughout the essay, Thoreau compares the government to a machine. He says that injustice may indeed be the friction of the machine. If that is the case, he advises, it is best to simply disengage from it. There is a chance that the machine itself may "wear smooth," and it will definitely "wear out" in time. In fact, it may be best to work to stop the machine if the injustice is too great to tolerate.

Thoreau asserts that it is not up to an individual to do everything to improve the world. However, it is necessary for decent people to do something to work for a better future. He is dismissive of the possibility that there are ways of working within the government to make this happen, stating that the entire basis of the government is flawed.

He next suggests a specific course of action for abolitionists living in the state of Massachusetts, saying that if they wish to end the institution of slavery in the United States, they should effectively cut off their involvement with the government on all levels, starting with the state government. Thoreau writes that the only way that he ever encounters the state government is in the person of the tax collector, so it is against this person that he must struggle for freedom from a corrupt government. Even though it might seem like a very small act of conscience, Thoreau proposes that all true revolutions start in this way, with a single determined individual acting in a morally upright manner.

Thoreau next puts forth his famous argument that the only true place for an honest man living in a society ruled by an unjust government is in prison. He explains that incarceration is the main tactic that the state knows to use to combat those who are against it, and anyone who honestly opposes the immoral actions of the state should be willing to be arrested. He asserts that being locked up as a prisoner of conscience is a way to clog up the prison system and convince those people charged with administering the functions of the state that they should quit their positions.

Thoreau envisions this as a nonviolent revolutionary tactic. However, he is quick to point out that he is not altogether opposed to the use of violence in reforming the government. He argues that it is a kind of violence to make people live contrary to their consciences, and this kind of metaphorical bloodshed is already taking place.

After acknowledging that the state sometimes chooses to take away property instead of incarcerating individuals who do not pay tax, Thoreau segues into a brief but powerful discussion of wealth in general. Overall, he believes, wealth is a corrupting force. As he puts it, "the more money, the less virtue," meaning that people of economic means often forget the importance of living according to their principles as they accumulate wealth by working within a corrupt state.

Thoreau devotes a significant portion of the essay to recounting his own experience with not paying taxes.

He first mentions that he refused to pay a tax that was being collected on behalf of the church. Although the tax man threatened him with jail if he did not pay, Thoreau wrote a letter to the town clerk stating that he did not wish to be known as a member of the church and that he would not pay any taxes to it.

The next incident Thoreau describes is his far more famous run-in with the law over his refusal to pay poll taxes for six years. He says that during the night he spent in jail, he did not feel constrained and in fact considered himself to be freer than the people on the outside. He recounts how he talked at length with his cellmate, learning all he could about the people who had previously dwelt within the cell, and was surprised to learn what a rich history the modest jail cell had. He describes it as a lot like traveling a foreign country, with unusual things to see and experience.

When he was released the next day because someone "interfered" and paid his tax, he writes, he felt himself to be a changed man. His resolve to resist the state was strengthened rather than weakened, and he no longer felt he could tolerate the company of his neighbors who professed to be against slavery and the Mexican-American War but were not willing to do anything about it. He recounts how he found solace from his ill feelings toward his fellow townspeople by going off into the countryside and picking berries.

Thoreau concludes "Resistance to Civil Government" by discussing the actual role that government can play in effecting meaningful change. He says that the American government, though it bears significant flaws, such as a constitution that allows slavery, is not a particularly bad one. However, he argues, it is not possible to rely on government alone to make a better world. Although the citizens of the United States should insist on improvements to their government, politicians are too limited in their understanding of what matters in life to bring about true reforms. Ultimately, Thoreau asserts, meaningful change comes from the creative force of individuals. Someday government may progress to the point that it respects the individual as the basis of its power, but such a state has yet to exist.

Essential Themes

Thoreau wrote "Resistance to Civil Government" with two specific, related grievances in mind: the continuation of the slave trade in the United States and the Mexican-American War. However, the impact of this work transcended his lifetime and the particular issues of his day. Later activists drew upon the main concepts he laid out in this groundbreaking work to further their own movements. As such, it is possible to consider Thoreau as an important pioneer in the field of social activism.

The key lesson of "Resistance to Civil Government" is that people of conscience should not simply work within the existing political system to change legislation but should instead disengage from an immoral government altogether. Thoreau envisioned government as a kind of machine and insisted that it is important for socially conscious people to refuse to be part of the machine if it is causing harm to society. By completely withdrawing their support from the machine, by not giving it their labor or taxes, morally astute individuals can help break down the corrupt machine.

Of course, Thoreau acknowledged that governments do not approve of people who refuse to participate in their smooth functioning. They will invariably react by punishing such activists, usually by placing them under arrest. As he learned from his own experience of being briefly incarcerated for refusing to pay poll tax, being put in prison is not necessarily such a terrible fate, and a person of strong convictions should take pride in being jailed by an immoral government, since this is the most honorable place for an honest person living in a corrupt state.

Although Thoreau did not entirely reject the possibility of supporting a violent revolution, his essay laid out a sort of template for nonviolent social protest that was used by some of the best-known social activists of the twentieth century. For instance, Mahatma Gandhi (1869–1948), who was the most influential leader of the movement to free India from British rule, was an avid reader of Thoreau's work. Gandhi first gained experience in the social-justice field through his civil rights work in South Africa. He described Thoreau as an important teacher in this period of his life, stating that "Resistance to Civil Government" affirmed the work he was doing to end racial oppression by the white South African government.

Another prominent figure in the history of nonviolent social change who greatly admired Thoreau was Martin Luther King Jr. (1929–68). America's best-known civil rights activist, King worked in the 1960s to improve conditions for African Americans. Like Gandhi, King was explicit about the important role that Thoreau's "Resistance to Civil Government" played in helping to shape his own philosophy and celebrated quest for social justice. King's struggle, Gandhi's, and the struggles of so many other activists who have been touched by "Resistance to Civil Government" and used the tactic of nonparticipation in corrupt governments stand as evidence of Henry David Thoreau's lasting legacy of innovative political philosophy.

Adam Berger, PhD

Bibliography

Cain, William. *A Historical Guide to Henry David Thoreau*. Oxford: Oxford UP, 2000. Print.

Coffman, George. *Studies in Language and Literature*. Chapel Hill: U of North Carolina P, 1945. Print.

Dillman, Richard. *The Major Essays of Henry David Thoreau*. Albany, NY: Whitston, 2001. Print.

Gandhi, Mahatma. *All Men Are Brothers: Life and Thoughts of Mahatma Gandhi As Told in His Own Words*. Paris: UNESCO, 1958. Print.

Harding, Walter. *Thoreau: Man of Concord*. New York: Holt, 1960. Print.

Pyatt, Sherman. *Martin Luther King, Jr.: An Annotated Bibliography*. New York: Greenwood, 1986. Print.

Smith, Harmon. *My Friend, My Friend: The Story of Thoreau's Relationship with Emerson*. Amherst: U of Massachusetts P, 1999.

Trent, William. *A History of American Literature, 1607–1865*. New York: Appleton, 1920. Print.

Additional Reading

Boller, Paul. *American Transcendentalism, 1830–1860: An Intellectual Inquiry*. New York: Putnam, 1974. Print.

Foos, Paul. *A Short, Offhand, Killing Affair: Soldiers and Social Conflict during the Mexican-American War*. Chapel Hill: U of North Carolina P, 2002. Print.

Moller, Mary Elkins. *Thoreau in the Human Community*. Amherst: U of Massachusetts P 1980. Print.

Murphy, Arthur. *Men and Movements in American Philosophy*. New York: Prentice, 1952. Print.

Thoreau, Henry David, and Brook Atkinson. *Walden and Other Writings*. New York: Modern Lib., 1950. Print.

Torr, James. *Slavery*. San Diego: Greenhaven, 2004. Print.

LESSON PLAN: **Resistance and Revolution**

Students analyze an essay by noted transcendentalist Henry David Thoreau to consider perspectives on the Mexican-American War, abolition, and the need for civil disobedience.

Learning Objectives

Consider multiple perspectives on the Mexican-American War; examine the influence of transcendentalist ideas on the abolition movement; compare and contrast differing sets of ideas over how to initiate change in the antebellum period.

Materials: Henry David Thoreau, "Resistance to Civil Government," (1849).

Overview Questions

What is Thoreau's opinion on the war with Mexico, and on slavery? Based on this opinion, why does he think citizens should resist civil government? How does he think such resistance can best be enacted? What does he hope this resistance will bring about, for individuals as well as society?

Step 1: Comprehension Questions

What does Thoreau think is the problem with government? Why does he think democracy cannot cure these evils? What kind of government would he like to see?

- **Activity:** Have students read aloud the first two sentences of the essay. Draw a two-column chart on the board labeled "Government" and "Democracy" and call on students to fill it in with Thoreau's complaints about both facets of America's political system. Use the chart and the opening sentences to discuss Thoreau's vision for ideal government.

Step 2: Comprehension Questions

Why does Thoreau oppose the Mexican-American War? What is his view of the American army, and why?

- **Activity:** Have students review the text for references to the Mexican-American War and to the army. Discuss Thoreau's reasons for opposition, citing passages that show his views.

Step 3: Context Questions

What is Thoreau's view of slavery? Why does he think many Northerners fail to act against slavery, even if they promote it? What does this suggest about Thoreau's view of human nature?

- **Activity:** Have students review paragraph eight and explain why Thoreau thinks many who are opposed to slavery do not rise against it. Ask students to evaluate Thoreau's opinion of his fellow man based on this paragraph, citing passages that support their ideas.

Step 4: Explorations Questions

What kind of revolution does Thoreau desire? Why does he think citizens should voice their opinions to the government? In what ways does he think meaningful change can come about? In his opinion, what sorts of actions will bring about meaningful change?

- **Activity:** Have students review the final paragraph and discuss the methods that Thoreau thought individuals could use to influence their government. Have students write a paragraph considering an example of resistance that abolitionists such as Thoreau employed or might have employed and explain how that act could have influenced others.

Step 5: Response Paper

Word length and additional requirements set by Instructor. Students answer the research question in the *Overview Questions*. Students state a thesis and use as evidence passages from the primary source document as well as support from the secondary historical document/s assigned in the lesson.

The Trial of John Brown

Date: October 19 and November 2, 1859
Author: Brown, John
Genre: speech; report

"Now, if it is deemed necessary that I should forfeit my life for the furtherance of the ends of justice . . . in this slave country whose rights are disregarded by wicked, cruel, and unjust enactments— I submit; so let it be done!"

Summary Overview

This article focuses on two excerpts from John Brown's interrogation, trial, and sentencing in the fall of 1859, after a failed slave rebellion led by Brown in Harpers Ferry, Virginia (today in West Virginia). The first section, set in Harpers Ferry, is from the interrogation and consists of a series of questions about his actions and motivations and Brown's answers to his captors. Arrested and eventually put on trial for treason and attempting to begin an insurrection and a slave rebellion, John Brown defended himself and the men he led, stating that he only did what he believed to be right and that slavery was wrong and needed to be stopped. The second section is his last speech to the court in Charlestown, Virginia, just before his execution. In this speech, he reprimands the court for its hypocrisy, but also praises the witnesses and those involved for their honest and fair treatment of his case. The two sections reveal John Brown's character and intent for the failed rebellion. Even his attempt was futile, his life and trial stand as a defining moment in American history.

Defining Moment

The trial of John Brown is one of the famous trials in American history. Before the Civil War started in 1861, the North and South had spent years passing legislation to promote their own interests and building their contempt for one another's way of life. John Brown grew up in this environment of unease and distrust between the two sections of the United States. While the Civil War was not fought over slavery alone, slavery was a defining issue that led to the South wanting to break away from the Union, and John Brown, as an extremist, contributed to the polarization of the Southern and Northern points of view. Instead of seeing slavery as simply an unjust part of life, Brown deemed slaveholders to be wicked and dedicated his life to stopping them from infringing on the rights of their slaves. This came to a head at in October 1859, when he and twenty-one other would-be liberators seized the federal arsenal at Harpers Ferry, Virginia, in an effort to arm enslaved blacks. While they were successful in taking over the town and arsenal, even taking sixty hostages, the insurrection never came to pass. Brown's small militant band was quickly decimated by local militia and federal troops, and the survivors were captured and tried for their crimes. At trial, Brown said that he was willing to die in order to shine light upon the injustices being done to slaves by "wicked, cruel, and unjust" laws. These excerpts from the trial show a man who was willing to die for what he believed in, and that fortitude rallied others with similar beliefs and terrified Southerners, who began to see all Northerners as supporters of John Brown.

The first excerpt in this section is a part of Brown's interrogation by the Marines who put down his revolt at Harpers Ferry; its intended audience was his interrogators, but the prosecutor, judge, and the rest of those who were trying him most likely had access to this information as well. The second part of the excerpt was his final speech to the court before he was executed; this intended audience seems to be broader than in the first part, as he addresses his prosecutors, as well as some of his own men and those who spoke for and against him. Through his words, it is clear that Brown lived by the "golden rule," to treat others as you wish to be treated, and that he valued honesty and truth. These values stemmed from his strict Calvinist upbringing and were driving forces behind his actions. They also created the situation that ultimately led to his death. Because he believed so strongly in those actions that he saw as just, he broke laws that he felt to be unjust and, when caught, was put to death. Through his sacrifice, Brown galvanized others into pushing for change and beginning to end unjust practices.

Author Biography

John Brown was a white man, born in Torrington, Connecticut, on May 9, 1800, to Owen and Ruth Mills Brown. His devoutly religious, strongly antislavery family was poor and spent much of Brown's young life moving from place to place. Among his various childhood experiences were living near American Indians and making friends with a slave boy in a household where he stayed briefly. The first taught him that all men are equal regardless of the color of their skin, and the second helped shape him into "a most determined Abolitionist," as he himself asserted (qtd. in Linder). From a very young age, Brown was determined to stop the injustices he saw committed against those around him. At seventeen, Brown publically affirmed his strict Calvinist beliefs and began to put his religion's teachings to practical use, first by aiding a runaway slave and hiding him in the Brown family home.

He passed on his mindset to his many children, seven of whom were born to his first wife, Dianthe Lusk, and thirteen of whom were born to his second wife, Mary Day. Unfortunately, most of his children died very young and did not live to become adults. His surviving children joined him in his passion for Christian values and freedom for enslaved peoples.

Throughout his life, Brown committed small acts in order to promote equalization of the races without fear of repercussions, such as when he was forbidden to return to his church after inviting black parishioners to sit in "whites-only" pews. This type of civil disobedience was quite common for Brown, but after Elijah Lovejoy, the editor of an antislavery newspaper in Illinois, was murdered by a proslavery mob in 1837, Brown began to take more overt and drastic measures to achieve his goals.

His trial is a direct result of this switch from individual, nonviolent disobedience to violent resistance. In 1839, Brown began to dream of starting a slave rebellion and spent the next twenty years trying to make it happen, driven in part by the increasing amount of proslavery legislation passed in Southern states and at the national level. Brown and some of his sons moved to the newly created territory of Kansas in 1855, during which time the proslavery and antislavery factions clashed for control. After the federal government proclaimed the state open to slavery in May 1856, Brown and six others armed themselves and killed five proslavery settlers. That fall he began to raise funds and recruits for his proposed attack on Harpers Ferry. In late 1858, Brown and his followers raided properties in slaveholding Missouri, leading the slaves they freed to Canada. In mid-October 1859, he and the eleven surviving members of his small "army" were captured by a dozen Marines after seizing the federal armory and arsenal in Harpers Ferry, Virginia. Tried in state court and pronounced guilty of treason, conspiracy, and murder, Brown was hanged on the morning of December 2, 1859.

HISTORICAL DOCUMENT

Harper's Ferry, Oct. 19, 1859.

Mr. Brown: No man sent me here; it was my own prompting and that of my Maker, or that of the devil, whichever you please to ascribe it to. I acknowledge no man in human form.

Mr. Vallandigham: Did you get up the expedition yourself?

Mr. Brown: I did.

Mr. Vallandigham: Did you get up this document that is called a constitution?

Mr. Brown: I did. They are a constitution and ordinances of my own contriving and getting up.

Mr. Vallandigham: How long have you been engaged in this business?

Mr. Brown: From the breaking of the difficulties in Kansas. Four of my sons had gone there to settle, and they induced me to go. I did not go there to settle, but because of the difficulties.

Mr. Mason: How many are engaged with you in this movement? I ask those questions for our own safety.

Mr. Brown: Any questions that I can honorably answer I will, not otherwise. So far as I am myself concerned I have told everything truthfully. I value my word, sir.

Mr. Mason: What was your object in coming?

Mr. Brown: We came to free the slaves, and only that.

A Young Man (in the uniform of a volunteer company): How many men in all had you?

Mr. Brown: I came to Virginia with eighteen men only, besides myself.

Volunteer: What in the world did you suppose you could do here in Virginia with that amount of men?

Mr. Brown: Young man, I don't wish to discuss that question here.

Volunteer: You could not do anything.

Mr. Brown: Well, perhaps your ideas and mine on military subjects would differ materially.

Mr. Mason: How do you justify your acts?

Mr. Brown: I think, my friend, you are guilty of a great wrong against God and humanity I say it without wishing to be offensive and it would be perfectly right in any one to interfere with you so far as to free those you wilfully and wickedly hold in bondage. I do not say this insultingly.

Mr. Mason: I understand that.

Mr. Brown: I think I did right, and that others will do right who interfere with you at any time and all times. I hold that the golden rule, "Do unto others as you would that others should do unto you," applies to all who would help others to gain their liberty. . .

A Bystander: Do you consider this a religious movement?

Mr. Brown: It is, in my opinion, the greatest service a man can render to God.

Bystander: Do you consider yourself an instrument in the hands of Providence?

Mr. Brown: I do.

Bystander: Upon what principle do you justify your acts?

Mr. Brown: Upon the golden rule. I pity the poor in bondage that have none to help them; that is why I am here; not to gratify any personal animosity, revenge or vindictive spirit. It is my sympathy with the oppressed and the wronged, that are as good as you and as precious in the sight of God.

Bystander: Certainly. But why take the slaves against their will?

Mr. Brown: I never did.

Bystander: You did in one instance, at least.

Stephens, the other wounded prisoner, here said, in a firm, clear voice— "You are right. In one case, I know the negro wanted to go back."

A Bystander: Where did you come from?

Mr. Stephens: I lived in Ashtabula county, Ohio.

Mr. Vallandigham: How recently did you leave Ashtabula county?

Mr. Stephens: Some months ago. I never resided there any length of time; have been through there.

Mr. Vallandigham: How far did you live from Jefferson?

Mr. Brown: Be cautious, Stephens, about any answers that would commit any friend. I would not answer that.

Stephens turned partially over with a groan of pain, and was silent.

Mr. Vallandigham (to Mr. Brown): Who are your advisers in this movement?

Mr. Brown: I cannot answer that. I have numerous sympathizers throughout the entire North.

Mr. Vallandigham: In northern Ohio?

Mr. Brown: No more there than anywhere else; in all the free States . . .

Reporter of the Herald: I do not wish to annoy you; but if you have anything further you would like to say I will report it.

Mr. Brown: I have nothing to say, only that I claim to be here in carrying out a measure I believe perfectly justifiable, and not to act the part of an incendiary or ruffian, but to aid those suffering great wrong. I wish to say, furthermore, that you had better—all you people at the South—prepare yourselves for a settlement of that question that must come up for settlement sooner than you are prepared for. The sooner you are prepared the better. You may dispose of me very easily; I am nearly disposed of now; but this question is still to be settled—this Negro question I mean—the end of that is not yet. These wounds were inflicted upon me—both sabre cuts on my head and bayonet stabs in different parts of my body some minutes after I had ceased fighting and had consented to a surrender, for the benefit of others, not for my own. [This statement was vehemently denied by all around.] I believe the major [meaning Lieut. J. B. Stuart, of the United States cavalry, would not have been alive; I could have killed him just as easy as a mosquito when he came in, but I supposed he came in only to receive our surrender. There had been loud and long calls of "surrender" from us as loud as men could yell but in the confusion and excitement I suppose we were not heard. I do not think the major, or any one, meant to butcher us after we had surrendered."

An Officer here stated that the order to the marines were not to shoot anybody; but when they were fired upon by Brown's men and one of them killed, they were obliged to return the compliment.

Mr. Brown insisted that the marines fired first.

An Officer: Why did not you surrender before the attack?

Mr. Brown: I did not think it was my duty or interest to do so. We assured the prisoners that we did not wish to harm them, and they should be set at liberty. I exercised my best judgment, not believing the people would want only sacrifice their own fellow citizens, when vat offered to let them go on condition of being allowed to change our position about a quarter of a mile. The prisoners agreed by vote among themselves to pass across the bridge with us. We wanted them only as a sort of guaranty of our own safety; that we should not be fired into. We took them in the first place as hostages and to keep them from doing any harm. We did kill some men in defending ourselves, but I saw no one fire except directly in self-defence. Our orders were strict not to harm any one not in arms against us.

Q.: Brown, suppose you had every nigger in the United States, what would you do

A.: Set them free.

Q.: Your intention was to carry them off and free them?

A.: Not at all.

A Bystander: To set them free would sacrifice the life of every man in this community.

Mr. Brown: I do not think so.

Bystander: I know it. I think you are fanatical.

Mr. Brown: And I think you are fanatical. "Whom the gods would destroy they first make mad," and you are mad.

Q.: Was it your only object to free the negroes?

A.: Absolutely our only object.

Q.: But you demanded and took Col. Washington's silver and watch?

A.: Yes; we intended freely to appropriate the property of slaveholders to carry out our object. It was for that, and only that, and with no design to enrich ourselves with any plunder whatever.

Q.: Did you know Sherrod in Kansas? I understand you killed him.

A.: I killed no man except in fair fight; I fought at Black Jack Point and Ossawatomie, and if I killed anybody it was at one of those places.

***

Charlestown, Va.
November 2, 1859.
John Brown's Last Statement to the Court,

I have, may it please the court, a few words to say.

In the first place, I deny everything but what I have all along admitted—the design on my part to free the slaves. I intended certainly to have made a clean thing of that matter, as I did last winter when I went into Missouri and there took slaves without the snapping of a gun on either side, moved them through the country, and finally left them in Canada. I designed to have done the same thing again on a larger scale. That was all I intended. I never did intend murder, or treason, or the destruction of property, or to excite or incite slaves to rebellion, or to make insurrection.

I have another objection; and that is, it is unjust that I should suffer such a penalty. Had I interfered in the manner which I admit, and which I admit has been fairly proved (for I admire the truthfulness and candor of the greater portion of the witnesses who have testified in this case)—had I so interfered in behalf of the rich, the powerful, the intelligent, the so-called great, or in behalf of any of their friends—either father, mother, brother, sister, wife, or children, or any of that class—and suffered and sacrificed what I have in this interference, it would have been all right; and every man in this court would have deemed it an act worthy of reward rather than punishment.

This court acknowledges, as I suppose, the validity of the law of God. I see a book kissed here which I suppose to be the Bible, or at least the New Testament. That teaches me that all things whatsoever I would that men should do to me, I should do even so to them. It teaches me, further, to "remember them that are in bonds, as bound with them." I endeavored to act up to that instruction. I say I am yet too young to understand that God is any respecter of persons. I believe that to have interfered as I have done—as I have always freely admitted I have done—in behalf of His despised poor was not wrong, but right. Now, if it is deemed necessary that I should forfeit my life for the furtherance of the ends of justice, and mingle my blood further with the blood of my children and with the blood of millions in this slave country whose rights are disregarded by wicked, cruel, and unjust enactments—I submit; so let it be done!

Let me say one word further.

I feel entirely satisfied with the treatment I have received on my trial. Considering all the circumstances it has been more generous than I expected. But I feel no consciousness of guilt. I have stated that from the first what was my intention and what was not. I never had any design against the life of any person, nor any disposition to commit treason, or excite slaves to rebel, or make any general insurrection. I never encouraged any man to do so, but always discouraged any idea of that kind.

Let me say also a word in regard to the statements made by some of those connected with me. I hear it has been stated by some of them that I have induced them to join me. But the contrary is true. I do not say this to injure them, but as regretting their weakness. There is not one of them but joined me of his own accord, and the greater part of them at their own expense. A number of them I never saw, and never had a word of conversation with till the day they came to me; and that was for the purpose I have stated.

Now I have done.

GLOSSARY

animosity: hatred, resentment, or antagonism that tends to be displayed in open hostility

bayonet: a dagger-like weapon attached to the muzzle of a gun and used in hand-to-hand combat

candor: frankness, openness, and sincerity of speech or other expression

constitution: written by Brown in 1858 to protect the "persons, property, lives, and liberties" of slaves and free men

fanatical: motivated or characterized by an extreme, uncritical enthusiasm or zeal

incendiary: tending to arouse strife or sedition; tending to inflame the senses

induce: to lead or move by persuasion or influence

ruffian: a tough, lawless person; roughneck; bully

sabre: a curved cavalry sword with a single edge; also spelled "saber"

Document Analysis

These two excerpts from John Brown's interrogation and trial mark a turning point in American history, as well as stand as a platform for a man to explain his beliefs and his felonious actions. John Brown could have used his trial as an opportunity to lay the blame on another, to explain his actions, or to try to find a way to escape with his life. Instead, Brown continued to uphold the values by which he had lived his life. He described his own religious fervor, his adherence to the "golden rule," and his ultimate goal of equality for all men both during the trial and in his final address to the court. Even though his court-appointed lawyer tried to portray him as crazy in an effort to have the case dismissed, Brown maintained a calm and collected manner during his questioning and even praised those who spoke against him for their honesty. His zeal for his cause is apparent in his word choice and the actions he took that landed him in jail, but overall he gives the appearance of a reasonable and well-educated man who was simply pursuing what he thought to be right. It was this contradiction between rational defense and treasonous actions that spurred such interest and controversy around his trial. The fallout from the trial was enormous and caused the breach between Northern and Southern views to widen even further. It even has been declared a cause for the Civil War's early beginning. Whether or not John Brown's life and trial altered the course of the nation, it was, without a doubt, a significant moment in history, with long-lasting effects.

The first section of the primary source is a partial transcript of Brown's interrogation, which took place immediately following his capture at Harpers Ferry. Wounded during the fighting, Brown was then interrogated for several hours by a Mr. Vallandigham, Mr.

Mason, and an unnamed "volunteer," during which time Brown revealed several details about his views and beliefs. These beliefs have caused him to be viewed by different people as either a hero or a terrorist. Even though many Southerners believed Brown to be crazy, his tone throughout his interrogation remains very calm and reasonable. He explains his actions, refuses to answer questions to which he does not know the answer, and even rebuffs the volunteer for criticizing him for his small number of followers. While his word choices reveal him to be an extremist, his demeanor indicates a composed individual who is capable and sound of mind.

Brown clearly lays out his reason for the attack as an interference with those who are "guilty of a great wrong against God and humanity," for they "wilfully and wickedly hold [others] in bondage." He further states that he is doing so in order to uphold the "golden rule" and believes himself to be "an instrument in the hands of Providence." He truly believed in his actions and that he was doing the right thing, upholding the intent of God. In his mind, equality should apply to everyone, not just white men, but black slaves too. This was a revolutionary concept in the South and was contravened by the existence of legal slavery there, as well as such federal laws as the Kansas-Nebraska Act of 1854 and the *Dred Scott v. Sandford* Supreme Court decision in 1857. These setbacks for the abolitionist cause spurred Brown to commit the attack on Harpers Ferry, because he saw the possibility of freedom for slaves through legal means slowly slipping away.

Although his intention was to help free slaves, or create an uprising of slaves, Brown did not want to force any man into doing something against his will. He states this himself as he says that he never "induced" anyone to join him and did not coerce slaves to leave their masters. One of his men who was also questioned during the interrogation, Mr. Stephens, and someone only recorded as a "bystander" made a statement to the contrary. Stephens said that he knew of at least one "negro" who wanted to turn back. While Brown did not reply directly to this statement, it seems unlikely that he would have forced anyone to do something that they were unwilling to do, simply because it would work against his cause. He saw himself as a liberator and a sort of freedom fighter. He could not perpetuate this image if he acted against the wishes of those he was supposed to be helping. Even later in the questioning, he says that he had no intention to "carry them off," for this phrase has a negative connotation. And later, during his final statement to the court, Brown returns indirectly to Stephens's statement and seems to chide him for giving false testimony concerning this point.

The diction of Brown, Stephens, and the interrogators is also a factor in understanding this excerpt. Brown and Stephens both refer to blacks as "negroes," which at the time was a common term with little derogatory meaning. One of the interrogators, on the other hand, asked Brown a question in which he referred to slaves as "niggers," a somewhat more pejorative term then and extremely offensive now. Furthermore, Brown is very formal in his speech and maintains a calm appearance, even under these accusations. When someone in the room calls him "fanatical," he simply turns the allegation around on that person. After he says, "'Whom the gods would destroy they first make mad,' and you are mad," there is no further movement on that line of questioning. No one responds to that statement, possibly because there is very little point in accusing a man who does not feel the need to defend his actions or explain away his guilt.

John Brown's Final Speech to the Court

For a man who was tried while lying in a bed due to the wounds he sustained at Harpers Ferry, John Brown made an impassioned and poignant final speech to the court. One of the characteristics that made John Brown so famous, or infamous, was his unfaltering dedication to his ideals. He begins his final address by freely admitting to his plan to free slaves and admitting to having done so previously. This was a man who felt no guilt for what he did and did not regret his actions, even though he knew that, having committed them, they were now going to cause his death. In one of his final moments before his execution, when he could express whatever emotions or thoughts he had without fear of further reprisal, Brown conducted himself with dignity and did not rage against those who had decided that he was to die. The only words he spoke were to highlight the hypocrisy behind their ruling, to speak of his submission before God, and to express his pity for the weakness of his coconspirators.

In Brown's second paragraph, he speaks directly to the motivation of his prosecutors. He tells them that they are wrong in their judgment of his actions—they do not actually want to punish him for attempting to free men, but rather for freeing the wrong men. If he had acted in the same way, but as a force for the Southerners, then he would have been praised and not punished. This understanding of his rivals reveals Brown's ability to truly know his opponents. It takes intelligence to be able to read people in such a way, and although it does not change the outcome of the trial, it helps to make Brown even more memorable. He must have known, during his years planning for the attack on Harpers Ferry, how he would be treated in any court if he was caught, and this may have made other men stop their plans, but not John Brown. Speaking before the court, he shows no fear, only a quiet conviction.

His religious dedication is apparent too in his speech, as is fitting considering what a large role religion played in his life and mindset. He conveys a sense of confusion that almost mocks the court as he talks about seeing a Bible in the room, but the men around it are ignoring the lessons within. As his life's work was heavily influenced by the Bible, especially such parts as the golden rule and the idea stated in his final speech that those who are in bondage are also bonded to their captors, he sees hypocrisy in the courtroom. Ultimately, he states that he cannot know God's will, but he is willing to go to his death if that is a necessary part of achieving justice for all men. This confirmed his fanaticism for Southerners at the same time that the Northern abolitionists would have commended him for his devotion to his cause.

Overall, Brown's speech reflects the individual; it is dignified, expresses his opinions and values, reiterates his motives and intentions, and does so without losing impact to unnecessary tangents and shifting of blame. In his last statements, Brown expresses his appreciation of the manner in which the trial was conducted, fairly and honestly. He also conveys his disappointment in the men who stated that their involvement was not of their own choosing, but that they had been coerced or induced in some way by Brown. All of this emotion, however, is confined and eloquently put into words in a way that most people would not be able to accomplish.

Lasting Impact of John Brown

John Brown lived in a time of great movement toward change. He predated the Civil War but was a part of the upheaval that would eventually culminate in the divide of the United States and its reformation. White supremacy dominated in the North as well as the South, even though many Northerners viewed slavery as wrong. The actual act of freeing the slaves was viewed as a scary and nearly impossible task—for what if the freed slaves moved North and overtook those states or stayed in the South and turned on their former owners? The "Negro question," as Brown calls it, fueled debate, legislation, violent protest, and more controversy than nearly any other issue. It would take a nearly legendary man, Abraham Lincoln, and a civil war to end slavery in the United States. But it took a man like John Brown to create enough tension and distrust between the different groups to polarize the North and South and bring the conflict to a head.

Slavery had been a part of American life since the mid-seventeenth century, and while many individuals as well as religious groups viewed the practice as wrong, not until 1780 were the first antislavery laws passed. Many Northern states followed this shift in legislation, but federal laws and Southern states did not move with this new turn in thought. This began the tension between the North and South, which only grew as new states entered the Union, having declared themselves to be either free or slave; the Missouri Compromise was outlined in 1820, delineating free and slave territories; and new taxes, seen as disproportionately targeting the South and benefitting the North, were added in the late 1820s and early 1830s. By the time of Brown's raid, the South had twice threatened to secede from the Union, first in 1832 and later in 1850, partially fueling the Compromise of 1850. This was the era into which John Brown was born, raised, and worked, an atmosphere in which slavery was one of the most visible social and political issues for all Americans. Slave rebellions, such as that led by Nat Turner in Virginia in 1831, and free blacks working to overcome slavery, as did Brown's friend Frederick Douglass, were not unknown, but Brown broke the mold when he, a white man, attacked a military post in order to arm the slaves he was trying to free. Many actions, both legislative and extralegal, led up to the outbreak of the Civil War, but these were fueled by distrust and dislike on both sides of the conflict. Brown's plot inflamed these emotions, putting true fear into Southerners and inspiring abolitionists.

John Brown's legacy took two very different avenues of expression. The first was in the way people viewed his actions, trial, and death. He became a folk hero of sorts and was idolized in song and poetry. Henry Wadsworth Longfellow, the famous nineteenth-century poet, even stated that John Brown's death would be remembered as "a great day in our history; the date of a new revolution" (Villard 563). Henry David Thoreau, the famous author, transcendentalist philosopher, and advocate of civil disobedience, even spoke on Brown's behalf to people in the North, because at first his militant action was poorly received and viewed as too violent. He even wrote the essay "A Plea for Captain John Brown," in an effort to stir Northern sympathy for Brown after his capture. With such well-known and beloved figures supporting his actions, John Brown became a symbol for the North and showed that, sometimes, drastic measures must be taken to overcome a government or an institution that did not support all of its people.

The second impact was much more immediate and worked with the first to create a paradigm shift in the way people worked for change. Before John Brown's attack on Harpers Ferry, white men had rarely instigated violence in order to help overturn slavery, and even passive, nonviolent abolitionism was considered extremist. After Brown, this type of nonviolence became the behavior of moderates, which tends to be the bulk of a population. Whether or not he had planned on this outcome, Brown's actions created shifts—some would say polarization—along the slavery–antislavery spectrum. Even though the North was originally aghast at his actions, Brown turned Northern public opinion more actively toward antislavery. In doing so, historian David S. Reynolds credits Brown with possibly having accelerated the start of the Civil War, following the election of the president who would issue the Emancipation Proclamation.

In these excerpts, John Brown's own words portray his character and the beliefs on which he based his life. With the combination of reasonable tone, thorough understanding of his adversaries, strict adherence to his own moral code, and nearly unprecedented violence, John Brown further divided the North and South—highlighted by the North turning Brown into a martyr while the South viewed him as a terrorist. He may be one of history's best-remembered examples of what a few men can do when they refuse to follow a system that they believe to be unjust and are willing to give their lives in the hope of making a significant change.

Essential Themes

In a time when white supremacy was prevalent and slavery was an accepted institution, a single man's trial was able to galvanize people into realizing that something was wrong with their tolerance of this society. The short- and long-term effects of John Brown's trial are much the same, the polarization of North and South, the beginning of the Civil War less than two years later, and the overwhelming understanding that no man is without the power to effect change. If a person believes in something enough and refuses to let injustice stand, then even with a few men, that person can make a difference. This was the heroic spirit that was admired in the North and the force of will that was feared in the South. Brown's unwavering calm, mixed with his utter devotion, made his message unstoppable, even though most people did not actually agree with the crimes he committed. His failed attack on Harpers Ferry is not the reason he is remembered a century and a half after his death. His presence and his effect on his friends, acquaintances, and even those he never met is what made him memorable. Without such people to instigate change, the world would look very different than it does today.

Anna Accettola, MA

Bibliography

American Experience: John Brown's Holy War. PBS Online/WGBH, 1999. Web. 19 Mar. 2013.

Linder, Douglas O. *Famous Trials: The Trial of John Brown, 1859*. University of Missouri–Kansas City School of Law, 2012. Web. 19 Mar. 2013.

Reynolds, David S. *John Brown, Abolitionist: The Man Who Killed Slavery, Sparked the Civil War, and Seeded Civil Rights*. New York: Knopf, 2005. Print.

Villard, Oswald Garrison. *John Brown, 1800–1859: A Biography Fifty Years After*. 1910. Charleston: BiblioBazaar, 2011. Print.

Additional Reading

Carton, Evan. *Patriotic Treason: John Brown and the Soul of America*. Lincoln: U of Nebraska P, 2009. Print.

DeCaro, Louis A., Jr. *Fire from the Midst of You: A Religious Life of John Brown*. New York: NYU, 2002. Print.

---. *John Brown: The Cost of Freedom*. New York: International, 2007. Print.

Du Bois, W. E. B. *John Brown*. 1909. New York: Sharpe, 1997. Print.

John Brown's Holy War. Dir. Robert Kenner. Narr. Joe Morton. WGBH Educational Foundation, 1999. DVD.

Oates, Stephen. *To Purge This Land with Blood: A Biography of John Brown*. New York: Harper, 1970. Print.

Peterson, Merrill D. *John Brown: The Legend Revisited*. Charlottesville: U of Virginia P, 2002. Print.

Redpath, James. *The Public Life of Capt. John Brown: With an Auto-Biography of His Childhood and Youth*. 1860. Charleston: Forgotten, 2012. Print.

Renehan, Edward J. *The Secret Six: The True Tale of the Men Who Conspired with John Brown*. Columbia: U of South Carolina P, 1997. Print.

Sanborn, F. B., ed. *The Life and Letters of John Brown: Liberator of Kansas, and Martyr of Virginia*. 1885. Charleston: BiblioBazaar, 2010. Print.

LESSON PLAN: **Rebellion at Harpers Ferry**

Students analyze a transcript of the trial of John Brown to consider disputes over slavery in the period leading up to the Civil War.

Learning Objectives

Analyze the causes and effects of John Brown's uprising, trial, and execution; compare and contrast different ideas about the institution of slavery; examine the influence of Brown's trial on the antislavery movement.

Materials: John Brown, "The Trial of John Brown," (1859).

Overview Questions

Why was John Brown put on trial? Why did he think his actions were justified, and why did others disagree? How does Brown's trial highlight areas of disagreement over "the Negro question"? In what ways might his trial and execution have been central to the buildup to the Civil War?

Step 1: Comprehension Questions

What happened in Harpers Ferry, Virginia? Why did Brown go there? What did he hope to accomplish?

- **Activity:** Ask students to reconstruct the events at Harpers Ferry and Brown's reasons for leading the raid, reading aloud key passages that highlight Brown's motivations.

Step 2: Comprehension Questions

How does Brown's account of the rebellion differ from that of the other speakers at the trial? Why do both Brown and his interrogator consider each other "fanatical"?

- **Activity:** Have students select a person involved in the trial, such as Brown, Mr. Mason, or the officer, and summarize that person's view of the events at Harpers Ferry. Have students share their summaries with the class and discuss why the perspectives differ so greatly.

Step 3: Context Questions

What arguments does Brown make to justify abolition? What reasons does he give for this view? Why do others disagree?

- **Activity:** Pair students to list Brown's arguments against slavery and then list the counterarguments raised during the trial. Have students use their lists to discuss whether they think Brown was right in organizing the raid.

Step 4: Historical Connections Questions

How might Brown's trial have intensified clashes over slavery during this period? How might his last statement and his execution have aided the antislavery cause? In what ways might these events have contributed to the outbreak of the Civil War?

- **Activity:** Ask students to consider what might have happened if Brown had been killed in the raid and therefore not brought to trial or allowed to voice his views. Discuss how it might have felt to hear Brown's last words and what kind of impact this might have had in the period leading up to war.

Step 5: Response Paper

Word length and additional requirements set by Instructor. Students answer the research question in the *Overview Questions*. Students state a thesis and use as evidence passages from the primary source document as well as support from supplemental materials assigned in the lesson.

Supplemental Historical Documents

HISTORICAL DOCUMENT

The Rights of Man to Property

Date: 1829
Author: Skidmore, Thomas
Genre: article; essay

Perhaps, among all the subjects that have received human investigation, there is none that has occupied so much of the time, and exercised so severely, the intellectual faculties of man, as his inquiries into the origin and nature of the rights of property. And perhaps it is equally true, that no enquiry whatever has been attended with so little success. It may seem to be the height of egotism, of vanity, of arrogance, of ignorance perhaps, and I know not what else, to make such a charge against the wisdom of past ages. But I confidently point to all that has been, and all that is, and ask if there be, or have been, any two governments of the world, that now have, or that ever have had their laws alike each other, on the subject of the rights of property? Not any two even of the States of our Union, can say as much; though among them, one would think, was the place to look for such a similarity, if it were any where to be found.

No wonder then, that Voltaire, on some occasion should have said that rights change character, as often as a traveller changes post-horses. It was, in truth, no exaggeration; for the fact is still worse than his representation makes it. In the same nation, even, those rights, at two different periods of time are not the same. And, as if this were not a sufficient satire upon our understanding of the subject, I believe, that there may be cases of the litigation of the rights of property in any country now known, where, if one hundred tribunals were simultaneously to try them, each of the greatest eminence for talents in judicial investigation, and each having before them precisely the same means of arriving at the facts, but having, however, no knowledge of each others' deliberations, they would, nevertheless, give a hundred different decisions.

This 'uncertainty of the law,' glorious as it has been proverbially called, by way of ridicule, I take it, is evidence, that the subject is not understood. If it were so, these varying decisions could never happen. Rights are like truths, capable of being understood alike by all men;—as much so, as the demonstrations of Euclid. If, what are called so, are not so understood, it is proof that they are not rights; for it is scarcely to be presumed that they could not be rendered apparent to our perception—

and that they are rather the arbitrary commands of power, than anything else.

But it is better to supply the deficiency of understanding on this subject, which seems to prevail, than to make it a matter of reproach. Let us see if it is possible to do it. It will be an achievement, of no small importance to mankind, inasmuch, as it will, in my apprehension, go far to exterminate all the moral and political evils, with which they are now afflicted.

There seem to be three things which have an intimate and inseparable connection with each other.

These are property, persons, and rights.

Out of these materials are built, or ought to be built, all the governments in the world. These are all the necessary and proper elements of their constitution; and these being applied as they have been, have caused, in my estimation, more evil to mankind, than anyone can pretend that governments have done good; and, being applied as they may be, will fulfil the destiny of man, by reversing the results of the past.

What, then, is property? I answer; the whole material world: just as it came from the hands of the Creator.

What are persons? The human beings, whom the same Creator placed, or formed upon it, as inhabitants.

What are Rights? The title which each of the inhabitants of this Globe, has to partake of and enjoy equally with his fellows, its fruits and its productions.

Let no one pretend, that there is yet other property. Let him ascend with me to the earliest ages; to periods of time, anterior to the formation of all governments; when our race existed, but when political institutions did not. For it is to these periods, we must ascend, if we mean to arrive at a true understanding of the theory of all just governments: And it is to these all my remarks, will apply, until I come to offer my sentiments as to the principles of property which ought to enter into their formation. Let no one, then, tell me that the labor, which the savage of the forest has employed, in the manufacture of his bow, is property. That only is *property*, which belongs to someone. Now it cannot belong to the race, collectively, for they did not produce it. It cannot belong to the individual, who prepared the bow—because, *it cannot be separated from it*; and because, if it could, it could have no physical existence whatever; and having no such existence, he would possess nothing more, than if he had never made it. Besides, the material, of which the bow is made, is the property of mankind. It is a property, too, which, previous to the existence of government, has never been alienated to anyone. If it has not been alienated, it cannot belong to another. Another cannot have any right to make use of it. Before he does, so, he must obtain the consent of all. What right then had that other to bestow his labor upon it? What right had he to convert it into a bow, or into anything else?

Instead of acquiring a right, thereby, to the bow, he has rather committed a trespass upon the great community of which he is a member. He is rather, of right, subject to punishment, than invested with title, to that which he has taken without consent, and appropriated to his own use. At least, then, it is evident, that *his labor*, bestowed upon the *material* of the bow, does not give him a title to the latter? Does the mere act of *taking possession* of it, give it? Most certainly not. For here, as well as elsewhere, consent is necessary. Otherwise, it would be quite as correct, for example, (all the members having put in an equal share of the capital) for a member of a banking company to appropriate to his own use, the contents or any part thereof, of the iron chest containing the gold and silver belonging to the whole. Nor is it an objection to the force of this argument, to say, that the iron-chest is already in possession of the company, by its agents or otherwise, while the domain of nature is not. It is here that I deny the truth of the declaration. The domain *is* in possession. The owners—and they are *equal* owners too, are already present, and upon it. They have not, it is true, *divided* it, among themselves, and given to each what he may call his own, anymore than the Banking Company mentioned has done the same thing: but they are nevertheless in possession. The analogy therefore is full and complete.

Will it be said, then, someone may ask, that if an Indian kill a deer, it is not, therefore, his? Most certainly it is not. What, in my turn I would ask, is to become of other Indians, if there be actually fewer deer, than are needed? Must the mere accidental, or even sought for, circumstance, of any Indian's meeting with, and killing a deer, make such Indian the owner of it, to the exclusion of his fellows, who have an equal claim to it by the right of nature? Shall one of the species feast upon it, and the remainder hunger? Besides, as in the case of the bow, may not trespass have been committed in killing the deer also? As, in that case, the *animal is the property of the whole*, and if consent have not been given, it still remains their property, whatever *one* of their number may have thought or done to the contrary. For the owners of this deer are only to be divested of their right and title to it, by their own act—and not by the act of another. . . .

In speaking of the consent which I require each individual to obtain of the whole community, let me not be understood, as considering such consent as being the origin of each person's right to his equal share of the whole property of the globe. By no means. This right he has in virtue of his existence, and in virtue of the existence of the property in question. They are inseparable, while one has vital life, or the other physical existence. But the consent I speak of is necessary, not for the purpose of granting rights, for these are born with the being to whom they belong, but, to define and locate his share; to say how much, what, and where it shall be; and to secure and defend its enjoyment exclusively to himself. Without such designation, he could not be assured of possession, to the exclusion of another; since that other has as good a natural right, to that which is artificially assigned to him, as he himself can pretend to have. As well might it be, contended that the pleasure of the executor, is the source of the right which the heir has, to the share he ultimately obtains, of the estate of the testator, as that the community in question, confers any right on its citizens.

The executor is only a trustee, for the benefit of the legatees; the testator, he who created the executor, furnishes the legacies. So, in the case of the great community of mankind. They in their general, or collective capacity, are trustees, for the benefit of each individual of the species—and the Creator of the Universe is the being, who has furnished the property, which is the subject-matter of the trust, and ordered it to be distributed to all equally. No act therefore, which either the heir to the estate, in the one case, or an individual of the great mass of mankind, in the other, is capable of committing, is competent to create rights for such individual; and for the plain and unanswerable reason, that, they are already created; in the first case, by the testator; and in the last, by the Being who made us and all we behold.

Nor, on the other hand, has the executor, or the great community referred to, any power to create rights, and for the same reason, that they are already created; and that there is no discretion given, to either of the agents or trustees in question, to alter or modify them in the smallest degree. If, as is often the case with legacies, the Divinity had specifically given, designated portions, of the fruits of his Works, to specified persons; then indeed, there would be no occasion for the great community in question to interfere. The work, which it is now their duty to perform, they would then find already achieved to their hands; and they would have nothing to do but to acquiesce. Besides, another reason, why neither the executor, or the community referred to, is able to confer rights, is, that they were not the creators, nor of course the owners, in their own original right, of the property in question. It necessarily existed previous to, and independent of their existence, and of course, came into their possession, subject to the conditions and the commands of a power who created both. . . .

LESSON PLAN: **The Distribution of Property**

Students analyze an excerpt from Thomas Skidmore's book on property, persons, and rights in order to learn about the early development of the US labor movement.

Learning Objectives

Explain Skidmore's ideas on property and wealth; analyze the causes and effects of an unequal distribution of wealth; describe Skidmore's solution and his views on property ownership and equality; hypothesize the influence of Skidmore's ideas on the labor movement in the United States and around the world.

Materials: Thomas Skidmore, "The Rights of Man to Property" (1829).

Overview Questions

What is Skidmore's perspective on property and wealth? Why has there been an unequal distribution of wealth? What factors have contributed to inequality? Is Skidmore's plan or solution possible? Why or why not? How might Skidmore's ideas have influenced later thinkers on property? How might they have influenced the development of national and international labor movements?

Step 1: Comprehension Questions

What is Skidmore's perspective on property and wealth? Who owns property?

- **Activity:** Select students to read aloud key passages from the selection. As students follow along, instruct them to underline or highlight phrases that indicate Skidmore's perspective on property and wealth. Invite students to share their findings and discuss them as a class.

Step 2: Comprehension Questions

Why has there been an unequal distribution of wealth? What factors have led to the imbalance and to inequality?

- **Activity:** Ask students to review Skidmore's ideas on what has caused an unequal distribution of wealth. Next, have students write a summary to describe the main factors that Skidmore claims have caused the imbalance.

Step 3: Context Questions

Is Skidmore's plan or solution possible? Why or why not? Evaluate its possible effects on people, property, and rights.

- **Activity:** Have students work in small groups to write down the plan or solution that Skidmore presents. Ask students to discuss how viable the plan is, then have each student write an evaluation of it, considering its effects on people, property, and rights.

Step 4: Exploration Questions

How might Skidmore's ideas have influenced later thinkers on ideas of property? How might they have influenced the development of national and international labor movements?

- **Activity:** Provide an opportunity for students to research other perspectives on property, such as those of Karl Marx, or on labor, such as Robert Owen. Ask students to compare and contrast both perspectives and to write two or three paragraphs explaining how Skidmore's ideas may have influenced those of later thinkers.

Step 5: Response Paper

Word length and additional requirements set by Instructor. Students answer the research question in the *Overview Questions*. Students state a thesis and use as evidence passages from the primary source document as well as support from supplemental materials assigned in the lesson.

HISTORICAL DOCUMENT

The Education of Free Men

Date: 1846; 1848
Author: Mann, Horace
Genre: essay

I believe in the existence of a great, immutable principle of natural law, or natural ethics,—a principle antecedent to all human institutions and incapable of being abrogated by any ordinances of man,—a principle of divine origin, clearly legible in the ways of Providence as those ways are manifested in the order of nature and in the history of the race,—which proves the absolute right of every human being that comes into the world to an education; and which, of course, proves the correlative duty of every government to see that the means of that education are provided for all.

In regard to the application of this principle of natural law,—that is, in regard to the extent of the education to be provided for all, at the public expense,—some differences of opinion may fairly exist, under different political organizations; but under a republican government, it seems clear that the minimum of this education can never be less than such as is sufficient to qualify each citizen for the civil and social duties he will be called to discharge;—such an education as teaches the individual the great laws of bodily health; as qualifies for the fulfillment of parental duties; as is indispensable for the civil functions of a witness or a juror; as is necessary for the voter in municipal affairs; and finally, for the faithful and conscientious discharge of all those duties which devolve upon the inheritor of a portion of the sovereignty of this great republic. . . .

In obedience to the laws of God and to the laws of all civilized communities, society is bound to protect the natural life; and the natural life cannot be protected without the appropriation and use of a portion of the property which society possesses. We prohibit infanticide under penalty of death. We practice a refinement in this particular.

The life of an infant is inviolable even before he is born; and he who feloniously takes it, even before birth, is as subject to the extreme penalty of the law, as though he had struck down manhood in its vigor, or taken away a mother by violence from the sanctuary of home, where she blesses her offspring. But why preserve the natural life of a child, why preserve unborn embryos of life, if we do not intend to watch over and to protect them, and to expand their subsequent existence into usefulness and happiness?

As individuals, or as an organized community, we have no natural right; we can derive no authority or countenance from reason; we can cite no attribute or purpose of the divine nature, for giving birth to any human being, and then inflicting upon that being the curse of ignorance, of poverty and of vice, with all their attendant calamities. We are brought then to this startling but inevitable alternative. The natural life of an infant should be extinguished as soon as it is born, or the means should be provided to save that life from being a curse to its possessor; and therefore every State is bound to enact a code of laws legalizing and enforcing Infanticide, or a code of laws establishing Free Schools! . . .

Under the Providence of God, our means of education are the grand machinery by which the "raw material" of human nature can be worked up into inventors and discoverers, into skilled artisans and scientific farmers, into scholars and jurists, into the founders of benevolent institutions, and the great expounders of ethical and theological science.

By means of early education, those embryos of talent may be quickened, which will solve the difficult problems of political and economical law; and by them, too, the genius may be kindled which will blaze forth in the Poets of Humanity. Our schools, far more than they have done, may supply the Presidents and Professors of Colleges, and Superintendents of Public Instruction, all over the land; and send, not only into our sister states, but across the Atlantic, the men of practical science, to superintend the construction of the great works of art. Here, too, may those judicial powers be developed and invigorated, which will make legal principles so clear and convincing as to prevent appeals to force; and, should the clouds of war ever lower over our country, some hero may be found,—the nursling of our schools, and ready to become the leader of our armies,—that best of all heroes, who will secure the glories of a peace, unstained by the magnificent murders of the battle-field. . . .

Without undervaluing any other human agency, it may be safely affirmed that the Common School, improved and energized, as it can easily be, may become the most effective and benignant of all the forces of civilization. Two reasons sustain this position. In the first place, there is universality in its operation, which can be affirmed of no other institution whatever. If administered in the spirit of justice and conciliation, all the rising generation may be brought within the circle of its reformatory and elevating influences. And, in the second place, the materials upon which it operates are so pliant and ductile as to be susceptible of assuming a greater variety of forms than any other earthly work of the Creator. The inflexibility and ruggedness of the oak, when compared with the lithe sapling or the tender germ, are but feeble emblems to typify the docility of childhood, when contrasted with the obduracy and intractableness of man. It is these inherent advantages of the Common School, which, in our own State, have produced results so striking, from a system so imperfect, and an administration so feeble. In teaching the blind, and the deaf and dumb, in kindling the latent spark of intelligence that lurks in an idiot's mind, and in the more holy work of reforming abandoned and outcast children, education has proved what it can do, by glorious experiments. These wonders, it has done in its infancy, and with the lights of a limited experience; but, when its faculties shall be fully developed, when it shall be trained to wield its mighty energies for the protection of society against the giant vices which now invade and torment it;—against intemperance, avarice, war, slavery, bigotry, the woes of want and the wickedness of waste,—then, there will not be a height to which these enemies of the race can escape, which it will not scale, nor a Titan among them all, whom it will not slay. . . .

Now, surely, nothing but Universal Education can counter-work this tendency to the domination of capital and the servility of labor. If one class possesses all the wealth and the education, while the residue of society is ignorant and poor, it matters not by what name the relation between them may be called; the latter, in fact and in truth, will be the servile dependants and subjects of the former. But if education be equably diffused, it will draw property after it, by the strongest of all attractions; for such a thing never did happen, and never can happen, as that an intelligent and practical body of men should be permanently poor. Property and labor, in different classes, are essentially antagonistic; but property and labor, in the same class, are essentially fraternal. The people of Massachusetts have, in some degree, appreciated the truth, that the unexampled prosperity of the State,—its comfort, its competence, its general intelligence and virtue,—is attributable to the education, more or less perfect, which all its people have received; but are they sensible of a fact equally important?—namely, that it is to this same education that two thirds of the people are indebted for not being, to-day, the vassals of as severe a tyranny, in the form of capital, as the lower classes of Europe are bound to in the form of brute force.

Education, then, beyond all other devices of human origin, is the great equalizer of the conditions of men—the balance-wheel of the social machinery. I do not here mean that it so elevates the moral nature as to make men disdain and abhor the oppression of their fellow-men. This idea pertains to another of its attributes. But I mean that it gives each man the independence and the means, by which he can resist the selfishness of other men. It does better than to disarm the poor of their hostility towards the rich; it prevents being poor. Agrarianism is the revenge of poverty against wealth. The wanton destruction of the property of others,—the burning of hay-ricks and corn-ricks, the demolition of machinery, because it supersedes hand-labor, the sprinkling of vitriol on rich dresses,—is only agrarianism run mad. Education prevents both the revenge and the madness. On the other hand, a fellow-feeling for one's class or caste is the common instinct of hearts not wholly sunk in selfish regards for person, or for family. The spread of education, by enlarging the cultivated class or caste, will open a wider area over which the social feelings will expand; and, if this education should be universal and complete, it would do more than all things else to obliterate factitious distinctions in society. . . .

But to all doubters, disbelievers, or despairers in human progress, it may still be said, there is one experiment which has never yet been tried. It is an experiment which, even before its inception, offers the highest authority for its ultimate success. Its formula is intelligible to all; and it is as legible as though written in starry letters on an azure sky. It is expressed in these few and simple words: "Train up a child in the way he should go, and when he is old he will not depart from it." This declaration is positive. If the conditions are complied with, it makes no provision for a failure. Though pertaining to morals, yet, if the terms of the direction are observed, there is no more reason to doubt the result, than there would be in an optical or a chemical experiment. . . .

But this experiment has never yet been tried. Education has never yet been brought to bear with one hundredth part of its potential force, upon the natures of children, and, through them, upon the character of men, and of the race. In all the attempts to reform mankind which have hitherto been made, whether by changing the frame of government, by aggravating or softening the severity of the penal code, or by substituting a government created, for a God-created religion;—in all these attempts, the infantile and youthful mind, its amenability to influences, and the enduring and self-operating character of the influences it receives, have been almost wholly unrecognized.

Here, then, is a new agency, whose powers are but just beginning to be understood, and whose mighty energies, hitherto, have been but feebly invoked; and yet, from our experience, limited and imperfect as it is, we do know that, far beyond any other earthly instrumentality, it is comprehensive and decisive. . . .

If, then, a government would recognize and protect the rights of religious freedom, it must abstain from subjugating the capacities of its children to any legal standard of religious faith, with as great fidelity as it abstains from controlling the opinions of men. It must meet the unquestionable fact that the old spirit of religious domination is adopting new measures to accomplish its work,—measures, which, if successful, will be as fatal to the liberties of mankind, as those which were practiced in by-gone days of violence and terror. These new measures are aimed at children instead of men. They propose to supersede the necessity of subduing free thought, in the mind of the adult, by forestalling the development of any capacity of free thought, in the mind of the child. They expect to find it easier to subdue the free agency of children, by binding them in fetters of bigotry, than to subdue the free agency of men, by binding them in fetters of iron. For this purpose, some are attempting to deprive children of their right to labor, and, of course, of their daily bread, unless they will attend a government school, and receive its sectarian instruction.

Some are attempting to withhold all means, even of secular education, from the poor, and thus punish them with ignorance, unless, with the secular knowledge which they desire, they will accept theological knowledge which they condemn. Others, still, are striving to break down all free Public School systems, where they exist, and to prevent their establishment, where they do not exist, in the hope, that on the downfall of these, their system will succeed. The sovereign antidote against these machinations is, Free Schools for all, and the right of every parent to determine the religious education of his children.

LESSON PLAN: **Universal Education**

Students analyze an essay by Horace Mann, combined from two reports to the Massachusetts State Board of Education, to consider education reform and arguments for universal public education in the antebellum period.

Learning Objectives

Consider multiple perspectives of reformers in the past; analyze how the reform movement affected the rise of public education in the United States; examine the importance of Horace Mann to contemporary education.

Materials: Horace Mann, "The Education of Free Men" (Tenth Annual Report to the Secretary of the Massachusetts State Board of Education, 1846; Twelfth Annual Report, 1848).

Overview Questions

Why did Mann think universal public education would benefit the United States? How did he think education would impact citizens and improve society? According to Mann, why does education lead to social equality? In what ways did Mann's reforms stand to reshape American society well into today?

Step 1: Comprehension Questions

Why does Mann think everyone deserves an education? What does he think the government's role should be in providing this education? What does he think students should learn in school?

- **Activity:** Have students state in their own words Mann's view of what education should be. Discuss how children had previously been educated and the alterations Mann proposes. Call on students to provide passages for support.

Step 2: Comprehension Questions

What changes to the education system does Mann want to implement? What oppositions exist to this plan? How does Mann argue against his opposition?

- **Activity:** Have students locate passages in which Mann argues against those opposed to public education. Have students discuss reasons why people might have resisted such sweeping changes. Ask students how Mann responds to his critics, citing passages to support their views.

Step 3: Context Questions

According to Mann, how will universal public education improve the nation? Why does he think a well-educated citizenry is necessary for a republic? What does he fear will happen if the United States fails to educate its children?

- **Activity:** Have students make a two-column chart listing the benefits Mann says will come of universal public education and the problems he fears will arise without it. Have students use their charts to discuss the ways Mann believed education would help develop prudent citizens.

Step 4: Historical Connections Questions

There are schools named after Horace Mann all over the country. How did Mann influence education in the United States? In what ways does his legacy live on?

- **Activity:** Ask students to consider what it would be like to grow up without universal schooling. Discuss whether students think the movement for universal public education achieved the results Mann hoped for, and what problems they think still need to be solved.

Step 5: Response Paper

Word length and additional requirements set by Instructor. Students answer the research question in the *Overview Questions*. Students state a thesis and use as evidence passages from the primary source document as well as support from supplemental materials assigned in the lesson.

HISTORICAL DOCUMENT

The New "Democratic" Doctrine

Date: 1856
Author: Young Men's Fremont and Dayton Central Union
Genre: political tract

The People of the Free States have so long yielded to the arrogant demands of the Slave Oligarchy in the South, that the latter has come to think it can carry any measure it sees fit, no matter how degrading it may be to the character of the free *white* men of the North.

Not many years ago the Southern slaveholders were contented to have their "human chattels" protected in the States where they held them.

Next, they demanded and secured *five* Slave States from acquired territory, (La., Fla., Ark., Mo., and Texas,) while the Free States have only secured *two*,—Iowa and California.

Next, the Slave power demanded all the territories, and broke down the Missouri Compromise, which secured a part of those territories to free labor.

Next, they demanded the right to come into the *free* States with their slaves whenever they choose, and stay as long as they please, and the United States Courts seem about to yield to them, and grant this outrageous demand.

But the last, the *crowning*, the *diabolical* assumption is, that Slavery is not to be confined to the NEGRO RACE, but must be made to include *laboring* WHITE MEN also. This doctrine, which is so monstrous and shocking as almost to seem incredible, is now openly avowed and defended by very many of the newspapers and of the public men of the South that support James Buchanan. The doctrine is also proclaimed by some Northern newspapers of the so-called Democratic party, but not generally with such boldness as in the South. . . .

"I call upon the opponents of Slavery to prove that the WHITE LABORERS of the North are as happy, as contented, or as comfortable, as the *Slaves* of the South. In the South the slaves do not suffer one-tenth of the evils endured by the white laborers of the North. Poverty is unknown to the Southern slave, for as soon as the masters of slaves becomes too poor to provide for them, he SELLS them to others who can take care of them. This, sir, is one of the excellencies of the system of Slavery, and this the superior condition of the Southern slave over the Northern WHITE laborer."

According to Mr. Downs, then, (good Democratic authority) all that the Northern *white laborer* requires is somebody to sell him when he falls into poverty. Admirable philanthropy! Beautiful Democracy!

Senator Clemens of Alabama declared in a speech in the U. S. Senate, that " the operatives of New England were not as well situated nor as comfortably off as the slaves that cultivate the rice and cotton fields of the South."

In a recent speech by Mr. Reynolds, Pierce Buchanan—Democratic candidate for Congress from Missouri, that gentleman distinctly asserted that—"The same construction of the power of Congress to exclude Slavery from a United States Territory, would justify the Government in excluding foreign-born citizens—GERMANS AND IRISH AS WELL AS NIGGERS."

Here a Missouri Democrat classes GERMANS and IRISH indiscriminately with NEGRO SLAVES.

Mr. L. H. Goode, another Atchison Democrat of Missouri, in a recent speech against the Free State men of Kansas, denounced the laboring men as "WHITE SLAVES."

These extracts are not taken from obscure prints, or obscure men. They are from the active, influential papers, and influential men who lead the Democratic party.

The Washington *Union*, the national organ of the "Democratic" party, says that the honest and heroic free LABORING MEN of Kansas—"Are a MISERABLE, BLEAR-EYED RABBLE, who have been transferred like SO MANY CATTLE to that country."

SENATOR BUTLER, (the uncle of "Assassin" Brooks) a shining light in the Democratic galaxy, declared in a speech in the U.S. Senate this session—"That men have no right to VOTE unless they are possessed of property as required by the Constitution of South Carolina. There no man can vote unless he owns *ten negroes*, or real estate to the *value of ten thousand dollars*."

And this is the doctrine which "Democracy," *so-called*, would introduce into the Free States.

JAMES BUCHANAN, the Presidential candidate of the men and of the party who hold these odious views, advocated the doctrine in the U. S. Senate, of reducing the WAGES of AMERICAN OPERATIVES and LABORERS to the European standard, which is known to be about TEN CENTS A DAY. What a fit candidate Mr. Buchanan is for those who would make WHITE MEN *slaves!*

JOHN C. FREMONT, the *true* Republican and true *Democrat*, who has worked his own way from poverty to greatness, pays the following high tribute to the dignity of FREE LABOR, and yet his enemies have the meanness to assert that he is a slave-holder. Col. Fremont *never* owned a dollar in human flesh. Hear what he says about "*free labor.*"

"FREE LABOR"—the natural capital which constitutes the *real wealth* of this great country, and creates that *intelligent power in the masses*, alone to be relied on as the bulwark of FREE INSTITUTIONS."

The New York *Day Book*, one of the two papers in New York City that support James Buchanan, proposes to enslave *poor* AMERICANS, GERMANS and IRISH, who may fall into poverty and be unable to support their families. Here are the *Day Book's* exact words in speaking of the POOR WHITE PEOPLE.

"Sell the parents of these children into SLAVERY. Let our Legislature pass a law that whoever will take these parents and take care of them and their OFFSPRING, in sickness and in health,—*clothe* them, *feed* them, and *house* them,—*shall be legally entitled to their services*; and let the same Legislature degree that whoever receives these parents and their CHILDREN, and obtains their services, shall take care of them AS LONG AS THEY SHALL LIVE."

JOHN C. FREMONT is the Representative and Advocate of the extension of FREE LABOR.

JAMES BUCHANAN and MILLARD FILLMORE are the Advocates of the extension of Slave Labor.

For which will you cast your votes, Lovers of Liberty?

LESSON PLAN: **A Vote for Liberty**

Students analyze a political pamphlet to consider the content and style of antebellum election campaigning.

Learning Objectives

Identify historical antecedents to the extension of white male political participation; compare and contrast regional views of slavery and free labor; analyze multiple causes that led to the rise of the Republican Party; evaluate the importance of political campaigning in the antebellum period.

Materials: Young Men's Fremont and Dayton Central Union, New York, "The New 'Democratic' Doctrine" (1856).

Overview Questions

Why was this short pamphlet published, and what did it hope to achieve? What fears do the authors have if James Buchanan is elected, and why? What were the causes and effects of the regional divisions expressed in John C. Fremont's campaign? How might this pamphlet and others like it have contributed to the rise of the Republican Party?

Step 1: Comprehension Questions

Why was this pamphlet written? What impact did its writers hope to have? What evidence does it marshal for support? How does it strive to influence voters?

- **Activity:** Discuss the persuasive elements of the pamphlet, such as the use of quotations, emphasis, and rhetorical questions. Ask students whether they would have found the pamphlet persuasive, explaining why or why not.

Step 2: Context Questions

How does the pamphlet contrast enslaved people in the South with white laborers in the North? What concerns does it raise about "white slaves"? What does it seek for white men?

- **Activity:** Pair students to list the contrasts between slavery and free white labor. Discuss any aspects of this comparison they find surprising. Have students use their lists to draw inferences about what the authors hoped to achieve for white men.

Step 3: Context Questions

What regional differences does the pamphlet expose? What caused these differences? What will be the effects?

- **Activity:** Have students list the complaints that the pamphlet makes against the Southern states. Write their responses on the board. Next, have students describe the causes of each conflict listed. Discuss what the effect of these divisions will be.

Step 4: Historical Connections Questions

What criticisms does the pamphlet launch against the Democratic and Know-Nothing Parties? What does this portend about the rise of the Republicans? What role might this pamphlet have played in swaying the political tide?

- **Activity:** Explain that Fremont loses the 1856 election, but that Republican Abraham Lincoln wins in 1860. Have students list the criticisms launched against the competing parties and use their lists to discuss what factors led to this political splintering.

Step 5: Response Paper

Word length and additional requirements set by Instructor. Students answer the research question in the *Overview Questions*. Students state a thesis and use as evidence passages from the primary source document as well as support from supplemental materials assigned in the lesson.